Lecture Notes in Artificial Intelligence 11502

Subseries of Lecture Notes in Computer Science

Series Editors

Randy Goebel
University of Alberta, Edmonton, Canada
Yuzuru Tanaka
Hokkaido University, Sapporo, Japan
Wolfgang Wahlster
DFKI and Saarland University, Saarbrücken, Germany

Founding Editor

Jörg Siekmann
DFKI and Saarland University, Saarbrücken, Germany

More information about this series at http://www.springer.com/series/1244

Mariana Montiel · Francisco Gomez-Martin ·
Octavio A. Agustín-Aquino (Eds.)

Mathematics and Computation in Music

7th International Conference, MCM 2019
Madrid, Spain, June 18–21, 2019
Proceedings

 Springer

Editors
Mariana Montiel ⓘ
Georgia State University
Atlanta, GA, USA

Francisco Gomez-Martin ⓘ
Technical University of Madrid
Madrid, Spain

Octavio A. Agustín-Aquino ⓘ
Technological University of the Mixteca
Oaxaca, Mexico

ISSN 0302-9743   ISSN 1611-3349   (electronic)
Lecture Notes in Artificial Intelligence
ISBN 978-3-030-21391-6   ISBN 978-3-030-21392-3   (eBook)
https://doi.org/10.1007/978-3-030-21392-3

LNCS Sublibrary: SL7 – Artificial Intelligence

Cover illustration: Maria Mannone

This Springer imprint is published by the registered company Springer Nature Switzerland AG
The registered company address is: Gewerbestrasse 11, 6330 Cham, Switzerland

Preface

The 7th Biennial International Conference for Mathematics and Computation in Music (MCM 2019) took place during June 18th–21st, 2019, at the Escuela Técnica Superior de Ingeniería de Sistemas Informáticos of the Universidad Politécnica de Madrid (UPM), in Madrid, Spain, (paper sessions) and at the Real Conservatorio Superior de Música de Madrid, RCSMM, (plenary talks and concerts). MCM 2019 continued the pattern, initiated in 2007 at the first MCM meeting, of biennial international conferences held on alternating sides of the Atlantic: Berlin in 2007, New Haven in 2009, Paris in 2011, Montreal in 2013, London in 2015, and Mexico City in 2017.

As the flagship conference of the Society for Mathematics and Computation in Music (SMCM), MCM 2019 provided a platform for the communication and exchange of ideas among researchers in mathematics, informatics, music theory, musicology, and related disciplines. It brought together researchers from around the world who combine mathematics or computation with music analysis, music cognition, composition, and performance.

The schedule is available at https://mcm19.etsisi.upm.es/schedules/the-schedule. The scientific program featured 28 paper presentations and five posters, as well as four plenary conferences There were two special sessions; Remanaging Riemann: Mathematical Music Theory as Experimental Philology and a Special Session on Pedagogy in Mathematical Music Theory. The other sessions were grouped around the following subjects: Algebraic and other Abstract Mathematical Approaches to Understanding Musical Objects; Octave Division; Computer Based Approaches to Composition and Score Structuring; Models for Music Cognition; Tilings, Canons and Maximal Evenness. There were four plenary conferences, held each evening at the Conservatory before the concerts. The first one was given by Guerino Mazzola, president of the SMCM (COMMUTE—Towards a Computational Musical Theory of Everything), the second by Octavio Alberto Agustín-Aquino (Counterpoint Worlds) the third by Emmanuel Amiot (The Unreasonable Efficiency of Algebra in Maths and Music (Musica Exercitia algebricae est?), and the fourth by Francisco Gómez (Outreach in Mathematical Music Theory).

Finally, there were three concerts that took place at the RCSMM by SMCM researchers. On the first evening, Moreno Andreatta and Giles Baroin, in the context of composing chansons based on texts by poets, added a mathematical dimension to this genre. By using permutational tools and graph-theoretical methods, they created an original universe where poetry and music meet in a new dialogue. On the second evening, Guerino Mazzola, together with Heinz Geisser and Naoki Kita, presented free jazz, faithful to their philosophy that music should transform gestures and thoughts into real sound structures. On the third evening of the conference, Emilio Lluis-Puebla y Octavio Alberto Augustín-Aquino, plenary speaker and member of the Scientific Program Committee, played Diabelli's integral work for piano and guitar.

We received forty-eight submissions of which twenty-two long papers were accepted (eight belonging to the special session on Riemann), five short papers corresponding to posters, and six short papers corresponding to the special session on pedagogy. All papers were reviewed by multiple reviewers. The submissions came from more than ten countries and four continents.

The chapters included in these proceedings correspond to long papers (half-hour talks at the conference), including the special session honoring Riemann, as well as short papers (corresponding to the posters) and short papers corresponding to the special session on pedagogy in mathematical music theory.

We thank the following institutions for providing their infrastructure and human resources for the organization and promotion of MCM 2019:

- Universidad Politécnica de Madrid
- Society for Mathematics and Computation in Music
- Conservatorio Superior de Música de Madrid
- Georgia State University

June 2019   Mariana Montiel
                                                 Francisco Gomez-Martin
                                                 Octavio A. Agustín-Aquino

The original version of the book frontmatter was revised: The designer of the logo was missing. The correction to the book frontmatter is available at
https://doi.org/10.1007/978-3-030-21392-3_37

Organization

General Organizing Committee

Francisco (Paco) Gómez — Technical University of Madrid, Spain
Mariana Montiel — Georgia State University, Georgia, USA
Emilio Lluis-Puebla — UNAM, Mexico
Guerino Mazzola — University of Minnesota, USA
Octavio Alberto Agustín Aquino — Instituto de Física y Matemáticas, Universidad Tecnológica de la Mixteca, Mexico
Thomas Noll — Escola Superior de Musica de Cataluña, Spain

Scientific Program Committee

Mariana Montiel — Georgia State University, Georgia, USA
Francisco (Paco) Gómez — Technical University of Madrid, Spain
Octavio Alberto Agustín Aquino — Instituto de Física y Matemáticas, Universidad Tecnológica de la Mixteca, Mexico

Local Organizing Committee

Francisco (Paco) Gómez — Technical University of Madrid, Spain
Víctor Pliego — Real Conservatorio Superior, Spain

Reviewers

Octavio A. Agustín-Aquino
Jean Paul Allouche
Emmanuel Amiot
Moreno Andreatta
Juan Sebastián Arias
Aitor Arronte Álvarez
Cristian Bañuelos
Gilles Baroin
Chantal Buteau
Olivia Caramello
Norman Carey
Rodrigo Castro López Vaal
David Clampitt
Darrell Conklin
Maxime Crochemore
Andrée Ehresmann

Michael Franklin
Harald Fripertinger
Emilia Gómez
Francisco (Paco) Gómez
Yupeng Gu
Gareth Hearne
Julian Hook
Franck Jedrzejewski
Maximos Kaliakatsos
Jeremy Kastine
Olivier Lartillot
Vicente Liern
Emilio Lluis-Puebla
Pedro Louzeiro
Maria Mannone
Dimitrios Margounakis

Guerino Mazzola

Brent Milam

Andrew Milne

Mariana Montiel

Javier Mora

Thomas Noll

Robert Peck

Richard Plotkin

Alexandre Popoff

David Rappaport

David Temperley

Petri Toiviainen

Isao Tokuda

Jason Yust

Marek Žabka

Fernando Zalamea

Collaborating Institutions

Technical University of Madrid

Real Conservatorio Superior de Música de Madrid

Georgia State University

Universidad Tecnológica de la Mixteca

Society for Mathematics and Music in Computation

Contents

Plenary Talks

Contrapuntal Aspects of the Mystic Chord and Scriabin's Piano Sonata No. 5

Octavio A. Agustín-Aquino[1]([✉]) [iD] and Guerino Mazzola[2]

[1] Instituto de Física y Matemáticas, Universidad Tecnológica de la Mixteca,
Huajuapan de León, Oaxaca, Mexico
octavioalberto@mixteco.utm.mx
[2] School of Music, University of Minnesota, Minneapolis, MN, USA
mazzola@umn.edu
http://www.utm.mx/~octavioalberto/
http://www.encyclospace.org

Abstract. We present statistical evidence for the importance of the "mystic chord" in Scriabin's Piano Sonata No. 5, Op. 53, from a computational and mathematical counterpoint perspective. More specifically, we compute the effect sizes and perform χ^2 tests with respect to the distributions of counterpoint symmetries in the Fuxian, mystic, Ionian and representatives of the other three possible counterpoint worlds in two passages of the work, which provide evidence of a qualitative change between the Fuxian and the mystic worlds in the sonata.

Keywords: Counterpoint · Scriabin · Mystic chord

1 Introduction

A prominent chord in Alexander Scriabin's late work is the so-called "mystic chord" or "Prometheus chord", whose pc-set when the root is C is $M = \{0, 6, 10, 4, 9, 2\}$ [7, p. 23]. It can be seen as a chain of thirds, and thus can be covered by an augmented triad followed by a diminished triad, together with a major triad followed by a minor triad (see Fig. 1). This surely evidences the strong tonal ambiguity of the chord, which is also associated to the Impressionism in music during the late 19th and early 20th centuries in Europe [15]. The mystic chord can be seen as an extension of the French sixth, which is completely contained in a whole tone scale; the mystic chord also has this property safe for a "sensible" tone [3, p. 278]. As we will see, this is an important feature from the perspective of the mathematical counterpoint theory developed by Mazzola [12, Part VII].

This work was partially supported by a grant from the *Niels Hendrik Abel Board*.

© Springer Nature Switzerland AG 2019
M. Montiel et al. (Eds.): MCM 2019, LNAI 11502, pp. 3–20, 2019.
https://doi.org/10.1007/978-3-030-21392-3_1

With respect to the structural role of the mystic chord in Scriabin's works, Gottfried Eberle states[1], for instance [8, p. 14],

> Alle musikalischen Ereignisse des Werks, harmonische wie melodische und kontrapunktische, seien im wesentlichen in diesem sechstönigen Komplex gegründet: "[...] alle melodischen Stimmen sind auf den Klängen der begleitenden Harmonie gebaut, alle Kontrapunkte sind demselben Prinzip untergeordnet" [Sabanajew, 1912].

and, moreover[2] [8, p. 16],

> Die Aussage trifft zu: Die Grundharmonie des Prometheus wird von Skrjabin nicht läger als Dissonanz begriffen und behandelt: "Das ist eine Grundharmonie, eine Konsonanz" [Sabaneev, 1925].

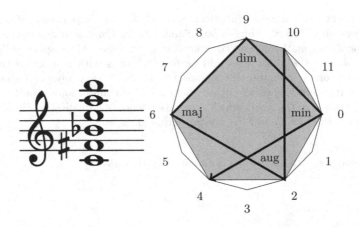

Fig. 1. Scriabin's mystic chord and four prominent triads (augmented, major, diminished, and minor) which cover it.

More specifically, in our contrapuntal interpretation, we view the mystic chord defining what is called a *strong dichotomy*, i. e., a bipartition of the pitch class set $\mathbb{Z}_{12}$ such that its only affine symmetry is the identity [12, Part VII, Chapter 30]. In particular, it[3] belongs to the class 78 in Mazzola's classification

---

[1] All the musical events of the work, harmonic as well as melodic and contrapuntal, are essentially within this six-tone complex: "[...] all the melodic voices are on the sounds of the accompanying harmony, all counterpoints are subordinated to the same principle".

[2] The statement is correct: The basic harmony of Prometheus is no longer understood and treated by Scriabin as dissonance: "This is a basic harmony, a consonance".

[3] It is interesting to note that the mystic chord can be seen as the first of a sequence of dichotomies that are always strong in microtonal equitempered tunings, as described in [2, Proposition 2.4 and Remark 3].

as it appears in his *Topos of Music* [12, Table L.1]. A strong dichotomy can be understood as a division of pitch classes in generalized consonances and dissonances, because the classical consonances of Renaissance counterpoint also define a strong dichotomy. There are four other bipartitions with the aforementioned mathematical properties (modulo affine symmetries). Here is a list of selected representatives of the strong dichotomies:

$$(K/D) = \Delta_{82} = (\{0, 3, 4, 7, 8, 9\}/\{1, 2, 5, 6, 10, 11\}),$$
$$(M/N) = \Delta_{78} = (\{0, 2, 4, 6, 9, 10\}/\{1, 3, 5, 7, 8, 11\}),$$
$$(I/J) = \Delta_{64} = (\{2, 4, 5, 7, 9, 11\}/\{0, 1, 3, 6, 8, 10\}),$$
$$\Delta_{68} = (\{0, 1, 2, 3, 5, 8\}/\{4, 6, 7, 9, 10, 11\}),$$
$$\Delta_{71} = (\{0, 1, 2, 3, 6, 7\}/\{4, 5, 8, 9, 10, 11\}),$$
$$\Delta_{75} = (\{0, 1, 2, 4, 6, 8\}/\{3, 6, 7, 9, 10, 11\}).$$

The subindex represents the class number in Mazzola's classification, whereas (K/D), (M/N) and (I/J) are the *Fuxian*, *mystic* and *Ionian*[4] dichotomies, respectively. The representatives Δ_{68}, Δ_{71}, Δ_{75} are the lexicographically smallest among their class, which we consider a reasonable choice until a musical one that is better can be found. But conversely: the musical one could be just that one which proves significant with respect to an analysis like the one we conducted. "Musical", anyhow, is mainly a historical criterion[5].

If we study the predicted allowed steps for a counterpoint distilled from M, we find that a favorable scale for cantus firmus pitches is one particular transposed mode of the whole-tone scale, namely the one with pc-set $\{1, 3, 5, 7, 9, 11\}$, with only eight forbidden transitions if we do not mind if the discantus leaves the selected whole-tone scale, or four if the discantus has to remain within the scale. Thus, we may consider two representatives of mystic chord: one, like M, which shares most of its tones with the "even" whole-tone scale $\{0, 2, 4, 6, 8, 10\}$, and the other[6] one $T^1 M$ that is closer to the "odd" whole-tone scale.

Hence, in general, for the even mystic chord, a very good scale for counterpoint is the odd whole-tone scale, and vice versa.

Unfortunately, for the whole-tone scale there is no analogue of Noll's theorem connecting a harmony based on triads and counterpoint (as explained in [12, Section 30.2.1]), since among all possible triads there is none whose set of endomorphisms is such that their linear part yields a strong dichotomy. This, by the way, is in accordance with classical musicological opinion on the scale of its poor harmonic possibilities (at least from the tonal harmony perspective [11, p. 486]), and perhaps it was an attractive characteristic for Scriabin to use it in his music.

---

[4] This name stems from the fact that this representative consists in all proper (non-vanishing) intervals in the Ionian mode, when counted from the tonic.

[5] Historical musical objects may not be relevant in terms of this counterpoint model. For example, the Lydian dichotomy induced by the pc-set $\{2, 4, 6, 7, 9, 11\}$ could be seen as a good candidate for a system of consonances, but is not strong because it has as a non-trivial inner affine symmetry.

[6] We denote with T^x the transposition by x.

These facts lead us to study the role of the strong dichotomies as possible contrapuntal principles in a one section of Scriabin's Piano Sonata No. 5, op. 53, in contrast to another section of the same work. The plan for the remaining of the paper is the following: first, in Sect. 2, we summarize Mazzola's counterpoint theory, which only deals with first-species counterpoint. Then, in Sect. 3, we explain how it can be extended to more general transitions of intervals and not only the ones between consonances, so we can perform a sufficiently general analysis of the passages. Apart from strong dichotomies which place us in different *counterpoint worlds*, Mazzola's theory is based on affine invertible transformations or *symmetries*. It turns out that different numbers of symmetries mediate in valid transitions between two intervals in different worlds. The musical meaning of these quantities is that, since the symmetries model tension, then the number of different instances of tension is a measure for the structural justification of a transition. Hence the number of symmetries measures the quantified tension, not only its existence. Furthermore, this number can be considered as an statistic whose properties are summarily described in Sect. 4, and used for hypothesis testing in Sect. 5 in order to detect the salience of different representatives of the counterpoint worlds. In Sect. 6 section we offer further counts of consonances and transitions that reinforce our conclusions, as well as more examples of the interplay of the mystic chord as a set of consonances and the whole tone scale displayed in the sonata. We provide some conclusions in the last section.

2   A Quick Overview of Mazzola's Counterpoint Model

Before we proceed, let us make a remark on notation: we denote a *counterpoint interval* by (x, y), where x is the *cantus firmus* and y is the interval that separates it from the *discantus*. Thus, $(2, 7)$ represents a counterpoint interval where the cantus firmus is 2 and the discantus is 9, because the separation between them, modulo octaves, is $(9 - 2) \bmod 12 = 7$.

In Mazzola's counterpoint model all the pitches are considered modulo octave. Thus the intervals between two tones reduces to $\mathbb{Z}_{12}$. In particular, as far as Renaissance counterpoint and the famous Fux's treatise *Gradus ad Parnassum* [9] are concerned, the set of consonances is $K = \{0, 3, 4, 7, 8, 9\}$ and thus dissonances are $D = \mathbb{Z}_{12} \setminus K = \{1, 2, 5, 6, 10, 11\}$. The bipartition of intervals (K/D) is an example of a *strong dichotomy*, which we shall define now. First, the group of affine symmetries between pitch classes in $\mathbb{Z}_{12}$ consists of those of the form

$$T^u.v(x) = vx + u$$

where v is coprime with 12, i. e., $v = 1, 5, 7, 11$ and $u \in \mathbb{Z}_{12}$. Note that the affine symmetry $p = T^2.5$ is such that $p(K) = D$ (acting pointwise) and it is the only one with this property. It is called the *polarity* of the set of consonances. Precisely those dichotomies that possess a unique polarity are called *strong*. As we have already mentioned, there is a total of six strong dichotomies with these properties up to equivalence under the action of the group of affine symmetries.

Counterpoint intervals can be endowed with the structure of dual numbers[7] $\mathbb{Z}_{12}[\epsilon] \in \mathbb{Z}_{12} \times \mathbb{Z}_{12}$, defining the sum

$$(x_1, y_1) + (x_2, y_2) = (x_1 + x_2, y_1 + y_2)$$

and the multiplication

$$(x_1, y_1)(x_2, y_2) = (x_1 x_2, x_1 y_2 + x_2 y_1). \tag{1}$$

The group of symmetries for counterpoint intervals consists of symmetries of the form

$$T^{(u_1, u_2)}.(v_1, v_2)$$

with (v_1, v_2) an invertible element with respect to the multiplication defined by (1), which amounts to require v_1 to be invertible. We denote them with $\overrightarrow{GL}(\mathbb{Z}_{12}[\epsilon])$. For an arbitrary strong dichotomy (X/Y) such that its set of consonances and dissonances are X and Y, respectively, the set of all consonant intervals is

$$X[\epsilon] := \{(c, x) : c \in \mathbb{Z}_{12}, x \in X\}$$

and the set of dissonant intervals is $Y[\epsilon] := \mathbb{Z}_{12} \times \mathbb{Z}_{12} \setminus X[\epsilon]$. In particular, there exists a canonical symmetry p_c such that $p_c(X[\epsilon]) = Y[\epsilon]$ and leaves the intervals with cantus firmus c invariant, and it is called an *induced polarity*. We let the group $\overrightarrow{GL}(\mathbb{Z}_{12}[\epsilon])$ to act pointwise on subsets $S \subseteq \mathbb{Z}_{12}[\epsilon]$, and we call

$$gX[\epsilon] = \{g(c, x) : (c, x) \in X[\epsilon]\}$$

a set of *g-deformed consonant intervals*. The *g-deformed dissonant intervals* are, of course, $gY[\epsilon]$.

Now a *counterpoint symmetry* g for a consonant interval $\xi = (c, x)$ is one such that

1. the interval ξ is a g-deformed dissonant interval,
2. it commutes with the induced polarity p_x, that is, $p_x \circ g = g \circ p_x$, and
3. the set of consonances that are also g-deformed consonant intervals is as large as possible within the symmetries with the above properties.

The consonant intervals which are g-deformed consonant intervals simultaneously for a counterpoint symmetry g are called the *admitted successors*. The idea behind these definitions is that transitions from consonance to consonance do not exhibit tension explicitly. Mazzola's solution to reveal this concealed tension is to see the first consonance as a deformed dissonance, and then resolving it to a deformed consonance that it is also a consonance (the step from ξ_1 to ξ_2 in Fig. 2).

---

[7] The pairs (x, y) can also be written as $x + \epsilon.y$ with $\epsilon^2 = 0$ in commutative algebra. The reason to introduce this algebraic structure is that it describes tangent vectors (see [12, Section 7.5] for further details).

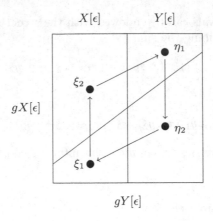

Fig. 2. Deformed consonant and dissonant intervals, and possible transitions.

It is important to mention that counterpoint symmetries can be calculated for cantus firmus $c = 0$ and then translated suitably [12, Section 31.3.1]. It is also relatively straightforward to adapt the calculations' results for other consonances and dissonances that are affinely equivalent to the (X/Y) dichotomy without redoing them entirely [12, Section 31.3.4]. We should stress that, when (X/Y) is the Fuxian dichotomy, then we recover many salient features of Renaissance counterpoint theory via counterpoint symmetries and admitted successors, for example: the fourth is classified as a dissonance, there is a general prohibition of parallel fifths, the tritone rules hold in the so-called reduced strict style (which is obtained to applying Fux's rules modulo octave), and the major scale is optimal for contrapuntal purposes, in the sense that it allows the largest number of allowed steps. See [1, Chapter 3] and [12, Section 31.4.1] for further details.

3   General Transitions in Mazzola's Counterpoint Model

The aforementioned model apparently only handles the transitions from consonances to consonances. But upon reflection we realize that it also handles the dissonance-to-dissonance steps (like the one from η_1 to η_2 in Fig. 2), by simply applying the induced polarity p_0 and translating the results accordingly[8]. More explicitly, the admitted successors of a dissonant interval $\eta_1 \in D[\epsilon]$ for a given counterpoint symmetry g are translates of

$$p_0(gK[\epsilon] \cap K[\epsilon]) = p_0 gK[\epsilon] \cap p_0 K[\epsilon]$$
$$= gp_0 K[\epsilon] \cap D[\epsilon] = gD[\epsilon] \cap D[\epsilon].$$

---

[8] This, by the way, leads to a natural concept of dissonant counterpoint [5].

Nevertheless, it is less obvious that dissonance-to-consonance steps or *resolutions* [9, p. 56] are also modeled[9], like the one from η_2 to ξ_1 in Fig. 2. In fact, we ought to define a "crossing" counterpoint symmetry g for a dissonance η_2 as one such that, apart from the obvious requirement of commuting with the induced polarity, η_2 is an appropriate deformation of a dissonant interval and maximizes the intersection of the original consonant intervals and g-deformed dissonant intervals. But the following result shows that no true generalization is needed.

Theorem 1. *Let $\eta \in Y[\epsilon]$. The symmetry $g' \in \overrightarrow{GL}(\mathbb{Z}_{12}[\epsilon])$ satisfies that*

1. *the interval η belongs to $g'Y[\epsilon]$,*
2. *it commutes with p_0 and*
3. *the set $g'Y[\epsilon] \cap X[\epsilon]$ has the largest cardinality among the symmetries with the previous two properties*

if, and only if, $g = p_0 \circ g'$ is a counterpoint symmetry for the interval $\xi = p_0(\eta) \in X[\epsilon]$.

Proof. Note first that p_0 is involutive, i.e., $p_0 = p_0^{-1}$. Thus g' commutes with p_0 if and only if $g = p_0 \circ g'$ does, since

$$g = p_0 \circ g' = g' \circ p_0 \iff g' = p_0 \circ g' \circ p_0 = g \circ p_0 = p_0 \circ g.$$

Thus

$$\xi \in gY[\epsilon] \iff \eta = p_0(\xi) \in p_0 \circ gY[\epsilon] = p_0 \circ p_0 \circ g'Y[\epsilon] = g'Y[\epsilon].$$

Finally, because

$$gX[\epsilon] \cap X[\epsilon] = g \circ p_0 Y[\epsilon] \cap X[\epsilon]$$
$$= g'Y[\epsilon] \cap X[\epsilon],$$

the maximization of the cardinality of the admitted successors $gX[\epsilon] \cap X[\epsilon]$ is equivalent to the maximization of $g'Y[\epsilon] \cap X[\epsilon]$.

In other words: in order to model the transition from dissonance to consonance with symmetries, we regard the dissonance η as a g-deformed dissonant interval and we admit as a successor a deformed dissonant interval that it is also a consonant interval, hence *dissolving* the contrast between dissonance and consonance via a deformation. The case for consonance-to-dissonance steps or *preparations* [4, p. 44], like the one from ξ_2 to η_1 in Fig. 2, is not only analogous: it is symmetrical, therefore we omit the details here.

---

[9] In Renaissance counterpoint the notion of resolution is understood only by stepwise movement of voices [10, p. 131], but the model can trivially be restricted to fulfill this requirement.

4   Some Statistical Contrapuntal Properties of the Counterpoint Worlds

In Table 1 we see the distribution of the number of contrapuntal symmetries between all intervals for the selected representatives mentioned in Sect. 1 of the *counterpoint worlds*[10].

If you have, for instance, the step $((0, 3), (2, 4))$ in the Fuxian world, there are two counterpoint symmetries that "allow" it. Contrariwise, the parallel fifths step $((0, 7), (2, 7))$ is forbidden, for it has 0 counterpoint symmetries. In the Fuxian world the maximum number of symmetries mediating in a step is 5. For the 12^4 possible steps (besides consonance to consonance also dissonance to dissonance, dissonance to consonance, and consonance to dissonance steps can be considered in the extended model), we have a total of 2400 inadmissible steps, 4992 steps with only one counterpoint symmetry, and so on within the Fuxian world. In Table 2 we find the mean and standard deviation of the distributions of Table 1, as well as the probability of a random pair of intervals to be valid.

It should be noted that the Fuxian world has the greatest liberty for counterpoint transitions, since it has the minimum of forbidden steps. It is followed by the Δ_{68}, mystic, Ionian, Δ_{75}, and Δ_{71}, in that order.

Let p_{Δ_1}, p_{Δ_2}, and $p_{\Delta_1 \cap \Delta_2}$ the probability of a random step to valid in worlds Δ_1, Δ_2, and in both, respectively. The absolute value of $|p_{\Delta_1} p_{\Delta_2} - p_{\Delta_1 \cap \Delta_2}|$, which measures the deviation of the events from independence, appears in Table 3. Notice that the highest deviation from independence occurs between the Ionian and Δ_{75} worlds. Nevertheless, most of the other pairs deviate from independence approximately by a 5% of this maximum value or even less.

Table 1. Distribution of the number of counterpoint symmetries for selected representatives of the counterpoint worlds.

Number of cpt. symmetries	Fuxian steps	Mystic steps	Ionian steps	Δ_{68} steps	Δ_{71} steps	Δ_{75} steps
0	2400	3840	4224	3744	4608	4320
1	4992	7296	11136	6912	6912	9120
2	9120	6720	4608	6624	6336	4992
3	384	0	768	3456	0	1440
4	2304	2880	0	0	2880	864
5	1536	0	0	0	0	0

---

[10] A counterpoint world is a directed graph, where each vertex is a counterpoint interval and there is an arrow connecting for each valid step. See [1, Chapter 4] for further details.

Table 2. Mean and standard deviation of the number of counterpoint symmetries in steps within the counterpoint worlds, and the probability that two random intervals to be a valid succession.

Counterpoint world	Mean	Std. dev.	Prob. of admissibility
Fuxian	1.99074	1.35401	0.88426
Mystic	1.55556	1.20444	0.81481
Ionian	1.09259	0.75202	0.79630
Δ_{68}	1.47222	0.97145	0.81944
Δ_{71}	1.50000	1.23606	0.77778
Δ_{75}	1.29630	1.00703	0.79167

Table 3. Absolute value of the difference between the product of the probabilities of being valid for a random step in two worlds and the probability of being valid in both worlds.

	Fuxian	Mystic	Ionian	Δ_{68}	Δ_{71}	Δ_{75}
Fuxian	—	0.0303	0.0154	0.0231	0.0113	0.0129
Mystic		—	0.0564	0.0036	0.0190	0.0000
Ionian			—	0.0067	0.6277	0.6373
Δ_{68}				—	0.0050	0.0006
Δ_{71}					—	0.0046

5   Fuxian and Mystic Worlds in Scriabin's Piano Sonata No. 5, Op. 53

We can find some explanatory power for the rationale behind contrapuntal transitions in a system of consonances and dissonances different from the Fuxian choice through Mazzola's model, particulary in the case of Scriabin's Piano Sonata No. 5, op. 53 [14]. We selected this work for a first exploration because of the explicit apparition of the mystic chord within it.

In the prologue section [17, Chapter IV], which we will call part 1, spanning measures 13 to 46, taking in most of the cases the cantus firmus as E (as suggested by standard musicological analysis of the work [18, pp. 2–3]), we have 37 contrapuntal transitions within measures 13–31. Next we isolate 36 possible transitions (omitting repetitions of certain patterns) for measures from 47 to 61, which are the initial measures of what is known as the first exposition of the sonata [17, Chapter IV], and that we will call part 2. In order to understand the codification of the input, which is done with the standard $\mathbb{Z}_{12}$ identification, the measures 13 to 15 (Fig. 3) in part 1 are codified as

```
[4 4 4;  8  3  8],
[4 4 4;10  8 10],
[4 4 4;  6 10  6],
[4 4 4;  3  6  3],
```

Fig. 3. Measures 13–15 from Scriabin's Piano Sonata No. 5, op. 53.

Fig. 4. Measures 48 and 49 from Scriabin's Piano Sonata No. 5, op. 53.

whereas the measures 48 and 49 (Fig. 4) in part 2 are codified as

```
[6 10 3;3 6 10],
[6 10 3; 11 3 6],
[3 6 3 11; 6 10 6 3],
[3 6 3 11; 11 3 10 8],
```

not taking the bass into account.

The average number of counterpoint symmetries per step and the standard deviation appears in Table 4.

We now compute the effect sizes[11] (ES) and the corresponding 95% confidence intervals for the two parts of the work under analysis (see Table 5), and we clearly observe a relatively large positive effect of the mystic world in the first part. For the second part, the presence of all the worlds reduces, except for

---

[11] The effect size we take is the so-called Cohen's d, which is the mean difference on the means between the two variables divided by the pooled standard deviation. See [6] for further details.

Table 4. Average number of symmetries per step and standard deviation in part 1 (measures 13–31) and part 2 (measures 47–61) of Scriabin's Sonata.

Cpt. world	Part 1		Part 2	
	Avg. # of sym.	Std. dev.	Avg. # of sym.	Std. dev.
Fuxian	2.10811	1.10010	1.94444	0.62994
Mystic	2.16216	1.34399	1.38889	1.20185
Ionian	1.02703	0.89711	0.88889	0.74748
Δ_{68}	1.54054	0.90045	1.77778	0.89797
Δ_{71}	1.59459	1.32202	1.27778	0.97427
Δ_{75}	1.13514	0.75138	1.08333	0.69179

Table 5. Effect size and 95% confidence intervals for part 1 (measures 13–31) and part 2 (measures 47–61) of Scriabin's Sonata.

Cpt. world	Part 1		Part 2	
	ES	95% conf. intvl.	ES	95% conf. intvl.
Fuxian	0.087	$[-0.236, 0.409]$	-0.034	$[-0.361, 0.293]$
Mystic	0.504	$[0.181, 0.826]$	-0.138	$[-0.465, 0.189]$
Ionian	-0.087	$[-0.410, 0.235]$	-0.271	$[-0.598, -0.056]$
Δ_{68}	0.070	$[-0.252, 0.393]$	0.315	$[-0.012, 0.642]$
Δ_{71}	0.077	$[-0.246, 0.399]$	-0.180	$[-0.507, 0.147]$
Δ_{75}	-0.160	$[-0.483, 0.162]$	-0.212	$[-0.539, 0.115]$

the Δ_{68} world, which is the only one whose effect size *increases*. This strange phenomenon, along with the apparent absence of the Fuxian world, is further clarified by the following tests.

If we perform χ^2 tests [16, Chapter 8] for the frequencies of number of symmetries, with p-values appearing in Table 6, we see that the only worlds that would pass a 95% test would be the distributions of the Fuxian and mystic worlds, which confirm that their presences are the only significant ones. If we now restrict the χ^2 test to the permitted versus allowed steps frequencies[12], we find the values in Table 7. Now we notice that the mystic world would pass a 89% test for part 1 and not for part 2, and the converse is true for the Fuxian world.

---

[12] In fact, the kurtosis of the distribution of the number of symmetries per step in the Fuxian world are 4.70239 and 7.55462 for part 1 and 2, respectively. This means that the second distribution deviates less from its mean, and thus in this case Cohen's d does not explain the change sufficiently because the mean of both distributions is very close to the general one. This was also observed in the first-species fragments of *Misae Papae Marcelli* by G. P. Palestrina against the general distribution; see [13] for details.

Table 6. List of p-values for χ^2 tests for part 1 (measures 13–31) and part 2 (measures 47–61) of Scriabin's Sonata.

Counterpoint world	p-value	
	Part 1	Part 2
Fuxian	3.1777×10^{-9}	2.7149×10^{-3}
Mystic	0.0219	0.0436
Ionian	0.2084	0.1809
Δ_{68}	0.6460	0.2669
Δ_{71}	0.7120	0.3535
Δ_{75}	0.5320	0.3007

Table 7. List of fractions of permitted steps per part and p-values for χ^2 tests for frequencies of permitted/forbidden steps in part 1 (measures 13–31) and part 2 (measures 47–61) of Scriabin's Sonata for the Fuxian and mystic worlds.

Cpt. world	Part 1		Part 2	
	Fraction of permitted steps	χ^2 statistic	Fraction of permitted steps	χ^2 statistic
Fuxian	0.92	0.5099	1.00	0.0300
Mystic	0.91	0.1031	0.83	0.7748

In other words: while part 2 does not use functional tonal harmony, it is much closer to the counterpoint of the standard consonances than to one stemming from the mystic chord heard in part 1, and no other counterpoint worlds are evident aside from these.

6 Some Additional Observations

Although it is not directly connected to Mazzola's counterpoint theory (since it only depends on the purely combinatorial classification of consonances and dissonances), it is very interesting to note that the highest count of consonances for part 1 under analysis corresponds to the mystic world, whereas the maximum occurs for the Fuxian consonances in part 2 (Table 8). If we calculate the number of transitions for the four possible transitions between consonances and dissonances (Table 9), we note that the maximum number of consonance-to-consonance steps in part 1 occurs for the mystic and Δ_{75} worlds (although the display of resolutions and preparations for the mystic world is evident, whereas it is totally absent for the world Δ_{75}). The maximum number of consonant transitions goes for the Fuxian world in part 2, as expected.

While not as explicit as an extraction of first species counterpoint from the sonata, we can find more evidences of the importance of the mystic chord as a choice of consonances and the role the whole tone scale has with respect to it.

For instance, from measure 102 to 103 Scriabin favors pitches within the even whole-tone scale and in 104 and 105 he states an odd mystic chord; then he suddenly changes the key and begins to stress the even whole-tone scale.

Another similar situation occurs in measures 130 and 131, where Scriabin displays an arpeggiated even mystic chord followed by an arpeggiated odd whole-tone scale in the following measure. Quite interestingly, this is continued by an odd mystic chord in measures 136 and 137, but preceding it with and ambiguity between the even and odd whole tone scale, anticipating another sudden change of mood in measure 140.

Table 8. Total number of consonances in each of the analyzed parts of Scriabin's sonata (total number of intervals is in parentheses).

Counterpoint world	Consonances in part 1 (57)	Consonances in part 2 (50)
Fuxian	24	44
Mystic	39	19
Ionian	31	32
Δ_{68}	17	24
Δ_{71}	22	17
Δ_{75}	24	23

Table 9. Total number of different transitions (DD: dissonance to dissonance; DC: dissonance to consonance; CD: consonance to dissonance; DD: dissonance to dissonance) for each of the analyzed parts of Scriabin's sonata.

Counterpoint world	Part 1				Part 2			
	DD	DC	CD	CC	DD	DC	CD	CC
Fuxian	14	8	6	9	4	0	0	32
Mystic	1	8	13	15	6	18	12	0
Ionian	5	12	11	9	0	15	9	12
Δ_{68}	17	11	7	2	7	10	16	3
Δ_{71}	15	8	8	6	13	10	13	0
Δ_{75}	22	0	0	15	19	0	0	17

A final explicit apparition of an even mystic chord in measure 262 is also associated with a dynamical fluctuation in the piece, but in this case its interaction with the whole scale is less apparent but seems to be in favor of the odd whole-tone scale, as expected.

7   Conclusions

As Eberle and other scholars who specialize in Alexander Scriabin have pointed out, the mystic or Prometheus chord has been a key architectural principle in some of his works but its relation to the contrapuntal aspect of them has largely been neglected or not understood. Through an extension of Mazzola's counterpoint model, where the mystic chord can literally (as Scriabin himself claimed) be taken as the consonances, a counterpoint theory emerges such that general transitions between consonances and dissonances can be handled, and thus we can compare the contrapuntal content of two different passages of Scriabin's fifth piano sonata not only across one but representatives of all the counterpoint worlds. The fact that we can perceive Scriabin's accomplishment of the combination of two counterpoint worlds within one composition attests the power of the mathematical model for understanding difficult works of art and project them into the future.

Acknowledgments. We thank Thomas Noll at Escola Superior de Música de Catalunya, Daniel Tompkins at Florida State University, and the anonymous referees for their valuable feedback.

Appendix: Source Code and Data

The following code implements a function in Octave (version 4.2.0) to calculate the number of counterpoint symmetries per step in a sequence of counterpoint intervals, encoded as columns of a matrix.

```
function R = analisis (M, K, simetrias)

% —— R = analisis (M, K, simetrias)
% Calculates the number of counterpoint symmetries
% that mediate between the counterpoint steps in M,
% where the first row corresponds to the cantus
% firmus and the second row to the intervals with
% the discantus. If the parameters K and simetrias
% are provided, it uses K as the consonances, and
% within the array simetrias they should appear in
% the format [a b c], corresponding to
% e^(0,a).(b,c).

if (nargin ()==1)

  K = [0 3 4 7 8 9];

  simetrias = {
    [6,1,6;  6,7,6;11,11,-4;11,11,4;11,11,0],
    [8,5,-4;8,5,4],
    [6,1,6;6,7,6],
    [0,7,0],
```

```
   [3 ,7 ,0;6 ,1 ,6;6 ,7 ,6;3 ,7 ,4;3 ,7 , −4] ,
   [8 ,5 ,8;8 ,5 ,4]
   };

end

ntonos = 2∗length (K);

R = zeros (1 ,columns (M) −1);

% Constructs the consonant intervals

Ke = [];
for s = K;
   Ke = [[[0: ntonos −1];ones (1 ,ntonos )∗s]  Ke];
end

D = setdiff ([0: ntonos −1],K);

De = [];
for s = D;
   De = [[[0: ntonos −1];ones (1 ,ntonos )∗s]  De];
end

for u=[0: ntonos −1]
  for v=[1:2: ntonos −1]
   if (((u!=0)||(v!=1))&&(sort (mod(K∗v+u ,ntonos))==D))
    plineal = v;
    pafin = u;
   end
  end
end

for w =  [1: columns (M) −1]

% Finds the appropiate set of counterpoint
% symmetries .

  if (ismember (M(2 ,w) ,K))
   cual = find (K==M(2 ,w));
   esconsonancia = 1;
  else
   cual = find (K==mod(M(2 ,w)∗ plineal+pafin ,ntonos ));
   esconsonancia = 0;
  end

  for l = [1: rows ( simetrias {cual })]

% Extracts symmetries as the matrix Q and the
% translation vector t .
```

```
Q = [simetrias{cual}(1,2)  0;
simetrias{cual}(1,3)  simetrias{cual}(1,2)];
t = [M(1,w);  simetrias{cual}(1,1)];

% Calculation  of  the  deformed  intervals.

consdeformadas = mod(Q*Ke+t*ones(1,length(Ke)),
ntonos);
disdeformadas = mod(plineal*Q*Ke+(t*plineal+
pafin)*ones(1,length(Ke)),ntonos);

% Adds  one  to  the  counter  if  the  next
% interval  is  an  admitted  successor.
  if(esconsonancia&&ismember(M(2,w+1),K))
    if(ismember(M(:,w+1)',consdeformadas','rows'))
    R(w) = R(w)+1;
    end
  elseif(esconsonancia&&ismember(M(2,w+1),D))
    if(ismember(M(:,w+1)',disdeformadas','rows'))
    R(w) = R(w)+1;
    end
  elseif(not(esconsonancia)&&ismember(M(2,w+1),D))
    if(ismember(M(:,w+1)',disdeformadas','rows'))
    R(w) = R(w)+1;
    end
  else
    if(ismember(M(:,w+1)',consdeformadas','rows'))
    R(w) = R(w)+1;
    end
  end
 end
end
end
```

The listed arrays contains the analyzed intervals extracted from Scriabin's sonata, one for each part.

```
contrapunto_scriabin_13_31 = {
[4  4  4;  8  3  8],
[4  4  4;10  8  10],
[4  4  4;  6 10  6],
[4  4  4;  3  6  3],
[4  4;  10  3],
[4  4;  8  11],
[6  6;  10  3],
[6  6;  8  11],
[4  4  4;  2  1  0],
[8  8  8  8  8;  4  0  1  2  8],
[4  4  4;  2  6  2],
[8  8  8;  2  6  2],
[8  8  8;  3  6  3],
```

```
[8  8  8;  1  6  1],
[4  4  4;  8  7  6],
[10  10  10;  8  7  6],
[5  4  3  2  1;  11  11  11  11  11];
[1  4;  7  7],
[10  7;  8  5],
[4  1;  8  5]
};
contrapunto_scriabin_47_61 = {
[6  10  3;3  6  10],
[6  10  3;  11  3  6],
[3  6  3  11;  6  10  6  3],
[3  6  3  11;  11  3  10  8],
[3  11  10  11;  6  3  3  3],
[3  11  10  11;  10  8  6  8],
[3  11  3;  6  3  6],
[3  11  3;  10  8  10],
[1  4  1  9;  4  8  4  1],
[1  4  1  9;  9  1  8  6],
[8  9  8;  1  1  1],
[8  9  8;  4  6  4],
[7  10  7  3;  10  2  10  8],
[7  10  7  3;  3  5  3  0]
};
```

References

1. Agustín-Aquino, O.A., Junod, J., Mazzola, G.: Computational Counterpoint Worlds. CMS. Springer, Cham (2015). https://doi.org/10.1007/978-3-319-11236-7
2. Agustín-Aquino, O.A.: Counterpoint in $2k$-tone equal temperament. J. Math. Music **3**(3), 153–164 (2009). https://doi.org/10.1080/17459730903309807
3. Ballard, L., Bengston, M., Young, J.B.: The Alexander Scriabin Companion. Rowman & Littlefield, Lanham (2017)
4. Benjamin, T.: The Craft of Modal Counterpoint. Routledge, New York (2005)
5. Cowell, H., Nicholls, D.: New Musical Resources. Cambridge University Press, Cambridge (1996)
6. Cumming, G.: Understanding The New Statistics. Routledge, New York (2012)
7. Dejos, V.: Analyse et interprétation des six dernières sonates pour piano d'Alexandre Scriabine. Ph.D. thesis, Université Paris-Sorbonne (2014)
8. Eberle, G.: Zwischen Tonalität und Atonalität: Studien zur Harmonik Alexander Skrjabins, Berliner Musikwissenschaftliche Arbeiten, vol. 14. Musikverlag Emil Katzbichler, München-Salzburg (1978)
9. Fux, J.J.: Gradus Ad Parnasum. W. W. Norton, New York (1965)
10. Jeppesen, K.: Counterpoint. Dover Publications Inc., New York (1992)
11. Kostka, S., Payne, D.: Tonal Harmony, 3rd edn. McGraw-Hill Inc., Boston (1995)
12. Mazzola, G.: The Topos of Music, vol. I: Theory. Springer, Heidelberg (2017). https://doi.org/10.1007/978-3-319-64364-9
13. Nieto, A.: Una aplicación del teorema de contrapunto. B. Sc. thesis, ITAM (2010)

14. Scriabine, A.: Cinquème sonate pour piano, Op. 53. Self-published, Lausanne (1907)
15. Trombley, R.: Impressionism in music. In: DiMartino, D., et al. (ed.) Music in the 20th Century, vol. 2, p. 305. Routledge (1999)
16. Warner, R.M.: Applied Statistics. SAGE, California (2012)
17. Wise, H.H.: The relationship of pitch sets to formal structure in the last six piano sonatas of Scriabin. Ph.D. thesis, University of Rochester (1987)
18. Zydek, S.: The harmonic and melodic language in Alexander Scriabin's Sonata No. 5, Op. 53 (2010). essay for Dr. Janners' course Music Theory II

ComMute—Towards a Computational Musical Theory of Everything

Guerino Mazzola[✉]

School of Music, University of Minnesota,
2106 Fourth Street South, Minneapolis, MN 55455, USA
mazzola@umn.edu
http://www.encyclospace.org

Abstract. This paper draws future perspectives of music as a comprising cultural achievement of humans. We discuss the role of music for mathematics and physics from Pythagoras to String Theory, its global human presence, transcending specific fields of knowledge in its synthetical force that unifies distant fields of knowledge and action in the concrete and abstract realms.

Keywords: Theory of Everything · Future music theory · String theory

1 The Physical Theory of Everything (ToE)

Before we discuss the idea of a musical Theory of Everything (ToE), we recall the physical ToE and its motivations. This theory claims the integration of the four fundamental physical force types: electromagnetic, weak, strong, and gravitation. The electromagnetic and weak are already united, and called "electro-weak". The still hypothetical integration of the electro-weak force with the strong force is called GUT: Great Unification Theory. Integration means that all these forces are special cases of a fundamental force, which splits into the four forces by a breaking of structural symmetries when energies are below a threshold.

Let us stress that even the reduction to those four forces is everything but evident. For example, would you guess that the mechanical forces of, say, a hammer hitting a nail, are the same type as the forces of adhesion of a glue? Or the forces of chemical reactions? Or the force of sunlight tanning your skin? They all pertain to the electromagnetic force type. The physical sciences and their outlets in chemistry have achieved an incredible reduction of the apparent variety of force types. This means that the surface of physical actions does not prevent a deep theory from unifying superficial diversities. We should keep in mind this fact when stepping over to the musical realm.

It is remarkable that "Everything" in physics relates to physical forces, but not to psychological or symbolic realities. This restriction is significant since it avoids any physicalist totalitarism. Physics does not claim a total explanation

© Springer Nature Switzerland AG 2019
M. Montiel et al. (Eds.): MCM 2019, LNAI 11502, pp. 21–30, 2019.
https://doi.org/10.1007/978-3-030-21392-3_2

of this world, physics deals with the outer nature and has never tried to reduce psychological or symbolic realities to physics. Quite the opposite: Prominent theoretical physicists, such as Roger Penrose (Fig. 1), argue that the innermost physical ontology might rely on mathematics. He also argues in [15] that physics has not yet included the psychological realm of the human mind in its basic conceptual architecture.

Fig. 1. Theoretical physicist Roger Penrose.

Despite the success of simplifying physical force types to three (electro-weak, strong, and gravitation), it is not clear why the ToE and even the weaker GUT should work. Physicists seem to believe in an ultimate unification, probably because of some monotheist paradigm: There is only one innermost, well yes: divine, entity that shapes the universe. The success gives them enough motivation to work in this direction with an impressive shared social, organizational,[1] and economic effort called "Big Science", see [4].

2   Why Would We Think About a Musical ToE?

In view of the fundamental role of music in all cultures,[2] it is not astonishing to think of a unified view of music in the spirit of the physical ToE:

Could it be that the variety of musical expressivity is the unfolding of a unique fundamental "force field"?

Before we delve into this hypothesis of musical unification, we should understand that the wording COMMUTE, meaning *Computational Music Theory of*

---

[1] The Internet was invented by Tim Berners-Lee at the CERN to coordinate nuclear research efforts globally.

[2] Even where music is virtually forbidden, with the Taliban, for example, its force is recognized, and that is why it is forbidden, sad irony.

Everything, would not, similar to ToE, include strictly everything. This is also why we add the adjective "computational". The idea is to think of a music theory that is computational; other theories might exist, but they are not addressed here.

Moreover, it is also, similar to ToE, not intended to subsume all realities, the physical, psychological, or symbolic. Nevertheless, recall that the musical idea has been a driving force in the development of physics and astronomy from Pythagoras to String Theory. It is not evident in how far a ComMute would connect to ToE, but one should keep in mind these deep relationships, especially when a composer wants to justify his/her overall motivation.

The physical ToE is a precise hypothesis, the unification of all physical force types, independently of how this would work. For a ComMute the analogy to physics is problematic. Music does not share the simple idea of forces which are embodied by quanta.[3] However, the core idea of Mazzola's modulation model (see Fig. 2) was an exact analogy to physical force quanta, musical symmetries being the analogy of forces, while modulation quanta (sets of pitches) are the analogy of physical quanta. But this is a special situation that cannot for the time being be generalized to general modulations.

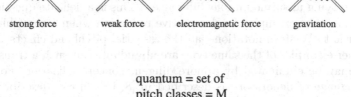

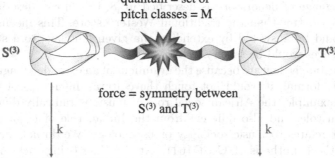

Fig. 2. Physical quanta and musical quantum M for a modulation from tonality S to tonality T; k is the cadence.

Another type of forces was used in the mathematical model of counterpoint (see [2]). Here, the dichotomy of consonances and dissonance was deformed by a symmetry in the role of an elastic force acting on the set of intervals.

---

[3] These are photons for the electromagnetic force, W and Z bosons for the weak force, gluons for strong force, and hypothetical gravitons for gravitation.

The idea of forces in music (theory) is not new, see [7]. Already Schoenberg used the metaphor of erotic (!) forces to explain harmonic tension in [17]. But there is no such universally acclaimed theoretical architecture as in physics, forces may show up (metaphorically or litteraly), but music has a number of very different structural paradigms, such as local-global duality, geometric ideas (the harmonic Moebius strip, for example), or gestural and topological approaches.

What are arguments against such a strong COMMUTE hypothesis? To begin with, the individual creativity of a musical composer or improviser seems to forbid any "universalist" background. This is the heritage of the Renaissance movement, which opposes to the Pythagorean "world formula" in an irreducible individual genealogy. This is however not stringent since a painter, for example, may create a deeply individual work of art with colors being completely described by the electromagnetic force that defines light and its action within the human eye. And on a higher level of structural abstraction, the variety of musical transformations can be described by a huge mathematical group, typically ranging within the cardinality[4] of 10^{40}. This is all comprised within a very clear and unified conceptual architecture of theory, but such a virtually infinite number guarantees an unlimited variety of individual utterances.

Another argument against COMMUTE would be the suspicion that this hypothesis is a consequence of the Western (Christian) colonialist mentality. Are we trying to unite all musical cultures under a big equalizing umbrella? And thereby destroying unsurmountable differences? This is a delicate question since we already have the example of a destructive reduction when transcribing Arab Maqam music to Western notation—all the essential pitchbend effects are eliminated. Other examples of the same type are abundant. But such a translational pathology may be eliminated by a more diligent conceptualization. For example, the language of denotators as described in [8, Ch. 6] can describe musical objects much better than the traditional Western score. This means that this question could be answered by extending the given language to a state where some differences would be taken care of.

This question is delicate because the argument of an extended language seems to be purely formal, it would not touch the cultural differences of the role of music. For example, the African social role of music is radically different from the Western role, and also different from the Indian role of Raga music, say. This aspect relates to music sociology or psychology. We do not include these aspects in the hypothesis of COMMUTE. At the time being such an inclusion seems too ambitious and also dangerous for the named reasons. But we shall see below in Sect. 3.3 that on the level of music theory, relations between European counterpoint and Raga music are appearing. Perhaps should one also reflect upon the idea of "fundamentally incomparable cultures" in view of a separation and

---

[4] The number of affine transformations on the local score of the software [8, Ch. 49] is

$$10'445'260'466'832'483'579'436'191'905'936'640'000 \approx 1.04453 \times 10^{37}.$$

even the famous "clash of civilizations". On the level of human rights the vast majority of cultures have agreed on a shared canon, such as the *habeas corpus* principle. In the movie *Teak Leaves at the Temples* [14], Mazzola argued that the language of gestures might be an approach to a non-divisional understanding of musical cultures.

Let us terminate this introduction with a discussion of the specification "computational" in CᴏᴍMᴜᴛᴇ. This means two things. First, such a music theory should be covering all that is accessible by mathematical methods and concepts. Second, it should be accessible via computational engines such as computers. This is a restriction of "everything" to "computational everything". It has the same function as in physics: What is not accessible in this way is not physically relevant. It is simply an expression of modesty, one only considers topics that are 'visible' to computation. Of course, as musical research progresses, more and more things may become 'visible'. But it is also risky to restrict one's views to what is actually computable. For example, Stephan Hawking claimed that the concept of a God is superfluous in physics. He did not consider the language and spirit of mathematics as being a *conditio sine qua non* for physics. The computational principle is pre-physical, and Hawking forgot to ask where we get that language from. Radical neuroscientists might argue that mathematics is an artifact of neurons, i.e., a product of physical reality. But any proof there of would use huge mathematical tools, which creates a circular argument, it would not explain anything.

In this sense, CᴏᴍMᴜᴛᴇ is a methodological limitation and should not be taken as a definition of music, but as a perspective, which can be tested and used to shape concrete progress. Nevertheless, the hypothesis is a very strong one, similar to ToE, or even more tricky because the conceptual landscape in music is less unified than in physics.

3   Some Directions Towards CᴏᴍMᴜᴛᴇ

In the following sections we want to describe a number of vectors towards such a CᴏᴍMᴜᴛᴇ, without claiming completeness.

3.1   Harmony and Rhythm

Harmony and rhythm have played very different roles in the history and cultural diversity of music. For example, recent research [13] stresses the fundamental difference in harmony and rhythm between classical European and African music. The complexity of Western harmony corresponds to the complexity of African polyrhythms, and vice versa: the simplicity of Western rhythms corresponds to the simplicity of African harmony. This difference however does not mean that rhythm cannot be dealt with like harmony. In fact, both phenomena deal with periodic sets of events, octave periodicity in harmony vs. time periodicity of rhythm. In mathematical music theory, Mazzola's modulation model is not limited to pitch, but can equally be applied to time, just rotate pitch by 90 degrees into time. This has been used for rhythmic modulation in the first movement of the composition *Synthesis*, but see [8, Ch. 50.2].

This double periodicity has also been used to investigate periodic structures in pitch or time using the finite Fourier decomposition of periodic functions. The classical theory of Fourier for time functions is a classical theory (partials, Fast Fourier Transform, etc.), but the (octave-)periodic pitch functions have been analyzed only recently by David Lewin, Ian Quinn, and Emmanuel Amiot [1]. This research proves that harmony and rhythm could converge to a unified theory of periodic functions in a number of parameter spaces. And such a unification could eventually create a less diversified perspective of Western and African musical cultures. Of course, the difference between music sociology of Europe and Africa remains untouched: The African music culture is shared by everybody, from childhood to adult life, Africans are musicians, whereas the European musician as a specifically educated person doesn't play that African standard role. This difference may vanish in the future if we learn to think in pitch and time according to the same theoretical and compositional paradigms.

3.2   Gestures for Harmony and Counterpoint

In Mazzola's mathematical music theory, modulation theory and counterpoint were developed using symmetries on pitch class spaces. This was not a topological approach and had its limits. For modulation theory the paring of tonalities was only permitted for tonalities in the same orbit of a symmetry group. Modulation from a major tonality to a gipsy tonality or even a pentatonic one was not conceived. A similar restriction happened to contrapuntal concepts. This model used a finite number of consonances selected by specific symmetries. It would crash if we had to consider an infinity of consonances in a continuous and therefore infinite interval model of counterpoint.

Both restrictions could be solved by a shared new language: musical gestures. Modulation could be remodeled as a gestural deformation of chords instead of a symmetric action [10]. Such a deformation does no longer require the two tonalities living in the same symmetry orbit. Using gestures and their homology theory, counterpoint could be remodeled independently of the number of consonant intervals at stake [2, Ch. 10].

This is an example of gesture theory being a unifier of music theory, an interesting parallel to physics, where string theory is a strong candidate for ToE. Strings are analogues to gestures in music theory, in other words: gestures are the musical analog to strings.

3.3   Counterpoint Worlds for Different Musical Cultures

The mathematical theory of counterpoint has not only embraced Fux tradition, but also opened with its five new worlds connections to Raga music and Scriabin's mystic chord. This theory is on its way to a global counterpoint theory. Connecting counterpoint models with Indian music is a sensational bridge between totally different musical cultures. We should recall here that connections between

Western and Raga music have been investigated by Robert Morris and Chitravina N. Ravikiran under the title of "Melharmony" [16]. This theory[5] "aims to create chords and counterpoints based on the melodic rules of evolved systems across the world." It could happen that our counterpoint worlds and melharmony converge to a new synthesis of two strong theoretical traditions.

3.4   Complex Time for Unification of Mental and Physical Realities in Music

The recent revolution of the time concept in physics was introduced by Stephen Hawking (among others) in order to solve singularity problems of the Big Bang model of the evolution of our universe in the initial moment some 13.8 billion years ago. Hawking's concept of time switches from the real time axis to the plane of complex numbers: Time now has two real coordinates $t = t_{Real} + i.t_{Im}$, it pronounces the real time t_{Real} and the imaginary time t_{Im}. This complex ontology has also been proposed and studied by physicists Bars and Terning [3]. This concept unifies Descartes' *res extensa*, the physical reality, with real time t_{Real}, with *res cogitans*, the thinking, mental reality, with imaginary time t_{Im}. This is a strong step towards a unification of a well-known duality in music: thinking and making, the physical utterance of performance vs. the mental construction in composition, performance, and improvisation. In [12, Ch. 78] were sketched ways of structurally connecting these two realities by means of world sheets, which are completely analogous to world sheets in physical string theory.

The duality of thinking and making in music has been a dividing force between theorists and performers in the Western music world. It is also present in the academic structure where "applied" scholars (teaching instrumental fields) are separated from "academic" scholars (music theory, musicology, education, ethnomusicology, music psychology). Their interaction is reduced to a poor "laissez vivre" and is not based on a shared reality, a fact that complex time theories might eliminate in the future.

3.5   Symbolic and Real Gestures

The idea of complex time has also been applied to connect symbolic gestures on the score to real gestures of the performing artist, see [12, Ch. 78]. This result fosters the unification of thinking and making. Eventually, this should help unify these two aspects of the art of music to a comprising reality.

3.6   Unifying Note Performance and Gestural Performance: Lie Operators

Computational performance theory was strongly developed by the Stockholm group around Sundberg [5]. This approach was concerned with the transformation of notes to sound events. It could be shown by the work of the Zurich group

---

[5] Citation form Wikipedia.

of Mazzola [11, Ch. 39.7] that important cases of such a performative transformation can be described by classical Lie operators from differential geometry. More precisely, the transition from a given performance stage to a more refined one is described by a Lie operator acting on the given performance vector field. When performance theory was extended to gestural performance, i.e., the transformation of symbolic gestures in the score to physical gestures of a musician, it could be shown that the same Lie operator formalism can be carried over to gestures [12, Ch. 78.2.13]. In other words, *there is now a unified formalism of performance theory for notes and for gestures*.

3.7 Unifying Composition and Improvisation?

It is an open question in how far composition and improvisation could be unified as special cases of a unique still hidden dynamics. We know of many famous composers, such as Beethoven or Mozart, that their compositions were often created from improvisation, see the genesis of Beethoven's Sonata Op. 109 [6], for example. In the Indian tradition of Raga, improvisation and composition are intimately related on the basis of mela scales. Perhaps the combination of flow concepts and gestures, as sketched in the free jazz book [9], could help find a unified understanding of musical creativity in composition and improvisation.

4   Imagining Big Science for ComMute

A future music theory that includes Big Science should above all change some of the dominating traditional characteristics of music theory and musicology as follows:

1. *Change "Meditative" into "Operational"!* We argue that it is wiser to try out several variants of a composition on a sequencer than to meditate on a fictitious best solution.
2. *Change "Metaphoric" into "Explicit"!* For example, it is advantageous to look for tempo curves instead of nebulous metaphors of movement.
3. *Change "Ubiquity" into "Topography"!* In fact, it is nonsense to postulate that the musical work has a monolithic omnipresence—and to be deceived if you won't find it that way round. Better look for topographically differentiated traces of what could contribute to a distributed concept of the musical work.
4. *Change "Ontological" into "Semiotic"!* Musicology often tries to find "the true and essential meaning" of something instead of distinguishing between layers of signification which are best described by semiotic categories such as denotation or connotation.
5. *Change "Magic" into "Communicative"!* The old-fashioned and absurd swearing to the genius of a great composer should be replaced by communication of ideas and perspectives.
6. *Change "Transcendence" into "Precision"!* It would be more interesting and scientific to publish detailed analyses of musical works instead of writing all those feuilletonistic books on composers. After all, the tools are ready; the minds should realize this.

This list might sound provocative, but without these changes no Big Science in music will be feasible. Perhaps are we now facing a transformation of music theory that is comparable to the Galilean transformation, which replaced reading Aristotelian philosophical books on physics by computational and experimental methods.

With this in mind, musical creativity will dramatically change its face with Big Science. With the elimination of the outdated genius paradigm, music will be more of a collaborative research with huge technological tools for its globally distributed realization. This collaborative style will also eliminate the strict separation between artist and audience. And the artistic virtuosity in the performance of musical works will become a niche exercise that can be performed better by robots. This does not mean that human instrumental virtuosity will disappear, but it will play the completely different role of a thinking-making research, not of a (however sophisticated) performance of given templates.

References

1. Amiot, E.: Music Through Fourier Space. Springer Series Computational Music Science. Springer, Heidelberg (2016). https://doi.org/10.1007/978-3-319-45581-5
2. Agustín-Aquino, O.A., Junod, J., Mazzola, G.: Computational Counterpoint Worlds. Springer Series Computational Music Science. Springer, Heidelberg (2015). https://doi.org/10.1007/978-3-319-11236-7
3. Bars, I., Terning, J.: Extra Dimensions in Space and Time. Springer, New York (2010). https://doi.org/10.1007/978-0-387-77638-5
4. http://www.cern.ch
5. Friberg, A., Bresin, R., Sundberg, J.: Overview of the KTH rule system for music performance. Adv. Exp. Psychol. **2**, 145–161 (2006). Special issue on Music Performance
6. Kinderman, W.: Artaria 195. University of Illinois Press, Urbana and Chicago (2003)
7. Larson, S.: Musical Forces. Indiana University Press, Bloomington (2012)
8. Mazzola, G., et al.: The Topos of Music—Geometric Logic of Concepts, Theory, and Performance. Birkhäuser, Basel (2002)
9. Mazzola, G., Cherlin, P.B.: Flow, Gesture, and Spaces in Free Jazz-Towards a Theory of Collaboration. Springer Series Computational Music Science. Springer, Heidelberg (2009). https://doi.org/10.1007/978-3-540-92195-0
10. Mazzola, G.: Gestural dynamics in modulation: (towards) a musical string theory. In: Pareyon, G., Pina-Romero, S., Agustin-Aquino, O.A., Lluis-Puebla, E. (eds.) The Musical-Mathematical Mind. Springer Series Computational Music Science, pp. 171–188. Springer, Heidelberg (2017). https://doi.org/10.1007/978-3-319-47337-6_18
11. Mazzola, G.: The Topos of Music II: Performance. Springer Series Computational Music Science. Springer, Heidelberg (2018). https://doi.org/10.1007/978-3-319-64444-8
12. Mazzola, G., et al.: The Topos of Music III: Gestures. Springer Series Computational Music Science. Springer, Heidelberg (2018). https://doi.org/10.1007/978-3-319-64481-3

13. Munyaradzi, G., Zimidzi, W.: Comparison of western music and African music. Creat. Educ. **3**(2), 193–195 (2012)
14. Nugroho, G.: Teak Leaves at the Temples. DVD, Trimax Enterprises Film, New York (2007)
15. Penrose, R.: The Road to Reality. Vintage, London (2002)
16. Ravikiran, C.N.: Robert morris and the concept of melharmony. Perspect. New Music **52**(2), 154–161 (2014)
17. Schönberg, A.: Harmonielehre (1911). Universal Edition, Wien (1966)

Algebraic and Other Abstract Mathematical Approaches to Understanding Musical Objects

Groupoids and Wreath Products of Musical Transformations: A Categorical Approach from poly-Klumpenhouwer Networks

Alexandre Popoff[1]([⊠]) [iD], Moreno Andreatta[2] [iD], and Andrée Ehresmann[3]

[1] 119 Rue de Montreuil, 75011 Paris, France
al.popoff@free.fr
[2] IRCAM/CNRS/Sorbonne Université and IRMA-GREAM,
Université de Strasbourg, Strasbourg, France
Moreno.Andreatta@ircam.fr, andreatta@math.unistra.fr
[3] Université de Picardie, LAMFA, Amiens, France
andree.ehresmann@u-picardie.fr

Abstract. Klumpenhouwer networks (K-nets) and their recent categorical generalization, poly-Klumpenhouwer networks (PK-nets), are network structures allowing both the analysis of musical objects through the study of the transformations between their constituents, and the comparison of these objects between them. In this work, we propose a groupoid-based approach to transformational music theory, in which transformations of PK-nets are considered rather than ordinary sets of musical objects. We show how groupoids of musical transformations can be constructed, and provide an application of their use in post-tonal music analysis with Berg's *Four pieces for clarinet and piano, Op. 5/2.* In a second part, we show how these groupoids are linked to wreath products through the notion of groupoid bisections.

Keywords: Klumpenhouwer network ·
Transformational music theory · Category theory · Groupoid ·
Wreath product

1 Groupoids of Musical Transformations

The recent field of transformational music theory, pioneered by the work of Lewin [7,8], shifts the music-theoretical and analytical focus from the "object-oriented" musical content to an operational musical process, wherein transformations between musical elements are emphasized. Within this framework, Klumpenhouwer networks (K-nets) [5,6,9] are network structures allowing both the analysis of musical objects through the study of the transformations between their constituents, and the comparison of these objects between them. A K-net can be informally defined as a labelled graph, wherein the labels of the vertices

© Springer Nature Switzerland AG 2019
M. Montiel et al. (Eds.): MCM 2019, LNAI 11502, pp. 33–45, 2019.
https://doi.org/10.1007/978-3-030-21392-3_3

belong to the set of pitch classes, and each arrow is labelled with a transformation that maps the pitch class at the source vertex to the pitch class at the target vertex. The K-net concept, anchored both in group theory and graph theory [12], has been later formalized in a more categorical setting, first as limits of diagrams within the framework of denotators [11], and later as a special case of a categorical construction called poly-Klumpenhouwer networks (PK-nets) [16–18]. K-nets are usually compared in terms of isographies, which correspond to isomorphisms of PK-nets in the categorical approach.

This paper proposes a groupoid-based approach to transformational music theory, in which transformations of PK-nets are considered rather than ordinary sets of musical objects. The first section shows how groupoids of musical transformations can be constructed, with an application to post-tonal music analysis. The second section shows how groupoids are linked to wreath products, which feature prominently in transformational music theory [4], through the notion of groupoid bisections, thus bridging the groupoid approach to the more traditional group-based approach of transformational music theory.

1.1   Introduction to PK-Nets

The groupoid-based approach to transformational music theory presented in this paper stems from the constitutive elements of poly-Klumpenhouwer networks which have been introduced previously [16,17]. We recall the categorical definition of a PK-net, which generalizes the original notion of K-nets in various ways. We assume that the basic notions of transformational music analysis are known, in particular with regards to the so-called T/I group and its action on the set of the twelve pitch classes (see [3] for additional information).

Definition 1. *Let* **C** *be a category, and* S *a functor from* **C** *to the category* **Sets** *of (small) sets. Let* Δ *be a small category and* R *a functor from* Δ *to* **Sets** *with non-empy values. A* PK-net *of form* R *and of support* S *is a 4-tuple* (R, S, F, ϕ), *in which* F *is a functor from* Δ *to* **C**, *and* ϕ *is a natural transformation from* R *to* SF.

A PK-net can be represented by the diagram of Fig. 1(a). The category **C** and the functor $S: \mathbf{C} \to \mathbf{Sets}$ represent the musical context of analysis.

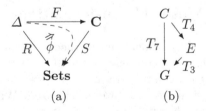

(a)   (b)

Fig. 1. (a) Diagrammatic representation of a PK-net (R, S, F, ϕ). (b) A K-net describing a major triad. The arrows are labelled with specific transformations in the T/I group indicating the transformations between pitch classes.

The morphisms of the category **C** are the musical transformations of interest. Any category **C** along with a functor $S\colon \mathbf{C} \to \mathbf{Sets}$ may be considered: transformational music theory often relies on a group acting on a given set of objects, the T/I group acting on the set of the twelve pitch classes being one of the most well-known examples. The category Δ serves as the abstract skeleton of the PK-net: as such, its objects and morphisms are abstract entities, which are labelled by the functor F from Δ to the category **C**. The objects of Δ do not represent the actual musical elements of a PK-net: these are introduced by the functor R from Δ to **Sets**. This functor sends each object of Δ to an actual set, which may contain more than a single element, and whose elements abstractly represent the musical objects of study. In the same way the morphisms of Δ represent abstract relationships which are given a concrete meaning by the functor F, the elements in the images of R are given a label in the images of S through the natural transformation ϕ, which ensures the transformational coherence of the whole diagram.

1.2   Reinterpreting the Constitutive Elements of a PK-Net

A basic Klumpenhouwer network describing a C major triad is shown in Fig. 1(b). In the framework of PK-Nets, this network corresponds to the data of

1. a category Δ_3 with three objects X, Y, and Z, and three non-trivial morphisms $f\colon X \to Y$, $g\colon Y \to Z$, and $g \circ f\colon X \to Z$ between them, and
2. a category **C** taken here to be the T/I group, with its usual action $S\colon T/I \to$ **Sets** on the set of the twelve pitch-classes, and
3. a functor $F\colon \Delta_3 \to \mathbf{C}$ such that $F(f) = T_4$, $F(g) = T_3$, and $F(g \circ f) = T_7$, and
4. a functor $R\colon \Delta_3 \to$ **Sets** sending each object of Δ_3 to a singleton, and a natural transformation ϕ sending these singletons to the appropriate pitch-classes in the image of **C** by S.

Upon examination of these constitutive elements, it readily appears that the "major triad" nature of this chord is entirely determined by the category Δ_3 and the functor $F\colon \Delta_3 \to \mathbf{C}$. The images of the morphisms of Δ_3 under F reflect the fact that a major triad is made up of a major third with a minor third stacked above it, resulting in a fifth. This observation is not specific to major triads. Consider for example the chord $\{D, E, G\}$, which is a representative of the set class $[0, 2, 5]$. This chord may be described by a PK-Net in which Δ_3 is the same as above, and in which we consider a different functor $F'\colon \Delta_3 \to \mathbf{C}$ such that $F(f) = T_2$, $F(g) = T_3$, and $F(g \circ f) = T_5$.

One may go further by considering pitch-class sets which are not necessarily transpositionnally related. Figure 2 shows an excerpt of Webern's *Three Little Pieces for Cello and Piano, Op. 11/2*, at bars 4–5, along with a PK-net interpretation of each three-note segment. These three-note segments are clearly not related by transposition, yet the corresponding represented networks share the same functor $\Delta_3 \to \mathbf{C}$. By abstracting this observation, one can consider that

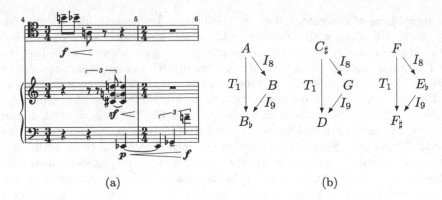

(a)   (b)

Fig. 2. (a) Webern, Op. 11/2, bars 4–5. (b) PK-nets corresponding to each of three-note segment of (a).

these three-note pitch-class sets belong to the same *generalized musical class for the PK-net*, which is defined by this particular functor $\Delta_3 \to \mathbf{C}$. The main point of this paper is to generalize further these observations by considering functors $F: \Delta \to \mathbf{C}$ as *generalized musical classes for a PK-net*.

Definition 2. *Let* $\mathbf{C}$ *be a category, and* Δ *be a small category. A* generalized musical class for a PK-net of diagram Δ *is a functor* $F: \Delta \to \mathbf{C}$.

As is well-known in category theory, functors $F: \Delta \to \mathbf{C}$ form a category, known as *the category of functors* $\mathbf{C}^{\Delta}$.

Definition 3. *The* category of functors $\mathbf{C}^{\Delta}$ *has*

1. *functors* $F: \Delta \to \mathbf{C}$ *as objects, and*
2. *natural transformations* $\eta: F \to F'$ *between functors* $F: \Delta \to \mathbf{C}$ *and* $F': \Delta \to \mathbf{C}$ *as morphisms.*

These natural transformations can be seen as generalized musical transformations between the corresponding generalized musical classes. The additional data of functors R and S, and of a natural transformation $\phi: R \to SF$, leads to individual musical sets derived from the generalized musical class $F: \Delta \to \mathbf{C}$ for a PK-net of diagram Δ. The purpose of this paper is to investigate the structure of $\mathbf{C}^{\Delta}$ and of specific functors from this category to **Sets**, and to relate these constructions with known group-theoretical results in transformational music analysis.

One may notice that different categories Δ and functors $F: \Delta \to \mathbf{C}$ may describe the same musical sets. For example, the major triad of Fig. 1(b) may also be described using a category Γ with three objects X, Y, and Z, and only two non-trivial morphisms $f: X \to Y$, $g: X \to Z$, between them, and a functor $F'': \Gamma \to \mathbf{C} = T/I$ sending f to T_4 and g to T_7. This alternative description focuses on the major third and the fifth without explicitly referencing the minor third. In a broader setting, one can even consider both transposition and inversion operations. For example, the functor F'' could instead send f to I_4 and g to I_7, emphasizing the inversions in the C major triad. Instead of being a limitation, this possibility allows for various transformations between chord types to be examined, as will be seen in the rest of the paper.

As stated previously, the category $\mathbf{C}$ is often a group in musical applications. The following proposition establishes the structure of the category of functors $\mathbf{C}^{\Delta}$ when Δ is a poset with a bottom element O and $\mathbf{C}$ is a group $\mathbf{G}$ considered as a single-object category.

Proposition 1. *Let Δ be a poset with a bottom element O and $\mathbf{G}$ be a group considered as a category. Then*

1. *the category of functors $\mathbf{G}^{\Delta}$ is a groupoid, and*
2. *for any two objects F and F' of $\mathbf{G}^{\Delta}$ the hom-set $Hom(F, F')$ can be bijectively identified with the set of elements of $\mathbf{G}$.*

Proof. Given two objects F and F' of $\mathbf{G}^{\Delta}$, i.e. two functors $F: \Delta \to \mathbf{G}$ and $F': \Delta \to \mathbf{G}$, any natural transformation $\eta: F \to F'$ between them is invertible, since the components of η are invertible morphisms of $\mathbf{G}$. Thus, the category of functors $\mathbf{G}^{\Delta}$ is a groupoid. Since Δ is a poset with a bottom element O, the natural transformation η is entirely determined by the component η_O, which can be freely chosen in $\mathbf{G}$. Thus the hom-set $Hom(F, F')$ can be bijectively identified with the set of elements of $\mathbf{G}$. $\square$

Since in such a case the elements of the hom-set $Hom(F, F')$ can be uniquely identified with the elements of $\mathbf{G}$, we will use the notation $g^{FF'}$, with $g \in \mathbf{G}$, to designate an element of $Hom(F, F')$ in $\mathbf{G}^{\Delta}$.

We now consider a functor $R: \Delta \to \mathbf{Sets}$ and a functor $S: \mathbf{G} \to \mathbf{Sets}$. For any object F of $\mathbf{G}^{\Delta}$, let $\mathrm{Nat}(R, SF)$ be the set of all natural transformations $\phi: R \to SF$.

Proposition 2. *There exists a canonical functor $P: \mathbf{G}^{\Delta} \to \mathbf{Sets}$ such that for any object F of $\mathbf{G}^{\Delta}$, $P(F) = Nat(R, SF)$.*

Proof. We consider the map $P: \mathbf{G}^{\Delta} \to \mathbf{Sets}$, which sends each object F of $\mathbf{G}^{\Delta}$ to the set $\mathrm{Nat}(R, SF)$. Then, given two objects F and F' of $\mathbf{G}^{\Delta}$ and any morphism $\eta: F \to F'$ between them, we can construct the image of η by P as the map $P(\eta): \mathrm{Nat}(R, SF) \to \mathrm{Nat}(R, SF')$ sending a natural transformation ϕ of $\mathrm{Nat}(R, SF)$ to the natural transformation $S\eta \circ \phi$ of $\mathrm{Nat}(R, SF')$. It is easily verified that P is a functor. $\square$

1.3 Transformations of Generalized Musical Classes for a PK-net

We now consider the specific case where the category $\mathbf{G}$ is the T/I group considered as a single-object category. We wish here to give examples of transformations of generalized musical classes for a PK-net, in the particular case where

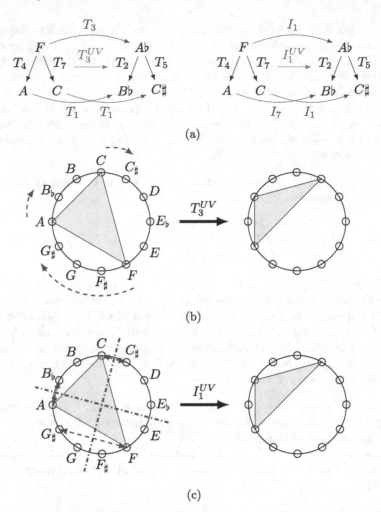

(a)

(b)

(c)

Fig. 3. (a) Action of the morphisms T_3^{UV} and I_1^{UV} of $(T/I)^\Gamma$ on the PK-net representing the F major chord, resulting in the $\{A\flat, B\flat, C\sharp\}$ chord. The constitutive elements of the PK-nets (the functor R, S, and the natural transformation ϕ) have been omitted here for clarity). (b) and (c) Graphical representation of the transposition and inversion components of the above morphisms, and their action on the individual pitch classes of the F major chord (dashed lines).

Δ is the category Γ introduced above, and with specific functors $U : \Gamma \to \mathbf{G}$ and $V : \Gamma \to \mathbf{G}$. Our goal is to detail the structure of the hom-set $\mathrm{Hom}(U, V)$. We consider the following objects of $(T/I)^\Gamma$:

- the functor $U : \Gamma \to T/I$ sending f to T_4 and g to T_7, and
- the functor $V : \Gamma \to T/I$ sending f to T_2 and g to T_5.

These functors model the set classes of prime form $[0,4,7]$ (major triad) and $[0,2,5]$. Let $\eta\colon U \to V$ be a natural transformation: it is uniquely determined by the component η_X, which is an element of T/I, from which we can derive the components η_Y and η_Z as follows.

- If $\eta_X = T_p$, with p in $\{0\ldots11\}$, then we must have $\eta_Y T_4 = T_2 T_p$, and $\eta_Z T_7 = T_5 T_p$. This leads to $\eta_Y = T_{p+10}$, and $\eta_Z = T_{p+10}$.
- If $\eta_X = I_p$, with p in $\{0\ldots11\}$, then we must have $\eta_Y T_4 = T_2 I_p$, and $\eta_Z T_7 = T_5 I_p$. This leads to $\eta_Y = I_{p+6}$, and $\eta_Z = I_p$.

Unlike the known action on triads of the transpositions and inversions of the T/I group, wherein the same group element operates on every pitch class of the chord, the two types of morphisms of $\mathrm{Hom}(U,V)$ have different components for each object of Γ. The morphisms T_p^{UV} can thus be considered as "generalized" transpositions, and the morphisms I_p^{UV} as "generalized" inversions between objects U and V. Figure 3 illustrates the action of these morphisms on the PK-net representing the F major chord, resulting in the $\{A\flat, B\flat, C\sharp\}$ chord.

1.4   An Application to Berg's Op. 5/2

To illustrate the above concepts, we will focus on a small atonal example from Berg's *Four pieces for clarinet and piano, Op. 5/2*. Figure 4 shows a reduction of the piano right hand part at bars 5–6. To analyse this progression, we consider the group $\mathbf{G} = T/I$, the category Γ described above, and the corresponding groupoid of functors $(T/I)^\Gamma$. In particular we consider the following objects of $(T/I)^\Gamma$:

- the functor $U\colon \Gamma \to T/I$ sending f to I_3 and g to I_{10},
- the functor $U'\colon \Gamma \to T/I$ sending f to I_7 and g to I_3,

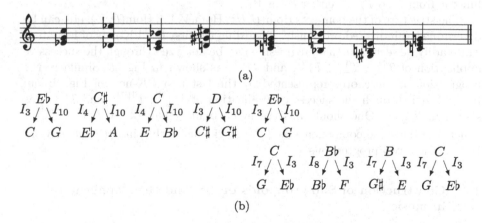

(a)

(b)

Fig. 4. (a) Berg, Op. 5/2, reduction of the piano right hand part at bars 5–6. (b) A PK-net interpretation of the first five chords (top row) and of the last four chords (bottom row) of the progression of (a).

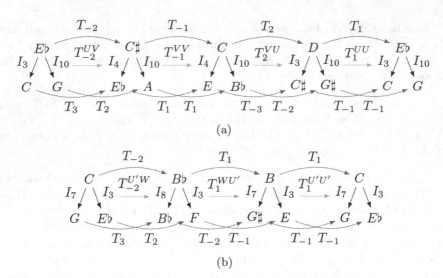

Fig. 5. Analysis of the progression of the (a) first five chords and of the (b) last four chords of Fig. 4(a) using morphisms of $(T/I)^{\Gamma}$.

- the functor $V: \Gamma \to T/I$ sending f to I_4 and g to I_{10}, and
- the functor $W: \Gamma \to T/I$ sending f to I_8 and g to I_3.

We also consider the functor $R: \Gamma \to \mathbf{Sets}$ sending each object of Γ to a singleton, and the functor $S: T/I \to \mathbf{Sets}$ given by the action of the T/I group on the set of the twelve pitch-classes. It can then easily be checked that the first five chords of the progression of Fig. 4a are instances of PK-nets using R and S, and whose functor from Γ to T/I is either U or V, as shown in Fig. 4b. Similarly, the last four chords of the progression of Fig. 4a are instances of PK-nets whose functor from Γ to T/I is either U' or W.

The structure of the hom-sets $\mathrm{Hom}(U, U)$, $\mathrm{Hom}(V, V)$, $\mathrm{Hom}(U, V)$, etc. can be determined as indicated previously. Regarding the first five PK-nets of Fig. 4b, it can readily be seen that this progression can be analyzed through the successive application of T_{-2}^{UV}, T_{-1}^{VV}, T_{2}^{VU}, and T_{1}^{UU}, as shown in Fig. 5a. Similarly the progression of the chords represented by the last four PK-nets of Fig. 4b can be analyzed through the successive application of $T_{-2}^{U'W}$, $T_{1}^{WU'}$, and $T_{1}^{U'U'}$, as shown in Fig. 5b. One should observe in particular that $T_{2}^{VU} \circ T_{-1}^{VV} = T_{1}^{VU}$, which has the same components as $T_{1}^{WU'}$, evidencing the similar logic at work behind these two progressions.

1.5 Construction of Sub-groupoids of $\mathbf{G}^{\Delta}$ and their application in music

In the examples considered in Sects. 1.3 and 1.4, for any object U of the groupoid $(T/I)^{\Gamma}$, the hom-set $\mathrm{Hom}(U, U)$ can be bijectively identified with elements of the

T/I group, and thus contains "generalized" transpositions and inversions. For transpositionally-related chords however, it may be useful to consider only a sub-category of $(T/I)^\Gamma$ wherein the hom-set $\mathrm{Hom}(U,U)$ only contains transposition-like morphisms. We show here how such a sub-category can be constructed by exploiting the extension structure of the T/I group.

We consider the general case where $\mathbf{G}$ is an extension $1 \to \mathbf{Z} \to \mathbf{G} \to \mathbf{H} \to 1$. This is the case for the T/I group for example, which is an extension of the form $1 \to \mathbb{Z}_{12} \to T/I \to \mathbb{Z}_2 \to 1$. Since $\mathbf{G}$ is an extension, the elements of $\mathbf{G}$ can be written as $g = (z, h)$ with $z \in \mathbf{Z}$, and $h \in \mathbf{H}$. Given a poset Δ, we define a functor $\Pi \colon \mathbf{G}^\Delta \to \mathbf{H}^\Delta$ induced by the homomorphism $\pi \colon \mathbf{G} \to \mathbf{H}$ as follows.

Definition 4. *For a given poset Δ with a bottom element, the functor $\Pi \colon \mathbf{G}^\Delta \to \mathbf{H}^\Delta$ induced by the homomorphism $\pi \colon \mathbf{G} \to \mathbf{H}$, is the functor which*

- *is the identity on objects, and*
- *sends any morphism $g^{FF'} = (z,h)^{FF'}$ in $\mathbf{G}^\Delta$ to $\pi(g)^{FF'} = h^{FF'}$ in $\mathbf{H}^\Delta$.*

By Proposition 1, we deduce immediately that the functor Π is full. We now consider a sub-category $\widetilde{\mathbf{H}^\Delta}$ of $\mathbf{H}^\Delta$ such that for any object U of $\widetilde{\mathbf{H}^\Delta}$, the group $\mathrm{End}(U)$ of endomorphisms of U is trivial, and such that the inclusion functor $\iota \colon \widetilde{\mathbf{H}^\Delta} \to \mathbf{H}^\Delta$ is the identity on objects. It is obvious to see that for any objects U and V of $\widetilde{\mathbf{H}^\Delta}$, the hom-set $\mathrm{Hom}(U,V)$ is reduced to a singleton which can be identified with one element of H. The choice of hom-sets $\mathrm{Hom}(U,V)$ is not unique and determines the sub-category $\widetilde{\mathbf{H}^\Delta}$. We now arrive to the definition of the desired category $\widetilde{\mathbf{G}^\Delta}$.

Definition 5. *The category $\widetilde{\mathbf{G}^\Delta}$ is defined as the pull-back of the following diagram.*

$$
\begin{array}{ccc}
\widetilde{\mathbf{G}^\Delta} & \dashrightarrow & \widetilde{\mathbf{H}^\Delta} \\
\downarrow & & \downarrow{\scriptstyle \iota} \\
\mathbf{G}^\Delta & \xrightarrow{\ \Pi\ } & \mathbf{H}^\Delta
\end{array}
$$

The following propositions are immediate from the definition.

Proposition 3. *For any object U of $\widetilde{\mathbf{G}^\Delta}$, the endomorphism group $\mathrm{End}(U)$ is isomorphic to $\mathbf{Z}$.*

Proposition 4. *For any objects U and V of $\widetilde{\mathbf{G}^\Delta}$, the hom-set $\mathrm{Hom}(U,V)$ is in bijection with a coset of $\mathbf{Z}$ in $\mathbf{G}$.*

In the specific case where $\mathbf{G}$ is the T/I group, there exists a projection functor $\Pi \colon T/I^\Delta \to \mathbb{Z}_2{}^\Delta$ induced by the homomorphism $\pi \colon T/I \to \mathbb{Z}_2$, and one can select an appropriate subcategory $\widetilde{\mathbb{Z}_2}^\Delta$. The subcategory $\widetilde{T/I}^\Delta$ obtained by the construction described above is then such that

- for any object U of $\widetilde{T/I}^\Delta$, the endomorphism group $\text{End}(U)$ is isomorphic to $\mathbb{Z}_{12}$ and its elements correspond to generalized transpositions as exposed in Sect. 1.3, and

- for any objects U and V of $\widetilde{T/I}^\Delta$, the elements of hom-set $\text{Hom}(U,V)$ correspond either to generalized inversions or to generalized transpositions (but not both). Their nature depends on the choice of the subcategory $\widetilde{\mathbb{Z}_2}^\Delta$.

2 Groupoid Bisections and Wreath Products

Wreath products have found many applications in transformational music theory [13,14], most notably following the initial work of Hook on Uniform Triadic Transformations (UTT) [4]. In this section, we show how groupoids are related to wreath products through *groupoid bisections*, thus generalizing the work of Hook.

2.1 Bisections of a Groupoid

Let $\mathbf{C}$ be a connected groupoid with a finite number of objects. By convention, we will index the objects of $\mathbf{C}$ by $i \in \{1,\ldots,n\}$, where n is the number of objects in $\mathbf{C}$. We denote by G the group of endomorphisms of any object i of $\mathbf{C}$. We first give the definition of a *bisection of a groupoid*. This notion, which has been studied in the theory of Lie groupoids, is a particular case of the notion of a local section of a topological category as introduced by Ehresmann [1], who later studied the category of such local sections [2]. The word *bisection* is due to Mackenzie [10].

Definition 6. *A* bisection *of* $\mathbf{C}$ *is the data of a permutation* $\sigma \in S_n$ *and a collection of morphisms* $a_{i\sigma(i)} \colon i \to \sigma(i)$ *of* $\mathbf{C}$ *for* $i \in \{1,\ldots,n\}$. *A bisection will be notated as* $(\ldots, a_{i\sigma(i)}, \ldots)$.

Bisections can be composed according to:

$$(\ldots, b_{i\tau(i)}, \ldots) \circ (\ldots, a_{i\sigma(i)}, \ldots) = (\ldots, b_{\sigma(i)\tau\sigma(i)} a_{i\sigma(i)}, \ldots),$$

and form a group $\text{Bis}(\mathbf{C})$. The main result of this section is the following theorem (which can be easily extended to all small connected groupoids), which establishes the structure of $\text{Bis}(\mathbf{C})$.

Theorem 1. *The group* $\text{Bis}(\mathbf{C})$ *is isomorphic to the wreath product* $G \wr S_n$.

Proof. We construct an explicit isomorphism from $\text{Bis}(\mathbf{C})$ to $G \wr S_n$. By an abuse of notation, we will denote by g_{ii} both an endomorphism of an object i of $\mathbf{C}$ and the corresponding element of G.

Let k be an object of $\mathbf{C}$, and let $\{c_{ki}, i \in \{1, \ldots, n\}\}$ be the set obtained by choosing a morphism c_{ki} of $\mathbf{C}$ for every object i of $\mathbf{C}$. This defines a collection of morphisms $\{c_{ij} = c_{kj}c_{ki}^{-1}, i \in \{1, \ldots, n\}, j \in \{1, \ldots, n\}\}$ such that for any objects p, q, and r of $\mathbf{C}$, we have $c_{qr}c_{pq} = c_{pr}$. The morphisms c_{ij} induce automorphisms ϕ_{ij} of G given by $\phi_{ij}(g_{ii}) = c_{ij}g_{ii}c_{ij}^{-1}$, with the added property that for any objects p, q, and r, we have $\phi_{qr} \circ \phi_{pq} = \phi_{pr}$.

Since $\mathbf{C}$ is a groupoid, any bisection $(\ldots, a_{i\sigma(i)}, \ldots)$ of $\mathrm{Bis}(\mathbf{C})$ can then be uniquely written as $(\ldots, c_{i\sigma(i)}g_{ii}, \ldots)$. Let $\chi \colon \mathrm{Bis}(\mathbf{C}) \to G \wr S_n$ be the bijective map which sends an element $(\ldots, a_{i\sigma(i)}, \ldots)$ of $\mathrm{Bis}(\mathbf{C})$ to the element $\langle (\ldots, \phi_{i1}(g_{ii}), \ldots), \sigma \rangle$ of $G \wr S_n$. It can be easily shown that the map χ is indeed an isomorphism (the technical proof is left to the reader). □

2.2 Application to Musical Transformations

The following proposition shows how can one pass from a groupoid action on sets to a corresponding group action.

Proposition 5. *Let $\mathbf{C}$ be a connected groupoid with a finite number of objects, with G the group of endomorphisms of any object, and let S be a functor from $\mathbf{C}$ to $\mathbf{Sets}$. There is a canonical group action of $G \wr S_n$ on the disjoint union of the image sets $S(i)$.*

Proof. Let $\bigsqcup S(i) = \bigcup \{(x, i), x \in S(i), i \in \{1, \ldots, n\}\}$ be the disjoint union of the image sets $S(i)$ and let $(\ldots, a_{i\sigma(i)}, \ldots)$ be a bisection of $\mathbf{C}$. The group action of $G \wr S_n$ on $\bigsqcup S(i)$ is directly given by the action defined as

$$(\ldots, a_{i\sigma(i)}, \ldots) \cdot (x, i) = (S(a_{i\sigma(i)})(x), \sigma(i)).$$

□

As a direct application to musical transformations, consider a subgroupoid $\widetilde{T/I^\Delta}$ as constructed in Sect. 1.5. Given a functor $R \colon \Delta \to \mathbf{Sets}$, we know from Proposition 2 that there exists a canonical functor $P \colon T/I^\Delta \to \mathbf{Sets}$, which extends to a functor $\widetilde{P} \colon \widetilde{T/I^\Delta} \to \mathbf{Sets}$. From Proposition 5, we thus deduce that there exists a group action of $\mathbb{Z}_{12} \wr S_n$ on the disjoint union of the image sets $\widetilde{P}(i)$, or in other words the set of all PK-nets (R, S, i, ϕ). In the case R is representable and $n = 2$, it is easy to see that one recovers a wreath product acting on two different types of chords analog to Hook's UTT group.

3 Conclusions

Building on the categorical framework of poly-Klumpenhouwer networks, this paper has introduced the notion of generalized musical class for a PK-net of diagram Δ as a functor $F \colon \Delta \to \mathbf{C}$, where Δ is a small category and $\mathbf{C}$ is a musically relevant category. In the case $\mathbf{C}$ is a group and Δ is a poset with a bottom element, it has been shown that generalized musical transformations emerge as morphisms of the groupoid of functors $\mathbf{C}^\Delta$. Through the example of Berg's *Four pieces for clarinet and piano, Op. 5/2*, an application to post-tonal music has been presented, extending the range of possibilities for analysis beyond transpositionally related pitch-class sets. In addition, the notion of groupoid bisection bridges this categorical approach with group-theoretical wreath products which have been introduced by previous authors. This categorical framework may readily be implemented in high-level programming languages [15] and would thus provide an opportunity for computer-aided music analysis and composition.

References

1. Ehresmann, C.: Catégories topologiques et catégories différentiables. In: Colloque de Géométrie Différentielle Globale. C.B.R.M. pp. 137–150. Librairie Universitaire, Louvain (1959)
2. Ehresmann, C.: Categories topologiques. iii. Indagationes Mathematicae (Proceedings) **69**, 161–175 (1966). https://doi.org/10.1016/S1385-7258(66)50023-3
3. Fiore, T.M., Noll, T.: Commuting groups and the topos of triads. In: Agon, C., Andreatta, M., Assayag, G., Amiot, E., Bresson, J., Mandereau, J. (eds.) MCM 2011. LNCS (LNAI), vol. 6726, pp. 69–83. Springer, Heidelberg (2011). https://doi.org/10.1007/978-3-642-21590-2_6
4. Hook, J.: Uniform triadic transformations. J. Music Theory **46**(1/2), 57–126 (2002). http://www.jstor.org/stable/4147678
5. Klumpenhouwer, H.: A Generalized Model of Voice-Leading for Atonal Music. Ph.D. thesis, Harvard University (1991)
6. Klumpenhouwer, H.: The inner and outer automorphisms of pitch-class inversion and transposition: some implications for analysis with Klumpenhouwer networks. Intégral **12**, 81–93 (1998). http://www.jstor.org/stable/40213985
7. Lewin, D.: Transformational techniques in atonal and other music theories. Persp. New Music **21**(1–2), 312–381 (1982)
8. Lewin, D.: Generalized Music Intervals and Transformations. Yale University Press (1987)
9. Lewin, D.: Klumpenhouwer networks and some isographies that involve them. Music Theory Spectr. **12**(1), 83–120 (1990)
10. Mackenzie, K.C.: General theory of Lie groupoids and Lie algebroids, London Mathematical Society Lecture Note Series, vol. 213. Cambridge University Press (2005). http://www.ams.org/mathscinet-getitem?mr=2157566
11. Mazzola, G., Andreatta, M.: From a categorical point of view: K-nets as limit denotators. Persp. New Music **44**(2), 88–113 (2006). http://www.jstor.org/stable/25164629
12. Nolan, C.: Thoughts on Klumpenhouwer networks and mathematical models: the synergy of sets and graphs. Music Theory Online **13**(3) (2007)
13. Peck, R.: Generalized commuting groups. J. Music Theory **54**(2), 143–177 (2010). http://www.jstor.org/stable/41300116
14. Peck, R.W.: Wreath products in transformational music theory. Persp. New Music **47**(1), 193–210 (2009). http://www.jstor.org/stable/25652406
15. Popoff, A.: Opycleid: a Python package for transformational music theory. J. Open Source Softw. **3**(32), 981 (2018). https://doi.org/10.21105/joss.00981

16. Popoff, A., Agon, C., Andreatta, M., Ehresmann, A.: From K-nets to PK-nets: a categorical approach. Persp. New Music **54**(2), 5–63 (2016). http://www.jstor.org/stable/10.7757/persnewmusi.54.2.0005
17. Popoff, A., Andreatta, M., Ehresmann, A.: A categorical generalization of Klumpenhouwer networks. In: Collins, T., Meredith, D., Volk, A. (eds.) MCM 2015. LNCS (LNAI), vol. 9110, pp. 303–314. Springer, Cham (2015). https://doi.org/10.1007/978-3-319-20603-5_31
18. Popoff, A., Andreatta, M., Ehresmann, A.: Relational poly-Klumpenhouwer networks for transformational and voice-leading analysis. J. Math. Music **12**(1), 35–55 (2018). https://doi.org/10.1080/17459737.2017.1406011

Fourier Phase and Pitch-Class Sum

Dmitri Tymoczko[1] and Jason Yust[2](✉)

[1] Princeton University, Princeton, NJ 08544, USA
dmitri@princeton.edu
[2] Boston University, Boston, MA 02215, USA
jyust@bu.edu

Abstract. Music theorists have proposed two very different geometric models of musical objects, one based on voice leading and the other based on the Fourier transform. On the surface these models are completely different, but they converge in special cases, including many geometries that are of particular analytical interest.

Keywords: Voice leading · Fourier transform · Tonal harmony · Musical scales · Chord geometry

1 Introduction

Early twenty-first century music theory explored a two-pronged generalization of traditional set theory. One prong situated sets and set-classes in continuous, non-Euclidean spaces whose paths represented voice leadings, or ways of moving notes from one chord to another [4,13,16]. This endowed set theory with a contrapuntal aspect it had previously lacked, embedding its discrete entities in a robustly geometrical context. Another prong involved the Fourier transform as applied to pitch-class distributions: this provided alternative coordinates for describing chords and set classes, coordinates that made manifest their harmonic content [1,3,8,10,19–21]. Harmonies could now be described in terms of their resemblance to various equal divisions of the octave, paradigmatic objects such as the augmented triad or diminished seventh chord. These coordinates also had a geometrical aspect, similar to yet distinct from voice-leading geometry.

In this paper, we describe a new convergence between these two approaches. Specifically, we show that there exists a class of simple circular voice-leading spaces corresponding, in the case of n-note nearly even chords, to the nth Fourier "phase spaces." An isomorphism of points exists for all chords regardless of structure; when chords divide the octave evenly, we can extend the isomorphism to paths, which can then be interpreted as voice leadings. This leads to a general technique for replacing individual components of a Fourier analysis with qualitatively similar voice-leading calculations.

2 Voice Leading and Fourier Phase

We begin by considering transpositions of a single n-note chord type lying in some c-note scale. We first explain how the nth Fourier component represents

© Springer Nature Switzerland AG 2019
M. Montiel et al. (Eds.): MCM 2019, LNAI 11502, pp. 46–58, 2019.
https://doi.org/10.1007/978-3-030-21392-3_4

chords on a circular space, sharing the same angular coordinate when related by O/n semitone transposition. (Here O is the size of the octave.) We then show that voice-leading spaces contain very similar subspaces, only now with *the sum of the chord's pitch classes* determining the angular coordinate. Thus when restricting our attention to the transpositions of a single chord, the nth Fourier phase is equivalent to pitch-class sum.

In what follows we represent pitches by real numbers in $\mathbb{R}$ rather than discrete values in $\mathbb{Z}$, as in much previous music-theoretical work.[1] Pitch classes arise by identifying octave-related pitches, and can be represented by real numbers in the range $0 \le p < O$; the collection of distinct pitch classes forms a one-dimensional circular space known as the "pitch class circle." These basic definitions are common to both theoretical approaches considered below. We will generally consider the octave to have size 12, with C corresponding to 0, C♯ to 1, and so on. In scalar contexts, it is useful to consider an octave of size n. This amounts to using the scale as a metric, so that, by definition, it divides the octave evenly [16].

The Fourier transform represents musical objects as a collection of complex numbers or components. The kth Fourier component of a pitch class is a vector with magnitude 1 and angular position $p \bmod c/k$; the resulting space can be understood as the quotient of the familiar pitch-class circle by rotation, as if the octave had been "reduced" to size O/k. The kth Fourier component of a chord is represented by the *vector sum* of its component pitch classes. For a finite collection of notes, $X = \{x_1, x_2, \ldots, x_n\} \in \mathbb{R}/c$, we have:

$$F_k(X) = \sum_{x \in X} e^{-2i\pi kx/c} \tag{1}$$

(Again many previous authors consider only equal-tempered pitches with values in $\mathbb{Z}_c$, but the approach extends naturally to continuous pitch classes.) The angle of the resulting chord, or $\arg(F_n)$ is its *phase*. The combination of reduced octave and vector sum gives rise to many of the Fourier transform's distinctive properties.

The left side of Fig. 1 presents the third Fourier component for single pitch classes and for major triads in the familiar twelve-tone chromatic universe. Because 3 divides 12 evenly, major-third transpositions leave angular position unchanged. The twelve equal-tempered triads occupy four separate angular positions dividing the circle into four equal parts; transposing a chord by descending semitone moves its angular position a quarter-turn clockwise. For some combinations of chord- and scale-size, the reduced octave may not be equivalent to an integer pitch-class interval, and no two distinct pitch-classes or transpositions of a chord have the same angular position. The right side of Fig. 1 shows the F_5 position of the twelve chromatic pitch classes, and minor ninth chords.

---

[1] Throughout this paper we assume that pitch classes are labeled with a continuous map from the space of notes' fundamental frequencies to $\mathbb{R}$, with the integer values of traditional music theory arising as a discretization of this mapping. This permits labelings like $f(C) = 0$, $f(C♯) = 1$, $f(D) = 2$, but not $f(C) = 0$, $f(G) = 1$, $f(D) = 2$.

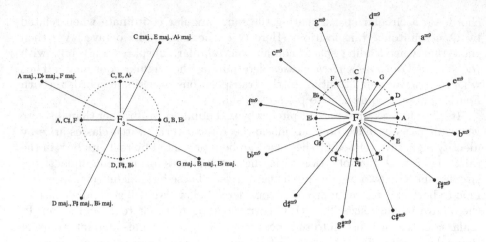

Fig. 1. The third Fourier component in complex space for pitch classes and major triads, and the fifth component for pitch classes and minor ninth chords.

Here the octave has size 12/5 and semitone transposition corresponds to rotation by $(5/12)2\pi$. The distinct transpositions of any 12-tone equal-tempered chord will therefore have unique angular positions, with fifth-related chords adjacent to one another.

On the surface, voice-leading spaces are very different from Fourier spaces, as they use neither the reduced octave nor vector summation of pitch classes. Instead, the theory of voice leading represents pitch classes as points on a circle whose size is equal to the octave O. The main objects of interest are *paths in pitch class space* which represent motion along the circle: thus $C \xrightarrow{4} E$ corresponds to the ascending major third, ascending by a quarter turn, while $C \xrightarrow{-8} E$ represents the descending minor sixth, moving three-quarters of a turn in the other direction. A *voice leading* is a multiset of paths in pitch-class space, representing a way of moving from one chord to another.

This situation can be modeled geometrically by *configuration spaces* in which points represent entire chords and paths represent voice leadings; distance in these spaces can therefore be understood as the aggregate physical distance required to move one set of notes to another on an instrument like the piano. Different paths between the same points correspond to different voice leadings. These spaces are quotients of R^n modulo octave equivalence and permutation of their coordinates: for an n-note chord, the configuration space is T^n/S_n, the n-torus modulo the symmetric group on n letters. (Starting with $\mathbb{R}^n$, with each dimension representing the pitch of one voice, we can derive these spaces by identifying octave-related pitches and permutationally related chords, or those with the same notes in different voices; the resulting orbifold is known as n-note chord space [13,16].) These chord spaces have one circular dimension representing transposition; the remaining ("horizontal") dimensions form an $(n-1)$-dimensional simplex with singular boundaries. These horizontal cross-sections can be taken to contain all chords whose pitch classes sum to the same value modulo O. For a c-note scale, there will be c distinct cross sections containing chords lying in that scale. (Here, pitch-class sum is computed by scalar addition modulo O, as opposed to vector addition.) A fundamental and counterintuitive fact is that the line containing transpositionally related n-note chords winds n times around the circular dimension, since transposition by $12/n$ leaves a chord's pitch-class sum unchanged. Since a complete turn along the circular dimension represents transposition by $12/n$, chords have the same circular coordinate if they are related by $12/n$ semitone transposition.

In other words, we find a role for the "reduced octave" O/n in both models. This quantity is manifest in the basic definition of Fourier space but arises as a non-obvious consequence of the fundamental geometry of voice-leading space. Figure 2 compares the two perspectives for the case of major triads in the chromatic scale. On the left we show the phases of the chords' F_3 component; on the right we represent them using a spiral diagram devised by Tymoczko [11,17], where the angular component corresponds to the circular dimension (with coordinates given by pitch-class sum) and the "line of transposition" is winds n times around it.

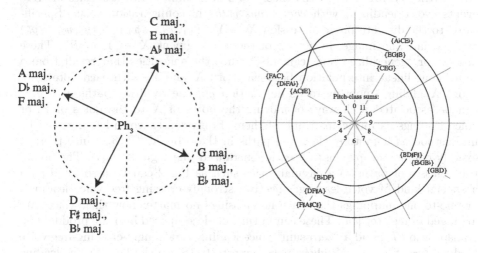

Fig. 2. Major triads in Ph$_3$ and the circular dimension of voice-leading space

This correspondence can be generalized.

Proposition 1. *Consider the collection $T = \{t_x\}$ consisting of the transpositions of any n-note chord, A, in any c-note scale. There is an equivalence between (a) differences between sum of the pitch classes for each t_x and (b) differences between their component-n phase values (Ph_n). That is, $\Sigma T_x(A) - \Sigma A =_{mod12} Ph_n(A) - Ph_n(T_x(A))$ (where Σ denotes pitch-class sum).*

Proof. Transposition by x is equivalent to multiplication by a unit vector in the Fourier space, so it changes Ph_n by nx mod 12. Similarly, T_x adds a constant of nx, mod 12, to the pitch-class sum. Therefore the change in Ph_n is the change of pitch-class sum.

This result also holds in continuous pitch space via the limit $c \to \infty$. The two different music-theoretical approaches thus converge on very similar graphs, so long as we restrict our attention to just a single chord type. Such graphs can be found throughout the analytical literature, as it is often useful to focus on e.g. diatonic triads or chromatic dominant sevenths. Historically, the circular coordinate was of crucial importance, as the initial exploration of both kinds of space was motivated by the goal of understanding set classes; in the Fourier realm this space can be constructed by ignoring phase while in the voice-leading case it involves focusing on (quotients of) the cross-sections with fixed pitch-class sum [2,9].

3   Glide Paths in Fourier Space

One of the central ideas in the theory of voice leading is to associate discrete events (voice leadings) with *continuous paths* in configuration space. Specifically, to the discrete pitch succession $X \to Y : (x_1, x_2, ..., x_n) \to (y_1, y_2, ..., y_n)$ we associate the image, in T^n/S_n of the line segment $X \to Y$ in R^n. These images, or "generalized line segments," trace the sonorities that result from a continuous linear interpolation between chord X and Y, with each note x_i of chord X gliding smoothly to its destination y_i. The resulting paths in T^n/S_n can be associated with ways of moving the notes of X to the notes of Y, or voice leadings as musicians think of them. Equivalently, voice leadings can be understood as homotopy classes of paths in the orbifold T^n/S_n, since there is exactly one homotopy class for each generalized line segment [6,7]. The homotopy classes of paths in a circular space such as Fig. 2 can be associated with a special kind of voice leading: bijective, strongly-crossing free voice leadings, or one-to-one mappings that have no crossings no matter how their voices are arranged in register [14]. These can in turn be decomposed into the product of a transposition T_x, and a "zero-sum" voice leading, or strongly-crossing-free voice leading $Z = X \to T_{-x}Y$ whose paths sum to 0. (Since the latter voice leading need not connect chords lying in the same scale, we need continuous space for this decomposition [16]). The angular component of a path in voice-leading space is given entirely by the transposition.

We can apply a similar approach in the Fourier domain as well, using voice leadings to define *glide paths* in the complex plane of the nth Fourier component. A continuous path $X \to Y$ is given by a vector sum $e^{ict}z_1(t) + e^{ict}z_2(t) + ... + e^{ict}z_n(t)$ in this space, where e^{ict} represents the voice leading's transpositional component, each $z_i(t)$ is a voice leading moving a single voice and $Z = \sum z_i(t)$ is a zero-sum voice leading. A question immediately arises whether the resulting paths are homotopically equivalent to those in circular voice-leading space.

By complex linearity, we can factor out the transpositional component e^{ict}, rewriting this vector sum as $e^{ict}Z(t)$; the total angular motion in Fourier space will be the sum of the angular motions of e^{ict} and $Z(t)$. From this it follows that we can restrict our attention to the zero-sum component: if a voice leading $X \to Y$ produces homotopically distinct paths in the two spaces, then its zero-sum component will do the same. Thus we ask whether we can find bijective voice leadings $Z(t)$ connecting transpositionally related chords, whose paths sum to zero (using standard addition), but which traverse one or more complete circles in Fourier space.

The answer is that we can, but only when the chord divides the octave some-what unevenly. For example, consider the voice leading $(C, D, E) \xrightarrow{(-4,2,2)} (G\sharp, E, F\sharp)$. Figure 3 shows that the two voices D→E and E→F$\sharp$ point in opposite directions in Ph$_3$, adding to 0 by vector addition; since both rotate counterclockwise one half-turn they contribute nothing to the vector sum. That sum is instead determined by the voice C→G$\sharp$, which makes a complete clockwise turn. So this is a bijective, zero-sum voice leading between transpositionally related chords that has no angular component in voice-leading space but makes a complete turn in Fourier space. The example generalizes to the case where $n - 1$ voices divide the circle equally (summing to 0); these can be moved by $O/(n - 1)$ in one direction while a final voice makes a complete circle in the other direction.

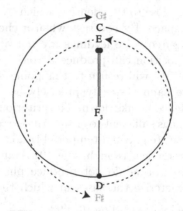

Fig. 3. The voice leading $(C, D, E) \xrightarrow{(-4,2,2)} (G\sharp, E, F\sharp)$ in F$_3$

By contrast, when chords divide the octave relatively evenly then paths will be homotopically equivalent. Figure 4 shows the paths corresponding to the voice leading $(C, E, G) \xrightarrow{-1,0,1} (B, E, G\sharp)$ in the third Fourier space. Here the vectors marked x_1 and x_3 simply switch positions, so that the chord's vector sum remains pointing in the upper right quadrant. It is clear that a complete circle will never result so long as all the chord's vectors remain pointing in the same half-plane throughout the voice leading. It follows from basic voice-leading geometry that

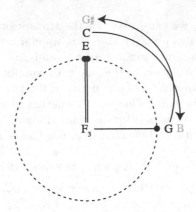

Fig. 4. The voice leading $(C, E, G) \xrightarrow{(-1,0,1)} (B, E, G\sharp)$ in F_3

the bijective, strongly crossing-free voice leadings of a nearly-even chord will always be of this form.

We can understand this phenomenon heuristically as follows: when a chord is nearly even, its bijective, strongly crossing free voice leadings are all transposition-like in the sense that they move all their notes by approximately the same distances [14, 16]. Thus when we factor out transpositional motion, what remains is something close to the identity, which by continuity will involve small changes in Fourier space. By contrast when a chord is very uneven, its bijective, strongly crossing-free voice leadings are not at all transposition-like; hence factoring out transposition can produce a voice leading that traverses a full circle in Fourier space. We will return to this point shortly.

As of this writing, we cannot specify precisely how uneven a chord may become before the equivalence breaks down. The criterion that all voice leadings remain in a single half-plane is sufficient to ensure the correspondence, and covers many common musical cases (e.g. equal-tempered triads and seventh chords). It is not necessary for convergence, though: the (025) and (015) trichords also have balanced voice leadings that do not produce phase-space cycles. Nor is it straightforward to characterize the cases in which the correspondence fails: the 18-tone equal-tempered voice leading $(0, \frac{16}{3}, 6) \xrightarrow{\frac{4}{3}, -\frac{10}{3}, 2} (\frac{4}{3}, 2, 8)$ results from a deformation of Fig. 3 above; even though no single voice makes a complete circle in phase space, the glide path does. Establishing precise bounds on the correspondence between the two spaces is thus a project for future work.

4   Crossfade Paths in Fourier Space

While some theorists [1, 3, 15] have applied the Fourier transform in continuous pitch-class space, the more common approach [1, 10, 20] assumes pitches lying in a particular equal division of the octave; these may be assigned real-valued weights representing musical salience. In this context, paths have been defined by gradually "fading out" some pitch classes while fading in others – a smooth interpolation of magnitudes that never leaves the equal-tempered domain.[2] That is, we define a crossfade path from chord X to X' as $(t)X + (1-t)X'$ for $t : 0 \rightarrow 1$ where the multiplication can be understood as applying to the weightings of either individual pitch classes or the resultant chordal vectors.[3] Such "crossfade paths" do not, on the surface, carry any implications about voice leading. Nevertheless, Yust, in [20] and subsequently in [21–23], has used the language of voice leading to interpret paths in these spaces. Here we consider the justification for this association.

Clearly, for non-antipodal points, "crossfade paths" will trace out a minimal trajectory through Fourier phase space. Figure 5, from [21], records the fifth Fourier phase of the twelve diatonic scales in the familiar chromatic universe; it is equivalent to the circular voice-leading space for equal tempered diatonic scales. Imagine fading out the F of C major (0♯) while fading in F♯ to move to G major (1♯); the phase of the resultant vector will move clockwise by one twelfth of a cycle. By our previous work, this is the same path in phase that would be traced out by a maximally efficient voice leading between the same scales, one in which F ascends by semitone to F♯. Thus there is indeed justification for associating "crossfade paths" with particular voice leadings.

However, one must be careful when drawing theoretical conclusions from this association, as the two forms of path arise in very different ways: changes of weighting rather than paths along the circle. Consider Yust's identification of enharmonicism with complete circles in Fig. 5. Tymoczko [12, 16] and Hook [5] have argued that notation reflects the logic of voice leading, with each letter

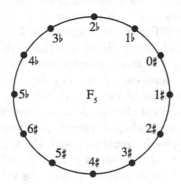

Fig. 5. Diatonic scales (labeled by number of accidentals) in Ph₅

---

[2] Such smoothly changing distributions might occur in algorithmic composition or in statistical analysis. Yust [20] touts this approach as a "cardinality-flexible," "common-tone-based" conception of musical distance, because it can relate chords of different sizes based on shared pitch-class content. It is possible that a something similar might be achieved by non-bijective cross-cardinality voice leading.

[3] Note that we define these crossfade paths for real-valued pitch classes, assuming each chord only has a finite number of non-zero weighted pitch classes.

name recording an abstract musical voice: when C major moves to G major, the "F voice" ascends by semitone to F♯. Yust [18] explains enharmonicism in exactly these (voice-leading-based) terms, using similar language to describe Ph₅ cycles [20, 22, 23]. In particular, he points out that a sequence of modulations that travels a full circle in this space will involve enharmonic respelling, sending C major to either B♯ major (for a clockwise path) or D♭♭ major (counterclockwise).[4] The subtle question is whether this phenomenon is to be explained by voice leading or the Fourier transform.

Here the important observation is that distinct voice leadings will generally produce different paths, whether in voice-leading space or using glide paths in Fourier space. Therefore, voice-leading methods can distinguish the modulation from C major to D♭ major, $C \to D♭$, that descends five semitones from the modulation $C \to C♯$ that ascends by seven semitones. (Note that we are making this point using notation, but as Tymoczko [16] argues, the notation serves to distinguish different voice leadings between background scales, and these can be present even in non-notated contexts.) The crossfade method will always choose the shortest way in Fourier phase space, so to make this kind of distinction requires, e.g., adding some other intermediary. We conclude that only voice-leading accurately represents enharmonicism as it can be modeled by scalar context, and hence that voice-leading provides a sufficient explanation of enharmonicism as we most commonly encounter it.[5]

5 Simulating Fourier Methods with Voice Leading

The correspondence we have been exploring is delicate one that arises only in certain special and limiting cases. This is illustrated by Fig. 6, which graphs the position of {CEG} and {C♯EF♯} in the two spaces; here chords with the same sum have different Fourier phases, a divergence that reflects differences between vector and scalar addition. The mere introduction of a second chord type thus breaks the correspondence between the two worlds.

However, from another point of view the connection is more robust. In earlier work Tymoczko [15] argued that there is a close correspondence between Fourier *magnitudes* and voice-leading distance: specifically the magnitude of the nth Fourier component is closely correlated with the voice-leading proximity to the nearest "doubled subset" of the nearest perfectly even n-note chord.[6] We can now give similar characterization of Fourier *phase* as well: the phase of a chord X's nth Fourier component is closely correlated with the transposition of E, the perfectly even n-note chord that is "nearest" to X, with distance measured by the size of the smallest voice leading from X to some *subset* of E's notes. (These subsets are represented by unisons in the nth Fourier space.) Fig. 7 plots

---

[4] This is a reflection of the fact that a loop enclosing the circular dimension of voice-leading space sends each note in a chord up or down by one chordal step.

[5] It remains an open question whether there exist forms of enharmonicism, perhaps arising from extended just intonation, that cannot be captured by scalar context.

[6] Amiot [1], pp. 145–9, subsequently demonstrated this analytically.

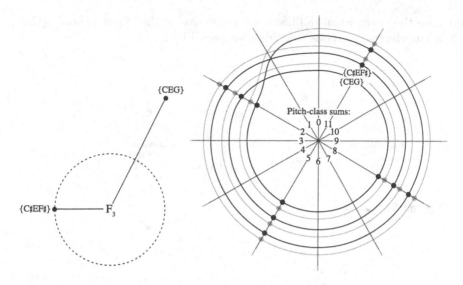

Fig. 6. Positions of {CEG} and {C♯EF♯} in F₃ and circular voice-leading space.

Fourier phase against the transposition of E for 100,000 randomly chosen trichords, tetrachords, and pentachords in continuous space. The correlation and its approximate nature are both clear: while the two quantities are generally related, it is possible for them to diverge substantially, particularly in the case of chords with small Fourier magnitude.

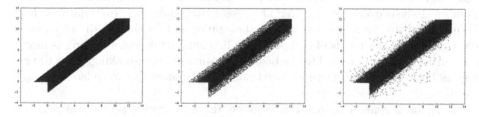

Fig. 7. Plots of Ph_n versus pitch-class sum for 100,000 randomly chosen trichords, tetrachords, and pentachords

The difference between the perspectives is largely attributable to the divergence between scalar and vector addition. In Fourier space we compute the magnitude and phases by adding the vectors representing the pitch classes of a chord; in voice-leading space, we can perform a similar calculation by asking what pitch class in the "reduced octave" of size O/n, has the smallest voice leading to the pitch classes of the chord; if we adopt the Euclidean metric, the resulting vector is one of the n vectors that can serve as the "average" of the n

points on the circle. Figure 8 illustrates in the case of the "fourth chord" (C, F, B♭), where the two methods coincide (compare Fig. 1).

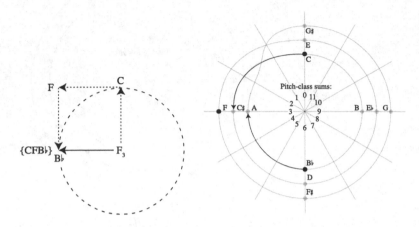

Fig. 8. Calculation of Ph₃ and the nearest subset of a perfectly even chord for {CFB♭}

This twofold correspondence gives us a general strategy for using voice leading to approximate the results of Fourier analysis: we replace the phase of the nth Fourier component with the transposition of the "nearest" perfectly even n-note chord (as just defined), and the magnitude with the voice-leading proximity (a decreasing function of distance) to that chord. While these quantities will not reproduce the Fourier transform exactly, they often provide an acceptable approximation. Furthermore, there is no obvious *musical* reason to privilege Fourier analysis over voice leading: at present, it remains controversial whether Fourier analysis, for all its mathematical elegance and familiarity, directly models anything in the minds of composers or listeners; while voice leading is more straightforwardly connected to the basic mechanics of music-making. Thus divergences between the two methods need not count against the voice-leading approach.

This more general connection between the two worlds provides a way to understand some puzzling features of the Fourier transform. Consider for example the divergence between pitch-class sum and Fourier phase noted at the beginning of this section: this results from the fact that chords with the same sum can be close to different subsets of the same perfectly even chord, or even different subsets of *different* perfectly even chords. For example, the first chord in Fig. 6, (C, E, G) is maximally close to the augmented triad a third of a semitone below C, while the second, (C♯, E, F♯) is maximally close to (C♯, F, F); in the context of our approximation, this is straightforward. Likewise, when we restrict our attention to a collection of *highly even* chords, all representing small perturbations of perfectly even chords, then we can expect a convergence between the methods. Thus for example, the positions of major and minor triads are consistent in both Ph₃ and circular voice-leading space.

Return now to the voice leading $(C, D, E) \xrightarrow{(-4,2,2)} (G\sharp, E, F\sharp)$, discussed in Sect. 3 above. Earlier we presented this as an case of divergence between the voice leading and Fourier worlds: a "balanced" voice leading that involves no change in pitch-class sum, but traverses a full circle in Ph_3. The voice-leading based approximation directs us, not to the sum of the pitch classes, but to the *nearest* perfectly even chord (represented by a unison in the reduced octave of 4 semitones). In the picture we have just described, this "nearest" chord indeed traverses a (discontinuous) circle in the reduced octave, much like Fourier phase. Thus what began as a delicate convergence between two fundamentally different ways of thinking leads, in the end, to a much more robust and general connection.

It thus appears that many music-theoretical uses of the Fourier transform can be reconceived in terms of voice leading. An interesting future project is specifying those musically relevant aspects of Fourier analysis that resist such reconceptualization – presumably, distinctively *harmonic* features that complement the broadly contrapuntal perspective we have been considering.

References

1. Amiot, E.: Music Through Fourier Space. Discrete Fourier Transform in Music Theory. Springer, Cham (2016). https://doi.org/10.1007/978-3-319-45581-5
2. Callender, C.: Continuous transformations. Mus. Theory Online **10**(3) (2004)
3. Callender, C.: Continuous harmonic spaces. J. Mus. Theory **51**(2), 277–332 (2007)
4. Callender, C., Quinn, I., Tymoczko, D.: Generalized voice-leading spaces. Science **320**(5874), 346–348 (2008)
5. Hook, J. Signature transformations. In: Hyde, M., Smith, C. (eds.) Mathematics and Music: Chords, Collections, and Transformations, pp. 137–60. University of Rochester Press (2008)
6. Hughes, James R.: Using fundamental groups and groupoids of chord spaces to model voice leading. In: Collins, Tom, Meredith, David, Volk, Anja (eds.) MCM 2015. LNCS (LNAI), vol. 9110, pp. 267–278. Springer, Cham (2015). https://doi.org/10.1007/978-3-319-20603-5_28
7. Hughes, J.R.: Orbifold path models for voice leading: dealing with doubling. In: Monteil, M., Peck, R.W. (eds.) Mathematical Music Theory: Algebraic, Geometric, Combinatorial, Topological and Applied Approaches to Understanding Musical Phenomena, pp. 185–94. World Scientific (2018)
8. Milne, A.J., Bulger, D., Herff, S.A.: Exploring the space of perfectly balanced rhythms and scales. J. Math. and Mus. **11**(3), 101–133 (2017)
9. Quinn, I.: A unified theory of chord quality in equal temperaments. University of Rochester, PhD dissertation (2004)
10. Quinn, I.: General equal-tempered harmony: parts two and three. Persp. New Mus. **45**(1), 4–63 (2006)
11. Sivakumar, A., Tymoczko, D.: Intuitive musical homotopy. In: Monteil, M., Peck, R.W. (eds.) Mathematical Music Theory: Algebraic, Geometric, Combinatorial, Topological and Applied Approaches to Understanding Musical Phenomena, pp. 233–51. World Scientific (2018)
12. Tymoczko, D.: Voice leadings as generalized key signatures. Mus. Theory Online **11**(4) (2005)
13. Tymoczko, D.: The geometry of musical chords. Science **313**, 72–74 (2006)

14. Tymoczko, D.: Scale theory, serial theory, and voice leading. Mus. Anal. **27**(1), 1–49 (2008)
15. Tymoczko, D.: Set class similarity, voice leading, and the Fourier transform. J. Mus. Theory **52**(2), 251–272 (2008)
16. Tymoczko, D.: A Geometry of Music: Harmony and Counterpoint in the Extended Common Practice. Oxford University Press, Oxford (2011)
17. Tymoczko, D.: Tonality: An owner's manual. Unpub. MS
18. Yust, J.: A space for inflections: following up on JMTs special issue on mathematical theories of voice leading. J. Math. Mus. **7**(3), 175–193 (2013)
19. Yust, Jason: Applications of DFT to the theory of twentieth-century harmony. In: Collins, Tom, Meredith, David, Volk, Anja (eds.) MCM 2015. LNCS (LNAI), vol. 9110, pp. 207–218. Springer, Cham (2015). https://doi.org/10.1007/978-3-319-20603-5_22
20. Yust, J.: Schubert's harmonic language and Fourier phase space. J. Mus. Theory **59**(1), 121–181 (2015)
21. Yust, J.: Special collections: renewing set theory. J. Mus. Theory **60**(2), 213–262 (2016)
22. Yust, J.: Organized Time: Rhythm, Tonality, and Form. Oxford University Press, Oxford (2018)
23. Yust, J.: Ganymed's heavenly descent. Mus. Anal. 38 (Forthcoming)

Categories, Musical Instruments, and Drawings: A Unification Dream

Maria Mannone[1(✉)] and Federico Favali[2]

[1] Department of Mathematics and Informatics,
University of Palermo, Palermo, Italy
mariacaterina.mannone@unipa.it, manno012@umn.edu
[2] Lucca, Italy
federicofavali@gmail.com

Abstract. The mathematical formalism of category theory allows to investigate musical structures at both low and high levels, performance practice (with musical gestures) and music analysis. Mathematical formalism can also be used to connect music with other disciplines such as visual arts. In our analysis, we extend former studies on category theory applied to musical gestures, including musical instruments and playing techniques. Some basic concepts of categories may help navigate within the complexity of several branches of contemporary music research, giving it a unitarian character. Such a 'unification dream,' that we can call 'cARTegory theory,' also includes metaphorical references to topos theory.

Keywords: Category theory · Gestural similarity · Classifying toposes

1 Introduction

Influences and mutual interactions between mathematics and music are connected by the abstract power of category theory [24]. A category is constituted of objects (points) and transformations between them (arrows), that verify associativity and invertibility properties. Transformations between categories (*functors*) map objects into objects, and arrows into arrows. Transformations between transformations[1] (*natural transformations*) are also defined. The formalism of categories is particularly suitable to the description of nested structures, and to the translation of structures from one context to another. Categories have been applied to music, especially in music theory [13, 20, 31, 34], and in the study of

---

[1] For example, we have an object A, and object B, and two transformations f, g such that $f : A \to B$, $g : A \to B$. A transformation between them is some η such that $\eta : f \to g$.

M. Mannone is an alumna of the University of Minnesota, USA.
F. Favali—Independent researcher.

M. Montiel et al. (Eds.): MCM 2019, LNAI 11502, pp. 59–72, 2019.
https://doi.org/10.1007/978-3-030-21392-3_5

musical gestures [3,4,20,32]. Recent developments [25,26] apply basic concepts (e.g., 2-categories, see [24]) to simple music structures,[2] as well as to more complex phenomena such as gestures of the gestures (nested and composed gestures; for 'gesture of gestures' see [32]) found in both conductors and performers in the orchestra, and 'gestural' communication between the conductor, the composer (who 'thinks of musical gestures'), and the listener, in terms of colimit (the conductor) and limit (the listener) [25]. This leads to the definition of gestural similarity within music to investigate analogies between the gestures of different performers, and the perception of these gestures musically. For example, two movements with increased energy that both produce the same transformations on their respective sound and sound spectra, such as an increase in loudness, are *similar*. Also, a simple musical sequence and a simple drawing with lines and points are 'gesturally similar' if they appear as being produced by the same gestural generator: e.g., a 'staccato' movement can generate either a sequence of staccato notes on the piano, or a sequence of points on a piece of paper [25]. This topic is connected with synesthesia, crossmodal correspondences, and the definition of audio-visual objects [23,37]. A detailed analysis of the implications of these studies in the psychology of perception, and of music perception [36], is outside of the scope of this paper. Nevertheless, problems such as the connection between the different art forms, or the extraction of 'essential information' from a visual or a musical object inclusive of the comparisons between them, are strongly related to psychology. In particular, a psychological experiment was recently run to assess the degree of similarity between a set of short musical sequences and visual shapes [8], validating gestural similarity [25]. Other studies have been focused on finding analogies between musical sequences and curves drawn by listeners [21] in the light of psychology. Music analysis can benefit from the mathematical theory of categories. For example, an analysis of a piece of Western music, and the listening to its performance, usually lead to different results, with a non-negligible difference between constructs and saliencies [30] that can be categorically described through non-commutative diagrams[3] [27]. The union of this information provides complete musical information, while their intersection gives essential information about the considered piece of music. Other applications include strategies to navigate complex piano scores, which may be modeled via categories [1,2].

In this paper, we present a new application of categories. In Sect. 2, we discuss the definition itself of a musical instrument from a categorical point of view. Then, we analyze the interaction between performers and non-classical instruments, such as augmented musical instruments, which include purely electronic, as well as acoustic instruments which have been augmented by

---

[2] For example, a *crescendo* is seen as a transformation from a loudness level to another, and the comparison between a faster and a slower crescendo is described via a comparison between transformations.

[3] In commutative diagrams, different arrows and combinations of arrows starting from the same object A reach the same object B, and the two different paths are equivalent.

electronics.[4] In this framework, there are also new instruments that involve muscular tension of the performer. Muscular tension, in this case, is not used to put into vibration a classical instrument, but acts as a direct source of information, opportunely detected, and mapped, into sound [11]. Moreover, there are some instruments that use embedded artificial intelligence, allowing transmission of information between them, and between audience and performers[5] [38]. This opens new paradigms in human-machine interactions, and it makes the diagram of Fig. 1 commutative. Of course, we can define new functors and natural transformations to connect all these areas (music theory, lower and higher structures, performance). Finally, in Sect. 3, we apply a metaphorical use of the concept of classifying topos, recently proposed as a bridge between different areas of mathematics [7], to investigate connections between music and the visual arts.

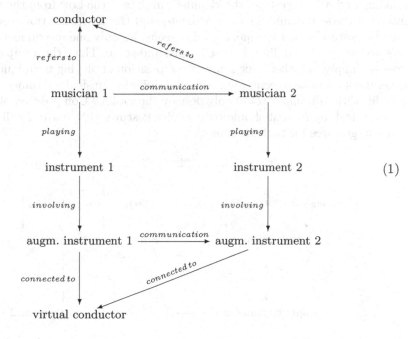

$$(1)$$

---

[4] With *augmented instrument*, we mean a musical instrument that has some sensors, electric connections or controllers, that enable the instrument play new sounds, enriched musical sequences, or even, in the case of the so-called *smart instruments* with embedded artificial intelligence [38], a 'dialogue' between a library of motifs and the played music, under the direct or indirect control of the performer. According to [38], smart instruments are more general than augmented ones. For an effective use of them, see [39].

[5] In particular, the connection between audience and performers via smart instruments and wearable devices allows the creation of isomorphisms in the diagrams of [25]. If also the conductor gets this kind of feedback through a smart device, categorically we could have a connection between colimit (the conductor) and limit (a listener in the audience). See [25] for details on the categorical description of the orchestra.

2 Definitions and Commutative Diagrams

A classical definition of a musical instrument is: 'a tool to make sounds/musical notes'. Thus, a musical instrument is characterized not only by its physical body but also by the performance techniques. This reminds us of the mathematical definition of a group: a set with operations defined on its elements, with the identity, the inverse element, and associativity. We may wonder if musical instruments might be seen as a group, with the physical body of an instrument as a set, and playing techniques as group operations. However, as we will see, there are some issues.

If the performer does not make any movement, he or she is making an 'identity' gesture; if the performer is playing and then stopping the sound, he or she is making an 'inverse' gesture: the violinist can detach the bow from the strings to interrupt the sound, and the flutist can interrupt the airstream. However, such an 'inverse gesture' is not unique: even if we consider only one instrument, gestures to stop the sound can differ in speed, time, and so on. Thus, the group definition does not apply. Another issue is about composition of playing techniques. It is in general not possible to compose gestures of different musical instruments: hitting a violin with a hummer could only destroy the violin.[6] Composition of gestures on a musical instrument should only involve gestures that naturally 'live' in the space of gestures for that instrument.[7]

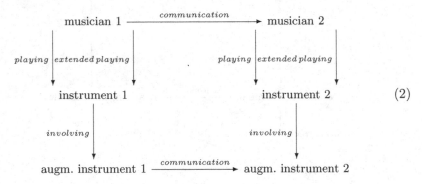

$$(2)$$

We may try to define musical instruments as a category, defined by objects (instruments) and morphisms (playing techniques). This is not a formal categorical definition, but a qualitative one. The same issue as before about techniques arises also here. Instead of considering generic 'playing techniques,' we should focus on musical gestures on each musical instrument: a violin is defined by the 'body' of the instrument and by the gestures (specific for the violin) the performer has to do in order to make the violin sound. We can still refer to playing

---

[6] See [25] for percussion and flute examples.

[7] We can still compare gestures of different spaces, with opportune changes: for example, a crescendo can be done with an increase of acceleration and pressure with hammer on a percussion, and with bow's movements on a violin [25].

techniques, but with this restriction: 'playing techniques for this or that specific instrument.' Composition of morphisms would involve specific gestures for the violin, for example a crescendo gesture (increased bow pressure/acceleration) followed by a staccato phrase (sudden interruption of the contact between bow and strings), or a staccato phrase played with a crescendo dynamics. Now, let us consider the whole orchestra. We can extend the categorical diagrams that include gestures of orchestral performers and conducting gestures presented in [25], by considering new instruments. Diagram 1 is made commutative through new techniques of electronically augmented instruments allowing for instrument-instrument communication. Additionally, we may hypothesize the existence of a virtual 'conductor' (not a robotic one that conducts human performers),[8] e.g., a control device that automatically, and autonomously, coordinates electronic instruments. If this is put in communication with a human conductor on the top of the diagram, the two vertices in Diagram 1 are connected, and the diagram assumes a ring shape. The reality of the musician-musician, and instrument-instrument communication, is more complex, involving feedback and thus two-sided arrows.

Communication between smart instruments may be made similar, or completely different, from communication between human performers. In general, it is not just a "copy" of human communication. Also, smart instruments may be programmed to be more autonomous, to allow a higher degree of control by human performers. Diagram 2 includes extended techniques,[9] that can be freely thought of as Kan extensions [24] of traditional techniques. The idea is then summarized in Diagram 3.

The diagram of Fig. 1 represents the relationships between the musical score, the performance, the body of the instrument, the playing techniques, the produced sound. The musical score and the physical body are 'static' elements, while both performance and playing techniques are 'dynamic' elements. The definition of a musical instrument not only as a physical body, but in terms of playing techniques, may be compared with the duality of music itself, such that music consists of scores (in the cases where a score is present or available) and performances. In fact, as pointed out by Gérard Genette, music can be seen as a "2-state immanency" that are, respectively, formed by the score and the performance [15]. Transitions from scores to performances have been mathematically investigated [33]. Both the physical body of an instrument and its playing techniques admit extensions, which may be investigated categorically. Also, we can wonder provocatively if a musical instrument can be considered as such only when played. Conversely, a generic object could be considered as a musical

---

[8] Examples of robotic conductors have been created at the University of Pisa and by the Music Conservatory of Palermo/University of Palermo, Engineering Department.

[9] A detailed discussion of extended techniques for voice and flute can be found in [10] and [18]. A smart version of the flute is not available yet; however, smart plucked instruments and percussions are available. Augmented flutes exist [17].

instrument if it is used as such. Duchamp's provocations about the concept of "art object," concrete music, and, earlier, futuristic 'intonarumori' [35] move in this direction.

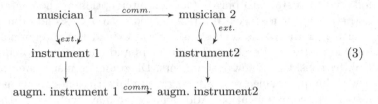

$$\text{augm. instrument 1} \xrightarrow{comm.} \text{augm. instrument2} \tag{3}$$

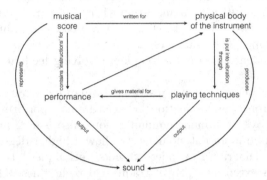

Fig. 1. Our investigation of musical instruments and their playing techniques can be compared with the dualism between musical scores and performances. Scores and physical bodies of the instruments belong to a static dimension, while performances and playing techniques belong to a dynamic dimension.

3   Classifying Topoi, Bridge Objects, and Music/visual Arts

We may generalize our analysis, including areas previously investigated, such as the relationship between music and visuals through categories [25]. A unifying concept is a 'bridge object' inspired by classifying topoi, used to unify geometrical theories[10] [5, 7]. Topoi have already been proposed in music [31]; however, our approach is meant to be more intuitive and interdisciplinary. We are introducing here topoi and not simply (small) categories to be able, at this level of generality, to borrow a connecting formalism between disciplines via a metaphorical use of

---

[10] In the words of Olivia Caramello, topoi (also called 'Toposes') "are mathematical objects which are built from a pair, called a site, consisting of a category and a generalized covering, called Grothendieck topology, on it in a certain canonical way (the process which produces a topos from a given site can be described as a sort of 'completion')." We can describe topoi as 'enhanced' categories, with a whiff of topology or a similarity to the category of sets.

topoi as bridges [5]. We may connect different objects, related the one to the other, via a third one, which may be built independently, or out of each. Also, we may solve problems in a field by using methods from another. We may associate a topos to any mathematical theory, the 'classifying topos of the theory.' According to Olivia Caramello, it "represents the framework in which the theory should be investigated, both in itself and in relationship to other theories." Classifying topoi may be metaphorically used as bridges to transfer information from one theory to another, and thus, topoi can also be considered as tools for dynamic unification (translations of objects, isomorphisms, structures) of mathematical theories. The 'transfer' operation is usually done in category theory via functors; here, we use the concept of bridge for transfers to contextualize the idea of 'general generator' of both sounds and images, as discussed later. Two theories having the same classifying topoi (or *toposes*) are called *Morita-equivalent* [7]. Two Morita-equivalent topoi have some common 'semantic content.' Such a semantic core would be constituted of "different manifestations of a unique property." The idea of topos as a 'translational tool' is based on the existence of multiple perspectives, and multiple representations for that topos, allowing for its use as a bridge and as a connecting object; we may then intuitively think of "different instances of a unique pattern" [6]. We also need to define a 'semantic core' when we wish to investigate analogies between different works of art, or analogies between techniques and strategies in different forms of art. This would constitute an extension of the concept of gestural similarity: not only the search for a common gestural generator — what Caramello would call a *static unification*, with a general item generating two other items through descending arrows — but a *dynamic unification*, through a path from item 1 (that is music in our analysis) to item 2 (that is visual arts in our analysis), see Fig. 2. Here, we use the terms 'bridge object' instead of 'classifying topos' to remark that we are not using this concept in a strict, technical way; instead, we use it as a metaphor [6] to extend the idea within an interdisciplinary framework. Also, as bridge objects are more general than topoi, we may define *invariants* — and in our artistic framework, we are strongly interested by invariants. We may imagine, for example, that Romantic music and Romantic paintings are metaphorically 'Morita-equivalent'. We may also wonder if new perspectives on artificial intelligence in music technology and visual images may also be, in some way, equivalent.[11] The use of a dynamic unification can be useful not only for the analysis of existing works, but also for the *making* of new works of art.

Here, we use a unifying concept, the 'bridge object,' inspired by the classifying topos, to connect music with visual arts. Actually, both music and visual arts have theories and the body of knowledge defined by techniques, styles, materials,

---

[11] In fact, a 'smart' technology, inspired by smart instruments and applied to visual arts, may consist in a smart tablet that takes as input a drawing gesture and gives as output a variegated, enriched visual representation. Thus, we can extend our comparison between extended sounds and extended visuals/drawings, and techniques developed in a field can be translated into new techniques to be applied into another field.

contents, and ideas. Topoi-inspired bridges may be general, and abstract tools to catch at once the variety within a given art form and transfer/translate it to another field, see Fig. 4. The elements of music and visual arts are described in Fig. 3. In Fig. 3, the same 'basic idea,' contained within the bridge/topos, can be represented and developed in the form of different artworks — we can think of artistic currents, where similar ideas may be present within visual arts, music, and also, literature. The essential idea can be caught by artists, and translated into specific gestures on canvas/paper (with brush or pencil) or on musical instruments.[12] Also, bridge objects 'indirectly' inform specific gestures the artist must make to produce the art object. Thus, we may compare the gestures between them, and we may also compare music/visual art which results from these gestures. In this sense, while investigating gestural similarity, we analyze arrows (gestures) and points (final results). At first, we can represent mental constructions with points, arrows, and commutative diagrams for the simple, 'practical' applications. Going higher with the abstraction, topoi can constitute a source of inspiration for the metaphor. However, underlying all these metaphors there are universal constructions. One of them is explored in

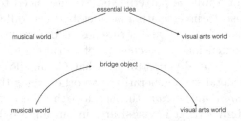

Fig. 2. Static unification (top) and dynamic unification (bottom) in Caramello's theory, with references to music and images. The 'essential idea' characterizes the common gestural generator that produces a sound or an image that are similar between them. Some detail of music and visual arts' worlds are given in Fig. 3; a possible relationship between essential ideas and bridge objects (inspired by classifying topoi) in this framework is described in Fig. 4. The unifying object, according to Caramello's theory, is the bridge object itself. Upper and lower diagrams can be connected, creating a commutative diagram, via an arrow joining the bridge object with the essential idea. We might dare to identify the bridge with the essential idea (and thus, that arrow would represent an identity), that could either be 'specified' into a specific artistic world (diagram above) or first obtained via an abstraction from a specific artistic world and then specified into another one (diagram below). With a unifying object such as a colimit the upper diagram implies the lower one; with a topos, also the reverse is true.

---

[12] For example, impressionistic painting uses imprecise contours and evident brush traces, and impressionistic music uses a lot of suspended chords and pedal piano effects. Might the 'imprecision' of a sketch, of an instant representation be at the core of impressionistic art? This could open a productive discussion on aesthetics, that is however out of the aim of this paper. Here, the word 'sketch' is used with its everyday meaning, and the term is not referred to the homonymous categorical construction.

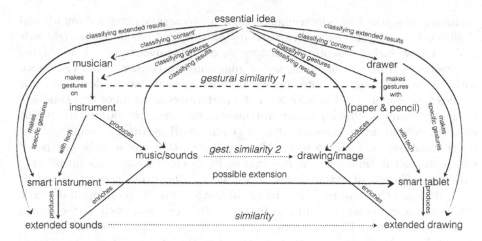

Fig. 3. An attempt to join musician's playing, traditional and smart musical instruments, visual artworks and visual artists' activity exemplified in drawing activity, and gestural similarity comparisons through the unifying power of bridge objects. The diagram here contains the 'essential idea;' how this is connected with bridge objects, is shown in Fig. 4. Smart instruments that enrich potentialities of traditional instruments may inspire smart tablet to enhance visual creation. As a 'categorical fractal' (a potentially nested structure) we can draw similar diagrams within each of the objects: for example, *music/sounds* and *drawing/image* can be analyzed in detail, comparing musical structures with visual shapes, analyzing their similarity, and the inner movements that ideally depict each melodic line or harmonic progression, obtaining a nested structure. We could also define essential ideas for smaller parts of the diagram with connections and transformations between them.

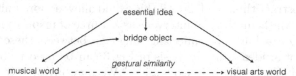

Fig. 4. The essential idea at the basis of musical or visual creation, that can be connected (see caption of Fig. 2) to gestural similarity studies, helps to build an intuitive concept of a bridge object — inspired by classifying topoi — that is meant to be a sort of 'bridge' to compare two different worlds, translating properties from one to another.

[25]: within the orchestral setup, the role of conductor can be seen as a colimit, and the role of the listener/audience as a limit. In this paper, we extended this approach to include not only gestures of musicians but also the instruments they use and the sounds they produce. Also, the 'gestural generator' cited in [25] for music and images is here extended to not only the gestures of visual artists but also to their tools and the drawings they produce. In the specific case of smart musical instruments, we have extended sounds, which enrich sounds obtained with traditional instruments. On the left side of the diagram of Fig. 3, there are

commutative squares with instruments, smart instruments, extended sounds and traditional sounds. A similar structure applies to visual media in the right side of Fig. 3. If we include robotic performers, we might analyze some robots playing traditional instruments, humans playing augmented instruments, and vice versa, with all their various and interconnected communication strategies. The same applies for a human which conducts robotic performers and a robot that conducts human performers. Playing smart instruments may require additional, specific gestures, which may be compared with (traditional) gestures through natural transformations (not shown in the diagram here), that can also be compared with extended techniques. The diagram in Fig. 3 can be made tridimensional, with the inclusion of external references, such as beautiful geometric and/or natural shapes that can inspire both visual images and the production of music [28]. The same geometric form can inspire visual studies as well as the design of new instruments. This is the case of the Telemetron [14], designed with the shape of a dodecahedron and able to sound in the absence of gravity. This is also the case of the CubeHarmonic [29], which embodies concepts from music theory such as the Tonnetz, as well as the permutation of Rubik's cube — a tonnetz with permutations. Also, the structure of musical instruments itself influences the necessary gestures, and the peculiarity of each instrument affects the expressive potential of music performed on it. Thus, some inverse arrows could be defined and investigated. The strength of this representation is the gradual connection between the 'matter' of music, the musical instruments, and its high-level content; that is, between instruments' physical bodies and playing techniques, the musical pieces, and their performers, and possible external music references within the other arts (or nature) as a source of inspiration, see Fig. 5. Actually, categories already inspired connections between objects and processes in nature and abstract thinking [12]. All this would allow a more unitary vision of different things. Mathematics can intervene as a source of inspiration or analysis, as well as provide a kind of connecting language between these elements. In Fig. 4, the 'essential idea'[13] at the basis of Fig. 3 can be used to build a topos-like bridge for a generic 'artistic expression.' We may investigate whether any structure would imply gestural similarity, making the diagram commutative, and expecting to find restrictive conditions — on the set underlying the category — for commutativity. In this way, we do not limit our investigation to the research of the 'general generator' of both sounds and visuals, as done in gestural similarity studies [25], but we may suggest how to translate constructions and knowledge from one area into another area.[14] As a practical example, any technology that augments the sound potential of musical instruments may be used to develop smart drawing devices to create complex visual structures from simple pencil movements. Also, teaching strategies that have been successfully exploited in

---

[13] The study of the 'essential idea' can profit from visual sketches [16], auditory sketches [19], and vocal imitations [9], acting as 'filters' to extract and/or reproduce some essential content from images and sounds.

[14] As suggested by a reviewer, we could restrict these categories to sub-cats to be endowed with topos structure.

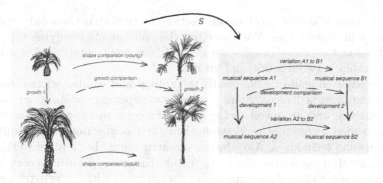

Fig. 5. Categorical formalism of functors can be applied to nature's forms and growth processes of different species [28]. A suitable mapping, as the action of a *sonification functor S*, can transform these forms, their comparisons, and their transformational processes into music, music variations, and developments [26]. Drawing by M. Mannone.

the framework of instrumental performance can be applied to other areas. In Fig. 4, arrows from the musical world to the visual-arts world may, of course, be inverted, obtaining another perspective on the 'topos.' The use of bridge objects could initiate a fertile debate about the problem of 'invariants'[15] and the concepts of the 'universal' in the arts, and it is no coincidence that mathematics often investigate invariant properties, and universal constructions play a decisive role in category theory.

4 Conclusion

In this paper, we extended current research between category theory and music to the definition of (traditional or augmented) musical instruments, and (traditional or extended) playing techniques, including the mutual interaction between performers and instruments, allowed by embedded artificial intelligence. The dialogue between instruments and musical performance practice/composing is two-fold: musical thinking influences the development of new instruments, but also the presence of new instruments stimulates musical thinking.[16] External

---

[15] In mathematics and physics, an entity can be invariant under certain transformations, thus being symmetric under a specific change. While dealing with transitions from a specific artistic expression to another, invariants can be nuclei of meaning that remain substantially unchanged. For example, we can wonder if there is some unchanged inner core behind artistic expressions belonging to the same artistic current.

[16] Category theory has also been used to describe the general process from the artistic production to the aesthetic contemplation [22]. The process from composition to performance/conducting and listening, described categorically in [25], can be seen as one of its possible 'concrete' applications, featuring several references to sounds and spectrograms. Curiously, both papers have been submitted on the same day.

influences to music do not involve composition/musical structures only, but also the instruments themselves. We also cited the concept of classifying topoi and their extension to 'bridge objects' to generalize current categorical studies on the relationship between music and visuals.

Future research could include both theoretical and computational developments of the proposed ideas. Some future, concrete applications may include musical analysis and improved pedagogical strategies to approach new instruments, extended techniques, and strengthen their connection with traditional instruments and techniques. Also, future research should be devoted to the connection of isolated applications of categories in the areas of music theory, music performance, score analysis, composition, comparisons with some extra-musical material, and musical instrument analysis. Thus, perhaps through the definition of suitable natural transformations, categories can be used not only to analyze topics from music but also to connect these topics from a unitarian perspective. Finally, taken as a whole, this may help us understand the richness of music and, in general, of the arts, and the potentialities of contemporary mathematics to describe in concrete terms the variety of human thinking. These ideas help overcome stereotypes of separation between disciplines, in the framework of research, and, in particular, of STEAM (Science, Technology, Engineering, the Arts and Mathematics) pedagogy.

The authors are grateful to Olivia Caramello for conversations and reading suggestions about classifying topoi.

References

1. Antoniadis, P., Bevilacqua, F.: Processing of symbolic music notation via multimodal performance data: Brian Ferneyhough's Lemma-Icon-Epigram for solo piano, phase 1. In: Hoadley, R., Nash, C., Fober, D. (eds.) Proceedings of TENOR 2016, pp. 127–136 (2016)
2. Antoniadis, P.: Embodied navigation of complex piano notation: rethinking musical interaction from a performer's perspective. Ph.D. thesis, Université de Strasbourg, pp. 274–278 (2018)
3. Arias, J.S.: Spaces of gestures are function spaces. J. Math. Music 12(2), 89–105 (2018)
4. Arias, J.S.: Gestures on locales and localic topoi. In: Pareyon, G., Pina-Romero, S., Agustin-Aquino, O.A., Lluis-Puebla, E. (eds.) The Musical-Mathematical Mind. CMS, pp. 29–39. Springer, Heidelberg (2017). https://doi.org/10.1007/978-3-319-47337-6_4
5. Caramello, O.: Theories, Sites, Toposes. Oxford University Press, New York (2018)
6. Caramello, O.: The theory of topos-theoretic 'bridges'-a conceptual introduction. Glass-bead (2016). http://www.glass-bead.org/article/the-theory-of-topos-theoretic-bridges-a-conceptual-introduction/?lang=enview
7. Caramello, O.: The unification of mathematics via topos theory. ArXiv arXiv:1006.3930 (2010)
8. Collins, T., Mannone, M., Hsu, D., Papageorgiou, D.: Psychological validation of mathematical gesture theory, Submitted (2018)
9. Delle Monache, S., Rocchesso, D., Bevilacqua, F., Lemaitre, G., Baldan, S., Cera, A.: Embodied sound design. Int. J. Hum.-Comput. Stud. 118, 47–59 (2018)

10. Dick, R.: The Other Flute. Lauren Keiser Music Publishing, Oxford (1989)
11. Di Donato, B., Bullock, J., Tanaka, A.: Myo Mapper: a Myo armband to OSC mapper. In: Dahl, L., Bowman, D., Martin, T. (eds.) Proceedings of NIME Conference, Blacksburg, USA, pp. 138–143 (2018)
12. Ehresmann, A., Gomez-Ramirez, J.: Conciliating neuroscience and phenomenology via category theory. Prog. Biophys. Mol. Biol. (JPMB) **19**(2), 347–359 (2016)
13. Fiore, T., Noll, T., Satyendra, R.: Morphisms of generalized interval systems and PR-groups. J. Math. Music **7**(1), 3–27 (2012)
14. Fish, S., L'Huillier, N.: Telemetron: a musical instrument for performance in zero gravity. In: Dahl, L., Bowman, D., Martin, T. (eds.) Proceedings of NIME Conference, Blacksburg, USA, pp. 315–317 (2018)
15. Genette, G.: L'opera dell'arte, two volumes. Clueb, Bologna (1999)
16. Guo, C., Song-Chun, Z., Wu, Y. N.: Towards a mathematical theory of primal sketch and sketchability. In: 9th IEEE Conference on Computer Vision (2003)
17. Heller, F., Cheung Ruiz, I.M., Borchers, J.: An augmented flute for beginners. In: Cumhur Erkut, C., De Götzen, A. (eds.) Proceedings of NIME Conference, Copenhagen, Denmark, pp. 34–37 (2017)
18. Isherwood, N.: The Techniques of Singing. Bärenreiter, Germany (2013)
19. Isnard, V., Taffou, M., Viaud-Delmon, I., Suied, C: Auditory sketches: very sparse representations of sounds are still recognizable. PloS One **11**(3) (2016). https://doi.org/10.1371/journal.pone.0150313
20. Jedrzejewski, F.: Hétérotopies musicales. Modéles mathématiques de la musique. Éditions Hermann, Paris (2019)
21. Kelkar, T., Jensenius, A.R.: Analyzing free-hand sound-tracing of melodic phrases. Appl. Sci. **8**(135), 1–21 (2018)
22. Kubota, A., Hori, H., Naruse, M., Akiba, F.: A new kind of aesthetics - the mathematical structure of the aesthetic. Philosophies **3**(14), 1–10 (2017)
23. Kubovy, M., Schutz, M.: Audio-visual objects. Rev. Philos. Psychol. **1**(1), 41–61 (2010)
24. Mac Lane, S.: Categories for the Working Mathematician. Springer, New York (1978). https://doi.org/10.1007/978-1-4757-4721-8
25. Mannone, M.: Introduction to gestural similarity. An application of category theory to the orchestra. J. Math. Music **12**(3), 63–87 (2018)
26. Mannone, M.: Knots, music and DNA. J. Creat. Music Syst. **2**(2), 1–23 (2018). https://www.jcms.org.uk/article/id/523/
27. Mannone, M., Favali, F.: Shared structures and transformations in mathematics and music: from categories to musicology. In: ESCOM-Italy Primo Meeting, Roma, Italy (2018)
28. Mannone, M.: Mathematics, Music, Nature (in Progress)
29. Mannone, M., Kitamura, E., Huang, J., Sugawara, R., Kitamura, Y.: CubeHarmonic: a new interface from a magnetic 3D motion tracking system to music performance. In: Dahl, L., Bowman, D., Martin, T. (eds.) Proceedings of NIME Conference, Blacksburg, USA, pp. 350–351 (2018)
30. Mastropasqua, M.: L'evoluzione della tonalità nel XX secolo. L'atonalità in Schoenberg. Clueb, Bologna (2004)
31. Mazzola, G., et al.: The Topos of Music, 2nd edn. Springer, Heidelberg (2018)
32. Mazzola, G., Andreatta, M.: Diagrams, gestures and formulae in music. J. Math. Music **1**(1), 23–46 (2007)
33. Mazzola, G., Mannone, M.: Global functorial hypergestures over general skeleta for musical performance. J. Math. Music **10**(7), 227–243 (2016)

34. Popoff, A.: Using monoidal categories in the transformational study of musical time-spans and rhythms. arXiv:1305.7192v3 (2013)
35. Russolo, L.: L'arte dei rumori. Edizioni futuriste di poesia, Milano (1910)
36. Sloboda, J.: Musical Mind. Oxford Science Publication, New York (2008)
37. Spence, C.: Crossmodal correspondences: a tutorial review. Atten. Percept. Psychophys. **73**(4), 971–995 (2011)
38. Turchet, L.: Smart musical instruments: vision, design principles, and future directions. IEEE Access **7**(1), 8944–8963 (2019)
39. Turchet, L.: Smart Mandolin: autobiographical design, implementation, use cases, and lessons learned. In: Cunningham, S., Picking, R. (eds.) Proceedings of the Audio Mostly Conference 2018, pp. 13:1–13:7, Wrexham Glyndwr University, Wrexham (2018). http://doi.acm.org/10.1145/3243274.3243280

Tropical Generalized Interval Systems

Giovanni Albini[1,2,3]($\boxtimes$) and Marco Paolo Bernardi[4]

[1] Conservatorio "Jacopo Tomadini", Udine, Italy
[2] Eesti Muusika- ja Teatriakadeemia, Tallinn, Estonia
[3] ISSM "Franco Vittadini", Pavia, Italy
mail@giovannialbini.it
[4] Università degli Studi di Pavia, Pavia, Italy
marco.bernardi@unipv.it

Abstract. This paper aims to refine the formalization of David Lewin's Generalized Interval System (GIS) by the means of tropical semirings. Such a new framework allows to broaden the GIS model introducing a new operation and consequently new musical and conceptual insights and applications, formalizing consistent relations between musical elements in an original unified structure. Some distinctive examples of extensions of well-known infinite GIS for lattices are then offered and the impossibility to build tropical GIS in the finite case is finally proven and discussed.

Keywords: Tropical semiring · Ordering · Generalized Interval System

1 Introduction

One of the most significant results achieved by the introduction of the Generalized Interval System (GIS) is to offer a consistent formal framework for musical elements and transformations between them. Although David Lewin's construction is very general and have been exploited for formalizing several different musical elements and transformations, one of its most straightforward use is for offering a formal framework for lattices, as the name itself suggests. Lattices have served as the basis of the ideas of this paper, thus, all the example that will be offered will be taken in their context. However, there may certainly be other possibilities and applications. In fact, the GIS notion in Lewin's own words "generalizes certain intuitions we have concerning traditional sorts of intervals that are directed from one pitch (or pitch class) to another. Generalized intervals are similarly directed, from one object of a GIS to another. These objects need not be pitches or pitch classes; they may have rhythmic, timbral, or other sort of character" [15].

According to [14], a Generalized Interval System can be defined as follows.

Definition 1. *A **Generalized Interval System (GIS)** is an ordered triple* (M, G, φ), *where* M *is a set of musical objects,* G *is a group and* φ *is an action of* G *on* M *which is free and transitive.*

© Springer Nature Switzerland AG 2019
M. Montiel et al. (Eds.): MCM 2019, LNAI 11502, pp. 73–83, 2019.
https://doi.org/10.1007/978-3-030-21392-3_6

Thus, for any $m \in M$, $\varphi(g, m) = m$ if and only if g is the identity element of G (free group action), and for any pair of elements $m_1, m_2 \in M$ there is one (and only one) $g \in G$ such that $\varphi(g, m_1) = m_2$ (transitive group action).[1]

It is important to underline the fundamental ontological and theoretical distinction that a GIS makes between the undertaken musical elements and the transformations among them: the former constituting a set of musical objects that per se are not ordered, and the latter being a set of transformations that forms a group and that acts on the aforesaid elements, defining and making explicit the structure of their set. This distinction is not obvious at all and was born as a generalization of Milton Babbitt and Allen Forte's ideas [7,12,13]. Furthermore, such an approach seems to meet neat structuralist criteria, in fact a GIS - misquoting Babbitt referring to a twelve tone-system - "like any formal system whose abstract model is satisfactorily formulable, can be characterized completely by stating its elements, the stipulated relation [...] among these elements, and the defined operations upon the so-related elements" [3].

In this framework, this paper aims to answer the following question: is it possible to refine the notion of the GIS so to find an even more detailed formalization that could represent in further detail musical elements and transformations among them?

There are certainly different ways to generalize GIS constructions, for instance by relaxing the simple-transitivity condition [18] or via the concept of groupoids and partial actions [16,17]. We have particularly investigated algebraic structures that might substitute the group one in the conventional definition of the GIS mainly in the context of lattices. The first apparently natural step has been to try to replace the group with a ring, keeping the group binary operation as the addition and introducing a multiplication that is distributive in respect to addition and under which the structure is a monoid.[2] As a result, in the specific case of lattices, this formalization leads to musical nonsense. If addition ends up representing the meaningful previously defined operation between transformation - that can be consistently seen as an ordered application of both the transformations - it is difficult to find a musical meaning for the multiplication, or to define it so to have one. For instance, let us consider the traditional case of intervals seen as a counting of semitones, hence constituting an algebraic structure that is isomorphic to the additive group $\mathbb{Z}$ in the case of pitches and to $\mathbb{Z}/12\mathbb{Z}$ in the case of pitch classes. Multiplying 3 by 2 ends in repeating the action of the interval 3 two times just for a mathematical contingency given by the numerical representation of intervals. In fact, in the aforesaid systems 2 is not a quantity but an interval, and multiplying two intervals has no acknowledged musical meaning. Therefore, due to the purpose of refinement of this paper, the

---

[1] According to Lewin's exact definition, as given in [14], the group action on the set is required to be "simply transitive". That is equivalent to the requirement of a free and transitive group action.

[2] The definition of a monoid requires only associativity and the existence of the identity element for the binary operation.

ring structure seems to be a dead end with respect to lattices.[3] Fortunately, if we stay close to the ring structure - dealing with semigroups and semirings - and we put the group binary operation of the GIS as the multiplication, we can find GIS refinements that fit our need and such as both operations are musically meaningful and could offer a more detailed insight of the undertaken musical elements.

Consequently, we shall introduce the mathematics of semirings, tropical semirings, min-plus and max-plus algebras, discussing then their implementation in the proposal for tropical Generalized Interval Systems both in the case of finite and infinite sets of musical elements.

2   Semirings and Tropical Algebras

Let us now introduce the algebraic structures that are going to be employed, in the order: semigroups, semirings, tropical semirings, min-plus and max-plus algebras. From a historical perspective, they are quite recent notions. Semirings have been introduced in 1934, in a short paper by Harry Schultz Vandiver [19], who gave them that name because of their ring-like structure. However, the same concept, although with a different name, has appeared in an earlier work by Richard Dedekind in 1884 [2,11]. The ideas that led to tropical algebra and tropical geometry can be traced back to the end of the fifties, as reported in 1979 in [5].

> In the past 20 years a number of different authors, often apparently unaware of one another's work, have discovered that a very attractive formulation language is provided for a surprisingly wide class of problems by setting up an algebra of real numbers (perhaps extended by symbols such as $-\infty$, etc.) in which, however, the usual operations of multiplication and addition of two numbers are replaced by the operations: (i) arithmetical addition, and (ii) selection of the greater (or dually, the less) of the two numbers, respectively.

Finally, "the adjective *tropical* was coined by French mathematicians, including Jean-Eric Pin, in honor of their Brazilian colleague Imre Simon, who was one of the pioneers in what could also be called min-plus algebra. There is no deeper meaning in the adjective tropical. It simply stands for the French view of Brazil" [20].

Let us now offer some formal definitions.

---

[3] However, outside the framework of lattices the ring structure can be successfully used to refine a GIS. Lewin gave in [15] an example of a GIS that calls out to be extended to a ring, although he did not carry out the extension himself. In fact, with respect to the GIS of Babbitt's lists investigated in the aforesaid paper, the transformation group can be easily and meaningfully extended to a ring. See Example 3 in Sect. 5 of this paper.

Definition 2. *A **semigroup** is an ordered pair* $(S, \bullet)$ *such that* S *is a non empty set and* $\bullet$ *is an associative binary operation; thus for any a, b, and c in* S:

$$(a \bullet b) \bullet c = a \bullet (b \bullet c). \tag{1}$$

Notice that no other restrictions are placed on a semigroup: it does not need an identity element and its elements do not need to have inverses within the semigroup. Only closure and associativity are preserved.

Definition 3. *A **semiring** is an ordered triple* $(S, \oplus, \otimes)$ *such that* S *is a non empty set,* $\oplus$ *and* $\otimes$ *are respectively called **addition** and **multiplication**, and* $(S, \oplus)$ *and* $(S, \otimes)$ *are semigroups such that multiplication left and right distributes over addition; thus for any a, b, and c in* S:

$$a \otimes (b \oplus c) = (a \otimes b) \oplus (a \otimes c) \quad and \quad (a \oplus b) \otimes c = (a \otimes c) \oplus (b \otimes c). \tag{2}$$

It should be emphasized that: (1) to avoid trivial examples, a semiring is hereby supposed to have at least two elements; (2) a semiring may or may not have identity elements for addition and/or multiplication, which may or may not coincide; (3) a semiring may or may not be additively and/or multiplicatively commutative, however, in case both the semigroups are abelian the semiring is said to be commutative [1]. For instance, $(\mathbb{N}, +, \times)$, with $\mathbb{N}$ the set of all the non-negative integers and $+$ and $\times$ the usual addition and multiplication of integers, is a commutative semiring with identity elements 0 and 1 for addition and multiplication respectively.

According to [11], let us now offer a general definition for tropical semirings.

Definition 4. *A **tropical semiring** is a semiring with idempotent addition; thus for any a in* S:

$$a \oplus a = a. \tag{3}$$

We can now introduce two of the most investigated tropical semirings.

Definition 5. *A **min-plus algebra** and a **max-plus algebra**, are the two tropical semirings* $(\mathbb{R} \cup \{\infty\}, \oplus, \otimes)$ *and* $(\mathbb{R} \cup \{-\infty\}, \oplus, \otimes)$, *with the operations as follows:*

$$x \oplus y = min\{x, y\} \quad or, \ respectively, \quad x \oplus y = max\{x, y\} \quad and \tag{4}$$

$$x \otimes y = x + y. \tag{5}$$

For them, the identity elements for the addition are ∞ and $-\infty$, respectively, and the multiplication is the usual addition of real numbers with 0 as the identity element. Commonly, min-plus and max-plus algebras are defined as such, but notice that in general in a tropical semiring the existence of an identity element is not a requirement, both for addition and multiplication. In order to extend the concept of a GIS, in which the elements of the algebras are - from a broader point of view - intervals and transformations between musical elements, the definition of an infinite one is thereby without any use, sense and practical application.

3 Extended and Tropical GIS

Considering the purpose of extending the notion of a Generalized Interval System, we shall then replace the group structure with a semiring one.

Definition 6. *An **Extended Generalized Interval System (eGIS)** is an ordered triple* (M, S, φ), *where* M *is a set of musical objects,* S *is a semiring* $(S, \oplus, \otimes)$ *such that with multiplication* $(S, \otimes)$ *constitutes a group, and* φ *is an action of* $(S, \otimes)$ *on* M *which is free and transitive.*

Notice that to preserve the feature of the binary operation between the intervals/transformations of a conventional GIS we have imposed the semiring multiplication to be a group. This way, it is possible to consider a standard GIS and to expand it in an extended one, keeping the group operation as the multiplication of the semiring and introducing a consistent addition that would satisfy its axioms. In this respect, idempotent operations - and in particular kind of minimum and maximum ones - ensure the definition of an order on the transformations, that to some extent one could read between the lines of the original idea of Lewin's GIS. In fact, in [14] Lewin refers to the transformations as "a family of directed measurements, distances, or motions of some sort". Therefore, the ordering of the elements of the transformation by the means of an idempotent binary operation lets explicit an otherwise not formally obvious metric of some musical meaning.

In fact, as is known, there is a strict correlation between the ordering of a set and some kinds of binary operations, as shown in the following two lemmas. Their proofs are simple and thus only sketched.[4]

Lemma 1. *To define a linear order in a set is equivalent to defining a binary operation that is associative, commutative and such that its outcome is always one of the two operands.*

Proof. Let a linear order be given. Define $a \oplus b = min\{a, b\}$. This is a binary operation. The required properties are obvious. Conversely, let be given a binary operation with those properties. Define $a \leq b$ if and only if $a \oplus b = a$. This is a binary relation. Since the outcome is always one of the two operands, the relation is reflexive and, if it is an order, it is a linear one. Antisymmetry is obvious. Since the operation is associative, the relation is transitive.

Lemma 2. *To define in a set a binary operation that is associative, commutative, and idempotent is equivalent to defining a (partial) order in which, for any two elements, there is a greatest lower bound, and also to defining a (partial) order in which, for any two elements, there is a least upper bound.*

Proof. If an order is given, define $a \oplus b = inf\{a, b\}$. The required properties are obvious. If, conversely, a binary operation is given, define $a \leq b$ if and only if $a \oplus b = a$. This relation is reflexive, owing to idempotency. It is obviously an order

---

[4] See also [8], Proposition 2.1.

relation, not necessarily linear. Anyway, it is easy to prove, using associativity and idempotency, that $(a \oplus b) \leq a$ and $(a \oplus b) \leq b$; moreover, if $c \leq a$ and $c \leq b$, then - again by associativity - $c \leq (a \oplus b)$, so $a \oplus b = inf\{a, b\}$, as required.

Notice that the hypotheses of Lemma 1 are a particular case of the ones of Lemma 2. Let us then narrow down the concept of the eGIS to one that considers only semirings with idempotent addition.

Definition 7. *A **Tropical Generalized Interval System (tGIS)** is an eGIS $(M, \mathbb{S}, \varphi)$ such that $\mathbb{S}$ is a tropical semiring.*

The advantage of introducing extended GIS and tropical GIS is not only of theoretical and explanatory nature in seeking new and more refined conceptual insights of a musical space, but it can offer also benefits on the application side. In a tropical GIS a kind of minimum or maximum binary operator works as the addition, as well as the composition between transformations works as the multiplication, and the two operations can be dealt together in long mathematical expressions of musical meaning that can be reduced and solved just as in traditional arithmetic. This is much different than simply requiring a linear order on the intervals of a GIS. In fact, it could be possible to define a linear order that implies a binary operation that could not satisfy the semiring features. The musical meaning of such an impasse will be discussed in Sect. 5.

Let us now study tropical Generalized Interval Systems both in the infinite and finite cases.

4   Infinite Tropical Generalized Interval Systems

Perhaps, the simplest example of a tropical GIS in the infinite case is the one obtained extending the conventional GIS $(P, \mathbb{Z}, \varphi)$ such as P is the infinite set of equal tempered pitches and its group of intervals is isomorphic to $\mathbb{Z}$. Let us define the two operations as follows:

$$x \oplus y = min\{x, y\} \quad \text{and} \quad x \otimes y = x + y \tag{6}$$

where $+$ is the usual addition in $\mathbb{Z}$. The tropical semiring structure of $(\mathbb{Z}, \oplus, \otimes)$ can be inferred from the min-plus algebra $(\mathbb{R} \cup \{\infty\}, \oplus, \otimes)$, of which $(\mathbb{Z}, \oplus, \otimes)$ is a subsemiring. Our tGIS is then $(P, (\mathbb{Z}, \oplus, \otimes), \varphi)$, for which there is no identity element for $\oplus$.

Another example can be given extending the GIS $(F, \mathbb{Q}, \varphi)$, where F are all the frequencies represented as positive rational numbers and the group is the multiplicative one $\mathbb{Q}$ of frequency ratios, that are positive rationals written as irreducible fractions as well. Its simplest tropical extension can be achieved defining the two operations such as:

$$x \oplus y = min\{x, y\} \quad \text{and} \quad x \otimes y = x \times y \tag{7}$$

where $\times$ is the usual multiplication in $\mathbb{Q}$. In this case, $\oplus$ simply outputs the shortest interval between the two operating ones.

However, different solutions embodying musical meaning can be defined for $\oplus$, keeping the multiplication from the group structure of $\mathbb{Q}$. For instance, reminded that we are dealing with irreducible fractions, it is possible to consider the following operation:

$$\frac{a}{b} \oplus \frac{c}{d} = \frac{GCD(a,c)}{LCM(b,d)}, \tag{8}$$

such as GCD stands for the greatest common divisor and LCM for the least common multiple of two integers. Consequently, such an operation outputs one of the two elements only if the multiplication of it by a natural number gives the other operand; in case it does not, it outputs the biggest element in $\mathbb{Q}$ such as the two operands can be obtained multiplicating it by natural numbers. It is an idempotent operation and multiplication left and right distributes over it. From the point of view of music, it outputs the biggest interval expressed as a ratio in respect of which the two operands can be seen as natural harmonics.

Let us now consider the GIS $(F(\sqrt[12]{2}), \mathbb{Q}^*(\sqrt[12]{2}), \varphi)$. $F(\sqrt[12]{2})$ is the set of all the frequencies that can be obtained as ratios combined with the ones in equal temperament. Thus, it is the set of all the frequencies that can be written as follows:

$$a_{11}(\sqrt[12]{2})^{11} \times a_{10}(\sqrt[12]{2})^{10} \times \cdots \times a_1 \sqrt[12]{2} \times a_0, \tag{9}$$

with $a_0, a_1, \ldots, a_{11} \in \mathbb{Q}$. Here $\mathbb{Q}^*(\sqrt[12]{2})$ is a subgroup of the multiplicative group of the algebraic number field $\mathbb{Q}(\sqrt[12]{2})$, generated by $\mathbb{Q}$ and $\sqrt[12]{2}$. Such a GIS can be extended with the semiring addition introduced in Eq. 7. On the contrary, the one offered in Eq. 8 does not work, because not all the elements of $F(\sqrt[12]{2})$ can be reduced to fractions, and, moreover, because a common submultiple between two elements in $\mathbb{Q}^*(\sqrt[12]{2})$ does not necessarily exist; hence not every couple of intervals can be seen as natural harmonics in a series.

In fact, regrettably, to extend an infinite GIS is not always as straightforward as it could appear. For instance, we have tried without success to consider a third proposal for $\oplus$ in order to extend $(F, \mathbb{Q}, \varphi)$ involving Euler's consonance degree value, *gradus suavitatis*, as it was described in [6] and investigated, amongst many others, in [4, 10]. First of all, given an irreducible fraction $\frac{a}{b}$ and following Euler's principles, let us define the function $C_e : \mathbb{Q} \to \mathbb{N}^*$ that associates a fraction with its degree of consonance as follows:

$$C_e\left(\frac{1}{2^n}\right) = n + 1 \tag{10}$$

otherwise, for $a, b \in \mathbb{N}^*$ such as $\frac{a}{b} \neq \frac{1}{2^n}$,

$$C_e\left(\frac{a}{b}\right) = C_e\left(\frac{1}{LCM\left(\frac{a}{GCD(a,b)}, \frac{b}{GCD(a,b)}\right)}\right)$$

$$= C_e\left(\frac{1}{p_1^{k_1} \times p_2^{k_2} \times \cdots \times p_m^{k_m}}\right) = \sum_{i=1}^{m}(p_i^{k_i} - k_i) + 1 \tag{11}$$

Thus, we have tried to define $\oplus$ accordingly:

$$\frac{a}{b} \oplus \frac{c}{d} = \begin{cases} \frac{a}{b}, & \text{if } C_e\left(\frac{a}{b}\right) < C_e\left(\frac{c}{d}\right); \\ \frac{c}{d}, & \text{if } C_e\left(\frac{c}{d}\right) < C_e\left(\frac{a}{b}\right); \\ min\{\left(\frac{a}{b}\right), \left(\frac{c}{d}\right)\} & \text{otherwise.} \end{cases} \tag{12}$$

In this case, $\oplus$ outputs the most consonant interval between the two (the one with the lowest degree of consonance); otherwise, if the two ratios share the degree, it outputs the smallest of them. Unfortunately, the distributive law does not work. In fact,

$$5 \otimes \left(\frac{1}{5} \oplus \frac{1}{8}\right) = 5 \otimes \frac{1}{8} = \frac{5}{8}, \tag{13}$$

but, at the same time,

$$\left(5 \otimes \frac{1}{5}\right) \oplus \left(5 \otimes \frac{1}{8}\right) = 1 \oplus \frac{5}{8} = 1. \tag{14}$$

A last successful example can be given extending the GIS (F_J, Q_J, φ), where F_J are all the pitches in 5-limit just intonation represented as frequencies and Q_J is the group of the just intonation ratios, i.e. the multiplicative subgroup of $\mathbb{Q}$ made up of all the numbers that can be expressed in the form $2^i 3^j 5^k$ such that $i, j, k \in \mathbb{Z}$. An idempotent addition can be defined as follows:

$$2^i 3^j 5^k \oplus 2^{i^*} 3^{j^*} 5^{k^*} = \begin{cases} 2^i 3^j 5^k, & \text{if } k > k^*, \\ & \text{if } k = k^* \text{ and } j > j^*, \\ & \text{if } k = k^*, j = j^* \text{ and } i > i^*, \\ 2^{i^*} 3^{j^*} 5^{k^*} & \text{otherwise.} \end{cases} \tag{15}$$

Therefore, for instance $\frac{8}{27} \oplus \frac{1}{5} = 2^3 3^{-3} 5^0 \oplus 2^0 3^0 5^{-1} = \frac{8}{27}$. Such an operation might be easily adjusted to be used to extend different GIS with n-limit extended just tuning intervals in the form $2^i 3^j \dots n^k$ with n prime.

Nevertheless, these are just a few examples of the multitude of potential extensions of infinite GIS that can be built for better or alternative insights and applications.

5   Finite Tropical Generalized Interval Systems

Considering our musical aims, it would be natural to try to apply the same structures to modular arithmetics, due to the importance of groups of intervals isomorphic to $\mathbb{Z}/12\mathbb{Z}$ and $\mathbb{Z}/7\mathbb{Z}$ in music theory. But, unfortunately, the following theorem (which is, perhaps, the main result of this paper) makes it impossible to build finite not trivial tropical GIS.

Theorem 1. *Given a finite set of at least two elements, it is not possible to define two binary operations such as one is associative, commutative and idempotent and the other is a group and is distributive over the first.*

Proof. Let us consider a finite set for which $\otimes$ is a group and $\oplus$ is associative, commutative and idempotent. Therefore, because of Lemma 2, there is an order in the set in which, for any two elements, there is a greatest lower bound, i.e., $a \oplus b$ is the greatest lower bound of a and b. Let 0 be the identity element for $\otimes$, $s \neq 0$, and $t = 0 \oplus s$. If $t \neq 0$, then $t \oplus 0 = t$ and, applying the distributive law, we get:

$$t \otimes t = t \otimes (t \oplus 0) = (t \otimes t) \oplus (t \otimes 0) = (t \otimes t) \oplus t. \tag{16}$$

Thus,

$$(t \otimes t) \oplus t = t \otimes t \tag{17}$$

and, because of order transitivity,

$$(t \otimes t) \oplus 0 = t \otimes t. \tag{18}$$

Let us consider $t^m = t \otimes t \otimes \cdots \otimes t$, m times, and such as $t^m = 0$ (m surely exists, because the group is finite). Then, by distributivity,

$$(t \otimes t^{m-1}) \oplus (t \otimes 0) = t \otimes t^{m-1}, \tag{19}$$

thus, $0 \oplus t = 0$, a contradiction. If $t = 0$, then $0 = 0 \oplus s$ and the proof is similar.

Let us discuss some related constructions which could be considered erroneously as counterexamples.

Example 1. Two-element Boolean algebra (also called Boolean semiring). This is not a counterexample to Theorem 1, because the two elements, with multiplication, do not form a group: 0 has no multiplicative inverse. All the other properties are verified [9].

Example 2. Finite fields (also called Galois fields). None of them is a counterexample. The addition is not idempotent (the only idempotent element is 0) and the element, with multiplication, do not form a group (the multiplicative group of any field contains the elements different from 0). Note that the field $(\mathbb{Z}/2\mathbb{Z}, +, \times)$ has two elements, as the Boolean algebra of Example 1. The only difference between these two algebraic structures is the sum $1 + 1$ (see next example).

Example 3. Direct product of finite fields. In [15] David Lewin uses the term "Boolean sum" for the sum modulo 2. In the above Example 1, the meaning is different: in the two-element Boolean algebra $1 + 1 = 1$; in the sum modulo 2, on the contrary, $1 + 1 = 0$. In the same paper, the author uses the group $((\mathbb{Z}/2\mathbb{Z})^4, +)$. So, let us consider for a moment also finite products of finite fields. None of them is a counterexample to Theorem 1 above. In fact, we can repeat what we have already shown in Example 2. Moreover, in such products there exist zero divisors, so the multiplicative group cannot even contain all the elements different from 0. Note that, if we consider a finite product of copies of $(\mathbb{Z}/2\mathbb{Z}, +, \times)$, we get a Boolean ring (i.e., the multiplication is idempotent). The group used by Lewin can be extended to such a ring.

The result offered by Theorem 1 is meaningful especially on the musical side. In fact, the sensitive requirement that cannot be satisfied is the distributive law, that de facto connects the two operations. Moreover, we have shown that to define on a set a binary operation that is associative, commutative, and idempotent is equivalent to defining an order in which, for any two elements, there is a greatest lower bound and also to defining an order in which, for any two elements, there is a least upper bound. As a matter of fact, cyclicity and linearity are not compatible concepts: if we try to deal with a finite - thus, in some sense, cyclical[5] - GIS from the point of view of a linear order we break its cyclical nature that made any combination of transformations meaningful. As a consequence, such linear orders could have only a theoretical significance on a taxonomic level[6], before any combination, and cannot offer any general systematic insight. Thus, a finite GIS cannot be extended to a tropical one.

6   Conclusions

We have introduced a refinement of David Lewin's Generalized Interval System by the means of tropical semirings, investigated the links between a tropical semiring addition and an ordering, studied some examples obtained extending well-known infinite GIS mainly in the context of lattices, and proven and discussed the impossibility to build tropical GIS in the finite case. Such new theoretical framework has shown the capability to embody a more detailed knowledge of the formalized musical elements in a unified structure. Moreover, we believe that the several possibilities in the definition of the semiring addition, both in the tropical and in the more general case of extended GIS, could trigger new ideas and conceptual insights in dealing with such elements, as we have shown in some of the examples offered. Therefore, further studies may be conducted in deepening the various extending possibilities. Finally, we have deepened finite and infinite tropical GIS, but the more general case of extended GIS is still open to further studies, especially about the finite case.

Acknowledgments. We thank Claudio Bernardi (Università di Roma "La Sapienza", Department of Mathematics) and the reviewers for their useful suggestions and remarks.

---

[5] In fact, every element of a finite group generates a cyclical subgroup.

[6] For instance, it would be meaningful to order the elements in $\mathbb{Z}/12\mathbb{Z}$ from 0, the minimum, to 11, the maximum, or, alternatively, in the following sequence: $0, 1, 11, 2, 10, 3, 9, 4, 8, 5, 7, 6$, in which it is taken the distance from 0 on both side, favoring the right one in case of the same value.

References

1. Adhikari, M.R., Adhikari, A.: Basic Modern Algebra with Applications. Springer, New Delhi (2014). https://doi.org/10.1007/978-81-322-1599-8
2. Ahsan, J., Mordeson, J.N., Shabir, M.: Fuzzy Semirings with Applications to Automata Theory. Springer, Heidelberg (2012). https://doi.org/10.1007/978-3-642-27641-5
3. Babbitt, M.: Twelve-tone invariants as compositional determinants. Music. Q. **46**, 246–259 (1960)
4. Bailhache, P.: Music translated into Mathematics: Leonhard Euler. In: Proceedings of Problems of Translation in the 18th Century, Nantes (1997)
5. Cuninghame-Green, R.: Minimax Algebra. Springer, Heidelberg (1979). https://doi.org/10.1007/978-3-642-48708-8
6. Euler: Tentamen novae theoriae musicae ex certissimis harmoniae principiis dilucide expositae (1737)
7. Forte, A.: The Structure of Atonal Music. Yale University Press, London (1973)
8. Gunawardena, J.: Idempotency. Cambridge University Press, Cambridge (1998)
9. Halmos, P., Givant, S.: Introduction to Boolean Algebras. Undergraduate Texts in Mathematics. Springer, New York (2009). https://doi.org/10.1007/978-0-387-68436-9
10. Hofmann-Engl, L.: Consonance/Dissonance - a historical perspective. In: Demorest, S.M., Morrison, S.J., Campbell, P.S. (eds.) Proceedings of the 11th International Conference on Music Perception and Cognition (ICMPC 2011), Seattle, Washington, USA (2011)
11. Krivulin, N.: Tropical optimization problems. In: Advances in Economics and Optimization: Collected Scientific Studies Dedicated to the Memory of L. V. Kantorovich, pp. 195–214. Nova Science Publishers, New York (2014)
12. Lewin, D.: A label free development for 12-pitch class systems. J. Music Theory **21**, 29–48 (1977)
13. Lewin, D.: On generalized intervals and transformations. J. Music Theory **24**(2), 243–251 (1980)
14. Lewin, D.: Generalized Musical Intervals and Transformations. Yale University Press, New Haven and London (1987)
15. Lewin, D.: Generalized interval systems for Babbitt's lists, and for Schoenberg's string trio. Music Theory Spectr. **17**(1), 81–118 (1995)
16. Popoff, A., Andreatta, M., Ehresmann, A.: A categorical generalization of Klumpenhouwer networks. In: Collins, T., Meredith, D., Volk, A. (eds.) MCM 2015. LNCS (LNAI), vol. 9110, pp. 303–314. Springer, Cham (2015). https://doi.org/10.1007/978-3-319-20603-5_31
17. Popoff, A., Agon, C., Andreatta, M., Ehresmann, A.: From K-nets to PK-nets: a categorical approach. Perspect. New Music **54**(2), 5–63 (2016)
18. Rahn, J.: Cool tools: polysemic and non-commutative nets, subchain decompositions and cross-projecting pre-orders, object-graphs, chain-hom-sets and chain-label-hom-sets, forgetful functors, free categories of a net, and ghosts. J. Math. Music **1**(1), 7–22 (2007)
19. Vandiver, H.S.: Note on a simple type of algebra in which the cancellation law of addition does not hold. Bull. Am. Math. Soc. **40**, 914–920 (1934)
20. Speyer, D., Sturmfels, B.: Tropical Mathematics. Math. Mag. **82**, 3 (2009)

Shall We (Math and) Dance?

Maria Mannone[1]([✉]) and Luca Turchet[2]

[1] Department of Mathematics and Informatics, University of Palermo, Palermo, Italy
mariacaterina.mannone@unipa.it, manno012@umn.edu
[2] Department of Information Engineering and Computer Science,
University of Trento, Trento, Italy
luca.turchet@unitn.it

Abstract. Can we use mathematics, and in particular the abstract branch of category theory, to describe some basics of dance, and to highlight structural similarities between music and dance? We first summarize recent studies between mathematics and dance, and between music and categories. Then, we extend this formalism and diagrammatic thinking style to dance.

Keywords: 2-categories · Music · Dance

1 Introduction: Why Mathematics for Dance

Joining the abstraction of mathematics with expressivity and passion in dance is possible. It means rationally exploring basic features of dance, and appreciating the flexibility of modern mathematics, for speculative investigation and practical purposes. A joint approach between music, dance, and mathematics would involve rational thinking upon the arts, as well as the 'translations' of ideas and transformational mechanisms between disciplines in a STEAM (Science, Technology, Engineering, Art, and Math) attitude.

'Concrete' applications can also involve pedagogy in one or more of these disciplines, giving amusing examples of applications of mathematical concepts and procedures, and investigating some hidden, theoretical roots of artistic practices. In particular, in the case of math and dance, an interplay between rationality and intuition may even help people learn dancing. This is the case of a software that helps tango learners to find the main pulse via a mathematical analysis of the underlying musical structures [1]. A way to compare underlying rhythms for dance is suggested in E. Amiot's book [2], where Fourier discrete transforms are used to give an idea of the distribution of durations of notes and rhythm patterns.

The world of dance includes different styles and techniques, each of them with inner symmetries. These symmetries may be thought of throught the lens

---

M. Mannone is an alumna of the University of Minnesota, USA.

M. Montiel et al. (Eds.): MCM 2019, LNAI 11502, pp. 84–97, 2019.
https://doi.org/10.1007/978-3-030-21392-3_7

of mathematics. An overview of mathematics for different dance styles is proposed in [24], with a focus on the geometry of figures ('poses'). The geometry of choreographies also includes connecting movements between poses of the group of dancers. One can analyze the geometry of poses of a single dancer, but a more complete investigation should also involve the analysis of the geometry generated by the entire group of dancers on stage. The audience of a ballet, and, in general, of a dance show, pays attention differently to dancers, dancers' groups, and parts of them. To investigate the relationship between attention and single dancers the concept of the *center of attention* has been used, an element already used in visual arts. It can be studied geometrically and statistically as a trajectory [23]. In analogy with the center of mass that connects form and mass, the center of attention has been connected with the ideal 'mass' of dancers, with the concept of 'center of attention mass.' The center of attention mass of an ensemble connects physics, group dancing schemes, and rhythm patterns. It is evaluated assigning weights to dancers' bodies based "on the type of movement performed and how likely the moves are to attract the audience's attention" [24].

A scientific perspective on choreography does not involve only analysis and understanding of dance practice: it can suggest new ideas sparkling creativity. Furthermore, specific geometric forms can be used as bases for choreography and other artistic applications; this is the case of the truncated octahedron[1] cited in [4], and the 'Apollonian circles'[2] from *The Daughters of Hypatia* by Karl Schaffer [23].

Dance involves figures as events in time continuously connected, and time – and expressivity – is shaped by music. Music does also influence not only the *when* of figures and movements but also their *how*, their style. Thus, a complete study of dance cannot prescind from the role of music. In fact, music and dance are tightly connected in several cultures [20].

One of the elements connecting music and dance is *gesture*, which influences expressive parameters of music. Gestures also contain information about pulse. The conductor communicates pulse and rhythm to orchestral musicians, as well as overall style and expressivity. Each musician performs specific gestures, according to the technique of the specific instrument he or she plays. Dancers do not take pulse directly from the conductor, but from performed music, via a 'filtering' operation; see [1]. Dancers' movements and gestures, especially in ballet, are linked with music and thus, indirectly, with musicians' gestures that produce that music.

We can wonder if it is possible to describe within some unitary vision the gestures of conductor, musicians, and dancers. To the best of our knowledge, there is not such a theory yet, but only a collection of experiences and case studies. A recent mathematical overview of the similarities between conducting and orchestral musicians' gestures uses the formalism of category theory [17]. In fact, the power of abstraction of categories allows for the schematization of

---

[1] An Archimedean solid.
[2] Families of circles where every circle of a family intersects every circle of the other family orthogonally.

similarities and similar transformations between different objects, relaxing the condition of 'equality' in favor of 'up to an isomorphism.'

The flexibility of categories and, more in general, of diagrammatic thinking is exemplified by the mathematical definition of *gesture*. While trying to sketch a general theory of music and dance, it is helpful to highlight common elements between different dance styles. Arrows and diagrams in categories can connect the discussed existing studies with current research in mathematical music theory. Figure 1 shows an intuitive and yet precise application of categorical formalism to dance. This schematization is inspired by the definition of musical gestures proposed in [19], that makes use of dance as a metaphor to understand music.

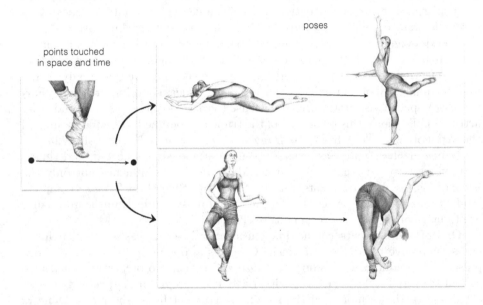

Fig. 1. A mapping from a simple diagram (with two points and an arrow) representing points in space and time touched by the foot of a dancer, and two different realizations of this scheme. The arrows between the two images of each pair of dancers represent the continuous movements to connect the two poses. The mapping consists of two (topological) functors from points in space-time (first category) to dance figures and movements (second category). This is a category of gestures, where objects are gestures, and morphisms are hypergestures. We are working with curves of gestures, that is, a particular instance of hypergestures. In the second category, the points are the figures (poses), and the arrows are the movements. We are using functors and not only functions because we need to map not only objects from a domain to a codomain but also the transformations between them, and functors map objects into objects, and morphisms into morphisms. Dancers are not usually aware of this, but the mathematics behind their art is the definition of gestures on topological categories [3,19]. Drawings by Maria Mannone.

In this paper, we briefly summarize mathematical theory of musical gestures [3,16,17,19] and basics of categories, and we show their possible application to dance. This approach may be useful to investigate formal and cognitive studies about dance [20].

2   Categories, Music, and Dance

Category theory can be applied to music [7,18], included musical gestures [3,8,18,19]. A category is given by objects (points or, to avoid a set-theoretic feeling, *vertices*) and morphisms between them (arrows), verifying associative and identity properties. We can define arrows between categories (*functors*) bringing objects of a category into objects of the other one, and morphisms of a category into morphisms of the other one. Considering categories themselves as vertices (to be connected via functors), we can easily build nested structures.[3]

In [19], a gesture is defined as a collection of vertices in space and time connected by a system of continuous curves.[4] Musical notes (vertices) are like 'the points touched by a dancer while moving continuously in the space' (arrows) [19]. This definition can be extended to visual arts, n-categories, and recursive gestures [16]. Musical gestures allow one to shape physical sound parameters for expressive reasons: a purely 'technical' gesture such as pressing a piano key can be shaped into, let us say, a delicate, caressing gesture.[5]

The most basic gesture is probably *breathing*, that can be seen in general as a couple of (inverted) curves between two points—a 'tense' state and a 'relaxed' state. In piano playing, we have the general idea of preparation and key-pressing. Breathing, in music and dance, is the starting point of both basic technique and expressive motion.[6] From conductor's hands to dancers' feet, all feelings are conveyed into muscular tension/release and drawing curves in space and time. 'Breathing' reminds of diaphragm movements for singers and wind players. More generally, breathing reminds of arsis and thesis, preparation and beat (conducting), inspiration and exhalation, dissonance and resolution in harmony. The dualism tension-relaxation is also relevant for dance [5]. In general, we can find *similarities* of gestures on different instruments—e.g., the necessary variations of movements to play a *forte* on violin and on piano [17]; these similarities also deform the basic metric gestures of a conductor.

In dance, we have poses/figures (vertices) and movements (arrows) connecting them. Movements can be seen as vertices, and transformations of these movements as arrows. Thus, both in music and dance we can categorically investigate

---

[3] We can define 2-categories and n-categories.

[4] More precisely, an abstract (and oriented) diagram is mapped into points and paths in a topological space.

[5] Conversely, the violent bow's movements of strings in the movie *Psycho* by Hitchcock well evoke the knife hitting.

[6] According to [9], "in the dance studio, conscious use of breathing patterns can enhance the phrasing and expressivity in movement."

basic technical gestures and their expressive deformations, as well as their compositions and groupings. Groupings and hierarchies of musical structures [13,18] and gestures [16] have a correspondence for dance: basic feelings represented via expressive gestures can be connected within a whole story, letting dance acquire a narrative dimension.

3   Diagrammatic Details

Gestures[7] in music and dance can be seen as two categories. In dance, the objects are the positions, and the morphisms are the movements to reach them.[8] We can define a functor from music to dance, involving metrical aspects in music to be connected with metrical aspects in dance, and expressive aspects of music with expressive aspects in dance. The 'vertices' would be isolated, remarkable points of the score or short sequences in music and figures in dance, and the 'arrows' would be the connecting passages in music and connecting gestures in dance.

The category *dance* is given by positions of the human body in space and time, called *figures*, connected via continuous movements:

$$\text{dance figure 1} \xrightarrow{movement} \text{dance figure 2}.$$

We can easily introduce 2-categories if we consider different ways to connect two figures, whose variation, represented by the double arrow, can embody changes in speed, amplitude, and expressivity; see diagram 1.

$$\text{dance figure 1} \quad \Downarrow \quad \text{dance figure 2} \qquad\qquad (1)$$

The identity corresponds to the absence of movement—keeping a static position. Horizontal composition is well-defined: the composition of two dance movements is another dance movement. Vertical composition is also well-defined: we can transform a movement into another, and the composition of two movement transformations leads to another movement. Vertical associativity is verified if we consider equivalence classes of movements connecting dance figures.[9]

---

[7] The category of gestures has gestures as objects and gestures of gestures (hypergestures) as the morphisms between them. The composition of hypergestures (paths) is associative up to a path of paths [16].

[8] From [5]: "The physical signal of dance consists of a change in position of the dancer body in space with respect to time." We can see positions as vertices and changes of positions as arrows. Also: "movement is physically created by an infinite sequence of continuous positions in space unfolding in time." We can represent the transition from a position to another one via an arrow representing a morphing.

[9] In fact, a transformation between movements requires a homotopy, and homotopy is not associative (it requires a reparametrization). However, homotopy classes are associative.

Horizontal associativity is also verified: similarly with (musical or generic) gestures, the composition of dance hypergestures (paths) is associative up to a path of paths. Diagrams help us compare figures and movements of different styles; see diagram 2. In fact, we can define, within the category 'dance,' a subcategory for dance-style 1, and another subcategory for dance-style 2. For sake of simplicity, we can just define a category for style 1 and a category for style 2.

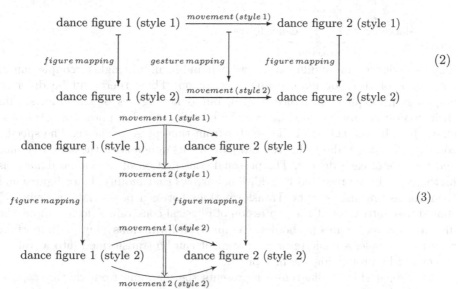

$$(2)$$

$$(3)$$

We can group movements in two, three, and so on, according to tempo. Dance teachers can ask their students to start clapping hands, letting them think of musical rhythm. Then, students will start making movements with their bodies according to the given rhythm. Mathematically, this is a mapping from the category of pulses to the category of basic dance movements; thus, we have a functor. In the category of pulses, objects are accents (beats), and arrows are time intervals between them. Beats are mapped into positions of the body in space and time, and time intervals are mapped into body movements to reach these positions;[10] see diagram 4, enriched with 2-categories. Diagram 2 is enriched in terms of 2-categories in diagram 3. In diagram 3, additional arrows, not shown for reasons of graphic clarity, map *movement* 1 (*style* 1) into *movement* 1 (*style* 2), *movement* 2 (*style* 1) into *movement* 2 (*style* 2), and double arrows into double arrows. The same applies to diagram 4, where 2-cells of 2-category pulse may represent the time variation between two consecutive pulses. We are using the formalism of 2-functors, that are morphisms between 2-cells[11] [14]. In fact, 2-cells give a metaphorical idea of the different ways to connect figures within

---

[10] In the case of total improvisation (music and dance), the diagram would be commutative.

[11] As defined in [14], a 2-functor between two categories A and B is a triple of functions that map objects, arrows, and 2-cells of A into objects, arrows, and 2-cells of B respectively, preserving "all the categorical structures."

the same style, to move hands in conducting between two pulses (diagram 5) for technical and expressive reasons, and so on.

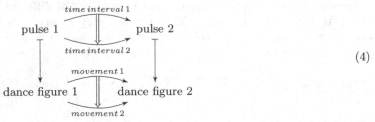

$$(4)$$

Figures in dance can be different for women and men, for single or couple dance, for groups of three or more people, and so on. Thus, there will be different mappings from pulse to dance figures, but dance figures of all dancers, and their connecting movements, have to be coordinated. Temporal consistency is guaranteed by the action of the functor from time pulse to dance. The specific connection between dance figures and movements depends on the style of dance and the role of each dancer. The personal contribution of individual dancers is mathematically represented by additional arrows that modify dance figures and their connecting movements. Transformations between poses (i.e., movements) should take into account the expression of physical constraints: for example, the distance between dancers' bodies. Tempo transformations play an important role: for example, a basic ternary movement can be transformed into a 'valzer' movement by prolonging the first pulse.

The upper side of diagram 5 represents the mapping from rhythmic pulse to conducting gestures (r. h. indicates right hand), where we consider the 2-cell given by two different right-hand's movements connecting two right-hand's positions; the lower side, the mapping from the same rhythmic pulse to basic dance movements (with a similar remark on 2-categories). Movements in conducting and dance are related because dancers hear the music, and they find conductor's beats through the music. If the dancers are dancing on their own without any music, they have to think tempo pulse in their own, too;[12] if there is music, dancers can rely on its pulse. Ideally, dancers, musicians, and of course the conductor, are thinking the same tempo pulse. For the sake of completeness, we should cite the Cunningham school, where dance is not connected with the pulse of music. In this case, we cannot define a functor from pulse to dance. We might describe diagram 5 as a simple functor from pulse to dance; however, it stresses the 'generator' role of pulse for both dance and conducting. We can imagine a 'pulse' that is first an abstract thought and then is embodied in conducting gestures and dance movements. In the practical reality, dancers extract,

---

[12] Dancers can move without any (external) music if they are able to think of their pulse and to communicate with each other via touch and non-verbal indications (and the leader should be particularly clear in such indications), especially for couple dancing; but this is an unstable situation. Permutations of roles should be clearly signaled via, for example, a variation in touch or visual communication.

as in a filter operation, the information about tempo pulse from music. Thus: pulse *is the basis of* (is mapped into) conducting gestures, that *are the basis of* orchestral playing, that *is the basis of* listening to music, *that helps* dancers catch pulse from music, *allowing them* to move accordingly; see diagram 6.

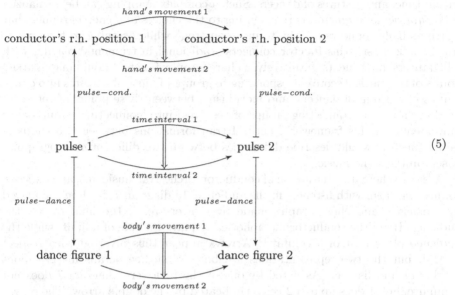

$$(5)$$

The arrow from conductor to dancer is dashed because the conductor does not directly give tempo to the dancer: he or she catches it from music, thus, from musicians' activity.

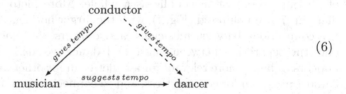

$$(6)$$

The mapping from tempo-pulse to dance can be formally described via a *pulse-dance functor*; see diagram 4.

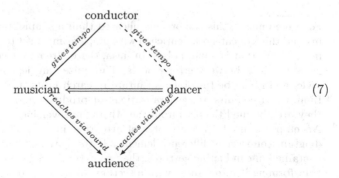

$$(7)$$

Overall musical character and expressivity shape expressive dance movements. For example, a sudden orchestral *forte* should imply a corresponding choreography variation for ballet dancers.[13] We can navigate through complexity of dance, by considering comparisons between gestures of orchestral musicians within time, and gestures of dancers. Such a complex mapping can be formalized as a *Choreography functor*, corresponding to the choices of a choreographer that instructs ballet dancers on how to move on stage while listening to the orchestra. In folk music, this functor connects traditional instruments' playing with folk dancers' movements. Intuitively, a choreography functor should map marked points of the musical score corresponding to groups of musical gestures into dance figures of a group of dancers, and morphisms between these points of the score (and the associate connecting groups of gestures) into 'connecting' group dance movements. In this framework, natural transformations between two choreography functors would describe differences between two different choreographies based on the same music.

We can schematize the action of conductor, orchestral musicians, and dancers, connecting them with listeners in the audience. In diagram 7, both music played by musicians and choreography made by dancers reach the final target, the audience. Here, the conductor metaphorically plays the role of a limit, while the audience plays that of a colimit.[14] Arrows appear thus inverted with respect to [17], but the two representations are both valid. See details in [17] about conductor and listener. As noted by one of the reviewers, diagram 7 does not commute, but it does up to a 2-cell as indicated by the double arrow. The reason is that impressions of the public with respect to musicians and with respect to dancers can be similar, but they will never be equal. The commutativity is verified if we consider a single listener, or if we consider the equivalence class of all impressions of the public as a whole. More pictorially, we can imagine diagram 7 as an ellipsoid (Fig. 2), with the larger horizontal section representing the connections between musicians' and dancers' movements, and the vertical one, the separation between music and dance worlds.[15] The conductor's role appears as being more relevant for a ballet than for other dance styles. Diagrams 2 and 7 are given for completeness, and to connect our study with former studies in mathematical theory of musical gestures of orchestral musicians [17].

---

[13] For tango music, this is more complicated than a simple 'pulse extraction.' We can instead think of categories enriched with maps from a beat to another beat containing inner maps, that is, inner pulses. In salsa, there often are recognizable patterns with clave rhythms between strong beats. The pulse can depend on the specific music style, and it can be the object of future research in itself.

[14] Limits and colimits are generalizations of products and coproducts, respectively; they are obtained the ones from the others via reversing arrows [12].

[15] An ellipse is used for the center of attention in [23]. The ellipsoid of Fig. 2 is a diagram connecting different elements. If the listener/audience recovers the pulse contained in conducting gestures, the two extremities of the ellipsoid can be joined, transforming it into a torus with a section collapsed into a point.

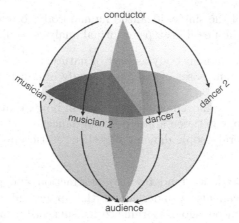

Fig. 2. Ellipsoid where conductor and audience can be thought of as limit and colimit, respectively.

4 Discussion

In this paper, we introduced the use of category theory, an abstract branch of mathematics, to the study of dance in relationship with music. The nested structures of categories help connecting different perspectives on dance, such as the relationship with musical pulse [1] and the geometry in dance [4]. Also, the 'trajectory,' that is, the change over space/time of the center of attention as a trajectory [23] can be schematized via an arrow, and the comparisons between centers of attention for different choreographies, via arrows between arrows. This would also allow for a comparison between the geometry of different choreographies, combining into a unitary vision the collection of examples proposed in literature [4, 23]. The geometry of choreographies can be investigated via connected categories.[16] In the case of the tango ball, we can also think of connected musical sequences, the so-called *tandas*, with their different styles.

Also, one can establish a connection between dancers' positions and movements and their center of attention mass [24], and one can compare variations of this center within a choreography with variations of this center within another choreography, quantitatively characterizing choreographers' styles and different editions/productions of the same ballet. More generally, a comparison between variations of the center of attention mass would well characterize differences and analogies of choreographies for different dance styles.

We can wonder if nested structures of categories may help connecting even more layers of understanding and aesthetic appreciation for dance. We can start

---

[16] A connected category J is a category where, for each couple of objects $j, k \in J$, there is a finite sequence of objects $j_0, j_1, ..., j_{2n}$ connecting them, that is: $j = j_0 \rightarrow j_1 \leftarrow j_2 \rightarrow ... \rightarrow j_{2n-1} \leftarrow j_{2n} = k$, where both directions are allowed [14]. Here, the morphisms are the arrows $f_i : j_i \rightarrow j_{i+1}$ or $f_i : j_{i+1} \rightarrow j_i$.

from the symmetry of the single, idealized human body to reach the most complex choreography. The possible steps of formal analysis would be:

1. the beauty[17] of the human body as part of nature;
2. the beauty of different poses of the human body in dance, as photographical shoots;
3. the beauty of dancing movements of the human body, that is, of the connections and transitions between static poses of dance;
4. the beauty of several people dancing together: 'static poses' as well as their connecting movements.

If, on the one hand, we tend towards abstraction and generalization, on the other hand we can also wonder about the applicability of our model in concrete setups and in pedagogical frameworks, suggesting categorical developments of recent research and maybe new software applications [1]. Both points and arrows are part of dance learning: dance students learn the poses and the way to smoothly, and expressively, reach them. The movements of each dancer have to be well-coordinated with movements of the other dancer of the couple, and with all the other dancers involved, if any. Thus, the formalism of monoidal categories[18] can catch the 'simultaneity' of transformations. We need monoidal categories and not just categories because, having more dancers dancing simultaneously, with monoidal categories we can easily model their different movements with different transformations.

In fact, next developments of this research can concern an abstract description of group dancing, from couples to larger groups. Diagram 8 refers to monoidal categories to represent the movements of a couple of dancers. Let A, B be two dancers, and P_i^A, P_i^B their i-th poses (or 'figures'), respectively. If dancer A changes figure while dancer B remains steady, the overall movement can be schematized by the action of the morphism $t \otimes 1$, where t indicates the movement, and 1 is the identity. Conversely, if A is steady and B moves, the movement will be represented by $1 \otimes t'$. In general, both dancers are moving, thus we have $t \otimes t'$ in the simplified case where A is moving via t and B via t'.

$$
\begin{array}{ccc}
P_1^A \otimes P_1^B & \xrightarrow{t\otimes 1} & P_2^A \otimes P_1^B \\
\downarrow{\scriptstyle 1\otimes t'} & & \downarrow{\scriptstyle 1\otimes t'} \\
P_1^A \otimes P_2^B & \xrightarrow{t\otimes 1} & P_2^A \otimes P_2^B
\end{array}
\tag{8}
$$

[17] The definition of *beauty* is beyond the scope of this paper, and it would start a philosophical debate. We can just say that a mixture of symmetry, balance, proportion, and smoothness of movements can be overall thought of and mathematically investigated as 'beauty' in dance.

[18] In a nutshell, a monoidal category, also called a tensor category, is a category C having a bifunctor $\otimes : C \times C \to C$, that verifies pentagonal and triangular identities [12]. See [8,16,21] for examples of monoidal categories in music.

Diagram 9 shows the action of a 'smoothness' operator s, that changes the movement of the first dancer—let us say, a beginner – from a *not smooth* movement to a *smooth* one. The complete operator, indicated in the diagram by the double arrow, is $s \otimes 1$, because it acts as an identity with respect to the second dancer, that is already moving smoothly. In diagram 9, the final poses are the same but the way to reach them are different. If dancers stop moving but music continues, we can describe dancers' movements via identities leading to the same positions. Also, if the leader role permutes during the show, we can use braids in monoidal categories. Finally, the formalism we developed for dance can be extended to other movements that 'have to be made in a specific way': a reviewer thought of a worker building a wall, or a tourist walking while visiting a church. This might raise a question: when is a movement 'dance'? We can think of formal characteristics, such as smoothness of movements and music-pulse following, but we can also think of aesthetics (and motivation) of movement in itself. According to [5], "Everyday movements are usually goal-oriented, which makes them fundamentally different from dance."

$$P_1^A \otimes P_1^B \quad \underset{smooth \otimes smooth}{\overset{not\ smooth \otimes smooth}{\rightrightarrows}} \quad {}_{s \otimes 1} P_2^A \otimes P_2^B \tag{9}$$

5   Conclusion

Summarizing, we applied to dance a categorical formalism formerly used for music [16,17], comparing gestures in music and dance, and highlighting some of their connections. We started from conceptual considerations in Sect. 2, we discussed metaphorical yet formal applications of functors and commutative diagrams to music and dance in Sect. 3, and we finally made some references to monoidal categories in Sect. 4. Previous work concerned mathematical description of gestures [19], connections of categorical and topological formalism with function spaces to investigate spaces of gestures [3], and application of 2-categories and n-categories to orchestral playing and to describe recursive musical gestures [16,17]. Former works about a formal and often mathematical description of dance topics [4,5,23,24] motivated us to include dance within the aforementioned diagrammatic and categorical formalism, trying to envisage general characteristics in different dance styles, and their general connection with music and musical gestures. This paper aimed to contribute towards a unified vision of gestures of conductor, musicians, and dancers. The mathematical reason behind that is to stress the importance of the unifying power of diagrammatic thinking to navigate within the complexity of the arts and to connect in a simple way things whose nature appears at first as deeply different. The artistic reason is to stress the importance of mutual knowledge between artistic roles, and the relevance of a well-working communication and continuous exchange via sounds, images, and gestures [6,10]. We can try to approach expressivity in the arts in a simple and rational way. We can do the same thing while admiring beauty of nature via scientific investigation. This is an attempt to find keys and hidden rules of aesthetics[19] and beauty, their hidden skeleta constituting the structure of a magnificent building. Future research may include a more detailed description of particular musical genres, such as tango, and its connection with tango music [1]. We can investigate if advanced topics in category theory do have a meaningful application in dance, and, vice versa, how essential topics in dance can be categorically described. Also, generative theories used to modeling natural language and dance [5,20] and natural forms (with their growth processes) [22] can be compared within a categorical framework, looking for formal analogies and differences, hoping to find hidden connections between beauty in dance (and music) and beautiful natural forms, looking for some natural 'roots' of beauty in the arts. And yes, let's (math and) dance!

Acknowledgments. The authors are grateful to the mathematician, musician, and tango dancer Emmanuel Amiot for his helpful suggestions.

References

1. Amiot, E., Lerat, J.-P., Recoules, B., Szabo, V.: Developing software for dancing tango in *Compás*. In: Agustín-Aquino, O.A., Lluis-Puebla, E., Montiel, M. (eds.) MCM 2017. LNCS (LNAI), vol. 10527, pp. 91–103. Springer, Cham (2017). https://doi.org/10.1007/978-3-319-71827-9_8
2. Amiot, E.: Music Through Fourier Spaces. Discrete Fourier Transform in Music Theory. Springer, Heidelberg (2016). https://doi.org/10.1007/978-3-319-45581-5
3. Arias, J.S.: Spaces of gestures are function spaces. J. Math. Music **12**(2), 89–105 (2018)
4. Borkovitz, D., Schaffer, K.: A truncated octahedron in dance, art, music, and beyond. Abstract at Joint Mathematics Meetings in San Diego (2018)
5. Charnavel, I.: Steps towards a Generative Theory of Dance Cognition. Manuscript, Harvard University (2016). https://ling.auf.net/lingbuzz/003137
6. Collins, T., Mannone, M., Hsu, D., Papageorgiou, D.: Psychological validation of the mathematical theory of musical gestures (2018, Submitted)
7. Fiore, T., Noll, T., Satyendra, R.: Morphisms of generalized interval systems and PR-groups. J. Math. Music **7**(1), 3–27 (2013)
8. Jedrzejewski, F.: Structures algébriques et topologiques de l'objet musical. Mathematics and Music. Journée Annuelle de la Société Mathématique de France **21**(21), 3–78 (2008)
9. Karin, J.: Recontextualizing dance skills: overcoming impediments to motor learning and expressivity in ballet dancers. Front. Psychol. **7**(431) (2016). https://www.ncbi.nlm.nih.gov/pmc/articles/PMC4805647/
10. Kelkar, T., Jensenius, A.R.: Analyzing free-hand sound-tracings of melodic phrases. Appl. Sci. **8**(135), 1–21 (2017)

---

[19] Categorical approaches on aesthetics of the arts [11] and of mathematics and the arts [15] can be joined with studies of nature.

11. Kubota, A., Hori, H., Naruse, M., Akiba, F.: A new kind of aesthetics – the mathematical structure of the aesthetic. Philosophies **3**(14), 1–10 (2017)
12. Lawvere, W., Schanuel, S.: Conceptual Mathematics. A First Introduction to Categories. Cambridge University Press, Cambridge (2009)
13. Lerdahl, F., Jackendoff, R.: Generative Theory of Tonal Music. MIT Press, Cambridge (1983)
14. Mac Lane, S.: Categories for the Working Mathematician. Springer, New York (1971). https://doi.org/10.1007/978-1-4757-4721-8
15. Mannone, M.: cARTegory theory: framing aesthetics of mathematics. J. Hum. Math. **9**(18), 277–294 (2019)
16. Mannone, M.: Knots, music and DNA. J. Creat. Music. Syst. **2**(2), 1–20 (2018). https://www.jcms.org.uk/article/id/523/
17. Mannone, M.: Introduction to gestural similarity in music. An application of category theory to the orchestra. J. Math. Music **18**(2), 63–87 (2018)
18. Mazzola, G., et al.: The Topos of Music: I-IV. Springer, Heidelberg (2018). https://doi.org/10.1007/978-3-319-64495-0
19. Mazzola, G., Andreatta, M.: Diagrams, gestures and formulae in music. J. Math. Music **1**(1), 23–46 (2010)
20. Patel-Grosz, P., Grosz, P.G., Kelkar, T., Jensenius, A.R.: Coreference and disjoint reference in the semantics of narrative dance. Proceedings of Sinn und Bedeutung **22**, 199–216 (2018)
21. Popoff, A.: Using monoidal categories in the transformational study of musical time-spans and rhythms (2013). arXiv:1305.7192v3
22. Prusinkiewicz, P., Lindenmayer, A.: The Algorithmic Beauty of Plants. Springer, New York (2004). https://doi.org/10.1007/978-1-4613-8476-2
23. Schaffer, K., Thie, J., Williams, K.: Quantifying the Center of Attention (CA) for Describing Dance Choreography. Abstract at the Joint Mathematics Meetings in San Diego (2018)
24. Wasilewska, K.: Mathematics in the world of dance. In: Proceedings of Bridges 2012: Mathematics, Music, Art, Architecture, Culture (2012)

Special Session: Remanaging Riemann: Mathematical Music Theory as "Experimental Philology"?

Special Section: Reimagining Riemann:
Mathematical Music Theory as
"Experimental Philosophy"

Decontextualizing Contextual Inversion

Jason Yust[✉]

Boston University, Boston, MA 02215, USA
jyust@bu.edu

Abstract. Contextual inversion, introduced as an analytical tool by David Lewin, is a concept of wide reach and value in music theory and analysis, at the root of neo-Riemannian theory as well as serial theory, and useful for a range of analytical applications. A shortcoming of contextual inversion as it is currently understood, however, is, as implied by the name, that the transformation has to be defined anew for each application. This is potentially a virtue, requiring the analyst to invest the transformational system with meaning in order to construct it in the first place. However, there are certainly instances where new transformational systems are continually redefined for essentially the same purposes. This paper explores some of the most common theoretical bases for contextual inversion groups and considers possible definitions of inversion operators that can apply across set class types, effectively de-contextualizing contextual inversions.

Keywords: Pitch-class set theory · Contextual inversion ·
Neo-Riemannian theory · Transformational theory

1 Standardizing Contextual Inversion

Contextual inversion was first defined by David Lewin and applied in various ways in many of his analyses [20, 21]. It has been an important analytical resource to many theorists in a variety of analytical contexts. Exemplary analysis using contextual inversions, as well as references to many other applications, can be found in articles by Lambert [16] and Straus [22] and Kochavi's dissertation [14].

Contextual inversion is most simply defined group-theoretically as an operation that maps pitch-class sets to their inversions and commutes with transpositions. Traditional inversion operations, defined as reflections of the pitch-class circle over some axis, do not commute with transpositions. This is often a desirable property; one normally considers, e.g., C major → F minor and D major → G minor to be the same type of progression, but as traditional inversions they are not, because the axis of inversion changes (C/F♯ in the first progression, D/G♯ in the second). The advantage of traditional inversion operations is that they are readily defined in the same way for all pitch-class sets.

There are two kinds of contextual inversion, those that apply to ordered and to unordered pitch-class sets. In the former category are serial operations like

© Springer Nature Switzerland AG 2019
M. Montiel et al. (Eds.): MCM 2019, LNAI 11502, pp. 101–112, 2019.
https://doi.org/10.1007/978-3-030-21392-3_8

Lewin's RICH operation. These are contextual inversions because they commute with transposition, but since they are typically defined by drawing upon aspects of the ordering, standardization across pitch-class sets is unproblematic. For instance, one can define a contextual inversion that uses the first note of the series as a common tone. This is, for instance, how Stravinsky often derives an I-form of a twelve-tone series from a P-form. This inversion readily applies to any kind of series, regardless of how long it is or what pitch-class set it is. Contextual inversion on serially ordered trichords has already been treated in excellent work by Fiore, Noll, and Satyendra [7–9] and Hall [10], and for twelve-tone music by Hook and Douthett [13]. The present work addressed the harder problem standardizing contextual inversion on unordered sets.

Another method of turning contextual inversions like P, L, and R into global operations is to redefine them using multiplication by *spectral units* as Amiot [3] does. Spectral units derived from a contextual inversion, however, do not necessarily consistently act as inversions, and in fact they can have infinite order (as do spectral units defined from the neo-Riemannian inversions). Nonetheless, Amiot's approach is related to the idea of directed inversions suggested below.

The difficulty of standardization might be understood as a virtue of contextual inversion. Many of Lewin's analyses [21] illustrate this well: a special inversion operator is defined for use only in the analysis at hand, requiring a mix of theoretical and analytical reasoning that itself serves as a crucial stage of the analytical process. The counterargument to this anti-standardization stance is that the same kinds of reasoning may frequently reappear, so that not only is it efficacious to establish a single standard, but it also advances the theoretical project by making the conceptual links across analyses apparent.

Common-tone content is frequently used as a basis for defining contextual inversions. The most prominent example of this is the paradigmatic contextual transformations, the Neo-Riemannian P, L, and R operations, which are defined as the inversions that preserve two common tones [5,12,20]. They have also been described, however, as minimal voice-leading transformations [5,6,24]. These two descriptions only happen to coincide for this particular set class but lead to distinct generalizations. I will consider each possibility below.

There are two principal criteria for a good standardization,

1. It applies to a large number of set classes
2. It is meaningful.

Of these, (2) is the most important. The primary value of contextual inversions, after all, is that they are often more meaningful as operations than standard inversions, and therefore the theoretical meaning of the operation is foremost. Criterion (1) is perfectly satisfied by a standard that applies to all set classes, which is easily possible if one completely ignores (2). For example, we could define an inversion around the first pitch class of a set's normal order. Since the normal order, however, is an essentially arbitrary convention, such an operation is of little value.

Straus [22] takes on the task of satisfying (1) perfectly while preserving some of the common-tone meaning of the neo-Riemannian transformations, by generalizing the two-common-tone property of P, L, and R to all trichords. An important flaw of this strategy was identified, however, by Fiore and Noll [7], which is that there is not a consistent group structure on P, L, and R so defined. For instance, the neo-Riemannian PL is an order 4 operation, PR is order 3, and LR is order 12, while for (016), Straus's PL, PR, and LR are orders 12, 12, and 2 respectively. Therefore, despite the nomenclature, these are not really the same operations from one trichord-type to another. Furthermore, Straus has to lean on the normal-order convention to satisfy criterion (1), leading to a degree of arbitrariness in which operation is called by which name. For instance, the operation that maps (012) to itself is P, whereas for (027), it is L.

It turns out to be quite difficult to satisfy criterion (1) perfectly without compromising on (2). Rather than pursue that holy grail here, I will instead prioritize criterion (2) and explore multiple possible kinds of contextual inversion that partially generalize and relate to voice-leading and common-tone properties.

2 Voice-Leading Standards

One potentially useful property in contextual inversions is minimal voice leading. Minimal voice leading by itself, however, is certainly not sufficient to define a contextual inversion on all set classes, since multiple voice leadings may be equally small, an example being the 1-semitone voice leadings given by the P and L operations on major and minor triads. Also, "minimal voice leading" is vague, since there might be a number of relevant metrics. Tymoczko and Hall [11,23] propose some limits on possible voice-leading metrics, but suggest that a number of metrics, in particular the L_p-norms, could be used. The choice between these will often change which voice leading would be considered minimal.

As an example consider the tetrachord {0147}. It has a unique maximal common-tone inversion: {1478}. However, considered as a voice leading, (C,D♭,E,G) → (A♭,D♭,E,G), this moves a single voice by the large distance of 4 semitones. On one commonly used voice leading metric, L_1, or the taxicab metric, there are a number of other inversions that have exactly the same size voice leading, such as (C,D♭,E,G) → (C,E♭,F♯,G), which moves two voices by two semitones, (C,D♭,E,G) → (B,D,E♯,F♯), which moves two voices up by semitone and two down by semitone. In fact, ten of the twelve inversions have a voice leading with this same distance of 4 on the L_1 metric. On an L_2 (Euclidean) or L_∞ metric, the smallest voice leading is the one that preserves zero common tones (moving every voice by one semitone), and there are three such inversions for each (0147).

Regardless of the voice-leading metric chosen, the minimal voice leading will often be achievable in multiple ways. Therefore minimal voice-leading does not generalize well as a contextual inversion standard. It is well defined for relatively few set classes, and it is difficult to predict which set classes it applies to.

Another voice-leading property of potential interest is sum class. It has been effectively applied in analysis by Cohn [6] and play an important role in recent theory of voice leading proposed by Dmitri Tymoczko [25].

A sum class standard satisfies criterion (2) effectively. If two sets have the same sum class, this means that there is a balanced voice leading from one to the other (and the converse is also true). Sum classes specify cross-sections of voice-leading spaces oblique to the line of transposition, and therefore are basic to the theory of voice-leading geometry.

When cardinality shares a factor with twelve, however, transposition by that factor preserves sum class. Therefore, only when cardinality is co-prime to twelve is there a unique inversion with the same sum class.

For sets of cardinality five or seven, there is a transposition (T_5 or T_7) that changes the sum class by 1, meaning that all transpositions have a unique sum class. This means that there is always exactly one inversionally related set in the same sum class, so that a sum class standard for contextual inversion is defined in just these cases, but not for other cardinalities. Thus, it is easy to know which set classes this inversional standard applies to, but ones that tend to be of the most analytical interest (trichords and tetrachords) are not included.

A balanced-voice-leading inversion will map inversionally symmetrical collections to themselves. But it is not necessarily a minimal voice-leading standard in any sense in other instances. Consider, for example, the pentatonic scale {CEFGB}. The balanced voice-leading inversion of this is {C♯DF♯GB}, a voice leading of (1, −2, 1, 0, 0). However, the smallest voice leadings are not balanced: (C,E,F,G,B) → (C,E,F,A,B) moves one note up by 2 and (C,E,F,G,B) → (C,E,F♯,G,B) moves one note up by 1.

3   Common-Tone Standards

Following Cohn [5], theorists often think first of maximal common-tone preservation as a way of defining contextual inversions. The inversions would then define a kind of proximity as reflected in the Tonnetz, or Cohn's generalization of it. The difficulty is that the maximal common-tone preserving inversion is rarely unique. Inversionally symmetrical trichords have a single maximal common-tone preserving operation, but other trichords have at least three inversions that preserve two pitch-classes (four if one of its intervals is a tritone). For this reason, Straus [22] defines three contextual inversions for all trichords. But defining multiple contextual inversions poses an additional danger: for two operations to be understood as the same when applied to different sets, they must generate the same groups. This is sometimes possible but limits generalizability. For instance, we could define two trichord inversions, I and J, that preserve a dyad other than ic1 or ic5. This can then only apply, however, to trichords with exactly one ic1/ic5 interval, i.e. (013), (014), (025), and (037), which is rather limited. To define three such operations, we can at best generalize over two trichord types, which is hardly a generalization.

We should therefore take a step back and investigate the phenomenon of common-tone preservation more systematically. Lewin observed the importance of common tones and treated them as a special case of his interval function [17,20], and also connected the interval function to the discrete Fourier transform (DFT) [18,19]. Specifically, the interval function is a cross-correlation and the number of common tones is its zeroeth entry. By the convolution theorem, which states that convolution of sets is equivalent to multiplication of their DFTs, we can derive the following expression for the number of common tones between a set A, and some inversion IA [28]:

$$\frac{1}{12} \sum_{k=0}^{11} |f_k(A)|^2 \cos(\varphi_k(A) - \varphi_k(IA)) \qquad (1)$$

Here, $f_k(A)$ refers to the kth Fourier coefficient of A and $\varphi_k(A)$ refers to its phase. When A is clear from context we can write simply f_k and φ_k. For a given pair of pitch-class sets, we can use δ_k to indicate the phase difference.

Equation (1) implies that a large number of common tones results when the phase values are close together, particularly on the larger DFT components. We may use this fact to define contextual inversions that relate to the sharing of common tones by using *distances in phase spaces*. Following [26] I will use the convention $Ph_k = \frac{u}{2\pi}\varphi_k$, where u refers to the universe (division of the octave), assumed to be 12 unless otherwise stated.

For example, Table 1 gives magnitudes of each component for major/minor triads, then cosines of phase differences for some inversions from C major.

Table 1. DFT for major and minor triads: phase differences and common tones from C major

Mag.^{2}		f_1	f_2	f_3	f_4	f_5	f_6	CTs
		0.27	1	5	3	3.7	1	
$\cos(\delta_k)$	E min	0.5	0.5	0.8	0.5	0.5	−1	2
	C min	0.5	0.5	0.8	0.5	0.5	−1	2
	A min	−0.87	−0.5	0.6	0.5	0.87	1	2
	G min	−0.87	−0.5	−0.6	0.5	0.87	1	1
	F min	0	1	0.6	−1	0	1	1
	G♯ min	−1	−1	0.8	−1	−1	−1	0
	B min	0	1	−0.6	−1	0	1	0
	D min	1	−1	−0.8	−1	1	0.5	0

According to (1), the last column of the table can be calculated from the previous six. For instance, for C major – E minor:

$$\frac{1}{12}(9(1) + 0.27(0.5) + 1(0.5) + 5(0.8) + 3(0.5) + 3.7(0.5) + 1(−1)$$
$$+ 3.7(0.5) + 3(0.5) + 5(0.8) + 1(0.5) + 0.27(0.5)) = 2 \qquad (2)$$

Notice that there are twelve terms to the calculation, the first representing the zeroth coefficient, which is simply the square of the cardinality, and the last five being the same as the ones corresponding to $f_1 - f_5$. Therefore, the common tones between C major and E minor are primarily attributable to their proximity in Ph$_3$, and secondarily Ph$_4$ and Ph$_5$. The calculation for C major – A minor on the other hand is:

$$\frac{1}{12}(9(1) + 0.27(-0.87) + 1(-0.5) + 5(0.6) + 3(0.5) + 3.7(0.87) + 1(1)$$
$$+ 3.7(0.87) + 3(0.5) + 5(0.6) + 1(-0.5) + 0.27(-0.87)) = 2 \tag{3}$$

The common tones here are attributable more to a close diatonic relationship, represented by the high $\cos(\delta_5)$, and less to the triadic similarity, $\cos(\delta_3)$, although generally f_3, f_4, and f_5 remain dominant. Note that the large difference in $\cos(\delta_1)$ is relatively immaterial given the small value of $|f_1|$ for triads. The C major – G minor relationship ("fifth-change") is similar in most respects to the C major – A minor (relative) relationship, but the reversal of the triadic proximity results in one fewer common tone.

Distances in phase spaces will typically not be completely generalizable because some set classes will either have undefined phases for certain Fourier coefficients, or will have equivalent distances with multiple inversions. For instance, we can see in Table 1 that the P relation of triads (e.g., C major – C minor) cannot be distinguished from the L relation (C major – E minor) at all using phase-space distances alone. Many kinds of inversion can nonetheless be defined that generalize to a large number of set classes. Consider, for example:

1. Minimum phase distance on a single component, such as Ph$_1$ or Ph$_5$
2. Minimum distance in a two-dimensional, or higher-dimensional, phase space, such as Ph$_{2/3}$
3. Minimum distance in a two-dimensional, or higher-dimensional, phase space, with values weighted by their coefficient size for the given set class.

For 12-tET, criterion (1) only works on Ph$_1$ or Ph$_5$, because when coefficient number k divides 12 (the size of universe), multiple transpositionally related chords will have the same phase values. All of these types of inversion, when applied to inversionally symmetrical sets, will map the set class to itself.

Of the 2-common-tone inversions, C minor (P) and E minor (L) can only be distinguished by taking into account direction of phase change. The other 2-common-tone inversion, A minor (R), is a nearest neighbor in a Ph$_{3/5}$ space, the tonal phase space defined by Amiot and Yust [1,2,27,29]. Or, an inversion maximizing a weighted sum $\sum |f_k|^2 \cos(\varphi_k)$ for just the high-numbered components $f_3 - f_6$, would also specify the relative relation for triads, and be generalizable to other set classes. A different two-dimensional phase space, Ph$_{2/3}$ would give C major – F minor as a minimum-distance inversion (if the dimensions are equally weighted). Just looking at a single phase value, Ph$_1$ or Ph$_5$, a 0-common-tone inversion, C major – D minor, would be the minimum-distance inversion. This inversion essentially splits the difference between the 2-common-tone inversions that are relatively close in both Ph_1 and Ph_5 (C minor and E minor), falling halfway between them on both the pitch-class circle and circle of fifths.

Defining an inversion that balances on either Ph_1 or Ph_5 has the advantage of being a relatively simple contextual inversion to understand across set classes, and can be defined for all set classes except only those that are *perfectly balanced*, or zero-valued on f_1 and f_5 [15]. In fact, complete systems of contextual inversions I_x^{ph1} and I_x^{ph5} can be defined where x indicates the change in phase (possibly non-integer valued) for the given inversion. The disadvantage is, as the previous example illustrates, the inversion that minimizes the phase change is not always actually high in common tones, because it is only one out of six distinct coefficients determining the total common tones in Eq. (1).

One interesting fact relevant to one-dimensional phase proximity is the following:

Proposition 1. *If set A has $f_1 \neq 0$ and an inversion IA with the same Ph_1 value (hence an integer value) then IA also has the same Ph_5 value as A, and the converse is also true.*

Proof. Assuming A and IA have the same Ph_1, then the pitch-class multiset sum of A and $T_6(IA)$ has a zero-valued f_1, because their f_1 values will be equal and opposite. As Amiot [2] shows, $f_1 = 0$ implies $f_5 = 0$ (and vice versa). Therefore A and $T_6(IA)$ must also have opposite Ph_5 (since they have equal $|f_5|$ and sum to $f_5 = 0$), so $Ph_5(A) = Ph_5(IA)$. The same argument works for the converse.

This proposition can be generalized to any f_j and f_k in any universe (u), by replacing T_6 with $T_{u/2}$, or, if u is odd, transferring into universe $2u$ by oversampling and using T_u. In combination with the common-tone formula in (1), this implies that if u is prime, then only inversionally symmetrical sets have integer-valued Ph_k for any k (because integer-valued Ph_k would mean that there is some inversion IA with *all* phase values equal to those of A, which means that the number of common tones is equal to the cardinality of A, and IA and A are therefore the same set).

As a case study, let us consider defining contextual inversions for major and minor triads that also can also be applied to dominant and half-diminished sevenths. Table 2 lists the phase differences for all of the inversions that retain at least one common tone. It is hard to define a PLR-type system of transformations in a principled way for seventh chords because the 2-common-tone case is so common (including half of all the possible inversions) and the 3-common-tone case only occurs one way. Childs [4], for example, generates the contextual inversion group using all seven 2–3 common-tone inversions, which, from a group-theoretic perspective, is rather extravagant for a 24-element group that requires only two generators. All seven 2–3 common-tone inversions are also minimal voice leadings of two semitones (with the possible exception of the 3-common-tone inversion, which would be larger on many metrics).

Consider then, the following possible types of inversion:

1. J_0 inverts to preserve Ph_1 and Ph_5.
   $J_0\{CEG\} = \{DFA\}$ and $J_0\{CEGB\flat\} = \{ACE\flat G\}$.

Table 2. DFT for dominant sevenths and half-diminished sevenths: phase differences and common tones from C^7

Mag.^{2}		f_1	f_2	f_3	f_4	f_5	f_6	CTs
		0.27	1	2	7	3.7	4	
Cos(δ)	$E^{\varnothing 7}$	−0.87	−0.5	0	0.79	0.87	1	3
	$A^{\varnothing 7}$	1	−1	1	0.14	1	−1	2
	$G^{\varnothing 7}$	0.5	0.5	−1	0.79	0.5	−1	2
	$C^{\varnothing 7}$	0	1	0	0.14	0	1	2
	$F\sharp^{\varnothing 7}$	0	1	0	0.14	0	1	2
	$C\sharp^{\varnothing 7}$	−0.5	0.5	1	0.79	−0.5	−1	2
	$B\flat^{\varnothing 7}$	0.87	−0.5	0	0.79	−0.87	1	2
	$D^{\varnothing 7}$	−0.87	−0.5	0	−0.93	0.87	1	1

2. J_f inverts to maximize $\cos(\delta_2)+\cos(\delta_3)$.
   $J_f\{\text{CEG}\} = \{\text{FA}\flat\text{C}\}$ and $J_f\{\text{CEGB}\flat\} = \{\text{C}\sharp\text{EGB}\}$.
3. J_t inverts to maximize $\cos(\delta_3)+\cos(\delta_5)$.
   $J_t\{\text{CEG}\} = \{\text{ACE}\}$ and $J_t\{\text{CEGB}\flat\} = \{\text{ACE}\flat\text{G}\}$.
4. J_h inverts to maximize $\sum_{k=3}^{6} |f_k|^2\cos(\delta_k)$.
   $J_h\{\text{CEG}\} = \{\text{ACE}\}$ and $J_f\{\text{CEGB}\flat\} = \{\text{EGB}\flat\text{D}\}$.

Two of these inversions, J_t and J_h, operate the same way on triads but differently on dominant seventh chords, while J_0 and J_t are equivalent on dominant sevenths but different on triads. These different kinds of inversions therefore give rise to distinct group actions when combined with contextual transposition to generate a 24-element contextual inversion group and applied across multiple set classes. However, they are all defined as involutions so that, when combined with contextual transpositions, they generate a group isomorphic to D_{12}, like standard inversions and the contextual inversion groups.

A different approach, which generates an inversion group of a distinct isomorphism class ($\mathbf{Z}_{24}$), is to define *directed* inversions, which go a particular direction in the phase spaces. For instance, let us use $Ph_{3/5}$, but instead of simply looking for the *nearest* chord, let J_{t+} be the chord that is the nearest in the ascending direction in Ph_3 and Ph_5. Figure 1 shows the triads in this space, and a line that corresponds to semitone transposition. Such lines representing some T_x in some phase space are known as intervallic axes [27]. In fact, this particular axis reflects an important sequential procedure for Schubert and other composers [6,27]. Because the triads fall close to the same line, J_{t+} is well-defined by proximity to it. This is not true of dominant and half-diminished sevenths, however, which coincide in the same point (via the inversion defined above as J_t), so J_{t+} is not well-defined for these.

The proximity of the chords to this line is related to a proposition proved in [27] and stated in a different form in [2] as proposition 6.8. Given any two inversionally symmetric sets, A, B, with well-defined phases in some phase space,

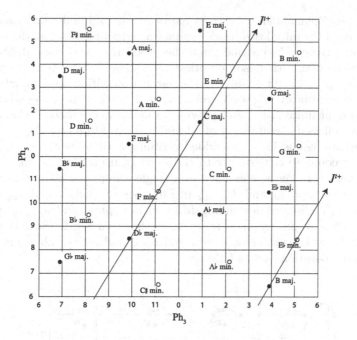

Fig. 1. J^{t+} in $Ph_{3/5}$-space.

we can draw a line connecting A to $T_x(A)$ such that some transposition of B will fall on the midpoint of that line. Specifically, it will be a transposition of B stabilized by the inversion that maps A to $T_x(A)$. Extending the line in either direction, then, all transpositions of A and B will fall regularly on such a line, ordered by T_x. The individual segments of such a line can be understood as inversions of one set over the center of symmetry of the other. The line in Fig. 1 connects minor thirds and individual pitch classes with $x = 1$, such that adjacent minor thirds and singletons always combine to give a major or minor triad. One could define similar lines using the other ways of partitioning the triad into symmetrical subsets. A partition into a perfect fifth plus a singleton gives an operation that alternates parallel and slide relationships: C minor → C major → C♯ minor → C♯ major → .... A partition into major third plus singleton gives an operation that alternates relative and fifth-change relationships: C major → A minor → D major → B minor → ....[1]

Another form of directed inversion is Amiot's [3] multiplication by a spectral unit, which can be defined for any contextual inversion, and also generalizes to any relation between homometric (AKA Z-related) sets. The spectral units

---

[1] The proximity of the triads to these lines can be calculated from the magnitude of the subsets on each Fourier component used to define the phase space, with perfect coincidence where the magnitudes are equal on each. Since all the subsets of major/minor triads are reasonably uniform in their $|F_3|$ and $|F_5|$, the triads fall quite close to all of these lines in $Ph_{3,5}$-space.

defined by neo-Riemannian operations happen to be of infinite order and when iterated beyond the initial two triads produce a series of pitch-class distributions that do not correspond to actual pitch class sets. However, these distributions could be correlated with triads or other pitch-class sets – seen this way, for instance, the spectral unit defined by the parallel operation approximates a P-L sequence ("hexatonic cycle": see [6]). Amiot, in [2] Chap. 3, proposes study of the spectral units of finite order, and provides a useful mathematical classification of these, as well as a classification of all finite spectral units for $\mathbf{Z}_{12}$.

Directed inversions have the added advantage that they may be defined so that they compose consistently to the same transposition, so that multiple directed inversions may be combined in a single group. For instance, we might define an inversion J_{-5th} and J_{-semit} in $\mathrm{Ph}_{3/4}$ space, such that J_{-5th} projects the chords onto a line of descending fifths in the space, and J_{-semit} projects them onto a line of descending semitones, as shown in Fig. 2. Since these compose to consistent (regular) transpositions, they can also be combined in a single group. These operations act as follows:

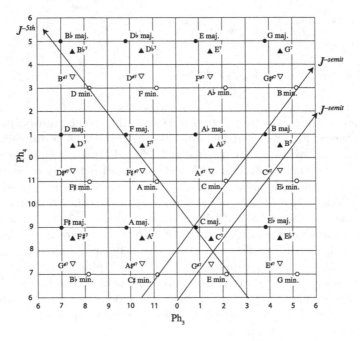

Fig. 2. J^{-5th} and J^{-semit} in $\mathrm{Ph}_{3/4}$-space.

$$\dot{\mathrm{C}}\text{ major} \xrightarrow{J_{-5th}} \mathrm{A}\text{ minor} \xrightarrow{J_{-5th}} \mathrm{F}\text{ major} \xrightarrow{J_{-5th}} \mathrm{D}\text{ minor} \ldots$$

$$\mathrm{C}\text{ major} \xrightarrow{J_{-semit}} \mathrm{C}\text{ minor} \xrightarrow{J_{-semit}} \mathrm{B}\text{ major} \xrightarrow{J_{-semit}} \mathrm{B}\text{ minor} \ldots$$

$$\mathrm{C}^7 \xrightarrow{J_{-5th}} \mathrm{F}\sharp^{\oslash 7} \xrightarrow{J_{-5th}} \mathrm{F}^7 \xrightarrow{J_{-5th}} \mathrm{B}^{\oslash 7} \ldots$$

$$\mathrm{C}^7 \xrightarrow{J_{-semit}} \mathrm{C}^{\oslash 7} \xrightarrow{J_{-semit}} \mathrm{B}^7 \xrightarrow{J_{-semit}} \mathrm{B}^{\oslash 7} \ldots$$

4   Conclusion

This paper has taken an expansive approach to the issue of generalizing contextual inversions on unordered sets, in recognition of the fact that contextual inversion groups can only be defined to apply across all set classes by abandoning the premise that the operations have a meaningful identity that is preserved regardless of what set-type it acts on. Instead, by prioritizing the premise of defining inversions through some meaningful music-theoretic construct, we have proposed a number of possibilities, though none that is well-defined across all set classes. Of the two kinds of properties most often used to explain contextual inversions, voice leading and common tones, the latter, through its mathematical relationship to Fourier phase, is the most promising for defining inversions that can be applied widely, if not to all set classes. That a single obvious standard does not emerge from this investigation may in fact be a virtue: it preserves the aspect of contextual inversions that Lewin turned from a seeming flaw into an asset, the fact that they must be chosen carefully to serve a specific analytical purpose. This forces the analyst or theorist to invest the operation with meaning, rather than rely on conventions. The present work opens the possibility that this aspect of contextual inversions may coexist with the possibility of generalizing these meanings across set types.

References

1. Amiot, E.: The torii of phases. In: Yust, J., Wild, J., Burgoyne, J.A. (eds.) MCM 2013. LNCS (LNAI), vol. 7937, pp. 1–18. Springer, Heidelberg (2013). https://doi.org/10.1007/978-3-642-39357-0_1
2. Amiot, E.: Discrete Fourier Transform in Music Theory. Springer, Heidelberg (2017). https://doi.org/10.1007/978-3-319-45581-5
3. Amiot, E.: Strange symmetries. In: Agustín-Aquino, O.A., Lluis-Puebla, E., Montiel, M. (eds.) MCM 2017. LNCS (LNAI), vol. 10527, pp. 135–150. Springer, Cham (2017). https://doi.org/10.1007/978-3-319-71827-9_11
4. Childs, A.: Moving beyond neo-Riemannian triads: exploring a transformational model for seventh chords. J. Music Theory **42**(2), 181–93 (1998)
5. Cohn, R.: Neo-Riemannian operations, parsimonious triads, and their 'Tonnetz' representations. J. Music Theory **41**(1), 1–66 (1997)
6. Cohn, R.: Audacious Euphony: Chromaticism and the Triad's Second Nature. Oxford University Press, Oxford (2011)
7. Fiore, T.M., Noll, T.: Voicing transformations and a linear representations of uniform triadic transformations. arXiv:1603.09636 (2016)
8. Fiore, T.M., Noll, T., Satyendra, R.: Incorporating voice permutations into the theory of neo-Riemannian groups and Lewinian duality. In: Yust, J., Wild, J., Burgoyne, J.A. (eds.) MCM 2013. LNCS (LNAI), vol. 7937, pp. 100–114. Springer, Heidelberg (2013). https://doi.org/10.1007/978-3-642-39357-0_8
9. Fiore, T.M., Noll, T., Satyendra, R.: Morphisms of generalized interval systems and PR-groups. J. Math. Music **7**(1), 3–27 (2013)
10. Hall, R.W.: Linear contextual transformations. In: Di Maio, G., Naimpally, S. (eds.) Theory and Applications of Proximity, Nearness, and Uniformity, pp. 101–29. Aracne Editrice, Rome (2009)

11. Hall, R.W., Tymoczko, D.: Submajorization and the geometry of unordered collections. Am. Math. Monthly **119**(4), 263–83 (2012)
12. Hook, J.: Uniform triadic transformations. J. Music Theory **46**(1–2), 57–126 (2002)
13. Hook, J., Douthett, J.: Uniform triadic transformations and the music of Webern. Perspect. New Music **46**(1), 91–151 (2008)
14. Kochavi, J.: Contextually defined musical transformations. Ph.D. diss., State University of New York at Buffalo (2002)
15. Milne, A.J., Bulger, D., Herff, S.A.: Exploring the space of perfectly balanced rhythms and scales. of Math. Music **11**(3), 101–33 (2017)
16. Lambert, P.: On contextual inversion. Perspect. New Music **38**(1), 45–76 (2000)
17. Lewin, D.: Forte's interval vector, my interval function, and Regener's common-note function. J. Music Theory **21**(2), 194–237 (1977)
18. Lewin, D.: Re: intervallic relations between two collections of notes. J. Music Theory **3**, 298–301 (1959)
19. Lewin, D.: Special cases of the interval function between pitch-class sets X and Y. J. Music Theory **45**, 1–29 (2001)
20. Lewin, D.: Generalized Musical Intervals and Transformations, 2nd edn. Oxford University Press, Oxford (2011)
21. Lewin, D.: Musical Form and Transformation: Four Analytic Essays. Yale University Press, New Haven (1993)
22. Straus, J.: Contextual-inversion spaces. J. Music Theory **55**(1), 43–88 (2011)
23. Tymoczko, D.: Scale theory, serial theory, and voice leading. Mus. Anal. **27**(1), 1–49 (2008)
24. Tymoczko, D.: The generalized Tonnetz. J. Music Theory **56**(1), 1–52 (2012)
25. Tymoczko, D.: Tonality: an owners manual. Unpub. MS
26. Yust, J.: Applications of DFT to the theory of twentieth-century harmony. In: Collins, T., Meredith, D., Volk, A. (eds.) MCM 2015. LNCS (LNAI), vol. 9110, pp. 207–218. Springer, Cham (2015). https://doi.org/10.1007/978-3-319-20603-5_22
27. Yust, J.: Schubert's harmonic language and Fourier phase space. J. Music Theory **59**(1), 121–81 (2015)
28. Yust, J.: Special collections: renewing set theory. J. Music Theory **60**(2), 213–62 (2016)
29. Yust, J.: Organized Time: Rhythm, Tonality, and Form. Oxford University Press, Oxford (2018)

From Schritte and Wechsel
to Coxeter Groups

Markus Schmidmeier[(✉)]

Florida Atlantic University, Boca Raton, FL 33431-0991, USA
markus@math.fau.edu

Abstract. The PLR-moves of neo-Riemannian theory, when considered as reflections on the edges of an equilateral triangle, define the Coxeter group $\widetilde{S}_3$. The elements are in a natural one-to-one correspondence with the triangles in the infinite Tonnetz. The left action of $\widetilde{S}_3$ on the Tonnetz gives rise to interesting chord sequences. We compare the system of transformations in $\widetilde{S}_3$ with the system of Schritte and Wechsel introduced by Hugo Riemann in 1880. Finally, we consider the point reflection group as it captures well the transition from Riemann's infinite Tonnetz to the finite Tonnetz of neo-Riemannian theory.

Keywords: Tonnetz · neo-Riemannian theory · Coxeter groups

1 PLR-Moves Revisited

In neo-Riemannian theory, chord progressions are analyzed in terms of elementary moves in the Tonnetz. For example, the process of going from tonic to dominant (which differs from the tonic chord in two notes) is decomposed as a product of two elementary moves of which each changes only one note.

The three elementary moves considered are the PLR-transformations; they map a major or minor triad to the minor or major triad adjacent to one of the edges of the triangle representing the chord in the Tonnetz. See [4,5].

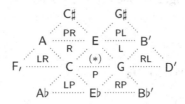

Fig. 1. Triads in the vicinity of the C-E-G-chord

Our paper is motivated by the observation that PLR-moves, while they provide a tool to measure distance between triads, are not continuous as operations on the Tonnetz:

© Springer Nature Switzerland AG 2019
M. Montiel et al. (Eds.): MCM 2019, LNAI 11502, pp. 113–124, 2019.
https://doi.org/10.1007/978-3-030-21392-3_9

Let s be a sequence of PLR-moves. Applying s to a pair of major chords results in a parallel shift of those two chords. However, applying the sequence s to a major chord and an adjacent minor chord makes the two chords drift apart. For example, applying the sequence $s = $ RL to the chord labeled $(*)$ in Fig. 1 yields the triad labeled RL on the right, while s applied to P gives RLP on the left, left of the triangle labelled LP.

In this paper we consider the three reflections s_1, s_2, s_3 on the edges of a fixed equilateral triangle, see Fig. 2.

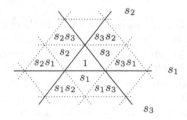

Fig. 2. The reflections s_1, s_2, s_3

The three reflections satisfy the relations

$$s_1^2 = s_2^2 = s_3^2 = 1, \quad (s_1 s_2)^3 = (s_2 s_3)^3 = (s_3 s_1)^3 = 1$$

which are the defining relations of the Coxeter group $\widetilde{S}_3$ corresponding to the affine irreducible Coxeter system $\widetilde{A}_2$ (Fig. 3).

Fig. 3. Affine Coxeter system $\widetilde{A}_2$

2　The Coxeter Group $\widetilde{S}_3$

We collect some results about the Coxeter group $\widetilde{S}_3$, most of the material is adapted from [1, Section 8.3]. The group $\widetilde{S}_3$ can be realized as the group of *affine permutations*,

$$\widetilde{S}_3 = \{f : \mathbb{Z} \to \mathbb{Z} : f \text{ bijective}, f(-1) + f(0) + f(1) = 0, \forall n : f(n+3) = f(n) + 3\},$$

with multiplication the composition of maps. Due to the last condition, it suffices to record the values of f on the window $\{-1, 0, 1\}$, so

$$\widetilde{S}_3 = \{[a, b, c] \in \mathbb{Z}^3 : a + b + c = 0, a, b, c \text{ pairwise incongruent modulo } 3\}.$$

Here, $1 = [-1, 0, 1]$, $s_1 = [0, -1, 1]$, $s_2 = [-1, 1, 0]$, $s_3 = [-2, 0, 2]$ and composition of affine permutations yields the multiplication rule

$$[a, b, c] \cdot s_i = \begin{cases} [b, a, c], & \text{if } i = 1 \\ [a, c, b], & \text{if } i = 2 \\ [c - 3, b, a + 3], & \text{if } i = 3. \end{cases}$$

Affine permutations, unlike sequences of reflections, provide a unique name for each element in $\widetilde{S}_3$. The following result permits us to write the group element into the triangle to which the corresponding sequence of reflections maps the identity element. In Fig. 4 we omit the brackets and place minus-signs under the numbers to improve readability.

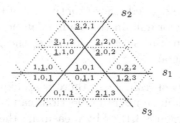

Fig. 4. Affine permutations

Proposition 2.1. *The elements in $\widetilde{S}_3$ are in one-to-one correspondence with the triangles in the Tonnetz.*

The result is well-known, in fact, the Tonnetz picture is commonly used to visualize the tesselation of the affine plane given by the Coxeter system $\widetilde{A}_2$, see for example [1, Figure 1.2]. We give the proof to obtain relevant details of this tesselation.

Using the correspondence in Proposition 2.1 we will identify the elements in $\widetilde{S}_3$ with the triangles in the Tonnetz. Thus, the group $\widetilde{S}_3$ acts on the Tonnetz via left multiplication and via right multiplication, and both actions are simply transitive.

Proof. The map given by sending a sequence of reflections to the triangle Δ obtained by applying the reflections to the triangle marked $(*)$ is an onto map: Unless Δ is the triangle $(*)$ itself, there exists at least one axis s_i between the two triangles. Reflecting Δ on s_i gives a triangle which is closer to $(*)$, hence the process of replacing Δ by $s_i(\Delta)$ terminates after finitely many steps.

Equivalent sequences modulo the relations give the same triangle, hence we obtain a map from $\widetilde{S}_3$ to the set of triangles. This map is injective since each triple $[a, b, c]$ records the coordinates of the triangle as described in the following lemma.   □

Lemma 2.2. *For an affine permutation $[a, b, c]$ and for $i = 1, \ldots, 3$, define*

$$c_i([a, b, c]) = \begin{cases} a + 1 & \text{if} \quad a \equiv i \mod 3 \\ b & \text{if} \quad b \equiv i \mod 3 \\ c - 1 & \text{if} \quad c \equiv i \mod 3. \end{cases}$$

Then the coordinate of the center of the triangle corresponding to the group element $[a, b, c]$ in the Tonnetz with respect to the axis s_i is c_i. (Here, the axis s_1 points to the left, s_2 to the top right and s_3 to the bottom right.)

For example, the three triangles in Fig. 4 above and below the intersection of the s_1- and the s_3-axis all have $a = -2$. Hence the s_1-coordinate of their center is $c_1 = -1$.

Proof. The numbers c_i are defined since exactly one of the entries a, b, c is congruent to i modulo 3. The formula in the lemma can be verified using induction on the length of a sequence $s_{i_1} s_{i_2} \cdots s_{i_n}$ defining the group element and the above multiplication formula.   □

We have seen that for a given triangle Δ, there is a unique group element which maps $(*)$ to Δ. The minimum number of reflections can be computed by counting inversions, see [1, Proposition 8.3.1] or by measuring the distance from $(*)$:

Corollary 2.3. *Suppose the triangle Δ corresponds to the affine permutation $[a, b, c]$. The minimum number d of reflections needed to map $(*)$ to Δ is the sum of the positive coordinates c_i, or $d = \frac{1}{2} \sum_{i=1}^{3} |c_i([a, b, c])|$.*   □

As a product of reflections, each group element gives rise to an operation on the Tonnetz which may be a translation, a rotation, a reflection or a glide reflection. In Fig. 5, we put a hook inside each triangle so that the type of operation given by an element of $\widetilde{S}_3$ can be read off from the position of the hooks in two corresponding triangles.

For example, going from $(*)$ in Fig. 5 to (1) is a reflection, to (2) a rotation, to (3) a glide reflection, and to (6) a translation.

3   The Fundamental Hexagon

It turns out that the Coxeter group $\widetilde{S}_3$ has a normal subgroup $\widetilde{T}$ of index 6 given by translations. The factor group $\widetilde{S}_3/\widetilde{T}$ is isomorphic to the symmetric group S_3. We call the fundamental domain with respect to the shift by a translation in $\widetilde{T}$ the fundamental hexagon. In the next section, we will discuss the role of this fundamental hexagon in music.

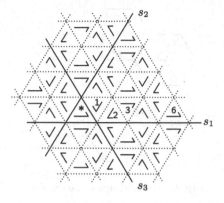

Fig. 5. Left multiplication by affine permutations

It would be desirable to have a "comma subgroup" in $\widetilde{S}_3$ to provide a link to the group generated by the PLR-moves on the finite Tonnetz, but the author was not able to detect a suitable normal subgroup in $\widetilde{S}_3$. However, there is a related group, the point reflection group P, which does have such a "comma subgroup", as we will see in Sect. 6.

Note that left multiplication by $s_2 s_3 s_2 = s_3 s_2 s_3$ is the reflection on the Tonnetz on the line one unit above the s_1-axis. Hence $t_1 = (s_2 s_3 s_2) s_1$ is the upwards translation by 2 units. Similarly, $t_2 = (s_3 s_1 s_3) s_2$ and $t_3 = (s_1 s_2 s_1) s_3$ are translations by 2 units towards the lower right and the lower left, respectively, as indicated in Fig. 6.

Proposition 3.1. *The group of translations* $\widetilde{T} = \langle t_1, t_2, t_3 \rangle = \langle t_1, t_2 \rangle$ *is a free abelian group of rank 2. Moreover, $\widetilde{T}$ is a normal subgroup of $\widetilde{S}_3$ of index 6, the factor group $\widetilde{S}_3/\widetilde{T}$ is isomorphic to the symmetric group S_3.*

Proof. From Euclidean geometry it is clear that $t_1 t_2 = t_3^{-1} = t_2 t_1$, it follows that $\widetilde{T} = \langle t_1, t_2 \rangle$ is an abelian group; moreover, the translations t_1, t_2 span a 2-dimensional lattice in the plane. The group $\widetilde{T}$ is a normal subgroup of $\widetilde{S}_3$ since $s_1 t_1 s_1^{-1} = t_1^{-1}$, $s_2 t_1 s_2^{-1} = t_3^{-1}$, $s_3 t_1 s_3^{-1} = t_2^{-1}$, and the index is 6 since the plane of the Tonnetz can be tiled with hexagons which are in one-to-one correspondence with the elements in $\widetilde{T}$.

For the last claim, consider $S_3 = \langle s_2, s_3 \rangle$ as a subgroup of $\widetilde{S}_3$. Since $S_3 \cap \widetilde{T} = \{e\}$, the composition

$$S_3 \to \widetilde{S}_3 \to \widetilde{S}_3/\widetilde{T}$$

is a one-to-one map, hence a group isomorphism.   □

Corollary 3.2. *As a group, $\widetilde{S}_3 = \widetilde{T} \cdot S_3$.*   □

We call the region in the Tonnetz corresponding to the subgroup $S_3 = \langle s_2, s_3 \rangle$ the **fundamental hexagon** (see Proposition 2.1). The left cosets $t S_3$ for $t \in \widetilde{T}$ form the tiling pictured in Fig. 6. Right multiplication by an element in S_3 yields

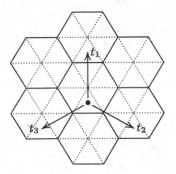

Fig. 6. Translations of hexagons

a permutation of the triangles within each hexagon, while left multiplication by an element of $\widetilde{T}$ is a parallel shift which preserves the hexagonal pattern.

We conclude this section by briefly listing the four types of elements in $\widetilde{S}_3$ in terms of their action on the Tonnetz given by left multiplication.

- The elements of order 2 are reflections on a line parallel to one of the axes. In particular, the reflection on the n-th line parallel to s_i is given by $t_i^n s_i$ $(n \in \mathbb{Z}, i = 1, 2, 3)$.
- Products of two reflections on lines which are not parallel are rotations by $\pm 120°$ about a vertex in the Tonnetz. Those are the elements of order 3 in $\widetilde{S}_3$.
- Products of two reflections on parallel lines are translations, they form the normal subgroup $\widetilde{T}$ considered above.
- The remaining elements are odd, they act as glide reflections on the Tonnetz; all have infinite order.

4   The Fundamental Hexagon in Music

The hexagon encapsulates fundamental concepts in music theory, and leads to some, perhaps weird, sequences of chords.

Each hexagon in the Tonnetz consists of six triangles which represent major and minor chords which have one note in common, see Fig. 7.

Consider the E-hexagon from Fig. 7. The three reflections $s_2, s_3, s_2 s_3 s_2$ in S_3 describe the PLR-moves locally.

Reflection on the s_3-axis is the leading tone exchange:

$$L:\quad C\text{-}E\text{-}G \longleftrightarrow E\text{-}G\text{-}B, \quad A\text{-}C\sharp\text{-}E \longleftrightarrow C\sharp\text{-}E\text{-}G\sharp$$

Reflection on the s_2-axis yields the relative major or minor:

$$R:\quad C\text{-}E\text{-}G \longleftrightarrow A\text{-}C\text{-}E, \quad E\text{-}G\sharp\text{-}B \longleftrightarrow C\sharp\text{-}E\text{-}G\sharp$$

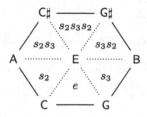

Fig. 7. Six major and minor chords

and reflection on the $s_2s_3s_2$-axis the parallel major or minor:

$$P: \quad \text{A-C}\sharp\text{-E} \longleftrightarrow \text{A-C-E}, \quad \text{E-G}\sharp\text{-B} \longleftrightarrow \text{E-G-B}.$$

The elements s_2s_3 and s_3s_2 in S_3 have order 3. Iterated multiplication by s_3s_2 gives rise to a 3-cycle of major chords within the E-hexagon:

$$\text{C-E-G} \longrightarrow \text{E-G}\sharp\text{-B} \longrightarrow \text{A-C}\sharp\text{-E} \longrightarrow \text{C-E-G}$$

and a 3-cycle of minor chords:

$$\text{C}\sharp\text{-E-G}\sharp \longrightarrow \text{A-C-E} \longrightarrow \text{E-G-B} \longrightarrow \text{C}\sharp\text{-E-G}\sharp.$$

The three steps in the cycle: The move to the upper left, then the horizontal move to the right and the move to the lower left, mark three stripes in the Tonnetz.

- The horizontal stripe given by a chord contains all possibly higher subdominant and dominant chords.
- The stripe in NE-SW direction pictures the (infinite) hexatonic system to which the chord belongs, see [2, Part III].
- The stripe in NW-SE direction represents the (infinite) octatonic system for the given chord, see [3].

We notice that while the rotations in S_3 mark the directions of the three stripes, the translations in $\widetilde{T}$ can be used to move between parallel systems.

We would like to point out that the three opening chords of Ludwig van Beethoven's *Moonlight Sonata* take place within the E-hexagon. The C$\sharp$-minor chord leads to the C$\sharp$-minor sept chord C$\sharp$-E-G$\sharp$-B (which contains the relative E-major chord), then to the (subdominant) A-major chord. The neighboring A-hexagon captures the transition from the A-major chord to the following subdominant D-major chord...

There are more, perhaps even weirder, chord sequences outside of the central hexagon. For example, the rotation by s_3s_2 permutes the major chords which have one edge in common with the E-hexagon:

$$\text{G-B-D} \longrightarrow \text{C}\sharp\text{-E}\sharp\text{-G}\sharp \longrightarrow \text{F-A-C} \longrightarrow \text{G-B-D}$$

and similarly the minor chords:

$$\text{C-E♭-G} \longrightarrow \text{G♯-B-D♯} \longrightarrow \text{F♯-A-C♯} \longrightarrow \text{C-E♭-G}.$$

Another type of chord sequence is obtained from translations of the hexagons in the Tonnetz. Consider the tiling pictured in Fig. 8.

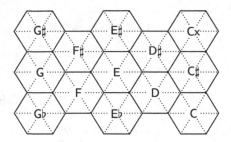

Fig. 8. The tiling by hexagons

The translations which define the tiling satisfy the identity $t_3 t_2 t_1 = e$. Applying successively $t_1, t_2 t_1, t_3 t_2 t_1$ to C-E-G yields the sequence of major chords

$$\text{C-E-G} \longrightarrow \text{C♯-E♯-G♯} \longrightarrow \text{B-D♯-F♯} \longrightarrow \text{C-E-G}$$

(in the E-, E♯-, and D♯-hexagons), and the sequence of minor chords

$$\text{A-C-E} \longrightarrow \text{A♯-C♯-E♯} \longrightarrow \text{G♯-B-D♯} \longrightarrow \text{A-C-E}$$

(also in the E-, E♯-, and D♯-hexagons).

A substantial collection of Tonnetz models can be found in [5]. An interesting musical case for the application of $\widetilde{S}_3$ are the "pitch retention loops" in which the chords in the hexagon occur in cyclical order, see in particular [5, Figure 6.3]. The Coxeter group $\widetilde{S}_3$ does not contain any elements of order 6, so the rotation by 60° may be difficult to explain. But the alteration of s_2 and s_3 is still a more effective description than the succession of L, P and R.

In the above, we have identified the infinite triadic Tonnetz with the Coxeter group $\widetilde{S}_3$ and studied the left action of the group $\widetilde{S}_3$ on itself. Considering the right action, note that alternating right multiplication by s_3 and s_2 generates the triads in each of the hexagons with base triad in $\widetilde{T}$, they are pictured in Fig. 8. The remaining hexagons in the Tonnetz have their base triad in either $s_3 s_2 \widetilde{T}$ or $s_2 s_3 \widetilde{T}$, there the triads in the cycle are generated by alternating right multiplication by s_1 and s_3, or by s_2 and s_1, respectively.

5   Schritte and Wechsel, Revisited

In [8], Hugo Riemann presents two kinds of operations on the Tonnetz, Schritte and Wechsel. Under a ***Schritt,*** each note in a major triad moves up or down

a certain number of scale degrees, while the notes in a minor triad move in
the opposite direction. For example, using neo-Riemannian terminology, the
Quintschritt is given by the RL-move, the Terzschritt by the PL-move. Under
a *Wechsel,* major and minor triads correspond to each other, for example the
Seitenwechsel w yields the parallel triad given by the P-move.

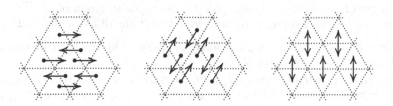

Fig. 9. Quintschritt RL, Terzschritt PL, and Seitenwechsel P

For a detailed description of Riemann's system of Schritte and Wechsel we
refer to [7] which also discusses the composition of Schritte and Wechsel. The
Schritte group T is generated by the Quintschritt RL and the Terzschritt PL, it
is isomorphic to the additive group $\mathbb{Z} \times \mathbb{Z}$. Note that under a Schritt, major and
minor triads move in opposite directions, see Fig. 9.

Each Wechsel can be obtained as a composition of a Schritt with the Seitenwechsel w, hence the product of a Wechsel with itself is the identity operation on the Tonnetz. More generally, if $t, t' \in T$ are Schritte, then the product
$(t'w) \cdot (tw) = t't^{-1}$ of two Wechsel is the composition of a Schritt t' with the
opposite of the Schritt t—hence the product of two Wechsel is always a Schritt.
The map $\varphi : T \to T, t \mapsto t^{-1}$ given by conjugation by w is an automorphism of
order two (since T is an abelian group), and the group R of Schritte and Wechsel
as described in [7, Appendix III] is the semi-direct product $\mathbb{Z}_2 \ltimes_\varphi T$.

We compare the Schritt-Wechsel group R and the Coxeter group $\widetilde{S}_3$.

As for the Coxeter group $\widetilde{S}_3$, the elements in R are in one-to-one correspondence with the triangles in the infinite Tonnetz. Using this identification,
the Schritt-Wechsel group R acts on itself via left multiplication and via right
multiplication; each action is simply transitive.

There is a normal subgroup N in $\widetilde{S}_3$ of index 2, it is given by all sequences
of reflections of even length. Under the identification of $\widetilde{S}_3$ with the triangles in
the Tonnetz, the subgroup N corresponds to the triangles of shape $\triangle$, which are
the triangles in even distance from $(*)$ (see Corollary 2.3). As a subset of $\widetilde{S}_3$, the
group N consists of the rotations and the translations.

For a reflection in $\widetilde{S}_3$, say s_1, the conjugation by s_1 defines a group automorphism $\psi : N \to N, n \mapsto s_1 n s_1^{-1}$. The group $\widetilde{S}_3$ is isomorphic to the semi-direct
product $\mathbb{Z}_2 \ltimes_\psi N$.

Despite these structural similarities, the groups R, $\widetilde{S}_3$ are not isomorphic.

6   The Point Reflection Group

To shed light on the interplay between Riemannian theory on the infinite Tonnetz and neo-Riemannian theory on the finite Tonnetz, we exhibit a third group (besides $\widetilde{S}_3$ and R), the point reflection group P. It has three main features:

- The group P is generated by three reflections (that is, elements of order 2).
- The group P is naturally isomorphic to the opposite group of R.
- There is a normal subgroup K in P with factor the dihedral group D_{12}.

Recall that D_{12} is the group of 24 elements, generated by the PLR-moves on the finite Tonnetz, see [6, Chapter 5].

The **point reflection group** P is the subgroup of the group of Euclidean plane isometries generated by the 180° rotations π_1, π_2, π_3, where each π_i is the point reflection about the midpoint of the edge of (*) on the s_i-axis, see Fig. 10.

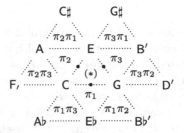

Fig. 10. Point reflections on the Tonnetz

The action on the Tonnetz given by left multiplication by point reflections is pictured in Fig. 11. By comparison, Fig. 5 in Sect. 2 shows the action by affine permutations.

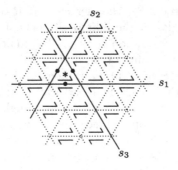

Fig. 11. Left multiplication by point reflections

The product of two point reflections is the translation by twice the difference between the centers, so for example, $\pi_3\pi_2$ is the shift by one unit to the right in parallel to the s_1-axis. Hence the collection of all products of an even number of point reflections forms the group of translations T.

Each remaining element in P is a product of a point reflection and a translation, hence a point reflection itself, about a vertex or about the midpoint of a triangle edge in the Tonnetz. Each such element has order 2.

Proposition 6.1. *The point reflection group P is in a natural way isomorphic to the opposite group of Riemann's Schritte-Wechsel group R.*

Proof. Identify the elements of P with the triads in the Tonnetz, as indicated in Fig. 11. Then right multiplication by $\pi_3\pi_2$ is the Quintschritt RL, by $\pi_3\pi_1$ the Terzschritt PL, and by π_1 the Seitenwechsel P, see Fig. 10. Quintschritt, Terzschritt and Seitenwechsel generate the group R, and the elements $\pi_3\pi_2$, $\pi_3\pi_1$ and π_1 generate P. Hence the left action of R on the Tonnetz coincides with the right action of P. Both actions are simply transitive; it follows that the groups R^{op} and P are isomorphic.   □

It seems to be well known that Riemann's Schritt-Wechsel group R has the Comma-Schritte subgroup as a normal subgroup such that the Schritt-Wechsel group of the finite Tonnetz, which is isomorphic to the dihedral group D_{12}, is a factor. The corresponding result for the (isomorphic) point reflection group can be obtained directly.

Definition. The *comma subgroup* K is the subgroup of the point reflection group P generated by $(\pi_3\pi_1)^3$ and $(\pi_1\pi_2)^4$.

One can see that K is the smallest subgroup of P which contains the "Lesser-Diesis-Schritt" $(\pi_3\pi_1)^3$, the "Greater-Diesis-Schritt" $(\pi_1\pi_2)^4$, the "Syntonic-Comma-Schritt" $(\pi_3\pi_2)^3\pi_1\pi_2$, and the "Pythagorean-Comma-Schritt" $(\pi_3\pi_2)^{12}$.

Proposition 6.2. *The comma subgroup K is a normal subgroup of P of index 24. The factor group P/K is isomorphic to the dihedral group D_{12}.*

Proof. Using the formula from the proof of Proposition 6.1, we obtain $\pi_i(\pi_3\pi_1)^3\pi_i^{-1} = (\pi_1\pi_3)^3 = ((\pi_3\pi_1)^3)^{-1} \in K$ and similarly, $\pi_i(\pi_1\pi_2)^4\pi_i^{-1} \in K$, so K is normal in P. The map $\psi : \mathbb{Z} \times \mathbb{Z} \to P, (a,b) \mapsto (\pi_3\pi_1)^a(\pi_1\pi_2)^b$ is one-to-one and has image T. The subgroup generated by $(3,0)$ and $(0,4)$ of $\mathbb{Z} \times \mathbb{Z}$ corresponds to K under ψ. Hence K has index 12 in T and index 24 in P.

Let $h = (\pi_1\pi_2)^{-1}(\pi_3\pi_1)$ (the semitone) and $\rho = \pi_1$. Then hK has order 12 in P/K, ρK has order 2, and $(\rho K)(hK)(\rho K)^{-1} = (hK)^{-1}$. Thus, hK and ρK generate a subgroup in P/K isomorphic to D_{12}.   □

7   Conclusion

In Riemannian theory, the vertices in the infinite Tonnetz are labeled by notes such that the fifth marks the horizontal direction. All operations on the Tonnetz perserve the horizontal direction: The Schritte are translations, and the Wechsel are products of a translation and a flip on the horizontal axis.

Neo-Riemannian theory purifies the Tonnetz by removing the labels attached to the vertices, and by identifying the triangles with chords. This allows to redefine the operations in terms of more basic reflections, which in turn give rise to new moves, in particular to rotations.

The group which defines the operations in Riemannian theory is the semi-direct product $R = \mathbb{Z}_2 \ltimes_\varphi T$ of the cyclic group of two elements by the group of affine translations in the plane.

By comparison, three reflections corresponding to PLR-moves generate the Coxeter group $\widetilde{S}_3$ which acts on the infinite Tonnetz. Like R, the group $\widetilde{S}_3$ contains a subgroup, say $\widetilde{T}$, of translations; actually $\widetilde{T}$ is isomorphic to T. Unlike R, the translation subgroup has index six, so there are many more elements in $\widetilde{S}_3$: reflections, 120°-rotations and glide reflections.

What has changed since Hugo Riemann introduced Schritte and Wechsel? We still visualize music in the Tonnetz... We still use algebra to describe the development of harmony... Yet, the building blocks are more fundamental and the operations have more variety. Riemannian theory is very much alive.

Happy 170th Birthday, Hugo Riemann!

Acknowledgements. The author would like to thank Benjamin Brück from Bielefeld, Germany, for helful comments regarding the Coxeter group. He is particularly grateful to Thomas Noll from Barcelona since his thoughtful advice, in particular regarding the action of interesting elements and subgroups of the Coxeter group on the Tonnetz, has led to substantial improvements of the paper (which about doubled in size).

References

1. Björner, A., Brenti, F.: Combinatorics of Coxeter Groups. GTM, vol. 231. Springer, Heidelberg (2005). https://doi.org/10.1007/3-540-27596-7
2. Cohn, R.: Maximally smooth cycles, hexatonic systems, and the analysis of late-romantic triadic progressions. Music Anal. **15**(1), 9–40 (1996)
3. Cohn, R.: Neo-Riemannian transformations, parsimonious trichords, and their Tonnetz representations. J. Music Theory **41**(1), 1–66 (1997)
4. Cohn, R.: Introduction to neo-Riemannian theory: a survey and a historical perspective. J. Music Theory **42**(2), 167–198 (1998)
5. Cohn, R.: Audacious Euphony: Chromaticism and the Triad's Second Nature: Oxford Studies in Music Theory. Oxford University Press, Oxford (2012)
6. Crans, A.S., Fiore, T.M., Satyendra, R.: Musical actions of dihedral groups. Am. Math. Mon. **116**(6), 479–495 (2009)
7. Klumpenhouwer, H.: Some remarks on the use of Riemann transformations. Music Theory Online **0**(9), 1–34 (1994)
8. Riemann, H.: Skizze einer Neuen Methode der Harmonielehre. Breitkopf und Haertel, Leipzig (1880)

Exploring the Syntonic Side of Major-Minor Tonality

Thomas Noll[1]([✉]) and David Clampitt[2]

[1] Departament de Teoria, Composició i Direcció,
Escola Superior de Música de Catalunya, Barcelona, Spain
thomas.mamuth@gmail.com
[2] School of Music, Ohio State University, Columbus, USA
clampitt.4@osu.edu

Abstract. The description of the Major and Minor modes as fillings of a triadic division of the octave offers the possibility to study them as Pairwise Well-Formed Modes. As a consequence one obtains two projections: the diatonic projection yields the well-known Ionian and Aeolian modes and provides a link between the triadic modes and the pseudo-classical modes. The syntonic projection looks unfamiliar at first sight, but closer inspection shows that these modes provide a common ground for the natural, harmonic, and melodic manifestations of both the Major and the Minor modes.

Keywords: Triadic mode · Diatonic and syntonic mode ·
Tonal and modal step intervals · Sturmian morphism ·
Algebraic combinatorics on words · Major/minor tonality

1 Introduction

In scale theory it is common to consider a generic layer of scale degrees together with a specific layer of notes or pitches. The specific layer is sometimes associated with the pitch parameter of actual musical tones in a psycho-acoustical sense. While this option is not always thematized, authors may still consider themselves to be safe in the light of this possibility. A challenging case in this regard is therefore the concept of a *Pairwise Well-Formed Scale*, in particular because our central idea is to conceive the major and minor modes as instances of pairwise well-formed modes. In our recent study [5] we emphasize the abstract context of the investigation, but the concept of pairwise well-formedness has radical consequences in itself, which should be further pursued. In fact, the definition of a *pairwise well-formed scale* involves a specific layer and the concrete realization of the major scale in just intonation with the step-interval pattern (a, c, b, a, c, a, b) and the specific interval sizes $a = log_2(9/8)$, $c = log_2(10/9)$, $b = log_2(16/15)$ turns out to be an instance of this concept. But the verification of the property of pairwise well-formedness involves acts of identification of pairs of these step intervals, i.e. $c = b$, $a = c$ and $a = b$. These identifications are hence situated half-way between the specific level where all three letters are different

© Springer Nature Switzerland AG 2019
M. Montiel et al. (Eds.): MCM 2019, LNAI 11502, pp. 125–136, 2019.
https://doi.org/10.1007/978-3-030-21392-3_10

and the generic level, where $a = b = c$. In one of these identifications the two instances of c are replaced by the letter a, which results in the step-interval pattern (a, a, b, a, a, a, b). As the definition requires, it turns out that this is the abstract step-interval pattern of a (non-degenerate) well-formed scale. It corresponds to the Ionian mode. The definition does not require one to single out specific values for c and b. But, although it is sufficient that there exist infinitely many possibilities, one may still consider oneself more safe by singling out either the step sizes $c = log_2(9/8)$ and $b = log_2(256/243)$ of Pythagorean tuning or $c = 2/12$ and $b = 1/12$ of 12-tone-equal temperament. Furthermore, the music-theoretical significance of an abstract Ionian mode seems beyond question. In other words, the music-theoretical postulate of an abstract diatonic layer, half-way between the generic scale degrees $\hat{1}, \dots, \hat{7}$ and the specific layer of the triadic major mode, seems quite reasonable.

The truly challenging case is the verification of the step-interval pattern (a, b, b, a, b, a, b), which results from the identification of the letters b and c. There are infinitely many possible solutions for a and b.[1] But even though it is by definition not necessary to single out specific values for a and b, the lack of a prominent instance for such a scale might seem disconcerting.

In search of a possibly hidden musical manifestation of the syntonic step-interval pattern (a, b, b, a, b, a, b), it is the goal of the present paper to think through the music-theoretical consequences of our approach in [5] more rigurously: if it is not the specific pitch-height differences which distinguish the step intervals of type a from those of type b, it must be some other musically relevant property. We see this difference in the syntactic behavior of these steps. The step intervals of type a could be called the *tonal* or *fixed* step intervals. Over a fixed tonic they remain unchanged in the typical inflections within major or minor modes and the processes of modal mixture (with respect to C-major and C-minor, step intervals $C - D$ and $F - G$, in major also $A - B$ and in natural minor also $Ab - Bb$). The step intervals of type b could be called the *modal* or *moveable* step intervals. They are the locations in the step-interval patterns where these processes take place. While through the identification of the letters b and c these alterations become unnoticeable, the step pattern *abbabab* still remembers the locations where they occur. In Sect. 3 we explore the typical alterations of the major and minor modes, such as their harmonic and melodic forms and show that the syntonic step-interval pattern *abbabab* remains unchanged under these alterations.

We may to some degree align ourselves in the history of theory with Hauptmann. Hauptmann's axioms are the "directly intelligible" intervals of the perfect octave, perfect fifth, and major third ([8], p. 5), which leads to the just major scale expressed by the word *acbacab*, and to the just (natural) minor scale, expressed as the word *abcabac*. The latter is not a conjugate of the major form, but a conjugate of its reversal. To wit, if *acbacab* represents the just C-major scale, then the circular reversal beginning from the fourth letter may represent

---

[1] For example the generator $g = (2 - \sqrt{2})/2$ yields a seven-note scale with the step intervals of sizes $a = 3 - 2\sqrt{2}$ and $b = 3/\sqrt{2} - 2$.

the just C-minor scale: take the prefix, *acba*, reverse it to form *abca*, and follow it by the reversal of the suffix *cab*, yielding *bac*. (The authentic division into perfect fifth and perfect fourth is in play here.) We will see below that transformationally the minor form is Twisted Triadic Aeolian. In this concrete expression of the scales we understand greater major steps ($a = log_2(9/8)$), lesser major steps ($c = log_2(10/9)$), and minor steps or diatonic semitones ($b = log_2(16/15)$). The chromatic alterations are the lesser and greater augmented primes, respectively $log_2(25/24)$ and $log_2(135/128)$. We will also call them the *modal* and *tonal* augmented primes, respectively. As between C-major and C-minor scales, we have alterations of modal step intervals by the lesser augmented prime at the locations represented in major and in minor by letters c and b. In fact, the most instructive way to describe the transformation from Major to Minor is the letter exchange $E_{(bc)}$, replacing each instance of *b* by *c* and vice versa: $E_{(bc)}((a, c, b, a, c, a, b)) = (a, b, c, a, b, a, c)$.[2] Hauptmann justifies these alterations in some situations via fixed mediating notes. f (see Sect. 3).

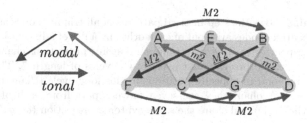

Fig. 1. Illustration of the tonal steps (horizontal) and the modal steps (diagonal either way) in a tone net representation of the Major scale.

2   The Two Sides of the Major and Minor Modes

Here we spare the reader negotiations about the quite abstract content of [5]. Instead we will focus on the main music-theoretical result in its concrete form, leaving generalities aside. The transformational orientation of that paper shall be only briefly recapitulated: the acts of filling the three triadic intervals with step intervals are studied as transformations on three-letter words. This ultimately motivates the coincidence of the number 3 of triadic intervals (major third, minor third and perfect fourth) with the number 3 of different step intervals

---

[2] In consideration of the fact that Dahlhaus ([7], e.g. p. 46), in his critical reflection on Hauptmann's dialectical concept of the Major and Minor keys, localizes traces of Dualism, it is worthwhile to highlight that these are not implied by the scalar structure. The flattening of scale degrees $\hat{3}, \hat{6}$ and $\hat{7}$ (by a lesser augmented prime) in a major scale leads to the corresponding minor scale. No triad needs to be turned upside down. This transformation corresponds to Hindemith's idea of *Trübung* (disturbance, turbidation), who emphatically rejects a dualistic concept. ([9], p. 78 and also [10], p. 147).

(traditionally called: greater major step, lesser major step, minor step). In several ways the transformations on three letters can be merged into transformations on two-letter words. Four of these mergings turn out to be Sturmian morphisms, as discussed in [5]. This finding constitutes the transformational formulation of the Pairwise Well-formedness Property. There are two main types of Sturmian mergings: diatonic morphisms and syntonic morphisms. They are defined on two-letter words and describe the acts of filling divisions of the octave into fifths and fourths (diatonic case), or into thirds and sixths (syntonic case). Here again the transformational setup motivates the coincidence of the number 2 of division intervals with the number 2 of step intervals.

For our purposes it suffices to describe the major and minor modes merely as triples of three-letter words and their mergings as pairs of two-letter words. The Table below shows the complete list of all 14 triadic modes. Its order appears as an interlocking of the separate Tables 3 and 5 in [5] and exemplifies a general property of (non-singular) pairwise well-formed scales: the existence of a Q-cycle (see [3]), analogous to Cohn's maximally smooth cycles [6].

Table 1. The table shows the step-interval patterns of all triadic modes as a Q-cycle of length 14. Consecutive modes arise out of each other by a flip of adjacent letters (under- and over-lined, respectively). The corresponding diatonic projections change only every other time. The syntonic projections traverse two cycles of length 7. The major and minor modes correspond to opposite positions in this long cycle (Plain Triadic Ionian vs. Twisted Triadic Aeolian; they are seven moves apart from each other in either direction along the cycle) and share the same syntonic projection $(ab, babab)$.

Triadic mode	Step intervals	Diatonic steps	Syntonic steps
Plain Triadic Ionian	$(\underline{ac}, \overline{b}a, cab)$	$(aaba, aab)$	$(ab, babab)$
Twisted Triadic Ionian	$(\overline{c}a, ba, c\underline{ab})$	$(aaba, aab)$	$(ba, babab)$
Plain Triadic Mixolydian	$(ca, b\underline{a}, c\overline{ba})$	$(aaba, aba)$	$(ba, babba)$
Twisted Triadic Mixolydian	$(c\underline{a}, \overline{bc}, \overline{a}ba)$	$(aaba, aba)$	$(ba, bbaba)$
Plain Triadic Dorian	$(\overline{cb}, \overline{a}c, ab\underline{a})$	$(abaa, aba)$	$(bb, ababa)$
Twisted Triadic Dorian	$(\overline{a}b, ac, a\underline{b}\overline{c})$	$(abaa, aba)$	$(ab, ababb)$
Plain Triadic Aeolian	$(ab, \underline{ac}, \overline{b}\overline{a}c)$	$(abaa, baa)$	$(ab, abbab)$
Twisted Triadic Aeolian	$(\underline{ab}, \overline{c}a, bac)$	$(abaa, baa)$	$(ab, babab)$
Plain Triadic Phrygian	$(\overline{b}a, ca, b\underline{ac})$	$(baaa, baa)$	$(ba, babab)$
Twisted Triadic Phrygian	$(ba, c\underline{a}, \underline{b}\overline{c}a)$	$(baaa, baa)$	$(ba, babba)$
Plain Triadic Locrian	$(b\underline{a}, \overline{c}b, \overline{a}ca)$	$(baab, aaa)$	$(ba, bbaba)$
Twisted Triadic Locrian	$(\overline{b}a, \overline{c}b, ac\underline{a})$	$(baab, aaa)$	$(bb, ababa)$
Plain Triadic Lydian	$(\overline{a}c, ab, a\underline{c}\overline{b})$	$(aaab, aab)$	$(ab, ababb)$
Twisted Triadic Lydian	$(ac, \underline{ab}, \overline{c}ab)$	$(aaab, aab)$	$(ab, abbab)$

The Major mode appears in the form of the *Plain Triadic Ionian* mode. The triple (ac, ba, cab) encodes the step-interval pattern $(M2\underline{M2}, \overline{m2}M2, \underline{M2}M2\overline{m2})$.

Diatonically, this reduces to the divided step-interval pattern $(aaba, aab)$, encoding the authentically divided Ionian mode in terms of major seconds and minor seconds $(M2M2m2M2, M2M2m2)$. Syntonically, this reduces to the step-interval pattern $(ab, babab)$, whose musical meaning shall be uncovered. The Minor mode appears in the form of the *Twisted Triadic Aeolian* mode. The triple (ab, ca, bac) encodes the step-interval pattern $(M2\overline{m2}, \underline{M2}M2, \overline{m2}M2\underline{M2})$. Diatonically, this reduces to the divided step-interval pattern $(abaa, baa)$, encoding the authentically divided Aeolian mode in terms of major seconds and minor seconds $(M2m2M2M2, m2M2M2)$. Syntonically, this reduces to the same step-interval pattern $(ab, babab)$, as in the case of the Major mode. The opposite positions of the major and minor modes on the long cycle of length 14 corresponds to the fact, that the letter exchange $E_{(bc)}$ represents the unique element of order 2 within the cyclic group of order 14. This is an interesting result and has been established in a quite general form in [5]. From a music-theoretical point of view the coincidence of the syntonic step-interval pattern of the Major and the Minor modes provides a common ground for the modes of triadic tonality. But at this point a potentially crucial objection must be raised: the "pure" major and minor modes can hardly be accepted as the only representatives of major and minor tonality. In particular the typical alterations of the 6th and 7th degrees must be taken into account as well.

Before proceeding with this task it is interesting to understand the musical meaning of the cyclic order in the table. It is evident from the third column, with the fifth-generated diatonic projections, that every other mode in the cycle appears to progress one step further with respect to circle-of-fifths order: Ionian - Mixolydian - Dorian - etc. If one keeps a fixed tonic, then the signature changes in the same way as in a modulation of the same mode to a new tonic at (downward) fifth-distance (as one moves downward on the table, from the C-major collection to F-major collection, etc.). The syntonic modes (in the fourth column), however, change with every new triadic mode along the cycle. Hauptmann describes these smaller changes as a *stretching out of the key-system to dominant or subdominant*. The dominant key shares the key signature with that of the Lydian mode, and the tonic of the dominant key corresponds to the fifth-divider of the Lydian-mode, i.e. with the framing note of the Hypo-Lydian mode. This is true for both forms of the triadic Lydian: the plain and the twisted. But the interesting observation to be made here is this: the step-interval pattern of Hauptmann's intermediate key between C-Major and G-Major coincides with the twisted Lydian mode (ac, ab, cab). The note F♯ replaces the F of the C-Plain-Triadic-Ionian, but the species of the fifth $cabc$ on D contains three modal steps and one tonal step. So it cannot serve as a dominant. But the signature and step-interval pattern of the twisted Lydian mode on C coincide with the twisted Aeolian mode on E (beginning on E in twisted C-Lydian yields the twisted Aeolian pattern $abcabac$). And E is the third-divider of the syntonic projection of the Plain Triadic Ionian mode. In other words, the Minor modes are half way between the Major modes and vice versa. Note, however that this does not correspond to the order in Heinichen's circle of keys.

This implies a two-fold concept of modulation, involving a diatonic and a syntonic component. Modulations between relative major and minor are purely syntonic (diatonically unnoticeable): when we move from plain triadic C-Ionian to twisted triadic C-Ionian, we have no change of signature, and to achieve the twisted A-Aeolian form it suffices to start on scale degree 6. We see no change in the diatonic steps column in Table 1, but we do see a change in the syntonic steps column. Conversely, modulations between parallel major and minor keys are purely diatonic (syntonically unnoticeable): when we move from plain triadic C-Ionian to twisted triadic C-Aeolian we change the signature, registering a change in the diatonic steps column, but no change in the syntonic steps column.

3   Alteration as Conjugation

Let $\mathcal{A}^*$ denote the free monoid generated by the letters of the finite alphabet $\mathcal{A}$. Within the free group $F_{\mathcal{A}}$, generated by the letters of $\mathcal{A}$ we consider all elements of the form $xz^{-1}y$, where x, y, z each run through the letters from $\mathcal{A}$. In addition we assume we have further letters at our disposal in order to denote all these elements with unique letters. In other words, we consider the subset $\tilde{\mathcal{A}} = \{xz^{-1}y \mid x, y, z \in \mathcal{A}\} \subset F_{\mathcal{A}}$ together with a bijection $\mathfrak{l} : \tilde{\mathcal{A}} \overset{\sim}{\to} \overline{\mathcal{A}}$ into a larger alphabet $\overline{\mathcal{A}}$ containing $\mathcal{A}$ and satisfying $\mathfrak{l}(x) = x$ iff $x \in \mathcal{A}$.

Definition 3.1. *Consider three letters $x, y, z \in \mathcal{A}$ together with the letter $t = \mathfrak{l}(xz^{-1}y)$. The two-letter words $\widetilde{x}\overset{z}{y} = tz$ and $\overset{z}{x}\widetilde{y} = zt$ are called the* right *and the* left z*-alteration of the two-letter word xy, respectively.*

The idea behind this definition is that in an alteration one has a two-letter word xy, whose commutative image remains unchanged, while one of the two letters is superceded by a third letter z. In the act conjugation of the replaced letter by either z or z^{-1} the letter z sneaks in while the concatenation of the replaced letter with z^{-1}, (the commutative image of which is their difference) are joined with the passive letter. The simplest and trivial case is an alteration which does not change the two-letter word xy.

Proposition 3.2. $\widetilde{x}\overset{z}{y} = xy$ *iff* $z = y$ *and* $\overset{z}{x}\widetilde{y} = xy$ *iff* $z = x$.

Proof. $\widetilde{x}\overset{z}{y} = xy$ iff $xz^{-1}y = x$ iff $z = y$. $\overset{z}{x}\widetilde{y} = xy$ iff $xz^{-1}y = y$ iff $z = x$.

The following examples are based on a three-letter alphabet $\mathcal{A} = \{a, b, c\}$ as well as on its two-letter subalphabet $\{a, b\}$. As the set $\tilde{\mathcal{A}}$ also contains those two elements $\{ab^{-1}a, ba^{-1}b\}$ which are built from this sub-alphabet, we may use the same letter-providing map $\mathfrak{l}$ on $\tilde{\mathcal{A}}$ in both cases without risking conflicts.

The first case is an exchange of the two letters a and b, namely $\overset{a}{b}a = a\overset{b}{b} = ab$.

Example 3.3. Consider the alphabet $\mathcal{A} = \{a, b\}$. With the interpretation $a = M2, b = m2$ the word *abaabaa* denotes the step-interval pattern of the Aeolian species of the octave. Applying the right b-alteration to the second occurrence of the factor ba yields *abaa* $\overset{\frown b}{ba}$ $a = abaaaba$, which is the Dorian species of the octave. Applying the right b-alteration again to the suffix ba in this pattern yields *abaaa* $\overset{\frown b}{ba} = abaaaab$, which can be recognized as the step interval pattern of the melodic minor mode (in terms of the intervals $a = M2$ and $b = m2$). Anticipating Example 3.5 we note, that we could go on to perform the unnoticeable alteration $\overset{\frown a}{aa}$ on the rightmost factor of type aa, without changing the pattern *abaaaab*.

The next interesting case is the (right- or left-) alteration of aa by another letter b. A third letter $d = \mathfrak{l}(ab^{-1}a)$ comes into play. The relevant musical example is the augmented second.

Example 3.4. Again starting from *abaabaa* we apply the right b-alteration to the suffix aa of the Aeolian species of the octave: *abaab* $\overset{\frown b}{aa} = abaabdb$. This can be recognized as the step-interval pattern of the harmonic minor mode in terms of the intervals $a = M2, b = m2$ and $d = A2$.

Now we turn to three letters. With the refined interpretation $a = M2, b = \overline{m2}, c = \underline{M2}$ we again go through the alterations from Examples 3.3 and 3.4.

Example 3.5. The starting point is the word *abcabac* denoting the step-interval pattern of the minor mode in the shape of the twisted triadic Aeolian species of the octave. Applying the right b-alteration to the second occurrence of the factor ba yields *abca* $\overset{\frown b}{ba}$ $c = abcaabc$. Applying the right b-alteration to its suffix bc yields *abcaa* $\overset{\frown b}{bc} = abcaacb$. The analogue to the redundant third alteration in Example 3.3 is not redundant here: we finally apply a left c-alteration to the factor ac and obtain *abca* $\overset{\frown c}{ac}$ $b = abcacab$, which we regard to be the step-interval pattern of the melodic minor mode in terms of the intervals $a = M2, c = \underline{M2}$ and $b = \overline{m2}$).

Example 3.6. Now consider the letter $\underline{d} = \mathfrak{l}(ab^{-1}c)$ and apply the right b-alteration to the suffix ac of the Minor species of the octave: *abcab* $\overset{\frown b}{ac} = abcab\underline{d}b$. This can be recognized as the step interval pattern of the harmonic minor mode in terms of the intervals $a = M2, b = \overline{m2}, c = \underline{M2}$ and $\underline{d} = \underline{A2}$.

4   Alteration and Letter Projection

Definition 4.1. *For any pair x and y of distinct letters of an alphabet $\mathcal{A}$ one has the associated* Letter Projection *with x in the role of the* abandoned letter *and y in the role of the* receiving letter*:*

$$\pi_{x \to y} : \mathcal{A} \to \mathcal{A} \backslash \{x\} \text{ with } \pi_{x \to y}(z) := \begin{cases} z \text{ if } z \neq x, \\ y \text{ if } z = x. \end{cases}$$

Letter projections $\pi_{x \to y} : \mathcal{A}^* \to \mathcal{A} \backslash \{x\}^*$ can be naturally extended to the larger letter domain and the words formed with them: $\overline{\pi}_{x \to y} : \overline{\mathcal{A}}^* \to \overline{\mathcal{A} \backslash \{x\}}^*$, where $\overline{\pi}_{x \to y}(rt^{-1}s) = \mathfrak{l}((\pi_{x \to y}(r)(\pi_{x \to y}(t))^{-1}\pi_{x \to y}(s))$. Thereby letter projections can be applied to alterations: If $\widehat{xy}^{z} = tz$ with $t = \mathfrak{l}((xy^{-1}x))$ one obtains $\overline{\pi}_{x \to y}(\widehat{xy}^{z}) = \overline{\pi}_{x \to y}(tz)$, and analogously $\overline{\pi}_{x \to y}(\widehat{xy}^{z}) = \overline{\pi}_{x \to y}(zt)$. This extension is natural in the sense that alteration and letter projection commute:

Proposition 4.2. *For any five letters* $x, y, r, s, t \in \mathcal{A}$ *one finds:*

$$\pi_{x \to y}(r)\pi_{x \to y}(s) = \overline{\pi}_{x \to y}(\widehat{rs}^{\pi_{x \to y}(t)}) \; and \; \pi_{x \to y}(r)\pi_{x \to y}(s) = \overline{\pi}_{x \to y}(\widehat{rs}^{\pi_{x \to y}(t)}).$$

The proof of this is straightforward. With this preparation we may now return to the Examples from Sect. 3 and inspect them with respect to letter projections.

4.1   Melodic Minor

Examples 3.3 and 3.5 provide two separate derivations of the step interval pattern of the melodic minor mode over the alphabets $\{a, b, c\}$ and $\{a, b\}$, respectively. In the upper and middle rows of Fig. 2 we can see, that they are connected under the letter projection $\overline{\pi}_{c \to a}$. Considering the aim of this paper, the most interesting insight can be drawn from the bottom row of Fig. 2, which shows the syntonic projections of these derivations. It turns out that the left- and the right-most interval patterns coincide *abbabab*. It is the unaltered step-interval pattern of the Standard syntonic mode. In other words, the melodic alteration of the Minor mode is diatonically noticeable and syntonically unnoticeable. The syntonic side offers itself as a common ground for the unaltered and the melodically altered Minor mode.

Hauptmann does not explicitly distinguish the two different kinds of alterations. But pursuing his principle that step intervals are mediated through two harmonic intervals he makes implicit decisions which we may interpret as choices. Tonal steps a have to be altered by tonal augmented primes and are always mediated through a fifth and a fourth. Modal steps have to be altered by modal augmented primes and are always mediated by a fourth and a third. The altered step interval in a tonal alteration can therefore not be mediated by the same tone, as the latter forms either a diminished fifth or an augmented fourth with one of the two tones of the altered step interval. But the altered step interval in a modal alteration can very well be mediated by the same tone, namely if the unaltered and the altered tone both form a third with that tone. Otherwise the mediation tone needs to be altered or replaced. The possibility to maintain the mediation tone may—theoretically—serve as a defining property for modal alterations. Hauptmann seems choose mediations tones by a criterium of key membership, as we will see below. In the key of C-major the tonal step from C to D as well as the modal step from D to E are both mediated through the tone G in the just described manner ([8], p. 37). The notes A and B on scale degrees $\hat{6}$ and $\hat{7}$ are mediated through the note E and form a tonal step interval a.

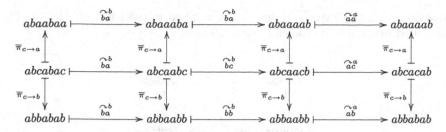

Fig. 2. Alteration chains for the derivation of the step-interval pattern of the melodic minor mode. The middle row starts with the octave species of the twisted triadic Aeolian mode *abcabac* and reaches the desired pattern *abcacab* on the right. The upper row shows the corresponding diatonic projection, starting from the octave species of the authentic Aeolian mode *abaabaa* and reaches *abaaaab*. The middle and upper rows are connected along the letter projection $\overline{\pi}_{c\to a}$. The bottom row shows the corresponding syntonic projection, starting from the octave species of the syntonic Standard mode *abbabab* and ends with the same mode. The middle and bottom rows are connected along the letter projection $\overline{\pi}_{c\to b}$.

With regard to the scale of the C-Minor key, we get into an interesting tension with Hauptmann's position. His starting point is not the natural minor scale, but the three-triad system constituted by the C-Minor, F-Minor and G-Major Triads. The implied scale is the harmonic minor scale, which we consider in the next subsection. But with regard to the *scale of the minor key* Hauptmann sees the need to close the gap between Ab and B though an alteration $Ab \to A$, resulting in a melodic minor scale. But precisely there we get into conflict with Hauptmann. The mediation for a tonal step between A and B must go though E. But Hauptmann discards this option, as the tone E does not belong to the key. Instead he chooses D as the mediating tone for a modal step, the same tone would serve to mediate between G and A as a tonal step. In other words, Hauptmann favors the step-interval pattern *abbaabb*, the penultimate node in the diagram of Fig. 2. As a drawback he gets a complicated alteration with a switch from the mediating tone Eb for the modal minor step $G - Ab$ to D.

We tend to regard harmonic and melodic minor to be both alterations of the natural minor mode, where we have a tonal step between Ab and Bb. In this perspective it seems more natural to expect a binding between the two altered notes, keeping the tonal step between them intact.[3]

4.2   Harmonic Minor, Harmonic and Melodic Major

Our position is further strengthened in the case of the harmonic alteration of the natural minor mode, as Fig. 3 shows. Under the diatonic projection $\overline{\pi}_{c\to a}$ the letter $\underline{d} = \mathfrak{l}(ab^{-1}c)$ is mapped to the letter $d = ab^{-1}a$. Under the syntonic

---

[3] In a separate paper we will have a closer look into this tension, collecting more arguments in favor and against both interpretations of the step pattern of melodic minor.

projection $\overline{\pi}_{c\to b}$ the letter $\underline{d} = \mathfrak{l}(ab^{-1}c)$ is mapped to the letter $ab^{-1}b = a$. The augmented prime $\underline{d}$ is syntonically unnoticeable.

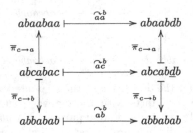

Fig. 3. Harmonic alteration of the minor mode. The middle row starts with the octave species of the twisted triadic Aeolian mode *abcabac* and yields $\underline{d}$ on the right. The upper row shows the corresponding diatonic projection, starting from *abaabaa* and reaches *abaabdb*. The middle and upper rows are connected along the letter projection $\overline{\pi}_{c\to a}$. The bottom row shows the corresponding syntonic projection, starting from the octave species of the syntonic Standard mode *abbabab* and ends with the same mode. The middle and bottom rows are connected along the letter projection $\overline{\pi}_{c\to b}$

Replacing all instances of the letters b and c in the middle rows of the two diagrams in Figs. 2 and 3 yields analogous derivations of the harmonic and melodic alterations of the major mode (c.f. Hauptmann's *Minor Major key*). While this letter-exchange leads to different diatonic projections it turns out that the syntonic projections are precisely the same as in Figs. 2 and 3.

In particular we can conclude that the (anti-standard) syntonic mode $(ab, babab)$ provides a unifying structure for the prominent forms of the major and minor keys.

5   Outlook: Embracing the Complete Syntonic Hierarchy

This outlook is inspired by Eytan Agmon's [2] discussion of the connection between counterpoint and harmony in harmonic tonality.

The "special structural status" of the perfect octave $P8$, perfect fifth $P5$ and perfect fourth $P4$ for the diatonic system can also be related to their role as periods. $P8$ is the main period of all diatonic modes. $P5$ and $P4$ are the periods of the doubly-periodic Guidonian hexachord *aabaa* (in the word-theoretic sense of periodicity). The corresponding prefixes *aaba* and *aab* are—at the same time— the Ionian species of the fifth and the fourth, whose concatenations yield the Ionian and Hypo-Ionian species of the octave.

When Agmon speaks of the thirds and sixths as cyclic generators, he thinks of the triads and seventh chords as chains of thirds within the generic layer of the diatonic scale, i.e. the cyclic group $\mathbb{Z}_7$ of the seven scale degrees. The third-generated structures have been motivated by the fact they afford smooth diatonic voice leading among themselves [1]. The concept of the *syntonic mode*

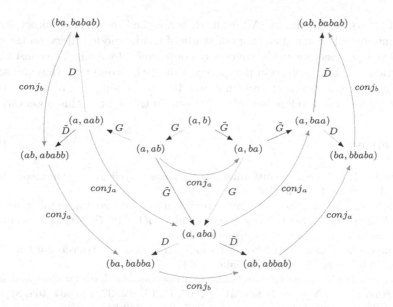

Fig. 4. The nodes along each of the concentric circular arcs form a complete conjugation class of special Sturmian morphisms. Each morphism f is represented by the pair $(f(a), f(b))$ of images of the letters a and b. The node (a, b) in the center represents the Identity map. Then from inside outwards the conjugation classes of G, GG, and DGG are displayed. The graph forms a subgraph of the Cayley graph of the automorphism group $Aut(F_2)$ with respect to the generators $G, \tilde{G}, D, \tilde{D}, conj_a, conj_b$. Each single conjugation class forms a linear graph, whose arrows are all labeled with one of the conjugations $conj_a$ or $conj_b$. The outward reaching arrows, connecting nodes on successive arcs, are labeled with the generators $G, \tilde{G}, D, \tilde{D}$ of the special Sturmian monoid (= monoid of special positive automorphisms).

is a refinement of this approach, in the sense that the syntonic modes are third-generated. We see in Fig. 4 six out of the seven syntonic modes, which form a complete conjugation class of Special Sturmian morphisms. The missing mode is the—so called—bad conjugate $(bb, ababa)$. They are shown along the outer arc of the diagram in Fig. 4 and form the syntonic analogoue of the six authentic Glarean modes. This analogy is—from the outset—a purely mathematical one. But the present paper is a first attempt to interpret them in musical terms. We may understand the interior arcs, moving inward, as the inversions of the seventh chords and of the triads, respectively. The inner node represents the basic division of the octave into the imperfect consonances third and sixth, and the divided words represent the filling-in of the third and the sixth. The missing elements—the bad conjugates—are the 6/4 triadic inversion (b, aa) and the 6/4/2 seventh-chord inversion (b, aaa).

On the one hand it is not surprising, that the innermost levels of the diatonic and the syntonic hierarchies are formed by the perfect and the imperfect consonances, respectively—perfect fifths and fourths as well as thirds and sixths:

pairs of octave complements. After all, they are the inner-triadic intervals. But this "tautological" consequence of our study of triadic modes offers, on the other hand, a new perspective on the concept of consonance, by itself. The consonances are particular simultaneities in polyphony. But at the same time they are spaces to be filled in subsequent transformations. It is a challenging project to review the emergence and development of polyphony in the light of this observation.

References

1. Agmon, E.: Linear transformations between cyclically generated chords. Musikometrika **3**, 15–40 (1991)
2. Agmon, E.: The bridges that never were: Schenker on the contrapuntal origin of the triad and seventh chord. Music Theory Online **3**(1) (1997). http://www.mtosmt.org/issues/mto.97.3.1/mto.97.3.1.agmon.html
3. Clampitt, D.: Pairwise Well-Formed Scales: Structural and Transformational Properties. Ph.D. diss, SUNY at Buffalo (1997)
4. Clampitt, D.: Mathematical and musical properties of pairwise well-formed scales. In: Klouche, T., Noll, T. (eds.) MCM 2007. CCIS, vol. 37, pp. 464–468. Springer, Heidelberg (2009). https://doi.org/10.1007/978-3-642-04579-0_46
5. Noll, T., Clampitt, D.: Kaleidoscope substitutions and pairwise well-formed modes: Major-Minor duality transformationally revisited. J. Math. Music **12**(3) (2018)
6. Cohn, R.: Maximally smooth cycles, hexatonic systems, and the analysis of late-romantic triadic progressions. Music Anal. **15**, 9–40 (1996)
7. Dahlhaus, C.: Untersuchungen über die Entstehung der harmonischen Tonalität. Bärenreiter, Kassel (1969)
8. Hauptmann, M. (W. E. Heathcote, trans.): The Nature of Harmony and Metre. Swan Sonnenschein & Co., London 1888 [1853]
9. Hindemith, P.: The Craft of Musical Composition. Schott, London (1940)
10. Mazzola, G.: The Topos of Music. Birkhäuser, Basel (2002)

Embedded Structural Modes: Unifying Scale Degrees and Harmonic Functions

Thomas Noll[1](✉) and Karst De Jong[1,2]

[1] Departament de Teoria, Composició i Direcció,
Escola Superior de Música de Catalunya, Barcelona, Spain
thomas.mamuth@gmail.com, karstdj@gmail.com
[2] Royal Conservatoire Den Haag, Hague, The Netherlands

Abstract. The paper offers an integration of the theory of structural modes, functional theory and diatonic scale degrees. In analogy to the parsimonious voice leading between generic diatonic triads we study parsimonious function leading between embedded structural modes. A combinatorics of diatonic embeddings of structural modes is given. In four analytical examples we study the interaction of relative minor and major modes within an encompassing diatonic collection. Finally we discuss alternative possibilities for the interpretation of the diminished fifth as a fundament progression.

Keywords: Structural modes · Functional harmony ·
Scale degree theory · Hierarchy · Diabolus in musica

1 Conciliation of Scale Degrees and Tonal Functions

The original foundation of tonal function theory is based on a system of triads. Thereby the status of the diatonic scale is downgraded to a mere aggregation of tones from these triads. Roman numeral analysis acts on the assumption that the basic vocabulary of tonal harmony is potentially formed by all seven diatonic triads. Some interesting efforts have been made to seek for a unification of tonal function and scale degrees [3,9,12]. In particular, Carl Dahlhaus provides a suitable anchor for our investigation (see also [11]).

In his studies on the origins of harmonic tonality, Carl Dahlhaus [3]—among many other things—aims to provide a definition of his subject: *harmonic tonality*. After a critical assessment of Sechter's theory of scale degrees and Riemann's theory of tonal functions, he comes to the conclusion that the two approaches have the potential to productively complement one another. He discards Riemann's motivations of the concept of *harmonic function* on the basis of a three-triad-system and proposes a seemingly structuralist perspective: Exploring the connection between tonal functions and scale-degree-intervals he characterizes chords related by seconds and fourths as *functionally different* and by thirds as *functionally indifferent*. Based on this observation he comes to the conclusion

© Springer Nature Switzerland AG 2019
M. Montiel et al. (Eds.): MCM 2019, LNAI 11502, pp. 137–148, 2019.
https://doi.org/10.1007/978-3-030-21392-3_11

that the largest number of pairwise functionally different scale degrees is three. As the first author [11] observes, these three pairwise functionally different scale degrees always form the same abstract set-class of scale degrees. Most prominently it is represented by the set $\{\hat{1}, \hat{4}, \hat{5}\}$, the roots of the tonic, subdominant and dominant triads, respectively.

In our own previous work [4,5], we incorporate only this part from our inspection of Dahlhaus' argument and propagate a renewed function theory on the basis of 3-tone modes. The tonal functions of structural bass notes (mainly chord fundaments) are controlled by *structural modes*, little chains of two fifths, connecting three notes, such as $F - C - G$. These notes are the carriers of the three tonal functions S, T, D, or T, S, D or D, S, T. Depending upon the location of the tonic function T on the flat side, in the middle or on the sharp side, we speak of the *first*, *second* and *third* mode, respectively. The alteration interval which allows to modulate from one mode to another is the minor third. We call it the *structural augmented prime* (the "little devil"). This interval is the starting point for a form of "structural chromaticism", namely the adding of one altered note and thereby extending the mode to a chain of three perfect fifths. The three modes differ in the functional degree (T, S or D), which is allowed to be altered:

1st mode C_1: $C - F - (D) - G - C$ with functional degrees $T - S - (\sharp S) - D - T$,
2nd mode C_2: $C - (A) - D - G - C$ with functional degrees $T - (\sharp T) - S - D - T$,
3rd mode C_3: $C - F - B\flat - (G) - C$ with functional degrees $T - S - D - (\sharp D) - T$.

We did not regard the marginal role of the diatonic scale as a shortcoming. In a special situation, which we will revisit more carefully in the present paper, we made instead the attempt to recover the full diatonic collection as a combination of two structural modes,—the "double-star constellation". The term stands for the interaction of two tonal regions in relative minor and major keys. And the particular challenge here is to align these two regions within a complete diatonic falling fifths progression.

$$
\begin{array}{ccccccc}
 & E\flat & B\flat & F & C & G & D & A \\
B\flat_1 : & S & T & D & \sharp S & & & \\
 & & & G_1 : S & T & D & \sharp S &
\end{array}
$$

This situation is challenging, as the complete diatonic progression of falling fifths is downright the epitome of Sechterian scale degree theory.

In the context of his attempt for a conciliation between scale degrees and harmonic function Dahlhaus [3] confesses that his concept of functional difference for seconds and fifths and functional indifference for thirds collapses in this case. It is simply impossible to label each of the seven degrees with either T, S or D in such a way that fifth- and step-related degrees receive different labels while third-related degrees identical labels. A serious problem arises from this fact only in situations where all seven degrees are actually used. Therefore Dahlhaus tries to tackle the problem with reference to the sequential character of the diatonic circle-of-fifths progression. And he refers to Fetis and Riemann arguing that sequences tend to suspend the elementary harmonic motion. We think, however, that this argument needs further differentiation. In Sect. 4 we inspect four popular songs for that matter.

Figure 1 shows our former analysis of the *Autumn Leaves* progression, as well as our former solution to this problem: Our trick is to decompose the diminished fifth into two structural augmented primes ("little devils"), each of which we consider to be functionally indifferent. The diminished fifth therefore also turns out to express of functional indifference. The complete diatonic cycle of fifths splits into a $B\flat$-Major half and a G-Minor half with consistent functional attributions.

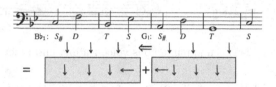

Fig. 1. Structural bass analysis of the *Autumn Leaves*-progression. The two gray boxes identify the structural modes $B\flat_1$ and G_1, respectively. The descending diminished fifth $E\flat - A$ is split into the structural augmented primes $E\flat - C$ ($= S - \sharp S$ in $B\flat_1$) and $C - A$ ($= \tilde{S} - \sharp S$ in G_1).

With regard to this perspective one may object that the specific difference between perfect and diminished fifths is being made absolute, while the homogeneous nature of the generic sequence of falling fifths is underexposed. We will revisit this solution in Sects. 4 and 5. After having established the connection between Dahlhaus' pairwise functionally different scale degrees on the one hand, and the structural modes on the other, we may now more faithfully return to Dahlhaus' original project by embedding the autonomous structural modes into the diatonic scale. In particular, our previous approach neglects interval triples, such as $\flat\hat{2}, \hat{5}, \hat{1}$ involving a semitone, an augmented fourth and perfect fourth/fifth. The present article sets out to elaborate further on these issues.

The two subsequent sections utilize a basic distinction in diatonic scale theory, namely firstly the study of structural modes as subsets of a generic diatonic scale, and secondly, their study as subsets of a specific diatonic scale, where precisely one of the seven fifths is a diminished one.

2   The Generic Embedding: Analogy Between Voice-Leading and Function-Leading

A useful starting point is the embedding of a generic structural mode into a generic diatonic scale, where all seven step intervals are regarded to be equal. This method has proven to be very useful for an understanding of the parsimonious voice-leading behaviour of generic diatonic triads and seventh-chords. Third-chains of length 3 and 4 have the property that the execution of a single step motion in one voice corresponds to a third-transposition of the entire chord

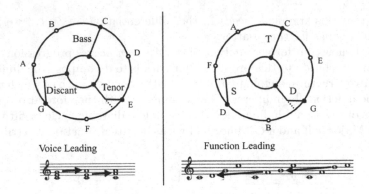

Fig. 2. Analogy between parsimonious voice-leading and function leading

up to inversion (see left side of Fig. 2). This fact is related to the maximally even distribution of triads (and seventh-chords) within the generic diatonic step cycle as well as with the fact, that the numbers 3 and 4 are multiplicative inverses modulo 7 (± 1) of the span 2 of the generating third: $3 \times 2 = -1 \bmod 7$ and $4 \times 2 = 1 \bmod 7$.

The right side of Fig. 2 illustrates that the same situation occurs with the generic structural modes embedded into the third-generated diatonic scale: The execution of a single third-motion in one function corresponds to a fifth-transposition of the entire structural mode. This observation ensures that the mechanics of structural modulation, as earlier described in [4,5] with respect to the autonomous structural modes, can also be faithfully performed within an encompassing diatonic scale.

When the principle of parsimonious voice leading among generic triads (as shown on the left side of Fig. 2) is applied to typical progressions in classical music, the sixth-fourth chord has usually to be skipped (see the upper example in Fig. 3, and refer to [14], Example 1). An analogous situation occurs in the application of function leading. In the opening measures of Chopin's Waltz in A minor the dominant and tonic functions of the first mode $A_1^{(3b)}$ move to the second mode $C_2^{(\natural)}$. As an intermediate stage one could first move only the (concealed) dominant E of $A_1^{(3b)}$ to that of the third mode $A_3^{(3b)}$, namely G. However, the third mode is the bad conjugate among the three structural modes and is untypical for the harmonic patterns of the classical repertoire, and so we skip it.[1]

---

[1] The first and second modes are refinements of the authentic division of the octave into fifth and fourth, while the third mode is not. Algebraically, this corresponds to the fact that $a \mapsto ba, b \mapsto b$ and $a \mapsto ab, b \mapsto b$ are both automorphisms of the free group F_2, while $a \mapsto bb, b \mapsto a$ is not. This is in strict analogy to the fact, that the sixth-fourth chord is the bad conjugate among the three triadic modes. The root position triad and the sixth chord are refinements of the division of the octave in third and sixth, while the sixth-fourth chord is not. Algebraically, $a \mapsto a, b \mapsto ab$ and $a \mapsto a, ba \mapsto b$ are both automorphisms, while $a \mapsto b, b \mapsto aa$ is not.

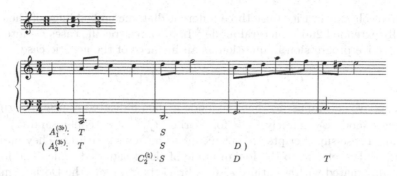

$A_1^{(3\flat)}$: T S
($A_3^{(3\flat)}$: T S D)
                $C_2^{(\natural)}:S$ D T

Fig. 3. Upper example: descending voice leading between a root position triad and a sixth-chord. Bottom example: simplified representation of Opening of Chopin's Waltz in A minor, B. 150, KK IVb/11 as an illustration of the principle of function leading.

Observe, how the principle of function leading differs from Riemann's principle of functional substitution: Riemann would acknowledge the d-minor chord as the proper representative of subdominant function in a-minor. In C-major, however, it would be degraded to the role of a substitute for the proper subdominant chord F. In our view we treat the retention of the subdominant function in analogy to that of a common tone in a chord progression. The fundament D is the proper subdominant degree in the 1st mode of A and likewise it is the proper subdominant degree in the 2nd mode of C. The same holds for the moving fundaments $E \rightsquigarrow G$ and $A \rightsquigarrow C$. They embody the dominant and tonic functions in A_1 and C_2, respectively.

3   Specific Regular and Irregular Embeddings

What distinguishes a specific diatonic scale from its generic form is the presence and the specific location of a diminished fifth. In this article we unbind ourselves from our previous rather rigid position, that perfect fifths embody functional difference, while diminished fifths are functionally indifferent.

A convincing example in favor of this decision can be found in the penultimate measure of Chopin's Prelude in C-Minor (Op. 28 No. 20) with harmonies $A_\flat$ $D_\flat$ G^7 Cm (see the note example in right column of Fig. 4). In the context of our previous autonomous treatment of the structural modes we would have been forced to either attribute dominant function to the fundament of $D_\flat$ or to postulate a change of key within this single measure. In order to illustrate the benefit of the distinction between the generic and specific embeddings of structural modes we present this example along with two slight modifications.

The three columns in Fig. 4 use three different diatonic embeddings of the chromatically extended 2nd structural mode.[2] In all three specific cases we interpret the respective progression in question as an instance of the generic case

$$C_2 : \sharp T \quad \downarrow \quad S \quad \downarrow \quad D \quad \downarrow \quad T.$$

The respective encompassing diatonic mode is then indicated as a superscript to the generic mode C_2, namely $C_2^{(2b)}$ for Dorian, $C_2^{(3b)}$ for Aeolian, and $C_2^{(4b)}$ for Phrygian. These superscripts are not meant to be key signatures. They indicate diatonic modes relative to the Ionian mode of the designated tonic. The Ionian mode is designated with a natural sign in brackets ($\natural$). Only the Dorian embedding $C_2^{(2b)}$ (left) entails three perfect fifths/fourths. We will therefore call it a *regular embedding*. The Aeolian $C_2^{(3b)}$ (middle) and Phrygian $C_2^{(4b)}$ (right) are *irregular embeddings*, as both contain one diminished fifth. They differ in their locations, which is shown in terms of a dotted line. The Phrygian embedding (right column) corresponds to the penultimate measure in Chopin's prelude.

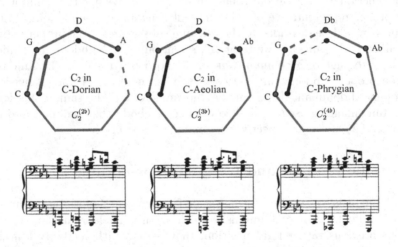

Fig. 4. Illustrations of three diatonic embeddings of the 2nd structural mode: $C_2^{(2b)}$, $C_2^{(3b)}$, and $C_2^{(4b)}$. The dotted lines indicate the location of the diminished fifth. Chopin's original version is shown in the right column.

The table in Fig. 3 gives an overview about the combinatorics of the possible configurations of embedded structural modes. The rather exotic Locrian embeddings are left out here.

---

[2] Of course we also adapt the chord tones in the other voices. But our concept of embedding applies to the horizontal dimension of fundament progressions, which may or may not coincide with the vertical dimension of the chords.

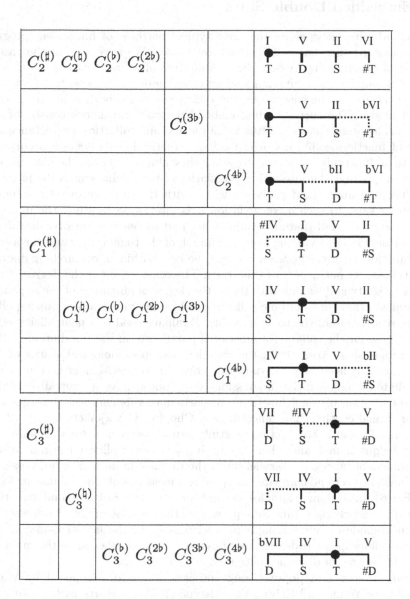

Fig. 5. For each of the three modes there are six diatonic embeddings. The respective diatonic modes are indicated as a superscript: (♯) = Lydian, (♮) = Ionian, (♭) = Mixolydian, (2♭) = Dorian, (3♭) = Aeolian, (4♭) = Phrygian (Here we dispense with the Locrian mode). In each case there are four regular embeddings and two irregular ones. The schemes on the right side of the table show the correspondence between functional degrees and Diatonic Scale Degrees. The irregular embeddings employ a diminished fifth. Its position is indicated through a dashed line.

4   Embedded Double-Stars

Major and minor keys share the same typical patterns of fundament progressions: namely either 1st or 2nd structural modes. We have seen in the case of the Chopin Waltz (Fig. 3) that the combination of a first with a second mode can be obtained with a function leading of two moving degrees. In this section we concentrate on the case where the relative keys are both realized in terms of 2nd modes. The corresponding embedded structural modes consist of disjoint, but adjacent chains of fifths within a diatonic collection (= distance 3 in terms of function-leading). Corresponding structural scale degrees occupy the same tonal functions. Moreover, together they almost exhaust the diatonic collection in question. An interesting peculiarity of the double star is the fact that the structural augmented prime coincides with the distance of relative major and minor keys. In such a constellation it is interesting to study the interplay of the structural and diatonic components and to see how an overall unity is being achieved. The swinging back and fourth of the tonal center and the associated functional degrees between two relative keys within an overarching diatonic collection marks one aspect of this study. The other aspect is the degree of diatonic contiguity and—along with that—the degree of obstinacy of the sequential mechanics within that diatonic collection, which may have a neutralizing effect on the articulation of the tonal meaning. Dahlhaus used this neutralizing effect as an excuse for the collapse of functional parallelism in the full diatonic falling fifths progression. Apart from the questionable epistemological status of this argument[3] it is necessary to study this effect in context. Under certain conditions diatonic falling fifths progressions may indeed have a neutralizing effect on the formation of tonal functions. In particular, this concerns passages with a clear formal continuation function (e.g. Chopin's C-Major etude Op. 12, No 1 mm. 42–45). But in this section we study situations where a tonal meaning can hardly be questioned, and where we are in two cases explicitly confronted with the problem of functional parallelism in the diatonic falling fifths progression.

We will inspect and compare the opening 8 measures of four popular melodies (see Fig. 6). In all four examples we find an interaction of a second structural mode A_2—underlying a 4-measure passage in the key of A-minor – with a second structural mode C_2 underlying a parallel passage in the key of C-major. The examples differ in the order of these passages, in their relation to the main key and in the degree of diatonic contiguity.

Beautiful love is a popular song and jazz standard, composed by Wayne King, Victor Young and Egbert Van Alstyne (1931). It starts with a four measure basic idea in minor, which is repeated in the relative major mode. In this piece the overall (and final) mode is minor. The structural bass is articulated

---

[3] Explicitly he writes: "Eine Theorie aber, die gerade dort versagt, wo auch das Phänomen, das sie erklären soll, ins Vage und Unbestimmte gerät, darf als adäquat gelten" ([3], p. 50). With this epistemological faux pas Dahlhaus threw the ball into Mazzola's court, who illustrates the collapse of functional parallelism through the combinatorial description of the seven diatonic triads in the form of a Moebius strip, which is known to be non-orientable [10].

Fig. 6. Embedded double-star configurations

in the embedded second modes $A_2^{(3b)} : S \quad D \quad T$ and $C_2^{(\natural)} : S \quad D \quad T$. Four of the five down-arrows in the annotation denote the structural progressions within these modes. The down-arrow $\downarrow$ connecting the fundaments A and D, is displayed slightly higher. It participates on the diatonic level of analysis and thereby contributes to the contiguity of the complete 8-measure phrase. It is not regarded an internal structural progression.

Love me or leave me is a popular song composed by Walter Donaldson (1928). It also starts in the minor mode with a repeated 2-measure idea which is then repeated once in major where the phrase concludes. The overall (and final) mode is major in this case. The 2nd modes are typically enriched by the structural alteration $\sharp T$ of the tonic degree T. This suggests a Dorian embedding $A_2^{(2b)}$. Here the connecting interval between the fundaments E and C is a third (notated by a right-down-arrow). The overarching diatonic contiguity is less strong and the two tonal centers are more clearly articulated as two poles. The repeat of the 8-measure phrase is launched by an inserted $II - V$.

The chanson and jazz standard *Les feuilles mortes/Autumn Leaves*, composed by Joseph Kosma (1945) is an instance where the aspect of diatonic contiguity is more salient. In the jazz tradition the A-part of the tune is harmonized as a complete falling fifths progression of diatonic seventh chords, entailing the incorruptible voice leading mechanics of a scheme called the *prolongational Prinner*[4]. So we have one interpretation of the progression as a flat quadripartite sequence with two measure units, competing with its higher order grouping into two halves (the first in relative major, the second in the home key). The grouping into two 4-measure units is strengthened by the original harmonization without scale degree VI. The subsequent insertion of scale degree VI in the jazz standard elicits a noticeable smoothening of the progression. The overall key is minor, but comparing with *Beautiful love* we see that the order of the relative key regions is reversed here. Hence the diatonic contiguity between the end of the A-part and its repeat is provided by the single fifth from A to D, while the contiguity between the first and the second halves is provided by two fifths (the perfect fifth from C to F and the diminished fifth from F to B). This analysis via embedded modes deviates from our earlier structural-mode analysis in [4] (see Fig. 1). One difference concerns the interpretation of the diminished fifth. In the earlier analysis the interval between VI and II was regarded as a structural double-alteration. In the new analysis we regard this progression simply as being non-structural alongside with the proceeding progression from III to VI. Another difference concerns the choice of the mode. The inclusion of scale degree VI leads to the choice of a first mode. But this choice is not quite supported by the music. The assumption of a second mode is much more convincing.

The idea of embedded modes is literally built upon the assumption of a coexistence of structural and diatonic layers. In this regard it is interesting that Martin Rohrmeier in his investigations into a generative syntax of tonal harmony [13] offers two hierarchical analyses of the A-part which are in good correspondence to the two aspects discussed above, i.e. as a complete falling fifths progression and as a double star constellation. It would be interesting to discuss the conditions for a coexistence of both hierarchies.

Fly me to the moon originally titled "In other words", is a popular song and jazz standard composed by Bart Howard (1954). With regard to the harmonic structure and the high degree of diatonic contiguity it resembles *Autumn leaves*. A notable difference is the occurrence of an A-minor-seventh chord at the downbeat of measure 1. What initially might suggest a tonic harmony in A-minor turns out to function as $\sharp T$ in a second structural mode $C_2^{(\natural)}$. The corresponding harmony at the downbeat of measure 5 is an F-major seventh chord, whose fundament can be interpreted as the structural scale degree $\sharp T$ in the irregular embedding $A_2^{(3\flat)}$ (c.f. Fig. 5). Due to the involvement of the scale degree $\sharp T$ in both modes, there is only one fifth (from C to F), which does not function as an internal structural progression.

---

[4] for reference and further discussion see Sect. 5.

5 Outlook

The present approach to the tonal analysis of fundament progressions via diatonically embedded structural modes provides a considerably higher amount of descriptive freedom compared to our previous approach using autonomous structural modes. The most sensitive spot of the analytical work is now the distinction between structural and non-structural progressions. Along with voice-leading/function-leading analogy we may compare non-structural diatonic fundament progressions with non-chord-tones. Along this analogy a possibly more adequate place is offered for the distinction between contrapuntal chords and proper harmonies within traditional Roman numeral analysis. One may envisage quite different analytical styles within the same descriptive framework.

We may test the productivity of the voice-leading/function-leading analogy even further. In the context of the Neo-Riemannian study of triadic progressions within the chromatic scale there is a controversy about the role of an intermediate diatonic level. The non-integrationist approach discards it, while the integrationist approach does not. The analogy of a non-integrationist approach would be a direct embedding of structural modes into the chromatic scale, which is in good accordance with Ernö Lendvai's treatment of tonal functions in the axis system. In particular, our previous interpretation of the diminished fifth as being composed from two functionally indifferent minor thirds would faithfully reflect this position.

A thorough continuation and elaboration of the explorations of the present paper should be guided by the analogy of an integrationist approach. A rich source to be studied is the annotated collection [7] of 230 jazz standards in terms of harmonic "LEGO bricks". These typical patterns are given in terms of Roman numerals and Chord symbols and offer themselves to be re-interpreted in terms of embedded structural modes (diatonically and chromatically). Elliot builds further on ideas that can be found in the original book by Conrad Cork [6].

Alone the differentiation of the possible meanings of perfect and diminished fifths is a demanding part of this project. We have seen that diminished fifths can be reasonably interpreted as structural progressions in irregular embeddings, while perfect fifths may also be seen as non-structural purely diatonic progressions. This includes the possibility to regard entire falling fifths progressions with a continuation function of high momentum as purely diatonic and a suspended structural level. A typical example would be Caplin's *prolongational Prinner*, a typical subspecies of Gjerdingen's Prinner scheme, serving a prolongational function (see [8], and [2]).

Further challenges on the interpretation of diminished fifths can be drawn from Nicole Biamonte's article about tritone substitutions [1]. She argues that there is a fundamental difference between the augmented 6th chords and tritone substitutions. This is a particular challenge, because tritone substitutions can be regarded as intervals/relations between real basses and fundaments, and hence are not located within the structural bass as such. Only an extended theory, which incorporates upper structures could possibly clarify these situations.

Acknowledgement. We wish to thank Jason Yust, David Clampitt and the anonymous reviewers for valuable feedback.

References

1. Biamonte, N.: Augmented-sixth chords vs. tritone substitutes. Music Theory Online **14**(2) (2008). http://www.mtosmt.org/issues/mto.08.14.2/mto.08.14.2.biamonte.html
2. Caplin, W.E.: Harmony and cadence in Gjerdingen's 'Prinner'. In: Neuwirth, M., Bergé, P. (eds.) What Is a Cadence? Theoretical and Analytical Perspectives on Cadences in the Classical Repertoire. Leuven University Press, Leuven (2015)
3. Dahlhaus, C.: Untersuchungen über die Entstehung der harmonischen Tonalität. Kassel et al.: Bärenreiter (1967)
4. de Jong, K., Noll, T.: Fundamental passacaglia: harmonic functions and the modes of the musical tetractys. In: Agon, C., Andreatta, M., Assayag, G., Amiot, E., Bresson, J., Mandereau, J. (eds.) MCM 2011. LNCS (LNAI), vol. 6726, pp. 98–114. Springer, Heidelberg (2011). https://doi.org/10.1007/978-3-642-21590-2_8
5. De Jong, K., Noll, T.: FFundamental bass and real bass in dialogue: tonal aspects of the structural modes. Music Theory Online **24**(4) (2018). http://mtosmt.org/issues/mto.18.24.4/mto.18.24.4.de_jong_noll.html
6. Cork, C.: The New Guide to Harmony with Lego Bricks: Revised and Extended Edition. Tadley Ewing Publications, Leicester (1996)
7. Elliott, J.: Insights In Jazz: An Inside View of Jazz Standard Chord Progressions. Jazzwise Publications, London (2009)
8. Gjerdingen, R.: Music in the Galant Style. Oxford University Press, New York (2007)
9. Harrison, D.: Harmonic Function in Chromatic Music. The University of Chicago Press, Chicago and London (1994)
10. Mazzola, G.: Die Geometrie der Töne. Birkhäuser, Basel (1990)
11. Noll, T.: Die Vernunft in der Tradition: Neue mathematische Untersuchungen zu den alten Begriffen der Diatonizität. ZGMTH 13. Special Issue (2016). https://doi.org/10.31751/864
12. Quinn, I.: Harmonic function without primary triads. Paper delivered at the annual meeting of the Society for Music Theory in Boston, November 2005
13. Rohrmeier, M.: Towards a generative syntax of tonal harmony. J. Math. Music **5**(1), 35–53 (2011)
14. Yust, J.: Distorted continuity: chromatic harmony, uniform sequences, and quantized voice leadings. Music Theor. Spectr. **37**(1), 120–143 (2015)

Non-Contextual JQZ Transformations

Franck Jedrzejewski[✉]

Atomic Energy Commission, Université Paris Lumières (CEA-CIPh), Paris, France
franckjed@gmail.com

Abstract. Initiated by David Lewin, the contextual PLR-transformations are well known from neo-Riemannian theory. As it has been noted, these transformations are only used for major and minor triads. In this paper, we introduce non-contextual bijections called JQZ transformations that could be used for any kind of chord. These transformations are pointwise, and the JQZ group that they generate acts on any type of n-chord. The properties of these groups are very similar, and the JQZ-group could extend the PLR-group in many situations. Moreover, the hexatonic and octatonic subgroups of JQZ and PLR groups are subdual.

Keywords: Neo-Riemannian group · PLR-group · JQZ-group · Generalized interval systems · Lewin · Parsimonious voice leading

In the neo-Riemannian theory, the use of algebraic structures provides a deep insight into the concept of musical structures and transformational processes. The contextual transformations P (*Parallel*), L (*Leading Tone*) and R (*Relative*) rediscovered by Lewin [15], Hyer [12,13] and Cohn [3–5] from the works of musicologist Hugo Riemann in the late 19th century [16], laid the foundations of the neo-Riemannian theory.

The present paper is organized as follows. After a reminder of some properties of the neo-Riemannian transformations P, L, and R we choose, as we did in 2005 (see [14]), three suitable generators J, Q, and Z for the T/I-group (formed by translations ($T_n(x) = x + n \mod 12$) and inversions ($I_n(x) = -x + n \mod 12$). The T/I-group is known to be isomorphic to the dihedral group D_{12} of 24 elements, the symmetry group of a 12-sided regular polygon [2,11]. In this paper we use the term *JQZ-group* synonymously to the term *T/I-group*. This is in analogy to the usage of the term *PLR-group* synonymously to the term *S/W-group* (Schritt/Wechsel group). This particular system of generators J, Q, and Z has not been systematiclly studied before, but its has very similar properties to the generators P, L and R of the Schritt-Wechsel group. They are not contextually defined and can be applied pointwise. Their definition is unique up to conjugation. Our concrete choice depends upon the choice of the C-major triad $\{0, 4, 7\}$ as a distinctive chord of reference. The choice of any other consonant triad $f(\{0, 4, 7\})$ in this role yields a conjugated triple $fJf^{-1}, fQf^{-1}, fZf^{-1}$ of generators. As in the case of the PLR-group, two subgroups of the JQZ-group are important: the *hexatonic group* generated by transformations J and Q, and the *octatonic group* generated by transformations J and Z.

© Springer Nature Switzerland AG 2019
M. Montiel et al. (Eds.): MCM 2019, LNAI 11502, pp. 149–160, 2019.
https://doi.org/10.1007/978-3-030-21392-3_12

1 PLR Transformations

As usual, we encode pitch classes using the standard model of $\mathbb{Z}_{12}$, where $c = 0$, $c\sharp = 1$, $d = 2$, and so on up to $b = 11$. Through this bijection, a major chord is a set of pitches consisting of three notes that has a root x, major third $x + 4$, and perfect fifth $x + 7$; a minor chord is a set of pitches consisting of three notes that has a root x, minor third $x + 3$, and perfect fifth $x + 7$, where the root of the chord ranges through $\mathbb{Z}_{12}$. Major and minor triads are identified with 3-element subsets of $\mathbb{Z}_{12}$ of the form $\{x, x + 4, x + 7\}$ and $\{x, x + 3, x + 7\}$, respectively. The set of the 24 major and minor chords is also called the set of *consonant triads*. Their interval structure can be expressed in terms of third chains $(4, 3)$ and $(3, 4)$, respectively. Rooted interval chains $((a, b), x)$ can be mapped to the associated pitch class sets via: $((a, b), x) \mapsto \{x, x + a, x + a + b\}$. Some neo-Riemannian approaches use *pitch-class segments* denoted by angular brackets. The set Σ of consonant triads then consists of the major segments $\langle x, x + 4, x + 7 \rangle$ and minor segments $\langle x, x - 4, x - 7 \rangle$ where the (dualistic) root x ranges over $\mathbb{Z}_{12}$. Properties on PLR groups have been established by Thomas Fiore et al. [1,7–10]. The PLR transformations on (dualistic) root position triads within Σ are defined by[1]

$$P \langle x, y, z \rangle = I_{x+z} \langle x, y, z \rangle \qquad (1)$$
$$R \langle x, y, z \rangle = I_{x+y} \langle x, y, z \rangle$$
$$L \langle x, y, z \rangle = I_{y+z} \langle x, y, z \rangle$$

The transformation P (*Parallel*) exchanges a major triad with the associated parallel minor triad. For instance, $P \langle c, e, g \rangle = P \langle 0, 4, 7 \rangle = \langle 7, 3, 0 \rangle = \langle g, e\flat, c \rangle$. The transformation R (*Relative*) exchanges a major triad with its relative minor triad (the real root of the *relative minor triad* is a minor third below the root of the major triad) $R \langle c, e, g \rangle = R \langle 0, 4, 7 \rangle = \langle 4, 0, 9 \rangle = \langle e, c, a \rangle$. And the transformation L (*Leittonwechsel, Leading tone exchange*) exchanges a major triad with a minor triad with its real root a major third above $L \langle c, e, g \rangle = L \langle 0, 4, 7 \rangle = \langle 11, 7, 4 \rangle = \langle b, g, e \rangle$. In other words, P relates triads that share a common fifth; L relates triads that share a common minor third; and R relates triads that share a common major third.

The PLR-transformations are involutions $P^2 = L^2 = R^2 = Id$, they are their own inverses. As noted, the group generated by P, L and R is called the *PLR-group*, the *Schritt/Wechsel* group or the neo-Riemannian group after the late 19th-century music theorist Hugo Riemann. Since $P = R(LR)^3$, the *PLR*-group is generated by L and R. It has been shown that the PLR-group is the dihedral group of 24 elements. And by corollary, the PLR-group acts simply transitively on the set of consonant triads. In the following, major and minor chords are

---

[1] Observe, however, that applying the formulae (1) to chord inversions leads to: $L \langle 0, 4, 7 \rangle = \langle 11, 7, 4 \rangle$ (Em), $L \langle 7, 4, 0 \rangle = \langle 9, 0, 4 \rangle$ (Am) and $L \langle 4, 7, 0 \rangle = \langle 3, 0, 7 \rangle$ (Cm). In this case, one can not use the equivalence of chord inversions. But these formulae can alternatively be interpreted as voicing transformations [10].

indicated by compact pitch class notations, with $A = 10$ and $B = 11$: 904 is the minor chord $\langle 9, 0, 4 \rangle = \langle e, c, a \rangle$ and 48B is the major chord $\langle 4, 8, 11 \rangle = \langle e, g\sharp, b \rangle$. The planar representation of the PLR group is a torus.

It is well known, that the transformations P, L, R are not defined on the 12 pitch classes themselves. P sends $e = 4$ in $< 0, 4, 7 >$ to 3 and in $< 9, 1, 4 >$ to 9. The transformations are contextually defined on the basis of the specific interval structure of the major and minor triads. There is no canonic way to define them in strict analogy on other single chord classes, and there are serious obstacles to extend them to all pitch class sets at once. Therefore it is the goal of the next section is to find non-contextual inversions as partners for P, L and R on $\mathbb{Z}_{12}$, which are then automatically valid for all k-chords.

2   JQZ Transformations

The purpose of this section is to select congenial inversions for the generators P, L and R among the 12 inversions I_k on $\mathbb{Z}_{12}$.

In a first step, we look for an inversion J that behaves like the Wechsel P for the C-major triad, i.e. which transforms the major chord $\{0, 4, 7\}$ into the minor chord $\{0, 3, 7\}$. The transformation $J = I_7$ fulfills this and is uniquely determined. For all $x \in \mathbb{Z}_{12}$, we get $J(\{x, x + 4, x + 7\}) = \{-x, -x + 3, -x + 7\}$. In other words, J transforms the major chord rooted at x into the minor chord rooted at $-x$ (mod 12). It can be interpreted as the permutation (in cyclic notation): $J = (0, 7)(1, 6)(2, 5)(3, 4)(8, 11)(9, 10)$.

In the second step, we look for an inversion Q that behaves like the Leiton-wechsel L on the C-major triad, i.e. transforming the major chord $\{0, 4, 7\}$ into the Leading-tone-exchange chord (Leittonwechselklang) $\{4, 7, 11\}$. The transformation $Q = I_{11}$ fulfills this and is uniquely determined. For all $x \in \mathbb{Z}_{12}$, we get $Q(\{x, x + 4, x + 7\}) = \{-x + 4, -x + 7, -x + 11\}$. In other words, Q transforms the major chord rooted at x into the minor chord rooted at $4 - x$ (mod 12). The transformation Q is the permutation $Q = (0, 11)(1, 10)(2, 9)(3, 8)(4, 7)(5, 6)$.

In the third and last step, we look for an inversion Z which behaves like the Wechsel R on the C-major triad, i.e. which transforms the major chord $\{0, 4, 7\}$ into the relative minor chord $\{9, 0, 4\}$. The transformation $Z = I_4$ fulfills this and is uniquely determined. For all $x \in \mathbb{Z}_{12}$, we get $Z(\{x, x + 4, x + 7\}) = \{-x + 9, -x, -x + 4\}$. In other words, Z transforms the major chord rooted at x into the minor chord rooted at $9 - x$ (mod 12). The transformation Z is the permutation: $Z = (0, 4)(1, 3)(5, 11)(6, 10)(7, 9)$.

Since JQZ transformations act pointwise, the order of the pitch classes does not matter.

As noted, the transformations J, Q, Z depend upon the choice of the C-major triad. But analogous transformations can be chosen with a different chord of reference, such that they behave like the transformations P, L, R on this chord. Introducing the transformations $J(x, +) = I_{2x+7}$, $Q(x, +) = I_{2x-1}$, $Z(x, +) = I_{2x+4}$ for a major chord, and the transformations $J(x, -) = I_{2x+7}$, $Q(x, -) = I_{2x+3}$, $Z(x, -) = I_{2x-2}$ for a major chord, we have the following result.

Theorem 1. *For the major chord $X = \{x, x+4, x+7\}$ we define the inversions:*

$$J(x, +) = I_{2x+7}, \quad Q(x, +) = I_{2x-1}, \quad Z(x, +) = I_{2x+4}$$

For the minor chord $X = \{x, x+3, x+7\}$ we define the inversions

$$J(x, -) = I_{2x+7}, \quad Q(x, -) = I_{2x+3}, \quad R = Z(x, -) = I_{2x-2}$$

In both cases $s = \pm$ we obtain $J(x, s)(X) = P(X), Q(x, s)(X) = L(X), Z(x, s)$ $(X) = R(X)$. Moreover, the transformations $J(x, s), Q(x, s), Z(x, s)$ are conjugates of J, Q and Z, respectively:

$$J(x, +) = T_x J T_x^{-1}, Q(x, +) = T_x Q T_x^{-1}, Z(x, +) = T_x Z T_x^{-1},$$
$$J(x, -) = I_x J I_x, \quad Q(x, -) = I_x Q I_x, \quad Z(x, -) = I_x Z I_x.$$

Proof. The proof is straightforward using Eq. (1). For instance, one has:

$$P\langle x, x + 4, x + 7 \rangle = I_{2x+7} \langle x, x + 4, x + 7 \rangle = J(x, +)$$

Using the properties (see Eq. (2) below), we have

$$T_x J T_x^{-1} = T_x I_7 T_{-x} = T_x I_{7+x} = I_{2x+7} = J(x, +) = J(x, -)$$

Other relationships are shown in the same way.

These conjugation relations allow us to choose a reference point (here $x = 0$), but it can be adapted for musical purpose. The Cayley-graph of the action of the neo-Riemannian group on the consonant triads with respect to the generators P, L, and R is known under the nickname "chickenwire torus". Analogously, the Cayley graph of the JQZ transformations is represented on Fig. 1. The torus is visualized by gluing the right border with the left side, and the top side with the bottom, according to the chords.

3   The JQZ and PLR Groups

The JQZ-transformations are involutions $J^2 = Q^2 = Z^2 = Id$. They generate the JQZ-group of order 24, with presentation:

$$\langle J, Q, Z \rangle = \langle J, Q, Z \mid J^2 = Q^2 = Z^2 = (JQ)^3 = (JZQ)^2 = (JZ)^4 = 1 \rangle$$

The toroidal representation was made by several authors including Richard Cohn in [3–5]. Derek Waller was one of the first authors to introduce the torus in musical representations [17]. The donut that is made by gluing the edges of the tonnetz was called the *chicken-wire torus* by Douthett and Steinbach [6]. Whether we start from the PLR network or from the JQZ network, we find the same topological figure (see Fig. 2).

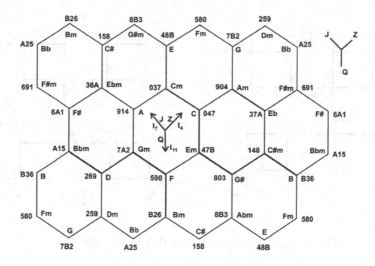

Fig. 1. Tonnetz of the JQZ-transformations

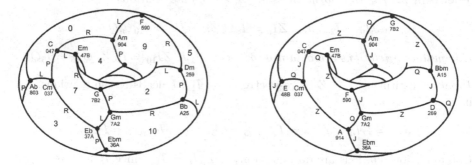

Fig. 2. Chicken-Wire Torus (left PLR, right JQZ)

In the *Cube Dance*, another figure introduced by Douthett and Steinbach in [6], each vertex represents a consonant triad or an augmented triad, and each solid edge is labeled by either P or L. A slightly differing figure can be obtained with the transformations J and Q: Observe, that four cubes dance in two pairs here (see Fig. 3).

Although there is an isomorphism between *PLR* and *JQZ* groups, this isomorphism is not obvious. In the T/I group, the transpositions commute $T_n T_m = T_m T_n = T_{m+n}$ but the inversions do not commmute. They satisfy the relations:

$$I_n I_m = T_{n-m} \quad T_n I_m = I_{n+m} \quad I_m T_n = I_{m-n} \quad (2)$$

PLR -Transformations commute with transpositions ($PT_n = T_n P$, $LT_n = T_n L$, $RT_n = T_n R$), while J, Q and Z anticommute ($JT_n = T_{-n}J$, $QT_n = T_{-n}Q$, $ZT_n = T_{-n}Z$).

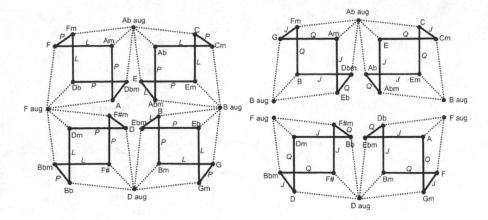

Fig. 3. Douthett's Cube Dance (left PLR, right JQZ)

Theorem 2. *The transformations J, Q, Z satisfy the relations*

$$JI_n = I_{2-n}J, \quad ZI_n = I_{8-n}Z, \quad QI_n = I_{10-n}Q$$

Commutation relations are obtained for $JI_1 = I_1J$, $ZI_{10} = I_{10}Z$, $QI_5 = I_5Q$.

Proof. Substituting J, Q, Z by respectively I_7, I_{11}, I_4 leads to the relations. For instance,

$$JI_n = I_7I_n = T_{7-n} = T_{2-n+5} = T_{2-n-7} = I_{2-n}I_7 = I_{2-n}J$$

Commutation relations are obtained only if $I_mI_n = T_6$. Since $I_mI_n = T_{m-n}$, n must be equal to $n = m + 6 \bmod 12$. Then for $m = 7$, $n = 1$, for $m = 10$, $n = 4$ and for $m = 4$, $n = 10$.

Theorem 3. *The transformations P, L, R on the set of consonant triads Σ satisfy the relations:*

$$T_{x-y}PL = T_{y-x}LP, \quad T_{z-y}PR = T_{y-z}RP, \quad T_{z-x}LR = T_{x-z}RL$$

Proof. We have $PL\langle x, y, z\rangle = P\langle y + z - x, z, y\rangle = \langle y, 2y - x, y + z - x\rangle$. On the other hand, the computation: $T_{2y-2x}LP\langle x, y, z\rangle = T_{2y-2x}L\langle z, x + z - y, x\rangle = T_{2y-2x}\langle 2x - y, x, x + z - y\rangle = \langle y, 2y - x, y + z - x\rangle = PL\langle x, y, z\rangle$ leads to the formula. The proof of the two other relations is similar.

In the following table, we give a dictionary between the two groups. already remarked, the JQZ transformations do not depend on element The transpositions T_n can be expressed as a combination of JQZ transformations. The correspondence of an element of the JQZ-group with an element in the PLR-group is given by their concordant behavior on a chosen triad. If this element $\langle x, y, z\rangle$ is a minor chord, the correspondance is given by $J \leftrightarrow P$, $Q \leftrightarrow L$, $Z \leftrightarrow R$.

But if the element is a minor chord, we have to inverse the element given by the minor chord. For instance, for the transposition T_3 up to a minor chord $T_3 = I_7 I_4 = JZ$, the corresponding element in PLR is PR for a minor chord and $(PR)^{-1} = RP$ for a major chord. The verification is straightforward:

$$PR \langle x, x+8, x+5 \rangle = P \langle x+8, x, x+3 \rangle = \langle x+3, x+11, x+8 \rangle$$
$$= T_3 \langle x, x+8, x+5 \rangle$$

For the inversions, the dependence is not only related to the major or minor chord but also to the root of the chord. For instance, we get

$$PRL \langle x, x+4, x+7 \rangle = PR \langle x+11, x+7, x+4 \rangle = P \langle x+7, x+11, x+2 \rangle$$
$$= \langle x+2, x+10, x+7 \rangle = I_{2x+2} \langle x, x+4, x+7 \rangle$$

In the following table, the index n in $2x+n$ must be computed first in order to use the PLR column. For instance, the passage from Ab (803) to Fm (085) is I_8. The chord Ab is a major chord rooted at $x-8$. It follows that $2x+n-8$ implies $n=4$. In the column *Major,* at line I_{2x+4} the corresponding PLR transformation is R. Thus the passage from Ab to Fm is the R transform. Moreover, since inversions are involution, the passage from Fm (085) to Ab (803) is also I_8. The chord root of the minor chord Fm is $x=0$ since the minor chord are of the form $\langle x, x+8, x+5 \rangle$. It follows from $2x+n=8$ and $x=0$ that $n=-4$. In the column *Minor* at line I_{2x-4}, the corresponding PLR transformation is R. Thus the passage from Fm to Ab is the R transform.

T/I	JQZ	$Major$	$Minor$	T/I	JQZ	$Major$	$Minor$	PLR
T_0	1	1	1	I_0	JQZ	I_{2x}	I_{2x}	PLR
T_1	$QJZJ$	$(LPRP)^{-1}$	$LPRP$	I_1	ZJZ	I_{2x+1}	I_{2x-1}	RPR
T_{11}	$(QJZJ)^{-1}$	$(PRPL)^{-1}$	$PRPL$	I_2	JZQ	I_{2x+2}	I_{2x-2}	PRL
T_2	$(QZ)^2$	$(LR)^{-2}$	$(LR)^2$	I_3	JQJ	I_{2x+3}	I_{2x-3}	PLP
T_{10}	$(QZ)^{-2}$	$(LR)^2$	$(LR)^{-2}$	I_4	Z	I_{2x+4}	I_{2x-4}	R
T_3	JZ	$(PR)^{-1}$	PR	I_5	$ZQZQJ$	I_{2x+5}	I_{2x-5}	$RLRLP$
T_9	$(JZ)^{-1}$	PR	$(PR)^{-1}$	I_6	QZQ	I_{2x+6}	I_{2x-6}	LRL
T_4	QJ	$(LP)^{-1}$	LP	I_7	J	I_{2x+7}	I_{2x-7}	P
T_8	$(QJ)^{-1}$	LP	$(LP)^{-1}$	I_8	QJZ	I_{2x+8}	I_{2x-8}	LPR
T_5	ZQ	$(RL)^{-1}$	RL	I_9	ZQZ	I_{2x+9}	I_{2x-9}	RLR
T_7	$(ZQ)^{-1}$	RL	$(RL)^{-1}$	I_{10}	JZJ	I_{2x+10}	I_{2x-10}	PRP
T_6	$(ZJ)^2$	$(RP)^{-2}$	$(RP)^2$	I_{11}	Q	I_{2x+11}	I_{2x-11}	L

A dictionnary between T/I, JQZ and PLR elements

With the presentation of the *PLR*-group and the *JQZ*-group, finding an isomorphism between the two groups which has a musical meaning is not obvious. However, there exists some isomorphisms between the *PLR* group and the *JQZ* group through the permutations of the symmetric group S_{24}. The calculation was done with the GAP software. It shows that if the PLR group is built with the generators:

$$P = (0,19)(1,15)(2,14)(3,11)(4,0)(5,18)(6,7)(8,22)(9,23)(12,21)(13,20)(16,17)$$
$$R = (0,16)(1,20)(2,21)(3,23)(4,22)(5,17)(6,19)(7,18)(8,13)(9,12)(10,15)(11,14)$$
$$L = (0,4)(1,2)(3,5)(6,8)(7,9)(10,12)(11,13)(14,16)(15,17)(18,20)(19,21)(22,23)$$

and the group JQZ is built with the generators:

$$J = (0,7)(1,6)(2,5)(3,4)(8,11)(9,10)$$
$$Q = (0,11)(1,10)(2,9)(3,8)(4,7)(5,6)$$
$$Z = (0,4)(1,3)(5,11)(6,10)(7,9)$$

then the group isomorphism is defined by $P \to J$, $L \to Q$ and $R \to Z$.

From the musical point of view, the JQZ and PLR paths in the tonnetz are very similar. The examples studied by Alissa S. Crans, Thomas M. Fiore, and Ramon Satyendra in [2] are reinterpreted here by JQZ relations. For instance, in the "Grail" theme of the *Prelude of Parsifal* (1882), the chord progression written under the compact form:

$$\underset{803}{A\flat} \to \underset{580}{Fm} \to \underset{158}{D\flat} \to \underset{A15}{B\flat m} \to \underset{803}{A\flat}$$

is interpreted in two ways. The PLR interpretation shows the importance of relative chords while the JQZ interpretation highlights the action of the octatonic subgroup, namely the inversion ZJZ between chords. The vertical arrows are not the same in the PLR transformations (one is R, and the other RLR) while they are perfectly symmetrical ($ZJZ = J^Z$) in the case of the group JQZ, representing the inversion I_1. Taking the chord $A\flat$ as a reference will lead to simpler relationships.

PLR Interpretation: JQZ Interpretation:

$$
\begin{array}{ccc}
A\flat & \xrightarrow{\ R\ } & Fm \\
\Big\downarrow{\scriptstyle RLR} & & \Big\downarrow{\scriptstyle L} \\
B\flat m & \xrightarrow[R]{} & D\flat
\end{array}
\qquad
\begin{array}{ccc}
A\flat & \xrightarrow{\ QJZ\ } & Fm \\
\Big\downarrow{\scriptstyle ZJZ} & & \Big\downarrow{\scriptstyle ZJZ} \\
B\flat m & \xrightarrow[QZQ]{} & D\flat
\end{array}
$$

In the *Lento occulto* of Feruccio Busoni's *Sonatina seconda*, the similarity between PLR and JQZ group is clear in the chord progression,

$$
\begin{array}{ccccccccc}
E\flat & \xrightarrow[RPRL]{ZJZQ} & C\sharp & \xrightarrow[PRPL]{ZJQJ} & D & \xrightarrow[PRPL]{ZJQJ} & E\flat & \xrightarrow[PRPL]{ZJQJ} & E \\
\Big\uparrow & & & & & & & & \Big\downarrow{\scriptstyle RL\,|\,QZ} \\
E\flat & \xleftarrow[PLPR]{JQJZ} & E & \xleftarrow[PL]{QJ} & C & \xleftarrow[RL]{QZ} & F & \xrightarrow[PRPR]{JZJZ} & B
\end{array}
$$

as well as in Debussy's *Danseuses de Delphes* (*Preludes* vol. 1):

$$B\flat \xrightarrow[L]{J} Dm \xrightarrow[RL]{ZQ} Gm \xrightarrow[PRL]{JQZ} C \xrightarrow[RLR]{ZQZ} Dm \xrightarrow[L]{J} B\flat \xrightarrow[RLRL]{ZQZQ} C \xrightarrow[LR]{ZQ} F$$

4   Dual and Subdual Groups

In this section, we study two particularly interesting subgroups: the hexatonic group and the octatonic group. The hexatonic group is the group generated by transformations J and Q. It has the presentation

$$\langle J, Q \rangle = \langle J, Q \mid J^2 = Q^2 = 1, \ JQJ = QJQ \rangle$$

The group has six elements: $\langle J, Q \rangle = \{T_0, I_7, T_4, I_3, T_8, I_{11}\} = \{1, J, QJ, JQJ, JQ, Q\}$. Each element of the group is compute using the relations $J = I_7$ and $Q = I_{11}$. For instance,

$$JQ(x) = J(-x + 11) = -(-x + 11) + 7 = x - 4 = x + 8 \ \text{mod} \ 12 = T_8(x)$$

The group acts on the major and minor chords, but likewise it acts on any other set class. The 3-chord $\{0, 6, 11\}$ has the 6-element orbit

$$\{\{0, 6, 11\}, \{1, 7, 8\}, \{3, 4, 10\}, \{3, 4, 9\}, \{2, 7, 8\}, \{0, 5, 11\}\}$$

within the set class 3–5 (Forte's nomenclature).

The octatonic group is generated by the transformations J and Z. It has the presentation: $\langle J, Z \rangle = \langle J, Z \mid J^2 = Z^2 = 1, \ (ZJ)^2 = (JZ)^2 \rangle$. The group has eight elements: $\langle J, Z \rangle = \{T_0, I_7, T_9, I_{10}, T_6, I_1, T_3, I_4\} = \{1, J, ZJ, JZJ, (ZJ)^2, ZJZ, JZ, Z\}$. For instance, we compute

$$JZ(x) = J(-x + 4) = -(-x + 4) + 7 = x + 3 \ \text{mod} \ 12 = T_3(x).$$

Since the groups T/I, PLR and JQZ are isomorphic, they have the same center. This centre is the group of ordre 2 consisting of $\{1, T_6\}$. The group Q of *quasi uniform triadic transformations* of order 1152 (GAP 1152#32554) introduced by Hook [11] is a refinement of the group U of *uniform triadic transformations* of order 288 (GAP 288#239). The group U is isomorphic to the wreath product of the cyclic group C_{12} of order 12 by the cyclic group C_2 of order 2. The group Q is the wreath product of the T/I group by the symmetric group of 2 elements S_2.

$$U = C_{12} \wr C_2 \quad Q = T/I \wr S_2 \simeq D_{12} \wr S_2$$

The notion of dual groups in the sense of Lewin has been introduced in [8].

Definition 1. *Two subgroups G_1, G_2 of a group $\mathfrak{S}$ are dual (in the sense of Lewin) if both act simply and transitively and are each others centralizers.*

$$C_{\mathfrak{S}}(G_1) = G_2 \quad and \quad C_{\mathfrak{S}}(G_2) = G_1$$

For instance, the centralizer of the T/I group in Q is the JQZ-group (or PLR-group) and the centralizer of the JQZ-group (or PLR-group) in Q is the T/I group. The computation is straightforward with the GAP software.

$$C_Q(T/I) = \langle J, Q, Z \rangle \quad and \quad C_Q(\langle J, Q, Z \rangle) = T/I$$

The same is true in the symmetric group $Sym(\Sigma) \simeq S_{24}$ of permutations of 24 elements [2] instead of Q: the JQZ-group and the T/I-group are subgroups of $Sym(\Sigma)$. The subduality of the hexatonic group and the octatonic group has been studied by Thomas Fiore and Thomas Noll in the same reference [8]. They define the concept of subduality in the following sense.

Definition 2. *Let G_1, G_2 be dual subgroups of the symmetric group S_{24} of the 24 triads and let H_1, H_2 be two subgroups of G_1, G_2 respectively. H_1 and H_2 are subdual groups if both act simply and transitively on a subset $X \subset S_{24}$ and are each others centralizers within the symmetric group S_X of this subset.*

$$C_{S_X}(H_1) = H_2 \quad and \quad C_{S_X}(H_2) = H_1$$

The hexatonic JQ-group $\langle J, Q \rangle$ has 4 orbits, namely two pairs of tritone-related sets of six triads each.

$\{C,\ Cm,\ E,\ Em,\ Ab,\ Abm\}$ and $\{D,\ Dm,\ F\sharp,\ F\sharp m,\ Bb,\ Bb\ m\}$ as well as $\{Db,\ Ebm,\ F,\ Gm,\ A,\ Bm\}$ and $\{Dbm,\ Eb,\ Fm,\ G,\ Am,\ B\}$. The orbits in the first pair are triads in proper hexatonic collections, i.e. they are also orbits of the hexatonic PL-group $\langle P, L \rangle$. The orbits in the second pair form orbits under a conjugate of $\langle P, L \rangle$, namely: $R \langle P, L \rangle R$. This leads to the following result.

Theorem 4. *With respect to the first two orbits the group $\langle J, Q \rangle$ is subdual to $\langle P, L \rangle$. With respect to the second two orbits $\langle J, Q \rangle$ is subdual to $R \langle P, L \rangle R$.*

The octatonic JZ-group $\langle J, Z \rangle$ has 3 orbits of 8 triads each. The first one $\{F\sharp m,\ F\sharp,\ Ebm,\ A,\ Cm,\ C,\ Am,\ Eb\}$ is also orbit of the octatonic PR-group. The two others $\{Bm,\ C\sharp,\ G\sharp m,\ E,\ Fm,\ G,\ Dm,\ Bb\}$ and $\{Bbm,\ D,\ Gm,\ F,\ Em,\ G\sharp,\ C\sharp m,\ B\}$ are orbits under conjuguation $(RL) \langle P, R \rangle (RL)^{-1}$. This lead to the following result.

Theorem 5. *With respect to the first orbit the group $\langle J, Z \rangle$ is subdual to $\langle P, R \rangle$. With respect to the second two orbits $\langle J, Z \rangle$ is subdual to $(RL) \langle P, R \rangle (RL)^{-1}$.*

5   The Atonal Triad

The study of the interplay of the PLR group and the JQZ group is helpful in atonal analysis. We will illustrate this for the atonal triad $\langle 0, 1, 6 \rangle$.

The main advantage of JQZ transformations is to be able to consider all types of chords and not only consonant chords. For instance, if the JQZ group acts on the atonal triad 016 $\{c, c\sharp, f\sharp\}$, the action leads to a new lattice. In the other hand, if we replace the set Σ of consonant triads by the set Γ of atonal triads rooted on x of the form $\langle x, x + 1, x + 6 \rangle$ and $\langle x, x - 1, x - 6 \rangle$ we get new relations

$$P \langle x, x + 1, x + 6 \rangle = \langle x + 6, x + 5, x \rangle, \ P \langle x, x + 11, x + 6 \rangle = \langle x + 6, x + 7, x \rangle$$
$$R \langle x, x + 1, x + 6 \rangle = \langle x + 1, x, x + 7 \rangle, \ R \langle x, x + 1, x + 6 \rangle = \langle x + 11, x, x + 5 \rangle$$
$$L \langle x, x + 1, x + 6 \rangle = \langle x + 7, x + 6, x + 1 \rangle, \ L \langle x, x + 11, x + 6 \rangle = \langle x + 5, x + 6, x + 11 \rangle$$

This allows us to interpret Georges Crumb's *Gargoyles*, a piano piece, extract from *Makrokosmos*, in both ways:

$$238 \xrightarrow[(PL)^3]{SZ} 56B \xrightarrow[PR]{QZ} 016 \xrightarrow[(PL)^4]{SZ} 349 \xrightarrow[LPRP]{QS} 781 \xrightarrow[RL]{(SZ)^2} 127$$

$$107 \xrightarrow[(LP)^3]{SZ} 43A \xrightarrow[RP]{QZ} BA5 \xrightarrow[(LP)^3]{SZ} 218 \xrightarrow[(LP)^4]{QS} 650 \xrightarrow[LR]{(ZS)^2} 0B6$$

The right hand evolves in the same way as the left hand: the atonal triads are linked by the transformations (JZ, QJ). The same transformations are used in both hands, except in the last triads. But if we consider a crossing of the hands: 781 goes to 0B6 by the transformation J, just as 650 goes to 127 by the same transformation.

Another interpretation is possible. As we saw for the PLR group, we can consider two kinds of atonal triads, one of structure $(1, 5)$ and the other of structure $(5, 1)$. From the relations of PLR seen above, we can introduce the transformations for atonal triads $\{x, x+1, x+6\}$,

$$J(x, +) = I_{2x+6}, \quad Q(x, +) = I_{2x+7}, \quad Z(x, +) = I_{2x+1}$$

and for the atonal triads $\{x, x+5, x+6\}$,

$$J(x, -) = I_{2x+6}, \quad Q(x, -) = I_{2x-7}, \quad Z(x, -) = I_{2x-1}$$

For $x = 0$, we have three new transformations $J = I_6, Q = I_7, Z = I_1$. The tritone (6) has replace the fifth (7) in the definition of J. Applying these transformations to Olivier Messiaen's *Regard de l'Onction terrible* (extract of *Vingt Regards de l'Enfant Jesus* #18), leads to the following chords progression, which evolves against the same chord A94, on the left hand. We use the following notation for the conjuguaison: $Z^J = JZJ$.

$$
\begin{array}{ccccccccccccc}
650 & \xrightarrow[PL]{JQ} & 54B & \xrightarrow[PL]{JQ} & 43A & \xrightarrow[PL]{JQ} & 329 & \xrightarrow[PL]{JQ} & 218 & \xrightarrow[PL]{JQ} & 107 & \longrightarrow & 107 \\
{\scriptstyle RPL}\downarrow{\scriptstyle Z^JQ} & {\scriptstyle JZ}\downarrow{\scriptstyle RP} & {\scriptstyle ZQ}\downarrow{\scriptstyle RL} & & {\scriptstyle ZJ}\downarrow{\scriptstyle RP^L} & {\scriptstyle (LP)^4}\downarrow{\scriptstyle ZQ^J} & {\scriptstyle (LP)^3}\downarrow{\scriptstyle Z^JJ^Q} & {\scriptstyle JQ}\downarrow{\scriptstyle (RP)^2} & & & & & \\
A94 & \longrightarrow & A94 & \longrightarrow & A94 & \longrightarrow & A94 & \longrightarrow & A94 & \longrightarrow & A94 & \xrightarrow[LP]{JQ} & 0B6
\end{array}
$$

This demonstrates the interest and power of these non-contextual transformations for the analysis of all kind of music, but especially for atonal music.

Acknowledgements. We thank anonymous reviewers for valuable remarks and Thomas Noll for comments that greatly improved the manuscript.

References

1. Berry, C.: Thomas fiore hexatonic systems and dual groups in mathematical music theory. Involve J. Math. **11**(2), 253–270 (2018)
2. Crans, A.S., Fiore, T.M., Satyendra, R.: Musical actions of dihedral groups. Am. Math. Mon. **116**(6), 479–495 (2009)
3. Cohn, R.: Neo-riemannian operations, parsimonious trichords, and their tonnetz representation. J. Music Theor. **41**(1), 1–66 (1997)
4. Cohn, R.: Introduction to neo-riemannian theory: a surveyand a historical perspective. J. Music Theory **42**(2), 167–180 (1998)
5. Cohn, R.: Audacious Euphony. Chromaticism and the Triad's Second Nature. Oxford University Press, New York (2012)
6. Douthett, J., Steinbach, P.: Parsimonious graphs: a study in parsimony, contextual transformation, and modes of limited transposition. J. Music Theor. **42**(2), 241–263 (1998)
7. Fiore, T., Satyendra, R.: Generalized contextual groups. Music Theory Online **11**(3) (2005)
8. Fiore, T.M., Noll, T.: Commuting groups and the topos of triads. In: Agon, C., Andreatta, M., Assayag, G., Amiot, E., Bresson, J., Mandereau, J. (eds.) MCM 2011. LNCS (LNAI), vol. 6726, pp. 69–83. Springer, Heidelberg (2011). https://doi.org/10.1007/978-3-642-21590-2_6
9. Fiore, T., Noll, T., Satyendra, R.: Morphisms of generalized interval systems and PR-Groups. J. Math. Music **3**, 3–27 (2013)
10. Fiore, T., Noll, T.: Voicing transformations and a linear representation of uniform triadic transformations. Siam J. Appl. Algebra Geom. **2**(2), 281–313 (2018)
11. Hook, J.: Uniform triadic transformations. J. Music Theory **46**(1/2), 57–126 (2002)
12. Hyer, B.: Tonal Intuitions in Tristan Und Isolde. PhD diss., Yale University (1989)
13. Hyer, B.: Reimag(in)ing riemann. J. Music Theory **39**(1), 101–138 (1995)
14. Jedrzejewski, F.: Permutation groups and chord tesselations. In: ICMC Proceedings, Barcelona (2005)
15. Lewin, D.: Generalized Musical Intervals and Transformations. Yale University Press, New Haven and London (1987)
16. Riemann, H.: Handbuch der Harmonielehre. Breitkopf & Härte, Leipzig (1887)
17. Waller, D.A.: Some combinatorial aspects of the musical chords. Math. Gaz. **62**, 12–15 (1978)

The Hierarchy of Rameau Groups

Franck Jedrzejewski[✉]

Atomic Energy Commission, Université Paris Lumières (CEA-CIPh), Paris, France
franckjed@gmail.com

Abstract. This paper contributes to the transformational study of progressions of seventh chords and generalizations thereof. PLR transformations are contextual transformations that originally apply only to consonant triads. These transformations were introduced by David Lewin and were inspired the works of musicologist Hugo Riemann. As an alternative to other attempts to define transformations on seventh chords, we define new groups in this article, called *Rameau groups*, which transform all types of seventh or ninth chords or more generally, any chords formed of stacks of major or minor thirds. These groups form a hierarchy for inclusion. We study on musical examples the ability of these operators to show symmetries in the progression of seventh chords.

Keywords: Neo-Riemannian group · PLR-group ·
Rameau-Schillinger operators · Rameau groups ·
Generalized interval systems · Lewin · Parsimonious voice leading

In addition to triads, seventh chords are most prominent in the harmonic vocabulary of tonal music. Initially, Neo-Riemannian theory was concerned only with the set of consonant triads. Later some authors have introduced new transformations to consider seventh chords and have developed new generalizations of the well known PLR transformations. Introduced by the musicologist Riemann [16], and reconsidered by Lewin [15], these transformations have been studied under many aspects. The goal of this paper is to propose a set of transformations based on third chains. We introduce new groups acting on seventh chords, ninth chords, or more generally on any chain of major and minor thirds. Considering stacks of thirds as Jean-Philippe Rameau did in 1722 to define chords, and taking into account that these stacks of thirds are defined in $\mathbb{Z}_{12}$, we introduce the *Rameau-Schillinger operators*, and study the hierarchy of groups that they generate.

1 The Seventh Chords

As we have just noticed, several authors proposed to extend the PLR transformations to the case of seventh chords. At the end of the 20th century, Gollin [9] and Childs [4] studied some relations between seventh chords in three-dimensional expansions of the tonnetz. They incorporated the dominant sevenths and the

M. Montiel et al. (Eds.): MCM 2019, LNAI 11502, pp. 161–171, 2019.
https://doi.org/10.1007/978-3-030-21392-3_13

half-diminished seventh chords into the scope of Neo-Riemannian theory. Childs considered examples from Chopin and Wagner. More recently, the case of seventh chords was also studied by Arnett and Barth [1], Kerkez [12] as well as by Sonia Cannas [2,3]. In 2012, Kerkez [12] proposed to extend PLR transformations to major and minor seventh chords. He defines two maps from the set H of major and minor seventh chords to itself,

$$P(x, y, z, t) = (z, y, x, 2\sigma(t) + t)$$
$$S(x, y, z, t) = (x - 2\sigma(t), t, z, y)$$

where $\sigma(t) = -1$ if t is a major seventh, and $\sigma(t) = +1$ if t is a minor seventh. The chords are supposed to be oriented and all computations are done modulo 12. Kerkek showed that the group generated by P and S is isomorphic to the dihedral group D_{12} of order 24.

Cannas found a group of operations between seventh chords capable to describe parsimonious voice leading, moving a single note by a semi-tone or a whole tone. She considered the PLRQ-group generated by 17 operators [2,3] acting on 5 types of seventh chords. She showed that the PLRQ group is isomorphic to the semi-product of the symmetric group of permutation S_5 by $\mathbb{Z}_{12}^4$. In addition, she proposed a new scheme for the *power towers graph*, introduced by Douthett and Steinbach in [8]. Moreover, she generalized her theory to 9 types of seventh chords and defined a new group $PLRQ^*$ generated by 37 operators. This group $PLRQ^*$ is isomorphic to $S_9 \ltimes \mathbb{Z}_{12}^8$. But these two groups, the $PLRQ$ and the $PLRQ^*$ groups, are very large.

In the following, we consider 7 types of seventh chords. These chords are stacks of major (4) or minor thirds (3). The chords are marked by their intervallic structure. For instance, 433 denotes dominant seventh chords.

Table 1. List of the seven types of seventh chords

Dominant seventh	433	C7	047A
Half-diminished seventh	334	$Cm^{7\flat5}$	036A
Major seventh	434	CM^7 or $C\Delta$	047B
Minor seventh	343	Cm^7	037A
Diminished seventh	333	$Cdim^7$	0369
Minor major seventh	344	Cm^{M7}	037B
Augmented major seventh	443	$Cmaj^{7\sharp5}$	048B

Transpositions T_n retain the intervallic structure of seventh chords. But the inversions I_n act differently depending on the type of seventh chords. Under the action of I_n, a dominant seventh chord (433) is transformed into a half-diminished seventh chord (334). A minor major seventh chord (344) is transformed into an augmented major seventh chord (443). The three other types of seventh chords retain their intervallic structure under the action of inversion. The set of diminished seventh chords forms a limited transposition set. There exist only 3 diminished seventh chords: 036A, 147A and 258B. They are their own inverses.

2 The Rameau-Schillinger Operators

Jean-Philippe Rameau was the first author to define chords as stacks of major or minor thirds. In the *Traité de l'harmonie* [13, p. 33], one reads:

> Pour te rendre les choses plus familières, l'on peut regarder à present les tierces comme l'unique objet de tous les accords. En effet, pour former l'accord parfait, il faut ajouter une tierce à l'autre, et pour former tous les accords dissonants, il faut ajouter trois ou quatre tierces les unes aux autres; la différence de ces accords disssonants ne provenant que de la différente situation de ces tierces; c'est pourquoi nous devons leur attribuer toute la force de l'harmonie, en la réduisant à ses premiers degrés; l'on peut en faire la preuve dans une quatri ème proportionnelle ajoutée à chaque accord parfait, d'où na îtront deux accords de septième; et dans une cinquième proportionnelle ajoutée à l'un de ces deux accords de septième d'où naîtra un accord de neuvième, qui renfermera dans sa construction les quatre accords précedents.

And in the *Nouveau système de musique théorique* [14], he takes again the definition of a chord:

> On appelle *Accord* l'union de trois ou quatre sons différents. L'ordre que ces trois ou quatre sons doivent tenir entre eux se borne dans son origine à une division par tierces; c'est-à-dire qu'ils doivent être arrangés à la distance d'une tierce les uns des autres.

In the long and ramified history of ideas about the study of chord progressions since Rameau there is one source which deserves to be explicitly acknowledged in the context of this article. In book *Book V: Special Theory of Harmony* of his posthumously published teaching material [17] Joseph Schillinger disentangles the combinatorics of third-chains from the combinatorics of fundament progressions and studies both structures on the one hand in a diatonic context and on the other hand in the *symmetric system*, i.e. within $\mathbb{Z}_{12}$. For example, the content of Table 1 can be found in [17, p. 447].

In the sequel we will interpret relations between the seven types of seventh chords in terms of transformations, which shall be called *split transpositions* or *Rameau-Schillinger operators* [11].

- R_1 exchange the first letter of the structure: $4 \to 3$ and $3 \to 4$, (R_1 is an involution $R_1^2 = 1$): $\widehat{3}34 \to \widehat{4}34$, $\widehat{4}33 \to \widehat{3}33$.
- R_2 exchange the second letter of the structure: $4 \to 3$ and $3 \to 4$, (R_2 is an involution $R_2^2 = 1$): $3\widehat{3}3 \to 3\widehat{4}3$.

- R_3 exchange the third letter of the structure: $4 \to 3$ and $3 \to 4$, (R_3 is an involution $R_3^2 = 1$): $34\widehat{3} \to 34\widehat{4}$.

The three Rameau-Schillinger operators verify the relations:

$$R_1^2 = R_2^2 = R_3^2 = 1$$
$$(R_1 R_2)^2 = (R_2 R_3)^2 = (R_1 R_3)^2 = 1$$

In the following, we will use to simplify the notations $R_{ij} = R_i R_j$, $R_{ijk} = R_i R_j R_k$, etc. Let us observe for the following that the only Rameau-Schillinger operator that is an inversion is the operator R_{13}. The group generated by R_1, R_2 and R_3 is commonly called the *elementary abelian group* of order 8. This group has the following presentation which uses precisely the relations found above.

$$E_8 = \langle R_1, R_2, R_3 \mid R_1^2 = R_2^2 = R_3^2 = (R_1 R_2)^2 = (R_2 R_3)^2 = (R_1 R_3)^2 = 1 \rangle$$

It acts on the set of the seven types of seventh chords through the transformation of their intervallic structures. Adding chord fundaments and the semitone transposition $T = T_1$, the group generated by R_1, R_2, R_3, T acts on the set of all seventh chords. The relationships of seventh chord types through Rameau-Schillinger operators are shown on Fig. 1. This figure shows how the action of Rameau-Schillinger operators on the seventh chord types is exemplified by those chords which are rooted on the pitch class 0.

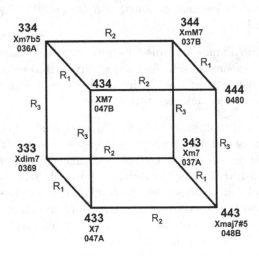

Fig. 1. Action of the Rameau-Schillinger operators on the seventh chords

As the augmented triad with 3 major thirds appears as a limit point (see Fig. 1), we need to add this chord and its transpositions to the seventh chord set. We therefore consider the set $\mathfrak{U}$ containing all 7 types of seventh chords as well as the four augmented triads. The set $\mathfrak{U}$ represents 8 types of intervallic structures and has 79 elements (since there are only 3 diminished seventh chords and 4 augmented triads). Elements X of $\mathfrak{U}$ are of the form $X = \{x, x + a, x + a + b, x + a + b + c\}$ with $a, b, c \in \{3, 4\}$. But in order to apply the operators $\{R_j\}_{j=1,2,3}$ consistently, we consider also the set $\widetilde{\mathfrak{U}}$ of *rooted third chains*

$$\widetilde{\mathfrak{U}} = \{3, 4\}^3 \times \mathbb{Z}_{12}$$

of 96 elements. This set represents seventh chords as third-chains $(a, b, c) \in \{3, 4\}^3$ which are rooted in some pitch class $x \in \mathbb{Z}_{12}$. We recover the set $\mathfrak{U}$ by the projection:

$$\pi : \widetilde{\mathfrak{U}} \longrightarrow \mathfrak{U}, \ \pi((a, b, c), x) = \{x, x + a, x + a + b, x + a + b + c\}$$

Consider now a simple example. In the seventh chords progression described as follows:

$$E\flat M^7 \xrightarrow{T_2 R_{123}} Fm^7 \xrightarrow{T_2} Gm^7 \xrightarrow{T_1 R_{123}} A\flat M^7 \xrightarrow{T_{11} R_{123}} Gm^7 \xrightarrow{T_{10}} Fm^7 \xrightarrow{T_{10} R_{123}} E\flat M^7$$

the axis of symmetry of the palindromic progression passing through the chord $A\flat M^7$ shares an ascending move from $E\flat M^7$ to $A\flat M^7$ and a descending move from $A\flat M^7$ to $E\flat M^7$. The moves from major seventh chord to minor seventh chord or from minor seventh chord to major seventh chord are represented by the operator R_{123} which among the Rameau-Schillinger operators is the only operator used in this excerpt (apart from the identity operator).

3   The Seventh Chords Groups

This section is divided in two parts. In Subsect. 3.1 we look at the transformations from the proceeding section more abstractly in group-theoretic terms and illustrate them in two musical examples. In Subsect. 3.2 we inspect another transformation group, which can alternatively be used to analyze progressions of seventh-chords.

3.1   The Seventh Chords Group $E_8 \times C_{12}$

Rameau-Schillinger operators act on the set $\widetilde{\mathfrak{U}}$. To see how the group acts, it is enough to transpose the Fig. 1 on each note of the 12 tone scale.

The seventh chord group $E_8 \times C_{12}$ is the direct product of the elementary abelian group E_8 by the cyclic group $C_{12} = \langle T \mid T^{12} = 1 \rangle$. The group has the following presentation:

$$
\begin{aligned}
RC_3 &= E_8 \times C_{12} \\
&= \left\langle \begin{array}{c} R_1, R_2, R_3, T \mid R_1^2 = R_2^2 = R_3^2 = T^{12} = (R_1 R_2)^2 = (R_2 R_3)^2 = (R_1 R_3)^2 \\ = T^{-1} R_1 T R_1 = T^{-1} R_2 T R_2 = T^{-1} R_3 T R_3 \end{array} \right\rangle
\end{aligned}
$$

Theorem 1. *The seventh chords group $E_8 \times C_{12}$ is an abelian group of order 96, isomorphic to $C_2 \times C_2 \times C_2 \times C_{12}$. The group acts simply and transitively on $\widetilde{\mathfrak{U}}$.*

Proof. As the product of two abelian groups, the group $E_8 \times C_{12}$ is abelian. The group has order

$$|RC_3| = |E_8| \times |C_{12}| = 8 \times 12 = 96$$

The group E_8 is isomorphic to $C_2 \times C_2 \times C_2$ implies that the group RC_3 is isomorphic to $C_2^3 \times C_{12}$.

The action of RC_3 on the set $\widetilde{\mathfrak{U}}$ can be understood as the repetition of Fig. 1 transposed 12 times and placed on a circle. But it can also be understood as a rectangle that is transposed 12 times, as a vast inflation by transpositions. After 12 transpositions, we recover the rectangle (in grey on Fig. 2) from which we left.

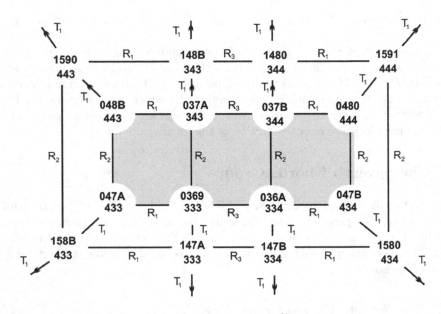

Fig. 2. Action of the group RC_3 on the set $\widetilde{\mathfrak{U}}$. (Color figure online)

In *Waltz for Debby* of Bill Evans, the music starts on a major seventh chord (434) and the transpositions are at the minor third down (T_9) or a fourth up (T_5). The analysis distinguishes the changes of chord types from simple transpositions or inversions. Up to transpositions, we stay in the grey rectangle of Fig. 2. Only one sequence from $Gm7\flat5$ to $C7$ (T_5R_{13}) is an inversion (I_5).

$$F^\Delta/A \xrightarrow{T_9R_{123}} Dm^7 \xrightarrow{T_5} Gm^7 \xrightarrow{T_9R_{12}} E^7/G\sharp \xrightarrow{T_5R_3} A^7/G \xrightarrow{T_5R_3} D^7/F\sharp$$

$$D^7/F\sharp \xrightarrow{T_5} C7/E \xrightarrow{T_5} F7/E\flat \xrightarrow{T_5} B\flat^\Delta/D \xrightarrow{T_9R_1} Gm^7\flat5 \xrightarrow{T_5R_{13}} C^7$$

$$C^7 \xrightarrow{T_9R_{12}} Am^7 \xrightarrow{T_5R_{123}} D7 \xrightarrow{T_5R_{123}} Gm^7 \xrightarrow{T_5R_{12}} C^7 \xrightarrow{T_5R_3} F^\Delta/A$$

In *Giant Steps* of John Coltrane, the dance of moves T_3R_3 or T_5R_3 leads each time to the moves T_6R_{123} followed by T_5R_{12}, except at the end where the transposition at the tritone is replaced by the transposition a tone lower $T_{10}R_{123}/T_5R_{12}$. This creates a kind of stability that is well highlighted by Rameau-Schillinger operator analysis

$$B\Delta \xrightarrow{T_3R_3} D7 \xrightarrow{T_5R_3} G\Delta \xrightarrow{T_3R_3} B\flat7 \xrightarrow{T_5R_3} E\flat\Delta \xrightarrow{T_6R_{123}} Am7 \xrightarrow{T_5R_{12}} D7$$

$$D7 \xrightarrow{T_5R_3} G\Delta \xrightarrow{T_3R_3} B\flat7 \xrightarrow{T_5R_3} E\flat\Delta \xrightarrow{T_3R_3} F\sharp7 \xrightarrow{T_5R_3} B\Delta \xrightarrow{T_6R_{123}} Fm7 \xrightarrow{T_5R_{12}} B\flat7$$

$$B\flat7 \xrightarrow{T_5R_3} E\flat\Delta \xrightarrow{T_6R_{123}} Am7 \xrightarrow{T_5R_{12}} D7 \xrightarrow{T_5R_3} G\Delta \xrightarrow{T_6R_{123}} C\sharp m7 \xrightarrow{T_5R_{12}} F\sharp7$$

$$F\sharp7 \xrightarrow{T_5R_3} B\Delta \xrightarrow{T_6R_3 123} Fm \xrightarrow{T_5R_{12}} B\flat7 \xrightarrow{T_5R_3} E\flat\Delta \xrightarrow{T_{10}R_{123}} C\sharp7 \xrightarrow{T_5R_{12}} F\sharp7$$

3.2   The Seventh Chords Group $E_4 \times D_{12}$

The elementary abelian group E_4 has order 4 and presentation:

$$E_4 = \left\langle R_1, R_2 \mid R_1^2 = R_2^2 = (R_1R_2)^2 = 1 \right\rangle$$

The seventh chords group $RD_3 = E_4 \times D_{12}$ is defined as the product of the elementary abelian group E_4 by the dihedral group D_{12}.

$$RD_3 = E_4 \times D_{12} = \left\langle \begin{array}{l} R_1, R_2, T, I \mid R_1^2 = R_2^2 = I^2 = T^{12} = (TI)^2 \\ = (R_1R_2)^2 = R_1TR_1T^{-1} = R_2TR_2T^{-1} \\ = (R_1I)^2 = (R_2I)^2 = 1 \end{array} \right\rangle$$

Theorem 2. *The seventh chords group $E_4 \times D_{12}$ is a non abelian group of order 96, isomorphic to $C_2 \times C_2 \times D_{12}$. The group does not act transitively on $\mathfrak{U}$.*

168　　F. Jedrzejewski

Proof. Since $I_n I_m \neq I_m I_n$, the group is not abelian. Its order is computed through the order of the product of two well-known groups: $|RD_3| = |E_4| \times |D_{12}| = 4 \times 24 = 96$. As the group has fixed points, it does not act transitively on $\widetilde{\mathfrak{U}}$.

The action of the group on the set $\mathfrak{U}$ leads to $6 \times 12 + 3 = 75$ seventh chords, and includes the transpositions of the 3-note chords 048 (444). Since by action of the dihedral group (which is isomorphic to the T/I group), dominant seventh chords (433) are transformed into half-diminished seventh chords (334) and minor major seventh chords (344) are transformed into augmented major seventh chords (443). The action on the basis rectangle of the 8 types of the set $\mathfrak{U}$ is shown on Fig. 3.

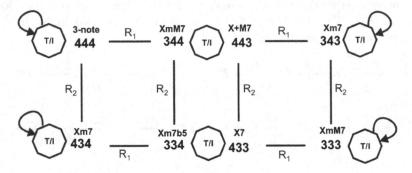

Fig. 3. Action of the group RD_3 on the set $\widetilde{\mathfrak{U}}$.

The following example shows how the chords evolve in Fig. 3. Starting from the upper right corner (343), the chord Gm^7 goes (R_{12}) to the major seventh E^7 (443), passes through the inversion I_1 and reaches the chord Bm7♭5 of structure 334. Then the chord moves up by R_2 to the chord Em^{M7} (344) crosses the T/I structure by the transposition I_0 in $A^\triangle$ and finaly returns to the upper right corner by R_1.

$$Gm^7 \xrightarrow{T_9 R_{12}} E^7 \xrightarrow{I_1} Bm7♭5 \xrightarrow{T_5 R_2} EmM7 \xrightarrow{I_0} A^\triangle \xrightarrow{T_3 R_1} Cm^7$$

4　The Ninth Chords Groups

The generalization of the previous results to the ninth chords is obvious. The presentation of the ninth chords group follows the same rules.

4.1 The Ninth Chords Group $E_{16} \times C_{12}$

The elementary abelian group E_{16} has order 16 and presentation

$$E_{16} = \left\langle \begin{array}{l} R_1, R_2, R_3, R_4 \mid R_1^2 = R_2^2 = R_3^2 = R_4^2 = (R_1 R_2)^2 = (R_2 R_3)^2 \\ = (R_1 R_3)^2 = (R_1 R_4)^2 = (R_2 R_4)^2 = (R_3 R_4)^2 = 1 \end{array} \right\rangle$$

The ninth chords group $RC_4 = E_{16} \times C_{12}$ is the product of the elementary abelian group E_{16} by the cyclic group C_{12}. RC_4 has order $16 \times 12 = 192$ and the following presentation:

$$RC_4 = E_{16} \times C_{12}$$
$$= \left\langle \begin{array}{l} R_1, R_2, R_3, R_4, T \mid R_1^2 = R_2^2 = R_3^2 = R_4^2 = T^{12} = (R_1 R_2)^2 = (R_2 R_3)^2 \\ = (R_1 R_3)^2 = (R_1 R_4)^2 = (R_2 R_4)^2 = (R_3 R_4)^2 = 1 \\ = T^{-1} R_1 T R_1 = T^{-1} R_2 T R_2 = T^{-1} R_3 T R_3 = T^{-1} R_4 T R_4, \end{array} \right\rangle$$

4.2 The Ninth Chords Group $E_8 \times D_{12}$

The elementary abelian group E_8 has order 8 and presentation:

$$E_8 = \left\langle R_1, R_2, R_3 \mid R_1^2 = R_2^2 = R_3^2 = (R_1 R_2)^2 = (R_2 R_3)^2 = (R_1 R_3)^2 = (R_1 R_3)^2 = 1 \right\rangle$$

The dihedral group D_{12} of order 12 has presentation:

$$D_{12} = \left\langle T, I \mid T^{12} = I^2 = (TI)^2 = 1 \right\rangle$$

The ninth chords group $RD_4 = E_8 \times D_{12}$ is the product of the elementary abelian group E_8 by the dihedral group. RD_4 has order $8 \times 24 = 192$ and the following presentation:

$$RD_4 = E_8 \times D_{12} = \left\langle \begin{array}{l} R_1, R_2, R_3, T, I \mid R_1^2 = R_2^2 = R_3^2 = I^2 = T^{12} = (TI)^2 \\ = (R_1 R_2)^2 = R_1 T R_1 T^{-1} = R_2 T R_2 T^{-1} = R_3 T R_3 T^{-1} \\ = (R_1 I)^2 = (R_2 I)^2 = (R_3 I)^2 = 1 \end{array} \right\rangle$$

5 The Hierarchy of the Rameau Groups

Seventh chords groups and ninth chords groups can be presented more broadly by introducing the notion of *Rameau groups* or *third chain transformations*. As we have seen in particular cases, there are two ways to define Rameau Groups: as a product by the cyclic group or as a product of the dihedral group. In both case, we introduce the elementary abelian group E_{2^n} of order 2^n. The group has presentation:

$$E_{2^n} = \left\langle R_1, ..., R_n \mid (R_i R_j)^2 = 1, \ i, j = 1, .., n \right\rangle$$

(1) The Rameau group RC_n is the product of the elementary abelian group E_{2^n} of order 2^n by the cyclic group C_{12}.

$$RC_n = E_{2^n} \times C_{12} = \langle R_1, ..., R_n, T \mid (R_i R_j)^2 = T^{12} = T^{-1} R_i T R_i = 1, \ i, j = 1, .., n \rangle$$

It acts on the set of n-note chords built with major or minor thirds: (words built with n letters on the alphabet $\{3, 4\}$, this could be interesting for an application of these groups to rhythmic structures). RC_n has order $|RC_n| = 2^n \times 12$. The groups are included in each other:

$$RC_1 \subset RC_2 \subset RC_3 \subset RC_4 \subset \cdots$$

(2) The Rameau group RD_n is the product of the elementary abelian group $E_{2^{n-1}}$ of order 2^{n-1} with the dihedral group D_{12}.

$$RD_n = E_{2^{n-1}} \times D_{12} = \left\langle \begin{array}{l} R_1, ..., R_{n-1}, T, I \mid (R_i R_j)^2 = I^2 = T^{12} \\ = R_i T R_i T^{-1} = (R_i I)^2 = (TI)^2, \ i, j = 1, .., n - 1 \end{array} \right\rangle$$

The group has order $|RD_n| = 2^{n-1} \times 24 = 2^n \times 12 = |RC_n|$. The groups are included in each other:

$$RD_1 \subset RD_2 \subset RD_3 \subset RD_4 \subset \cdots$$

Acknowledgements. We thank anonymous reviewers for valuable remarks and Thomas Noll for comments that greatly improved the manuscript.

References

1. Arnett, J., Barth, E.: Generalizations of the Tonnetz: tonality revisited. In: Proceedings of the 2011 Midstates Conference on Undergraduate Research in Computer Music and Mathematics (2011)
2. Cannas, S., Antonini, S., Pernazza, L.: On the group of transformations of classical types of seventh chords. In: Agustín-Aquino, O.A., Lluis-Puebla, E., Montiel, M. (eds.) MCM 2017. LNCS (LNAI), vol. 10527, pp. 13–25. Springer, Cham (2017). https://doi.org/10.1007/978-3-319-71827-9_2
3. Cannas, S.: Geometric representation and algebraic formalization of musical structures. Ph.D. Dissertation, University of Strasbourg and Università degli Studi di Pavia e di Milano-Biocca (2018)
4. Childs, A.: Moving beyond Neo-Riemannian triads: exploring a transformational model for seventh chords. J. Music Theory **42**(2), 191–193 (1998)
5. Cohn, R.: Neo-Riemannian operations, parsimonious trichords, and their Tonnetz representation. J. Music Theory **41**, 1–66 (1997)
6. Cohn, R.: Introduction to neo-riemannian theory: a survey and a historical perspective. J. Music Theory **42**(2), 167–180 (1998)
7. Cohn, R.: Audacious Euphony. Chromaticism and the Triad's Second Nature. Oxford University Press, Oxford (2012)
8. Douthett, J., Steinbach, P.: Parsimonious graphs: a study in parsimony, contextual transformation, and modes of limited transposition. J. Music Theory **42**(2), 241–263 (1998)

9. Gollin, E.: Some aspects of three-dimensional Tonnetze. J. Music Theory **42**(2), 195–206 (1998)

10. Fiore, T., Satyendra, R.: Generalized contextual groups. Music Theory. Online **11**(3), 1–27 (2005)

11. Jedrzejewski, F.: Hétérotopies musicales. Modèles mathématiques de la musique, Paris, Hermann (2019)

12. Kerkez, B.: Extension of Neo-Riemannian PLR-group to Seventh Chords. In: Bridges, Mathematics, Music, Art, Architecture, Culture, pp. 485–488 (2012)

13. Rameau, J.-P.: Traité de l'harmonie réduite à ses principes naturels, Paris (1722)

14. Rameau, J.-P.: Nouveau système de musique théorique, Paris (1726)

15. Lewin, D.: Generalized Musical Intervals and Transformations. Yale University Press, New Haven (1987)

16. Riemann, H.: Handbuch der Harmonielehre. Breitkopf, Leipzig (1887)

17. Schillinger, J.: The Schillinger System on Musical Compostion. C. Fischer, New York (1946)

Distant Neighbors and Interscalar Contiguities

Daniel Harasim[1]([✉]), Thomas Noll[2], and Martin Rohrmeier[1]

[1] Digital and Cognitive Musicology Lab, École Polytechnique Fédérale de Lausanne,
Lausanne, Switzerland
{daniel.harasim,martin.rohrmeier}@epfl.ch
[2] Departament de Teoria, Composició i Direcció,
Escola Superior de Música de Catalunya, Barcelona, Spain
thomas.mamuth@gmail.com

Abstract. This paper studies the "integration" problem of nineteenth-century harmony—the question whether the novel chromatic chord transitions in this time are a radical break from or a natural extension of the conventional diatonic system. We examine the connections between the local behavior of voice leading among diatonic triads and their generalizations on one hand, and the global properties of voice-leading spaces on the other. In particular, we aim to identify those neo-Riemannian chord connections which can be integrated into the diatonic system and those which cannot. Starting from Jack Douthett's approach of filtered point symmetries, we generalize diatonic triads as second-order Clough-Myerson scales and compare the resulting Douthett graph to the respective Betweenness graph. This paper generally strengthens the integrationist position, for example by presenting a construction of the hexatonic and octatonic cycles that uses the principle of minimal voice leading in the diatonic system. At the same time it provides a method to detect chromatic wormholes, i.e. parsimonious connections between diatonic chords, which are not contiguous in the system of second order Clough-Myerson scales.

Keywords: Diatonic theory · Hexatonic cycles ·
Neo-Riemannian transformations · Maximally even scales ·
Voice-leading parsimony

1 Introduction

Music exhibits complex structures across its various dimensions such as harmony, voice-leading, and rhythm. The structural relations are subject to cultural evolution observable in the historic development of music. A famous transition in

This project has received funding from the European Research Council (ERC) under the European Union's Horizon 2020 research and innovation programme under grant agreement No. 760081 PMSB. We thank Claude Latour for supporting this research through the Latour Chair in Digital Musicology.

The original version of this chapter was revised: the chapter was changed to open access retrospectively under a CC BY 4.0 license. The correction to this chapter is available at https://doi.org/10.1007/978-3-030-21392-3_37

harmony took place in the Western classical music of the 19th century when composers started to use triads and seventh-chords in novel chromatic connections that exceed the previous diatonic usage [6,10,16]. An ongoing debate concerns the nature of this transition, called the "integration" problem [18]: Was the novel usage of the chords a radical break from or a natural extension of conventional tonal harmony? This paper aims at supporting the latter position by reconstructing the advanced harmonic structures of late 19th century music—also found in Jazz—in a generalized diatonic framework. We draw from definitions and results of neo-Riemannian theory, mathematical scale theory, voice-leading spaces, and Fourier analysis and reveal connections between these approaches.

As a means of precise formalization, mathematical music theory comprises descriptions and propositions of musical objects and their relations. The strands of this discipline originated and evolved independently, concentrating on the characterization of particular musical phenomena. Many proposals have for example been made to explain the musical relevance of the triad from various different angles. These include its status as a building block of a three-triad-system in Hauptmann's concept of the major and minor keys [12], its voice-leading parsimony in connection to other triads [5,8], its status as a second-order maximally even set [4], its transformational stability properties as a pitch class set [13], and its position as a neighbor of the singularity on the orbifold of 3-chords [17]. The logical dependencies between these characterizations triggered an exciting process of integration between previously separated lines of research and constitute ongoing debates to date. The existence of structural connections between the different approaches would moreover have an interesting interpretation concerning the development of tonality in Western music of the 19th century: It would suggest that Romantic composers gradually widened the diatonic usage of triads and seventh-chords to explore a complex space of extended tonality. The contrary position argues for several independent utilizations of the triad as the basic building block of tonality. For instance, Richard Cohn interprets the "over-determined triad" [5,6] as the seed for the destruction of the tonal system from within and emphasizes triads as inhabitants of the chromatic system, released from their diatonic affiliations. The voice-leading connections within a hexatonic cycle, Cohn's paradigmatic example for the disengagement of the triad from diatonic control, exemplifies two distinct types of diatonically motivated chord connections. In the hexatonic cycle

$$ C \xmapsto{P} Cm \xmapsto{L} A\flat \xmapsto{P} A\flat m \xmapsto{L} E \xmapsto{P} Em \xmapsto{L} C, $$

the neo-Riemannian operations P and L are alternately applied to the respective triads in 12-tone equal temperament. The *leading-tone exchange* L is a parsimonious diatonic connection (e.g. $C \mapsto Em$). The *parallel* transformation P can be interpreted as the consequence of an alteration of the underlying scale ($\flat$ or $\sharp$, e.g. $Em \mapsto E$).

The present article examines the connections between the local voice-leading behavior of diatonic triads and their generalizations on one hand, and the global properties of voice-leading graphs on the other. We thereby identify those

neo-Riemannian chord connections which can be integrated into our generalization of the diatonic system and those which cannot. John Clough, Jack Douthett
and their co-authors made significant contributions to both local and global
aspects, which we take as our points of departure. Main results with respect to
characterizing properties of diatonic sets were achieved in their joint paper on
Maximally Even Sets [4]. Pathbreaking for the understanding of voice-leading
graphs was the joint paper of Douthett with Peter Steinbach on *parsimonious
graphs* [8] using neo-Riemannian approaches. Programmatic steps towards a systematic combination of both aspects can be found in Douthett's approach of
filtered point symmetry and dynamical voice leading [7].

2   Triads as Second-Order Clough-Myerson Scales

The goal of this section is to generalize diatonic triads and their PLR transformations in order to investigate the generalized triadic connections in the consequent
sections.

Definition 1 (Clough-Myerson Scale). *A* (first-order) *Clough-Myerson
scale is a maximally even scale of which its chromatic and diatonic cardinalities are co-prime.*

Notably, all Clough-Myerson scales are non-degenerate well-formed [2,3].[1]
Each such scale is thus uniquely determined (up to chromatic transposition) by
its cardinality d and the cardinality c of its ambient chromatic scale $(d < c)$.
Within the chromatic scale $\mathbb{Z}_c$, we have $d \cdot c$ different modes of the c scale
transpositions. Each mode is given by one instance of Clough and Douthett's
J-function $J_{c,d}^m : \mathbb{Z}_d \to \mathbb{Z}_c$, where the mode index m varies from 0 to $d \cdot c - 1$.
Note that in this terminology, modes have more structure than scales, as they are
scales with a distinguished root tone just like C Ionian, F Lydian, and E Phrygian
are modes of the diatonic scale $\{C, D, E, F, G, A, B\}$. The specific pitch class of
scale degree k of the mode with index m is given by

$$J_{c,d}^m(k) := \left\lfloor \frac{ck + m}{d} \right\rfloor \mod c.$$

Clough-Myerson scales are well-formedly generated by the specific interval $\bar{d}$,
which is the multiplicative inverse of the scale cardinality d modulo the chromatic
cardinality c, $\bar{d}d = 1 \mod c$. The following proposition shows how each Clough-
Myerson mode can be expressed in generation order.

Proposition 1. *Each mode first-order Clough-Myerson mode $J_{c,d}^m$ can be
expressed in generation order by virtue of the map $G_{c,d}^m : \mathbb{Z}_d \to \mathbb{Z}_c$ where*

$$G_{c,d}^m(k) := \bar{d}(m - k) \mod c.$$

---

[1] Clough and Meyerson [3] show that Clough-Myerson scales have Myhill's property,
i.e. every non-zero generic interval appears in two species. Carey and Clampitt [2]
show that Myhill's property is equivalent to non-degenerate well-formedness.

Proof. For each mode index m, the well-formedness property can be expressed by a commutative triangle as follows.

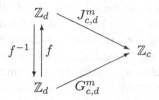

The affine automorphism $f : \mathbb{Z}_d \to \mathbb{Z}_d$ and its inverse f^{-1} are given by $f(k) = g(m - k) \bmod d$ and $f^{-1}(k) = m - wk \bmod d$. The linear factor $g \in \mathbb{Z}_d$ in the automorphism f is the residue class mod d of the step span ($=$ generic size) of the generator and can be calculated as $\left\lfloor \dfrac{d\bar{d}}{c} \right\rfloor$. The inverse linear factor $w = g^{-1} \in \mathbb{Z}_d$ (in the inverse automorphism f^{-1}) is the winding number of the scale, i.e. the number of covered octave ambits in the scale generation. Obviously, the formulae represent mutually inverse morphisms: $f^{-1}(f((k)) = m - wg(m - k) = m - m + k = k$. We check the commutativity of the diagram by verifying that $J^m_{c,d} \circ f = G^m_{c,d}$ for $m \in \{0, ..., d \cdot c - 1\}$ and $k \in \{0, ..., d - 1\}$. This follows from the following equalities in $\mathbb{N}$:

$$\left\lfloor \frac{c \left\lfloor \frac{d\bar{d}}{c} \right\rfloor (m - k) + m}{d} \right\rfloor = \left\lfloor \frac{(d\bar{d} - 1)(m - k) + m}{d} \right\rfloor = \left\lfloor \bar{d}(m - k) + \frac{k}{d} \right\rfloor = \bar{d}(m - k).$$

Definition 2. *Consider three natural numbers $0 < e < d < c$ such that the greatest common divisors $(e, d) = (d, c) = 1$. A second-order Clough-Myerson mode $J^{m,n}_{c,d,e} := J^m_{c,d} \circ J^n_{d,e} : \mathbb{Z}_e \to \mathbb{Z}_c$ is defined as the concatenation of the two Clough-Myerson modes $J^n_{d,e} : \mathbb{Z}_e \to \mathbb{Z}_d$ and $J^m_{c,d} : \mathbb{Z}_d \to \mathbb{Z}_c$.*

3   Diatonic Contiguity and Its Violation

Observation. Whenever there is a most parsimonious connection between two diatonic triads (one voice moves by one semitone), they either belong to a common diatonic collection (leading tone exchange) or they belong to a pair of neighboring diatonic collections along the circle of fifths (parallel transformation, e.g. C in F major to Cm in B♭ major). This shall be called the property of *diatonic contiguity.*

The observation is relevant, because its general formulation would strengthen the integrationist position of Yust [18] as described in Sect. 1. In the controversy on the autonomy or the diatonic dependency of triads, it is therefore interesting to know whether this property holds for a broader family of second-order Clough-Meyerson scales. The contiguity notably does not hold for all configurations of second-order Clough-Myerson scales. The following is a counter-example.

We consider a generic seven-note scale $\mathbb{Z}_7$ in the role of the generalized chromatic space and use the note names C, D, E, F, G, A, and B. Therein, we have the parsimonious cycle of the fourth-generated pentatonic scales and within each scale we have the complete parsimonious cycle of all five chords with four tones. In other words, we consider the second-order Clough-Myerson scales for $c = 7$, $d = 5$, and $e = 4$. In each of the seven 4-chord cycles, there is exactly one diatonic-seventh chord being maximally even in $\mathbb{Z}_7$. These diatonic seventh chords violate the—in this case—"pentatonic" contiguity. They have most parsimonious voice leading (one voice moves by one diatonic step), but the pentatonic distance (generalized key distance) between them is 3, as shown in the array below using the Manhatten (or taxicab) distance. Consider for instance the seventh-chords $F^{\text{maj}7}$ and Dm^7. They have a generalized chromatic distance of 1 implying that they are most parsimonious, but the pentatonic scales in which they occur ($\{C, E, F, A, B\}$ and $\{C, D, F, G, A\}$) are not neighboring scales.

$$\{C, D, F, G, A\} : \{C, D, F, G\}, \underline{\{C, D, F, A\}}, \{C, D, G, A\}, \{C, F, G, A\}, \{D, F, G, A\}$$
$$\{C, D, E, G, A\} : \{C, D, E, G\}, \{C, D, E, A\}, \{C, D, G, A\}, \underline{\{C, E, G, A\}}, \{D, E, G, A\}$$
$$\{D, E, G, A, B\} : \underline{\{D, E, G, B\}}, \{D, E, A, B\}, \{D, G, A, B\}, \{E, G, A, B\}, \{E, G, A, B\}$$
$$\{D, E, F, A, B\} : \{D, E, F, B\}, \{D, E, A, B\}, \underline{\{D, F, A, B\}}, \{E, F, A, B\}, \{D, E, F, A\}$$
$$\{C, E, F, A, B\} : \{C, E, F, B\}, \{C, E, A, B\}, \{C, F, A, B\}, \{E, F, A, B\}, \underline{\{C, E, F, A\}}$$
$$\{C, E, F, G, B\} : \{C, E, F, B\}, \underline{\{C, E, G, B\}}, \{C, F, G, B\}, \{E, F, G, B\}, \{C, E, F, G\}$$
$$\{C, D, F, G, B\} : \{C, D, F, B\}, \{C, D, G, B\}, \{C, F, G, B\}, \underline{\{D, F, G, B\}}, \{C, D, F, G\}.$$

The construction used to derive the counter-example can be generalized to arbitrary second-order Clough-Myerson configurations using the concept of Douthett graphs, similar to coordinate spaces [14,15] or configuration spaces [19].

Definition 3 (Douthett Graph). *For given cardinalities* $0 < e < d < c$, *the Douthett graph* $\mathcal{D}_{c,d,e}$ *has second-order Clough-Myerson scales as nodes, and edges between any two* intrascalar neighbors $J_{c,d}^m(J_{d,e}^{n+1}(\mathbb{Z}_e))$ *and* $J_{c,d}^m(J_{d,e}^n(\mathbb{Z}_e))$, *as well as between any neighbors under chromatic alteration. This is whenever* $J_{c,d}^{m+1}(J_{d,e}^n(\mathbb{Z}_e)) \neq J_{c,d}^m(J_{d,e}^n(\mathbb{Z}_e))$.

Intrascalar neighbors generalize chords that are related by the neo-Riemannian transformations L and R while neighbors under chromatic alteration generalize chords that are related by the transformation P.[2]

4   Distant Neighbors and Interscalar Contiguities

This section compares Douthett graphs with their corresponding betweenness graphs using the concepts of distant (intrascalar) neighbors and interscalar

---

[2] Here we have to dispense with a transformational treatment of chord progressions. The Douthett graph for the diatonic triads contains the chicken-wire graph (being the Cayley-graph of the action of the Schritt-Wechsel group on the 24 major and minor triads with respect to the generators P, L and R). The diminished triads and the corresponding voice leading connections are not included.

contiguities as defined below. Figure 1 (top) shows the Douthett graph $\mathcal{D}_{12,7,3}$ of the major, minor, and diminished triads in 12-tone equal temperament. Edges are colored black if they are also edges of the corresponding betweenness graph (see below) or colored orange otherwise. The chords of the diatonic scales go from left to right. For example, the triads of the C major scale Em, C, Am, F, Dm, Bdim, and G form an intrascalar (in this case diatonic) voice-leading cycle of the graph. The chords C and Cm, represented by $\{0, 4, 7\}$ and $\{0, 3, 7\}$, are an example of neighbors under chromatic alteration. The following concept of voice-leading distance (also known as taxicab metric [17] or voice-leading work [6]) is used to consequently define betweenness graphs.

Definition 4 (Voice-Leading Distance). *For each* $c \in \mathbb{N}$, *the generalized chromatic scale* $\mathbb{N}_c = \{0, 1, \ldots, c-1\}$ *(here used as a set of integers) forms a metric space together with the* Lee *distance*

$$d(x, y) = \min(|x - y|, c - |y - x|),$$

where $x, y \in \mathbb{N}_c$. *The* (minimal) *voice-leading distance between to chords (or scales)* $X, Y \subseteq \mathbb{N}_c$ *is then defined as the summed movement of a minimal bijection,*

$$D(X, Y) = \min_{f: X \overset{\cong}{\to} Y} \sum_{x \in X} d(x, f(x)).$$

A minimal bijection is also called minimal voice leading *from* X *to* Y.

Note that the voice-leading distance is a metric on any set of equally sized chords. There is in particular always a minimal voice leading which fixes all notes in the intersection of the chords. For proofs and examples see [11].

Definition 5 (Betweenness Graph). *A chord* $Y \subseteq \mathbb{Z}_c$ *is in between* two *chords* $X, Z \subseteq \mathbb{Z}_c$ *if* $D(X, Z) = D(X, Y) + D(Y, Z)$. *The betweenness graph of a set of equally sized chords* $\mathcal{X} \subseteq 2^{\mathbb{N}_c}$ *(where* $2^{\mathbb{N}_c}$ *denotes the powerset of* $\mathbb{N}_c$) *has an edge between two chords* X *and* Z *iff there is no other chord in between them. For given cardinalities* $0 < e < d < c$, *the betweenness graph of second-order Clough-Myerson scales is denoted by* $\mathcal{B}_{c,d,e}$.

Figure 1 (bottom) shows the betweenness graph $\mathcal{B}_{12,7,3}$ that corresponds to the Douthett graph $\mathcal{D}_{12,7,3}$ shown in Fig. 1 (top). In Fig. 1 (bottom), edges are colored black if they are also edges of $\mathcal{D}_{12,7,3}$ or colored orange otherwise. Since the chord pairs Dm and Bdim as well as Bdim and G are not connected directly, but through the out-of-scale chords B♭ respectively Bm, the triads of the C major scale form a different cycle in the betweenness graph than the intrascalar voice-leading cycle in the Douthett graph $\mathcal{D}_{12,7,3}$.

Douthett graphs focus on the local aspect of voice-leading transformations. From the definition, the path distance of two given chords cannot be obtained directly, but for any given chord, its neighbors can be accessed directly. In contrast, betweenness graphs focus on the global aspect of minimal voice-leading.

The voice-leading distance of two given chords can be calculated using the definition, but it is not straightforward to decide if two chords are adjacent in the betweenness graph. In general, Douthett graphs and betweenness graphs have overlapping edges, but neither of them is a subgraph of the other. To compare them, we name edges that are in the Douthett graph $\mathcal{D}_{c,d,e}$, but not in the betweenness graph $\mathcal{B}_{c,d,e}$ and vice versa.

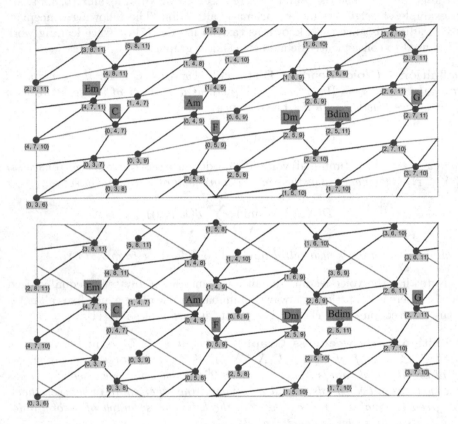

Fig. 1. Douthett and Betweenness graphs for $c = 12, d = 7$ and $e = 3$. (Color figure online)

Definition 6 (Distant Neighbors). *Edges of a Douthett graph $\mathcal{D}_{c,d,e}$ which are not edges of the corresponding betweenness graph $\mathcal{B}_{c,d,e}$ are called* distant (intrascalar) *neighbors.*

The orange edges in Fig. 1 (top) show the distant neighbors of the second-order Clough-Myerson scales with cardinalities $c = 12, d = 7$ and $e = 3$. Consider for example the chords Dm and Bdim. They are both chords in the C major scale, but not adjacent in the betweenness graph $\mathcal{B}_{12,7,3}$ shown in Fig. 1 (bottom), because the chord B♭ (represented by $\{2, 5, 10\}$) is located between them with respect to the voice-leading distance.

Definition 7 (Interscalar Contiguities). *Edges of the betweenness graph* $\mathcal{B}_{c,d,e}$, *which are not edges of the Douthett graph* $\mathcal{D}_{c,d,e}$ *are called* interscalar contiguities.

The orange edges in Fig. 1 (bottom) show the interscalar contiguities of the second-order Clough-Myerson scales with cardinalities $c = 12, d = 7$ and $e = 3$. Consider for example the chords Cm and G, represented by $\{0, 3, 7\}$ and $\{2, 7, 11\}$, respectively. Since there is no triad Y such that $D(Cm, G) = D(Cm, Y) + D(Y, G)$, Cm and G are adjacent in the betweenness graph $\mathcal{B}_{12,7,3}$, but they are neither intrascalar neighbors nor neighbors under chromatic alteration.

5   Path Characterization of Hexatonic and Octatonic Cycles in Betweenness Graphs

As described in the introduction, hexatonic cycles are commonly defined using the neo-Riemannian transformations L and P in the Douthett graph $\mathcal{D}_{12,7,3}$ of diatonic triads. In the corresponding betweenness graph $\mathcal{B}_{12,7,3}$, hexatonic cycles can be characterized as cycles of toggling voice leadings with voice-leading distance 1 (zigzag voice leadings with alternating voice-movement direction). In the cycle of C, Cm, Ab, Abm, E, and Em for example, the tone E is moving *down* to Eb, G is moving *up* to Ab, C is moving *down* to Cb, etc. The characterization in terms of toggling voice leadings is, in particular, independent of the inner structure of the chords. It is an outer characterization that can be applied to any space of equally sized chords. For example in the case of 12-7-4 second-order Clough-Myerson scales (diatonic seventh-chords), the cycles of toggling voice leadings with voice-leading distance 1 are exactly the octatonic cycles such as C^7 Am^7 A^7 $F\sharp m^7$ $F\sharp^7$ Ebm^7 Eb^7 Cm^7 C^7. In general, however, toggling voice-leading cycles with voice-leading distance 1 do not always exists in second-order Clough-Myerson spaces. The betweenness graph $\mathcal{B}_{17,8,3}$ does for instance not contain any.

The observed characterization of hexatonic and octatonic cycles moreover allows for their construction using solely the principle of minimal voice leading and the set of diatonic triads and seventh-chords, respectively. If taken as a definition of a *generalized hexatonic cycle*, this characterization allows for the investigation of sufficient and necessary conditions for Clough-Myerson configurations c-d-e to have a generalized hexatonic.

6   Chromatic Saturation

Distant intrascalar neighbors occur when a scale-external chord sneaks in between neighbor chords of a scale. These intermediate chromatic passing chords can easily be detected in terms of their voice-leading behavior. They are reached and left with motions in one and the same voice. It is therefore a consistent further step in the modelling of voice-leading connections to include these passing chords, which we do not require to be second-order Clough-Myerson scales.

Recalling the fact that second-order Clough-Myerson scales are in particular *second order maximally even*, we find that such single-voice-motion passing chords turn out to be at least as even as the less even one among the two connected chords. To make this explicit we subscribe to Emmanuel Amiot's proposal to measure the evenness of chords or scales $X \subset \mathbb{Z}_c$ in terms of the magnitude of the 1st Fourier coefficient of its representation on the unit circle [1].

For every chromatic pitch class space $\mathbb{Z}_c$, consider the embedding $\iota : \mathbb{Z}_c \to \mathbb{T} \subset \mathbb{C}$ via c-th roots of unity into the unit circle $\mathbb{T}$ within the complex numbers $\mathbb{C}$, $\iota(k) := \exp(2\pi i k/c)$ for any integral representative $k \in \mathbb{Z}$ of the residue classes in $\mathbb{Z}_c$. For every e-tone mode $\sigma : \mathbb{Z}_e \to \mathbb{Z}_c$, we have the concatenation $\iota \circ \sigma : \mathbb{Z}_e \to \mathbb{C}$. Recall that for any map $\phi : \mathbb{Z}_e \to \mathbb{C}$ we may consider its finite Fourier transform $\widehat{\phi} : \mathbb{Z}_e \to \mathbb{C}$ by virtue of the formula

$$\widehat{\phi}(t) = \frac{1}{e} \sum_{k=0}^{e-1} \phi(k) \exp\left(-\frac{2\pi i k t}{e}\right).$$

Definition 8. *For a given sequence $X : \mathbb{Z}_e \to \mathbb{T}$ of points $X_k = \exp(2\pi i t_k), t_k \in [0,1)$ on the unit circle we define its* evenness *in terms of the absolute value* $\mathrm{evenness}(X) = |\widehat{X}(1)|$. *For an e-tone mode $\sigma : \mathbb{Z}_e \to \mathbb{Z}_c$, we define its evenness as the evenness of the concatenation: $\iota \circ \sigma : \mathbb{Z}_e \to \mathbb{C}$.*

Our finding on the passing chords is in fact of more general nature and can be best understood with a continuous moving voice.

Definition 9. *For a given sequence $X = (\exp(2\pi i t_1), \ldots, \exp(2\pi i t_{e-1})) \in \mathbb{T}^{e-1}$ of $e-1$ points on the unit circle, consider the continuous family $X_- : [0,1) \to \mathbb{T}^e$ with $X_t := (\exp(2\pi i t), \exp(2\pi i t_1), \ldots, \exp(2\pi i t_{e-1}))$, together with the Single-Zero-Padding of X, namely the vector*

$$X^0 := (0, \exp(2\pi i t_1), \ldots, \exp(2\pi i t_{e-1})) \in \mathbb{C}^e.$$

The family X_t is called a chord with a sliding voice *and the vector X^0 shall be called the "muted slider."*

Proposition 2. *Consider a chord with a sliding voice $X_t : [0,1) \to \mathbb{T}^e$ and the associated "muted slider" X^0. Then the associated one-parameter family $\{\widehat{X_t}(1) \in \mathbb{C} \mid t \in [0,1)\}$ of the first Fourier-Coefficients of the vectors X_t forms a circle of radius $1/e$ around the first Fourier-Coefficient $\widehat{X^0}(1)$ of X^0. The most even and uneven chords X_v and X_u correspond to the parameters $v = \arg(\widehat{X^0}(1))/2\pi$ and $u = v + \frac{1}{2} \bmod 1$, respectively.*

Proof. For $t \in [0,1)$ one finds:

$$\widehat{X_t}(1) = \frac{1}{e}\left(\exp(2\pi i t) + \sum_{k=1}^{e-1} \exp(2\pi i(t_k - k/e))\right) = \frac{\exp(2\pi i t)}{e} + \widehat{X^0}(1). \qquad (1)$$

Let $l = |\widehat{X^0}(1)|$ and $\psi = \arg(\widehat{X^0}(1))$ denote the magnitude and the phase of the first Fourier-coefficient of X^0, respectively. Then we obtain the first Fourier-Coefficient of the most even chord X_v by adding the radius $1/e$ to the magnitude l, while keeping the same phase ψ, $\widehat{X_v}(1) = (l+1/e)\exp(i\psi)$. Likewise, we obtain $\widehat{X_u}(1) = (l-1/e)\exp(i\psi)$, for the most uneven chord. In order to see that the parameter of X_v is actually $v = \psi/2\pi$ we insert this value for t in Eq. (1).

$$\widehat{X_{\psi/2\pi}}(1) = \frac{\exp(\frac{2\pi i\psi}{2\pi})}{e} + \widehat{X^0}(1) = \frac{\exp(i\psi)}{e} + l\exp(i\psi) = (l+\frac{1}{e})\exp(i\psi) = \widehat{X_v}.$$

$$(1)$$

Moving the sliding voice from $\exp(2\pi i\psi)$ about half the unit circle to the opposite point $\exp(2\pi i(\psi + 1/2))$ corresponds to a half circle movement of the Fourier-coefficient $(l + 1/e)\exp(i\psi)$ in the small circle around $\widehat{X^0}(1)$ to the opposite point $(l - 1/e)\exp(i\psi)$, and hence $u = v + \frac{1}{2}$.

This proposition has the following consequence for passing chords.

Corollary 1. *Consider two instances X_r and X_s of a chord with a sliding voice $X_t : [0,1) \to \mathbb{T}^e$, such that all other points (the fixed tones) are located in the circular segment between s and r and no points between r and s, i.e. $0 \leq s < t_1 < \ldots t_{e-1} < r < 1$. Consider the corresponding 1st Fourier coefficients $\widehat{X_r}(1)$ and $\widehat{X_s}(1)$. If the location of the 1st Fourier coefficient $\widehat{X_u}(1)$ of the most uneven chord X_u in the family X_t is not between $\widehat{X_r}(1)$ and $\widehat{X_s}(1)$ in counter-clockwise direction, then for any t between r and s ($r \leq t < 1$ or $0 \leq t \leq s$), we have $|\widehat{X_t}(1)| \geq \min(|\widehat{X_r}(1)|, |\widehat{X_s}(1)|)$.*

Proof. The assertion is an immediate consequence of the fact that the curve $\{\widehat{X_t}(1) \,|\, t \in [0,1)\}$ is a circle. Within any segment of the circle that does neither contain $\widehat{X_v}(1)$ nor $\widehat{X_u}(1)$, the magnitude $|\widehat{X_t}(1)|$ is monotonously increasing (or decreasing). If only $\widehat{X_v}(1)$ is contained in a segment, but not $\widehat{X_u}(1)$, the magnitude $|\widehat{X_t}(1)|$ will pass through the maximum, and satisfies $|\widehat{X_t}(1)| \geq \min(|\widehat{X_r}(1)|, |\widehat{X_s}(1)|)$ throughout.

In the light of Corollary 1, we have to study the remaining case where the location of the 1st Fourier coefficient $\widehat{X_u}(1)$ of the most uneven chord X_u in the family X_t is actually between $\widehat{X_r}(1)$ and $\widehat{X_s}(1)$ (in counter-clockwise direction). We will first show in the case $e = 3$ that such chords have one very large step interval, which implies that this situation can not occur with second order Clough-Myerson chords (scales).

Proposition 3. *Consider a 3-chord with a sliding voice $X_t : [0,1) \to \mathbb{T}^e$, such that the pair $X = (\exp(2\pi i t_1), \exp(2\pi i t_2)) \in \mathbb{T}^2$ of its fixed tones satisfies $0 \leq t_1 < t_2 < 1$. Further suppose that $X_u = X_0$ is the most uneven chord. Then the fixed tones satisfy $t_1 < \frac{1}{12}$ and $t_2 > \frac{11}{12}$. i.e. the three tones of X_u are located within a segment of the angle $\frac{2\pi}{6}$.*

Proof. As $u = 0$ is the parameter of the most uneven chord, it follows from Proposition 2 that $\arg(\widehat{X^0}(1)) = 2\pi v = \pi$, since $v = u - \frac{1}{2}$. In other words: the 1st Fourier coefficients $\widehat{X^0}(1)$ and $\widehat{X_0}(1) = \widehat{X^0}(1) + \frac{1}{3}$ are both located on the real line and the coefficient $\widehat{X^0}(1)$ must be negative. This implies that the two (non-zero) summands of $3\widehat{X^0}(1) = (\exp(2\pi i(t_1 - \frac{1}{3})) + \exp(2\pi i(t_2 - \frac{2}{3})))$ must be conjugated with a shared negative real part. Hence, $t_2 = 1 - t_1$ and this implies $t_1 \leq \frac{1}{2}$, because $t1 \leq t_2$. We have $Re(\exp(2\pi i(t_1 - \frac{1}{3})) < 0$ iff $\frac{1}{4} < (t_1 + \frac{2}{3}) \bmod 1 < \frac{3}{4}$ iff $0 < t_1 < \frac{1}{12}$ or $\frac{7}{12} < t_1 < 1$. The latter inequality is out of question, because $t_1 < \frac{1}{2}$, Hence we obtain $t_1 < \frac{1}{12}$ along with $t_2 > \frac{11}{12}$.

An analogous statement is most likely true also for chords of cardinality $e > 3$ and should be proven with the help of an estimate for $|\widehat{X_0}(1)|$ in dependence of the size of circular segment around 1 covered by the points of X_0. An estimation for the size of the largest step interval follows also from the following conjecture about the distribution of the summands of the 1st Fourier-Coefficient for a consecutive sequence of points on the unit circle.

Conjecture 1. Consider a sequence $X = (\exp(2\pi i t_1), \ldots, \exp(2\pi i t_{e-1})) \in \mathbb{T}^{e-1}$ of consecutive points on the unit circle in counter-clockwise order with the property that the first Fourier-Coefficient of $X^0 = (0, \exp(2\pi i t_1), \ldots, \exp(2\pi i t_{e-1})) \in \mathbb{C}^e$ is a negative real number, more precisely $\widehat{X^0}(1) \in (-1, 0)$. Then the sequence $Y^0 = (\exp(2\pi i(t_1 - 1/e)), \ldots, \exp(2\pi i(t_k - k/e)))$ of the $e - 1$ (non-zero) summands of $e \cdot \widehat{X^0}(1)$ is formed by (clockwise) consecutive points on the unit circle.

According to this conjecture the parameters $t_1, \ldots, t_{e-1}$ must fit into an interval of size $(1 - \frac{e-1}{e}) - \frac{1}{e} = 1 - \frac{e-2}{e} = \frac{2}{e}$. For $e \geq 4$ this excludes all instances of second order Clough-Myerson Chords.

7   Conclusion and Future Research

This paper studied the "integration" problem by proposing a generalization of diatonic triads using second-order Clough-Myerson scales in the role of the triads. It further compared the resulting chord connections to the globally defined voice-leading distance utilizing the novel concepts of distant neighbors and interscalar contiguities. The property of diatonic contiguity does not hold in this general case, as a counterexample demonstrates. The paper particularly presented a generalization of hexatonic cycles that is integrated into the diatonic system.

There are three main directions in which future work will build upon this paper. In order to further understand the relationship between Douthett graphs and betweenness graphs, one utilizes the evenness measure of the first Fourier coefficient to define, study and compare the saturations of the Douthett graphs and the betweenness graphs with passing chords. The second direction brings transformations back into play and aims to interpret suitable subgraphs of these voice-leading graphs as Cayley-graphs of group actions with respect to musically meaningful generators. The third direction interprets the findings of this paper as a potential integrationist enrichment of *Tonfeld* analysis [10,16] and aims to bring this area in closer contact with the discourse on neo-Riemannian approaches.

Acknowledgement. The authors would like to thank Fabian C. Moss, Christoph Finkensiep, and the two anonymous reviewers for their constructive, and helpful comments.

References

1. Amiot, E.: Music Through Fourier Space, Discrete Fourier Transform in Music Theory. Springer, Heidelberg (2016). https://doi.org/10.1007/978-3-319-45581-5
2. Carey, N., Clampitt, D.: Self-similar pitch structures, their duals, and rhythmic analogues. Perspect. New Music **34**, 62–87 (1996)
3. Clough, J., Myerson, G.: Variety and multiplicity in diatonic systems. J. Music Theory **29**(2), 249–270 (1985)
4. Clough, J., Douthett, J.: Maximally even sets. J. Music Theory **35**, 93–173 (1991)
5. Cohn, R.: Neo-Riemannian operations, parsimonious trichords, and their "Tonnetz" representations. J. Music Theory **41**(1), 1–66 (1997)
6. Cohn, R.: Audacious Euphony: Chromatic Harmony and the Triad's Second Nature. OUP USA, Oxford (2012)
7. Douthett, J.: Filtered point-symmetry and dynamical voice-leading. In: Douthett, J., et al. (eds.) Music Theory and Mathematics: Chords, Collections, and Transformations, pp. 72–106. University of Rochester Press, New York (2008)
8. Douthett, J., Steinbach, P.: Parsimonious graphs: a study in parsimony, contextual transformations, and modes of limited transposition. J. Music Theory **42**(2), 241–263 (1998)
9. Fiore, T.M., Noll, T., Satyendra, R.: Incorporating voice permutations into the theory of neo-Riemannian groups and Lewinian duality. In: Yust, J., Wild, J., Burgoyne, J.A. (eds.) MCM 2013. LNCS, vol. 7937, pp. 100–114. Springer, Heidelberg (2013). https://doi.org/10.1007/978-3-642-39357-0_8. (Including Subseries Lecture Notes in Artificial Intelligence and Lecture Notes in Bioinformatics)
10. Haas, B.: Die neue Tonalität von Schubert bis Webern. Hören und Analysieren nach Albert Simon. Noetzel, Wilhelmshaven (2004)
11. Harasim, D., Schmidt, S.E., Rohrmeier, M.: Bridging scale theory and geometrical approaches to harmony: the voice-leading duality between complementary chords. J. Math. Music **10**(3), 193–209 (2016)
12. Hauptmann, M.: Die Natur der Harmonik und der Metrik. Breitkopf und Härtel, Leipzig (1853)
13. Noll, T.: The topos of triads. In: Colloquium on Mathematical Music Theory. Grazer Math. Ber., vol. 347, pp. 103–135. Karl-Franzens-Univ. Graz (2005)
14. Plotkin, R.: Transforming transformational analysis: applications of filtered point-symmetry. Dissertation. University of Chicago (2010)
15. Plotkin, R., Douthett, J.: Scalar context in musical models. J. Math. Music **7**(2), 103–125 (2013)
16. Polth, M.: The individual tone and musical context in Albert Simons Tonfeldtheorie. Music Theory Online **24**(4), (2018)

17. Tymoczko, D.: The geometry of musical chords. Science **313**(5783), 72–74 (2006)
18. Yust, J.: Distorted continuity: chromatic harmony, uniform sequences, and quantized voice leadings. MTS **37**(1), 120–143 (2015)
19. Yust, J.: A space for inflections: following up on JMM's special issue on mathematical theories of voice leading. J. Math. Music **7**(3), 175–193 (2013)

Constraint-Based Systems of Triads and Seventh Chords, and Parsimonious Voice-Leading

Matt Klassen[(✉)]

DigiPen Institute of Technology, Redmond, WA 98052, USA
mklassen@digipen.edu
http://www.digipen.edu

Abstract. This paper presents a generalization of the neo-Riemannian PLR group to the set of triads with inversions (major, minor, diminished and augmented). A second generalization is proposed, using an extended system of seventh chords with inversions. Both the sets of triads and seventh chords are defined with constraints on semitone separation of voices. In the case of triads, the set of parsimonious transformations is shown to have the structure of a semi-direct product of groups of the form $S_n \ltimes \mathbb{Z}_{12}^{n-1}$, where n is the number of chord types in the set.

Keywords: Constraint-based · Seventh · Triad · Parsimonious · Neo-Riemannian

1 Introduction

1.1 Constraint-Based Systems

In this paper we consider voicings of triads and seventh chords from the viewpoint of semitone separation constraints.

Constraint-based definitions of chords are meant to yield a collection of chords which are close together in the sense of parsimonious voice-leading. In particular, such chords should have spacing between voices which are somewhat similar. We choose to specify such spacing by focusing on the total spread between the highest and lowest pitches, and also the vector of spreads between adjacent pitches. This method also seems to capture some of the well-known and useful chord collections in the case of triads and seventh chords.

The cost of this approach is that we consider systems of chord-types in an absolute sense, not as pitch-class sets. Each chord type is a root position or chord inversion which can be described by the semitone separation type. The benefit of this approach is that we can include chords which have different numbers of inversion types into one system for the purpose of parsimonious voice-leading.

Supported by DigiPen Institute of Technology.

M. Montiel et al. (Eds.): MCM 2019, LNAI 11502, pp. 185–198, 2019.
https://doi.org/10.1007/978-3-030-21392-3_15

For example, the augmented triad has only one separation type, unlike the other triads. Similarly, the dominant seventh chord with flat fifth has only two separation types, unlike the other seventh chords.

The two systems of constraints can be described simply as follows. For the system of major, minor, diminished, and augmented triads, we constrain the separation between pairs of consecutive notes to be from 3 to 6 semitones, and the separation between the upper and lower notes to be from 6 to 9 semitones. All of these triads and their chord inversions are recovered precisely in this way. A similar system of sevenths chords can be defined with separation between pairs of consecutive notes to be from 1 to 4 semitones, and the separation between the upper and lower notes to be from 8 to 11 semitones. All of the standard seventh chords and their chord inversions are recovered in this way, as well as two additional chords obtained from the dominant seventh by lowering or raising the fifth by one semitone.

In order to explore the transformations between these chord types, we consider chords to be ordered tuples of integers such as (a, b, c) or (a, b, c, d), with $a < b < c < d$. This distinguishes a root position chord from its inversions, as separate chord types. In this context, the concept of pitch class set can still be invoked on these chord collections as an equivalence relation. It is also convenient to work with equivalence classes of chord types modulo twelve, but still preserving the types. For example, the set of triad types modulo 12, with C as 0, includes the B major triad in root position, represented as $(11, 15, 18)$ or as $(-1, 3, 6)$, but not as $(3, 6, 11)$. The latter is of course the first inversion, which in this context is not equivalent as a chord type to the previous two.

What is gained from this point of view is a simple approach to parsimonious voice-leading, and the induced groups of transformations. We recover the PLR group for triads as a subgroup of the larger parsimony group, which we show to be isomorphic to $S_{10} \ltimes \mathbb{Z}_{12}^9$.

These methods can be put into a wider context, where we start with a system of chord types and consider the group generated by basic parsimonious transformations which swap chord types by changing only one voice by one semitone. If there are n chord types which are defined with a system of constraints similar to the two cases we describe, then it is interesting to investigate whether it is possible to describe the parsimony group as $S_n \ltimes \mathbb{Z}_{12}^{n-1}$.

1.2   Background

In his foundational work, David Lewin [7] explored music theory and composition from the perspective of transformational theory. In this context, algebraic structures, such as groups, play an important role in defining and elucidating musical content. In this branch of transformational music theory, known as *neo-Riemannian theory*, voice-leading between chords plays an important role. The canonical example of this is the PLR group, originally introduced by the 19th-century music theorist Hugo Riemann [8]. The transformations P, L, and R each represent the chord change between a major and minor triad by moving one voice of each chord by one or two semitones. Moreover, these transformations relate the important pairs of such triad relationships such as *Parallel*, *Relative*, or *Leading-Tone Exchange*. These types of voice-leading involving small steps between voices are often called *parsimonious*.

Transformations between voicings of triads are also considered in [4], where the authors consider extensions of P, L and R to linear functions defined on all of $\mathbb{Z}_{12}^3$.

In addition to the algebraic action of the PLR group on the set of major and minor triads, a geometric model called the Tonnetz is central to the study of neo-Riemannian transformations. For a full description of the Tonnetz and operations in the PLR group as Dihedral group, we refer the reader to [1] and [3].

In Sect. 2 we recall some facts about the PLR group, in particular its structure as a semi-direct product of groups. In Sect. 3 we identify the structure of the parsimony group G for the constraint-based system of triads with inversions. In Sect. 4 we describe the constraint-based system of seventh chords, and in Sect. 5 we propose some future work.

2   The *PLR* Group as a Semi-direct Product of Groups

The well-known PLR group is a group of transformations on the set of 24 consonant (major and minor) triads. Here we consider triads as pitch-class sets, each consisting of three elements: root, third, and fifth. We will label the sets M and m of major and minor triads as:

$$M = \{M_0, M_1, \ldots, M_{11}\}, \quad m = \{m_0, m_1, \ldots, m_{11}\}$$

where $M_0 = C$ major, $M_1 = C\sharp$ major ... $M_{11} = B$ major, and $m_0 = C$ minor, $m_1 = C\sharp$ minor ... and $m_{11} = B$ minor.

Next recall the three neo-Riemannian transformations:

- P (parallel) swaps major and minor triads by lowering the third (of major triads) or raising the third (of minor triads) by one semitone
- L (leading tone) swaps major and minor triads by moving the root (of major triads) down a semitone, or the fifth (of minor triads) up a semitone
- R (relative) swaps major and minor triads by moving the fifth (of major triads) up a whole tone, or moving the root (of minor triads) down a whole tone

The set of all transformations on the set of major and minor triads which are generated from these is called the PLR group, which we label here as:

$$G_{PLR} = \langle P, L, R \rangle.$$

We can also represent these transformations with indices as follows:

P: $M_i \mapsto m_i$, $m_i \mapsto M_i$ L: $M_i \mapsto m_{i+4}$, $m_i \mapsto M_{i-4}$ R: $M_i \mapsto m_{i+9}$, $m_i \mapsto M_{i-9}$

These transformations can be described by an ordered pair $(s, \mathbf{t})$, where s takes the value σ if the transformation swaps M and m, and 1 (the identity permutation) if the transformation does not swap M and m. The value $\mathbf{t}$ is an integer vector $(t, -t)$ which indicates the shift (or translation) t (modulo twelve) on the index i of a major triad, and the shift $-t$ (modulo 12) on the index j of a minor triad.

For instance, we describe the three transformations as:

$$P : (\sigma, (0, 0)), \quad L : (\sigma, (4, -4)), \quad R : (\sigma, (9, -9))$$

Note: We differ slightly from Hook's notation in [5] where the symbols $+$ and $-$ are used instead of 1 and σ to describe the mode of his Uniform Triadic Transformations, or UTT's.

If $S_2 = \{1, \sigma\}$ is the symmetric group consisting of permutations of the two symbols M and m, and $\mathbb{Z}_{12}$ is the group of integers modulo 12, then we can represent any element of G_{PLR} as an ordered pair $(s, \mathbf{t})$ in the set product:

$$S_2 \times \mathbb{Z}_{12} \times \mathbb{Z}_{12}.$$

Finally, we quote here the well-known structure theorem for G_{PLR} (see [5] for a proof).

Theorem 1. *The neo-Riemannian group G_{PLR} is isomorphic to a semi-direct product $S_2 \ltimes \mathbb{Z}_{12}$.*

Note: Since the semi-direct product $S_2 \ltimes \mathbb{Z}_{12}$ is isomorphic to the dihedral group of order 24 (see for instance [3]), we also get the standard representation of the PLR group as a dihedral group of order 24.

3   Constraint-Based System of Triads

Triads can be obtained in root position by stacking major or minor thirds. This produces the four triad types: major, minor, diminished and augmented. In music theory it is often preferred to think in terms of pitch class sets, so the chord inversions of these four triads are taken to be equivalent to their root position versions. In this paper, we consider each inversion as a separate entity. In order to distinguish them, we identify each chord by its "successive-interval array". This notion is first defined by Chrisman in [2], in a more general context. For our purpose, we include only the semitone gaps between successive notes, leaving out Chrisman's inclusion of the semitone gap between the highest pitch and one octave above the lowest pitch. In this paper we refer to this simplified array of semitone gaps as *si-type*, for "successive interval type".

We will refer to chords (in equal temperament) by integer tuples which indicate pitches relative to some fixed starting value. For example, if middle C is represented as 0, then a piano with 88 keys is represented by the values -39 (A_0) to 48 (C_8). The triple $(0, 4, 7)$ then represents a C Major triad in root position, with root middle C. We will always assume that such a triple (a, b, c) of integers satisfies $a < b < c$, or equivalently that the pitch values are increasing from left to right.

The si-type $[x, y]$ describes a triad (a, b, c) where $x = b - a$ and $y = c - b$. Thus the si-type of the C Major triad above, or any other Major triad in root position, is $[4, 3]$. The first inversion of this triad then is represented by $(4, 7, 12)$ and has si-type $[3, 5]$. The four types of triad, together with their chord inversions, yield 10 different si-types, which are listed in the following Table 1:

Table 1. si-types of triads

chord name (and symbol)	Root	1st Inv	2nd Inv
Major triad (M)	[4, 3]	[3, 5]	[5, 4]
minor triad (m)	[3, 4]	[4, 5]	[5, 3]
diminished triad (o)	[3, 3]	[3, 6]	[6, 3]
augmented triad ($+$)	[4, 4]	[4, 4]	[4, 4]

Constraint-based definition of triad (based on si-type): We define a triad (a, b, c), given with integers $a < b < c$, to be one with si-type $[x, y] = [b - a, c - b]$ satisfying the following constraints:

$$3 \leq x, y \leq 6 \quad \text{and} \quad 6 \leq x + y \leq 9.$$

It is easy to check that the above 10 si-types in the table are the only ones which satisfy these constraints.

Now consider parsimonious voice-leading transformations from one triad to another which are of the simplest type: changing one of a, b, or c by only one semitone. (Note: we refer to the three voices of the chord based on their position, not their function as root, third or fifth.)

The following table lists all such transformations which yield another chord in this collection. Here we indicate the transformation with the notation a_+ to mean that the note value a is replaced with $a + 1$:

$$a_+ \; : \; (a, b, c) \rightarrow (a + 1, b, c)$$

and a_- to mean that a is replaced with $a - 1$:

$$a_- \; : \; (a, b, c) \rightarrow (a - 1, b, c),$$

and so on for b and c (Table 2).

Triads modulo 12

We define the set T of triads (a, b, c) mod 12, according to their si-type and lowest pitch value a. We take the value $a = 0$ to be the pitch C, etc. Since there are 10 si-types and 12 possible values for a, we have 120 elements in T. It is important to note that these elements are not pitch class sets, since we are still distinguishing between inversions as separate triads. We will use the common notations but add superscripts and subscripts to indicate chord types

Table 2. Parsimonious Transformations on si-types

symbol	si-type	a_-	a_+	b_-	b_+	c_-	c_+
M	[4, 3]	[5, 3]	[3, 3]	[3, 4]			[4, 4]
M_1	[3, 5]	[4, 5]			[4, 4]	[3, 4]	[3, 6]
M_2	[5, 4]		[4, 4]	[4, 5]	[6, 3]	[5, 3]	
m	[3, 4]	[4, 4]			[4, 3]	[3, 3]	[3, 5]
m_1	[4, 5]		[3, 5]	[3, 6]	[5, 4]	[4, 4]	
m_2	[5, 3]	[6, 3]	[4, 3]	[4, 4]			[5, 4]
o	[3, 3]	[4, 3]					[3, 4]
o_1	[3, 6]				[4, 5]	[3, 5]	
o_2	[6, 3]		[5, 3]	[5, 4]			
$+$	[4, 4]	[5, 4]	[3, 4]	[3, 5]	[5, 3]	[4, 3]	[4, 5]

and inversions. (Since lower case letters are already being used for voices, we write Cm for a C minor triad instead of c.) For example, one could list:

$$C = (0, 4, 7), Ab_1 = (0, 3, 8), F_2 = (0, 5, 9), Cm = (0, 3, 7), Am_1 = (0, 4, 9),$$

$$Fm_2 = (0, 5, 8), C^o = (0, 3, 6), A_1^o = (0, 3, 9), F\sharp_2^o = (0, 6, 9), C^+ = (0, 4, 8)$$

for chords occuring in the ten different si-types having starting pitch C, or $a = 0$.

Each of the si-types determines a subset of T, so we use the symbol or the si-type for subsets as well. For example:

$$M = [4, 3] = \{C = (0, 4, 7), C\# = (1, 5, 8), D = (2, 6, 9), \ldots, B = (11, 15, 18)\}$$

is the subset of 12 major triads, and

$$o_1 = [3, 6] = \{A_1^o = (0, 3, 9), Bb_1^o = (1, 4, 10), B_1^o = (2, 5, 11), \ldots, Ab_1^o = (11, 14, 20)\}$$

is the subset of 12 first inversion diminished triads, etc. (Note that we maintain the order $a < b < c$, and that we consider (a, b, c) as representative of an equivalence class modulo 12. So we could use $Ab_1^o = (-1, 2, 8)$ but not $(11, 2, 8)$ since it is an ordered triple but not a pitch-class set.)

Next, we define transformations between si-types, in particular the swaps of order two between si-types which are induced by raising or lowering one voice a, b, or c, by one semitone. As permutations on the set T, these are *involutions* since they swap all triads of one si-type with triads of another si-type, and performing this swap twice results in the identity permutation. (Note the usual P and L transformations are now factored into three swaps on si-types.) We indicate each transformation with its corresponding pair of adjustments to one voice (Table 3).

Table 3. Parsimonious transformation labels

$P_0: M \longleftrightarrow m, \quad b_-, b_+$	$P_1: M_1 \longleftrightarrow m_1, \quad a_-, a_+$	$P_2: M_2 \longleftrightarrow m_2, \quad c_-, c_+$
$L_0: M \longleftrightarrow m_2, \quad a_-, a_+$	$L_1: M_1 \longleftrightarrow m, \quad c_-, c_+$	$L_2: M_2 \longleftrightarrow m_1, \quad b_-, b_+$
$f_0: M \longleftrightarrow o, \quad a_+, a_-$	$f_1: M_1 \longleftrightarrow o_1, \quad c_+, c_-$	$f_2: M_2 \longleftrightarrow o_2, \quad b_+, b_-$
$g_0: m \longleftrightarrow o, \quad c_-, c_+$	$g_1: m_1 \longleftrightarrow o_1, \quad b_-, b_+$	$g_2: m_2 \longleftrightarrow o_2, \quad a_-, a_+$
$\alpha_0: M \longleftrightarrow +, \quad c_+, c_-$	$\alpha_1: M_1 \longleftrightarrow +, \quad b_+, b_-$	$\alpha_2: M_2 \longleftrightarrow +, \quad a_+, a_-$
$\beta_0: m \longleftrightarrow +, \quad a_-, a_+$	$\beta_1: m_1 \longleftrightarrow +, \quad c_-, c_+$	$\beta_2: m_2 \longleftrightarrow +, \quad b_-, b_+$

These transformations are pictured (as swaps of chord types) in the following diagram:

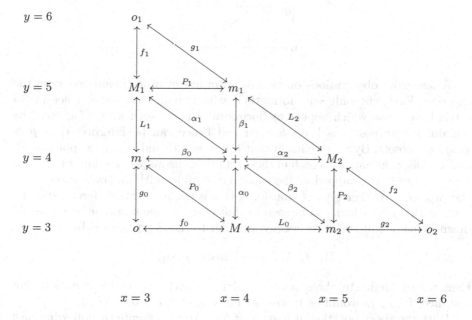

Fig. 1. Parsimonious transformation diagram

Note that in any small triangle of the following shape, if we start with any chord, then follow the arrows *clockwise*, this results in an increase by one semitone to each of the voices, resulting in a transformation which affects this one chord type as:

$$(a, b, c) \longrightarrow (a+1, b+1, c+1).$$

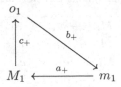

Similarly, if we follow the arrows *counterclockwise* this results in:

$$(a, b, c) \longrightarrow (a - 1, b - 1, c - 1).$$

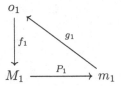

A few more observations on this diagram are in order before we state the theorem. First, the only transformations which change the lower voice (a) of a triad are those which appear as horizontal arrows, such as f_0, L_0, etc. The remaining transpositions leave a fixed and hence can be interpreted as *pure swaps* of subsets. By this we mean that if the sets M and m are swapped by P_0 and we index the entries of each of these sets then the major and minor triads (in root position) are swapped at the same index value, with no translation inside the two sets. Another type of transformation is the *pure translation* on subsets, such as $P_0 f_0 g_0 f_0$, which can be seen to shift m up by one semitone, and shift M down by one semitone. If we specify an order to the si-types, or subsets, as:

$$(M, M_1, M_2, m, m_1, m_2, o, o_1, o_2, +)$$

then we can indicate these pure translations with the vector notation. For instance, $P_0 f_0 g_0 f_0$ would be represented as $(-1, 0, 0, 1, 0, 0, 0, 0, 0, 0)$.

With the above notation, it is straight-forward to generate the following such pure translations:

$$(-1, 1, 0, 0, 0, 0, 0, 0, 0, 0), (-1, 0, 1, 0, 0, 0, 0, 0, 0, 0), (-1, 0, 0, 1, 0, 0, 0, 0, 0, 0),$$

$$(-1, 0, 0, 0, 1, 0, 0, 0, 0, 0), (-1, 0, 0, 0, 0, 1, 0, 0, 0, 0), (-1, 0, 0, 0, 0, 0, 1, 0, 0, 0),$$

$$(-1, 0, 0, 0, 0, 0, 0, 1, 0, 0), (-1, 0, 0, 0, 0, 0, 0, 0, 1, 0), (-1, 0, 0, 0, 0, 0, 0, 0, 0, 1)$$

This can be achieved by conjugation, or simply preceeding and following $P_0 f_0 g_0 f_0$ by a series of transpositions which are in reversed orders. For example, we obtain

$$(-1, 1, 0, 0, 0, 0, 0, 0, 0, 0) = L_1(P_0 f_0 g_0 f_0) L_1$$

and

$$(-1, 0, 1, 0, 0, 0, 0, 0, 0, 0) = L_2 g_1 f_1 L_1(P_0 f_0 g_0 f_0) L_1 f_1 g_1 L_2.$$

Next, we define the *parsimony group* G to be the group of transformations generated by all of the above defined transformations, acting as involutions on the set T of 120 triads modulo 12.

$$G = \langle P_0, P_1, P_2, L_0, L_1, L_2, f_0, f_1, f_2, g_0, g_1, g_2, \alpha_0, \alpha_1, \alpha_2, \beta_0, \beta_1, \beta_2 \rangle.$$

We will show that G is isomorphic to a semi-direct product of two groups:

$$G \cong S_{10} \ltimes \mathbb{Z}_{12}^9.$$

The first of these is the full permutation group S_{10} on 10 symbols, in this case on the chord symbols or si-types. The second factor in the semidirect product is $\mathbb{Z}_{12}^9$, obtained from the action of the group $\mathbb{Z}_{12}$ on subsets of chords in one si-type. This factor can be seen as the subgroup Z of $\mathbb{Z}_{12}^{10}$ consisting of all vectors $\mathbf{t} = (t_1, \ldots, t_{10})$ satisfying $\sum_{i=1}^{10} t_i = 0$.

We need to specify the group operation in G which is given by the homomorphism

$$\phi : S_{10} \longrightarrow Aut(Z)$$

with $\phi(s) = s(\mathbf{t})$, or in other words, the action of $\phi(s)$ on a vector $\mathbf{t}$ in Z is to simply permute the vector components of $\mathbf{t}$. We can represent any element of G as a pair $(s, \mathbf{t})$ and then the product is given as:

$$(s, \mathbf{t}) \cdot (s', \mathbf{t}') = (ss', \mathbf{t} + s(\mathbf{t}')),$$

where

$$s(\mathbf{t}') = (t'_{s(1)}, t'_{s(2)}, \ldots, t'_{s(10)}).$$

To see this, let the vector of si-types be relabeled with superscripts so that

$$(M, M_1, M_2, m, m_1, m_2, o, o_1, o_2, +) = (T^1, T^2, \ldots, T^{10}).$$

Each of the twelve chords inside each si-type can then be indicated with subscripts, so that C major root position is now T_0^1, and B augmented, or B^+, is now T_{11}^{10}. With this notation we can see that

$$(s, \mathbf{t})(T_j^i) = T_{j+t_i}^{s(i)}.$$

This product then satisfies the properties:

Lemma 1. *For any elements* $(s, \mathbf{t})$ *and* $(s', \mathbf{t}')$ *in the parsimony group* G, *we have:*

- $(s, \mathbf{t}) \cdot (s', \mathbf{t}') = (ss', \mathbf{t} + s(\mathbf{t}'))$
- $(s, \mathbf{t})^{-1} = (s^{-1}, s^{-1}(-\mathbf{t}))$
- $(s, \mathbf{t})(1, \mathbf{t}')(s, \mathbf{t})^{-1} = (1, s(\mathbf{t}'))$

Proof. The product (with first factor acting first) is verified by:

$$((s,\mathbf{t})\cdot(s',\mathbf{t}'))(T_j^i) = (s',\mathbf{t}')(T_{j+t_i}^{s(i)}) = T_{j+t_i+t'_{s(i)}}^{s'(s(i))} = T_{j+t_i+s(t'_i)}^{(ss')(i)},$$

and the form of the inverse follows directly. The last property is verified as:

$$(s,\mathbf{t})(1,\mathbf{t}')(s,\mathbf{t})^{-1} = (s,\mathbf{t})(1,\mathbf{t}')(s^{-1}, s^{-1}(-\mathbf{t})) = (s,\mathbf{t})(s^{-1}, \mathbf{t}' + s^{-1}(-\mathbf{t}))$$

$$= (1, \mathbf{t} + s(\mathbf{t}' + s^{-1}(-\mathbf{t}))) = (1, s(\mathbf{t}')).$$

□

From the last property of the Lemma we obtain:

Corollary 1. *The group Z of pure translations is a normal subgroup of G.*

Next, we recall that a group G is a semi-direct product, written $K \ltimes_\phi H$ if the following hold:

- K and H are subgroups of G
- H is normal in G
- $KH = G$
- $\phi : K \longrightarrow Aut(H)$ is a homomorphism, $k \mapsto \phi_k$
- The product in G is $(k,h)(k',h') = (kk', h\phi_k(h'))$

Theorem 2. *The parsimony group G defined above is isomorphic to $S_{10} \ltimes \mathbb{Z}_{12}^9$.*

Proof. The proof follows the outline of the proof of Theorem 1 in [1]. There are two steps: (1) We show that the permutation part of this group contains all transpositions on the sets of triad types, and (2) We show that the vectors of integers modulo 12 contain all elements of the type

$$(t_1, t_2, \ldots, t_{10})$$

satisfying $\sum_{i=1}^{10} t_i = 0$, which shows that the subgroup of pure translations Z is isomorphic to $\mathbb{Z}_{12}^9$. The first part follows from Fig. 1 where we can identify a sequence of transpositions which generate all of S_{10}. In fact, we can generate all transpositions, or swaps of two si-types, where we avoid any translations. This is done simply by following arrows in the diagram from one si-type to another but avoiding the horizontal arrows. For example, the swap between type o (diminished triad in root position) and type m_2 (minor triad second inversion) can be obtained as:

$$g_0 L_1 \alpha_1 \beta_2 \alpha_1 L_1 g_0.$$

Since the transpositions generate the full symmetric group, the first part is done. It is evident that the generators of G satisfy the property that the translation vector has sum of its components equal to zero. The second part follows by noting that we can express any element of the specified type as a sum of the elements generated above, in particular:

$$(t_1, t_2, \ldots, t_{10}) = t_2(-1, 1, 0, 0, 0, 0, 0, 0, 0, 0) + \cdots + t_{10}(-1, 0, 0, 0, 0, 0, 0, 0, 0, 1)$$

where the first coordinate is automatically correct since $t_1 = -(t_2 + \cdots + t_{10})$.

□

We can immediately identify the PLR group as a subgroup of the parsimony group G. In particular, since each operation now factors as a product of three transpositions, we have:

$$G_{PLR} \cong \langle P_0 P_1 P_2, L_0 L_1 L_2, R_0 R_1 R_2 \rangle.$$

4   Constraint-Based System of Seventh Chords

Extensions of the PLR group to seventh chords are explored in several recent papers. In [6] Kerkez defines a PS-group, isomorphic to G_{PLR}, which acts on the major and minor seventh chords. In [1] Cannas, Antonini, and Pernazza, define a group called $PLRQ$ which generalizes the PLR group to five types of seventh chords: dominant, minor, half-diminished, major, and diminished, and they show that this group is isomorphic to the semi-direct product $S_5 \ltimes \mathbb{Z}_{12}^4$. Continuing in this vein, we now extend these results to a larger constraint-based system of seventh chords.

A typical definition of seventh chord might be: *"A four-note chord obtained by stacking thirds based on a major or minor scale."* One should also add that such a chord can be inverted in the usual way, giving three other equivalent four-note chords. If we are interested primarily in pitch classes, then of course these all represent the same pitch-class set. In this paper we consider these as individual chords in their own right, and note that their structure gives way to a very simple constraint-based description of seventh chords.

If seventh chords are assumed to come from the major or minor scale construction alluded to above, then we have the following seven types, which we call the classical types of seventh chords.

Dominant seventh (7), minor seventh (m7), half-diminished seventh (⌀7), Major seventh (M7), minor-Major seventh (mM7), augmented Major seventh (+M7), diminished seventh (o7).

As we did for triads, recalling Chrisman's "successive-interval array" in [2], we introduce the "successive-interval type", or si-type: $[x, y, z]$ for a seventh chord. In equal temperament, we can represent a four-note chord by an integer vector of values (a, b, c, d). Here we will assume that the note values are listed in increasing order $a < b < c < d$.

We define the successive-interval type, or si-type: $[x, y, z]$ for a seventh chord (a, b, c, d) to be:

$$[x, y, z] = [b - a, c - b, d - c],$$

or simply the numbers of semitones separating the notes of the chord, from left to right.

For example, if we use 0 to represent middle C, then the chord $(0, 4, 7, 10)$ would be C Dominant seventh chord in root position. The si-type for this chord is then $[4, 3, 3]$. The first inversion of this chord is $(4, 7, 10, 12)$, with si-type $[3, 3, 2]$. Note: The si-type describes a chord inversion, but is not an invariant of the pitch class set.

It is easy to see that there are 25 si-types associated to these classical seventh chords with all of their inversions. The only chord whose inversions do not generate new si-types is the full diminished chord. It is also easy to check that the semitone separation variables x, y, z exhibited in these classical seventh chord types always assume values $1, 2, 3$ or 4, and that any such chord (a, b, c, d) with one of these types must have total spread $x + y + z$ to be at least 8 semitones (a minor sixth) and at most 11 semitones (a Major seventh). Next, we take the above description of si-types and turn it into a definition of seventh chord:

Constraint-based definition of seventh chord (based on si-type): We define a seventh chord (a, b, c, d), given with integers $a < b < c < d$, to be one with si-type $[x, y, z] = [b - a, c - b, d - c]$ satisfying the following constraints:

$$1 \leq x, y, z \leq 4 \quad and \quad 8 \leq x + y + z \leq 11.$$

Practiclly speaking, we are defining a seventh chord to be one which can be played on the piano by simply choosing four notes in such a way that: (1) any two adjacent notes are separated by a major third, a minor third, a whole step, or a half step, and (2) the spread from the first to the last notes is at least a minor sixth, and at most a major seventh.

An obvious question to ask is whether the above constraints are a description of precisely the above collection of 25 si-types, or have we introduced something new? The answer is that indeed there are precisely two new chords in this family: the flat 5 seventh (7♭5) and the sharp 5 seventh (7♯5).

The si-types of the classical seventh chords as well as these two additional chords are listed in the following Table 4:

Table 4. si-types of constraint-based system of seventh chords

chord name (and symbol)	Root	1st Inv	2nd Inv	3rd Inv
Dominant seventh (7)	[4, 3, 3]	[3, 3, 2]	[3, 2, 4]	[2, 4, 3]
minor seventh (m7)	[3, 4, 3]	[4, 3, 2]	[3, 2, 3]	[2, 3, 4]
half-diminished seventh (∅7)	[3, 3, 4]	[3, 4, 2]	[4, 2, 3]	[2, 3, 3]
Major seventh (M7)	[4, 3, 4]	[3, 4, 1]	[4, 1, 4]	[1, 4, 3]
minor-Major seventh (mM7)	[3, 4, 4]	[4, 4, 1]	[4, 1, 3]	[1, 3, 4]
augmented Major seventh (+M7)	[4, 4, 3]	[4, 3, 1]	[3, 1, 4]	[1, 4, 4]
diminished seventh (o7)	[3, 3, 3]	[3, 3, 3]	[3, 3, 3]	[3, 3, 3]
flat 5 seventh (7♭5)	[4, 2, 4]	[2, 4, 2]	[4, 2, 4]	[2, 4, 2]
sharp 5 seventh (7♯5)	[4, 4, 2]	[4, 2, 2]	[2, 2, 4]	[2, 4, 4]

Since the 7♭5 chord only generates two si-types, while the 7♯5 generates four types, we have a total of 31 si-types for this constraint-based system of seventh chords. We label the set of these 31 si-types S_7:

$$S_7 = \{[x, y, z] : 1 \leq x, y, z \leq 4, 8 \leq x + y + z \leq 11\}.$$

Let's call the set of integer vectors (a, b, c, d) representing a seventh chord as above C_7, which is a subset of $\mathbb{Z}^4$:

$$C_7 = \{(a, b, c, d) : a < b < c < d, x = b - a, y = c - b, z = d - c, 1 \le x, y, z \le 4,$$
$$8 \le x + y + z \le 11\}.$$

Finally, we consider C_7 modulo translation by the group $\mathbb{Z}_{12}$. By this we mean that two chords (a, b, c, d) and (a', b', c', d') are considered equivalent if they have the same si-type $[x, y, z]$ and $a \equiv a'$ (mod 12). We can represent each of these equivalence classes by a chord (a, b, c, d) with $0 \le a \le 11$. Denote the equivalence class of a chord (a, b, c, d) by simply $(a, b, c, d)_{12}$. Then we define:

$$X_7 = \{(a, b, c, d)_{12} : (a, b, c, d) \in C_7\}.$$

The size of X_7 is $31 \cdot 12 = 372$.

We define the parsimony group G_7 for this set X_7 of seventh chords to be the group generated by all parsimonious transformations which raise or lower one of the four voices, a, b, c or d, of the seventh chord by one semitone, but only allowing such transformations in the case where the resulting chord is in the same set X_7. Just as with the parsimony group G for triads, each such transformation can be seen as a swap of two s-types, with a possible shift modulo 12.

5   Future Work

We propose to investigate the following question in a continuation of this work:

Is the parsimony group G_7 defined above isomorphic to $S_{31} \ltimes \mathbb{Z}_{12}^{30}$?

We can define an infinite graph on the constraint-based system of seventh chords with edges which exist if there is a parsimonious voice-leading transformation between the two chords. We have developed software to play random walks on this graph, and propose to use this type of system for generative music.

X_7 breaks up naturally into some subsets which can be described as stabilizers of permutation actions on the si-type. Such subsets are:

$$X_1 = \{7, m7, \varnothing 7\}, \; X_2 = \{M7, mM7, +M7\}, \; X_3 = \{o7\}, \; \text{and} \; X_4 = \{7\flat 5, 7\sharp 5\}.$$

We propose to study further these subsets, and the corresponding subgroups of the parsimony group G_7, and their significance for voice-leading and generative music.

Acknowledgements. We would like to thank the referee and the organizer Thomas Noll for their very helpful comments and suggested references.

References

1. Cannas, S., Antonini, S., Pernazza, L.: On the group of transformations of classical types of seventh chords. In: Agustín-Aquino, O.A., Lluis-Puebla, E., Montiel, M. (eds.) MCM 2017. LNCS (LNAI), vol. 10527, pp. 13–25. Springer, Cham (2017). https://doi.org/10.1007/978-3-319-71827-9_2

2. Chrisman, R.: Describing structural aspects of pitch-sets using successive-interval arrays. J. Music Theory **27**(2), 181–201 (1979)
3. Crans, A., Fiore, T.M., Satyendra, R.: Musical actions of dihedral groups. Am. Math. Monthly **116**(6), 479–495 (2009)
4. Fiore, T.M., Noll, T.: Voicing transformations of triads. SIAM J. Appl. Algebra Geom. **2**(2), 281–313 (2018)
5. Hook, J.: Uniform triadic transformations. J. Music Theory **46**(1/2), 57–126 (2002)
6. Kerkez, B.: Extension of Neo-Riemannian PLR-group to Seventh Chords. Bridges 2012: Mathematics, Music, Art, Architecture, Culture (2012)
7. Lewin, D.: Generalized Musical Intervals and Transformations. Yale University Press, New Haven (1987)
8. Riemann, H.: Handbuch der Harmonielehre. Breitkopf und Härtel, Leipzig (1887)

Octave Division

Distributional Analysis of n-Dimensional Feature Space for 7-Note Scales in 22-TET

Gareth M. Hearne[✉], Andrew J. Milne, and Roger T. Dean

The MARCS Institute for Brain, Behaviour and Development,
Western Sydney University, Penrith, Australia
G.Hearne@westernsydney.edu.au

Abstract. Many scale features have been defined in an effort to account for the ubiquity of the diatonic scale in tonal music. In 12-TET, their relative influences have been difficult to disentangle. In 22-TET however, the features are spread differently across different scales. We sought here to to establish a set of 7-note scales in 22-TET that represent the major clusters within the whole population of scales. We first calculate numerous features of every 7-note scale in 22-TET that may relate to their perception in harmonic tonality. This feature space is then reduced by the step-by-step removal of features which may be most completely expressed as linear combinations of the others. A k-medoids cluster analysis leads finally to the selection of 11 exemplar scales, including approximations of four different tunings of the diatonic scale in just intonation.

Keywords: Diatonic scale features · K-medoids cluster analysis · 22-TET

1 Introduction

This paper details the selection of a small set of scales that in further research will be used to tease apart the psychological effect of the features that have been ascribed to the diatonic scale. It achieves this through first collecting appropriate features from a review of the literature and defining some more, then by calculating the value of each of these features for the set of 7-note scales of 22-TET, choosing an appropriate subset of values, and conducting a k-medoids clustering of the scales in this feature space, resulting in the selection of a small set of exemplar scales that represent distinct clusters from an optimal clustering of the set, that we see as best representative of the entire space. Outside the scope of this paper, this exemplar set is to be used in a perceptual experiment, testing for the effect of these features on the cognition of harmonic tonality using the scales as stimulus.

The features may be divided into six groups: Generator complexity, R-ad entropy, redundancy, coherence and evenness, consonance, and tetrachordality.

© Springer Nature Switzerland AG 2019
M. Montiel et al. (Eds.): MCM 2019, LNAI 11502, pp. 201–212, 2019.
https://doi.org/10.1007/978-3-030-21392-3_16

Given that almost all of these features are defined based on the diatonic scale, it shows extreme values for all of them. It boasts equal lowest generator complexity and R-ad entropy and equal highest redundancy for 7-note scales in 12-TET. It is also the maximally even 7-note scale in 12-TET, and 12-TET's only omnitetrahordal scale. The diatonic scale also maximises the number of constituent consonant triads. Since in 12-TET the diatonic scale holds a monopoly on many of these features, we need to look elsewhere if we are to tease them apart. 22-TET is chosen as it is the simplest tuning wherein a single scale no longer holds a monopoly, but where all the features we define exist across an appropriate range of values in some scales. We choose also to limit our analysis to scales of 7 notes to minimise the size of our set and simplify our analysis. Beginning our review with redundancy, we first introduce how we will be discussing scales in this article.

2   Review

In this paper a scale is considered to be an equivalence class by rotation of ordered sets of specific intervals called steps, where the different rotations of a scale are its modes. Scales in equal temperaments (ETs) are written in their "brightest" mode (the mode in which the larger steps are most concentrated towards the beginning; the lexicographically highest mode), unless otherwise indicated, with step sizes written in degrees of the equal temperament. For example, the diatonic scale in 12-TET is represented as 2221221.

2.1   Redundancy

Carey suggests that a pitch class set can be considered a scale, 'when its generic intervals efficiently organize and encode its specific intervals. Put simply, a scale is that kind of pitch-class set in which it makes sense to think about intervals generically' [4].

Redundancy and coherence concern the relationship between specific and generic intervals. *Redundancy* concerns the certainty with which a generic interval infers a specific interval, while *coherence* concerns the inverse: the certainty with which a specific interval infers a generic interval.

Considering redundancy, Rothenberg defines the *variety* of a generic interval as the number of specific sizes it comes in. *Mean variety* [19] and *maximum variety* follow directly from this, considering all the generic intervals of the scale (up to N-1, where N is the cardinality of the scale). Wilson notes that some *generated scales* – scales that can be produced from the iterated addition of a specific interval modulo the period [11] – possess the property that the maximum variety is two. He calls these scales *Moment of Symmetry* or *MOS* scales [21,22].

Clough and Douthett defined *maximally even (ME) scales* as scales in which each generic interval has either one or two adjacent specific intervals, meaning that it is 'distributed as evenly as possible' [9]. ME scales are a subset of *Distributionally even (DE scales)*, where each generic interval comes in either one or two specific intervals [11].

Similarly, Carey and Clampitt [6] define a *well-formed (WF)* scale as a generated scale in which the generator is of invariant generic size. They divide WF scales into two types: *degenerate*, the set of equal temperaments, and *non-degenerate*, the set of scales that possess *Myhill's property* – that each generic interval comes in exactly two specific sizes [12]. In non-equal scales of prime cardinality, WF, DE and MOS are equivalent. We refer henceforth to these scales as WF.

After Myhill's property for well-formed scales, *trivalent scales* are defined such that each generic interval comes in three specific sizes. Consider the JI major scale 9/8 5/4 4/3 3/2 5/3 15/8 2/1. With steps of 9/8 10/9 16/15 9/8 10/9 9/8 16/15, it is trivalent [5,7]. In meantone temperament, the minor and major tones – 10/9 and 9/8 – are tempered to equivalence (tempering out their difference, 81/80). This leads us back to the well-formed meantone diatonic, which may be described, in the major mode, as LLsLLLs. If we take any other pair of step sizes to be equivalent, we also are led to well-formed scales. i.e., taking 10/9 to be equivalent to 16/15 (tempering out 25/24) leads to LssLsLs, and taking 9/8 to be equal to 16/15 (tempering out 135/128) leads to sLssLss. This property is described by Clampitt as *pairwise well-formedness* [8].

Carey later introduces the concept of *strong n-valence* as a generalisation to a consequence of Myhill's property: 'Let n represent the number of distinct step sizes per span. If the set of $(n)(n-1)/2$ (positive) differences between the n step sizes is the same for each span, the set has strong n-valence' [5]. He conjectures that 'iff a set of odd cardinality has strong trivalence then it is pairwise well-formed'.

An instance of a pair of intervals of the same generic size which differ in specific size is called a difference. Carey's sameness quotient gives a continuous measure of the infrequency of difference in a scale, which is where a pair of intervals of the same generic size differs in specific size [4].

Another similar feature, which will here be called n-chord entropy, introduced recently by Milne and Dean [17] considers the entropy of the distribution of n-chords, which are n note factors/segments of the scale (we are most familiar with n-chords when n is 4; i.e., tetrachords). The probability mass function

$$P_i(n)$$

is the number of occurrences of each different n-chord, divided by the number of notes in the scale. Then the n-chord entropy in bits is as follows:

$$E(P) = -\sum_i P_i log_2 P_i \qquad (1)$$

n-chord entropy is defined in a scale of N notes for

$$2 \leq n \leq N - 1$$

2.2   Coherence and Evenness

Rothenberg [18] introduced the concept of propriety, where a scale is considered *proper* if no specific interval of generic interval n is larger than any specific interval of generic interval $n+1$. The diatonic scale in 12-TET is proper, but not strictly proper, where a scale is considered to be *strictly proper* if no specific interval of generic size n is *equal to* or larger than any specific interval of generic size $n+1$. A pair of intervals for which strict propriety fails for a scale is called a failure. Failures may be *contradictions*, when propriety also fails, or *ambiguities*, where only strict propriety fails.

Balzano [3] independently introduced the concept of *coherence*, equivalent to strict propriety. He then then defined a weaker version of coherence which the diatonic scale in 12-TET passes, in which ambiguity is allowed an interval of half an octave (the tritone).

Tuned as it was for centuries to Pythagorean intonation, the diatonic scale is improper, where the Aug 4 is sharper than the dim 5. With Meantone tempering it is strictly proper. Clearly a scale does not need to be strictly proper or even proper to be tonal, and accordingly we do not include binary coherence features in our analysis. Non-binary measures for coherence have also been defined, by which the various tunings of the diatonic scale recieve extreme values.

Similar to his sameness quotient, in the same paper Carey introduced a coherence quotient as a continuous measure for the infrequency of failures of coherence (ambiguity or contradiction) [4].

Along with propriety, Rothenberg introduced *stability*, with which proper scales can be compared, defined as the portion of unambiguous intervals, out of all $N(N\text{-}1)$ possible intervals [18]. Unlike Carey's coherence quotient which considers both ambiguities and contradictions, Rothenburg stability concerns only ambiguities (of any degree). Given that it is only defined for proper scales, we do not include it in our analysis.

Thus far no feature directly concerns the relative size of intervals in the scale. Lumma introduces two concepts intended to take this into account. The first of these – Lumma stability – is an extension of Rothenberg's stability. Lumma stability is the portion of the octave that is not covered with the spans of each generic interval class. The portion of the octave more than singly covered by the spans of each generic interval class is defined as Lumma impropriety [13].

Evenness also directly concerns the relative sizes of intervals of a scale, measuring the similarity the scale to an ET of the same cardinality. For more thorough definitions and formulae see [1,2]. Evenness can be seen as a continuous generalization of the binary measure of maximal evenness.

2.3   *R*-ad entropy

We define R-ad entropy as the entropy of the distribution of subsets of R notes – "R-ads" – from a scale of cardinality N where R ranges from 2 to $N\text{-}1$. We consider however only R-values of 2 and 3, corresponding to dyads and triads, as we consider larger subsets of notes to less important to tonality. The entropy in bits is calculated as in n-chord entropy above, using the probability mass function of the number of occurences of each different R-ad, divided by the total number of R-ads.

2.4   Generator Complexity

Generator complexity considers the compactness with which the scale can be represented in a minimum number of dimensions. Where the *Graham complexity*, after Graham Breed, is the number of generators needed to reach an interval in a scale or a 2-dimensional tuning system, we define *scalar Graham complexity (SGC)* as the minimum number of generators of a given size needed to cover a scale, across all possible sizes of generator. It follows that the scalar Graham complexity or SGC of any generated scale of n notes is n-1. Carey [4] suggests that both the minimum number of different generators for which it may be considered a generated scale (for which we were unable to build an algorithm) and the acoustic dissonance of the generators affects its scale candidacy.

2.5   Consonance and Tetrachordality

Consonance has received more definitions than there are researchers who write about it. We do not wish to give any definition of consonance, but to simply observe that the diatonic scale contains the highest number of triads and dyads generally considered to be consonant (e.g., perfect intervals, major and minor thirds and sixths, major and minor triads) out of any 7-note scale in 12-TET.

In tonal-harmonic music the tonic function belongs not only to a note but to a consonant triad (either major or minor). Major and minor triads are *tertian* in the diatonic scale, meaning that above the notes are separated by thirds in the scale. Since the consonance of triads in 22-TET is unknown, an experiment was run to collect such data. Added to our analysis are measures of the maximum, median and minimum perceived consonance of the tertian triads of each scale.

In terms of dyads, we assume that in 22-TET, as in 12-TET, the perfect fifth remains the strongest consonance (other than the octave). Tetrachordal scales maximize similarity at intervals of a perfect fifth and fourth, combining consonance with redundancy. A mode of a scale is said to be *tetrachordal* if it consists of two identical non-overlapping tetrachords that span an approximation of 4/3 (along with, necessarily, a step of an approximation of 9/8 as a remainder). Erlich [15] defined a *tetrachordal* scale as a scale all of whose modes are tetrachordal. Such scales are now referred to more clearly as *omnitetrachordal* [16]. The diatonic scale is the only omnitetrachordal scale in 12-TET. We define tetrachordality as the number of modes of a scale of N notes that are tetrachordal, divided by the total number of modes, N.

3   Analysis

In order of mention, our features for analysis, according to their classification, are:

- Redundancy:
  1. mean variety
  2. maximum variety
  3. trivalence
  4. well-formedness
  5. pairwise well-formedness
  6. strong trivalence
  7. sameness quotient
  8. bichord entropy
  9. trichord entropy
  10. tetrachord entropy
  11. pentachord entropy
  12. hexachord entropy

- Coherence and evenness:
  13. coherence quotient
  14. Lumma stability
  15. Lumma impropriety
  16. evenness
- R-ad entropy:
  17. dyad entropy
  18. triad entropy
- Generator complexity:
  19. scalar Graham complexity
- Consonance:
  20. min consonance
  21. max consonance
  22. median consonance
- Tetrachordality:
  23. tetrachordality

3.1   Reduction

We assume that, especially given the classification of these features into 6 groups, many may not be linearly independent of each other. 23 is also a large number of features to consider in a cluster analysis and so we reduce the dimensionality. A dimensional reduction could be used, however in order to later test the extent to which these features may mediate the ability of a scale to support harmonic tonality, we instead select a subset of features that are least able to be expressed as linear combinations of the others. In order to achieve this, the features are calculated for every 7-note scale in 22-TET. The variance inflation factor (the factor by which the variance of a predictor is inflated compared to what you would expect if there was no multicollinearity; no correlation between predictors) is calculated for all the features, measuring the extent to which they may be predicted by a linear combination of the other features. The feature with the highest variance inflation factor is removed, and the processes is iterated until the variance inflation factor for all remaining features is less than 2.

We found immediately that some of our features correlated 100% with each other: Hexachord entropy had only two values, depending on whether or not the scale was WF. It might be worth looking into n-chord entropy then, in future work, as a generalisation of well-formedness. Strong trivalence, we found, correlated 100% with trivalence. Where strong trivalence did not correlate 100% with pairwise well-formedness we have disproven Carey's conjecture: For example, 4334332 is an example of a strongly trivalent scale that is not pairwise well-formed. Though Carey proves by example that not all trivalent scales are strongly trivalent, we found that all trivalent 7-note scales in 22-TET are strongly trivalent. Removing hexachord entropy and strong trivalence first, our procedure leads us to the following features:

- Redundancy:
  1. maximum variety
  2. well-formedness
  3. pairwise well-formedness
  4. trichord entropy
  5. pentachord entropy
- Coherence and evenness:
  6. Lumma stability
  7. Lumma impropriety
- R-ad entropy:
  8. triad entropy
- Generator complexity:
  9. scalar Graham complexity
- Consonance:
  10. min consonance
  11. max consonance
  12. median consonance
- Tetrachordality:
  13. tetrachordality

The feature of evenness, we suspect, is captured, along with coherence, in Lumma stability and impropriety, given that they involve direct measures of relative interval size.

3.2 Cluster Analysis

Considering that our features are of different types of values – binary and continuous – we use Mahalanobis distance as our distance measure for our clustering. K-medoids clustering is used (via *Partitioning Around Medoids* in R) rather than k-means clustering given that exemplar scales from the original set are needed.

In order to test for the appropriateness of different numbers of clusters, we measure the average silhouette width for each clustering. The silhouette width for a single object is a measure of how similar it is to the cluster to which it is assigned, compared to the other clusters. It ranges from -1 to 1, where a high value indicates that the object is well classified in its cluster and a value below 0 indicates it is closer to another cluster, and may be misclassified [20].

The clustering algorithm leads us to a maximum at 9 clusters, with an average silhouette width of 0.26. We observed however that the average silhouette width, and therefore the clustering may be substantially improved by leaving the vast majority of scales in a single cluster rather than splitting them into multiple clusters. Accordingly, from the initial clustering solutions for 3 to 40 clusters we combined clusters such that the average silhouette width most improved. Further, misclassified scales (those with negative silouette width) were moved into the cluster they are closest to when appropriate. Via these processes, we find a maximum average silhouette width of 0.9877 at 2 clusters, where one cluster is the scale 76 (4441441) and the other cluster is every other scale. We know from this that the scale 4441441 is the most distinct scale in terms of our features. 3 clusters give the second best solution, consisting of 4441441, scale 1 (4333333) and the remainder, with average silhouette value 0.9857. Following this, the other 5 well-formed scales split from the remainder group as a cluster (for an average silhouette width of 0.9806), followed by scales 50 and 32 (for an average silhouette value of 0.9729) followed by scale 11 (4342432) and its inverse, scale 13 (4342342) the pairwise well-formed (PWF) JI major scale (for an average silhouette width of 0.9606). The average silhouette width decreases incrementally for each larger number of new clusters until 12 clusters, in which the decrement from 11 clusters is substantially larger (0.9018 to 0.7646).

A principal component analysis is run in order to reduce the dimensionality of the space such that we may visualize the clustering solution. The following diagrams show rotations of a plot of the clustering in the first three principal components (which account for 22%, 18% and 10% of the variance respectively). For interpretability, the representation of the 13 features in the principal components are plotted as vectors with labels at 15 standard deviations from the origin, though PWF is mostly hidden (you can kind of see it in the maroon cluster, which comprises PWF scales). 11 clusters seems quite appropriate looking at the clustering, and 11 scales is already pushing towards, or possibly through the limit on how many scales we can test in an experiment. Accordingly we take 11 clusters to be a stopping point. For supplementary material, including an interactive 3D PCA plot of the clustering, data for all 7752 scales, and sound files for the exemplar scales, follow this link: https://en.xen.wiki/w/User:Gareth.hearne/Analysis22-7

3.3   Exemplar Scales

Table 1 displays the exemplar scales in hexadecimal, along with their scale ID, so they can be located in the cluster diagram. They are ordered such that the first n scales are the exemplars for the best n-cluster solution, and the size of each new cluster, and the average silouette value for each associated successive clustering is also shown.

Tables 2 and 3 display the values of the 13 features and their z-scores for these scales.

Table 1. Exemplar scales associated with each successive cluster added.

Number of clusters	Added cluster	Exemplar scale ID	Exemplar scale	Cluster size	Average silhouette width
NA	magenta	4866	8113621	NA	NA
2	pink	76	4441441	1	0.9877
3	red	1	4333333	1	0.9857
4	brown	1739	6226222	5	0.9806
5	teal	50	4432432	2	0.9729
6	orange	13	4342432	2	0.9606
7	green	17	4343332	18	0.9374
8	lavender	1405	6142612	18	0.9340
9	cyan	4397	7414141	14	0.9243
10	blue	7367	B122222	34	0.9068
11	maroon	4954	8121811	40	0.9018

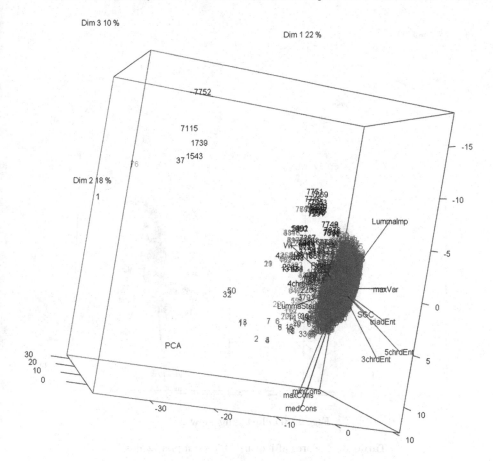

Fig. 1. 3D clustering view 1

Table 2. Values of features for exemplar scales.

Scale	SGC	triad ent	max var	WF	PWF	3chrd ent	5chrd ent	Lumma stability	Lumma imprty	max cons	min cons	med cons	4chrdlty
8113621	12	7.26	5	0	0	2.81	2.81	0	1	0.54	1.90	1.03	0
4441441	6	6.29	2	1	0	1.56	2.24	0	5/22	0.74	1.96	1.25	1
4333333	6	6.29	2	1	0	1.15	2.13	8/11	0	0.95	3.23	1.83	3/7
6226222	6	6.23	2	1	0	1.56	2.24	0	1	0.80	1.07	0.81	0
4432432	11	7.12	4	0	0	1.95	2.52	2/11	2/11	1.04	3.23	1.83	5/7
4342432	11	7.04	3	0	1	2.24	2.81	9/22	1/22	1.04	3.23	1.83	3/7
4343332	11	7.31	4	0	0	2.24	2.81	3/11	0	0.95	3.23	1.43	0
6142612	11	7.37	5	0	0	2.24	2.81	0	21/22	0.80	3.23	1.25	3/7
7414141	11	7.04	3	0	1	1.84	2.52	0	1	0.74	1.96	1.17	0
B122222	11	7.04	4	0	0	1.66	2.52	0	1	0.39	1.79	0.86	0
8121811	12	6.99	3	0	1	2.24	2.81	0	1	0.54	1.90	1.03	0

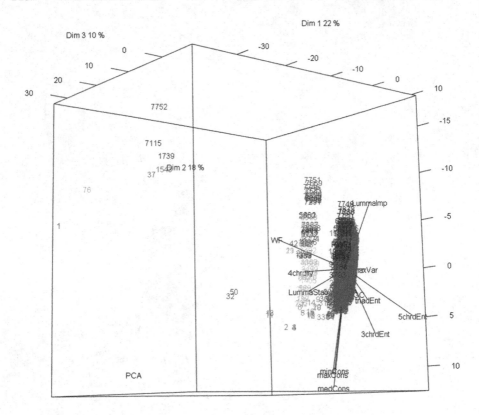

Fig. 2. 3D clustering view 2

Table 3. Z-scores of features for exemplar scales.

Scale	SGC	triad ent	max var	WF	PWF	3chrd ent	5chrd ent	Lumma stability	Lumma imprty	max cons	min cons	med cons	4chrd -lty
8113621	−0.13	−0.79	−0.71	−0.03	−0.09	0.68	0.08	−0.07	0.40	0.17	−0.13	−0.11	−0.05
4441441	−4.00	−6.09	−4.15	33.26	−0.09	−5.44	−19.31	−0.07	−3.69	0.72	−0.05	0.72	36.31
4333333	−4.00	−6.09	−4.15	33.26	−0.09	−7.43	−22.97	30.40	−4.90	1.29	1.71	2.92	15.53
6226222	−4.00	−6.40	−4.15	33.26	−0.09	−5.44	−19.31	−0.07	0.40	0.88	−1.29	−0.94	−0.05
4432432	−0.77	−1.54	−1.86	−0.03	−0.09	−3.51	−9.62	7.55	−3.93	1.54	1.71	2.92	25.92
4342432	−0.77	−1.97	−3.01	−0.03	11.42	−2.11	0.08	17.07	−4.66	1.54	1.71	2.92	15.53
4343332	−0.77	−0.48	−1.86	−0.03	−0.09	−2.11	0.08	15.16	−4.90	1.29	1.71	1.40	−0.05
6142612	−0.77	−0.17	−0.71	−0.03	−0.09	−2.11	0.08	−0.07	0.16	0.88	1.71	0.72	15.53
7414141	−0.77	−1.97	−3.01	−0.03	11.42	−4.04	−9.62	−0.07	0.40	0.72	−0.05	0.42	−0.05
B122222	−0.77	−1.97	−1.86	−0.03	−0.09	−4.91	−9.62	−0.07	0.40	−0.24	−0.29	−0.76	−0.05
8121811	−0.13	−2.28	−3.01	−0.03	11.42	−2.11	0.08	−0.07	0.40	0.17	−0.13	−0.11	−0.05

The scale 8113621 represents the vast majority of scales (magenta), and for which all features are valued within 1 standard deviation of the mean. The scale 4441441 (pink), the WF scale generated by the approximation of 3/2, is the most exceptional (and probably the most similar to 12-TET's diatonic scale), and the scale 4333333 (red), the maximally even scale, the second most exceptional. The scale 6226222 represents the other 5 WF scales (brown). 4432432 represents itself and its inverse 4423423 (teal), the two scales with tetrachordality of 5/7. 4342432 represents itself and its inverse 4342342 (orange), the PWF scales with tetrachordalty value 3/7. 4343332 represents the remaining scales that are relatively consonant, with Lumma stability above 0 and low Lumma impropriety (green). 6142612 represents the other scales with tetrachordality 3/7 (lavender). The remaining PWF scales are split between the clusters represented by 7414141 (cyan), and 8121811 (maroon), the first being those with pentachord entropy 2.52, and the second, 2.81, which is very close to the mean for all scales. The final exemplar scale B122222 represents the scales with pentachord entropy 2.52 that are not PWF (blue) (Figs. 1 and 2).

The clustering seems to be dominated by WF, PWF and tetrachordality, the variables for which the few possible values other than 0 are very rare. This is probably because extreme values of these features can cause scales to "stand out" more overall than extreme values of other features.

We note that scales 1, 13, 50 and 76 can be thought of as 22-TET's approximations of 4 different JI representations of the diatonic scale. We'll begin with scale 13, 4342432, which, in its mode 4324342, is 22-TET's approximation of the JI major scale, 9/8 5/4 4/3 3/2 5/3 15/8 2/1, which is PWF. Scale 50 is very similar. In its mode 4324432 its 22-TET's approximation of an alternative JI major scale, 9/8 5/4 4/3 3/2 27/16 15/8 2/1. This scale is not PWF, but it has tetrachordality 5/7, rather than 3/7. If we take its steps to be of 22 (unequal) śruti of early Indian music, rather than of degrees of 22-TET, these two scales are (modes of) the two basic scales of early Indian music, *Ma grāma* and *Sa grāma*, respectively [10,14,15]. A third scale, '*Ga grāma*', though less frequently discussed, also existed. Though the tuning is quoted differently across sources, Daniélou [14] suggests that it is 3334333, which in 22-TET is scale 1, 22-tET's approximation of the PWF JI dorian scale 10/9 6/5 4/3 3/2 5/3 9/5 2/1.

Finally, scale 76 in its mode 4414441 we already know is 22-TET's approximation of the Pythaogrean diatonic scale 9/8 81/64 4/3 3/2 27/16 243/128 2/1. It can also be though of as approximating the scale 9/8 9/7 4/3 3/2 27/16 27/14 2/1, in a similar way to how in 12-TET the scale 2212221 approximates both Pythaogrean and JI major scales.

The last two scales (4414441 and 4333333), the most distinct in 22-TET, are probably the most popular among musicians who use 22-TET, referred to as 'Superpyth [7]' and 'Porcupine [7]' respectively. This analysis suggests we should not be surprised by this.

References

1. Amiot, E.: David Lewin and maximally even sets. J. Math. Music 1(3), 157–172 (2007)
2. Amiot, E.: Discrete Fourier transform and Bach's good temperament. Music Theory Online 15(2), (2009). http://www.mtosmt.org/issues/mto.09.15.2/mto.09.15.2.amiot.html. Accessed 10 Jan 2019

3. Balzano, G.J.: The pitch set as a level of description for studying musical pitch perception. In: Clynes, M. (ed.) Music, Mind, and Brain, pp. 321–351. Springer, Boston (1982). https://doi.org/10.1007/978-1-4684-8917-0_17
4. Carey, N.: On coherence and sameness, and the evaluation of scale candidacy claims. J. Music Theory 46(1/2), 1–56 (2002)
5. Carey, N.: Coherence and sameness in well-formed and pairwise well-formed scales. J. Math. Music 1(2), 79–98 (2007)
6. Carey, N., Clampitt, D.: Aspects of well-formed scales. Music Theory Spectr. 11(2), 187–206 (1989)
7. Clampitt, D.: Mathematical and musical properties of pairwise well-formed scales. In: Klouche, T., Noll, T. (eds.) MCM 2007. CCIS, vol. 37, pp. 464–468. Springer, Heidelberg (2009). https://doi.org/10.1007/978-3-642-04579-0_46
8. Clampitt, D.L.: Pairwise Well-formed Scales: Structural and Transformational Properties (1998)
9. Clough, J., Douthett, J.: Maximally even sets. J. Music Theory 35(1/2), 93–173 (1991)
10. Clough, J., Douthett, J., Ramanathan, N., Rowell, L.: Early indian heptatonic scales and recent diatonic theory. Music Theory Spectr. 15(1), 36–58 (1993)
11. Clough, J., Engebretsen, N., Kochavi, J.: Scales, sets, and interval cycles: a taxonomy. Music Theory Spectr. 21(1), 74–104 (1999)
12. Clough, J., Myerson, G.: Variety and multiplicity in diatonic systems. J. Music Theory 29(2), 249–270 (1985)
13. Op de Coul, M.: Scala. http://www.huygens-fokker.org/scala/
14. Daniélou, A.: Music and the Power of Sound: The Influence of Tuning and Interval on Consciousness. Inner Traditions/Bear, Rochester (1995)
15. Erlich, P.: Tuning, tonality, and twenty-two-tone temperament. Xenharmonikon 17, 12–40 (1998)
16. Erlich, P.: Private communication (2017)
17. Milne, A.J., Dean, R.T.: Computational creation and morphing of multilevel rhythms by control of evenness. Comput. Music J. 40(1), 35–53 (2016)
18. Rothenberg, D.: A mathematical model for perception applied to the perception of pitch. In: Storer, T., Winter, D. (eds.) Formal Aspects of Cognitive Processes. LNCS, vol. 22, pp. 126–141. Springer, Heidelberg (1975). https://doi.org/10.1007/3-540-07016-8_8
19. Rothenberg, D.: A model for pattern perception with musical applications part II: the information content of pitch structures. Math. Syst. Theory 11(1), 353–372 (1977)
20. Rousseeuw, P.J.: Silhouettes: a graphical aid to the interpretation and validation of cluster analysis. J. comput. Appl. Math. 20, 53–65 (1987)
21. Wilson, E.: Letter to John Chalmers petertaining to Moments of Symmetry/Tanabe Cycle (1975). http://www.anphoria.com/meruone.pdf
22. Wilson, E.: On the development of intonational systems by extended linear mapping. Xenharmonikon 3 (1975). http://www.anaphoria.com/xen3b.pdf. Accessed 10 Jan 2019

Filtration of Pitch-Class Sets Complexes

Louis Bigo[1]($\boxtimes$)(iD) and Moreno Andreatta[2](iD)

[1] CRIStAL, UMR 9189, CNRS, Université de Lille,
Lille, France
louis.bigo@univ-lille.fr
[2] IRCAM/CNRS/Sorbonne Université, IRMA-GREAM, Université de Strasbourg,
Strasbourg, France
Moreno.Andreatta@ircam.fr, andreatta@math.unistra.fr

Abstract. A pitch-class set complex is a multidimensional object that spatially represents a collection of pitch-class sets and the intersections between them. If we consider the pitch classes within short time slices a piece can be divided into, we can evaluate for how long some combinations of pitch-classes sound simultaneously and then filter the piece according to the most relevant ones. This filtration process is performed by considering the superlevel sets of the function that computes the cumulative duration of pitch-class sets during the piece. Experiments show that musical sequences in the same style can exhibit similar subcomplexes in the filtration of their pitch-class set complexes. Filtered pitch-class set complexes also provide original informations on the use of the tonality and on the notion of centricity within a piece.

Keywords: Pitch-class sets · Harmonic similarity ·
Simplicial complexes · Pitch-class set complexes · Filtration ·
Persistent homology

1 Introduction

Pitch-class set theory, as a part of music set theory introduced by A. Forte [11], is largely used in musical analysis via a number of approaches. While mostly used for the study of atonal music, pitch-class set theory provides efficient tools for systematic study of any kind of music that can be represented with collections of pitch-classes. We propose in this paper a method to organize pitch-class sets occurring over a musical piece. Organizations resulting from different pieces can be compared to evaluate harmonic similarity and perform stylistic classification.

Harmonic similarity in symbolic musical data has been studied with various approaches including compression methods [1] and geometrical distances [8]. The idea of reducing a musical sequence by keeping only the structurally more important elements is a fundamental principle in Schenkerian analysis. Automatizing Schenkerian analysis however raises problems of multiple outputs and high computation times [15]. Rather, the reduction method proposed here is systematic and does not face any complexity issue.

M. Montiel et al. (Eds.): MCM 2019, LNAI 11502, pp. 213–226, 2019.
https://doi.org/10.1007/978-3-030-21392-3_17

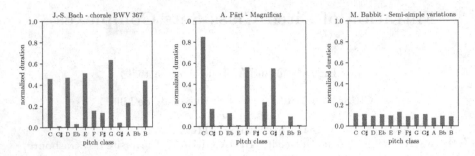

Fig. 1. Pitch-Class distributions computed on different pieces.

In this work, pitch-class sets represent groups of notes that sound simultaneously.[1] A musical piece is reduced to a sequence of successive *slices*, each slice being labelled by a pitch-class set. The *cumulative duration* of a pitch-class set over a musical piece is computed by summing the durations of the slices labelled by this pitch-class set. This value gives an indication of the importance of the pitch-class set over the whole piece. We use it as a *filtration function* to keep only predominant pitch-class sets.

Experiments show that two collections of predominant pitch-class sets, computed from distinct musical pieces, can be equivalent up to transposition. This equivalence indicates a similarity regarding the relative importance of pitch-classes and pitch-class sets in the two pieces and more generally regarding the way tonality is implemented in these pieces.

1.1 Pitch-Class Distributions and Centricity

Pitch-class distributions enable to compare the cumulative duration of the 12 pitch-classes over a musical sequence. These distributions are computed by counting the number of occurrences of each pitch-class, generally weighted by their duration. Figure 1 displays pitch-class distributions of three musical pieces and illustrates different composition strategies in terms of pitch-class use: a tonal piece by J.-S. Bach, a tonal piece in the minimalist style by A. Pärt, and an atonal piece by M. Babbitt. Pitch-class cumulative durations are normalized by the duration of the piece.

Pitch-class distributions are used in a wide variety of applications, both in symbolic and audio music information retrieval. They are particularly used for chord recognition [14] and key detection, for which they can be compared to pre-defined pitch-class profiles [20].

Pitch-class distributions also constitute an efficient tool for studying centricity in a musical sequence. As discussed by D. Tymoczko [21], *centricity* relates to the idea that "a particular note is felt to be more prominent, important, or stable than the others." In this work, we extend the notion of centricity to

---

[1] Pitch-class sets in music set theory sometimes represent notes occurring close to each other but not necessarily simultaneously.

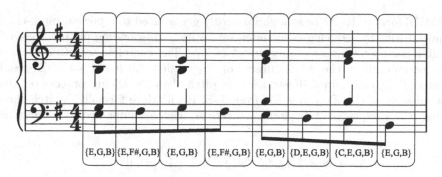

Fig. 2. Pitch-class set slicing of the first measure of chorale BWV 259 from J.-S. Bach. In this example, all slices have the duration of a eighth note.

sets of simultaneous pitch-classes. As the number of pitch-class sets appearing along a musical sequence can be large, we introduce the notion of *filtration* that enables to keep only the most relevant collections of pitch-class sets, based on their cumulative duration along the sequence. We use spatial representations of pitch-class sets to provide an intuitive understanding of these concepts.

1.2 Spatial Representations

Musical objects and their relations are frequently represented as spatial structures that give intuitive interpretations of music-theoretical principles. The (generalized) *Tonnetz* [7,12,22] and voice-leading spaces [21] are examples of such representations and have been used in a wide variety of applications in music theory, analysis, and composition.

Geometrical simplicial complexes have been used to represent musical objects, in particular pitch-class sets [5,6,18] and largely applied to stylistic and transformational analysis [4].

Recent studies into musical simplicial complexes and persistent homology [3,13] and the increasing field of *Topological Data Analysis* have opened new perspectives for these approaches.

2 Cumulative Duration of Pitch-Class Sets

2.1 Slicing Musical Sequences

We represent musical sequences as ordered collections of consecutive *pitch slices*, each slice having a proper duration. Every time a new pitch starts or stops being played, the current slice ends and a new one begins. The process applies systematically for every note encountered within the score, including embellishments. This segmentation method, widely used in computational musicology, also goes under the name of pitch simultaneities or *salami slicing* [23]. It can be applied to any musical sequence of any genre as long as the sequence can be represented in the MIDI format. It can be straightforwardly generalized to represent pitch-class simultaneities by reducing every pitch set to its corresponding pitch-class set.[2] A pitch-class set consists of any subset of $\mathbb{Z}_{12}$. The complete set of pitch-class sets corresponds to the set of subsets of $\mathbb{Z}_{12}$, called the *power set* of $\mathbb{Z}_{12}$ and notated $\mathcal{P}(\mathbb{Z}_{12})$. Figure 2 illustrates this pitch-class set slicing process on the first measure of chorale BWV 259 from J.-S. Bach. More formally, a pitch-class slicing $\mathcal{S}$ is a sequence of N pitch-class sets A_i each accompanied by a duration d_i:

$$\mathcal{S} = [(A_0, d_0), (A_1, d_1), ..., (A_N, d_N)]$$

where the durations d_i sum up to the duration D of the whole musical sequence.

2.2   Cumulative Duration

Let $\mathcal{S}$ be a pitch-class slicing and X any arbitrary pitch-class set. The *cumulative duration* $\mathcal{D}_\mathcal{S}(X)$ corresponds to the sum of the durations of the slices of $\mathcal{S}$ whose pitch-class set includes X, normalized by the length of the entire pitch-class slicing D:

$$\mathcal{D}_\mathcal{S}(X) = [\sum_{\{(A_i, d_i) \in \mathcal{S} | X \subseteq A_i\}} d_i]/D$$

The value $\mathcal{D}_\mathcal{S}(X)$ therefore indicates how much the pitch-class set X appears in total along $\mathcal{S}$ and ranges between 0 (if the pitch-class set X is absent from the sequence) and 1 (if the pitch-class set X is played in each slice). The inclusion between pitch-class sets induces an ordering on their cumulative duration:

$$\forall(X_1, X_2), X_1 \subseteq X_2 \Rightarrow \mathcal{D}_\mathcal{S}(X_2) \leq \mathcal{D}_\mathcal{S}(X_1)$$

Figure 3 displays the 10 pitch-class sets having the highest cumulative durations within the 50 first slices of three musical excerpts. In order to facilitate the comparison between the examples, three sequences in the same key (G major) have been selected.

2.3   Ranking Pitch-Class Sets

We call α_i^n the pitch-class set of size n (or n-pitch-class set) having the i-th highest cumulative duration within a given musical sequence. For example, α_1^1 is the most prevalent pitch-class and α_2^3 is the second most prevalent 3-pitch-class set in the sequence. Therefore, the sequence $\alpha_1^n, \alpha_2^n, \ldots, \alpha_m^n$ gathers all n-pitch-class sets appearing in the sequence, sorted by decreasing cumulative duration, meaning that for every $i \in [0, m-1]$, we have $\mathcal{D}_\mathcal{S}(\alpha_i^n) \geq \mathcal{D}_\mathcal{S}(\alpha_{i+1}^n)$.

---

[2] In this work we restrain to twelve tone equal temperament in which pitch-classes are represented by integers modulo 12.

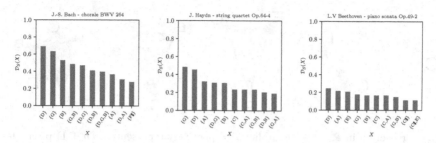

Fig. 3. 10 pitch-class sets having highest cumulative duration over the 50 first slices of 3 musical excerpts. The three excerpts are in the key of G Major.

3 Pitch-Class Set Complexes

3.1 Representing Pitch-Class Sets

We use labelled geometric simplices to represent pitch-class sets and labelled geometric simplicial complexes to represent collections of pitch-class sets. This approach goes back to Guerino Mazzola's Mathematical Music Theory [17,18] which has been enriched recently to study aspects of *generalized Tonnetze* [5,6].

A simplex of dimension n, or n-simplex, represents a pitch-class set of size $n + 1$. In particular:

- a single pitch-class is represented by a 0-simplex (a vertex),
- a 2-pitch-class set is represented by a 1-simplex (an edge),
- a 3-pitch-class set is represented by a 2-simplex (a triangle),
- a 4-pitch-class set is represented by a 3-simplex (a tetrahedron),
- a 5-pitch-class set is represented by a 4-simplex (a pentatope)

We say that a simplex is *labelled* by a pitch-class set and we denote by $\lambda(\sigma)$ the pitch-class set labelling the simplex σ. As in this work a simplex is systematically labelled by a unique pitch-class set, we will simplify the notation $\mathcal{D}_S(\lambda(\sigma))$ by writing $\mathcal{D}_S(\sigma)$ to designate the cumulative duration of the pitch-class set labelling the simplex σ.

The *faces* of a n-simplex σ are the simplices incident to σ whose dimension is lower than n. Simplices verify the *closure condition* which requires that a n-simplex is systematically bounded by $n + 1$ faces of dimension $n - 1$, and recursively. For instance, a 2-simplex (a triangle) is bounded by three 1-simplices (edges) which are each bounded by two 0-simplices (vertices). The faces of a simplex σ represent subsets of the pitch-class set labelling σ. The closure condition results in the systematic representation of every subsets of pitch-classes included in a pitch-class set, which also fits with a perceptual and cognitive assumption. In fact, one could argue that during the listening process, a listener is hearing all possible subsets of notes included in a played chord.

Figure 4 displays simplices representing pitch-class sets of various size. The goal of these representations of pitch-class sets is to highlight inclusions between

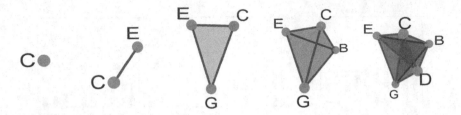

Fig. 4. Projection in $\mathbb{R}^3$ of 5 n-simplices, respectively representing $(n+1)$-pitch-class sets, with $n = 0, 1, 2, 3$ and 4.

subsets via incidence relationships between simplices. The coordinates of the vertices in the figure do not matter and have been arbitrarily chosen to facilitate the visualization.

3.2   Representing Collections of Pitch-Class Sets

A pitch-class set slicing $\mathcal{S}$ can be represented by a *pcs-complex* $\mathcal{K}_\mathcal{S}$ which is obtained by:

1. representing every pitch-class set included in $\mathcal{S}$ by a simplex,
2. merging simplex faces that represent the same pitch-class set.

The merging step ensures that a given pitch-class set can label one simplex at most [5]. Figure 5 illustrates two pcs-complexes. The right pcs-complex gathers the pitch-class sets included in the pc-slicing of Fig. 2. It consists in 3 3-simplices (tetrahedra) that share a common 2-simplex (a triangular face) labelled by the pitch-class set $\{E, G, B\}$ (in dark gray in the figure).

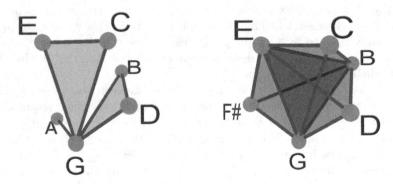

Fig. 5. On the left, a pcs-complex representing the collection of pitch-class sets $\{(C,E,G), (D,G,B), (G,A)\}$. On the right, the pcs-complex representing the collection of pitch-class sets included in the slicing illustrated on Fig. 2.

3.3   Filtration of Pcs-Complexes

In this section, we introduce the idea of applying a *filtration* on a pcs-complex in order to keep only pitch-class sets that sound the most frequently over a musical piece. This process can be formalized by *filtration functions*.

A *filtration function* is a function $f : \mathcal{K} \to \mathbb{R}$, that associates a real number to any simplex of a simplicial complex $\mathcal{K}$ and that is non-increasing[3] on increasing sequences of faces. This means that $f(\sigma_1) \geq f(\sigma_2)$ whenever σ_1 is a face of σ_2 in $\mathcal{K}$.

Given a filtration function f and a constant value $c \in \mathbb{R}$, we define the *superlevel complex* $\mathcal{L}_c^+(f)$ as the sub-complex of $\mathcal{K}$ that includes simplices for which f attributes a value superior or equal to c:

$$\mathcal{L}_c^+(f) = \{\sigma \in \mathcal{K} \mid f(\sigma) \geq c\}$$

The monotonicity of f on increasing sequences of faces ensures that any superlevel complex will respect the closure condition on its simplices. The set of superlevel complexes produced by a filtration function can be ordered as a sequence of nested complexes, that starts with the empty complex and ends with the complete complex $\mathcal{K}$:

$$\emptyset = \mathcal{K}_0 \subseteq \mathcal{K}_1 \subseteq \cdots \subseteq \mathcal{K}_n = \mathcal{K}$$

We may think of a filtration process as a description of how to construct $\mathcal{K}$ by adding chunks at a time [9].[4] As the simplices forming pcs-complexes are labelled by pitch-class sets, any function that systematically attributes a real value to a pitch-class set and that is non-increasing on sequences of increasingly inclusive pitch-class sets, can potentially be used as a filtration function on a pcs-complex. In Sect. 3.4 we will use the cumulative duration of pitch-class sets as a filtration function on the pcs-complex representing the slicing of a musical sequence.

3.4   A Filtration Based on Cumulative Durations

When applied to pitch-class sets that label a pcs-complex, cumulative duration is a non increasing function on increasing sequences of faces. It can therefore be used as a filtration function on pcs-complexes.

---

[3] Note that filtration functions can equally be defined as *non-decreasing* on increasing sequences of faces as long as f is monotonic. In this paper we define filtration functions as non-increasing since this enables a more intuitive comprehension of the notion of filtering pitch-class sets over a musical piece depending on their cumulative duration as presented in Sect. 4.

[4] This may appear counter-intuitive as the notion of filtration is usually seen as a process that consists in removing elements as opposed to adding them. We will nevertheless keep this property to stick with the standard notation used in simplicial complex filtration [9].

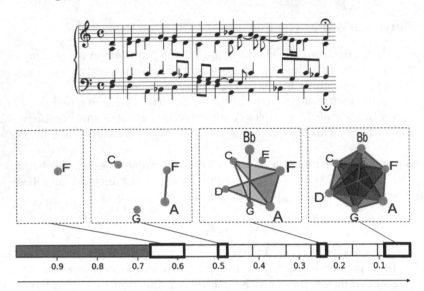

Fig. 6. The four superlevel complexes $\mathcal{L}_{0.66}^+$, $\mathcal{L}_{0.5}^+$, $\mathcal{L}_{0.25}^+$, and $\mathcal{L}_0^+$, induced by the filtration of the pcs-complex representation of the first phrase of J.-S. Bach chorale BWV 254. The bottom arrow represents the evolution of the filtration.

As the cumulative duration $\mathcal{D}_S$ is the only filtration function considered in this work, we take the liberty to simplify the superlevel complex notation from $\mathcal{L}_c^+(\mathcal{D}_S)$ to $\mathcal{L}_c^+$:

$$\mathcal{L}_c^+ = \{\sigma \in \mathcal{K} \,|\, \mathcal{D}_S(\sigma) \geq c\}$$

Over the filtration of a pcs-complex based on cumulative duration, the first non-empty nested sub-complex $\mathcal{K}_1$ generally consists of one single 0-simplex (a vertex) labelled by α_1^1 which is the most prevalent pitch-class.[5] $\mathcal{K}_2$ generally consists of the 0-simplex of $\mathcal{K}_1$ plus an additional 0-simplex labelled by the second most prevalent pitch-class α_2^1. $\mathcal{K}_3$ will generally either add a third 0-simplex labelled by the third most prevalent pitch-class α_3^1, or a 1-simplex (edge) labelled by the most prevalent 2-pitch-class set α_1^2 which necessarily is $\{\alpha_1^1, \alpha_2^1\}$.

Figure 6 illustrates four superlevel complexes resulting from the filtration of the pcs-complex representing the first phrase of the chorale BWV 254 by J.-S. Bach. The horizontal bar represents the sequence of nested complexes resulting from the filtration. The filtration process goes from left to right. The first complex of the sequence is the empty complex $\mathcal{K}_0$ which appears in the leftmost region of the bar (gray). When the filtration level passes below 0.66, a 0-simplex ($\mathcal{K}_1$) labelled by the most prevalent pitch-class (F) appears. At the end of the

---

[5] It can still happen, especially in short musical sequences, that the highest cumulative duration is equally attributed to two or more pitch classes. $\mathcal{K}_1$ therefore corresponds to a n-simplex with $n > 0$.

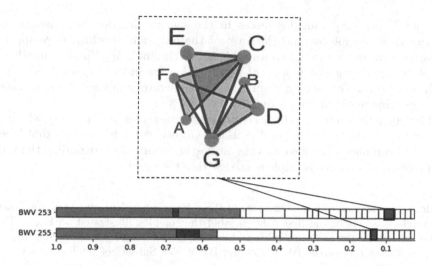

Fig. 7. Equivalence up to transposition of two superlevel complexes in the filtration of J.-S. Bach's chorales BWV 253 and BWV 255.

filtration (right extremity of the bar) the complete collection of pitch-class sets that sound during this extract have appeared within the complex.

Filtering pitch-class sets that occur predominantly across a musical sequence provides a condensed representation of the pitch-class set material used in the sequence. In Sect. 4, we try to identify and interpret similarities between super-level complexes resulting from the filtration of different musical pieces.

4   Analyzing Filtrations

4.1   Transpositionally Equivalent Superlevel Complexes

Figure 7 illustrates a superlevel complex that appears during the course of the filtration of both chorales BWV 253 and BWV 255. For the sake of clarity, the pcs-complex in the top of the figure has been transposed into a form that only exhibits pitch-class sets in the key of C major although the corresponding superlevel complexes in the filtration of BWV 253 and BWV 255 respectively gather pitch-class sets in the keys of A major and G major (see Table 1).

This common trait in the filtration of the two pcs-complexes can be interpreted in the following way: the collection of all pitch-class sets that are heard more than 10% of the time in the chorale BWV 253 is equivalent (up to a trans-position) to the collection of all pitch-class sets that are heard more than 14% of the time in the chorale BWV 255.

Intuitively, a similar superlevel complex illustrates the fact that a collection of pitch-class sets, that all occur predominantly in one sequence, is equivalent up to transposition to a collection of pitch-class sets that all occur predominantly in one other sequence. This property that shows a similarity between both harmonic contents, is not surprising for pieces in the same style. However, the size of the superlevel complexes and the level of the filtration at which they appear enable to measure in an original way this harmonic similarity. Similar superlevel complexes appearing at low level of the filtration are indeed especially striking as they demonstrate a strong similarity in the hierarchy linking the pitch-class sets appearing along the two sequences.

The pitch-class sets in Table 1 confirm a strong presence of tonality which is characteristic of the repertory of J.-S. Bach. Observing pitch-class sets that label superlevel complexes can also provide interesting information regarding the way the principle of tonality is implemented within the piece.

Table 1. A collection of pitch-class sets in three forms equivalent up to transposition. The pitch-class sets in the first column label the complex illustrated on Fig. 7. The pitch-class sets in the next two columns label superlevel complexes appearing respectively in filtration of pieces BWV 253 and BWV 255. Subsets of pitch-class sets are omitted to lighten notations.

	BWV 253 (T_9)	BWV 255 (T_7)
$\{0, 4, 7\}$	$\{1, 4, 9\}$	$\{2, 7, 11\}$
$\{0, 5, 9\}$	$\{2, 6, 9\}$	$\{0, 4, 7\}$
$\{2, 7, 11\}$	$\{4, 8, 11\}$	$\{2, 6, 9\}$
$\{5, 7\}$	$\{2, 4\}$	$\{0, 2\}$
$\{2, 5\}$	$\{2, 11\}$	$\{0, 9\}$

Figure 8 illustrates the appearance of almost the same complex than the one in Fig. 7, $\{\{C, E, G\}, \{C, F, A\}, \{D, F, G, B\}\}$, in a low level of filtration of three movements of quartets by J. Haydn. The corresponding collection of pitch-class sets consists of three essential degrees of a major tonality (I, IV and V^7) and provides a sign of a strong tonal context within these pieces. Next appearing simplices in the filtration are (after the same transposition) $\{\{D, A\}, \{D, F, A\}\}$ for Haydn Op. 33 No. 3-iii, $\{\{G, A\}, \{C, G, A\}\}$ for Haydn Op. 17 No. 1-i and $\{\{G, A\}, \{C, G, A\}, \{C, B\}, \{C, G, B\}\}$ for Haydn Op. 17 No. 6-i.

This experiment shows that looking at the superlevel complexes of the filtration of a musical piece can provide elements, in addition with pitch-class sets distributions, to study the prevalence of some underlying tonality.

4.2   Discussion on Filtration Features

Measuring the similarity between two filtrations is not straightforward and can be performed in different ways. We propose some filtration features that can be used as a distance measure to compare musical pieces.

The filtration of a pcs-complex $\mathcal{K}_S$ can first be described by some features unrelated to the values of its pitch-class sets:

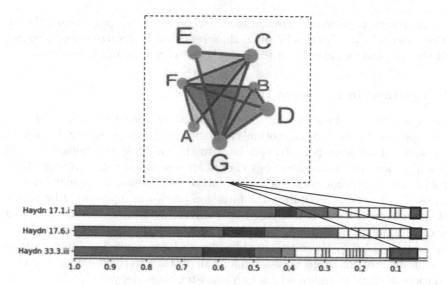

Fig. 8. Equivalence up to transposition of three superlevel complexes in the filtration of three movements of Haydn quartets.

- the level from which the filtration provides a non-empty complex. This level corresponds to the cumulative duration of the most prevalent pitch-class set ($\mathcal{D}_\mathcal{S}(\alpha_1^1)$), which is likely to be a single pitch-class.
- the maximum level at which the filtration of $\mathcal{K}_\mathcal{S}$ includes a 2-simplex which represents a minor or major triad. This feature indicates how present is the most frequent triad.

A more extensive study could focus on step sizes between successive levels during a filtration process. For example, the difference of levels between the two first non-empty complexes gives an idea of how much more prevalent is the most prevalent pitch-class set over the remaining pitch-class sets. This measure closely relies to the notion of *centricity* which indicates how much a selected pitch-class (more generally a pitch-class set) is prevalent over all the others. Filtration of pcs-complexes therefore provides a collection of original tools to study centricity in musical sequences.

4.3   Persistence of Musical Properties

Experiments described in Sect. 4.1 could be extended to track music similarity between two musical sequences for example by measuring the lowest filtration level exhibiting two superlevel complexes that are equivalent up to transposition.

The way tonality is implemented in a musical piece could also be studied by measuring the lowest level at which the filtration of its pcs-complex includes pitch-class sets that all belong to one usual tonality.

Large intervals between filtration levels, wherever they occur during the filtration, highlight a collection of pitch-class sets that is strongly more frequent than the rest and can also reach to original approaches for music analysis.

4.4 Relations to Persistent Homology

Looking at the "life duration" of a musical property during the course of a filtration process relates to the notion of "persistence" in persistent homology. In persistent homology, persistence relates to the life-cycle of a homology class over a filtration [10]. These homology classes are associated with topological features of the filtered complex, such as connected components, circular holes or cavities. Their persistence during the filtration process is represented by *persistent diagrams* which can be compared by using the *bottleneck distance*. Different experiments following this approach have proven to be promising for musical classification [2,3,13]. However, the difficulty to bring a musical interpretation of the life cycle of homotopy classes remains an obstacle to the full understanding of music-analytical techniques based on persistent homology.

Extending analysis approaches inspired by persistent homology would undoubtedly benefit from a number of tools and methods that have been elaborated in this field of mathematics and, more specifically, in the community of Topological Data Analysis (TDA).

5 Code Implementation and Visualization

The code developed for this research has been written in Python3 and is freely available online.[6] 3D representations of pcs-complexes have been produced with a dedicated tool accessible through any internet browser.[7] Musical sequences are uploaded in this tool as MIDI files. The browser displays a 3D representation of the pcs-complex gathering every set of pitch classes that happen to sound simultaneously at some point of the sequence. The analysis can be reduced to any time window within the sequence thanks to the double horizontal cursor. A vertical cursor enables the user to select a filtration level that determines the displayed simplices. The values taken by the cursor run from 0 to 1 to stick with the definition of the normalized cumulative duration of pitch-class sets.

6 Conclusion

This work presents some experiments on filtration of pcs-complexes as a structural way to retrieve music information. We suggested some preliminary features to describe and compare filtrations. Future works include measuring the ability of these features to reveal musical similarities between different pieces, and more generally to provide some insights on the musical style of the represented piece.

---

[6] https://gitlab.com/lbigo/pitchsalami.

[7] http://lbigo.gitlab.io/ChordComplexViz.

Future works also include a more systematic and in-depth study of the persistence of transposition relation between two filtered complexes, as the persistence of other musical relations such as inversion, diatonic transposition and, more generally, transformational operators.

Filtrations of pcs-complexes could also benefit from being reduced to selected temporal windows within a musical piece in order to exhibit changes of strategies in the use of pitch-class sets during the piece. Such approaches could undoubtedly benefit from multi-timescale visualization techniques that have been elaborated for various tasks including key detection [19] or set-class analysis [16].

Future experiments will also include the possibility to filter a pcs-complex reduced to a particular type of pitch-class set. For example, keeping only major and minor triads (and their subsets of pitch-classes) in a pitch-class slicing might more easily produce common superlevel complexes over the filtration of tonal musical sequences.

Acknowledgments. We would like to thank friends and colleagues for fruitful discussions and careful proofreading including Mattia Bergomi, Paul Ladyman, members of the spatial computing project and the Algomus team. We also thank Antoine Lafrance for his contribution on the online visualization application.

References

1. Ahonen, T.E., Lemström, K., Linkola, S.: Compression-based similarity measures in symbolic, polyphonic music. In: ISMIR, pp. 91–96 (2011)
2. Bergomi, M.G., Baratè, A., Di Fabio, B.: Towards a topological fingerprint of music. In: Bac, A., Mari, J.-L. (eds.) CTIC 2016. LNCS, vol. 9667, pp. 88–100. Springer, Cham (2016). https://doi.org/10.1007/978-3-319-39441-1_9
3. Bergomi, M.G.: Dynamical and topological tools for (modern) music analysis. Ph.D. thesis, Université Pierre et Marie Curie-Paris VI (2015)
4. Bigo, L., Andreatta, M.: Topological Structures in Computer-Aided Music Analysis. Computational Music Analysis, pp. 57–80. Springer, Cham (2016). https://doi.org/10.1007/978-3-319-25931-4_3
5. Bigo, L., Andreatta, M., Giavitto, J.-L., Michel, O., Spicher, A.: Computation and visualization of musical structures in chord-based simplicial complexes. In: Yust, J., Wild, J., Burgoyne, J.A. (eds.) MCM 2013. LNCS (LNAI), vol. 7937, pp. 38–51. Springer, Heidelberg (2013). https://doi.org/10.1007/978-3-642-39357-0_3
6. Catanzaro, M.J.: Generalized tonnetze. J. Math. Music **5**(2), 117–139 (2011)
7. Cohn, R.: Neo-riemannian operations, parsimonious trichords, and their "tonnetz" representations. J. Music Theor. **41**(1), 1–66 (1997)
8. De Haas, W.B., Wiering, F., Veltkamp, R.C.: A geometrical distance measure for determining the similarity of musical harmony. Int. J. Multimedia Inf. Retrieval **2**(3), 189–202 (2013)
9. Edelsbrunner, H.: Geometry and Topology for Mesh Generation, vol. 7. Cambridge University Press, Cambridge (2001)
10. Edelsbrunner, H., Harer, J.: Computational Topology: An Introduction. American Mathematical Society (2010)
11. Forte, A.: The Structure of Atonal Music, vol. 304. Yale University Press, New Haven (1973)

12. Gollin, E.: Some aspects of three-dimensional "tonnetze". J. Music Theor. **1**, 195–206 (1998)
13. Lascabettes, P.: Homologie Persistante Appliquée à le reconnaissance de genres musicaux. Master's thesis, École Normale Supérieure Paris-Saclay/Irma (2018)
14. Lee, K.: Automatic chord recognition from audio using enhanced pitch class profile. In: ICMC (2006)
15. Marsden, A.: Schenkerian analysis by computer: a proof of concept. J. New Music Res. **39**(3), 269–289 (2010)
16. Martorell, A., Gómez, E.: Contextual set-class analysis. In: Meredith, D. (ed.) Computational Music Analysis, pp. 81–110. Springer, Cham (2016). https://doi.org/10.1007/978-3-319-25931-4_4
17. Mazzola, G.: Geometrie der Töne: Elemente der Mathematischen Musiktheorie. Birkhäuser (1990)
18. Mazzola, G.: The topos of music: geometric logic of concepts, theory, and performance. Birkhäuser (2012)
19. Sapp, C.S.: Harmonic visualizations of tonal music. In: ICMC, vol. 1, pp. 419–422. Citeseer (2001)
20. Temperley, D., Marvin, E.W.: Pitch-class distribution and the identification of key. Music Percept.: Interdisc. J. **25**(3), 193–212 (2008)
21. Tymoczko, D.: A Geometry of Music: Harmony and Counterpoint in the Extended Common Practice. Oxford University Press, Oxford (2010)
22. Tymoczko, D.: The generalized tonnetz. J. Music Theor. **1**, 1–52 (2012)
23. White, C.W., Quinn, I.: The yale-classical archives corpus. Empirical Musicology Rev. **11**(1), 50–58 (2016)

Computer-Based Approaches to Composition and Score Structuring

Synesthesizer: Physical Modelling and Machine Learning for a Color-Based Synthesizer in Virtual Reality

Giovanni Santini[✉]

Hong Kong Baptist University, Kowloon Tong, Hong Kong
info@giovannisantini.com
http://www.giovannisantini.com/

Abstract. The *Synesthesizer* is a software synthesizer inspired to *chromesthesia*, that kind of synesthesia that connects sounds and colors. While chromesthesia usually produces color perception in response to sound stimulation, this synthesizer does the opposite: sound is generated according to color detection. More precisely, RGB (Red Green Blue) values are detected (one pixel at a time) and used to determine the behaviour of five physical models for virtual instruments. The motivation for creating such a synthesizer arose from the will to generate a timbral continuum out of the color continuum, allowing to explore the relation between color spectrum and sound spectrum. The Synesthesizer has two additional possible applications:

- A picture can become a sort of score; graphic scores can have a different source of interpretation;
- Given its intuitiveness, it might allow even non-experts to explore the possibilities of sound synthesis.

The current version has been developed in a Virtual Reality (VR) environment.

Keywords: Synesthesia · Synthesizer · Physical modeling · Machine Learning · Virtual reality

1 Introduction and Background

Synesthesia (joined perception, from the Greek *syn*, together, and *aisthesis*, perception) is produced by the simultaneous trigger of two or more sensorial responses as the result of the stimulation of just one sense [1].

In particular, *chromestesia* (color-related perception, from the Greek *chroma*, color, and *aisthesis*) links sight to hearing, producing color in response to sound.

The application of such phenomenon to the artistic field has been realized at least since the 18th Century, with the *Color Organ* by Louis Bertrand Castel (1740) [2].

While a full review of the literature on the topic is far beyond the scope of this paper, it is worth pointing out some works, realized in the past twenty

© Springer Nature Switzerland AG 2019
M. Montiel et al. (Eds.): MCM 2019, LNAI 11502, pp. 229–235, 2019.
https://doi.org/10.1007/978-3-030-21392-3_18

years, related to the generation of sound from color detection (or from other sets of information that can be derived from images). Such applications (in fact reverting the usual sensory pathway of chromestesia), are closely related to the presented synthesizer, where the author applied a color-to-sound strategy.

The work described in [3] shows the use of a metaphoric interface (shapes and colors used as controllers for generating timbres). In this case, beyond the artistic interest, the reduced difficulty of musical production (thanks to the simplified interface) can let music-making be available to a larger set of users.

[4] shows a strategy for converting pixels and images into melodies (not simple events). Its implementation is based on a system of rules (based on a chromaticism index) essentially linking color to pitch (or set of pitches).

Color-to-sound relations have been also applied in market oriented production, e.g. [5] and [6].

In the cited cases, the idea of translation of color into pitch (and brightness or saturation into loudness) seems to be the most researched. A clearer focus on timbre can be found in other applications, like *Hue Music* [2], based on color-averaging across sub-sections of a picture. The software associates 8 different colors to 7 timbres (white is equated to silence).

2   The Synesthesizer

2.1   Color-to-Sound Mapping

The presented synthesizer is exclusively focused on timbre production. Pitch can be changed manually but is not controlled algorithmically.

A conspicuous part of the background literature implemented scientifically grounded procedures. However, even when using close relationships (e.g., color wavelength to pitch wavelength, as in [7]), the final result is dependent (to some extent) on an arbitrary mapping of values. In fact, the wavelength of the visible light, as perceived by an average individual, ranges from 380 to 750 nm (i.e., slightly less than one octave). Consequently, re-mapping colors to pitches (even reducing the pitch range to one single octave) requires some strategy that is extraneous to the direct relationship of color and light wavelengths (thus resulting, at some point, in an arbitrary decision).

In the Synesthesizer, the author decided to follow the concept of synesthesia as a cognitive process that produces different results in different subjects [8]. The user decides (arbitrarily) the connection between five physical models developed with Modalys (snare-drum, tube, gong, bowed string, plucked string, with customizable parameters) and five colors (chosen by the user). Even if the Synesthesizer provides a timbral correspondence[1] for each one of the possible colors producible with the RGB representation (16,777,216 combinations), it requires

---

[1] More specifically, a different set of values of parameters of the physical models. Depending on the RGB values, two instruments are chosen and cross-synthesized. The processe is explained more in detail in 2.5.

the user to decide only few relationships. Every other correspondence is produced by the output values of a Machine Learning (ML) algorithm (described in 2.4).

2.2   Components

In its current version, the Synesthesizer is based upon three different programs linked through OSC protocol:

- A software developed in Unity[2] by the author for color detection in VR;
- A Wekinator[3] project, mapping the three incoming RGB values to 35 output values;
- A Max/MSP patch managing five physical models developed with Modalys (Ircam tools).

2.3   The VR Color Scanning Software

The software for color analysis consists in a Virtual Room containing different pictures (customizable). It is meant to be used with an *HTC Vive* headset.

The user is asked to hold two controllers. The right one is used for triggering a *Raycaster*[4] (Fig. 1). If the line collides with one virtual object, such as a picture,

Fig. 1. A Raycaster (violet line) is sent towards the picture (H. Bosch's *De hooiwagen*). The color of the pixel intercepted by the Raycaster is used to color the panel attached to the left controller and sent through OSC to the Wekinator. (Color figure online)

---

[2] A programming framework providing a solid environment for graphic intensive applications [9].

[3] The Wekinator is a software for the application of Machine Learning in the arts field [10].

[4] A virtual straight line drawn from the controller towards infinity.

the color of the point of incidence on the surface (pixel) is extracted and used to color a virtual panel attached to the left controller (Fig. 2).

RGB values (ranging from 0 to 255) are also sent through OSC to the Wekinator project described in the next paragraph.

```
void Update()
{
    if (controller.triggerPressed)
    {
        eventsHandler = true;

        Ray ray = new Ray(controller.transform.position, controller.transform.forward);
        RaycastHit hit;
        Debug.DrawRay(controller.transform.position, controller.transform.forward, Color.green);

        if(Physics.Raycast(ray, out hit))
        {
            var rend = hit.collider.GetComponent<Renderer>();

            if (rend == null || rend.lightmapIndex > 253)
                return;

            var pixelUV = hit.lightmapCoord;
            var tex = rend.material.mainTexture as Texture2D;
            var colors = tex.GetPixelBilinear(pixelUV.x, pixelUV.y);
            var rd = objToColor.GetComponent<Renderer>();

            rd.material.color = colors;

            colorDetected = colors;
        }
    }
    else
    {
        eventsHandler = false;
    }
}
```

Fig. 2. The code of the *Update* function in the class responsible for RGB data extraction. Another class is responsible for sending those data through OSC to the Wekinator.

2.4   The Wekinator Project

The linear regression algorithm of the Wekinator has been trained on 5 different colors (each one related to one physical model in the Max patch described later).

For each of these 5 colors (i.e. a vector of three values), 35 output values (related to the 5 physical models) have been manually inserted and the model have been trained accordingly. For every other color, the output values are predicted (i.e. interpolated) by the model.

In other words, the Wekinator is used for generating continuously different values of the 35 output parameters according to color changes (each of the 16,777,216 possible RGB vectors creates a different combination of those 35 parameters).

It is to be noted that such extreme richness can be achieved through the production of a training set of just 5 colors, thanks to the Machine Learning tool.

Output values are sent to the Max/MSP patch through OSC connection.

2.5   The Sound Processing

The Max/MSP patch has two main functions:

- Running the 5 Modalys models;
- Performing cross-synthesis between "adjacent" models.

The first incoming parameter is used for deciding which instruments are play-ing. In the Max patch (see Fig. 3), all the models (except for the Tube) present a "Cross with" bar. According to the first parameter, two adjacent instruments are activated and merged through cross-synthesis. The position along the "Cross with" bar determines the balance in the mix of the two instruments and their cross-synthesis (in the picture, the mix is perfectly balanced; in case the bar would be completely blue, only the sound of the Tube would be produced: both the Snare and the cross-synthesis would be silenced).

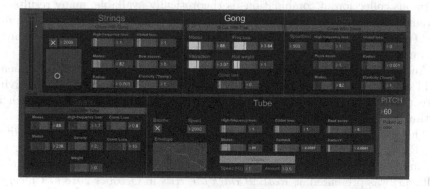

Fig. 3. The Max/MSP interface.

The other 34 parameters are used to regulate in real-time all the values of the different models. One important point of the overall process is that by changing the training set of the Wekinator the overall collection of results can be entirely changed. Such possibility is to be considered a key feature and derives from the consideration that synesthesic perception is linked to individual differences.

3   Uses, Limitations and Future Work

The project is aimed at three main results:

- Constructing an intuitive and easy-to-use interface providing a facilitated artistic experience even to non-musicians;
- Exploring the possible links between different senses (pictures can be scores);
- Creating a tool for timbral research, finalized to compositional use.

As shown before, RGB coding provides more than 16 million possibilities. In addition, results depend exclusively on how the Wekinator is trained, i.e. by changing the parametrical output values for the training, the timbral outcome can totally change as well: the use of colors can introduce an intuitive, fast-to-program way to navigate across timbral spaces.

The implementation in a VR environment responds to a series of practical reasons:

- Pictures can be easily changed and a scene can include more than one picture;
- No need to calibrate a sensor for different lighting conditions;
- The use of Raycasters allows to reach and scan even far pictures.

Among the limitations, the most impactful one is probably the impossibility to change the pitch algorithmically. As the application is strongly focused on timbre, timbral differences related to pitches are crucial.

The differentiation of timbral combinations is another limit. Even if an enormous collection of combinations is theoretically available, many results are extremely similar (and sometimes indistinguishable). Increasing the training size[5] (more than 5 colors) and/or the number of physical models might improve the variety of results.

Another limitation is the pixel-by-pixel color analysis. Future improvements could consist in the implementation of image analysis techniques[6] for deriving more complex musical textures and evolved compositional elements (such as rhythm, multilayered textures and time development).

The described tool was presented and demoed during the *First Annual AR/VR Retreat* in December 2018 in Berkeley. A previous version, not in VR and making use of a physical color sensor (with the contribution of Jonathan Rullman) was presented at *RedBull Hack the Hits* in October 2018 at Chicago's *MLab*. In both cases, no evaluation experiment was designed. A future study should be addressed to an evaluation of the Synesthesizer in terms of usability, engagement and perceived appropriateness of color-to-sound correspondences.

4   Conclusions

This paper has presented an application that translates color into timbre by using Machine Learning (through the use of Wekinator) and physical modelling for virtual instruments (by using Modalys).

The process has not been based on physical similarities between light and sound and has not made use of algorithms directly making a conversion without human intervention. The initial decision of color-to-instrument mapping is crucial, as it constitutes the training set of the Machine Learning algorithm,

---

[5] For the sake of clarity, it is worth pointing out that the model is here used only as a way to fastly produce interpolated values. Therefore, its prediction accuracy is not a main concern in this specific case.

[6] Strategies of data extraction could include spectrographic analysis, image segmentation (by grouping sets of pixels) and feature extraction.

responsible for interpolating parameters for the remaining colors (more than 16 million combinations). The use of arbitrary decision is considered coherent with the principle of individuality of synaesthesic experiences.

By providing an intuitive and simplified interface, the program can be used for timbral research at different levels, from people with no musical education to composers. It might also provide an additional way of interpretation for pictures and graphic scores.

Future improvements (by implementing pitch-changing strategies and image analysis techniques) could further expand the potentialities of this application.

An evaluation, obtained by designing experiments with musicians, non-trained users and synesthesic subjects, will be the object of a future research.

References

1. Cytowic, E.R.: Synesthesia: A Union of the Senses, 2nd edn. MIT Press, Cambridge (2002). https://doi.org/10.1007/978-1-4612-3542-2
2. Payling, D.: Visual Music Composition with Electronic Sound and Video. Staffordshire University (2014)
3. Shatter, G., Zueger, E., Nitschke, C.: A synaesthetic approach for a synthesizer interface based on genetic algorithm and fuzzy sets. In: Proceedings of International Computer Music Conference 2005 (ICMC 2005), pp. 664–667 (2005)
4. Margounakis, D., Politis, D.: Converting images to music using their colour properties. In: Proceedings of the 12th International Conference on Auditory Display (ICAD06), pp. 198–205 (2006)
5. Specdrums on Kickstarter. https://www.kickstarter.com/projects/364756202/specdrums-music-at-your-fingertips. Accessed 4 Jan 2019
6. McClard, P.T.: Music generating system and method utilizing control of music based upon displayed color. US Brevetto US5689078A (1995)
7. Macedo, A.R.: Visible and audible spectrums-a proposal of correspondence. Proc. Artech **5**, 168–171 (2010)
8. Rogowska, A.: Synaesthesia and Individual Differences. Cambridge University Press, Cambridge (2015)
9. Unity. https://www.unity3d.com. Accessed 4 Jan 2019
10. Wekinator - Instructions. http://www.wekinator.org/instructions/. Accessed 4 Jan 2019

Mercury®: A Software Based on Fuzzy Clustering for Computer-Assisted Composition

Brian Martínez–Rodríguez[1] and Vicente Liern[2(✉)]

[1] Universidad Politécnica de Valencia, Valencia, Spain
brian.martinez.rodriguez@gmail.com
[2] Dep. Matemáticas para la Economía y la Empresa,
Universidad de Valencia, Valencia, Spain
vicente.liern@uv.es

Abstract. We present MERCURY, a new software for computer-assisted composition based on fuzzy clustering algorithms. This software is able to generate a big number of transitions between any two different melodies, harmonic progressions or rhythmical patterns. Mercury works with symbolic music notation. The software is, therefore, able to read music and to export the generated musical production into MusicXML format. This paper focusses on some theoretical aspects of the CFT algorithm implemented in the software in order to create those complete transitions, overviewing not only the structure of the program but the user's interface and its music notation module. Finally, the wide variety of compositional possibilities of Mercury are shown by means of several computational examples.

Keywords: Algorithmic composition · Computer · Fuzzy · Clustering

1 Introduction

The first public performance of the *Illiac Suite* on 9th August of 1956 at the Illionis University [1], is considered to be the starting point of computer-assisted composition. During the last six decades, a big number of programs have been developed bringing new technical possibilities and widening the compositional abilities of the computers. The main disciplines that have been extensively explored have been summarized in [15]: creation of Markov models for musical structures or sequences generation [6], creation of generative grammars for the production of musical structures [16], algorithmic composition based on chaos theory and self-similarity [5], approach to composition and variation using genetic algorithms [3], use of cellular automata [13], neural networks and, more recently, artificial intelligence and machine learning techniques [9].

Data clustering techniques, either crisp or fuzzy, have been successfully applied to the field of computer-assisted musical analysis for mode recognition

© Springer Nature Switzerland AG 2019
M. Montiel et al. (Eds.): MCM 2019, LNAI 11502, pp. 236–247, 2019.
https://doi.org/10.1007/978-3-030-21392-3_19

[18], musical patterns analysis [4], style classification [12], etc. In the MCM 2017 Conference, we proposed the Fuzzy Ordered C-Means (FOCM) algorithm allowing comparison of some ordered sequences of notes [11]. The software that is presented now is able to generate variations and transitions from two given musical materials, an initial and a final one. For that purpose, we have expanded FOCM into a new technique denominated Fuzzy Complete Transition (FCT) algorithm that, given any two sequences, gradually transforms the initial into the final one. A transition is generated by the accumulation of all the intermediate states. The musical adaptation of this algorithm has been implemented in the software Mercury, that provides the users with three basic kinds of transitions, according to the three tradicional characteristics of music: melodic transition, harmonic transition and rhythmical transition. Once the user has selected one of them, Mercury reads the input data from *MusicXML* files and parses the information that at any case is required. After parameters have been set by the user, experimentation with transitions has been conducted and the results have been evaluated, the music material generated by the computer can be exported to a new MusicXML file, and subsequently loaded into any music notation software (e.g. *Musescore, Finale, Sibelius,* etc.) where the composer can continue with the art of music composition.

2   Theoretical Background

Following the definition included in the FOCM algorithm given in [11], we can express the sequence of notes as:

Definition 1. *Let x be a musical note determined by q characteristics (pitch, intensity, duration, silence, etc.) expressed as a vector in $\mathbb{R}^q$. A melody of n notes is a sequence $\mathscr{M} = \{x_i\}_{i=1}^n$ where each $x_i \in \mathbb{R}^q$ is a musical note.*

As in this work we will use harmonic sequences, harmony will be treated in a similar way to the previously defined sequence of notes. Moreover, as in this case we are only interested in the pitch, the notes can be expressed as real numbers and, consequently, a chord of k notes will be an element of $\mathbb{R}^k$.

Definition 2. *Let $y \in \mathbb{R}^k$ be a chord defined by a k-tuple of MIDI pitch values $\in [0, 127]$ expressed as a vector in $\mathbb{R}^k$. A k-harmony $\mathscr{H}$ is the sequence $\mathscr{H} = \{y_i\}_{i=1}^n$ where each $y_i \in \mathbb{R}^k$ is a chord of k MIDI pitches.*

A rhythmical element z_i is defined by three characteristics: the duration compared with a quarter, which will be expressed by means of a duration coefficient $\delta_i \in]0, \infty[$, the silence which will be expressed by a binary variable, and the MIDI velocity taking values between 0 and 127. The duration coefficient was obtained in [11] as

$$\delta_i = \sum_{k=1}^{m_i} \left[\frac{1}{2^{a_k^i}} \cdot \frac{2^{b_k^i+1} - 1}{2^{b_k^i}} \cdot \frac{d_k^i}{c_k^i} \right], \tag{1}$$

where m_i is the number of figures in z_i, $a_k^i \in \{-1, \dots, 7\}$ expresses the k-th figure of z_i ($-1 =$ whole, $0 =$ half, etc.), b_k^i is the number of dots of z_i, and d_k^i/c_k^i modifies the duration when there exists a tuplet (c_k^i notes in the time of d_k^i).

Definition 3. *A rhythm pattern of n elements $\mathcal{R}$ is a sequence $\mathcal{R} = \{z_i\}_{i=1}^n$ where each $z_i \in \mathbb{R}^3$ is a rhythmical element.*

2.1 The Main Algorithm

Mercury is able to generate complete transitions between two different melodies, harmonies or rhythmical patterns by means of an iterative technique that we have denominated FCT algorithm. The process works in the following way: once the two melodies (or two harmonic sequences or rhythmical patterns) have been represented as two sequences of elements in the metric space $\mathbb{R}^q$, the algorithm will initialize the set of centroids $c \geq 2$ with the sequence that we want to change. In our paper, this sequence will be the shortest one, denominated as S_0. The final sequence with n elements, our goal, is denoted as S_f, being assigned to the points of the data set about which the partition will be calculated. Then we run the FOCM algorithm. Once it has finished, a new centroid will be added to the set of centroids. This process will be repeated until the number of centroids (S_0) is equal to the number of points of the data set (S_f). At that point, the algorithm totally converges and S_0 becomes equal to S_f.

STEP 1. Choose any convenient neighbourhood function.

STEP 2. Choose any convenient distance function d in $\mathbb{R}^q$. Establish the fuzziness parameter $\lambda > 1$. Set $c_0 = c$.

STEP 3. Initialize the centroids: assign c_0 to the values of the initial sequence S_0. For each iteration l do:

STEP 4. If $c_l > n$ then stop; else if $c_l \leq n$ do:

STEP 5. If $c_l = n$ select the discrete neighbourhood function (see Table 1), otherwise continue with the initial neighbourhood function.

STEP 6. Update the partition matrix $\widehat{U}^{(l)} := \left(\hat{u}_{ij}\right)^{(l)}$ and the centroids $\{\mathbf{v}_j^{(l)}\}$ using equations

$$u_{ij} = \frac{1}{\sum_{k=1}^c \left(\frac{d(\mathbf{x}_i, \mathbf{v}_j)}{d(\mathbf{x}_i, \mathbf{v}_k)}\right)^{\frac{2}{\lambda-1}}}, \; \hat{u}_{ij} = \frac{u_{ij} \cdot f(i,j)}{\sum_{k=1}^c u_{ik} \cdot f(i,k)}, \; \mathbf{v}_j = \frac{\sum_{i=1}^n \hat{u}_{ij}^\lambda \cdot \mathbf{x}_i}{\sum_{i=1}^n \hat{u}_{ij}^\lambda}. \tag{2}$$

STEP 7. Compare $\widehat{U}^{(l)}$ with $\widehat{U}^{(l+1)}$ using any convenient matrix norm, being $\epsilon \in (0,1)$ an arbitrary termination criterion. If $\| \widehat{U}^{(l+1)} - \widehat{U}^{(l)} \| \leq \epsilon$ then go to STEP 8. Otherwise set $l = l + 1$, calculate the centroids $\{\mathbf{v}_j^{(l)}\}$ with $\widehat{U}^{(l)}$ and $\hat{u}_{ij}$ given in (2) and go back to STEP 6.

STEP 8. Choose the two consecutive points h, $h + 1$ with $1 \leq h \leq c_l - 1$ for which the distance between them is maximum. In other words, for the current iteration l select a point h such that

$$\max_{1 \leq h \leq c_l - 1} [d(\mathbf{v}_h^l, \mathbf{v}_{h+1}^l)]. \tag{3}$$

STEP 9. Set $l = l + 1$. Add to $\mathbf{V}^l$ a new centroid in the position $h + 1$ of the sequence of the centroids, with the attributes calculated as the average: $(\mathbf{v}_h^l + \mathbf{v}_{h+1}^l)/2$. Update $c_l = c_l + 1$. Go back to STEP 4.

2.2 Global Fuzzy Transition States

The set of all the intermediate states through which the set of centroids crosses constitutes a complete transition from the initial state $\mathbf{V}^0$ to the final state $\mathbf{V}^k$, in which the number of centroids c_k is equal to the number of points n. At the same time, any centroid i is equal to any element i, accomplishing this condition

$$\mathbf{v}_i^k = \mathbf{x}_i, \quad 1 \leq i \leq n. \tag{4}$$

We denote $\mathbf{v}_i^l$, a musical element (note, chord or rhythm element) in the l-th iteration, $0 \leq l \leq k$, $1 \leq i \leq c_l$. A state in the l-th iteration is given by the sequence $\mathbf{V}^l = \{\mathbf{v}_1^l, \mathbf{v}_2^l, \ldots, \mathbf{v}_{c_l}^l\}$. We asume that $\mathbf{V}^0 = \{\mathbf{v}_1^0, \mathbf{v}_2^0, \ldots, \mathbf{v}_{c_0}^0\}$ is the initial state. The set of all the iterated states is given by a Global Fuzzy Transition.

Definition 4. *A Global Fuzzy Transition $\widehat{\mathscr{T}}$ from the initial centroids $\mathbf{V}^0$ to the final centroids $\mathbf{V}^k$ is defined by the sequence*

$$\widehat{\mathscr{T}} = \{\mathbf{V}^0, \mathbf{V}^1, \mathbf{V}^2, \ldots, \mathbf{V}^k\} = \{\mathbf{V}^l\}_{l=0}^k. \tag{5}$$

2.3 Neighbourhood and Distance Functions

The concept of neighbourhood functions is the key point in our technique. It allows us to introduce the order of a sequence in the clustering process. It sets the weight that every point of the data set will be given when comparing it to each point of the centroids set. In this way, if an appropriate function is defined, we can easily relate the first elements of the data set to the first elements of the centroids set with highest weight values and, at the same time, eliminate the relation of the first elements of the data set with the last elements of the centroids set just setting zero the weight values. In Table 1 we show the more usual neighbourhood functions for sequences with n elements and c centroids (Fig. 1).

Table 1. Usual neighbourhood functions.

Name	Formula
1. Gaussian	$f(i,j) = \frac{1}{\sqrt{2\pi\sigma^2}} e^{-\left[\frac{1}{2\sigma^2}\left(i-\mu j\right)^2\right]}$
2. Triangular	$f(i,j) = \begin{cases} \frac{i}{\mu j}, & j \neq 0 \text{ and } 0 \leq i \leq \mu \\ 1 - \frac{(i-\mu j)}{(n-\mu j-1)}, & \text{otherwise} \end{cases}$
3. Exponential*	$f(i,j) = e^{-\frac{1}{\tau}\lvert i-\mu j\rvert}$
4. Sigmoidal*	$f(i,j) = \frac{1}{1+e^{[a\cdot b(i-c)]}}, \quad a = \frac{-2j}{(c-1)}+1, b = \frac{\tau}{(n-1)}, c = \frac{(n-1)}{2}$
5. Discrete	$f(i,j) = \begin{cases} 1, & i = j \\ 0, & i \neq j \end{cases}$

* The parameter τ denotes the width of the function and $\mu = (n-1)/(c-1)$.

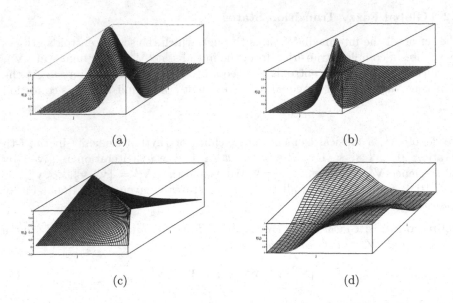

(a)   (b)

(c)   (d)

Fig. 1. Neighbourhood functions used in Mercury: (a) Gaussian, (b) Exponential, (c) Triangular, (d) Sigmoidal.

Table 2. Several distance functions implemented in Mercury.

Distance function	Expression for $\mathbf{x}, \mathbf{y} \in \mathbb{R}^q$
1. Euclidean	$d_{\mathrm{euc}}(\mathbf{x}, \mathbf{y}) = \left[\sum_{k=1}^{q} (x_k - y_k)^2 \right]^{\frac{1}{2}}$
2. Average Euclidean	$d_{\mathrm{euc}}(\mathbf{x}, \mathbf{y}) = \frac{1}{q} \left[\sum_{k=1}^{q} (x_k - y_k)^2 \right]^{\frac{1}{2}}$
3. Manhattan	$d_{\mathrm{man}}(\mathbf{x}, \mathbf{y}) = \sum_{k=1}^{q} |x_k - y_k|$
4. Minkowski	$d_{\mathrm{min}}(\mathbf{x}, \mathbf{y}) = \left[\sum_{k=1}^{q} |x_k - y_k|^r \right]^{\frac{1}{r}}, \quad r \geq 1$
5. Chebyshev	$d_{\mathrm{max}}(\mathbf{x}, \mathbf{y}) = \max_{k=1}^{q} |x_k - y_k|$
6. Chord	$d_{\mathrm{chord}}(\mathbf{x}, \mathbf{y}) = \left[2 - 2 \frac{\sum_{k=1}^{q} x_k y_k}{\|\mathbf{x}\|_2 \|\mathbf{y}\|_2} \right]^{\frac{1}{2}}$
7. Geodesic	$d_{\mathrm{geo}}(\mathbf{x}, \mathbf{y}) = \arccos \left(1 - \frac{d_{chord}(\mathbf{x}, \mathbf{y})}{2} \right)$
8. Canberra metric	$d_{\mathrm{can}}(\mathbf{x}, \mathbf{y}) = \sum_{k=1}^{q} \frac{|x_k - y_k|}{|x_k| + |y_k|}$
9. Divergence coefficient	$d_{\mathrm{div}}(\mathbf{x}, \mathbf{y}) = \frac{1}{q} \left[\sum_{k=1}^{q} \left(\frac{x_k - y_k}{x_k + y_k} \right)^2 \right]^{\frac{1}{2}}$
10. Discrete metric	$d_{\mathrm{dis}}(\mathbf{x}, \mathbf{y}) = \begin{cases} 1, & \text{if } \mathbf{x} = \mathbf{y} \\ 0, & \text{if } \mathbf{x} \neq \mathbf{y} \end{cases}$

Mercury allows the user to select one among several distance functions in order to proceed with the calculations. This function, due to its specific definition, returns very different computational results, providing a high degree of musical variety. The distance functions [7] that have been implemented are shown in Table 2.

2.4 The Quantization Process

It is necessary to establish a criterium in order to determine the equivalence between the real numbers generated by the CFT Algorithm and the symbolic music notation. In the case of the pitch attribute, the notes are chosen enharmonically by means of the selection of the closest integer MIDI pitch value. In a similar way, the intensity, represented musically with the following symbols ppp, pp, p, mp, mf, f, ff, and fff, will be approximated to the closest MIDI velocity value of the previous symbols (see [17]), according to Table 3:

Table 3. MIDI velocity values for the dynamic symbols used in musical notation.

Dynamic	Velocity	Dynamic	Velocity
$pppp$	8	mf	64
ppp	20	f	80
pp	31	ff	96
p	42	fff	112
mp	53	$ffff$	127

In the case of the duration coefficient, a wide variety of possible symbolic rhythmical notations exist, whose duration coefficient is exactly the same. In order to approximate the numerical result obtained for the duration attribute to its closest symbolic notation, the user has to specify which of the possible combinations of durations (whole, half, quarter, quaver, semiquaver, etc.), number

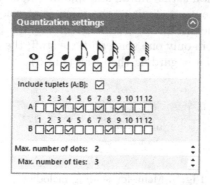

Fig. 2. Example of setting up for quantization.

of tied notes, number of dots and kinds of tuplets (3:2, 5:4, 7:4, etc.) are possible. To achieve this, Mercury offers the user the *Quantization Settings Menu*. Figure 2 shows an example of a user-defined quantization:

Once the setting has been established, Mercury calculates the duration coefficient for all the possible allowed combinations, removing the repeated ones, sorting the final results by an increasing order and storing them in RAM memory just in case the quantization settings do not change in following calculations. When the CFT algorithm has finished and the program needs to search for the most appropriate symbolic rhythmical notation, it will simply choose from the list the closest one to the numerical value of the duration coefficient generated by CFT.

3   Structure of the Program

Mercury is composed of four basic modules: the calculation kernel, the input/output module, the user interface module and the graphical music notation library. All these modules work in an independent way and communicate themselves by a set of domain classes capable to represent and share all the symbolic information that music needs. The calculation kernel is written in object-oriented programming language *C#* and implements both FOCM and CFT algorithms. It also contains an architecture of classes to map the symbolic music notation objects that can represent melodies, harmonies, chords, etc. into matrices of real numbers with which the algorithm will work. In addition, each neighbourhood and distance function is represented by classes that perform the required calculations within the process of the algorithm. Mercury receives as an input, scores in format *musicXML* that can be easily generated with standard music edition software. The program parses the information included in the tagged XML format and translates it into its musical object system. In this version, melody is restricted to monophonic lines written only in one staff, but there is no other restriction in terms of duration, rhythmical patterns, articulation, dynamics, silences, etc. Mercury is able to work and create transitions between two melodies of any kind and length. In the case of the harmonic transition, the only restriction is that initial and final harmonies must have the same number of voices, without any limit to the number of voices and length of any of the harmonic sequences. Finally, in the case of loading rhythmical structures, they should be written in only one voice and one staff; the program in that case will omit any information regarding the pitch (Fig. 3).

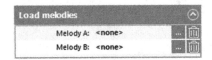

Fig. 3. Menu for loading melodies.

All the results generated by Mercury can be easily exported to a MusicXML file, given the user the possibility of using them as a musical material for the composition process. Furthermore, the program allows the user to listen, directly from the program by means of the MIDI playing, the melodies, chords or rhythms generated. With this functionality the user can evaluate the musical interest of the results and choose those that better fit with the desired compositional goals.

3.1   The User Interface

The user interface has been developed under VB.NET, using the free controls library *Syncfusion* for .NET programming, running at the moment under Windows operating system with .NET framework 4.5 technology. The main form allows the user to create, edit and save projects. Each project includes as many tabs as the user would need to experiment with the possibilities that Mercury offers. The music information can be easily edited or moved between tabs so the work of the composer becomes more flexible. In the *Play menu*, the user can specify the MIDI settings for playing the music in real time from the *Microsoft GS Wavetable Synth* or any other MIDI device connected to the computer like a MIDI digital piano (Fig. 4).

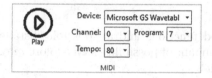

Fig. 4. Menu for MIDI settings: device, channel, program, tempo.eps

The CFT algorithm requires the user to establish several parameters that are direct and strongly related with the musical results obtained, and the *Fuzzy Settings Control* allows to control them. As explained in [2,11], the higher the *Fuzzy Coefficient* λ is, the fuzzier the process of clustering will be, so the individual elements of the intermediate steps will show more tendency to share their attributes. The *Stop Criterion* is an arbitrary value that will stop the convergence process. High values force the algorithm to stop without having converged. On the other hand, low values generate unnecessary states with no musical changes, making the process slower and increasing the requirements of memory (Fig. 5).

The menu also facilitates the possibility to choose among several neighbourhood functions (three from the gaussian family, three from the exponential family, four triangular, one rectangular, one trapezoidal and one sigmoidal), and also the possibility to choose among several distance functions (Euclidean, Average Euclidean, Manhattan, Average Manhattan, Minkowsky, Chebyshev, Chord, Geodesic, Canberra metric, Divergence Index and Discrete metric). Each of these neighbourhood or distance functions will provide very different intermediate states. The combination of all possible values for Fuzzy Coefficient, all

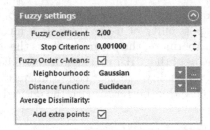

Fig. 5. Menu for setting the CFT parameters.

Fig. 6. A melody, a chord sequence and a rhythmical pattern displayed in the graphic music notation library of Mercury.

possible neighbourhood functions and all possible distance functions provides the user with a huge amount of possibilities to explore in order to search for the desired musical material.

3.2   The Graphic Music Notation Library

The library used for displaying the music is based on *PSALMControlLibrary* (Polish System for Archivising Music Control Library), an open-source control developed for *.NET Framework* in 2010 by *Jacek Salamon*. It has been strongly modified to fit the requirements of our program. In Fig. 6, three examples of a melody, a harmonic sequence and a rhythmical pattern are displayed.

4   Computational Examples

In this section we present three simple examples that illustrate the applicability of the method in three different scenarios: melody, harmony and rhythm. Each example is configured with different fuzzy coefficient λ, distance function and neighbourhood function, showing some of the intermediate musical states generated by the algorithm in each transition from element B to the objective element A. Each intermediate state is notated with its corresponding step number on the left. Notice that at the last state of each transition the element A is reached. The examples have been run on Mercury and finally exported in MusicXML format to a score edition software.

Fig. 7. Initial state and iterations number 1, 5, 9, 13, 17 and 21.

Fig. 8. Complete harmonic transition from S_0 to S_f.

Example 1. Intermediate states of the complete fuzzy transition calculated with CFT between two birdsongs transcribed by composer *Olivier Messiaen* [14]. The fuzzy settings are $\lambda = 3$, exponential neighbourhood and chord metric (Fig. 7).

Example 2. Intermediate states of the complete fuzzy transition calculated with CFT between two harmonic sequences S_0 and S_f. The fuzzy settings are $\lambda = 1.5$, gaussian neighbourhood and Manhattan distance (Fig. 8).

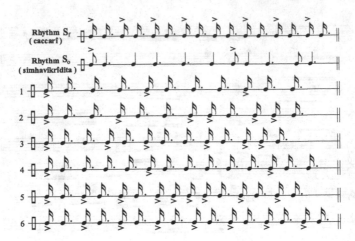

Fig. 9. Complete rhythmical transition from *simhavikrîdita* to *caccarî*.

Example 3. Intermediate states of the complete fuzzy transition calculated with CFT between rhythms *caccarî* and *simhavikrîdita*, belonging to 120 deçi-tâlas [8]. The fuzzy settings are $\lambda = 5$, exponential neighbourhood and chord metric (Fig. 9).

5   Conclusions

In this paper we have explored the possibilities of our software Mercury® in the field of the symbolic computer-assisted composition. The use of Mercury by several classical music composers shows the software as a useful tool to generate transitions and variations of melodic, harmonic and rhythmical material, widening the number of creative options that may fit with the aesthetic requirements of their artistic criteria. In some of these tests the algorithm proved to converge too much quickly, loosing swiftly the characteristics of the initial sequence. This issue may decrease the musical interest of the transition, so it will be fixed in future works. The limitations of the first version of the software include the restriction to monophonic melodic lines and the use of only one staff for the music material used as input data. Besides, the transitions between harmonies only work if all chords belonging to the initial and final ones have the same number of notes. Future versions of the software will improve these limitations and implement the CFT algorithm for other characteristics of music: for example, is it possible to create transitions between the timbre of two sounds (as shown in [12]) offering promising results for sound synthesis in the field of electroacoustics or spectral music. Is it possible, as well, to create transitions between two different tuning systems defined in [10]. The present version of Mercury works only under *Windows* operative system. Following developments will include *iOS* and *Android* distributions. The software is currently available at www.futurewebofmercury. com.

References

1. Ariza, C.: Two pioneering projects from the early history of computer-aided algorithmic composition. Comput. Music J. **35**(3), 40–56 (2011)
2. Bezdek, J.C.: Pattern Recognition with Fuzzy Objective Function Algorithms. Plenum Press, New York (1981)
3. Biles, J.: GenJam: a genetic algorithm for generating jazz solos. In: Proceedings of International Computer Music Conference ICMC 1994, pp. 131–137. Michigan Publishing (1994)
4. Buteau, C.: Melodic clustering within topological spaces of Schumann's Träumerei. In: Proceedings of International Computer Music Conference ICMC 2006, pp. 104–110. Tulane University, New Orleans (2006)
5. Dodge, C.: Profile: a musical fractal. Comput. Music J. **12**(3), 10–14 (1988)
6. Farbood, M., Schoner, B.: Analysis and synthesis of Palestrina-style counterpoint using Markov Chains. In: Proceedings of International Computer Music Conference ICMC 2001, pp. 1–4. Michigan Publishing (2001)
7. Gan, G., Ma, C., Wu, J.: Data Clustering: Theory, Algorithms, and Applications. SIAM, Philadelphia (2007)
8. Johnson, R.: Messiaen. University of California Press, Paris (1989)
9. Krzyzaniak, M.: Interactive learning of timbral rhythms for percussion robots. Comput. Music J. **42**(2), 35–51 (2018)
10. Liern, V.: Fuzzy tuning systems: the mathematics of musicians. Fuzzy Sets Syst. **150**(1), 35–52 (2005)
11. Martínez, B., Liern, V.: A fuzzy-clustering based approach for measuring similarity between melodies. In: Agustín-Aquino, O.A., Lluis-Puebla, E., Montiel, M. (eds.) MCM 2017. LNCS (LNAI), vol. 10527, pp. 279–290. Springer, Cham (2017). https://doi.org/10.1007/978-3-319-71827-9_21
12. Martínez, B., Liern, V.: Comparación y transiciones espectrales mediante el algoritmo fuzzy c-means. In: Tecniacústica 2017: 48° Congreso Español de Acústica; Encuentro Ibérico de Acústica; European Symposium on Underwater Acoustics Applications, European Symposium on Sustainable Building Acoustics: A Coruña, 3–6 Octubre 2017, pp. 1169–1175. Sociedad Española de Acústica (2017)
13. Miranda, E.: Cellular automata music: an interdisciplinary project. J. New Music. Res. **22**(1), 3–21 (1993)
14. Messiaen, O.: The Technique of My Musical Language. Alphonse Leduc, Paris (1956)
15. Nierhaus, G.: Algorithmic Composition: Paradigms of Automated Music Generation. Springer, New York (2009). https://doi.org/10.1007/978-3-211-75540-2
16. Roads, C.: Composing grammars. In: Proceedings of International Computer Music Conference ICMC 1977, pp. 54–132. University of California, San Diego (1977)
17. Selfridge-Field, E.: Beyond MIDI: The Handbook of Musical Codes. MIT Press, Cambridge (1997)
18. Tompkins, D.C.: A cluster analysis for mode identification in early music genres. In: Agustín-Aquino, O.A., Lluis-Puebla, E., Montiel, M. (eds.) MCM 2017. LNCS (LNAI), vol. 10527, pp. 312–323. Springer, Cham (2017). https://doi.org/10.1007/978-3-319-71827-9_24

A Parse-Based Framework for Coupled Rhythm Quantization and Score Structuring

Francesco Foscarin[1](✉), Florent Jacquemard[2], Philippe Rigaux[1], and Masahiko Sakai[3]

[1] CNAM Paris, Paris, France
francesco.foscarin@cnam.fr
[2] INRIA Paris, Paris, France
[3] Nagoya University, Nagoya, Japan

Abstract. We present a formal language-based framework for MIDI-to-score transcription, the problem of converting a sequence of symbolic musical events with arbitrary timestamps into a structured music score. The framework aims at solving in one pass the two subproblems of rhythm quantization and score production. It relies, throughout the process, on an apriori hierarchical model of scores given by generative grammars.

We show that this coupled approach helps to make relevant and interrelated decisions, and we present an algorithm computing transcription solutions optimal with respect to both the fitness of the quantization to the input, and a measure of complexity of music notation.

1 Introduction

Music transcription is the act of converting a music performance into music notation (*i.e.*, a score). Several aspects of this problem are studied in the literature, according to the variety of music representation format considered. One of the most studied is the conversion of an audio recording into an unquantized MIDI file (*audio-to-MIDI*, A2M) [2], *i.e.* the extraction, from an audio signal, of a symbolic representation with explicit event descriptors such as pitch, onset and offset, expressed in a real-time unit (seconds). We focus on the complementary problem of converting unquantized MIDI into a music score (*MIDI-to-score*, M2S). M2S transcription can itself be divided into two subproblems:

(*i*) *Rhythm Quantization* (RQ) is the conversion of time values from real-time units to musical-time units (beats, or fraction of bars) [4,16,18]. RQ alone is generally achieved via the manipulation of linear data structures (e.g., sequences of messages in MIDI files).

(*ii*) *Music score production* (MSP) involves the determination of higher level information: voices, bars, grouping of events with tuplets and beams, encoding of durations with ties and dots *etc*, see [6]. A salient feature of music

© Springer Nature Switzerland AG 2019
M. Montiel et al. (Eds.): MCM 2019, LNAI 11502, pp. 248–260, 2019.
https://doi.org/10.1007/978-3-030-21392-3_20

notation is its hierarchical nature, already advocated by the models such as Rhythm Trees [1]. An accurate MSP procedure thus requires the manipulation of hierarchical data structures.

Traditionally, subproblems (*i*) and (*ii*) are considered independently, in sequence. This allows to delegate subproblem (*ii*) to the MIDI import module of a score editor. Such an approach to M2S transcription might be satisfying in simple cases. It strongly depends, however, on how the quantized MIDI input fits the specifics of the music notation language. To put it differently, the linear structure produced by step (*i*) might be hardly compatible with the hierarchical notational structures of music scores used by step (*ii*). Even if each step yields quite satisfying results regarding its specific goal, their combination might therefore exhibit a discrepancy, and possibly yield poor transcription results. This is particularly true for complex rhythms with *e.g.* deep nesting, mixed tuplets, rests, grace notes, *etc.*

In the present paper, we propose a framework for M2S where subproblems (*i*) and (*ii*) are tightly coupled: the structural information needed for score construction in (*ii*) is built during step (*i*), and takes into consideration an apriori music notation model. More precisely, (*i*) is solved by a *parsing algorithm*, and the parse tree defines a rhythmic structure of the output score, similar to Rhythm Tree representations [1, 10].

This framework offers several distinctive advantages that contribute to improve the result quality. First, it makes it possible to jointly consider all the decisions made along the transcription process, and to model it as a *multicriteria optimization problem*, for two criterias: *fitness* between output to input, and of *rhythmic complexity*, in the sense of [17].

Second, we can leverage on expressive and powerful computational formalisms. On the one hand, we rely on *weighted context-free grammars* (WCFG), a standard formalism for modeling and ranking hierarchical constituent structure in computational linguistics. WCFG are used to describe an *a priori* music notation language. On the other hand, optimal tree representation can be obtained by efficient parsing algorithms [9] using Dynamic Programming. One of the main contribution of the paper is to show that this formal machinery can be adapted to solve M2S accurately and efficiently.

We expose the formal background of M2S in Sect. 2. The algorithmic part is developed in Sect. 3. Section 5 concludes the paper by describing experiments and further work.

2 Framework Definition and Objective

M2S takes as input a sequence of (unquantized) events and returns a music notation of this sequence. This section presents the formalisms used to represent these input and output and to model the framework.

Time Units and Tempo Curves. Timestamps can be expressed either in *real-time unit* (*rtu*), used for unquantized events, or *musical-time unit* (*mtu*) for music score events. In both cases, the temporal domain is $\mathbb{Q}_+$. In the rest of the paper, we assume a *rtu* of 1 s and a *mtu* of 1 bar. Given a time signature, every time value in mtu can be converted to a value in *beats*.

A *tempo curve* is monotonically increasing function $\theta : \mathbb{Q}_+ \to \mathbb{Q}_+$, converting rtu values into mtu values see *e.g.* [8]. Let $\bar{\tau} = \langle \tau_0, \dots, \tau_m \rangle$ be a sequence of rtu values with $\tau_0 = 0$ (typically the timestamps of input events). A *tempo model* $\mathcal{M}$ compatible with $\bar{\tau}$ is a set of tempo curves piecewise linear, with slope changing at the timestamps of $\bar{\tau}$. More precisely, every $\theta \in \mathcal{M}$ is defined by a sequence $\langle T_0, \dots, T_{m-1} \rangle$ such that for all $0 \leq i \leq m-1$, the restriction of θ to $[\tau_i, \tau_{i+1}[$ is a line of slope $T_i \in \mathbb{Q}_+$ (expressed in bars per second in our case, instead of bpm). Typically $\mathcal{M}$ expresses restrictions on the changes of T_i, according to the real durations $\tau_{i+1} - \tau_i$, in order to ensure a certain smoothness of the tempo curves. We skip unnecessary details about the specification of $\mathcal{M}$.

Timelines. A *time interval* is a right-open interval $I = [\tau, \tau'[\subset \mathbb{Q}_+$. I is called *unbounded* when $\tau' = +\infty$ and *bounded* otherwise. The left bound τ is called the *start* of I and denoted $start(I)$. We call *partition* of a time interval I a sequence of disjoint time intervals $I_1, \dots, I_k$, with $k \geq 1$, such that $\bigcup_{j=1}^{k} I_k = I$. We also write $I = I_1 + \dots + I_k$ in this case. The k-*split* of a bounded time interval I (for $k > 0$) is a partition of I of size k such that the duration of each component is $\frac{dur(I)}{k}$. In the case of a 2-split I_1, I_2 of I, we write $left(I)$ for I_1 and $right(I)$ for I_2.

We assume given a *notational alphabet* $\mathbb{E}$, which is a finite set of symbols to encode musical artifacts.

Example 1. A possible choice for $\mathbb{E}$ is the set of MIDI message symbols extended for explicit representation of rests. Pitch values are in $[0, 128]$, 128 being for rests, velocity in $[0, 127]$, and a flag distinguishes onsets/offsets. This flag, useful for polyphonic music, can be skipped in monophonic case.   ◊

An *event* e is a pair $\langle \eta, \tau \rangle$ made of a symbol $\eta \in \mathbb{E}$, denoted $symb(e)$, and a *timestamp* $\tau \in \mathbb{Q}$, denoted $date(e)$. A *timeline* $\mathcal{I}$ is a pair $\langle I, \bar{e} \rangle$, where I is a time interval denoted $carrier(\mathcal{I})$ and $\bar{e} = e_1, \dots, e_m$ is a finite sequence of events denoted $events(\mathcal{I})$, with increasing timestamps and such that $date(e_i) \in I$ for all $1 \leq i \leq m$. A timeline with timestamps in *rtu* (resp. *mtu*) is called a *real-timeline* (resp. *musical*-timeline). Operations on time intervals, like *e.g.* +, are extended to timelines as expected.

Example 2 (Toy running example). Let $\mathcal{I}_1$ and $\mathcal{I}_2$ be timelines defined by: $carrier(\mathcal{I}_1) = [0, 1[$ and $events(\mathcal{I}_1) = \langle e_1, e_2, e_3 \rangle$, with respective timestamps $0.07, 0.72, 0.91$; $carrier(\mathcal{I}_2) = [1, 2[$ and $events(\mathcal{I}_2) = \langle e_4, e_5, e_6 \rangle$ with respective timestamps $1.05, 1.36, 1.71$.   ◊

Semirings. Domains of weight used to rank solutions to transcription are abstractly defined as semirings, that can be instantiated into several concrete domains (*e.g.* probabilities or costs). A *semiring* $\mathcal{S} = \langle \mathbb{S}, \oplus, \mathbb{0}, \otimes, \mathbb{1} \rangle$ is a structure with a domain $\mathbb{S} = dom(\mathcal{S})$, two associative binary operators $\oplus$ and $\otimes$, and neutral elements $\mathbb{0}$ and $\mathbb{1}$; $\oplus$ is commutative, $\otimes$ distributes over $\oplus$: $\forall x, y, z \in S$, $x \otimes (y \oplus z) = (x \otimes y) \oplus (x \otimes z)$, and $\mathbb{0}$ is absorbing for $\otimes$: $\forall x \in S$, $\mathbb{0} \otimes x = x \otimes \mathbb{0} = \mathbb{0}$. Components of a semiring S may be subscripted by S when needed. We simply write $x \in S$ to mean $x \in \mathbb{S}$.

Intuitively, in the application presented below, $\oplus$ selects an optimal value amongst two values and $\otimes$ combines two values into a single value.

A semiring S is *commutative* if $\otimes$ is commutative. It is *idempotent* if for all $x \in S$, $x \oplus x = x$. It is *monotonic wrt* a partial ordering $\leq$ iff for all x, y, z, $x \leq y$ implies $x \oplus z \leq y \oplus z$, $x \otimes z \leq y \otimes z$ and $z \otimes x \leq z \otimes y$. Every idempotent semiring S induces a partial ordering $\leq_S$ called the *natural ordering* of S and defined by: for all x and y, $x \leq_S y$ iff $x \oplus y = x$. It holds then that S is monotonic *wrt* $\leq_S$. S is called *total* if it is idempotent and $\leq_S$ is total *i.e.* when for all x and y, either $x \oplus y = x$ or $x \oplus y = y$.

In practice, we use two kinds of total semirings: Viterbi semiring defining *probability models*, whose domain $[0, 1] \subset \mathbb{R}_+$, $\oplus$ is max, $\mathbb{0} = 0$, $\otimes$ is real product, and $\mathbb{1} = 1$, and tropical semirings, defining *cost models* whose domain $\mathbb{R}_+ \cup \{+\infty\}$, $\oplus$ is min, $\mathbb{0} = +\infty$, $\otimes$ is sum, and $\mathbb{1} = 0$.

Weighted Context-Free Grammars. A WCFG over a semiring S and an alphabet $\mathbb{E}$ is a tuple $\mathcal{G} = \langle Q, init, P, weight, mus \rangle$ where: Q is a finite set of non-terminal symbols (nt), $init \in Q$ is an initial non-terminal, P is a set of production rules in one of the following forms:

(k–div) $q \to \langle q_1, \ldots, q_k \rangle$ with $q, q_1, \ldots, q_k \in Q$, and rank $k > 1$, or
(term) $q \to \bar{e}$ with $q \in Q$ and $\bar{e} \in \mathbb{E}^*$ ($\bar{e}$ is called *terminal* symbol).
weight assigns to each production rule in P a weight value in S,
mus assigns to each (k–div) production rule in P a function associating to a musical-time interval O a partition $O_1, \ldots, O_k$ of O.

The components of a WCFG $\mathcal{G}$ may be subscripted by $\mathcal{G}$ when needed. We use the respective notations $q \xrightarrow{w} \langle q_1, \ldots, q_n \rangle$ and $q \xrightarrow{w} \bar{e}$ for (k–div) and (term) productions rules of weight $w \in S$. The (k–div) rules (for $k \geq 2$) define the possible divisions of musical time intervals, *e.g.* the division of a quarter note into 2 eight notes or into a triplet. The weight associates a *rhythmic complexity* in S to each division. The recursive application of (k–div) rules represents nested divisions. Their complexity values will be composed using $\otimes$.

Example 3. The following $(2-, 3-\text{div})$ production rules, with weight values in a tropical semiring, define two possible divisions of a bounded time interval represented by the nt q_0, into respectively a duplet and a triplet.

$$\rho_1 : q_0 \xrightarrow{0.06} \langle q_1, q_2 \rangle, \quad \rho_2 : q_0 \xrightarrow{0.12} \langle q_1, q_2, q_2 \rangle.$$

In those rules, q_1 represents the first event in a division, and q_2 the others. Further binary divisions of time sub-intervals are possible with:

$$\rho_3 : q_2 \xrightarrow{0.1} \langle q_3, q_3 \rangle, \quad \rho_4 : q_3 \xrightarrow{0.11} \langle q_4, q_4 \rangle. \qquad \Diamond$$

The (term) production rules specify the musical symbols of $\mathbb{E}$ that can occur in a time interval. An empty sequence in the right-hand-side of such rule represents the *continuation* of an event started before and not yet released – notated with a tie or a dot in a score.

In practice, in order to keep $\mathcal{G}$ reasonably small, we use as set of terminal symbols a finite abstraction of $\mathbb{E}^*$, like in the following example.

Example 4. In the case of monophonic input, simultaneous events are interpreted as grace notes: a singleton sequence $\langle \eta_1 \rangle$ represents a single note, $\langle \eta_1, \eta_2 \rangle$ represents a grace note η_1 followed by a note η_2, $\langle \eta_1, \eta_2, \eta_3 \rangle$ represents two grace notes η_1, η_2 followed by a note η_3, *etc.* The set $\mathbb{F} = \{0, 1, 2, 3\}$ is a finite abstraction of $\mathbb{E}^*$ where the symbols 0, 1, 2 represent resp. a continuation, one and two symbols of $\mathbb{E}$ and 3 represents a sequence of $\mathbb{E}^*$ of length ≥ 3. In the following, we assign a weight value (in a tropical semiring) to (term) productions rules of a grammar $\mathcal{G}$, depending on the number of grace notes.

$$\rho_5 : q_0 \xrightarrow{0.15} 0, \quad \rho_6 : q_0 \xrightarrow{0.01} 1, \quad \rho_7 : q_0 \xrightarrow{0.79} 2, \quad \rho_8 : q_0 \xrightarrow{1.02} 3,$$
$$\rho_9 : q_1 \xrightarrow{0.02} 0, \rho_{10} : q_1 \xrightarrow{0.01} 1, \rho_{11} : q_1 \xrightarrow{0.25} 2, \rho_{12} : q_1 \xrightarrow{0.64} 3,$$
$$\rho_{13} : q_2 \xrightarrow{0.02} 1, \rho_{14} : q_3 \xrightarrow{0.04} 0, \rho_{15} : q_3 \xrightarrow{0.01} 1, \rho_{16} : q_4 \xrightarrow{0.01} 1$$

The *nt* q_0 represents a whole bar, with a single event in ρ_6 (*e.g.* a whole note in a $\frac{4}{4}$ bar), as a tied note in ρ_5 or preceded by 1 or 2 grace notes in ρ_7 and ρ_8; q_1 represents a first note in a division with a rule of Example 3 (preceded by 1 or 2 grace notes in ρ_{11} and ρ_{12}); q_2 represents the next notes in the same divisions and q_3 and q_4 further levels of divisions (grace notes are not allowed for q_2, q_3, q_4, ties are not allowed for q_4).   ◇

Symbols in abstractions of $\mathbb{E}^*$ may embed more information, like *e.g.* pitch-contour for sequences of grace notes, or velocity, or on/off flag.

Parse Trees and Serialization. Given a WCTG $\mathcal{G}$ over a semiring $\mathcal{S}$, the set $\mathcal{T}(\mathcal{G})$ of *parse trees* is the smallest set of trees labelled by production rules of $\mathcal{G}$ such that:

– for all (term) rule ρ in $\mathcal{G}$, $\rho \in \mathcal{T}(\mathcal{G})$, with root ρ,
– for all (k–div) rule $\rho = q \xrightarrow{w} \langle q_1, \ldots, q_k \rangle$ in $\mathcal{G}$, and all $t_1, \ldots, t_k \in \mathcal{T}(\mathcal{G})$ whose respective roots have heads $q_1, \ldots, q_k$,
  $\rho(t_1, \ldots, t_k) \in \mathcal{T}(\mathcal{G})$ with root ρ.

In the second case, we call head of a rule its *left-hand-side nt*. We write $\mathcal{T}(\mathcal{G}, q)$ for the subset of parse trees of $\mathcal{T}(\mathcal{G})$ whose root is headed with *nt* q. The weight of a parse tree is obtained by recursively applying $\otimes$.

– $weight(t) := weight(\rho)$ when the label of t is of type (term),
– $weight(\rho(t_1, \ldots, t_k)) := weight(\rho) \otimes \left[\bigotimes_{i=1}^{k} weight(t_i) \right]$.

parse tree t	$\|t\|_{[0,1[}$ (timestamps)	$weight(t)$	notation
$t_1 = \rho_1(\rho_{10}, \rho_3(\rho_{14}, \rho_{15}))$	$0, \frac{3}{4}$	0.22	♩♪♩
$t_2 = \rho_1(\rho_{10}, \rho_3(\rho_{14}, \rho_4(\rho_{16}, \rho_{16})))$	$0, \frac{3}{4}, \frac{7}{8}$	0.34	♩♫
$t_3 = \rho_2(\rho_{10}, \rho_{13}, \rho_{13})$	$0, \frac{1}{3}, \frac{2}{3}$	0.17	♫♪
$t_4 = \rho_2(\rho_{11}, \rho_{13}, \rho_{13})$	$0, 0, \frac{1}{3}, \frac{2}{3}$	0.41	♪♫♪

Fig. 1. Some parse trees and their linearization (Example 5).

We associate to every parse tree t of $\mathcal{T}(\mathcal{G})$ and every (output) mtu interval O a musical-timeline denoted $\|t\|_O$ and defined by:

- $\|q \xrightarrow{w} a\|_O = \langle O, \langle \eta_1, start(O)\rangle, \ldots, \langle \eta_p, start(O)\rangle\rangle$, when $a = \langle \eta_1, \ldots, \eta_p\rangle$,
- $\|\rho(t_1, \ldots, t_k)\|_O = \|t_1\|_{O_1} + \ldots + \|t_k\|_{O_k}$ when $O_1, \ldots, O_k = mus(\rho)(O)$.

This mapping, called *serialization*, defines the timestamps for the symbols of $\mathbb{E}$ labeling the leaves of t. Moreover, t also yields a grouping structure for the resulting events. In other terms, t is a consistent representation of music events with respect to the notation defined by the grammar, and a music score can be constructed straightforwardly from it.

Example 5. Taking the rules of Examples 3 and 4, assuming that $mus(\rho_1)$, $mus(\rho_2)$, $mus(\rho_3)$, $mus(\rho_4)$ return respectively 2-, 3-, 2- and 2-splits of bounded intervals, Fig. 1 presents parse trees and their serialization in a 1 bar *mtu*-interval. Note that t_1 has 3 leaves, but $\|t_1\|_{[0,1[}$ contains only 2 events, because its second leaf is a continuation with 0 event. ◇

Example 6. We extend the grammar of Example 5 with (2−div) rules $\rho_0 = q \xrightarrow{1} \langle q_0, q_0\rangle$, $\rho'_0 = q \xrightarrow{1} \langle q_0, q\rangle$ for partitioning a *mtu* interval $O = [\tau, \tau'[$ into one bar (nt q_0) and its right part (nt q). These binary rules can be used to recursively divide a musical-time interval into several bars. The function $mus(\rho'_0)$ maps O to the partition made of $[\tau, \tau + 1[$ (first bar) and $[\tau + 1, +\infty[$ (rest of O), providing that $\tau' > \tau + 1$ or $\tau' = +\infty$. For O of duration 2 bars, the serialization $\|\rho_0(t_2, t_3)\|_O$ is a timeline with 6 events, with timestamps $0, \frac{3}{4}, \frac{7}{8}, 1, \frac{4}{3}, \frac{5}{3}$. This tree corresponds to the notation ♩♩♫ ♫♫, assuming a time signature of $\frac{1}{4}$. ◇

Input-Output Fitness Measure. We model expressive timing of human performance [8] by a composed application of a *global tempo curve* θ and *local time-shifts* for individual events. The *distance* δ measures time shifts between written and played events. It is computed in a semiring $\mathcal{S}$ based on a given $\delta_0 : \mathbb{Q}_+ \times \mathbb{Q}_+ \to \mathcal{S}^1$.

$$\delta(e_1, e_2) = \begin{cases} \delta_0(date(e_1), date(e_2)) & if\, symb(e_1) = symb(e_2) \\ \mathbb{0} & otherwise \end{cases}$$

---

[1] $\mathbb{0}$ is the worse (and absorbing) value in the semiring models that we consider.

We extend δ to sequences of events $\bar{e} = \langle e_1, \ldots, e_m \rangle$ and $\bar{e}' = \langle e'_1, \ldots, e'_n \rangle$ by $\delta(\bar{e}, \bar{e}') = \bigotimes_{i=1}^{m} \delta(e_i, e'_i)$ if $m = n$ and $\mathbb{0}$ otherwise, and to timelines by $\delta(\mathcal{I}, \mathcal{O}) = \delta(events(\mathcal{I}), events(\mathcal{O}))$.

Example 7. For a tropical semiring, let $\delta_0(\tau_1, \tau_2) = |\tau_1 - \tau_2|$. Its extension δ is a measure of the accumulation of time-shifts of events, in rtu. $\Diamond$

We also use a measure γ of *tempo variations* defined by a tempo curve, based on a given $\gamma_0 : \mathbb{Q} \times \mathbb{Q}_+ \to \mathcal{S}$. Given a real-timeline $\mathcal{I}$, and a tempo curve θ in a model $\mathcal{M}$ compatible with $events(\mathcal{I})$, γ is defined as

$$\gamma(\theta) = \bigotimes_{i=0}^{m-1} \gamma_0(T_{i+1} - T_i, \tau_{i+1} - \tau_i)$$

where $\langle T_0, \ldots, T_{m-1} \rangle$ is the sequence of slope values defining θ (see page 2), and $\langle \tau_0, \ldots, \tau_m \rangle$ are the timestamps in $events(\mathcal{I})$.

Example 8. For a $\mathcal{S}$ tropical, we can define γ_0 as the ratio between the variation of slopes $\gamma_0(dT, d\tau) = \frac{dT}{d\tau}$ when $d\tau \neq 0$, and $\gamma_0(dT, 0) = 0$. $\Diamond$

Altogether, we define the *fitness* of a quantized musical-timeline $\mathcal{O}$ (a score) to the real-timeline $\mathcal{I}$ (a performance), *wrt* a tempo curve θ, as

$$fit(\mathcal{I}, \mathcal{O}, \theta) = \delta(\theta(\mathcal{I}), \mathcal{O}) \otimes \gamma(\theta).$$

In our settings, the output timeline $\mathcal{O}$ will be the serialization $\|t\|_O$ of a parse tree t of a WCFG $\mathcal{G}$ over $\mathcal{S}$ (for a given mtu time interval O).

Transcription Objective. Assuming an alphabet $\mathbb{E}$, a commutative, idempotent and total semiring $\mathcal{S}$ and a fitness measure based on δ_0 and γ_0 as above, the M2S problem is defined as follows.

INPUT: – a real-timeline $\mathcal{I}$, non-empty (*i.e.* with $|events(\mathcal{I})| > 0$),
            – a WCFG $\mathcal{G} = \langle \mathbb{E}^*, Q, init, P, weight, mus \rangle$ over $\mathcal{S}$,
            – a musical-time interval $O = [0, N[$ with $N \in \mathbb{N}_+ \cup \{+\infty\}$,
            – a tempo model $\mathcal{M}$ compatible with $events(\mathcal{I})$.

OUTPUT: – a tempo curve $\theta \in \mathcal{M}$ defined on $carrier(\mathcal{I})$,
            – a parse tree $t \in \mathcal{T}(\mathcal{G})$, such that
            $weight(t) \otimes fit(\mathcal{I}, \|t\|_O, \theta)$ is minimal *wrt* $\leq_{\mathcal{S}}$.

Therefore, the objective of M2S is to find a parse tree t representing a score that optimizes a combination of its *rhythmic complexity* (weight *wrt* $\mathcal{G}$), and its *fitness* to the input $\mathcal{I}$. The two criteria are antinomic, in the sense that improving the fitness generally increases the complexity of the tree and viceversa. Let us discuss the relevance of the above combination with $\otimes$ by reviewing two concrete domains used for $\mathcal{S}$.

(*i*) If $\mathcal{S}$ is a Viterbi semiring, then the weight *wrt* $\mathcal{G}$ and the fitness are probability values and we want to maximize their product with $\otimes$.

(ii) If $\mathcal{S}$ is a tropical semiring, then the weight and the fitness can be seen as two unrelated quality criteria, and one can resettle M2S as a multicriteria optimization problem [11].

Let $\mathcal{P} = \mathcal{T}(\mathcal{G}) \times \mathcal{M}$ be the solution space for M2S, and let us consider the two objective functions c and d of $\mathcal{P}$ into the tropical semiring $\mathcal{S}$ defined, for $p = (t, \theta) \in \mathcal{P}$, by $c(p) = weight(t)$ and $d(p) = fit(\mathcal{I}, \|t\|_O, \theta)$ (for the given $\mathcal{I}$ and O). By monotonicity of $\mathcal{S}$, we can restrict our search to so-called *Pareto-optimal* points $p \in \mathcal{P}$, i.e. such that there is no $p' \in \mathcal{P}$ with $c(p') <_\mathcal{S} c(p)$ and $d(p') <_\mathcal{S} d(p)$.

M2S is expressed as the minimization of the combination $c(p) \otimes d(p)$, where $\otimes$ is interpreted as a sum in $\mathbb{R}_+$. This is similar to a technique of scalarization by weighted sum, selecting a point p with minimal $\alpha.c(p) + d(p)$ (in $\mathbb{R}_+$) called *scalar optimal*. Intuitively, α can be seen as a user parameter setting how much one want to favour the rhythmic complexity against the fitness. In practice, one can apply the coefficient α to $weight(t)$ by multiplying by α all the weight values in productions of $\mathcal{G}$. This approach is correct and complete in the following sense: every scalar optimal point $p \in \mathcal{P}$ (for some α) is Pareto-optimal and for all Pareto-optimal point $p \in \mathcal{P}$ there exists a coefficient α such that p is a scalar optimal for α (Theorem 11.17 and Corollary 11.19 of [11], chapter 11.2.1).

Example 9. Let $\mathcal{I} = \mathcal{I}_1 + \mathcal{I}_2$ (see Example 2), $\mathcal{G}$ be the WCFG from the Examples 3, 4 and 6, a musical-time interval $O = [0, 1[$ and a tempo model containing a single tempo curve θ_0 mapping 1 s to 1 measure. Two possible solutions to M2S are the parse trees $t_5 = \rho_0(t_2, t_3)$ (Example 6) and $t_6 = \rho_0(t_1, t_4)$. Their serialization $\|t_5\|_O$ and $\|t_6\|_O$ have both six events with respective timestamps $(0, \frac{3}{4}, \frac{7}{8}, 1, \frac{4}{3}, \frac{5}{3})$ and $(0, \frac{3}{4}, 1, 1, \frac{4}{3}, \frac{5}{3})$; and t_5 and t_6 respectively correspond to ♩ ♫ ♫ and ♩ ♫ ♫.

Using the distance defined in the Example 7 we obtain $weight(t_5) \otimes fit(\mathcal{I}, \|t_5\|_O, \theta_0) = 0.51 + 0.265 = 0.775$ and $weight(t_5) \otimes fit(\mathcal{I}, \|t_6\|_O, \theta_0) = 0.63 + 0.32 = 0.95$. That means that t_5 is preferred over t_6, and actually the algorithm of Sect. 3.2 will return t_5 as optimal solution. The reason is that in $\mathcal{G}$ the weight for having a grace note (rule ρ_{11}) is quite high compared to the other rules. If we lower the weight of ρ_{11} to 0.07, then $weight(t_6) \otimes fit(\mathcal{I}, \|t_6\|_O, \theta) = 0.77$ and t_6 becomes the optimal solution. This illustrates the notation preferences defined in $\mathcal{G}$, e.g. for favouring grace-notes or precise rhythmic notation.   ◊

3   Transcription Algorithm

We now present a transcription algorithm that works in two steps: it computes first a WCFG $\mathcal{K}$ by augmenting $\mathcal{G}$ with some information from the input $\mathcal{I}$ (Sects. 3.2 and 3.3 describe two examples of construction of such $\mathcal{K}$, corresponding to different use cases) and then it solves M2S by computing an optimal parse tree for $\mathcal{K}$, using a Dynamic Programming algorithm presented in next Sect. 3.1.

3.1   Viterbi 1-Best Algorithm

Let $\mathcal{K}$ be a WCFG with nt set $\mathbb{K}$ over a total semiring $\mathcal{S}$. The following recursive function $best_\mathcal{K}$ associates to every nt $k \in \mathbb{K}$ a parse tree $t \in \mathcal{T}(\mathcal{K}, k)$ with a weight optimal $wrt \geq_\mathcal{S}$. By abuse, we make no distinction below between a parse tree $t \in \mathcal{T}(\mathcal{K})$ and its weight value $weight(t) \in \mathcal{S}$. Since $\mathcal{S}$ is total, it means that $\oplus$, applied to parse trees of $\mathcal{T}(\mathcal{K})$, selects the tree with minimal weight $wrt \leq_\mathcal{S}$.

$$best_\mathcal{K}(k) = \bigoplus_{\rho_0 = k \xrightarrow[\mathcal{K}]{w_0} a} \rho_0 \oplus \left[\bigoplus_{\rho = k \xrightarrow[\mathcal{K}]{w} \langle k_1, \dots, k_n \rangle} \rho \big(best_\mathcal{K}(k_1), \dots, best_\mathcal{K}(k_n) \big) \right]$$

If $\mathcal{K}$ is acyclic, then the above definition is well founded and the following results holds (*e.g.* by induction on k following a topological sort of $\mathbb{K}$).

Lemma 1. *For all* $k \in \mathbb{K}$, $best_\mathcal{K}(k) = \displaystyle\bigoplus_{t' \in \mathcal{T}(\mathcal{K},k)} t' = \min_{\leq_S} \{t' \in \mathcal{T}(\mathcal{K}, k)\}$.

Remember that the weight of a parse tree is the product of all the weights of the productions rules labeling its nodes. Therefore, the above formula can be understood as an alternation of sums with $\oplus$ (selection of one parse tree of optimal weight) and products with $\otimes$ (of weights of all subtrees). The function $best$ can be computed by a straightforward adaptation of a Viterbi-like Dynamic Programming algorithm returning the best derivations for weighted acyclic hypergraphs ([9], Sect. 5.1). With a tabulation over $\mathbb{K}$, in order to avoid recalculation of solution for subproblems, this algorithm runs in time linear in the size of $\mathcal{K}$.

In the case where $\mathcal{K}$ is not acyclic, one can use a generalization by Knuth of the Dijkstra shortest path algorithm (Algorithm 6 of [9])[2].

We apply this algorithm to a WCFG $\mathcal{K}$ built on the top of $\mathcal{G}$ from an input timeline $\mathcal{I}$. Two particular computations of $\mathcal{K}$ corresponding to different case studies are presented below.

3.2   Constant Tempo

In this first case study, we assume a constant tempo. This case study, illustrated in Example 9, corresponds to performances recorded with a metronome. The tempo model is $\mathcal{M} = \{\theta_0\}$, where a single tempo curve θ_0 represents the constant tempo value T which, for the sake of simplicity, we assume below to be the identity ($T = 1$).

In this case, the purpose of M2S transcription is essentially to correct local time-shifts of events. A parse tree t defines a partition of a given time interval O, by recursive application of the division rules labeling the nodes of t (see the definition of $\|t\|_O$). This partition can be seen as a *"grid"* containing the time positions of the bounds of the sub-intervals. M2S then consists in the *realignment*

---

[2] Acyclic WCFG are however sufficient for our purpose.

of the events of $\mathcal{I}$ to the nearest bound in the grid. The cost of this alignment is then the distance, with δ, between $\mathcal{I}$ and the score represented by t.

$\mathcal{K} = \langle \mathbb{E}^*, \mathbb{K}, \mathit{init}, P, \mathit{weight}, \mathit{mus} \rangle$ is built to represent all the time sub-intervals defined from $\mathit{carrier}(\mathcal{I})$ by recursive divisions, according to the rules of $\mathcal{G}$. For this purpose, every nt $k \in \mathbb{K}$ contains two components accessible with the following attributes:

- $k.nt$: a nt of $\mathcal{G}$,
- $k.car$: a real-time interval embedded in $\mathit{carrier}(\mathcal{I})$.

(div) productions rules of P are of the form $\rho = k \xrightarrow{w} \langle k_1, \ldots, k_n \rangle$, where

1. $\rho' = k.nt \xrightarrow[\mathcal{G}]{w} \langle k_1.nt, \ldots, k_n.nt \rangle$ is a rule of $\mathcal{G}$, $\mathit{mus}(\rho) = \mathit{mus}(\rho')$,
2. $k_1.car, \ldots, k_n.car$ is the application of $\mathit{mus}(\rho')$ to $k.car$,
3. $\mathit{events}(\mathcal{I}|_{k.car}) \neq \emptyset$, meaning that k is $\mathit{inhabited}$[3].

The last condition drastically reduces the size of $\mathcal{K}$ in practice, *wlog* since it is useless to divide empty intervals.

(term) rules of P deal with the realignment of the events of $\mathcal{I}$ to the bounds defined by a parse tree of $\mathcal{K}$, and compute the input-output distance as in Sect. 2. For a nt k, we know the events of $\mathcal{I}$ inside $C = k.car$. Some of these events (those in the first half of C, called *early*) will be aligned to the left bound of C. The others (those in the second half of C, called *late*) will be aligned to the right bound of C, *i.e.* actually to the left bound of the interval defined by the next leaf in a parse tree. To deal with this situation correctly, we add two components to every nt $k \in \mathbb{K}$, accessible with the following attributes:

- $k.post$: the late events of $\mathcal{I}$ in $k.car$ (*i.e.* those in its second half),
- $k.pre$: a buffer memorizing the *post* for the previous leaf.

And we add the following conditions for every (div) production rule:

4. $k_1.pre = k.pre, \forall 1 \leq i \leq n \; k_{i+1}.pre = k_i.post, k_n.post = k.post$.

This ensures a correct bottom-up propagation of *pre* and *post* values.

The other rules of P have the form (term) $k \xrightarrow{w} \bar{e}$, where $\bar{e} = k.pre + \mathit{events}(\mathcal{I}|_{left(k.car)})$ (concatenation of the *pre* buffer and the vector of events of $\mathcal{I}$ early in $k.car$), $\mathit{events}(\mathcal{I}|_{right(k.car)}) = k.post$ and $w = w_0 \otimes [\bigotimes_{i=1}^{|\bar{e}|} \delta_0(\mathit{start}(k.car), \mathit{date}(e_i))]$, with $q \xrightarrow{w_0} \bar{e}$ in $\mathcal{G}$.

The weight of the above (term) rule combines with $\otimes$ the weight w_0 of the corresponding rule in $\mathcal{G}$ (*i.e.* a complexity value) with the distance for the realignment of the points of $\bar{e}$ from their positions in $\mathcal{I}$ to new positions defined by the bounds of $k.car$. Moreover, $k_0 = \mathit{init}_\mathcal{K}$ is defined by $k_0.nt = \mathit{init}_\mathcal{G}$, $k_0.car = \mathit{carrier}(\mathcal{I})$, $k_0.pre = k_0.post = 0$.

---

[3] The restriction $\mathcal{I}|_C$ of $\mathcal{I}$ is such that by $\mathit{carrier}(\mathcal{I}|_C) = C$ and $\mathit{events}(\mathcal{I}|_C)$ is the sub-sequence of events of $\mathit{events}(\mathcal{I})$ inside C.

258   F. Foscarin et al.

Correctness and Completeness of Construction. Let us now sketch a proof that from $best_{\mathcal{K}}(k_0)$, one can build a solution for M2S conform to the definition in Sect. 2. First, one can observe that every parse tree $t \in \mathcal{T}(\mathcal{K})$ can be projected onto a parse tree $\pi_{\mathcal{G}}(t) \in \mathcal{T}(\mathcal{G})$. Indeed, by condition (1.) for (div) rules of $\mathcal{K}$, it is sufficient to replace, in every label of t, every nt k by $k.nt$ and, for (term) rules, to replace the rule's weight by the weight defined in $\mathcal{G}$. Next, for $k \in \mathbb{K}$, let use us define $\mathcal{I}|_k$ by $carrier(\mathcal{I}|_k) = carrier(\mathcal{I}|_{k.car})$ and $events(\mathcal{I}|_k) = k.pre + events(\mathcal{I}|_{left(k.car)})$ (using the above notations).

Proposition 1. *For all $k \in \mathbb{K}$ and $t \in \mathcal{T}(\mathcal{K},k)$, it holds that $weight(t) = weight(t') \otimes fit(\mathcal{I}|_k, \|t'\|_{k.car}, \theta_0)$, where $t' = \pi_{\mathcal{G}}(t)$.*

This can be showed by induction on t, using the above conditions (2–4) for inductions steps. It follows from Proposition 1 and the fact that $\mathcal{I}|_{k+0} = \mathcal{I}$ that $(\pi_{\mathcal{G}}(best_{\mathcal{K}}(k_0)), \theta_0)$ is a solution of M2S for $\mathcal{G}$ and $\mathcal{I}$.

3.3 Coupled Tempo Inference and Rhythm Quantization

In this second case, we sketch a construction of grammar $\mathcal{K}$ that permits a joined evaluation of a tempo curve θ and a parse tree t. Instead of realigning late events to the right bound of the current real-time interval, we move the right bound of the interval, such that the modified interval contains only early events. The new interval length induces the definition of a piecewise linear tempo curve θ like in Sect. 2.

In addition to the attributes $k.nt$ and $k.car$ (Sect. 3.2), every nt k of $\mathcal{K}$ has a third attribute $k.mod$ for a real-time interval modified from $k.car$. The latter is defined in (term) production rules $k \xrightarrow{w} \bar{e}$, such that events $\bar{e}$ in $k.mod$ are all early in this interval. The propagation of mod values for (div) rules is similar to that of pre and $post$ (Sect. 3.2).

Moreover, the nts of $\mathcal{K}$ also store the slope values induced by the $k.mod$, and the (div) rules also verify that the corresponding tempo curve θ (defined as in Sect. 2) belongs to the given model $\mathcal{M}$.

Fig. 2. Two extracts of transcription experiments; the output of our framework (qparse) is compared with the output of commercial softwares (See footnote 7).

4 Experiments

The above framework for M2S transcription has been fully implemented[4] in C++. We ran manual experiments with a dataset composed of monophonic extracts from the classical repertoire, chosen from a progressive textbook for learning rhythmic reading [12]. The extracts have a length of about 15 bars on average, different time signatures (assumed known in the experiments), and contain rhythmic notations of various style and complexity. They were recorded with a MIDI keyboard by several players of different levels (non-pianist, semi-professional and professional pianists) and processed using a command line executable. The WCFGs used for experiments, ranged from generic grammars crafted manually, to specific grammars learned from the score [5].

These experiments gave promising results, especially in cases that are traditionally complex to handle (Fig. 2), *e.g.* complex rhythms with mixed tuplets or alternations between short and long notes, grace notes, *etc.* The transcription time for each extract was below 100ms. Several optimisations (out of the scope of this paper) on the internal representation of grammars (with attributes) and scores (by binary trees instead of sequences) permitted important efficiency gains.

We are currently developing a general framework for automated evaluation, that stores MIDI inputs along references scores, trains WCFGs [5] from style-consistent corpus, and identifies errors in transcription output.

5 Conclusion

We have presented a modular framework for M2S transcription. It relies on a parsing algorithm for a given weighted grammar $\mathcal{G}$, and handles the problem of complex rhythms and grace notes. Grammar models contrast with the linear Markovian models used in [4,16,18]. Using hierarchical models is a trend sucessfully explored for rhythmic notation processing *e.g.* [1,10,17], meter detection [14], melodic search [3], and music analysis [7,13,15,19]. The approach is founded on the conviction that music structure complexity exceeds linear models.

An application of the same framework to polyphonic inputs is also under study, applying our framework to note-on and note-off input events to couple the voice separation problem with rhythm quantization.

References

1. Agon, C., Haddad, K., Assayag, G.: Representation and rendering of rhythm structures. In: Proceedings of the 2nd International Conference on WEB Delivering of Music (CW), pp. 109–113. IEEE Computer Society (2002)
2. Benetos, E., Dixon, S., Giannoulis, D., Kirchhoff, H., Klapuri, A.: Automatic music transcription: challenges and future directions. J. Intell. Inf. Syst. 41(3), 407–434 (2013)

---

[4] See https://qparse.gitlabpages.inria.fr for sources and complete examples.

3. Bernabeu, J.F., Calera-Rubio, J., Iñesta, J.M., Rizo, D.: Melodic identification using probabilistic tree automata. J. New Music Res. **40**(2), 93–103 (2011)
4. Cogliati, A., Temperley, D., Duan, Z.: Transcribing human piano performances into music notation. In: Proceedings of the ISMIR, pp. 758–764 (2016)
5. Foscarin, F., Jacquemard, F., Rigaux, P.: Modeling and Learning Rhythm Structure https://hal.inria.fr/hal-02024437, (2019)
6. Gould, E.: Behind bars: the definitive guide to music notation. Faber Music (2011)
7. Granroth-Wilding, M., Steedman, M.J.: Statistical parsing for harmonic analysis of jazz chord sequences. In: Proceedings of the ICMC (2012)
8. Honing, H.: From time to time: the representation of timing and tempo. Comput. Music J. **25**(3), 50–61 (2001)
9. Huang, L.: Advanced dynamic programming in semiring and hypergraph frameworks. In: COLING (2008)
10. Jacquemard, F., Donat-Bouillud, P., Bresson, J.: A structural theory of rhythm notation based on tree representations and term rewriting. In: Collins, T., Meredith, D., Volk, A. (eds.) MCM 2015. LNCS (LNAI), vol. 9110, pp. 3–15. Springer, Cham (2015). https://doi.org/10.1007/978-3-319-20603-5_1
11. Jahn, J.: Vector Optimization. Theory, Applications, and Extensions. Springer, Heidelberg (2011). https://doi.org/10.1007/978-3-642-17005-8
12. Lamarque, E., Goudard, M.J.: D'un rythme à l'autre, vol. 1–4. Henry Lemoine, Paris (1997)
13. Marsden, A., Tojo, S., Hirata, K.: No longer 'somewhat arbitrary': calculating salience in GTTM-style reduction. In: Proceedings of the 5th International Conference on Digital Libraries for Musicology, pp. 26–33. ACM (2018)
14. McLeod, A., Steedman, M.: Meter detection in symbolic music using a lexicalized PCFG. In: Proceedings of the SMC (2017)
15. Nakamura, E., Hamanaka, M., Hirata, K., Yoshii, K.: Tree-structured probabilistic model of monophonic written music based on the generative theory of tonal music. In: Proceedings of the ICASSP (2016)
16. Nakamura, E., Yoshii, K., Sagayama, S.: Rhythm transcription of polyphonic piano music based on merged-output HMM for multiple voices. IEEE/ACM TASLP abs/1701.08343 (2017)
17. Nauert, P.: A theory of complexity to constrain the approximation of arbitrary sequences of timepoints. Perspect. New Music **32**(2), 226–263 (1994)
18. Raphael, C.: A hybrid graphical model for rhythmic parsing. Artif. Intell. **137**(1–2), 217–238 (2002)
19. Rohrmeier, M.: Towards a generative syntax of tonal harmony. J. Math. Music **5**(1), 35–53 (2011)

Reinterpreting and Extending Anatol Vieru's Periodic Sequences Through the Cellular Automata Formalisms

Paul Lanthier[1]($\boxtimes$), Corentin Guichaoua[2]($\boxtimes$), and Moreno Andreatta[2,3]($\boxtimes$)

[1] Université de Rouen, LMRS (UMR 6085), Mont-Saint-Aignan, France
paul.lanthier@etu.univ-rouen.fr
[2] Université Strasbourg, USIAS/IRMA (UMR 7501), Strasbourg, France
{guichaoua,andreatta}@math.unistra.fr
[3] IRCAM/CNRS/Sorbonne Université, Paris, France
moreno.andreatta@ircam.fr

Abstract. In this paper we focus on Anatol Vieru's periodic sequences that we approach with the formalism of the theory of cellular automata. After extending previous results about the action (in the image direction) of one particular cellular automaton on periodic sequences we show the existence of a second one which is its complementary (or *dual*). The main idea of the paper is that the study of preimages of one of those two automata is the study of the images of the other one and vice versa. By using the duality, we have been able to show explicitly the evolution of the period and the form of the preimages for both automata. In order to illustrate the theoretical constructions, a musical composition is presented using the two automata both in the image and preimage directions.

1 Introduction

The theory of periodic sequences has been introduced by the Romanian composer Anatol Vieru (1926–1998) in the 1980's [7] as an original way to approach "modalism" as a third World [5] between tonality and atonality. This approach has been firstly formalized by mathematician Dan T. Vuza in his systematic mathematical study of the modal theory of Anatol Vieru [8]. Vieru's constructions have been successively investigated and developed at the end of the Twentieth Century, thanks to increasing collaborations between mathematicians, computer sciences and computational musicologists [3,4].

Our study tries to follow this path by taking into account the most recent results on the algebraic formalization of Vieru's Periodic sequences [1] and confronting the traditional group- and module-theoretical approach with the computational framework provided by cellular automata. This new formalism also applies to the algebraic formalization of the equal-tempered system assuming that a given cyclic group of order n may represent, at the same time, the collection of pitches (or pitch classes) and intervals (or interval classes).

© Springer Nature Switzerland AG 2019
M. Montiel et al. (Eds.): MCM 2019, LNAI 11502, pp. 261–272, 2019.
https://doi.org/10.1007/978-3-030-21392-3_21

The finite difference calculus applied to periodic sequences taking values in a cyclic group is not the only natural construction enabling the composer to explore the intimate relation between notes and intervals. There is a similar operator which is widely used in cellular automata theory and which considers additions between consecutive elements of a periodic sequence taking value in a given cyclic group.

One of the main ideas of this paper is to explore the existing duality between those two automata, using some ideas coming both from the classical algebraic approach and from the new framework based on cellular automata. The main problem, which has been partially solved, concerns the complete characterization of reducible and reproducible components of a periodic sequence in the case of the additive operator as well as study of the inverse temporal process of both the difference and additive finite calculus. This question has rarely been addressed in the previous literature despite its natural compositional application. The study of the preceding layers of a given periodic sequence musically corresponds to the search of a melodic patterns which are able to generate a given musical theme after a given number of iterations of the finite additive or difference calculus operator. These layers depend on the choice of the initial element of every preceding sequence and this can be done in a deterministic or a random way.

In order to illustrate the music-theoretical and computational properties of this inverse construction, a microtonal fugue has been composed. The subject, or main theme of the fugue, and its imitations structurally interact thanks to the action of the main automata (associated respectively with the finite difference and finite addition calculus) in the past and the future history of the main theme. This shows the reappearance of some elements of the main theme and their imitations at different preceding layers and permits to make use of them in the development of the canonic process.

2   Background

2.1   Cellular Automata

Cellular automata are specific transformations acting on a finite or infinite grid of cells. The fondamental principle is that each cell interacts with its close neighbourhood according to the rule of the cellular automaton. Let $\mathcal{A}$ be a finite set called alphabet and E the grid, a countable set. We call "full-shift" $\mathcal{X} = \mathcal{A}^E$ the set of all the possible configurations. We will choose $E = \mathbb{Z}$.

Let $\mathcal{N} \subset \mathbb{Z}$ finite be our neighbourhood, it describes the size of the interaction between cells over the action of the automaton.

A basic transformation is called the "shift", $\sigma : \mathcal{X} \to \mathcal{X}$ defined locally by:

$$(\sigma x)(i) = x(i+1), \text{ for } x \in \mathcal{X}.$$

A determinist cellular automaton is a continuous transformation $F : \mathcal{X} \to \mathcal{X}$ defined by a neighbourhood $\mathcal{N} = \{k_0, ..., k_n\}$, a finite subset of $\mathbb{Z}$ and a local transformation $f : \mathcal{A}^{\mathcal{N}} \to \mathcal{A}$ which commutes with the shift σ: $\sigma \circ F = F \circ \sigma$ and defined by

$$\forall i \in \mathbb{Z} : (Fx)(i) = f\left(x(i + k_0), \ldots, x(i + k_n)\right) := f\big(x(i + \mathcal{N})\big). \qquad (1)$$

We note DCA the set of deterministic cellular automata.

Definition 1 (Spatial dependence cone). *Let $Y := (X_n(i)_{i \in \mathbb{Z}})_{n \in \mathbb{Z}} \subset \mathcal{X}$ a given family of configurations. We define the spatial dependence cone of Y for a given neighbourhood $\mathcal{N} := \{k_0, \ldots, k_n\}$, noted $\mathcal{S}^Y_{\mathcal{N}}$, localised by a spatial point $(i, n) \in \mathbb{Z}^2$ and bounded by a length $\ell \in \mathbb{N}$ as follows:*

$$\mathcal{S}^Y_{\mathcal{N}}(i, n, \ell) := \{(m, j)/m \in [\![n, n + \ell]\!] : (m - n)k_0 + i \leq j \leq (m - n)k_n + i\}.$$

Property 1 (Trivial property). Let $F : \mathcal{X} \to \mathcal{X} \in \mathrm{DCA}$ with f its local rule and $\mathcal{N}$ its neighbourhood. Let $Y := (X_n(i)_{i \in \mathbb{Z}})_{n \in \mathbb{Z}} \subset \mathcal{X}$ with $\mathcal{S}^Y_{\mathcal{N}}$ its dependence cone. If $\forall(j, m) \in \mathcal{S}^Y_{\mathcal{N}}(i, n, \ell) : X_m(j) = f(X_{m-1}(j + \ell)_{\ell \in \mathcal{N}})$, then $X_n(i) = F^\ell X_{n-\ell}(i)$.

We shall now define an automata class that we will study hereafter.

Definition 2 (σ-polynomial deterministic cellular automata). *We note $\mathbb{Z}[\sigma^{\pm 1}]$ the set of σ-polynomial automata, i.e., of the form $F = \sum_{i \in \mathbb{Z}} a_i \sigma^i$, where a finite number of $a_i \in \mathbb{Z}$ are non-zero and σ^i is the ith self-composition of σ.*

The automata belonging to $\mathbb{Z}[\sigma^{\pm 1}]$ are linear: Let $F_1, F_2 \in \mathbb{Z}[\sigma^{\pm 1}]$ from a set $\mathcal{X}$ in itself, then $\forall x \in \mathcal{X} : (F_1 + F_2)(x) = F_1(x) + F_2(x)$ and as $\mathbb{Z}[\sigma^{\pm 1}] \subset \mathrm{DCA}$ we have that $\forall F_1, F_2 \in \mathbb{Z}[\sigma^{\pm 1}] : F_1 \circ F_2 = F_2 \circ F_1$ as $F \circ \sigma = \sigma \circ F$.

Two of these automata will be of particular focus to our work:

$$\begin{cases} \Delta = \sigma - Id \\ f_\Delta : \mathcal{A} \times \mathcal{A} \to \mathcal{A} \\ (a, b) \mapsto b - a \end{cases} \qquad \text{and} \qquad \begin{cases} \tau = \sigma + Id \\ f_\tau : \mathcal{A} \times \mathcal{A} \to \mathcal{A} \\ (a, b) \mapsto b + a \end{cases}$$

Both are of neighbourhood $\mathcal{N} = \{0, 1\}$, the first one beeing the discrete derivative (the one studied by A.Vieru) and the other one the well-known Ledrappier's one.

However, the first few properties we show apply to all such automata.

Property 2 (Isomorphism with the ring of Laurent polynomials). $(\mathbb{Z}[X^{\pm 1}], +, \times) \sim (\mathbb{Z}[\sigma^{\pm 1}], +, \circ)$, thus $(\mathbb{Z}[\sigma^{\pm 1}], +, \circ)$ is a commutative ring.

Proof. We exhibit the isomorphism:

$$\varphi : \mathbb{Z}[X^{\pm 1}] \to \mathbb{Z}[\sigma^{\pm 1}]$$

$$\left(\sum_i a_i X^i\right) + \left(\sum_i b_i X^i\right) \mapsto \left(\sum_i a_i \sigma^i\right) + \left(\sum_i b_i \sigma^i\right)$$

$$\left(\sum_i a_i X^i\right) \times \left(\sum_i b_i X^i\right) \mapsto \left(\sum_i a_i \sigma^i\right) \circ \left(\sum_i b_i \sigma^j\right)$$

We can see that this isomorphism is compatible with the two laws of the ring of Laurent polynomials.

We now present on which space of state $\mathcal{X}$ we want to work on.

2.2   Periodic Sequences

This section introduces the notation we will use throughout the article.

For the purpose of this article, a sequence will be a function $X : \mathbb{Z} \to \mathbb{Z}_N$, and $(\mathbb{Z}_N^{\mathbb{Z}}, +, \times)$ is the ring of $\mathbb{Z}_N$-valued sequences.

Definition 3 (Periodic sequence). *A sequence X is periodic if there exists a positive integer τ such that $\forall i$, $X(i) = X(i + \tau)$. The set of periodic sequences is noted $\mathcal{C}_N$.*

Definition 4 (Cyclicity and period). *Let $X \in \mathcal{C}_N^{\pi}$. Any positive integer π such that $\forall i$, $X(i) = X(i + \pi)$ is called a* cyclicity *of X. The smallest such integer τ is its* period. *We will say that X is π-cyclic and τ-periodic respectively[1]. The set of π-cyclic sequences is noted $\mathcal{C}_N^{\pi}$.*

Definition 5 (Reducibility). *Let $F \in \mathbb{Z}[\sigma^{\pm 1}]$. A sequence $X \in \mathcal{C}_N^{\pi}$ is said to be* reducible *over F if and only if there is an integer δ such that $F^{\delta} X = 0^{\mathbb{Z}}$. The set of such sequences is $Red_F(\mathcal{C}_N^{\pi}) = \bigcup_{i \in \mathbb{N}} \ker(F^i)$.*

Definition 6 (Reproducibility). *Let $F \in \mathbb{Z}[\sigma^{\pm 1}]$. A sequence $X \in \mathcal{C}_N^{\pi}$ is said to be* reproducible *over F if and only if there is a positive integer δ such that $F^{\delta} X = X$. The set of such sequences is $Rep_F(\mathcal{C}_N^{\pi}) = \bigcup_{i \in \mathbb{N}} \ker(F^i - id)$ (Fig. 1).*

(a)

$$
\begin{array}{c|ccc}
X & 1 & 1 & 0 \\
\Delta X & 0 & 1 & 1 \\
\Delta^2 X & 1 & 0 & 1 \\
\Delta^3 X & 1 & 1 & 0
\end{array}
$$

(b)

$$
\begin{array}{c|cccc}
X & 1 & 3 & 5 & 1 \\
\Delta X & 2 & 2 & 2 & 2 \\
\Delta^2 X & 0 & 0 & 0 & 0
\end{array}
$$

Fig. 1. (a) A reproducible sequence on $\mathbb{Z}_2$ (b) A reducible sequence on $\mathbb{Z}_6$

Theorem 1. *Let $F \in \mathbb{Z}[\sigma^{\pm 1}]$ and $\pi \in \mathbb{N}^*$. Any periodic sequence $X \in \mathcal{C}_N^{\pi}$ can be decomposed uniquely as $X = X_{red} + X_{rep}$, where $X_{red} \in Red_F(\mathcal{C}_N^{\pi})$ and $X_{rep} \in Rep_F(\mathcal{C}_N^{\pi})$. In other terms, $\mathcal{C}_N^{\pi} = Rep_F(\mathcal{C}_N^{\pi}) \oplus Red_F(\mathcal{C}_N^{\pi})$.*

Proof. The proof of [3, th3] generalises directly, replacing occurrences of Δ by any polynomial automaton F.

3   Summary of Previous Results and Extensions on the Automata τ and Δ

We will henceforth focus on the automata τ and Δ. To maintain brevity for shared properties, we will assume F to stand for either.

---

[1] This is slightly contrasting with conventional terminology in which saying a sequence is τ-periodic does not imply minimality.

3.1   Existing Results on Images of Δ

Now that we have defined the notions of reproducibility and reducibility, a topic of interest is their characterisation. Several results exist on Δ, but τ has yet to be studied extensively.

Theorem 2 ([3, th. 7]). *Let X be a $\mathbb{Z}_{p^k}$ valued sequence, with p prime. X is reducible if and only if it is p^m-periodic.*

While in appearance this result only applies to some cases, because $\mathbb{Z}_N$ (and by extension C_N^π) can be decomposed as a direct sum of its p-maximal subgroups, any sequence can be decomposed as one or more such case. [1] refined this result with the addition of bounds on the number of steps needed to reduce the sequence, which we do not detail here.

We note $\eta_{a,b}$ such that $\forall X \in \mathbb{Z}_N^{\mathbb{Z}}, \eta_{a,b}X(i) = X(ai + b)$.

Theorem 3. *Let $X \in C_N^\pi$. If X is reducible over Δ, then $\eta_{a,b}X$ is also reducible over Δ. Furthermore, if a and π are coprime, then the converse holds.*

Proof. The first part is a corollary of the previous theorem. The second part follows from the fact that if a and π are coprime, then $\eta_{a,b}X$ is a permutation of X, so $X = \eta_{a,b}^n \eta_{a,b}X$ for some n.

Theorem 4. *Let $X \in C_{p^k}^\pi$ with p prime. X is reproducible if and only if $\forall b \in [\![1, \pi]\!], \eta_{p^r,b}X$ is reproducible, with r the maximum integer such that p^r divides π.*

Proof. This is essentially a reformulation of corollary 15 of [3], with the added step of re-applying the parent theorem to the condition in order to express it in terms of reproducibility of its subsequences.

3.2   New Results on Preimages

We now consider the preimages of a given sequence through Δ and τ. We can rewrite the local relation defined by Δ as $X(i+1) = X(i) + \Delta X(i)$ and that defined by τ as $X(i+1) = X(i) - \tau X(i)$, thus determining a single value of an antecedent of a given sequence determines all of its values.

We will note Δ_a^{-1} (respectively τ_a^{-1}) the function that maps a sequence to its preimage through Δ (respectively τ) with value a at index 0. By extension, we will note Δ_A^{-n} with $A = (a_1, \ldots, a_n)$ the function that maps X to X' such that $\Delta^n X' = X$ and $\forall j \in [\![1, n]\!], \Delta^{n-j}X'(0) = a_j$. We also note for $X \in \mathbb{Z}_N^{\mathbb{Z}}$:

$$F_X^n = \begin{cases} F^n & \text{if } n \geq 0 \\ F_{X(n)}^{-1} \circ F_X^{n+1} & \text{if } n < 0 \end{cases} \tag{2}$$

For n increasingly negative the process can be either deterministic or random depending on how the initial values of the preimages are chosen (Fig. 2).

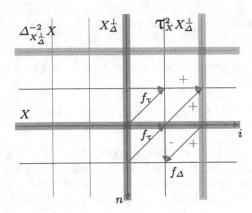

Fig. 2. Illustration of the notations. The short arrows show the local rules of automata, and wide coloured lines are sequences.

Theorem 5 (Duality of Δ and τ). *Let $X_F^{\perp} \in \mathbb{Z}_N^{\mathbb{Z}}$ be a sequence such that $X_F^{\perp}(i) = F^i X(0)$ for all positive i. We call it a dual of X. Then $\forall i, n \in \mathbb{Z}$, we have $\Delta_{X_\Delta^{\perp}}^n X(i) = \tau_X^i X_\Delta^{\perp}(n)$ and $\tau_{X_\tau^{\perp}}^n X(i) = \Delta_X^i X_\tau^{\perp}(n)$.*

Proof. We write the proof for $F = \Delta$ but it also stands for $F = \tau$ as well. Let $Y := (\Delta_{X_\Delta^{\perp}}^n X(i)_{i \in \mathbb{Z}})_{n \in \mathbb{Z}}$ and $Y^{\perp} := (\Delta_{X_\Delta^{\perp}}^n X(i)_{n \in \mathbb{Z}})_{i \in \mathbb{Z}}$. Let $\mathcal{S}_N^Y$ be the dependence cone of Y and let $\mathcal{S}_N^{Y^{\perp}}$ be the dependence cone of $Y^{\perp}$. We first remark that $\forall i, n \in \mathbb{Z}, \ell \in \mathbb{N}: \mathcal{S}_N^Y(i, n, \ell) = \mathcal{S}_N^{Y^{\perp}}(n, i, \ell)$. $\forall (j, m) \in \mathcal{S}_N^X(i, n, l)$ we have:

$$\Delta_{X_\Delta^{\perp}}^m X(j) = f_\Delta(\Delta_{X_\Delta^{\perp}}^{m-1} X(j), \Delta_{X_\Delta^{\perp}}^{m-1} X(j+1))$$
$$= \Delta_{X_\Delta^{\perp}}^{m-1} X(j+1) - \Delta_{X_\Delta^{\perp}}^{m-1} X(j)$$

So $\Delta_{X_\Delta^{\perp}}^{m-1} X(j+1) = f_\tau(\Delta_{X_\Delta^{\perp}}^{m-1} X(j), \Delta_{X_\Delta^{\perp}}^m X(j))$.

By Property 1 we can conclude that $\forall i, n \in \mathbb{Z}$, we have $\Delta_{X_\Delta^{\perp}}^n X(i) = \tau_X^i X_\Delta^{\perp}(n)$.

Corollary 1. *Let $X \in \mathcal{C}_N^\pi$ reproducible over Δ (respectively τ) in δ steps. Then there exists a unique periodic dual sequence $X_\Delta^{\perp}$ (respectively $X_\tau^{\perp}$); this sequence is of cyclicity δ and is reproducible over τ (respectively Δ) in π steps.*

Property 3. Let $X \in \mathcal{C}_N$. We have, $\forall n \in \mathbb{N}, i \in \mathbb{Z}$:

$$\Delta^n X(i) = \sum_{j=0}^{n} (-1)^{n-j} \binom{n}{j} X(i+j) \tag{3}$$

$$\tau^n X(i) = \sum_{j=0}^{n} \binom{n}{j} X(i+j) \tag{4}$$

Proof. Since $(\mathbb{Z}[\sigma^{\pm 1}], \circ)$ is commutative, we can use the binomial theorem:

$$\Delta^n = (\sigma - id)^n = \sum_{j=0}^{n}(-1)^{n+j}\binom{n}{j}\sigma^j$$

$$\tau^n = (\sigma + id)^n = \sum_{j=0}^{n}\binom{n}{j}\sigma^j$$

and the formulae follow by the left distributivity of application.

Lemma 1.

$$\forall k \geq 0, \forall i, n \text{ such that } i \geq n : \sum_{j=n}^{i}(-1)^j\binom{i}{j}\binom{j-n}{k} = (-1)^{n+k}\binom{i-k-1}{n-1}.$$

Proof.

$$A_{i,k} := \sum_{j=n}^{i}(-1)^j\binom{i}{j}\binom{j-n}{k} = \sum_{j=n}^{i}(-1)^j\left[\binom{j}{i-1} + \binom{j-1}{i-1}\right]\binom{k}{j-n}$$

$$= \sum_{j=n}^{i}(-1)^j\binom{j}{i-1}\binom{k}{j-n} + \sum_{j=n-1}^{i-1}(-1)^{j+1}\binom{j}{i-1}\binom{k}{j+1-n}$$

$$= \sum_{j=n}^{i-1}(-1)^j\binom{j}{i-1}\left[\overbrace{\binom{k}{j-n} - \binom{k}{j+1-n}}^{-\binom{k-1}{j-n}}\right] + \overbrace{(-1)^n\binom{n-1}{i-1}\binom{0}{k}}^{:=b_{i,k}}$$

$$= -A_{i-1,k-1} + b_{i,k} = \sum_{q=0}^{k}(-1)^q b_{i-q,k-q} = (-1)^k b_{i-k,0}$$

$$= (-1)^{k+n}\binom{n-1}{i-k-1} \text{ by definition.}$$

Note that $A_{i-q,q} = 0$ when $q > k$ and that $\forall i : b_{i,k} = 0$ for $k \neq 0$.

Property 4. Let $X \in \mathcal{C}_N$ and $A = (a_1, \ldots, a_n) \in \mathbb{Z}_N^n$. The values of antecedents are given by the following formulae:

$$\Delta_A^{-n}X(i) = \sum_{j=0}^{n-1}\binom{i}{j}X_{\underset{\Delta}{\perp}}(n-j) + \sum_{k=0}^{i-n}\binom{i-k-1}{n-1}X(k) \qquad (5)$$

$$\tau_A^{-n}X(i) = \sum_{j=0}^{i}(-1)^{i+j}\binom{i}{j}X_{\underset{\tau}{\perp}}(n-j) + \sum_{k=0}^{i-n}(-1)^{k+i+n}\binom{i+k-1}{n-1}X(k) \qquad (6)$$

Proof. By the duality of τ and Δ, we have:

$$\Delta_A^{-n} X(i) = \tau^i X_{\Delta}^{\perp}(0) = \sum_{j=0}^{i} \binom{i}{j} X_{\Delta}^{\perp}(j) = \sum_{j=0}^{n-1} \binom{i}{j} X_{\Delta}^{\perp}(n-j) + \sum_{j=n}^{i} \binom{i}{j} \Delta^{j-n} X(0)$$

$$= \sum_{j=0}^{n-1} \binom{i}{j} X_{\Delta}^{\perp}(n-j) + \sum_{j=n}^{i} \binom{i}{j} \sum_{k=0}^{j-n} (-1)^{j-n+k} \binom{j-n}{k} X(k)$$

$$= \sum_{j=0}^{n-1} \binom{i}{j} X_{\Delta}^{\perp}(n-j) + \sum_{k=0}^{i-n} (-1)^{-n+k} \left[\sum_{j=n}^{i} \binom{i}{j} (-1)^j \binom{j-n}{k} \right] X(k)$$

Similarly, we have:

$$\tau_A^{-n} X(i) = \Delta^i X_{\tau}^{\perp}(0) = \sum_{j=0}^{i} (-1)^{i+j} \binom{i}{j} X_{\tau}^{\perp}(j)$$

$$= \sum_{j=0}^{n-1} (-1)^{i+j} \binom{i}{j} X_{\tau}^{\perp}(n-j) + \sum_{j=n}^{i} (-1)^{i+j} \binom{i}{j} \tau^{j-n} X(0)$$

$$= \sum_{j=0}^{n-1} (-1)^{i+j} \binom{i}{j} X_{\tau}^{\perp}(n-j) + \sum_{j=n}^{i} (-1)^{i+j} \binom{i}{j} \sum_{k=0}^{j-n} \binom{j-n}{k} X(k)$$

$$= \sum_{j=0}^{n-1} (-1)^{i+j} \binom{i}{j} X_{\tau}^{\perp}(n-j) + \sum_{k=0}^{i-n} (-1)^i \left[\sum_{j=n}^{i} \binom{i}{j} (-1)^j \binom{j-n}{k} \right] X(k)$$

By applying Lemma 1 to the expression in square brackets in both equations, we obtain the aforementionned formulae.

Unlike through F, $\mathcal{C}_N^\pi$ is not stable through F_a^{-1}, as the period may grow, in a fashion we will now characterise.

Theorem 6. *Let $X \in \mathcal{C}_N$ of period τ. Then $\Delta_a^{-1} X$ is of period $o_N(\overline{X})\tau$, where $o_N(x)$ denotes the (additive) order of x in $\mathbb{Z}_N$, and $\overline{X} = \Delta_a^{-1} X(\tau) - \Delta_a^{-1} X(0)$.*

Proof. Since X is τ-periodic, $\forall i, k \in \mathbb{Z}$, $X(i) = X(i + k\tau)$, therefore $\Delta_a^{-1} X(i + k\tau) = \Delta_a^{-1} X(i) \iff \Delta_a^{-1} X(i + k\tau + 1) = \Delta_a^{-1} X(i+1)$ and by induction $\Delta_a^{-1} X$ is $k\tau$-cyclic. We also know that τ divides the period of $\Delta_a^{-1} X$ so in order to find it we need to find the minimal integer $k > 0$ such that $\Delta_a^{-1} X(k\tau) = \Delta_a^{-1} X(0)$.

From the formula above, we can see that $\Delta_a^{-1} X(i+\tau) - \Delta_a^{-1} X(i) = \Delta_a^{-1} X(i + n\tau) - \Delta_a^{-1} X(i + (n-1)\tau)$, therefore $\Delta_a^{-1} X(k\tau) - \Delta_a^{-1} X(0) = k(\Delta_a^{-1} X(k\tau) - \Delta_a^{-1} X(0))$. By definition, the smallest $k > 0$ such that this product is 0 is the order of $\overline{X}$ (as defined above), hence $\Delta_a^{-1} X$ is $o_N(\overline{X})\tau$-periodic.

Theorem 7. *Let $X \in \mathcal{C}_N$ of period τ. Then $\tau_a^{-1} X$ is of period (Fig. 3):*

- $o_N(\overline{X})\tau$, *where* $\overline{X} = \tau_a^{-1} X(\tau) - \tau_a^{-1} X(0)$, *if τ is even.*
- τ *if $\overline{X} = 0$ or 2τ otherwise, if τ is odd.*

$$X \mid 1\,3\,5\,5\,1\,0\,1\,3\,5\,5\,1\,0\,1\ldots$$
$$\Delta_2^{-1}X \mid 2\,3\,0\,5\,4\,5\,5\,0\,3\,2\,1\,2\,2\ldots$$

Fig. 3. Period growth on a $\mathbb{Z}_6$-valued sequence.

Proof. Through the same argument as above, we need to find the smallest integer $k > 0$ such that $\tau_a^{-1}X(k\tau) = \tau_a^{-1}X(0)$. From there two cases arise:

- τ is even: from the formula, we get $\Delta_a^{-1}X(i+\tau) - \Delta_a^{-1}X(i) = \Delta_a^{-1}X(i+n\tau) - \Delta_a^{-1}X(i + (n-1)\tau)$ and the rest of the proof follows as above;
- τ is odd: we get $\Delta_a^{-1}X(i+\tau) - \Delta_a^{-1}X(i) = -(\Delta_a^{-1}X(i+2\tau) - \Delta_a^{-1}X(i+\tau))$, therefore $\Delta_a^{-1}X(i+2\tau) = \Delta_a^{-1}X(i)$ and k is 2, unless $\overline{X} = 0$, in which case k is 1.

This last result has interesting corollaries that allow us to partially characterise reproducible and reducible sequences over τ.

Corollary 2. *If a sequence $X \in \mathcal{C}_N$ is reducible over τ, then it is either constant or its period is of the form $2\prod_k q_k$, where q_k divides N.*

Proof. Any reducible sequence is an antecedent of the zero sequence, which is of period 1, and the order of an element of $\mathbb{Z}_N$ always divides N.

Corollary 3. *If a sequence $X \in \mathcal{C}_N^\pi$ is reducible over τ and π is odd, then it is constant and $X(0) \in \frac{N}{2^k}\mathbb{Z}_N$ with 2^k the largest power of 2 dividing N.*

Proof. X is constant according to the previous corollary. The value of constant sequences doubles with each iteration of τ, and $\frac{N}{2^k}\mathbb{Z}_N$ are the solutions to the equation $\exists l : 2^l \times x = 0 \mod N$.

Corollary 4. *Let $X \in \mathcal{C}_N^\pi$. If N and π are odd, then X is reproducible over τ.*

Proof. From the previous corollary, if both N and π are odd, the only reducible sequence is the zero sequence. Therefore, $\mathcal{C}_N^\pi = \operatorname{Rep}_\tau(\mathcal{C}_N^\pi) \oplus \{0^{\mathbb{Z}}\} = \operatorname{Rep}_\tau(\mathcal{C}_N^\pi)$.

4   Musical Example

The search of the preimages leads to a natural question from a compositional point of view: can we find elements of our initial periodic sequence by going in its past with the two automata or do we forget totally our initial configuration?

The chosen example is linked to that question, being a fugue, whose sheets[2] and audio[3] are available online. In fact in a fugue, a leading element is present, the so called subject that may be accompanied by one or more countersubjects.

After the exposition where the subject and countersubjects move from one part to another, a special moment arises: the development. This moment is interesting and one of the main possible challenges is to bring something new but still inherited from the subject and countersubjects.

The alphabet $\mathcal{A} = \mathbb{Z}_{16}$ was chosen with the scale represented in Fig. 4.

---

[2] http://repmus.ircam.fr/_media/moreno/score_lanthier_duality.pdf.
[3] http://repmus.ircam.fr/_media/moreno/audio_lanthier_duality.mp3.

Fig. 4. The octave divided in 16 equal parts which is used for the composition.

A subject α was chosen to lead this experience and the original thing was to take two countersubjects being the images of this subject by the two automata (Figs. 5 and 6).

To find elements of α, $\Delta\alpha$ and $\tau\alpha$ in the preimages, the search of permutations (noted p), transpositions ($\alpha + a$), subsequences (η) and "similar" elements were used, for instance $10, 13, 1$ is considered close to $10, 12, 1$ which we indicate by $10, 13, 1 \simeq 10, 12, 1$. Another symbol was used to describe the "head" of a thema, noted $\wedge$ (Fig. 7).

Fig. 5. The thema "Alpha"

Fig. 6. First countersubject

Fig. 7. Second countersubject

Fig. 8. 2 Extracts [29,39] and [46,53] bars from the development with preimages

We can clearly see that the density of elements of α, $\Delta\alpha$ and $\tau\alpha$ in the development is high in respect to the transformations we spoke about. This clearly leads to think that there is a weaker notion than reproducibility in the past to investigate and that the initial value is not forgotten in a sense. The preimages were chosen for the period to remain constant or to double in order to not have too long thema, it constrained the number of possibilities (Fig. 8).

5 Perspectives

An important open question would be to demonstrate if by choosing some specific initial values preimages can be obtained containing more elements of the initial configuration than some other paths. From a probabilistic point of view, it would be interesting to see if by choosing randomly the initial values of the preimages, we forget the initial configuration. The main difficulty lies in the evolutionary character of the period of the Markov process that the preimages describe. But in the case of a non-exploding period evolution we can conjecture that the initial condition is eventually forgotten, as the uniform measure on the alphabet used to choose initial values for preimages is preserved by the two automata combined with the duality result. Do other pairs of cellular automata share a similar duality? Is it possible to generalize Vieru's theory via wider classes of automata?

References

1. Ancellotti, N.: On Some Algebraic Aspects of Anatol Vieru Periodic Sequences. Master, Università degli studi di Padova (2015)
2. Andreatta, M., Agon, C., Noll, T., Amiot, E.: Towards pedagogability of mathematical music theory. In: Bridges: Mathematical Connections in Art, Music and Science, pp. 277–284 (2006)
3. Andreatta, M., Vuza, D.T.: On some properties of periodic sequences in Anatol Vieru's modal theory. Tatra Mt. Math. Publ. **23**(1), 1–15 (2001)
4. Andreatta, M., Vuza, D.T., Agon, C.: On some theoretical and computational aspects of Anatol Vieru's periodic sequences. Soft Comput. **8**(9), 588–596 (2004)
5. Vieru, A.: Modalism-a "Third World". Perspect. New Music **24**, 62–71 (1985)
6. Vieru, A.: Generating modal sequences (a remote approach to minimal music). Perspect. New Music **30**, 178–200 (1992)
7. Vieru, A.: The Book of Modes (I, II): From Modes to a Model of the Intervallic Musical Thought: from Modes to Musical Time. Editura Muzicală (1993)
8. Vuza, D.: Aspects mathématiques dans la théorie modale d'Anatol Vieru. Editura Academiei Republicii Socialiste România (1982)

Models for Music Cognition and Beat Tracking

Surprisal, Liking, and Musical Affect

Noah R. Fram$^{(\boxtimes)}$

CCRMA, 660 Lomita Drive, Stanford, CA 94305, USA
nfram@ccrma.stanford.edu
http://ccrma.stanford.edu

Abstract. Formulation and processing of expectation has long been viewed as an essential component of the emotional, psychological, and neurological response to musical events. There are multiple theories of musical expectation, ranging from a broad association between expectation violation and musical affect to precise descriptions of neurocognitive networks that contribute to the perception of surprising stimuli. In this paper, we propose a probabilistic model of musical expectation that relies on the recursive updating of listeners' conditional predictions of future events in the musical stream. This model is defined in terms of cross-entropy, or information content given a prior model. A probabilistic program implementing some aspects of this model with melodies from Bach chorales is shown to support the hypothesized connection between the evolution of surprisal through a piece and affective arousal, indexed by the spread of possible deviations from the expected play count.

Keywords: Affect · Entropy · Music · Perception ·
Probabilistic programming · Surprisal

1 Introduction

Meyer's seminal work, *Emotion and Meaning in Music* (1956) formed the basis of a widely held conceptualized of musical expectation as a cognitive process in a broadly Bayesian mold. Meyer described the crucial role that expectation violations play in constructing musical affect, thus implying that expectation mediates between musical perception and emotional response. Other scholars soon incorporated this claim into their own approaches to a cognitive analysis of musical expectation and surprisal. Narmour's implication-realization model, which was crafted as an alternative to the Schenckerian orthodoxy in music analysis, represents the first such theory to explicitly draw on Gestalt principles of perception (Narmour 1989). It would later be amended to include distinctions between "top-down" (or semantic) and "bottom-up" (or phonetic) expectations (Narmour 1991).

Since then, theorists have also begun representing musical expectation using analogies to physical processes or established measures from information theory. Margulis's delineation of three distinct kinds of musical tension (Margulis 2005)

© Springer Nature Switzerland AG 2019
M. Montiel et al. (Eds.): MCM 2019, LNAI 11502, pp. 275–286, 2019.
https://doi.org/10.1007/978-3-030-21392-3_22

and Larson's representation of melodies as obeying the musical equivalent of gravity, inertia, and magnetism (Larson 2002; 2004) are indicative of this trend, and offer ample room for computational exploration. Other researchers have taken more directly computational approaches. For instance, Temperley applied Bayesian probability theory directly to describe the cognitive process by which humans predict underlying structural features from musical surfaces (Temperley 2004) and devised a musical version of Shannon entropy (Temperley 2007), and Margulis and Beatty investigated its usefulness as an analytic tool (Margulis and Beatty 2008).

Recently these two general approaches have converged. Agres, Abdallah, and Pearce demonstrated that information-theoretic measures such as those developed by Margulis and Temperley are related to musical memory (Agres et al. 2018). Bayesian modelling has been applied, with varying amounts of success, to neurological correlates of surprisal, notably the mismatch negativity (MMN) (Lieder et al. 2013) and early right anterior negativity (ERAN) (Broderick et al. 2018). In addition, there is a theorized inverse-U relationship between musical complexity and reported preference (Güçlütürk et al. 2016; McMullen and Arnold 1976), and recent research has led to descriptive models of this correlation (Agres et al. 2017). However, a generative model capable of directly predicting behavioral correlates of musical liking or preference based on measures of musical expectation and surprisal is lacking.

This study aims to fill precisely this gap. Its specific aims are twofold: to devise a Bayesian model on a cognitive level of analysis that will capture both the underlying construction of musical expectations and how those expectations relate to behavior surrounding liking; and to determine what measures of liking or preference are feasible and useful for training and assessing such a two-level model.

2   Model Foundations

Extant theories suggest four primary characteristics of musical expectation: it is recursive, in that the match or mismatch between an expectation and an observed event is used to construct future expectations; it is dynamic, in that the mental model used to make predictions is not fixed; it is based on musical tendencies, as opposed to physical or cultural pressures; and it is related to information content. Furthermore, as indicated both by neurophysiological research and theories of musical semiotics, music is perceived as a sequence of events, rather than a continuous stream of sound. Given the symbolic nature of musical perception, two approaches to modelling music expectation – Huron's ITPRA model from his book *Sweet Anticipation* (2006), and Agres, Abdallah, and Pearce's two-level model of informational expectation (2018) – offer advances in this area of scholarship that are particularly relevant to the present project.

2.1 The ITPRA Model

Huron (2006) theorizes that musical expectations are constructed in five over-lapping stages that are organized into two epochs: the pre-event epoch, consisting of the imagination and tension stages; and the post-event epoch, consisting of the prediction, reaction, and appraisal portions. This structure is shown in Fig. 1. First, listeners imagine possible outcomes of an event. The approach of the imagined event leads to an increase in tension, as the listener waits to discover whether or not their prediction is valid. Once the event occurs, there is an immediate assessment of the accuracy of the prediction and an immediate reactive assessment, followed by a more thorough appraisal and adjustment of the predictive parameters.

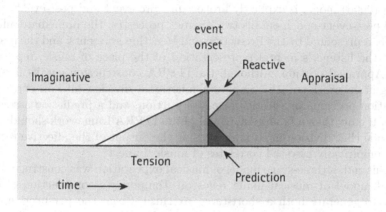

Fig. 1. The ITPRA model of musical expectation

This approach highlights both the affective nature of musical expectation proposed by Meyer (1956) and the plasticity of prediction. To Huron, expectation is based more on the listener's beliefs about musical structure than the music's actual structure; to borrow from Lerdahl (1988), expectation has more to do with the listener's grammar than with the composer's. Therefore, Huron's construction of musical expectation is fundamentally Bayesian, as it entails a listener making non-deterministic inferences about a piece of music and, by extension, about its creator.

2.2 Probabilistic Expectation

As described by Margulis and Beatty (2008), entropy and other information-theoretic measures have become increasingly popular in music analysis. These measures were shown by Agres et al. (2018) to be related to musical expectation. Specifically, they showed that a probabilistic model relying on measures of information content, coding gain, and predictive information could accurately simulate memory for musical sequences. In addition, they demonstrated the benefits of training both a long-term (top-down) and a short-term (bottom-up) predictive model simultaneously, and using both to generate an expectation.

This approach is not necessarily resource-rational, and does not reflect abstract perception of musical types. But it does represent an important advance in modelling musical expectation. Most notably, it recasts the problem of building expectation, which had previously been a question of pure prediction, as an optimization problem on information-theoretic measures of musical structure. This approach is potentially much more efficient, and lends itself very well to expansions into more ecologically-valid models of musical expectation.

3   Surprisal Model of Musical Liking

Huron's (2006) model is explicitly broken into pre-event and post-event epochs, but the post-event epoch entails two distinct processes: the immediate affective response, represented by the Prediction and Reaction segments; and the reassessment of the listener's mental representation of the piece of music, represented by the Appraisal portion. Although the ITPRA construction entails five separate cognitive processes, this implies a functional division into an expectation formulation portion, an affective response portion, and a prediction assessment portion. If true, then a functional model of the ITPRA framework should explicitly encode that division in such a way that the output of the affective response mirrors empirically assessed correlates of musical affect.

To this end, a three-stage model of musical expectation was constructed. This surprisal model of musical liking relies on Temperley's construction of cross-entropy to generate both a short-term, extrinsic (from the perspective of the listener) model of musical expectation and a long-term, intrinsic collection of models for expectations on inferred musical types.

3.1   Mathematical Formulation

Extrinsic Model. For a naïve listener, the initial condition is assumed to be generated from a flat Dirichlet distribution:

$$\mathbf{p} = (p_0, ..., p_{k-1})$$
$$\sum \mathbf{p} = 1 \tag{1}$$

Here, $\mathbf{p}$ is any element of the open standard $k - 1$-simplex.

$$P_0(x|\mathbf{p}) = \prod_{i=0}^{k-1} p_i^{[x=i]} \tag{2}$$

This initial distribution is used in the pre-event epoch to generate an intrinsic musical expectation. The initial (empty) sequence of musical events is denoted

D_0, and the sequence of the first n events is D_n. At each musical event, the listener makes an observation and assesses its surprisal given this expected intrinsic distribution:

$$H_{n-1}(D_n, P_{n-1}) = -\frac{1}{n} \log P_{n-1}(D_n | D_{n-1}), \ n = 1, 2, \ldots \tag{3}$$

The surprisal vector $\mathbf{H} = (H_0, \ldots, H_{k-1})$ will be used to generate a liking rating at the end of the process. During the post-event epoch, the probability distribution is updated within the bounds of a malleability tolerance r, to prevent over-fitting early in the process:

$$P_n = \underset{|P - P_{n-1}| < r}{\arg \min} \ H_{n-1}(D_n, P) \tag{4}$$

Here, $|P - P_{n-1}|$ is determined by a distance measure on distributions such as the Kullbach-Liebler divergence, and r governs how much the intrinsic distribution can change in any time-step.

Intrinsic Model. This intrinsic process runs in parallel to an extrinsic, long-term process, which operates according to similar principles. The primary mathematical difference between the extrinsic and intrinsic models is that while the intrinsic model constructs an expectation based on observed data from *within* a piece of music, the extrinsic model predicts which type or category of music a piece belongs to and constructs an expectation based on an archetypal distribution for that type. Since pieces are sorted into categories, if the observed dataset consists of only one piece, there is by definition only one available type. As a result, the distribution over the number of categories is initialized after encountering a second piece. For a näive listener, this distribution is sampled from a Dirichlet distribution where, for piece k with the distribution over n categories at time step $k - 1$ denoted $\mathbf{q}_{k-1} = (q_0, \ldots, q_{n-1})$, the following holds:

$$\alpha = (\alpha_0, \ldots, \alpha_n)$$

$$\alpha_i^{[x<n]} = \frac{1}{(n-1)q_i}, \ \alpha_n = 1 \tag{5}$$

$$\mathbf{q}_k = \text{sample}(\text{Dir}(\alpha))$$

This construction maintains a bias toward the same number of categories as in the previous step, with a neutral possibility of adding another category. The distribution over the number of categories is optimized after each piece of music, so the expected number of categories $E(\mathbf{q}_k)$ remains constant while a piece of music is playing.

Each category has an associated probability distribution, denoted Q_i. At each time step, the listener selects the most likely category C_i given the musical context by minimizing cross-entropy:

$$i = \underset{i \in 0, \ldots, E(\mathbf{q}_k)}{\arg \min} \ H_{n-1}(D_n, Q_i) \tag{6}$$

After a musical piece concludes, the number of categories is inferred. If a category is added, the new piece is assumed to be the seed. If there are fewer categories than before, the most similar pair (by Kullbach-Leibler divergence) are combined:

$$\mathbf{P} = (p_0, ..., p_j), \quad \mathbf{Q} = (q_0, ..., q_j)$$

$$\mathbf{R} = \left\{ \left(\frac{p_i + q_i}{2} \right) \right\}_{i \in 0, ..., j} \tag{7}$$

After the categories are set, the last categorization choice C_i is preserved and the corresponding distribution is updated using the last short-term distribution P to minimize distribution cross-entropy:

$$Q_i^* = \underset{|Q - Q_i| < R}{\arg \min} \left| \sum_{x \in X} Q_i(X = x) \log Q(X = x) \right| \tag{8}$$

This intrinsic model reaches a series of locally stable sets of categories, which are only perturbed by unusual or uncategorizable pieces of music. However, the terms of genres drift over time, which reflects the fundamentally dynamic nature of genre proposed by contemporary theorists such as Brackett (2016), Sturm (2014), Frow (2005), and Bhatia (2004; 2016).

Musical Resolution. Since D_n is a sequence of events, where "events" are arbitrarily defined, this structure allows for variation in perceptual resolution depending on what kind of events are analyzed. Some *a priori* possibilities include onsets (isochronous or otherwise), beats, harmonic shifts, phrases, or melodic cycles. In human cognition, these "events" are likely even more abstract, as they are learned subdivisions of continuous auditory signals.

Liking. The relationship between musical affect and liking is complicated by the strong connection between preference for certain categories or genres of music and exemplars of those categories or genres (Rentfrow and Gosling 2007). However, the inverse-U relationship discussed earlier indicates a relationship between surprisal and preference may emerge when controlling for other extramusical associations or characteristics of music. One possible explanation, which will be assessed in the experimental portion of this paper, is that features of the surprisal vector are related to affective arousal, but not valence. This would imply that information content and the accuracy of expectations are connected to the strength of the affective response, but not necessarily its direction.

3.2   Bayesian Formulation

This procedure is somewhat simpler to depict using a Bayesian network, such as the one in Fig. 2. In this depiction, the precise probabilistic descriptions of the inference steps are hidden in favor of showing the connections among the various

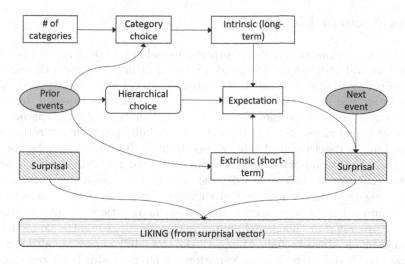

Fig. 2. Schematic of the Bayesian model connecting liking with musical surprisal.

models. Two notable features of this approach stand out: first, although the extrinsic and intrinsic models are probabilistically dependent, there is no causal dependence between the two; second, the only decision made by the listener is the hierarchical choice between the extrinsic and intrinsic predictions. Since music unfolds in time, the network in Fig. 2 represents the activity in one time-step, and does not include the process of adjusting the extrinsic model after a piece has concluded.

Since there is limited data being passed, and the resource-heavy portion occurs after the piece has concluded, this framework is likely resource-rational, especially since the only preserved information is a finite set of distributions.

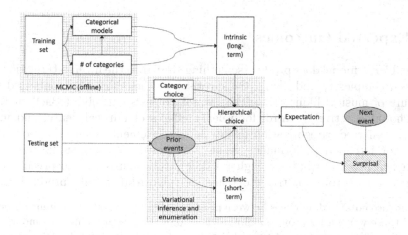

Fig. 3. Visual schematic of implementation in Python and WebPPL.

4   Assessment Methods

The explicit implementation of the surprisal model in this study, shown in Fig. 3, required several restrictions. First and foremost, rather than learn the extrinsic and intrinsic portions in parallel, the intrinsic model was implemented offline and then applied as a static set of distributions. This was to avoid determining an order in which the melodies in question were encountered. Second, the domain of "musical events" was restricted to melodic pitch onsets, rather than a more general description of musical possibilities. Third, the number of possible categories in the extrinsic model was assumed to be between 1 and 10, and the length of a musical "word" was held to two consecutive onsets when constructing the melodic language of thought. These restrictions were to conserve computational power, and do not reflect assumptions about the genuine cognitive process that this model approximates. Lastly, the intrinsic model was trained using a Markov chain Monte Carlo (MCMC) approach, although the theorized methodology is closer to variational inference. This last alteration was due to interference between the inferences on the number of categories and the distributions that characterize those categories.

The adjusted model was implemented in WebPPL using a data management and cross-validation procedure written in Python. Once finished, this process generates a series of surprisal vectors, with a new cross-entropy value generated for each melodic onset.

The probabilistic program described above was applied to a set of 371 melodies from Bach chorales, extracted from the KernScores database hosted by the Center for Computer-Assisted Research in the Humanities (CCARH) at the Stanford University Music Department (Sapp 2005). Post-hoc statistical methods, most notably hierarchical cluster analysis, were used to analyze the resulting data. These methods are not thought to reflect actual cognitive behavior, but are rather an attempt to uncover structures that are embedded in the surprisal vectors.

5   Expected Outcomes

If the ITPRA model does produce something similar to the inverse-U relationship between complexity and liking, the surprisal vectors should be connected to a measure of musical liking. Since the dataset consists entirely of Bach chorales, this should effectively control for valence effects of musical genre, and imply that the inferred categorization relates more to elements such as key or mode, meter, or intended performance venue.[1] Without making assumptions about which features contribute to higher liking values, clustering surprisal vectors using a time-warping or trajectory analysis algorithm should produce groups

---

[1] There are notable differences between pieces written for casual or amateur musicians and those written for professional musicians, and the rise in virtuosic compositional practice was contemporaneous with Bach's career (Baron 1998; Lott 2015; Radice 2012).

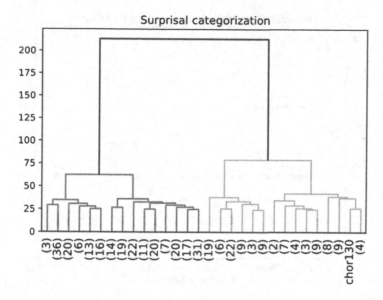

Fig. 4. Dendrogram showing clusters in the surprisal vectors for Bach chorale melodies.

of pieces with different preference ratings. These preference ratings should then be reflected in behavioral measures such as consumption or recommendation frequency.

6   Results

As the melodies are all of different lengths, the surprisal vectors were resampled to include the same number of data points. Distance between surprisal vectors was then calculated using the Keogh lower bound on the dynamic time-warping distance to preserve contour features of their development in time, and those distances were used to cluster the melodies with Ward's algorithm (Fig. 4).

This clustering approach has been used in automatic genre recognition (AGR) research, and has been shown to have a favorable accuracy over other methods when dealing with pieces of significantly different tempi (Holzapfel and Stylianou 2008). In addition, time-warping methods have been shown to ameliorate the effects of noise when searching for periodicity in time series signals (Elfeky et al. 2005), which provides further support for its validity as an analytical method here. Play counts for a subset of these chorales were extracted from Spotify. Since the play counts decay logarithmically as the album progresses, deviation from the expected play count was computed and plotted against category in the surprisal analysis (Fig. 5).

This plot indicates that categories 1 and 3 were much more concentrated around no deviation, while categories 2 and 4 were more likely to overshoot the expectation. However, an ANOVA indicated no significant shift in the mean deviation from expected play time by category.

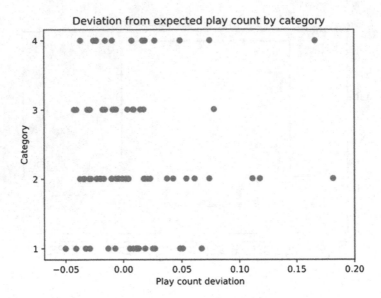

Fig. 5. Plot of $\log(\text{playCount}) - E(\log(\text{playCount}))$ against surprisal vector category.

7   Discussion

Although these data are imprecise, and the results are not statistically clear, there are a few potentially interesting conclusions that may be drawn. Most notably, these data suggest a relationship between features of the surprisal vector and the variation in liking, especially upwards variability. This specific connection is derived from the distance metric used; dynamic time-warping distance preserves similarities in trajectories that are not preserved by more standard metrics such as Euclidean distance. Such expanded variability suggests a possible link between features of surprisal's movements in time and affective arousal, although further study is necessary for confirmation.

Most promising is that these trends follow the theoretical prediction that expectation violation is directly related to musical affect, and that this effect is visible even with the severe limitations of this particular implementation. The dataset in this case, consisting solely of soprano melodies from Bach chorales, is limited in size, does not have much internal variation, and is underconsumed in the current musical market. Similarly, using deviation from expected play counts as a proxy for liking suffers from multiple assumptions, most notably the assumptions that more-played tracks are better-liked and that deviation from a logarithmic trendline is a robust measure of deviation in play counts.

Further research requires a more complete dataset, including a larger range of musical idioms and a more thorough language of musical symbols, and a more accurate measure of liking. One possibility is to use MIDI realizations of pop songs, build symbols consisting of note simultaneities (a generalization of chords and harmonies), dynamic levels or motion, and basic instrumentation, and correlate the resulting surprisal categories with measures of chart performance. This would allow the model to train sequentially rather than building the intrinsic model offline, much like a real listener would.

Acknowledgments. My thanks to Noah Goodman, Ben Peloquin, Robert Hawkins, Malcolm Slaney, and Jonathan Berger for their assistance in the development and implementation of this research.

References

Agres, K., Abdallah, S., Pearce, M.: Information-theoretic properties of auditory sequences dynamically influence expectation and memory. Cogn. Sci. **42**(1), 43–76 (2018)

Agres, K., Herremans, D., Bigo, L., Conklin, D.: Harmonic structure predicts the enjoyment of uplifting trance music. Front. Psychol. **7**, 1999 (2017)

Baron, J.H.: Intimate Music: A History of the Idea of Chamber Music. Pendragon Press, Stuyvesant (1998)

Bhatia, V.K.: Worlds of Written Discourse: A Genre-Based View. Continuum International, London (2004)

Bhatia, V.K.: Genre as interdiscursive performance in public space. In: Reiff, M.J., Bawarshi, A. (eds.) Genre and the Performance of Publics, pp. 25–42. University Press of Colorado, Boulder (2016)

Brackett, D.: Categorizing Sound. University of California Press, Oakland (2016)

Broderick, M.P., Anderson, A.J., Di Liberto, G.M., Cross, M.J., Lalor, E.C.: Electrophysiological correlates of semantic dissimilarity reflect the comprehension of natural, narrative speech. Curr. Biol. **28**(5), 803–809 (2018)

Elfeky, M.G., Aref, W.G., Elmagarmid, A.K.: WARP: time warping for periodicity detection. In: Fifth IEEE International Conference on Data Mining (ICDM 2005), p. 8, November 2005. https://doi.org/10.1109/ICDM.2005.152

Frow, J.: Genre: The New Critical Idiom. Routledge, New York (2005)

Güçlütürk, Y., Jacobs, R.H.A.H., van Lier, R.: Liking versus complexity: decomposing the inverted U-curve. Front. Hum. Neurosci. **10**, 112 (2016)

Holzapfel, A., Stylianou, Y.: Rhythmic similarity of music based on dynamic periodicity warping. In: 2008 IEEE International Conference on Acoustics, Speech and Signal Processing, pp. 2217–2220, March 2008. https://doi.org/10.1109/ICASSP.2008.4518085

Huron, D.: Sweet Anticipation: Music and the Psychology of Expectation. The MIT Press, Cambridge (2006)

Larson, S.: Musical forces, melodic expectation, and jazz melody. Music Percept. **19**(3), 351–385 (2002)

Larson, S.: Musical forces and melodic expectations: comparing computer models and experimental results. Music Percept. **21**(4), 457–498 (2004)

Lerdahl, F.: Cognitive constraints on compositional systems. Contemp. Music Rev. **6**(2), 97–121 (1988)

Lieder, F., Klaas, S.E., Daunizeau, J., Garrida, M.I., Friston, K.J.: A neurocomputational model of the mismatch negativity. PLoS Comput. Biol. **9**(11), e1003288 (2013)

Lott, M.S.: The Social Worlds of Nineteenth-Century Chamber Music: Composers, Consumers, Communities. University of Illinois Press, Urbana (2015)

Margulis, E.H.: A model of melodic expectation. Music Percept. **22**(4), 663–714 (2005)

Margulis, E.H., Beatty, A.P.: Musical style, psychoaesthetics, and prospects for entropy as an analytic tool. Comput. Music J. **32**(4), 64–78 (2008)

McMullen, P.T., Arnold, M.J.: Preference and interest as functions of distributional redundancy in rhythmic sequences. J. Res. Music Educ. **24**(1), 22–31 (1976)

Meyer, L.B.: Emotion and Meaning in Music. University of Chicago Press, Chicago (1956)

Narmour, E.: The "genetic code" of melody: cognitive structures generated by the implication-realization model. Contemp. Music Rev. **4**(1), 45–63 (1989)

Narmour, E.: The top-down and bottom-up systems of musical implication: building on Meyer's theory of emotional syntax. Music Percept. **9**(1), 1–26 (1991)

Radice, M.A.: Chamber Music: An Essential History. The University of Michigan Press, Ann Arbor (2012)

Rentfrow, P.J., Gosling, S.D.: The content and validity of music-genre stereotypes among college students. Psychol. Music **35**(2), 306–326 (2007). https://doi.org/10.1177/0305735607070382

Sapp, C.S.: Online database of scores in the Humdrum file format. In: ISMIR, pp. 664–665 (2005)

Sturm, B.L.: The state of the art ten years after a state of the art: future research in music information retrieval. J. New Music Res. **43**(2), 147–172 (2014)

Temperley, D.: Bayesian models of musical structure and cognition. Musicae Scientiae **8**(2), 175–205 (2004)

Temperley, D.: Music and Probability. The MIT Press, Cambridge (2007)

Autocorrelation of Pitch-Event Vectors in Meter Finding

Christopher Wm. White[✉]

The University of Massachusetts Amherst, Amherst, USA
cwmwhite@umass.edu

Abstract. Computational researchers often use autocorrelation techniques to identify the meter of a musical passage, tracking the ebs and flows of loudness or –if using symbolic data– peaks and valleys of note attacks. This paper investigates the relative success of various harmonic and pitch events compared to a note-attack model when identifying musical meter using autocorrelation. This study implements such a process using several different parameters: note attacks, pitch class change, set class probabilities, and scale-degree set probabilities. These outputs are measured against a ground truth derived from each piece's notated time signature. The relative success of each parameter is tracked using F scores. While the study shows that loudness-oriented parameters are overall more successful, the paper discusses how its findings add to our understanding of musical meter and the role played by pitch parameters in metric accents.

Keywords: Computation · Corpus analysis · Modeling · Meter

1 Introduction

For some decades, computational researchers have used autocorrelation to identify meter in music [1–4]. These approaches represent musical passages as timelines that –if using sound signals– track peaks and nadirs of loudness. In the case of symbolic representations (specifically of polyphonic music), these approaches generally track the numbers of note onsets (i.e., note attacks) occurring at each moment. Using the logic that greater numbers of note attacks should create louder moments, these approaches treat note attacks as a proxy for loudness [5, 6].

Figure 1a shows a vector of note attacks for the first two measures of a harmonization of "O Canada," with the beginnings of measures 1 and 2 highlighted. The autocorrelation method modulates the prime vector through each possible rotation and correlates those rotations with the prime vector. Equation 1 shows the formula for r_k, the autocorrelation at rotation k, in terms of the input vector x with $\bar{x}$ serving as the mean of x. Below Fig. 1b's prime vector, I show three example rotations of the series. Figure 1c shows the resulting correlation coefficients for all rotations, with the x-axis metered in quarter-note durations (i.e., each rotation offsets events sequentially by an eighth-note, and therefore axis's units progress by .5). The process shows that rotations corresponding to 2 quarter notes return the highest correlation, followed by quarter-note, with the intervening eighth-note rotations returning negative correlations.

© Springer Nature Switzerland AG 2019
M. Montiel et al. (Eds.): MCM 2019, LNAI 11502, pp. 287–296, 2019.
https://doi.org/10.1007/978-3-030-21392-3_23

a)

b)   c)

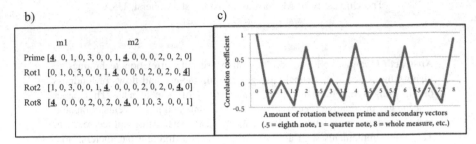

Fig. 1. (a) A harmonization of the first two measures of "O Canada," (b) a note-onset vector drawn from the harmonization with three sample rotations, (c) autocorrelations resulting from each rotation

$$r_k = \frac{\sum_{t=k+1}^{n-k}(x_{t-k} - \bar{x})(x_t - \bar{x})}{\sum_{t=1}^{n}(x_t - \bar{x})^2} \tag{1}$$

High autocorrelation values indicate recurrent similarities. The half-note peaks (i.e., peaks at multiples of 2) in Fig. 2 not only indicate that the same sorts of events happen at half-note intervals, but that the entire series of events looks similar when rotated by half note. Conversely, the negative correlations corresponding to the eighth-note off-beat pulses not only indicate that different things occur on pulses separated by those intervals, but that the surrounding events also do not align with the prime vector. (Importantly, high autocorrelation values do *not* mean that the process has identified peaks in the signal: Fig. 2's spikes do not necessarily mean those moments are metrically accented, but rather simply mean that the vector has similar properties when rotated by that interval.)

However, other parameters besides note attacks recur at predictable periodicities in Fig. 1. For instance, both measure's downbeats begin with the same tonic harmony, while dominant harmonies populate the second halves of both measures. These sorts of connections between harmony and meter have not gone unnoticed by computational researchers, with some models using pitch height [7] or harmonic changes [8–11] as potential indicators of metric emphasis. Additionally, corpus research [12, 13] shows that certain chords and cadences tend to occur on metrically-accented pulses within tonal repertoires.

But while important work has been done to test the relative efficacy of loudness versus note onsets [14] and loudness versus the arrival of certain chords and cadences [15], little work has focused on comparing loudness-oriented parameters (like note onsets) to multiple pitch-based and harmonic parameters (like chordal and pitch-class change). What pitch parameters most contribute to metric accents? Do certain kinds of harmonic events recur with sufficient regularity to identify a piece's meter? And how successful at meter finding are pitch-based parameters when compared to loudness-based parameters?

This paper investigates the relative success of various harmonic and pitch events compared to a note-attack model when identifying musical meter. In what follows, I implement the autocorrelation process using several different parameters, and measure the models' output against a ground truth derived from the piece's notated time signatures. I end by discussing how this investigation adds to our understanding of musical meter.

2 Method

2.1 The Corpus and Ground Truth

This study relies on the *music21* corpus [16]. Several desiderata needed to be considered when selecting portions of this corpus. First, files with reliable metric metadata were required in order to construct a ground truth: therefore, only *musicXML* files were selected, since their time signature data is generally more reliable (being entered by the encoder rather than set as a default). Second, given the focus on harmony and note onsets, only polyphonic pieces were considered. Third, in order to incorporate different styles and textures, multiple composers were used; however, in order for these composers' sub-corpora to be usable in the ensuing analyses, only composers with more than nine xml files were selected. This yielded four composers: Monteverdi, Haydn, Beethoven, and Bach. The corpus was compiled using Python version 2.6 and the music21 software package [17].

The file's time signatures were used to construct a metric ground truth. The signature's denominator was used to identify a pulse level below which duple groupings were expected. In both 2/8 and 6/8 signatures, for instance, eighth notes would be expected to divide into two sixteenths. The numerator was then used to expect duple or triple groupings of the denominator's pulses. 2/8 would expect duple groupings of the eighth-note pulse, while 6/8 would expect triple groupings. The ground truth was agnostic as to broader hypermetric groupings (i.e., there was no expectation that two measures of, say, 6/8 or 2/4 would or would not group together into pulses larger than the measure).

Note that the concept of "meter" is complicated and multifaceted. I turn to some of these complications below, but for the purposes of this computational study, I heuristically equate meter with the pulses and divisions suggested by a piece's time signature. While a piece's time signature does not account for moments of metrical ambiguity and complexity (e.g., hemiolas and hypermeter), it does capture *something* about the music's pulse divisions, and it is that information on which this study relies.

2.2 The Meter-Finding Algorithm

For each file, the quickest/most-frequent pulse is identified. This is done by (a) identifying each pulse layer and (b) discarding fastest divisions that occur with less than

10% of the frequency of the next broader division. This mean that while pieces in, say, a duple meter might use a handful of sixteenth-note triplets (or even just a handful of sixteenth notes), those values would be disregarded as a viable baseline pulse. Next, a four-measure vector is extended from the beginning of the piece, with events represented as an n-dimensional vector, where n is the number of quickest/most frequent pulses present in the excerpt. For instance, Fig. 1's excerpt heuristically uses the eighth note as its baseline pulse: since there are 16 eighth-note pulses within the excerpt's two measures, the vector has 16 members.

An autocorrelation is run on each piece in the corpus, returning correlation coefficients for each rotation. Periodic peaks in the coefficients are identified. This is done by (a) identifying the highest retrieved correlation, (b) finding other equally-space peaks with similarly high correlations, (c) discounting those peaks from the signal and repeating the process to find the next-highest series of correlations. Peaks are "similar" when they are within 1/10 of the standard deviation of the entire set of correlations (in principle, the choice of fraction depends on how strict one wants to be).[1] The periodicity of those peaks are then associated with note values from the source file, and are compared with the ground truth. Figure 2, for instance, would notice that eighth-note, quarter-note, half-note, and even whole-note peaks recur, indicating those pulses to be salient, and aligning with the excerpt's ground truth.

2.3   F Scores

A fully successful assessment would identify all pulse layers indicated or suggested by the signature, while partially successful assessments identify some subset of the possible layers. Results are represented as F scores, calculated by combining *precision* and *recall*. Precision is calculated as the number of correct pulses identified given divided by all answers given. Recall is calculated as the number of correct answers given divided by the number of correct answers expected. The value runs between 0 and 1, with 1 indicating a model that perfectly identifies all possible correct answers with neither false positives nor incorrect answers. (For more, see [19].) Following musical intuition, assessments were not penalized if they missed some potential intermediate pulse between some smaller and larger duple grouping. That is, if a model identified the whole-note and quarter-note pulses within a piece notated in 4/4, yet neglected to return the half-note pulse, there was no penalty. (However, if the model had identified a dotted-half-note pulse in that context, it would be penalized.) Since there was no ground truth available for hypermeters, answers larger than the notated measure (i.e., the numerator's grouping) were ignored.

---

[1] There is no a standard way of undertaking this task, and the parameters for doing so depend on how sensitive a meter-finder one desires. On the one hand, we could simply define a "peak" as a moment higher than surrounding values (see [1, 2]), or we could undertake a Fourier transform to identify salient periodicities in our peaks [18].

2.4   Parameters Used

Six parameters were used in separate implementations of the model: (1) amounts of note onsets/attacks, (2) whether note onsets occur, (3) amounts of pitch-class change, (4) whether pc-change occurs, (5) set-class probabilities, and (6) scale-degree set probabilities. The note-onset approach was designed to best approximate the above-cited loudness-based models. This approach populated each vector with the number of notes struck at the corresponding moment in the music. The second implementation is a binary version of the first, with 1 representing events on which any note attack occurs and zero representing moments with no new note events: this approach essentially represents whether we should expect a spike of loudness at that event rather than the magnitude of the spike. The pitch-class change vectors capture how different the pitch-class content of a particular moment is from the preceding moment. (Moving from a C major triad to an F major triad would register a change of 2 pcs, since the latter triad contains one pc in common with former while introducing two new pcs.) The fourth implementation is a binary version of the pc-change vector, simply indicating whether an event introduces a new pitch class or not. In other words, this approach shows whether or not an event hosts a harmonic change.

The last two approaches use frequencies of occurrence within the overall corpus to populate the vectors with probabilities. Set-class probabilities capture the relative frequency of a particular chord structure within the larger corpus. Octave, permutational, cardinal, and transpositional equivalencies were used for the sets, but not inversional equivalence [20]. The "salami slice method" was used to parse the corpus into chord events [21]: in this method, each time a note was added or subtracted from the texture a new chord event was registered. As an example: major triads (set class [0, 4, 7]) occupy 17% of the corpus's set distribution, and therefore pulses hosting a major triad were assigned a value of .17. Finally, the probabilities of scale degree sets were similarly used, with key orientations from the files' metadata used to assign scale degrees. (Local key information was used, thereby accounting for modulations.) Sets employed modulo-12 chromatic scale degrees, such that 0 would represent tonic, 11 would represent the leading tone, and so on. Order and doublings were ignored. As an example: tonic triads make up 9% of the corpus's harmonies, and so such a chord event would be assigned a value of .09 within a vector.

To further isolate the role of pitch and harmony in metric modeling, the non-binary approaches were implemented using two versions. In the first "with zeros" approach, if no new event occurred on a pulse, the corresponding moment in that vector received a zero. A parallel vector was also used, having each value continue within the vector until replaced by another event. These "no-zeros" vectors represent the piece's timeline as only a series of sustained events, constraining the autocorrelation process to only use the events themselves rather than intervening *lacks of events*. Figure 2 and Table 1 show each version of the prime vector from another excerpt from O Canada, again using eighth-note pulses for each value in the vectors, adapted to each approach. The table also includes intermediary rows describing the pc changes and the sets used.

Fig. 2. A harmonization of "O Canada," measure 3

Table 1. Vectors drawn from Fig. 2 using each parameter, with additional notations describing pc changes, the observed set-classes, and the constituent scale-degree sets

Note-attacks	4	0	1	0	3	0	3	0
NA Binary	1	0	1	0	1	0	1	0
NA no zeros	4	4	1	1	3	3	3	3
PCs that change			A→Bb		Bb→A		{FAC}→{GBD}	
PC change	–	–	1	0	1	0	3	0
PC binary	–	–	1	0	1	0	1	0
PC no zeros	–	–	1	1	1	1	3	3
OPTC Set class	[0, 4, 7]		[0, 2, 7]		[0, 4, 7]		[0, 3, 6, 8]	
SC probs.	.17	0	.02	0	.17	0	.05	0
SC no zeros	.17	.17	.02	.02	.17	.17	.05	.05
SD Set (mod 12)	{0, 4, 7} tonic triad		{0, 5, 7} passing ^4		{0, 4, 7} tonic triad		{0, 2, 6, 9} V^7/V	
SD probs.	.09	0	.01	0	.09	0	.01	0
SD no zeros	.09	.09	.01	.01	.09	.09	.01	.01

3   Results

Table 2 presents the *F* scores for each composer using each parameter under the with-zeros treatment; Table 3 presents scores using the no-zeros approach. The with-zeros approach performs higher overall, with many of the no-zeros scores dipping below a score of .5. The most successful parameter is note attacks with average scores of .76 and .52 in the with-zeros and no-zeros conditions, respectively. The scale-degree probabilities then have the lowest average scores, yielding .70 and .44 in their respective conditions.

Table 2. Average *F* score results for each composer using each of the parameters under the with-zeros condition

Composer	Note attack	NA binary	PC change	PC binary	SC probability	Scale-degree probability
Monteverdi	.80	.73	.78	.66	.72	.71
Bach	.75	.69	.74	.64	.74	.75
Mozart	.78	.73	.74	.69	.68	.67
Beethoven	.72	.69	.68	.59	.69	.66

Table 3. Average *F* score results for each composer using each of the parameters under the no-zeros condition

Composer	Note attack	PC change	SC probability	Scale-degree probability
Monteverdi	.48	.45	.44	.42
Bach	.60	.61	.58	.48
Mozart	.51	.40	.44	.44
Beethoven	.52	.42	.46	.41

4 Discussion

These results indicate that, in most cases, a note-attack (with zeros) approach outperforms other models. Indeed, it would seem that the more harmonically oriented a parameter, the lower its scores in Tables 2 and 3, with parameters relying on chord identities performing worst. Loudness –at least as approximated by note attacks– appears to be the most salient metrical parameter. However, these results yield several interesting findings, including the importance of zeros to the models, the interconnection of the parameters, as well as some suggestive interactions with broader theories of meter.

4.1 The Importance of Zeros and Contour

Comparing Tables 2 and 3 makes the importance of zeros obvious: removing null values dramatically handicaps the model. It would seem that this model of meter is more about tracking moments where *nothing* happens than where *something* happens. The method, then, appears to align periods of stasis as much as it aligns moments of accent when identifying periodicities. This suggests both that the relative strength of accents are not in-and-of-themselves sufficient to determine a piece's meter, and that points of stasis and silence might be necessary to meter finding.

Additionally, the binary versions of the note-attack and pc-change vectors returned relatively high scores, but not as high as the non-binary versions. This suggests that the relative amount of loudness or the amount of pc change –not only whether there is a change– is an important factor to meter finding (at least as constructed in this study).

4.2 Harmony's Role in Meter Finding

The relative success rates of the three harmonic parameters –pc change, set-class probabilities, and chord probabilities– potentially indicate which aspects of harmony most align with metric accents. From historical theories like those of Koch and Kirnberger [22], to contemporary studies of tonal prolongation [23, 24], to music cognition experimentation [15, 25], research suggests that dramatic harmonic changes tend to align with metric accents. The relatively successful performance of the pc-change model, coupled with the poor performances of the set-class and chord-probability model, suggests that the most important parameter of harmony when communicating metric accents is specifically the amount of pc change. That is, rather than metric accents being derived from the identities of particular chords or from the use of particular harmonic structures, this study suggests that harmonic progressions that change relatively more pcs align with metric emphases.

Importantly, however, note attacks are not *always* the most successful parameter. The Bach corpus, for instance, favors the harmonic parameters over the note-attack implementation. This is likely because this sub-corpus is comprised primarily of Bach's four-voice chorales, a texture with consistently equal numbers of note attacks, and the close-to-homophonic textures of hymnody do not offer fluctuations in note attacks. This finding suggest, however, that in styles and textures in which note attacks are not a useful metric parameter, harmony potentially provides an outsized role in expressing musical meter.

4.3 Autocorrelation and the Definition of Meter

These findings, of course, have potential connections to the ways listeners attribute meter, or how composers imagine meter expressed in their musical choices. For instance, parameters that perform relatively well in the current implementation might be proportionately more salient to listeners' perception of metric accents. While such explicit connections remain for future work, we might speculate as to how these results interact with larger definitions of meter.

Music theorists define "meter" in a number of subtly different ways; however, we can imagine the general concept dividing into three suppositions: meter (1) arises from a series of consistently paced accents [24, 26], (2) involves listeners expecting that this pacing will continue into the future [27], and (3) groups adjacent pulses by either twos or threes to form a hierarchy of stronger and weaker pulses [28]. The autocorrelation method itself is aligned to these suppositions in several ways. To the first, it identifies consistently-paced similar events; to the second, it compares current, future, and past events by its vector rotations; to the third, it identifies periodicities at varieties of timescales.

But, this study suggests two ways that these suppositions might be loosened while still accurately predicting a meter. The first supposition might be extended to include moments of non-accent, since vectors with consistently-paced zeros improved each model's performance. Also, given that the autocorrelation method has no fealty to duple and triple divisions, the third supposition might be treated a norm or expectation rather than a rule. That is, this study's method could easily identify a quarter-note pulse and a whole-note pulse without an intervening half-note pulse and still accurately reflect a quadruple time signature.

5 Limits and Future Work

Of course, this work is incomplete. The model could and should be more sophisticated, incorporating more information than merely the beginning of each piece. More composers and more diverse repertoires should also be incorporated into further studies. The observations drawn from this work would also need more behavioral and psychological study to move from the realm of speculation to testable arguments. Additionally, the density of note onsets interacts with several other musical parameters, including texture, instrumentation, and chord change. Future work might investigate how the extent to which note onsets might be a proxy for events in these other domains. Finally, when applied to pitch-based parameters, the autocorrelation approach can potentially identify non-metric musical segmentations like grouping, phrasing and formal boundaries, and potentially engages with previous work on these topics [23, 28–30]. Indeed, false positives returned by the model are reacting to *some* kind of regularity on the musical surface, regularities that might reflect phrases and motives not aligned with the notated meter; such regularities might be studied in more depth in future work. Regardless, this study does provide a first step in investigating the role of recurrent pitch events in expressing musical meter.

References

1. Palmer, C., Krumhansl, C.: Mental representations of musical meter. J. Exp. Psychol. Hum. Percept. Perform. **16**, 728–741 (1990)
2. Brown, J.C.: The determination of meter of musical scores by autocorrelation. J. Acoust. Soc. Am. **94**(4), 1953–1957 (1993)
3. Eck, D.: Identifying metrical and temporal structure with an autocorrelation phase matrix. Music Percept. **24**(2), 167–176 (2006)
4. Gouyon, F., Dixon, S.: A review of automatic rhythm description systems. Comput. Music J. **29**, 34–54 (2005)
5. Boone, G.M.: Marking mensural time. Music Theor. Spect. **22**(1), 1–43 (2000)
6. Zikanov, K.: Metric properties of mensural music: an autocorrelation approach. Paper presented at the National Meeting of the American Musicological Society, Milwaukee, WI (2014)
7. Dixon, S., Cambouropoulos, E.: Beat tracking with musical knowledge. In: Proceedings of the 14th European Conference on Artificial Intelligence, pp. 626–630. IOS Press, Amsterdam (2000)
8. Goto, M., Muraoka, Y.: Real-time beat tracking for drumless audio signals: chord change detection for musical decisions. Speech Commun. **27**, 311–335 (1999)
9. Temperley, D., Sleator, D.: Modeling meter and harmony: a preference-rule approach. Comput. Music J. **23**(1), 10–27 (1999)

10. Dixon, S.: Automatic extraction of tempo and beat from expressive performances. J. New Music Res. **30**, 39–58 (2001)
11. Rosenthal, D.F.: Machine rhythm: computer emulation of human rhythm perception. Doctoral dissertation. MIT, Cambridge (1992)
12. Rosenthal, M.A., Hannon, E.H.: Cues to perceiving tonal stability: the role of temporal structure. Music Percept. **33**, 601–612 (2016)
13. White, C.Wm.: A corpus-sensitive algorithm for automated tonal analysis. In: Collins, T., Meredith, D., Volk, A. (eds.) MCM 2015. LNCS (LNAI), vol. 9110, pp. 115–121. Springer, Cham (2015). https://doi.org/10.1007/978-3-319-20603-5_11
14. Gouyon, F., Widmer, G., Serra, X., Flexer, A.: Acoustic cues to beat induction: a machine learning perspective. Music Percept. **24**(2), 177–188 (2006)
15. London, J., Himberg, T., Cross, I.: The effect of structural and performance factors in the perception of anacruses. Music Percept. **27**(2), 103–120 (2009)
16. Cuthbert, M.S., Ariza, C.: music21: a toolkit for computer–aided musicology and symbolic music data. In: Proceedings of the International Symposium on Music Information Retrieval, pp. 637–642 (2011)
17. Yust, J.: Organized Time: Rhythm, Tonality, and Form. Oxford University Press, New York (2018)
18. Chinchor, N.: MUC-4 evaluation metrics. In: Proceedings of the Fourth Message Understanding Conference, pp. 22–29. Association for Computational Linguistics, Stroudsburg (1992)
19. Callender, C., Quinn, I., Tymoczko, D.: Generalized voice-leading spaces. Science **320**, 346 (2008)
20. Quinn, I.: What's 'Key for Key': A Theoretically Naive Key–Finding Model for Bach Chorales. Zeitschrift der Gesellschaft für Musiktheorie, 7/ii, pp. 151–63 (2010)
21. Mirka, D.: Metric Manipulations in Haydn and Mozart: Chamber Music for Strings, 1787–1791. Oxford University Press, New York (2009)
22. Yeston, M.: The Stratification of Musical Rhythm. Yale University Press, New Haven (1976)
23. Lerdahl, F., Jackendoff, R.: A Generative Theory of Tonal Music. MIT Press, Cambridge (1983)
24. Prince, J.B., Thompson, W.F., Schmuckler, M.A.: Pitch and time, tonality and meter: how do musical dimensions combine? J. Exp. Psychol. **35**(5), 1598–1617 (2009)
25. Krebs, H.: Fantasy Pieces: Metrical Dissonance in the Music of Robert Schumann. Oxford University Press, New York (1999)
26. London, J.: Hearing in Time: Psychological Aspects of Musical Meter. Oxford University Press, New York (2004)
27. Cohn, R.: Complex hemiolas, ski-hill graphs and metric spaces. Music Anal. **20**(3), 295–326 (2001)
28. Meredith, D., Wiggins, G.A., Lemström, K.: Pattern induction and matching in polyphonic music and other multidimensional datasets. In: Proceedings of the 5th World Multi-Conference on Systemics, Cybernetics, and Informatics, vol. X, pp. 61–66 (2001)
29. Cambouropoulos, E.: The local boundary detection model (LBDM) and its application in the study of expressive timing. In: Proceedings of the International Computer Music Conference, San Francisco, pp. 17–22 (2001)
30. Pearce, M.: The construction and evaluation of statistical models of melodic structure in music perception and composition, Ph.D. thesis, School of Informatics, City University, London (2005)

The Envelopes of Consonant Intervals and Chords in Just Intonation and Equal Temperament

Luis Nuño[✉][iD]

IUI ITACA Polytechnic University of Valencia,
Camino de Vera S/N, 46022 Valencia, Spain
lnuno@dcom.upv.es, harmonicwheel@gmail.com

Abstract. Musical consonances are most times assumed to be associated with the absence of beats or roughness, which can only be achieved, in a strict sense, in just intonation. In this paper, signals representing consonant intervals and chords are analyzed, both in just intonation and in an arbitrary slight deviation from it. Analytical approximate formulas for their envelopes are obtained and then applied to the particular case of equal temperament. It was found that, in just intonation, the envelopes are flat but, in the other cases, the envelopes have a ripple which corresponds to beats or roughness, thus indicating a loss of consonance. Both the amplitudes and periodicities of the ripples are obtained for all types of consonances.

Keywords: Consonance · Beat · Roughness · Envelope ·
Just intonation · Equal temperament

1 Introduction

Searching for the basis of musical consonances has grabbed the attention of many musicians, musical instrument manufactures, and all kind of scientists for centuries... and is still under discussion. Relevant answers to this phenomenon have been given from different areas of knowledge, such as: mathematics, physics, biology, psychology or sociology [1–8]. Apart from the theoretical models, also experimental results, based on tests and surveys, have been obtained. Unfortunately, most of the studies have been carried out on intervals and not on chords.

In spite of the difficulty to give an answer covering every point of view, it is generally accepted that there are 6 basic types of consonances: 4 related to the intervals and 2 to the chords. In the first case, they are the octave, perfect fifth, major and minor thirds (the unison is not here considered, because it is a trivial consonance); and, in the second case, the major and minor chords (which are, in fact, combinations of consonant intervals). As well, the inversions both of the intervals and chords are considered consonant, too.

This study has been carried out for pure tones, that is, simple sinusoids, in contrast to complex tones, which are formed by a series of harmonics that

© Springer Nature Switzerland AG 2019
M. Montiel et al. (Eds.): MCM 2019, LNAI 11502, pp. 297–308, 2019.
https://doi.org/10.1007/978-3-030-21392-3_24

affect the sensation of consonance differently. Then, in our case, all types of consonances will be combinations of (pure) tones whose frequencies are small multiples of a fundamental one, that is, tones belonging to a harmonic series, particularly the harmonics 2 (octave), 3 (perfect fifth) and 5 (major third). But, additionally, there is another important characteristic of the consonances that is pointed out in many studies: the absence of beats or roughness, which are rhythmical fluctuations of the amplitude as a result of constructive and destructive interferences.

In parallel to those discussions there is another ancient problem: the tuning of musical instruments. Thus, in [9], more than 180 systems are described, which fortunately can be reduced to about 20 basic ones. As well, [10] is a good reference on this matter in Spanish. Among those systems, the Pythagorean tuning perfectly matches the harmonics 2 and 3, while the just intonation also matches the harmonic 5. Other systems, called temperaments, slightly deviate from those harmonics in order to meet other requirements. For example, the meantone temperament reduces the Pythagorean fifths in a quarter of syntonic comma in order to match the major thirds, that is, the harmonic 5, but at the expense of deviating from harmonic 3. Another important example is the 12-tone equal temperament (12-TET) or, simply, equal temperament, which divides the octave into 12 equal parts (in a logarithmic frequency scale), thus resulting in a uniform and closed system. As a matter of fact, most tuning systems tend to approach the just intonation.

Then, on the one hand, the consonances are combinations of harmonics 2, 3 and 5 from a harmonic series and, on the other hand, those harmonics are perfectly matched by the just intonation. Therefore, the following question arises: how consonant is a consonance with respect to its deviation from just intonation? This paper is devoted to answer that question. To do that, signals containing 2 or 3 pure tones corresponding to a consonance are analyzed, both in just intonation and in an arbitrary slight deviation from it. It was found that, in just intonation, the envelopes of those signals are flat, but when there is a slight deviation from it, the envelopes have a ripple which corresponds to beats or roughness. This fact is closely related to the above-mentioned characteristic of the consonances, which indicates that the ripple is a measure of the loss of consonance. The ripple resembles a vibrato in amplitude and is characterized by its amplitude and its "periodicity", which may include one or more periods.

The simplest type of beat arises from the combination of two tones with similar frequencies, and is well-known. However, in this study the beats correspond to the combination of two or three tones whose frequencies are "almost multiples" of a fundamental one, and obtaining analytical expressions of their envelopes is not an easy task. Thus, in Sects. 2 and 3, approximate formulas for those envelopes are obtained, which represents the main contribution of this paper. In Sect. 4, these formulas are applied to just intonation and equal temperament, although they are general formulas that can be applied to most tuning systems. To keep this study under a reasonable extension, the inversions of the consonances were not analyzed. As well, the octave was not considered here, because it is perfectly matched by practically all tuning systems.

2   Consonant Intervals

The combination of two pure tones whose frequencies are almost multiples of a fundamental one, f_0, gives rise to the signal

$$s(t) = \cos k\omega_0 t + \cos(l\omega_0 t + \alpha)$$
$$\alpha = at + \theta \tag{1}$$

$\omega_0 = 2\pi f_0$ being the fundamental angular frequency and θ the initial angle or phase. In just intonation, $a = 0$ and the overall period of $s(t)$ is $T_0 = 2\pi/\omega_0 = 1/f_0$ divided by the greatest common divisor of (k, l), which will be 1 in all cases here considered. In other tuning systems, the angular frequency a represents a slight deviation from it, which gives rise to the period $T_a = 2\pi/a$. Throughout this paper, it will be assumed that $T_a \gg T_0$. This condition assures that $T_a \gg T_0/k$, T_0/l, as well.

Excluding the unison and the octave, there are 3 types of consonant intervals (apart from their inversions): the perfect fifth, where the pair $(k, l) = (2, 3)$, the major third, where $(k, l) = (4, 5)$, and the minor third, where $(k, l) = (5, 6)$.

As explained in [11], the "force" (loudness) of a sound is related to the amplitude of the oscillations. In our case, except in just intonation, the amplitude of $s(t)$ varies with time, giving rise to an envelope formed by the maximum and minimum values of $s(t)$ in each period T_0. For the perfect fifth, those maximum and minimum values will be represented by functions $E_1^5(\alpha)$ and $E_2^5(\alpha)$, respectively. The solid line in Fig. 1 named $(2, 3)$ shows the upper envelope $E_1^5(\alpha)$ of $s(t)$ as a function of $\alpha/\pi \in [0, 2]$. The graph was obtained with 200 points for α/π; and, for each of them, 2000 values of t were used to obtain the maximum of $s(t)$.

Due to the shape of this graph, the function $|\cos x|$ will be used to approximate $E_1^5(\alpha)$, in the following form

$$F_1(\alpha) = A + B|\cos\alpha| \tag{2}$$

To obtain the coefficients A, B, the function $F_1(\alpha)$ is forced to have the same maximum and minimum values as $E_1^5(\alpha)$. The result is

$$A = 1.6342, \qquad B = 0.3658 \tag{3}$$

The same procedure was followed to approximate the lower envelope $E_2^5(\alpha)$ of $s(t)$, the final formulas being

$$F_1(\alpha) = 1.6342 + 0.3658|\cos\alpha|$$
$$F_2(\alpha) = -1.6342 - 0.3658|\sin\alpha| \tag{4}$$

Regarding the major and minor thirds, and in order to distinguish their formulas from those of the perfect fifth, the following expression for $s(t)$ will be used:

$$s(t) = \cos k\omega_0 t + \cos(m\omega_0 t + \beta)$$
$$\beta = bt + \varphi \tag{5}$$

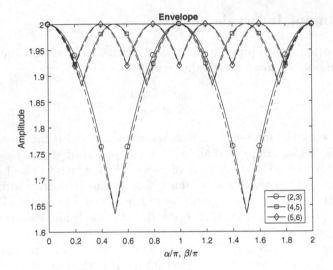

Fig. 1. Upper envelopes of $s(t)$ for consonant intervals (solid lines), along with their approximating functions (dashed lines). Curve $(2,3)$ corresponds to the perfect fifth, $(4,5)$ to the major third, and $(5,6)$ to the minor third.

Let us first consider the major third. The upper and lower envelopes will be represented by functions $E_1^3(\beta)$ and $E_2^3(\beta)$, respectively. The solid line in Fig. 1 named $(4,5)$ shows the upper envelope $E_1^3(\beta)$ of $s(t)$ as a function of $\beta/\pi \in [0,2]$, obtained as in the previous case. Following the above procedure, the approximating function for the upper envelope now takes the form

$$G_1(\beta) = A + B|\cos 2\beta| \tag{6}$$

The coefficients A, B are obtained by imposing the same conditions as in the previous case, the result being

$$A = 1.8809, \qquad B = 0.1191 \tag{7}$$

and the final formulas for approximating the upper and lower envelopes are, respectively,

$$G_1(\beta) = 1.8809 + 0.1191|\cos 2\beta|$$
$$G_2(\beta) = -1.8809 - 0.1191|\sin 2\beta| \tag{8}$$

With respect to the minor third, the upper and lower envelopes will be represented by functions $E_1^{b3}(\beta)$ and $E_2^{b3}(\beta)$, respectively. The solid line in Fig. 1 named $(5,6)$ shows the upper envelope $E_1^{b3}(\beta)$ of $s(t)$ as a function of $\beta/\pi \in [0,2]$, obtained as in the previous cases. Following the same procedure, the approximating function for the upper envelope now takes the form

$$H_1(\beta) = A + B|\cos 2.5\beta| \tag{9}$$

The coefficients A, B are obtained by imposing the same conditions as in the previous cases, the result being

$$A = 1.9197, \qquad B = 0.0803 \tag{10}$$

and the final formulas for approximating the upper and lower envelopes are, respectively,

$$H_1(\beta) = 1.9197 + 0.0803|\cos 2.5\beta|$$
$$H_2(\beta) = -1.9197 - 0.0803|\sin 2.5\beta| \tag{11}$$

In order to assess the accuracy of this approximation, Fig. 1 also includes the graphs of $F_1(\alpha)$, $G_1(\beta)$ and $H_1(\beta)$ (dashed lines), and good agreement between every two paired curves is observed. In the three types of intervals, the envelope has a ripple whose amplitude equals the coefficient B, and its period is defined by α or β.

3   Consonant Chords

The combination of three pure tones whose frequencies are almost multiples of a fundamental one, f_0, gives rise to the signal

$$s(t) = \cos k\omega_0 t + \cos(m\omega_0 t + \beta) + \cos(l\omega_0 t + \alpha)$$
$$\alpha = at + \theta, \qquad \beta = bt + \varphi \tag{12}$$

$\omega_0 = 2\pi f_0$ being the fundamental angular frequency and θ, φ the initial angles or phases. Letters k, l, m, as well as α, β, are assigned following the order of harmonics, while the addends in (12) follow the order of notes in the chord. In just intonation, $a = b = 0$ and the overall period of $s(t)$ is $T_0 = 2\pi/\omega_0 = 1/f_0$ divided by the greatest common divisor of (k, m, l), which will be 1 in all cases here considered. In other tuning systems, the angular frequencies a and b represent slight deviations from it, which give rise to the periods $T_a = 2\pi/a$ and $T_b = 2\pi/b$, respectively. Throughout this paper, it will be assumed that $T_a, T_b \gg T_0$. This condition assures that $T_a, T_b \gg T_0/k, T_0/l, T_0/m$, as well.

There are 2 types of consonant chords: the major chord, where the triplet $(k, m, l) = (4, 5, 6)$, and the minor chord, where $(k, m, l) = (10, 12, 15)$.

As in last section, except in just intonation, the amplitude of $s(t)$ varies with time, giving rise to an envelope formed by the maximum and minimum values of $s(t)$ in each period T_0. For major chords, those maximum and minimum values will be represented by functions $E_1^M(\alpha, \beta)$ and $E_2^M(\alpha, \beta)$, respectively. Solid lines in Fig. 2 show the upper envelope $E_1^M(\alpha, \beta)$ of $s(t)$ as a function of $\beta/\pi \in [0, 2]$ for different values of $\alpha/\pi \in [0, 0.5]$. Each graph was obtained with 200 points for β/π; and, for each of them, 2000 values of t were used to obtain the maximum of $s(t)$. The corresponding graphs for $\alpha/\pi \in [0.5, 1]$ are shown in Fig. 3.

As in the previous section, the function $|\cos x|$ will be used for approximating $E_1^M(\alpha, \beta)$, which now takes the form

$$P_{11}(\alpha, \beta) = A + B|\cos(\beta - 0.6\alpha)| + C|\cos\alpha|, \quad 0 \le \alpha \le \pi/2$$
$$P_{12}(\alpha, \beta) = A + B|\cos(\beta - 0.6\alpha + 0.1\pi)| + C|\cos\alpha|, \quad \pi/2 \le \alpha \le \pi \tag{13}$$

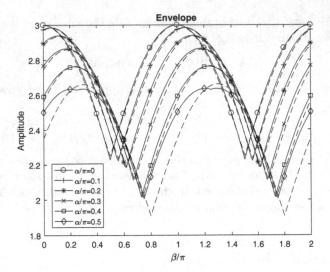

Fig. 2. Upper envelope $E_1^M(\alpha, \beta)$ of $s(t)$ as a function of β/π for $\alpha/\pi \in [0, 0.5]$ (solid lines), along with its approximating function $P_1(\alpha, \beta)$ (dashed lines)

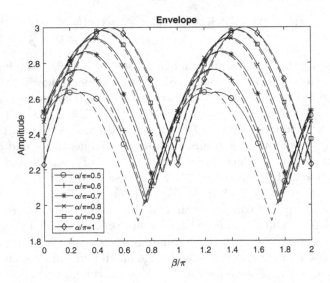

Fig. 3. Upper envelope $E_1^M(\alpha, \beta)$ of $s(t)$ as a function of β/π for $\alpha/\pi \in [0.5, 1]$ (solid lines), along with its approximating function $P_1(\alpha, \beta)$ (dashed lines)

The phase shift between $P_{11}(\alpha, \beta)$ and $P_{12}(\alpha, \beta)$, which occurs at $\alpha = \pi/2$, can be expressed by the sawtooth function $\arctan(\tan x)$, thus allowing to combine the two formulas (13) in just one:

$$P_1(\alpha, \beta) = A + B|\cos[\beta - 0.5\alpha - 0.1\arctan(\tan\alpha)]| + C|\cos\alpha| \qquad (14)$$

Note that Figs. 2 and 3 correspond to half a period in the variable α. For the other half, however, the graphs of $E_1^M(\alpha, \beta)$ are the same, but moved $\beta/\pi = 0.5$ to the right. Therefore, the formula (14) is valid for all α, β.

To obtain the coefficients A, B, C, a first condition is $A + B + C = 3$, so that the maximum value $P_{1,\max}(\alpha, \beta) = 3$. Then, in order to achieve a good approximation for most values of α, the function $P_1(\alpha, \beta)$ is forced to have the same maximum and minimum values as $E_1^M(\alpha, \beta)$ for $\alpha = 0.4\pi$. The result is

$$A = 1.91, \qquad B = 0.75, \qquad C = 0.34 \tag{15}$$

Since this is a different kind of approximation compared to the one used in last section, in this case it was considered exact enough to use coefficients to two decimal places. The same procedure was followed to approximate the lower envelope $E_2^M(\alpha, \beta)$ of $s(t)$, the final formulas being

$$
\begin{aligned}
P_1(\alpha, \beta) &= 1.91 + 0.75|\cos[\beta - 0.5\alpha - 0.1\arctan(\tan\alpha)]| + 0.34|\cos\alpha| \\
P_2(\alpha, \beta) &= -1.91 - 0.75|\cos[\beta - 0.5\alpha + 0.1\arctan(\cot\alpha)]| - 0.34|\sin\alpha|
\end{aligned}
\tag{16}
$$

In order to assess the accuracy of this approximation, Figs. 2 and 3 also include the graphs of $P_1(\alpha, \beta)$ (dashed lines), and good agreement between every two paired curves is observed. The greatest error occurs for $\alpha/\pi = 0.5$ at the minimum values, which is less than 5%. The value of $\arctan(\tan\alpha)$ for $\alpha/\pi = 0.5$ in Fig. 2 was obtained from the left (0.5^-) and in Fig. 3 from the right (0.5^+).

Regarding the minor chords, the upper and lower envelopes will be represented by functions $E_1^m(\alpha, \beta)$ and $E_2^m(\alpha, \beta)$, respectively. Following the above procedure, which again requires the use of the sawtooth function, the approximating function for the upper envelope now takes the form

$$Q_1(\alpha, \beta) = A + B|\cos[2.5\beta - 1.4\arctan(\tan\alpha)]| + C|\cos\alpha| \tag{17}$$

which is valid for all α, β. The coefficients A, B, C are obtained by imposing the same conditions as in the previous case, the result being

$$A = 2.53, \qquad B = 0.13, \qquad C = 0.34 \tag{18}$$

and the final formulas for approximating the upper and lower envelopes are, respectively,

$$
\begin{aligned}
Q_1(\alpha, \beta) &= 2.53 + 0.13|\cos[2.5\beta - 1.4\arctan(\tan\alpha)]| + 0.34|\cos\alpha| \\
Q_2(\alpha, \beta) &= -2.53 - 0.13|\sin[2.5\beta + 1.4\arctan(\cot\alpha)]| - 0.34|\sin\alpha|
\end{aligned}
\tag{19}
$$

Now, the greatest error also occurs for $\alpha/\pi = 0.5$ at the minimum values, which in this case is less than 2.5%.

In both types of chords, the envelope has a ripple whose amplitude is the sum of the coefficients B and C, and its periodicity is defined by α and β.

4 Results

Formulas obtained in Sects. 2 and 3 are valid for any kind of tuning or temperament, with the only condition that $T_a, T_b \gg T_0$. In this section, results are given for just intonation and equal temperament. In the first case, $a = b = 0$, while in the second one, $a = k\omega_0(2^{7/12} - 3/2) = -1.693 \cdot 10^{-3} k\omega_0$ (perfect fifth) and $b = k\omega_0(2^{4/12} - 5/4) = 9.921 \cdot 10^{-3} k\omega_0$ (major third) or $b = k\omega_0(2^{3/12} - 6/5) = -10.793 \cdot 10^{-3} k\omega_0$ (minor third). Then, the periods defined by a and b range from $T_a = 295 T_0$ (perfect fifth) to $T_b = 9.27 T_0$ (minor chord). Therefore, in all cases, the required condition is fulfilled. Additionally, we can obtain the corresponding values for other tuning systems. For example, in Pythagorean

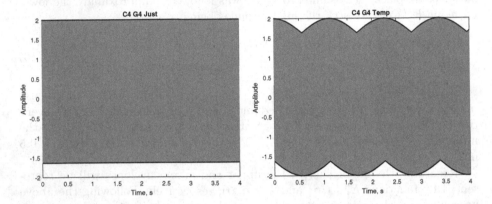

Fig. 4. Perfect fifth C4G4 in just intonation for $\theta = 0$ **Fig. 5.** Perfect fifth C4G4 in equal temperament for $\theta = 0$

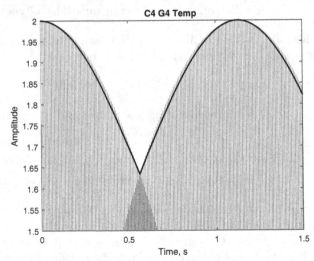

Fig. 6. Perfect fifth C4G4 in equal temperament for $\theta = 0$ (detail)

tuning, $a = 0$ and $b = k\omega_0(81/64 - 5/4) = 15.625 \cdot 10^{-3}k\omega_0$ (major third) or $b = k\omega_0(32/27 - 6/5) = -14.815 \cdot 10^{-3}k\omega_0$ (minor third). And in meantone temperament, $a = k\omega_0[(3/2)(81/80)^{-1/4} - 3/2] = -4.651 \cdot 10^{-3}k\omega_0$ (perfect fifth) and $b = 0$ (major third) or $b = k\omega_0[(32/27)(81/80)^{3/4} - 6/5] = -3.721 \cdot 10^{-3}k\omega_0$ (minor third). Therefore, the only period being less than previous ones is obtained for the Pythagorean tuning, minor chord, where $T_b = 6.75T_0$, the approximation being still acceptable.

All signals in the following examples last 4 s and their graphs were obtained by sampling them at 44,100 Hz, as in the WAV audio format. In fact, the corresponding audio files were generated, too. For simplicity, all the examples will start with note C4, whose frequency is 261.626 Hz and, therefore, $k\omega_0 = 1643.842$ rad/s.

Regarding the consonant intervals, Figs. 4 and 5 show $s(t)$ and its envelopes $F_1(\alpha)$ and $F_2(\alpha)$ for the perfect fifth C4G4, in just intonation and equal temper-

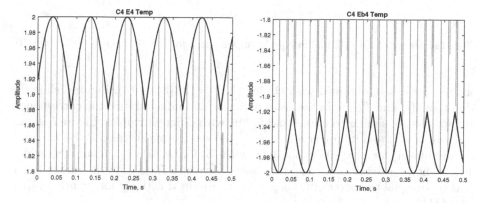

Fig. 7. Major third C4E4 in equal temperament for $\varphi = -0.7\pi$ (detail)

Fig. 8. Minor third C4Eb4 in equal temperament for $\varphi = 0.3\pi$ (detail)

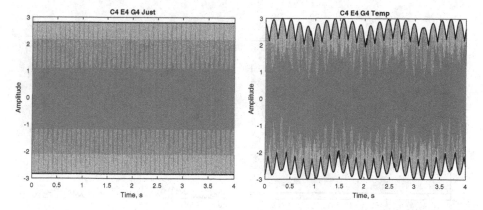

Fig. 9. Major chord C4E4G4 in just intonation for $\theta = 0.3\pi$, $\varphi = -0.7\pi$

Fig. 10. Major chord C4E4G4 in equal temperament for $\theta = 0.3\pi$, $\varphi = -0.7\pi$

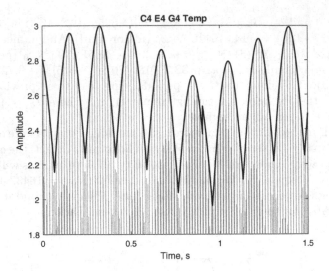

Fig. 11. Major chord C4E4G4 in equal temperament for $\theta = 0.3\pi$, $\varphi = -0.7\pi$ (detail)

ament, for $\theta = 0$, obtained with (1) for $(k,l) = (2,3)$ and (4). Figure 6 shows a detail of $s(t)$ and $F_1(\alpha)$. In the cases of major and minor thirds, the corresponding graphs are similar to Figs. 4 and 5, but with different ripples. Figure 7 shows a detail of $s(t)$ and its upper envelope $G_1(\alpha)$ for the major third C4E4 in equal temperament, for $\varphi = -0.7\pi$, obtained with (5) for $(k,m) = (4,5)$ and (8), while Fig. 8 shows a detail of $s(t)$ and its lower envelope $H_2(\alpha)$ for the minor third C4Eb4 in equal temperament, for $\varphi = 0.3\pi$, obtained with (5) for $(k,m) = (5,6)$ and (11).

With respect to consonant chords, Figs. 9, 10 and 11 show $s(t)$ and its envelopes $P_1(\alpha, \beta)$ and $P_2(\alpha, \beta)$ for the major chord C4E4G4, in just intona-

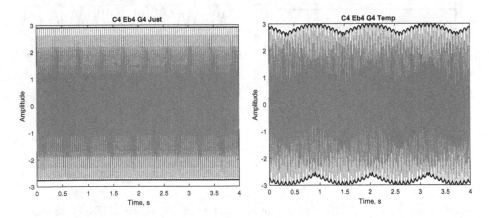

Fig. 12. Minor chord C4Eb4G4 in just intonation for $\theta = -0.2\pi$, $\varphi = 0.6\pi$

Fig. 13. Minor chord C4Eb4G4 in equal temperament for $\theta = -0.2\pi$, $\varphi = 0.6\pi$

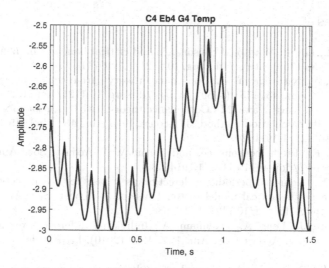

Fig. 14. Minor chord C4Eb4G4 in equal temperament for $\theta = -0.2\pi$, $\varphi = 0.6\pi$ (detail)

tion and equal temperament, for $\theta = 0.3\pi$, $\varphi = -0.7\pi$, obtained with (12) for $(k, m, l) = (4, 5, 6)$ and (16). And Figs. 12, 13 and 14 show $s(t)$ and its envelopes $Q_1(\alpha, \beta)$ and $Q_2(\alpha, \beta)$ for the minor chord C4Eb4G4, in just intonation and equal temperament, for $\theta = -0.2\pi$, $\varphi = 0.6\pi$, obtained with (12) for $(k, m, l) = (10, 12, 15)$ and (19). Since in equal temperament $a \ll b$, the ripples in these graphs include a fast variation with a short period, defined by b, superimposed to a slow variation with a large period, defined by a.

5   Conclusions

Signals corresponding to consonant intervals and chords have been analyzed. They were combinations of 2 or 3 pure tones whose frequencies are almost multiples of a fundamental one. The procedure for obtaining approximate formulas for the envelopes of those signals has been developed. In just intonation, the envelopes are flat, but when there is a slight deviation from it, they have a ripple which corresponds to beats or roughness, thus indicating a loss of consonance. Both the amplitudes and periodicities of the ripples have been obtained for all types of consonances. It has been found that the amplitude of a ripple is determined by the type of consonance itself, while its periodicity is defined by the frequency deviations from just intonation. In the case of intervals (2 tones), the ripple includes one period, while in the case of chords (3 tones) the ripple includes two periods superimposed.

Conducting a survey to evaluate the human perception of ripples in consonant intervals and chords is now under consideration, but preliminary results indicate that ripples with small amplitudes (as in minor third intervals) or large periods (as in perfect fifth intervals) are hardly perceived, while ripples with greater amplitudes and lesser periods (as in major chords) are clearly perceived.

References

1. Plomp, R., Levelt, W.: Tonal consonance and critical bandwidth. J. Acoust. Soc. Am. **38**, 548 (1965). https://doi.org/10.1121/1.1909741
2. Kameoka, A., Kuriyagawa, M.: Consonance theory part I: consonance of dyads. J. Acoust. Soc. Am. **45**, 1451 (1969). https://doi.org/10.1121/1.1911623
3. Kameoka, A., Kuriyagawa, M.: Consonance theory part II: consonance of complex tones and its calculation method. J. Acoust. Soc. Am. **45**, 1460 (1969). https://doi.org/10.1121/1.1911624
4. Terhardt, E.: Pitch, consonance, and harmony. J. Acoust. Soc. Am. **55**, 1061 (1974). https://doi.org/10.1121/1.1914648
5. Ebeling, M.: Neuronal periodicity detection as a basis for the perception of consonance: a mathematical model of tonal fusion. J. Acoust. Soc. Am. **124**, 2320 (2008). https://doi.org/10.1121/1.2968688
6. McDermott, J., Lehr, A., Oxenham, A.: Individual differences reveal the basis of consonance. J. Acoust. Soc. Am. **127**, 1949 (2010). https://doi.org/10.1121/1.3384926
7. Bowling, D., Purves, D.: A biological rationale for musical consonance. Proc. Natl. Acad. Sci. **112**(36), 11155–11160 (2015). https://doi.org/10.1073/pnas.1505768112
8. Trulla, L., Di Stefano, N., Giuliani, A.: Computational approach to musical consonance and dissonance. Front. Psychol. **9**, 381 (2018). https://doi.org/10.3389/fpsyg.2018.00381
9. Barbour, J.: Tuning and Temperament: A Historical Survey. Dover Publications, Mineola (2004)
10. Goldáraz, J.: Afinación y temperamento en la música occidental. Alianza Editorial, S. A., Madrid (1998)
11. Helmholtz, H.: On the Sensations of Tone as a Physiological Basis for the Theory of Music. Longmans, Green, and Co., London; New York (1895)

Maximally Even Tilings

Jeremy Kastine[1,2]([✉])

[1] Georgia State University, Atlanta, GA, USA
[2] Georgia Highlands College, Rome, GA, USA
jkastine@highlands.edu

Abstract. Rhythmic tiling canons tend to feature highly regular, periodic rhythms which, from a musical standpoint, can be quite monotonous and lacking in character. Allowing for "holes", we can compose "partial tiling canons" that feature more irregular/interesting rhythms. In this paper, we will investigate the construction of partial tiling canons in which the composite rhythm is maximally even.

Keywords: Tiling · Maximally even sets · Canon · Music composition

1 Introduction

Rhythmic tiling canons have been the subject of much research since Vuza's seminal papers on the subject [8–11]. For example, special issues on the topic have been released by the Journal of Mathematics and Music [1] and Perspectives of New Music [2]. The following is a typical example of a rhythmic tiling canon.

	0 1 2 3 4 5 6 7 8 9 10 11 12 13 14 15
Part 1	1 2 3 · 4 · · · 5 · · · · · · · : ‖
Part 2	· · · · · 1 2 3 · 4 · · · 5 · · : ‖
Part 3	· · · 5 · · · · · · 1 · 2 · 3 · 4 : ‖

This canon can be described as consisting of $\{0,5,10\}$-shifted copies of the rhythmic theme $\{0,1,2,4,8\}$ modulo 15. In this paper, this will be expressed more compactly as $(\{0,5,10\},\{0,1,2,4,8\})_{15}$. One of the most important results about rhythmic tiling canons $(A,B)_n$ is that most of them are periodic in the sense that $\mathrm{mod}_n(A+p) = A$ or $\mathrm{mod}_n(B+p) = B$ for some $p < n$ (e.g., $\{0,5,10\}$ in the example above). In particular, the only lengths n that permit aperiodic tiling are 72, 108, 120, 144,... (OEIS A102562, [3]).

From a musical standpoint, periodic rhythmic tiling canons are often quite monotonous and lacking in character. The composer of rhythmic canons has the following three options available:

1. settle for the monotonous rhythms of periodic tilings,
2. employ aperiodic tilings, the length of which may surpass the audience's capacity for processing, or
3. seek greater rhythmic variety by allowing "holes".

© Springer Nature Switzerland AG 2019
M. Montiel et al. (Eds.): MCM 2019, LNAI 11502, pp. 309–321, 2019.
https://doi.org/10.1007/978-3-030-21392-3_25

We explore the third option in this paper. So as not to stray too far from the spirit of tiling though, we still want the composite rhythms of our canons to consist of a relatively evenly distributed pattern of notes and rests, as in the following example.

	0	1	2	3	4	5	6	7	8	9	10	11	12	13
Part 1	1 ·	2 ·	3 ·	·	·	4	5 ·	·	·	:	‖
Part 2	·	·	·	1 ·	2 ·	3 ·	·	·	4	5	:	‖

The composite rhythm in this example $\{0, 2, 3, 4, 5, 7, 8, 9, 11, 12\}$ is "maximally even" modulo 13, as described in the following section.

2   Maximally Even Sets and Cycles

There exists a surprising variety of equivalent characterizations of maximal evenness [6]. We will review two characterizations that will be useful to us in this paper. Then we will introduce cycle graphs as an alternative context for studying maximal evenness. This will allow us to define a new operation on maximally even sets/cycles that will be useful in our study of maximally even tilings.

Definition 1. The following notation will be used.

- Let $\mathrm{mod}_n(a)$ denote the least non-negative number equivalent to a modulo n.
- We will use $\equiv_n$ to denote equivalence modulo n.
- Define $[a, b)_\mathbb{Z}$ to be the set of integers x such that $a \leq x < b$.
- We will denote the floor of a real number x as $\lfloor x \rfloor$ and its ceiling as $\lceil x \rceil$.

Definition 2. Let $k \leq n$. Let $A = \{a_0, a_1, ..., a_{k-1}\} \subseteq [0, n)_\mathbb{Z}$, where $a_0 < a_1 < ... < a_{k-1}$. We will say that A is maximally even modulo n if either of the following equivalent conditions hold [5].

1. $\mathrm{mod}_n(a_j - a_i) \in \{\lfloor \mathrm{mod}_k(j - i)\frac{n}{k} \rfloor, \lceil \mathrm{mod}_k(j - i)\frac{n}{k} \rceil\}$ for $i, j \in [0, k)_\mathbb{Z}$.
2. There exists some $i \in [0, n)_\mathbb{Z}$ such that $A = \mathrm{mod}_n(B + i)$ where $B = \{\lfloor \frac{jn}{k} \rfloor : j \in [0, k)_\mathbb{Z}\}$.

A reader who is unfamiliar with the notion on maximal evenness is encouraged to verify that $\{0, 2, 3, 4, 5, 7, 8, 9, 11, 12\}$ is maximally even modulo 13 using each of these characterizations.

Definition 3. If $V = \{v_0, v_1, ..., v_{k-1}\}$ and $E = \{(v_0, v_1), (v_1, v_2), ..., (v_{k-1}, v_0)\}$, then we will say that $C = (V, E)$ is a directed cycle on V. In this paper, all cycles will be directed, so the word "directed" will often be omitted. Define $\begin{bmatrix} v_1 \\ v_2 \end{bmatrix}_C$ to be the path (set/sequence of edges) leading from v_1 to v_2 in C.

Let w be a positive integer-valued function on E. We will say that w is a weight function on C and that (C, w) is a weighted cycle on V. Define $w(E') = \sum_{e \in E'} w(e)$ for any $E' \subseteq E$. We will say that $w(E)$ is the total weight of (C, w). Let 1_E be the weight function defined by $1_E(e) = 1$ for all $e \in E$.

Definition 4. Let (C, w) be a weighted cycle with $C = (V, E)$ and $w(E) = n$. We will say that w is a maximally even weight function on C provided that $\left\{ w\left(\begin{bmatrix} v_0 \\ v \end{bmatrix}_C \right) : v \in V \right\}$ is a modulo n maximally even set for some (or equivalently, all) $v_0 \in V$. In this case, we will also say that (C, w) is a maximally even cycle.

Proposition 5. Let (C, w) be a weighted cycle with $C = (V, E)$, $w(E) = n$, and $|V| = k$. Then (C, w) is maximally even if and only if

$$ w\left(\begin{bmatrix} v_1 \\ v_2 \end{bmatrix}_C \right) \in \left\{ \left\lfloor 1_E\left(\begin{bmatrix} v_1 \\ v_2 \end{bmatrix}_C \right) \frac{n}{k} \right\rfloor, \left\lceil 1_E\left(\begin{bmatrix} v_1 \\ v_2 \end{bmatrix}_C \right) \frac{n}{k} \right\rceil \right\} $$

for all $v_1, v_2 \in V$. (This result follows directly from the preceding definitions.)

Proposition 6. Let (C, w) be a weighted cycle where $C = (V, E)$, $w(E) = n$, and $|V| = k$. Let w' be a positive weight function on E of the form $j1_E + w$ or $j1_E - w$, where $j \in \mathbb{Z}$. Then (C, w') is a maximally even cycle of total weight $n' = w'(E) = jk \pm n$ if and only if (C, w) is maximally even.

Proof. We will prove this result in the case that w' is of the form $j1_E + w$. The case in which w' is of the form $j1_E - w$ can be proved in a similar way.

Suppose that (C, w) is maximally even. Then for $v_1, v_2 \in V$ we have the following.

$$ \left\lfloor 1_E\left(\begin{bmatrix} v_1 \\ v_2 \end{bmatrix}_C \right) \frac{n'}{k} \right\rfloor = \left\lfloor 1_E\left(\begin{bmatrix} v_1 \\ v_2 \end{bmatrix}_C \right) \frac{jk + n}{k} \right\rfloor $$

$$ = j1_E\left(\begin{bmatrix} v_1 \\ v_2 \end{bmatrix}_C \right) + \left\lfloor 1_E\left(\begin{bmatrix} v_1 \\ v_2 \end{bmatrix}_C \right) \frac{n}{k} \right\rfloor $$

$$ \leq j1_E\left(\begin{bmatrix} v_1 \\ v_2 \end{bmatrix}_C \right) + w\left(\begin{bmatrix} v_1 \\ v_2 \end{bmatrix}_C \right) $$

$$ = w'\left(\begin{bmatrix} v_1 \\ v_2 \end{bmatrix}_C \right). $$

In an analogous way, it can be shown that

$$ w'\left(\begin{bmatrix} v_1 \\ v_2 \end{bmatrix}_C \right) \leq \left\lceil 1_E\left(\begin{bmatrix} v_1 \\ v_2 \end{bmatrix}_C \right) \frac{n'}{k} \right\rceil. $$

Therefore, (C, w') is maximally even, since

$$ w'\left(\begin{bmatrix} v_1 \\ v_2 \end{bmatrix}_C \right) \in \left\{ \left\lfloor 1_E\left(\begin{bmatrix} v_1 \\ v_2 \end{bmatrix}_C \right) \frac{n'}{k} \right\rfloor, \left\lceil 1_E\left(\begin{bmatrix} v_1 \\ v_2 \end{bmatrix}_C \right) \frac{n'}{k} \right\rceil \right\}. $$

The converse can be show in a similar way. $\square$

Example 7. Let (C, w) be the maximally even cycle given below, and let $C = (V, E)$. (This cycle corresponds to the modulo 18 maximally even set $\{0, 4, 8, 11, 15\}$.)

$$(1) \xrightarrow{\;4\;} (2) \xrightarrow{\;4\;} (3)$$

with edges 3 (from (5) to (1)), 3 (from (4) to (3)), and $(5) \xleftarrow{\;4\;} (4)$.

Let $w' = -2 \cdot 1_E + w$. This operation reduces the weight of each edge by 2. Note that (C, w'), given below, is a maximally even cycle. (This cycle corresponds to the modulo 8 maximally even set $\{0, 2, 4, 5, 7\}$.)

$$(1) \xrightarrow{\;2\;} (2) \xrightarrow{\;2\;} (3)$$

with edges 1, 1, and $(5) \xleftarrow{\;2\;} (4)$.

Now let $w'' = 3 \cdot 1_E - w'$. This operation swaps the 1's and 2's of w'. Note that (C, w''), given below, is a maximally even cycle. (This cycle corresponds to the modulo 7 maximally even set $\{0, 1, 2, 4, 5\}$.)

$$(1) \xrightarrow{\;1\;} (2) \xrightarrow{\;1\;} (3)$$

with edges 2, 2, and $(5) \xleftarrow{\;1\;} (4)$.

In this example we see that maximally even cycles/sets come in families that are related via the operation described in the previous proposition. Most importantly, we should notice that through "reducing" and "swapping", we can arrive at a member of each family that has a relatively small total weight. This is made more precise in the following proposition.

Proposition 8. Let (C, w) be a weighted cycle where $C = (V, E)$, $w(E) = n$, and $|V| = k$. If (C, w) is maximally even, then it can be expressed in the one of the forms $(C, j1_E + w_0)$ or $(C, j1_E - w_0)$ where (C, w_0) is a maximally even cycle with $n_0 = w_0(E) \leq 1.5k$.

Proof. For now, suppose that $\frac{n}{k}$ is closer to its ceiling than to its floor. In other words, $\left\lceil \frac{n}{k} \right\rceil - \frac{n}{k} \leq 0.5$. Let $w_0 = \left(\left\lceil \frac{n}{k} \right\rceil + 1 \right) 1_E - w$. Note that w_0 is strictly positive since

$$w_0(e) = \left(\left\lceil \frac{n}{k} \right\rceil + 1 \right) 1_E(e) - w(e) \geq \left(\left\lceil \frac{n}{k} \right\rceil + 1 \right) - \left\lceil \frac{n}{k} \right\rceil = 1$$

for all $e \in E$. By Proposition 6, (C, w_0) is a maximally even cycle. Note that (C, w) can be expressed as $\left(C, \left(\left\lceil \frac{n}{k} \right\rceil + 1\right) 1_E - w_0\right)$ and that

$$w_0(E) = \left(\left\lceil \frac{n}{k} \right\rceil + 1\right) k - n = \left(\left\lceil \frac{n}{k} \right\rceil k - n\right) + k \leq 0.5k + k = 1.5k.$$

In the case that $\frac{n}{k}$ is closer to its floor than to its ceiling, (C, w) can be expressed as $\left(C, \left(\left\lfloor \frac{n}{k} \right\rfloor - 1\right) 1_E + w_0\right)$ where $w_0 = \left(1 - \left\lfloor \frac{n}{k} \right\rfloor\right) 1_E + w$.   □

3   Partial Tiling Pairs and Cycles

Example 9. Consider the following rhythmic canon.

	0	1	2	3	4	5	6	7	8	9	10	11	12	13	14
Part 1	1	·	·	·	2	·	3	·	·	·	4	·	·	·	:‖
Part 2	·	4	·	·	·	1	·	·	·	2	·	3	·	·	:‖

This canon can be described as consisting of $\{0, 5\}$-shifted copies of the rhythmic theme $\{0, 4, 6, 10\}$ modulo 14. This method of describing rhythmic canons will be formalized in Definition 10.

Another way to describe this rhythmic canon is as the following weighted cycle.

$$(1,1) \xrightarrow{\ 1\ } (2,4) \xrightarrow{\ 3\ } (1,2) \xrightarrow{\ 1\ } (2,1)$$

with $3 \uparrow$ on the left and $\downarrow 1$ on the right,

$$(2,3) \xleftarrow{\ 1\ } (1,4) \xleftarrow{\ 1\ } (2,2) \xleftarrow{\ 3\ } (1,3)$$

Each vertex labeled (i, j) corresponds to the j-th note of part i. The edges of the cycle are determined by the order in which the notes occur. The edge weights are determined by the amount of time between successive notes. This method of describing rhythmic canons will be formalized in Proposition 11 and Definition 12.

Definition 10. Let n be a positive integer, and let $A, B \subseteq [0, n)_{\mathbb{Z}}$ with $0 \in A \cap B$. If $(a, b) \to \mathrm{mod}_n(a + b)$ defines a bijection from $A \times B$ to $\mathrm{mod}_n(A + B)$, then we will say that $(A, B)_n$ is a partial tiling pair. We will refer to $\mathrm{mod}_n(A+B)$ as the range of $(A, B)_n$. If its range is maximally even, then we say that $(A, B)_n$ is a maximally even tiling pair. If its range is all of $[0, n)_{\mathbb{Z}}$, then we will say that $(A, B)_n$ is a full tiling.

Proposition 11. Let A and B be finite sets, let $C = (A \times B, E)$ be a cycle, and let w be a weight function on C. The following are equivalent.

1. For all $a_1, a_2 \in A$ and $b_1, b_2 \in B$, we have

$$w\left(\begin{bmatrix} (a_1, b_1) \\ (a_1, b_2) \end{bmatrix}_C\right) = w\left(\begin{bmatrix} (a_2, b_1) \\ (a_2, b_2) \end{bmatrix}_C\right).$$

2. For all $a_1, a_2 \in A$ and $b_1, b_2 \in B$, we have

$$w\left(\begin{bmatrix}(a_1, b_1)\\(a_2, b_1)\end{bmatrix}_C\right) = w\left(\begin{bmatrix}(a_1, b_2)\\(a_2, b_2)\end{bmatrix}_C\right).$$

Proof. Suppose that (C, w) satisfies the first condition. Let $n = w(E)$. Then for all $a_1, a_2 \in A$ and $b_1, b_2 \in B$ we have the following.

$$w\left(\begin{bmatrix}(a_1, b_1)\\(a_2, b_1)\end{bmatrix}_C\right) \equiv_n w\left(\begin{bmatrix}(a_1, b_1)\\(a_1, b_2)\end{bmatrix}_C\right) + w\left(\begin{bmatrix}(a_1, b_2)\\(a_2, b_2)\end{bmatrix}_C\right) + w\left(\begin{bmatrix}(a_2, b_2)\\(a_2, b_1)\end{bmatrix}_C\right)$$

$$= w\left(\begin{bmatrix}(a_2, b_1)\\(a_2, b_2)\end{bmatrix}_C\right) + w\left(\begin{bmatrix}(a_1, b_2)\\(a_2, b_2)\end{bmatrix}_C\right) + w\left(\begin{bmatrix}(a_2, b_2)\\(a_2, b_1)\end{bmatrix}_C\right)$$

$$= n + w\left(\begin{bmatrix}(a_1, b_2)\\(a_2, b_2)\end{bmatrix}_C\right)$$

$$\equiv_n w\left(\begin{bmatrix}(a_1, b_2)\\(a_2, b_2)\end{bmatrix}_C\right).$$

Since the first and last values are between 0 and $n - 1$ and equivalent modulo n, they are equal.

The converse can be proved in an analogous way. $\qquad\square$

Definition 12. If either of the equivalent conditions in Proposition 11 hold, then we will say that (C, w) is a partial tiling cycle. If $w = 1_E$, then we will say that (C, w) is a full tiling cycle.

Definition 13. Let $(A, B)_n$ be a partial tiling pair, and list the elements of its range in increasing order: $0 = \rho_0 < \rho_1 < \dots < \rho_{k-1} < n$. For each i there is a unique $(\alpha_i, \beta_i) \in A \times B$ such that $\mathrm{mod}_n(\alpha_i + \beta_i) = \rho_i$. Define the weighted cycle corresponding to $(A, B)_n$ as follows.

$$(\alpha_0, \beta_0) \xrightarrow{\rho_1 - \rho_0} (\alpha_1, \beta_1) \xrightarrow{\rho_2 - \rho_1} (\alpha_2, \beta_2) \cdots\cdots\cdots\cdots\rightarrow$$
$$n - \rho_{k-1} \uparrow \qquad\qquad\qquad\qquad\qquad\qquad\qquad\qquad\downarrow$$
$$(\alpha_{k-1}, \beta_{k-1}) \leftarrow\cdots\cdots\cdots\cdots\cdots\cdots\cdots\cdots\cdots\cdots$$

Example 14. Note that $(A, B)_n = (\{0, 4, 10\}, \{0, 2, 7, 9\})_{14}$ is a partial tiling pair. Its corresponding weighted cycle is as follows.

$$(0, 0) \xrightarrow{2} (0, 2) \xrightarrow{1} (10, 7) \xrightarrow{1} (4, 0) \xrightarrow{1} (10, 9) \xrightarrow{1} (4, 2)$$
$$1 \uparrow \qquad\qquad\qquad\qquad\qquad\qquad\qquad\qquad\qquad\qquad\qquad \downarrow 1$$
$$(4, 9) \xleftarrow{1} (10, 2) \xleftarrow{1} (4, 7) \xleftarrow{1} (10, 0) \xleftarrow{1} (0, 9) \xleftarrow{2} (0, 7)$$

Definition 15. Let (C, w) be a weighted cycle on $A \times B$. Let $n = w(E)$, and choose $(a_0, b_0) \in A \times B$. Define the following.

$$A' = \left\{ w\left(\begin{bmatrix} (a_0, b_0) \\ (a, b_0) \end{bmatrix}_C \right) : a \in A \right\}$$

$$B' = \left\{ w\left(\begin{bmatrix} (a_0, b_0) \\ (a_0, b) \end{bmatrix}_C \right) : b \in B \right\}$$

We will say that $(A', B')_n$ is the pair generated by (C, w) starting at (a_0, b_0).

Example 16. Let (C, w) be the following partial tiling cycle.

$$(1,1) \xrightarrow{\;1\;} (2,3) \xrightarrow{\;1\;} (3,2) \xrightarrow{\;1\;} (1,2) \xrightarrow{\;2\;} (2,1)$$

with $(3,1) \xleftarrow{\;3\;} (1,3) \xleftarrow{\;1\;} (3,3) \xleftarrow{\;1\;} (2,2)$, $(1,1) \xleftarrow{\;1\;} (3,1)$, $(2,1) \xrightarrow{\;3\;} (2,2)$.

The pair generated by (C, w) starting at $(1,1)$ is $(\{0, 5, 13\}, \{0, 3, 10\})_{14}$.

Proposition 17. Let $(A, B)_n$ be a partial tiling pair. Let (C, w) be the weighted cycle corresponding to $(A, B)_n$. The following hold.

1. (C, w) is a partial tiling cycle with total weight n.
2. The pair generated by (C, w) starting at $(0,0)$ is the same as $(A, B)_n$.

These results follow directly from the relevant definitions. The reader is encouraged to verify them in the particular case given in Example 14.

Proposition 18. Let (C, w) be a partial tiling cycle on $A \times B$, and choose $(a_0, b_0) \in A \times B = C$. Let $(A', B')_n$ be the pair generated by (C, w) starting at (a_0, b_0). The following hold.

1. $(A', B')_n$ is a partial tiling pair.
2. Let (C', w') be the partial tiling cycle corresponding to $(A', B')_n$. Then (C', w') is the same as (C, w) up to a relabeling of its vertices which is induced by bijections from A' to A and B' to B.

These results follow directly from the relevant definitions. The reader is encouraged to verify them in the particular case given in Example 16.

Proposition 19. Let $C = (A \times B, E)$ be a cycle, and let w_1 and w_2 be weight functions on C. Let $j_1, j_2 \in \mathbb{Z}$ such that $w = j_1 w_1 + j_2 w_2$ is strictly positive. If (C, w_1) and (C, w_2) are partial tiling cycles, then (C, w) is a partial tiling cycle.

Proof. Let $a_1, a_2 \in A$ and $b_1, b_2 \in B$.

$$w\left(\begin{bmatrix} (a_1, b_1) \\ (a_1, b_2) \end{bmatrix}_C \right) = j_1 w_1 \left(\begin{bmatrix} (a_1, b_1) \\ (a_1, b_2) \end{bmatrix}_C \right) + j_2 w_2 \left(\begin{bmatrix} (a_1, b_1) \\ (a_1, b_2) \end{bmatrix}_C \right)$$

$$= j_1 w_1 \left(\begin{bmatrix} (a_2, b_1) \\ (a_2, b_2) \end{bmatrix}_C \right) + j_2 w_2 \left(\begin{bmatrix} (a_2, b_1) \\ (a_2, b_2) \end{bmatrix}_C \right)$$

$$= w\left(\begin{bmatrix} (a_2, b_1) \\ (a_2, b_2) \end{bmatrix}_C \right)$$

So (C, w) is a partial tiling cycle. $\qquad\square$

Example 20. Let (C, w_1) be the following partial tiling cycle.

$$(1,1) \xrightarrow{\;1\;} (3,3) \xrightarrow{\;2\;} (2,1) \xrightarrow{\;1\;} (1,2) \xrightarrow{\;2\;} (1,3)$$

$$(1,1) \searrow^{1} \qquad\qquad\qquad\qquad\qquad (1,3) \swarrow^{1}$$

$$(3,2) \xleftarrow{\;3\;} (2,3) \xleftarrow{\;1\;} (3,1) \xleftarrow{\;1\;} (2,2)$$

Let (C, w_2) be the following partial tiling cycle.

$$(1,1) \xrightarrow{\;2\;} (3,3) \xrightarrow{\;2\;} (2,1) \xrightarrow{\;2\;} (1,2) \xrightarrow{\;3\;} (1,3)$$

$$\searrow^{1} \qquad\qquad\qquad\qquad\qquad \swarrow^{1}$$

$$(3,2) \xleftarrow{\;5\;} (2,3) \xleftarrow{\;1\;} (3,1) \xleftarrow{\;2\;} (2,2)$$

Note that $(C, -2w_1 + 3w_2)$, given below, is a partial tiling cycle.

$$(1,1) \xrightarrow{\;4\;} (3,3) \xrightarrow{\;2\;} (2,1) \xrightarrow{\;4\;} (1,2) \xrightarrow{\;5\;} (1,3)$$

$$\searrow^{1} \qquad\qquad\qquad\qquad\qquad \swarrow^{1}$$

$$(3,2) \xleftarrow{\;9\;} (2,3) \xleftarrow{\;1\;} (3,1) \xleftarrow{\;4\;} (2,2)$$

4   Regular Maximally Even Tilings

We now turn our focus to maximally even tiling pairs and cycles. In this section, we will study maximally even tiling canons that can be derived from full tilings simply by inserting rests.

Definition 21. We will say that a cycle $C = (A \times B, E)$ is regular if $(C, 1_E)$ is a partial tiling cycle. We will say that a partial tiling cycle (C, w) is regular if C is. We will say that a partial tiling pair is regular if its corresponding partial tiling cycle is regular. If a partial tiling cycle or pair is not regular, we will say that it is irregular.

Proposition 22. Let (C, w) be a partial tiling cycle where $C = (A \times B, E)$. Choose $j_1, j_2 \in \mathbb{Z}$ such that $w' = j_1 1_E + j_2 w$ is strictly positive. Then the following hold.

1. If (C, w) is regular, then (C, w') is a regular partial tiling cycle.
2. If $j_1 \neq 0$ and (C, w') is a partial tiling cycle, then C is regular.

Proof. The first result follows directly from Proposition 19 and the definition of regularity.

To prove the second result, note that

$$-\operatorname{sgn}(j_1) j_2 w + \operatorname{sgn}(j_1) w' = \operatorname{sgn}(j_1) j_1 1_E$$

is strictly positive. By Proposition 19, $(C, \operatorname{sgn}(j_1) j_1 1_E)$ is a partial tiling cycle. It is easy to see that if $(C, h 1_E)$ is a partial tiling cycle for $h \in [1, \infty)_{\mathbb{Z}}$, then $(C, 1_E)$ is too. Therefore, $(C, 1_E)$ is a partial tiling cycle. So C is regular. $\square$

The operation introduced in the previous proposition can be used to induce an equivalence relation on regular partial tiling cycles. The following example and proposition show how we can pick a representative from each equivalence class with a relatively small total weight.

Example 23. Let (C, w) be the following regular partial tiling cycle.

$$
\begin{array}{ccc}
(1,1) \xrightarrow{\ 7\ } (2,1) \xrightarrow{\ 6\ } (1,2) \\
7\uparrow \qquad\qquad\qquad\qquad \downarrow 7 \\
(2,3) \xleftarrow{\ 7\ } (1,3) \xleftarrow{\ 7\ } (2,2)
\end{array}
$$

Let $w' = -5 \cdot 1_E + w$. Then (C, w') is the following regular partial tiling cycle.

$$
\begin{array}{ccc}
(1,1) \xrightarrow{\ 2\ } (2,1) \xrightarrow{\ 1\ } (1,2) \\
2\uparrow \qquad\qquad\qquad\qquad \downarrow 2 \\
(2,3) \xleftarrow{\ 2\ } (1,3) \xleftarrow{\ 2\ } (2,2)
\end{array}
$$

Let $w'' = 3 \cdot 1_E - w'$. Then (C, w'') is the following regular partial tiling cycle.

$$
\begin{array}{ccc}
(1,1) \xrightarrow{\ 1\ } (2,1) \xrightarrow{\ 2\ } (1,2) \\
1\uparrow \qquad\qquad\qquad\qquad \downarrow 1 \\
(2,3) \xleftarrow{\ 1\ } (1,3) \xleftarrow{\ 1\ } (2,2)
\end{array}
$$

This example shows that we can use "reducing" and "swapping" operations to write any regular partial tiling cycle in terms of one with a relatively small total weight. This is made more precise in the following proposition.

Proposition 24. Let (C, w) be a regular maximally even partial tiling cycle where $C = (A \times B, E)$, $w(E) = n$, and $|A \times B| = k$. Then (C, w) can be expressed in the form $(C, j1_E \pm w_0)$ where (C, w_0) is a regular maximally even partial tiling cycle with $n_0 = w_0(E) \le 1.5k$. (This result follows directly from Propositions 8 and 22.)

Algorithm 25. Given a fixed $k \in \mathbb{N}$, the procedure below will produce a list of every regular maximally even tiling pair $(A, B)_n$ with $|A \times B| = k$ and $n \le 1.5k$.

- Set LIST to $\emptyset$.
- Find all full tiling pairs $(A, B)_k$ with $|A \times B| = k$. (This can be accomplished using a procedure given in [7].) For each of these,
    - Let $((A \times B, E), 1_E)$ be its corresponding full tiling cycle.
    - For each $n \in [k, 1.5k]_{\mathbb{Z}}$, modulo n maximally even set X, and weight function w on $(A \times B, E)$ corresponding to X, do the following.
        - If $((A \times B, E), w)$ is a partial tiling cycle, then
            - Let $(A', B')_n$ be the pair generated by $((A \times B, E), w)$ starting at $(0, 0)$.
            - Add $(A', B')_n$ to the LIST.

5 Irregular Maximally Even Tilings

In this section, we will give a necessary condition on n and k for the existence of irregular maximally even tilings. This condition significantly narrows our search for such tilings. Then we look at a couple of methods for actually producing them.

Lemma 26. Let $n \geq k$, and let $\gcd(n, k) = g$. Then

$$\left\lceil \frac{in}{k} \right\rceil = \left\lfloor \frac{(i+1)n}{k} \right\rfloor$$

for some $i \in [0, k)_\mathbb{Z}$ if and only if $n \leq 2k - 2g$.

Proof. Suppose that $\left\lceil \frac{in}{k} \right\rceil = \left\lfloor \frac{(i+1)n}{k} \right\rfloor = j$ for some $i \in [0, k)_\mathbb{Z}$. Let $n' = n/g$ and $k' = k/g$. Then we have the following.

$$j - 1 < \frac{in}{k} = \frac{in'}{k'} \leq j \leq \frac{(i+1)n'}{k'} = \frac{(i+1)n}{k} < j + 1$$

So we can write

$$\frac{in'}{k'} = j - 1 + \frac{r_i}{k'} \quad \text{and} \quad \frac{(i+1)n'}{k'} = j + \frac{r_{i+1}}{k'}$$

where $0 < r_i \leq k'$ and $0 \leq r_{i+1} < k'$. Now note that

$$
\begin{aligned}
\frac{n}{k} = \frac{n'}{k'} \\
= \frac{(i+1)n'}{k'} - \frac{in'}{k'} \\
= \left(j + \frac{r_{i+1}}{k'} \right) - \left(j - 1 + \frac{r_i}{k'} \right) \\
= 1 + \frac{r_{i+1}}{k'} - \frac{r_i}{k'} \\
\leq 1 + \frac{k'-1}{k'} - \frac{1}{k'} \\
= 2 - \frac{2}{k'}
\end{aligned}
$$

which yields $n \leq 2k - 2g$.

Now suppose that $n \leq 2k - 2g$. Choose $h, j \in \mathbb{Z}$ such that $hn + jk = g$. Use the division algorithm to write $h = kq + i$ where $0 \leq i < k$. Note that

$$\frac{in}{k} = \frac{(h - kq)n}{k} = \frac{hn - kqn}{k} = \frac{g - jk - kqn}{k} = \frac{g}{k} - j - qn.$$

Since $1 \leq g \leq k$, we have $\left\lceil \frac{in}{k} \right\rceil = 1 - j - qn$. Also,

$$
\begin{aligned}
1 - j - qn \leq \frac{n}{k} - j - qn \\
< \frac{g + n}{k} - j - qn \\
= \frac{(i+1)n}{k}
\end{aligned}
$$

and

$$\frac{(i+1)n}{k} = \frac{g+n}{k} - j - qn$$

$$\leq \frac{g+2k-2g}{k} - j - qn$$

$$= 2 - \frac{g}{k} - j - qn$$

$$< 2 - j - qn$$

So we have $\left\lfloor \frac{(i+1)n}{k} \right\rfloor = 1 - j - qn$. Thus, $\left\lceil \frac{in}{k} \right\rceil = \left\lfloor \frac{(i+1)n}{k} \right\rfloor$. □

Proposition 27. Let (C, w) be a maximally even tiling cycle with $C = (A \times B, E)$, $|A \times B| = k$, and $w(E) = n$. If (C, w) is irregular, then $n \leq 2k - 2\gcd(n, k)$.

Proof. Since (C, w) is irregular, $(C, 1_E)$ is not a partial tiling. So we can choose $a_1, a_2 \in A$, and $b_1, b_2 \in B$ such that

$$1_E \left(\begin{bmatrix} (a_1, b_1) \\ (a_1, b_2) \end{bmatrix}_C \right) \neq 1_E \left(\begin{bmatrix} (a_2, b_1) \\ (a_2, b_2) \end{bmatrix}_C \right).$$

Define the following.

$$i = 1_E \left(\begin{bmatrix} (a_1, b_1) \\ (a_1, b_2) \end{bmatrix}_C \right)$$

$$j = 1_E \left(\begin{bmatrix} (a_2, b_1) \\ (a_2, b_2) \end{bmatrix}_C \right)$$

Without loss of generality, we can assume $i < j$. Since (C, w) is maximally even we have the following (by Proposition 5).

$$w \left(\begin{bmatrix} (a_1, b_1) \\ (a_1, b_2) \end{bmatrix}_C \right) \in \left\{ \left\lfloor \frac{in}{k} \right\rfloor, \left\lceil \frac{in}{k} \right\rceil \right\}$$

$$w \left(\begin{bmatrix} (a_2, b_1) \\ (a_2, b_2) \end{bmatrix}_C \right) \in \left\{ \left\lfloor \frac{jn}{k} \right\rfloor, \left\lceil \frac{jn}{k} \right\rceil \right\}$$

Now note that

$$w \left(\begin{bmatrix} (a_1, b_1) \\ (a_1, b_2) \end{bmatrix}_C \right) \leq \left\lceil \frac{in}{k} \right\rceil \leq \left\lfloor \frac{(i+1)n}{k} \right\rfloor \leq \left\lfloor \frac{jn}{k} \right\rfloor \leq w \left(\begin{bmatrix} (a_2, b_1) \\ (a_2, b_2) \end{bmatrix}_C \right)$$

Since (C, w) is a partial tiling cycle,

$$w \left(\begin{bmatrix} (a_1, b_1) \\ (a_1, b_2) \end{bmatrix}_C \right) = w \left(\begin{bmatrix} (a_2, b_1) \\ (a_2, b_2) \end{bmatrix}_C \right).$$

Therefore,

$$\left\lceil \frac{in}{k} \right\rceil = \left\lfloor \frac{(i+1)n}{k} \right\rfloor.$$

By Lemma 26, $n \leq 2k - 2\gcd(n, k)$. □

Definition 28. For a partial tiling pair $(A, B)_n$ and unit $u \in \mathbb{Z}_n$, let

$$\text{MULT}_u[(A, B)_n] = (\text{mod}_n(uA), \text{mod}_n(uB))_n.$$

We will say that $\text{MULT}_u[(A, B)_n]$ is a unit multiple of $(A, B)_n$.

Proposition 29. Let u be a unit in $\mathbb{Z}_n$. Then $\text{MULT}_u[(A, B)_n]$ is partial tiling pair if and only if $(A, B)_n$ is a partial tiling pair.

Example 30. Note that $(\{0, 2, 4\}, \{0, 1\})_7$ is a regular partial tiling pair and

$$\text{MULT}_2[(\{0, 2, 4\}, \{0, 1\})_7] = (\{0, 1, 4\}, \{0, 2\})_7$$

is an irregular partial tiling pair. In addition to demonstrating the previous result (that unit multiplication preserves tiling), this example demonstrates that unit multiplication does not necessarily preserve regularity! The following algorithm takes advantage of this fact.

Algorithm 31. Given a fixed $k \in \mathbb{N}$, the procedure below will produce every irregular maximally even tiling pair $(A, B)_n$ with $|A \times B| = k$ that is a unit multiple of a regular partial tiling pair.

- Set LIST to $\emptyset$.
- Find all full tiling pairs $(A, B)_k$ with $|A \times B| = k$. (This can be accomplished using a procedure given in [7].) For each of these,
  - Let $((A \times B, E), 1_E)$ be its corresponding full tiling cycle.
  - For each $n \in [k, 2k - 2\gcd(n, k)]_{\mathbb{Z}}$, modulo n maximally even set X, modulo n unit u, and weight function w on $(A \times B, E)$ corresponding to $\text{mod}_n(uX)$, do the following.
    - If $((A \times B, E), w)$ is a partial tiling cycle, then
      - Let $(A', B')_n$ be the pair generated by $((A \times B, E), w)$ starting at $(0, 0)$.
      - If $\text{MULT}_{u^{-1}}[(A', B')_n]$ is irregular, then add it to the LIST.

Example 32. The algorithm above does not produce all irregular maximally even tiling pairs. For example, $(\{0, 1, 4, 7, 20\}, \{0, 2, 12, 14\})_{24}$ is an irregular maximally even tiling pair that is not a unit multiple of any regular partial tiling pair.

Definition 33. We define the multiplexation of partial tilings $(A_i, B)_n$ for $i = [0, j)_{\mathbb{Z}}$ to be $(\cup_{i=0}^{j-1}(jA_i + i), jB)_{jn}$. (This operation is discussed in [4] in the context of full tilings.)

Proposition 34. The multiplexation of partial tilings $(A_i, B)_n$ for $i = [0, j)_{\mathbb{Z}}$ is a partial tiling. Also, the partial tiling pairs $(A_i, B)_n$ must be maximally even if their multiplexation is to be maximally even.

Example 35. Note that $(\{0, 1, 4, 7, 20\}, \{0, 2, 12, 14\})_{24}$ from Example 32 is the multiplexation of the regular maximally even tiling pairs $(\{0, 2, 10\}, \{0, 1, 6, 7\})_{12}$ and $(\{0, 3\}, \{0, 1, 6, 7\})_{12}$.

6   Conclusion

In this paper we have seen how to construct all regular maximally even tilings, as well as irregular ones that are unit multiples or multiplexations of regular partial tilings. Through an exhaustive search, it has been verified that these techniques are sufficient to produce all maximally even tilings with $|A \times B| \leq 24$. More work will be necessary to determine whether these techniques are sufficient in general.

It is exciting to bring together two formerly unrelated branches of mathematical music theory, tiling and maximal evenness, in such a natural way. It is equally (if not more) exciting to think of the musical compositions that may result from this study.

References

1. J. Math. Music 3(2) (2009). https://doi.org/10.1080/17459730903086140
2. Perspect. New Music 49(2) (2011). http://www.perspectivesofnewmusic.org/TOC492.pdf
3. A102562 (2014). http://oeis.org/A102562. Accessed 24 Nov 2018
4. Amiot, E.: New perspectives on rhythmic canons and the spectral conjecture. J. Math. Music 3(2), 71–84 (2009). https://doi.org/10.1080/17459730903040709
5. Clough, J., Douthett, J.: Maximally even sets. J. Music Theory 35(1/2), 93–173 (1991). http://www.jstor.org/stable/843811
6. Demaine, E.D., et al.: The distance geometry of music. Comput. Geom. 42(5), 429–454 (2009). https://doi.org/10.1016/j.comgeo.2008.04.005. http://www.sciencedirect.com/science/article/pii/S0925772108001156. Special Issue on the Canadian Conference on Computational Geometry (CCCG 2005and CCCG 2006)
7. Kolountzakis, M.N., Matolcsi, M.: Algorithms for translational tiling. J. Math. Music 3(2), 85–97 (2009). https://doi.org/10.1080/17459730903040899
8. Vuza, D.T.: Supplementary sets and regular complementary unending canons (part one). Perspect. New Music 29, 22–49 (1991)
9. Vuza, D.T.: Supplementary sets and regular complementary unending canons (part three). Perspect. New Music 30, 102–124 (1992)
10. Vuza, D.T.: Supplementary sets and regular complementary unending canons (part two). Perspect. New Music 30, 184–207 (1992)
11. Vuza, D.T.: Supplementary sets and regular complementary unending canons (part four). Perspect. New Music 31, 270–305 (1993)

Short Papers

Distributed Vector Representations
of Folksong Motifs

Aitor Arronte Alvarez[1] and Francisco Gómez-Martin[2(✉)]

[1] Center for Language and Technology,
University of Hawaii at Manoa, Honolulu, USA
arronte@hawaii.edu
[2] Applied Mathematics Department,
Technical University of Madrid, Madrid, Spain
fmartin@etsisi.upm.es

Abstract. This article presents a distributed vector representation model for learning folksong motifs. A skip-gram version of word2vec with negative sampling is used to represent high quality embeddings. Motifs from the Essen Folksong collection are compared based on their cosine similarity. A new evaluation method for testing the quality of the embeddings based on a melodic similarity task is presented to show how the vector space can represent complex contextual features, and how it can be utilized for the study of folksong variation.

Keywords: Folksong motifs · Melodic context · Motif embedding · Word2vec

1 Introduction

Vector representations of words have been widely used in Natural Language Processing (NLP) tasks [18]. Following the distributional hypothesis [5,9], vector space models represent, or embed, words that are semantically related to each other closer in a continuous vector space [24]. A recent development in vector space models is word2vec [8,13,15], developed for learning high-quality word vectors from large corpora.

A neural network language model for learning word-embeddings was first proposed to learn a statistical language model and a word vector representation [1]. A simpler model using a neural net with a single hidden layer to learn word vector representations, and then train a language model was later developed [14]. Word2vec follows this simpler approach in two steps: first, continuous word vectors are learned using the simpler model [14], and then an n-gram is trained using these representations.

The relation between music and language has been studied in the cognitive science literature. Even though they are treated as different cognitive faculties, both share structural characteristics and generate similar expectations on the

M. Montiel et al. (Eds.): MCM 2019, LNAI 11502, pp. 325–332, 2019.
https://doi.org/10.1007/978-3-030-21392-3_26

listener [2]. NLP methods have been adapted and adopted in Music Information Retrieval (MIR) contexts [3,4,6]. More specifically, word2vec was used to
model musical contexts in western classical music works [10], and for chord rec-
ommendations [11]. In both cases the music compositions studied were complex
polyphonic works. The work presented in this article uses a much less data intensive material: monophonic songs.

Following the distributional hypothesis in semantics, the goal of this research
is to adopt the skip-gram version of the word2vec model for the distributional
representation of melodic units. Several melodic features such as contour, grouping, and small size motifs seem to be part of the so called 'Statistical Music Universals' [17,19]. This sequential processing of melodic units may be related to
the human capacity to group and comprehend motifs as units within a melodic
context. Our hypothesis is that these units may relate to each other in a melody
in similar ways as words do in sentences. If that is the case, the distributional
hypothesis should hold true for folksong melodies.

In the following sections a description of the skip-gram version of word2vec to
learn motifs from the Essen Folksong Collection [20] is presented. We will present
different similarity measures to determine how melodic context can capture the
similarity of folksong motifs.

2 Word2vec: Representing Folksong Motifs in a Distributed Vector Space

2.1 Word2vec Model

In the skip-gram version of the word2vec model, the goal is to find word embeddings that can predict the surrounding words of a target word in a sentence
or document [15]. Formally, the model can be defined in the following terms:
given a corpus W of words w and contexts c, the network tries to predict the
surrounding words of a target in a context. The objective of the skip-gram is to
maximize the following log probability:

$$\arg\max_{\theta} \prod_{w \in W} \left[\prod_{c \in C} p(c \mid w; \theta) \right] \tag{1}$$

where $p(c \mid w; \theta)$ is calculated by the softmax function:

$$p(c \mid w; \theta) = \frac{e^{v_c \cdot v_w}}{\sum_{c' \in C} e^{v_{c'} \cdot v_w}} \tag{2}$$

where v_c and $v_w \in R^d$ are vector representations of v and c, and C is the set of
all possible contexts. The set of parameters θ is composed of v_{c_i}, v_{w_i} for $w \in W$.

Since the term $p(w; \theta)$ involves a summation over all possible contexts c'
becomes computationally very intensive, and it is normally replaced with negative sampling [15]. This article uses this sampling technique.

The cosine similarity measure is used to determine the relatedness of two embeddings. The metric for a pair of words w_1 and w_2 can be defined as [22]:

$$cos(w_1, w_2) = \frac{\overrightarrow{w_1} \cdot \overrightarrow{w_2}}{\|\overrightarrow{w_1}\| \|\overrightarrow{w_2}\|} \tag{3}$$

for all similarity computations in the embedding space, where $\overrightarrow{w}$ is a real-valued vector embedding of word w.

2.2 Melodic Context and Motif Representation

We are interested in studying how word2vec can model melodic context using small musical motifs instead of words. In the present research context is understood as the sequential organization of melodic units that establish statistically relevant relationships with one another in a melodic segment.

Melodic similarity and classification methods depend strongly on melodic representation [23]. Motifs from the Essen folksong collection are represented by using strings. First, intervals are codified for each song by using Music21 [7] chromatic step values from the original Kern format, and encode interval direction with Boolean values (1 for ascending and 0 for descending). For instance, the string 21 represents an ascending major second, and the string 30 a descending minor third. Repeated notes are encoded as 00.

Once the entire folksong corpus is encoded using this scheme, motifs are extracted as multi-words [15]. A multi-word is then a concatenation of two or more intervals or durations that are found in a melody adjacent to each other. For example, an intervallic multi-word of size 3 30_00_21 represents a descending minor third, followed by a repeated note, and by an ascending major second.

The multi-word representation of motifs is obtained following these steps:

- From a corpus of intervals we create a vocabulary of multi-word M with multi-words mw of length 2. Only those mw that occur at least 10 times are kept, based on the quality of the results from ad-hoc queries.
- For each mw in M intervals in the corpus are substituted with their corresponding mw.

The same procedure is used for mw of size 3, with the only difference that the minimum number of occurrences of mw in a corpus is set to 5. The word2vec model is run based on the corpora created obtaining vector representations for all the motifs.

2.3 Evaluation Methods

Evaluation of Word Embeddings (WE) falls into two categories: intrinsic and extrinsic evaluation [22]. Intrinsic evaluation methods test for syntactic or semantic relationships between words using predefined queries. Then, methods are evaluated by aggregating correlation scores. Extrinsic evaluations are performed by using WE as the input feature for another task, and then embeddings are evaluated based on the changes in the performance of that particular task.

This study concentrates on intrinsic evaluations, more specific on relatedness and analogy. Relatedness in WE is the cosine similarity between two words. Pairs of words should have higher correlation scores when compared with human annotated semantic similarity scores [22]. Analogical reasoning was first used for testing semantic relationships between pairs of words given specific phrases: given a term x and a term y so that x:y resembles a sample relationship i:j [13]. All these evaluation methods are language specific, and have not being adapted for MIR tasks.

Given the non-linguistic nature of music, and the difficulty of interpreting WE, more so when they represent melodic motifs, a new method is presented for evaluating Melodic Embeddings (ME) based on variations of motifs and similarity measures for those motifs in relation to a reference one. The method proceeds as follows:

1. For each multi-word mw_i, where $i = 1, 2, ..., l$ and l is the cardinality of the vocabulary M from corpus C, we compute $max(cos(mw_i, mw_j))$ for all j, and obtain the most related multi-word mw_i^+ of mw_i, so that $mw_i : w_i^+$, and an unrelated multi-word mw_i^-, where $cos(mw_i, mw_i^-) < h$, where h is an acceptable similarity threshold.

2. Chose from C a melodic segment c and replace mw_i with mw_i^+ and mw_i^-, obtaining a related c^+ and an unrelated c^- melodic segments. This action is performed for all segments in C.

3. Obtain $sim(c, c^+)$ and $sim(c, c^-)$, where $sim()$ is a function that computes a measure of melodic similarity between pairs of melodic segments.

The idea behind this evaluation method is that, if vector representations of motifs are of good quality, when a motif mw_i is replaced with its most similar motif mw_i^+ in a melodic segment c obtaining c^+, then a melodic similarity measure should indicate that segment c is more similar to c^+ than to c^-.

To measure intervallic similarity, sequences are evaluated using the mean absolute difference in intervals (*diffint*) [16]. Since this study deals with equal-length sequences, note sequences are evaluated with city block distance (*citydist*) [21], and for duration-weighted pitch sequences correlation distance (*corrdist*) [12]. In order to compute distance measures based on note sequences, a vector of pitches represented as numerical MIDI values is used.

2.4   Evaluating Motif Embeddings

A sample of 2000 melodic segments is randomly selected from the European subcollection from the Essen folksong corpus. Multi-word embeddings of size 2 and 3 are obtained using the skip-gram version of word2vec with context size of 5 and vector dimension of 150. We measure melodic similarity using *diffint*, *citydist*, and *corrdist* for related and unrelated multi-word melodic segments using the method presented in Sect. 2.3, and compare their means.

Wilcoxon rank sum test is performed on related and unrelated melodic segments for all similarity measures, resulting on significant differences in means for all measures (p-$value$<0.01). Ad-hoc queries of intervallic motif embeddings of size 2 show similarity between motifs based on the context. For instance, Fig. 1 shows similar motifs from mw of size 2 (transposed to C), and Fig. 2, shows melodic examples where those motifs are present in similar melodic contexts: all three fragments contain the target motif, either 00_20 or 20_00 preceded by a melodic unison and followed by an ascending major second.

Fig. 1. Similar intervallic motifs from mw of size 2

Fig. 2. Fragments of European folksongs with similar intervallic motifs colored in red (Color figure online)

Next, closely related and unrelated melodic segments variations from a reference segment using the procedure described in Sect. 2.3 are computed. We compare the similarity between a reference melodic segment with its most related variation and the same reference segment with a close variation, and with a non related (or distant) variation. The cosine similarity for multi-words of size 2 and

Table 1. Euclidean distance between similarity scores

Results			
Measure	ref_var_ref_close_var	ref_var_ref_distant_var	mw_size
diffint	**6.231**	7.853	2
citydist	**8.836**	11.213	2
corrdist	**0.503**	2.378	2
diffint	**2.163**	4.782	3
citydist	**4.556**	7.181	3
corrdist	**0.713**	4.044	3

3 is used to select closely related and unrelated motifs. We utilize the Euclidean distance for comparing the average similarity scores of the 2000 segments and all the variants described.

The results in Table 1 show that the distance of the similarity scores between the reference segments and their variations, and the reference segments and closely related variants (*ref_var_ref_close_var*) yield better results than when we compare the reference segments and their variants, with the reference segments with distantly related variants (*ref_var_ref_distant_var*).

Overall, the results of the motif embeddings show that vector representations of folksong motifs capture contextual melodic features. Query results show how motifs can be modeled with the skip-gram version of the word2vec from monophonic contexts. One of the advantages of this method is that motifs can be easily modeled in a complete unsupervised manner given a context, and they can be retrieved using the cosine distance. At the same time, with large corpora the algorithm tends to discover multiple motifs, some of which may be irrelevant for the musicological analysis.

3 Conclusions

Word2vec has been used to model complex Western polyphonic classical music [10]. In this article the skip-gram version of word2vec is used to learn rich representations of monophonic motifs from the Essen folksong collection. The proposed approach shows how motifs from folksongs can be learned from a large corpus and compared with each other using the cosine similarity. This approach can be very useful for the musicological study of folksong variation using small melodic units such as motifs. It also shows, how word2vec is able to capture and model melodic contexts from monophonic songs. Future work should concentrate on the filtering of motifs based on different musicological criteria, to avoid a combinatorial explosion and to select relevant motifs for the musical analysis.

The evaluation of WE is an important research topic in the NLP literature [22]. In this article a novel computational method for evaluating the quality of motif embeddings is proposed. The approach presented shows how the model captures different degrees of motif similarity. This evaluation method can be very useful for studying the similarity of melodic segments based on motifs and their related variants. Future work in this area should include a cognitive similarity evaluation task performed by human participants to test the quality of the embeddings.

References

1. Bengio, Y., Ducharme, R., Vincent, P., Jauvin, C.: A neural probabilistic language model. J. Mach. Learn. Res. **3**(Feb), 1137–1155 (2003)
2. Besson, M., Schön, D.: Comparison between language and music. Ann. New York Acad. Sci. **930**(1), 232–258 (2001)
3. Boom, C.D., et al.: Large-scale user modeling with recurrent neural networks for music discovery on multiple time scales. Multimed. Tools Appl. **77**, 15385–15407 (2017)
4. Boulanger-Lewandowski, N., Bengio, Y., Vincent, P.: Modeling temporal dependencies in high-dimensional sequences: application to polyphonic music generation and transcription. arXiv preprint arXiv:1206.6392 (2012)
5. Clark, S.: Vector space models of lexical meaning. In: Lappin, S., Fox, C. (eds.) The Handbook of Contemporary Semantic Theory, pp. 463–472. Wiley-Blackwell, Hoboken (2015)
6. Conklin, D., Witten, I.H.: Multiple viewpoint systems for music prediction. J. New Music Res. **24**(1), 51–73 (1995)
7. Cuthbert, M.S., Ariza, C.: Music21: A toolkit for computer-aided musicology and symbolic music data. In: ISMIR. Utrecht, The Netherlands (2010)
8. Goldberg, Y., Levy, O.: word2vec explained: deriving mikolov et al'.s negative-sampling word-embedding method. arXiv preprint arXiv:1402.3722 (2014)
9. Harris, Z.S.: Distributional structure. Word **10**(2–3), 146–162 (1954)
10. Herremans, D., Chuan, C.H.: Modeling musical context with word2vec. arXiv preprint arXiv:1706.09088 (2017)
11. Huang, C.Z.A., Duvenaud, D., Gajos, K.Z.: Chordripple: recommending chords to help novice composers go beyond the ordinary. In: Proceedings of the 21st International Conference on Intelligent User Interfaces, pp. 241–250. ACM, Sonoma (2016)
12. Janssen, B., van Kranenburg, P., Volk, A.: Finding occurrences of melodic segments in folk songs employing symbolic similarity measures. J. New Music Res. **46**(2), 118–134 (2017)
13. Mikolov, T., Chen, K., Corrado, G., Dean, J.: Efficient estimation of word representations in vector space. arXiv preprint arXiv:1301.3781 (2013)
14. Mikolov, T., Kopecky, J., Burget, L., Glembek, O., et al.: Neural network based language models for highly inflective languages. In: 2009 IEEE International Conference on Acoustics, Speech and Signal Processing, ICASSP 2009, pp. 4725–4728. IEEE, Taipei (2009)
15. Mikolov, T., Sutskever, I., Chen, K., Corrado, G.S., Dean, J.: Distributed representations of words and phrases and their compositionality. In: Advances in Neural Information Processing Systems, pp. 3111–3119. Lake Tahoe, Nevada (2013)
16. Müllensiefen, D., Frieler, K., et al.: Cognitive adequacy in the measurement of melodic similarity: algorithmic vs. human judgments. Comput. Musicology **13**(2003), 147–176 (2004)

17. Nettl, B.: An ethnomusicologist contemplates universals in musical sound and musical culture. In: Brown, S., Nils, L., Wallin, B.M. (eds.) The Origins of Music, pp. 463–472. MIT Press, Cambridge (2000)
18. Rumelhart, D.E., Hinton, G.E., Williams, R.J.: Learning representations by back-propagating errors. Nature 323(6088), 533 (1986)
19. Savage, P.E., Brown, S., Sakai, E., Currie, T.E.: Statistical universals reveal the structures and functions of human music. Proc. National Acad. Sci. 112(29), 8987–8992 (2015)
20. Schaffrath, H., Huron, D.: The essen folksong collection in the humdrum kern format. Technical report, Center for Computer Assisted Research in the Humanities, Menlo Park, CA, USA (1995)
21. Scherrer, D.K., Scherrer, P.H.: An experiment in the computer measurement of melodic variation in folksong. J. Am. Folklore 84(332), 230–241 (1971)
22. Schnabel, T., Labutov, I., Mimno, D., Joachims, T.: Evaluation methods for unsupervised word embeddings. In: Proceedings of the 2015 Conference on Empirical Methods in Natural Language Processing, pp. 298–307. Lisbon, Portugal (2015)
23. Toiviainen, P., Eerola, T.: A computational model of melodic similarity based on multiple representations and self-organizing maps. In: Proceedings of the seventh international conference on music perception and cognition, Sydney. Causal Productions, Adelaide, pp. 236–239 (2002)
24. Turney, P.D., Pantel, P.: From frequency to meaning: vector space models of semantics. J. Artif. Intell. Res. 37, 141–188 (2010)

Visualizing Temperaments: Squaring the Circle?

Gilles Baroin[1,2](✉) and André Calvet[3]

[1] Laboratoire ENAC, Université Fédérale de Toulouse, Toulouse, France
Gilles@Mathemusic.net
[2] Laboratoire LLA Créatis, Université Fédérale de Toulouse, Toulouse, France
[3] IRCAM, Paris, France
http://www.Mathemusic.net

Abstract. Since our hearing system is accustomed to the equal temperament system, best applied to modern western musical instruments, we perceive the other tuning systems as unfamiliar, without being able to describe exactly how and what sounds weird and seems dissonant.

This paper describes the construction of new mathemusical models and visualization concepts: Two dimensional static and dynamic models, 3D and 4D animated objects.

These tools are designed to graphically compare temperaments and generate visualizations that reinforce/augment the auditory impression. We discuss limits and applications for our models and their different applications.

All videos will be available on www.mathemusic.net.

Keywords: Temperament · Visualization · Hypersphere

1 Introduction

1.1 Definitions

A temperament refers to a specific tuning system for the subdivision of the octave. Tempering is the process of adjusting intervals in tuning a piano or other musical instruments. We do not take inharmonicity into account and consider that each octave has an exact ratio of 2:1, hence the temperaments are therefore defined within one octave. For comparison purpose, temperaments are transposed to the same reference C (Note #0).

We furthermore assume that the reader is familiar with Set Theory [1].

In just intonation, each interval between two pitches corresponds to a whole number ratio between their frequencies whereas, in equal temperament, the octave is divided into 12 equal semitones. Therefore the frequency of the nth pitch is $f_n = f_0.2^{n/12}$ with f_0, the frequency of the reference note.

For history and details on temperamentology please refer to Jedrzejewski [2] Calvet [3].

© Springer Nature Switzerland AG 2019
M. Montiel et al. (Eds.): MCM 2019, LNAI 11502, pp. 333–337, 2019.
https://doi.org/10.1007/978-3-030-21392-3_27

1.2   Context

At the time of just intonation, temperament (i.e. Pythagorean) was designed so that musical instruments could sound as "in tune" in a few some keys, but seem "dissonant" in other keys. The listener identifies dissonances and vaguely feels a distance between a specific temperament and the equal one, which is nowadays the reference. Over time, the distance of pure temperament gradually gave way to the distance of equal temperament. Our static tools are used to quantify, visualize and compare temperaments between them. Our dynamic approach helps identify the tonalities for which the temperament is intended and which chordal context produces the most pleasing (displeasing), usual (unusual) sounds to the ear.

We have applied the methods to well-known temperaments, such Zarlino, Bach by Kellner, Mesotonic by Aaron and the Pythagorean ones. All studies are available on www.mathemusic.net.

2   Visualization Tools

2.1   Definitions

For static comparison, we superimpose the drawing of the studied temperament to that of the equal one and observe the differences in shape.

For dynamic visualization, we reduce the local harmony as a triad made of three intervals: m3, M3, P5, (international shorthand notation) and compare the values of these intervals to the theoretical frequencies of a just intonation ($m3_p = 5/6$, $M3_p = 5/4$, $P5_p = 3/2$).

These three parameters are used as the lengths of the sides of a triangle or a box for the 2D or 3D models, respectively.

We use the same music score to illustrate all temperaments, the soundtracks [4] are MIDI generated and played with the software Pianoteq [5] that enables personal tuning.

In order to have a smooth journey through all 24 tonalities, the music follows a regular Hamiltonian path on the Tonnetz: a succession of L and R Transformations: CMaj, Amin, FMaj, Dmin,.... Emin, CMaj. See Andreatta [6], Albini [7].

2.2   One Dimension

One can represent the log of frequencies of each note of the considered temperament along a circle. The equal temperament is represented by a regular dodecagon; however, because the differences between temperaments are so slight in frequencies, the superimposition of the drawings will not be pertinent enough. That is the reason why we have developed higher dimensional models.

2.3   Two Dimensions

We use the chromatic circle as a basis and associate, this time, each pitch class n, to a complex number p_n : $p_n = r_n e^{i\theta_n}$. In polar coordinates we have: $r_n = r_0 f_n/f_0$, $\theta_n = n\pi/6$.

The equal temperament will still be plotted as a regular dodecagon, whereas the drawing of other temperaments will result in an equiangular non-regular polygon: It gives the impression of stretching the chromatic circle along its radius.

By superimposing different temperament drawings, we are now able to compare them. See Fig. 1.

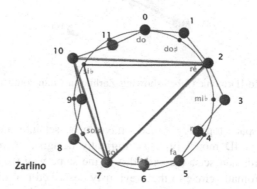

Fig. 1. The "Tempered Chromatic Circle" showing Mesotonic vs equal temperaments. (Color figure online)

Dynamic Visualization. Our Hamiltonian song reveals a rotating and deforming triangle [6]; each side relates to a constituting interval of the triad. In order to indicate the ratio to a pure interval, we use coloration for each side of the triangle: Green stands for pure interval, red stands for the most distant ones. As expected, the coloration remains constant while illustrating the equal temperament. Temperaments featuring pure intervals enclose some full green sequences while the music plays in the tonality they are designed for.

2.4 Three Dimensions

We model each triad as a box with sides l_x, l_y, l_z such as

$$l_x = f(m3/m3_p), \quad l_y = f(M3/M3_p), \quad l_z = f(P5/P5_p)$$

With f in the form of $a + b^{m/m_p}$, function used for visualization scaling.

The color of the box varies from green to red, accordingly to the human perception [8]. A triad made of pure intervals will therefore appear as a green cube (Fig. 2).

2.5 Four Dimensions

The set of pitch classes $@Z_{12} \Rrightarrow @(Z_3 \otimes Z_4)$, is usually considered as a product of circles, which is topologically a torus. But when the usual picture of a torus is drawn, distances are distorted, it can be proved that there is no way to embed $Z_3 \otimes Z_4$ isometrically in 3D-space, The use of points on the surface of a hypersphere permits us to preserve the correlation between musical interval and euclidian distance [10].

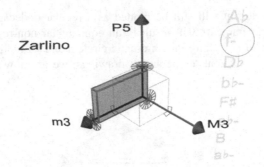

Fig. 2. The "Tempered Harmonic Cube" showing Zarlino in f min compared to pure intervals. (Color figure online)

Due to the 4D space topology, objects have to be set into motion to be understandable. The Planet-4D model [9] was originally designed to represent tempered tonal or atonal, chords and sets. We extend it in the same way we have extended the one dimensional chromatic circle to the previously described two-dimensional model. We also use the same coloration principle, preserve the equiangularity and alter the distance of each pitch class to the hypersphere center according to its ratio to an equal tempered tone.

The quaternionic coordinates of each tempered pitch class become: $Q_{nt} = Q_n f_n/f_0$ with

- $Q_n = \left(\frac{1}{\sqrt{3}} e^{i\frac{2n\pi}{3}}, \frac{1}{\sqrt{2}} e^{i\frac{2n\pi}{4}}\right), n \in [0.11]$: the original coordinates of pitch class n in the Planet-4D Model,
- f_n, f_0: frequencies of the note in the studied and equal temperaments, respectively (Fig. 3).

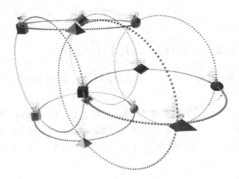

Fig. 3. The "Tempered Hypersphere" appears as a deformation of the Planet-4D (in gray)

As expected, the 4D representation of the equal temperament will be the standard hypersphere of the Planet-4D model featuring constant color; whereas other temperaments will be shown as a stretched sphere with changing color.

3   Conclusions

In this study we have observed that, due to the topology of each space, our models have different applications.

The static "Tempered Chromatic Circle" provides a global instant impression of regularity and enables direct comparison between temperaments. On the other hand, dynamic models are suitable to following the evolution of experienced dissonance while playing a song.

The dynamic "Tempered Chromatic Circle" provides the observer with the ability to follow the parsimonious voice leading in our Hamiltonian song sample.

The 3D dynamic "Tempered Harmonic Cube" facilitates the perception of harmonically similar chords, because they are displayed in similar color. Moreover, the user gets an efficient global perception of the variation of the dissonance.

In the "Tempered Planet-4D Hypersphere" model, even if we are unable by design to compare temperaments in a static way, the perception of symmetry is maximized.

This model was designed to answer the recurring question: what if the temperament is not equal? In the next studies we could try to represent the deformation in 4D of the two geodesics: the chromatic circle and the circle of fifths. We would like to try visualization for atonal music on non-equal temperament.

References

1. Forte, A.: The Structure of Atonal Music. Yale University Press, New Haven and London (1973). ISBN 0-300-01610-7
2. Jedrzejewski, F.: Mathématiques des systèmes acoustiques. Tempéraments et modèles contemporains. L'Harmattan (2002)
3. Calvet, A.: Le clavier bien obtempéré, Essai de Tempéramentologie (2019, to be published)
4. Dessault, H.: Improvised arpeggiated suites #1 and #4 (2015)
5. Guillaume, P., et al.: Pianoteq software (2005)
6. Andreatta, M., Baroin, G.: An introduction on formal and computational models in popular music analysis and generation. In: Kapoula, Z., Vernet, M. (eds.) Aesthetics and Neuroscience, pp. 257–269. Springer, Cham (2016). https://doi.org/10.1007/978-3-319-46233-2_16
7. Albini, G., Antonini, S.: Hamiltonian cycles in the topological dual of the tonnetz. In: Chew, E., Childs, A., Chuan, C.-H. (eds.) MCM 2009. CCIS, vol. 38, pp. 1–10. Springer, Heidelberg (2009). https://doi.org/10.1007/978-3-642-02394-1_1
8. Andreatta, M.: On group-theoretical methods applied to music: some compositional and implementational aspects. In: Perspectives in Mathematical Music Theory (2004)
9. Baroin, G.: The planet-4D model: an original hypersymmetric music space based on graph theory. In: Agon, C., Andreatta, M., Assayag, G., Amiot, E., Bresson, J., Mandereau, J. (eds.) MCM 2011. LNCS, vol. 6726, pp. 326–329. Springer, Heidelberg (2011). https://doi.org/10.1007/978-3-642-21590-2_25
10. Amiot, E., Baroin, G.: Looking at old and new isometries between pc-sets in the Planet-4D model. In: Music Theory Online. Society for Music Theory (2015)

Music Corpus Analysis Using Unwords

Darrell Conklin[1,2](✉)

[1] Department of Computer Science and Artificial Intelligence,
University of the Basque Country UPV/EHU, San Sebastian, Spain
darrell.conklin@ehu.es
[2] IKERBASQUE, Basque Foundation for Science, Bilbao, Spain

Abstract. Discovering patterns reoccurring within a collection of pieces is a fundamental type of music corpus analysis. The inverted task is to discover patterns that are surprisingly infrequent in a corpus, including completely absent patterns or unwords. The key issue in mining unwords is evaluating whether a specific pattern is merely statistically absent from the corpus, or is prohibited in the style exemplified by the corpus. This paper describes a statistical method for evaluating unwords and applies it to reveal interesting unwords for counterpoint and chord sequences.

Keywords: Unwords · Music analysis · Statistics · Pattern discovery

1 Introduction

Discovering patterns in data is a fundamental form of exploratory data analysis. For computational music analysis, *inter-opus* patterns reoccurring in a corpus may signify interesting musical aspects including stylistic schema, motifs in tune families, and features of diachronic style change. Though most research has focused on positive patterns, the discovery of negative patterns, rules, and constraints in data is an area of growing interest [3]. For this type of analysis one inverts the task and asks: what are the patterns that *do not occur* in a corpus?

The signification of absent patterns must be viewed with caution, because the absence of most long patterns is not surprising, due to the finite, even small, size of a corpus. Such patterns do not have a signification because their absence is expected. On the other hand, the absence of some short patterns may be statistically surprising and this may indicate a structural constraint of the broad music style exemplified by the corpus. In the field of bioinformatics, short absent patterns have been called variously *minimal absent words* [13], *unwords* [11], *nullomers* [10], and *minimal forbidden words* [8]. These are absent patterns that are not contained in any other absent pattern.

The methods described in this paper differ from the bioinformatics applications cited above in three ways. First, we have a *set* of pieces for analysis, not just one long sequence. Second, the components of words have internal structure, being sets of features rather than single letters. Third, we are interested in *individual unwords* as targets of analysis, rather than a large unstructured set of

© Springer Nature Switzerland AG 2019
M. Montiel et al. (Eds.): MCM 2019, LNAI 11502, pp. 338–343, 2019.
https://doi.org/10.1007/978-3-030-21392-3_28

all possible unwords. The fact that a corpus comprising a total of L events will have $O(\sigma L)$ unwords (σ the alphabet size) [8] necessitates some method to filter and rank the set of all unwords.

In this paper, the significance of an unword is measured using a p-value, indicating the probability that a pattern is not found in a corpus. Low p-values can be interpreted as evidence of absence rather than merely absence of evidence. This recalls the fact that a positive corpus alone can provide negative evidence [14]. The use of p-values here is appropriate and intuitive: the intuition being that unwords having a high expected count (i.e., that are short, and general) have low p-values and are interesting.

2 Methods

This section defines the representation for patterns, defines the concept of an unword, and concludes by defining p-values for unwords.

2.1 Patterns

To represent patterns, a *viewpoint* function is used to map events in sequences to abstract features. A *feature* of an event is a pair $\tau{:}v$ comprised of a viewpoint name τ paired with a value v. For example, for a viewpoint that computes the chord root movement (crm) of successive chords in terms of their diatonic interval, the values are elements of the set $\{\mathsf{d}, \mathsf{P}, \mathsf{m}, \mathsf{M}, \mathsf{A}\} \times \{1, \ldots, 7\}$, and example features are crm:M6 and crm:P1. A *feature set* is a set of features, and a *pattern* is a sequence of feature sets. A pattern *subsumes* a piece or another pattern if it can be placed such that subset relations hold between all aligned components.

A *corpus* is a collection of pieces. The *piece count* $n(\Phi)$ of a pattern Φ in a corpus is the number of pieces in the corpus subsumed by the pattern. An *unword* is any pattern Φ for which $n(\Phi) = 0$ and which does not subsume any other unword (i.e., unwords are minimal absent patterns).

2.2 Statistics of Unwords

Let X be a random variable modelling the piece count of a pattern, so $P(X = k)$ is the probability that the observed count of the pattern is exactly k (≥ 0). In the following the p-value $P(X = 0)$ of an unword will be defined.

To compute a p-value for a pattern, a generative model must be used to define the background distribution of pattern occurrences. This can be done by assuming that sequences in the background population have the same zero-order distribution of event features as the corpus. Under these assumptions, the probability p that a pattern $s_1, \ldots, s_m$ subsumes a random event sequence (also of length m) is the product of the probabilities of the feature sets of the pattern:

$$p = \prod_{i=1}^{m} \frac{n(s_i)}{L}, \tag{1}$$

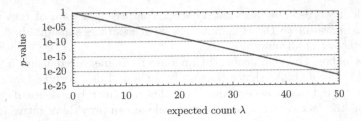

Fig. 1. Diminishing unword p-value with increasing expected count.

where $n(s_i)$ is the number of events in the dataset that match the feature set s_i. This probability p can then be used to compute the expected number of pieces subsumed by a pattern. The number of positions where a pattern of length m can occur in a piece σ of length $\ell(\sigma)$ is:

$$t(\sigma) = \ell(\sigma) - m + 1, \tag{2}$$

and therefore the probability that the pattern *does not occur* in the piece is $(1 - p)^{t(\sigma)}$, and the probability that it occurs *at least once* in the piece is $1 - (1 - p)^{t(\sigma)}$. Its expected piece count in the corpus Γ is:

$$\lambda = \sum_{\sigma \in \Gamma} 1 - (1 - p)^{t(\sigma)}, \tag{3}$$

and the probability of observing no pieces containing the pattern is:

$$P(X = 0) = \prod_{\sigma \in \Gamma} (1 - p)^{t(\sigma)}, \tag{4}$$

which can be simplified using a Poisson approximation to $P(X = 0) = \exp(-\lambda)$. These formulae define the expectation λ (Eq. 3) and the p-value (Eq. 4) of an unword. Figure 1 shows how the p-value of an unword evolves for different values of λ: as desired, unwords that are expected (high λ) obtain low p-values (are more likely to be structural rather than statistical absent words).

3   Results

This section illustrates a selection of unwords discovered in two different corpora. Both use features derived in some way from a multivoice music surface (counterpoint, chord sequences).

3.1   Counterpoint

The Bach chorale harmonizations are an ideal music application of unwords, as some structures rarely or never appear, guided by the language of counterpoint. From 185 Bach chorale harmonizations [1] the soprano and bass voices are extracted, and a contrapuntal pattern representation [5] is used to investigate voice-leading movements that are absent and potentially prohibited between the two voices in the chorales. A common way to deal with a polyphonic music surface is to slice the surface at every unique note onset, transforming the score from a set of voices to a sequence of slices. Here the two-voice texture given by the extracted soprano and bass voices was sliced. These sequences were analyzed for unwords using viewpoints expressing melodic contour of the top and bottom voices (tvc, bvc), vertical interval (vint) (folded to within one octave) and a temporal relation with the possible values {bv-sw, tv-sw, st} (bottom voice starting while top sounding, top voice starting while bottom sounding, and starting together).

Table 1 (top) shows a selection of highly significant (low p-values) unwords discovered in the analysis corpus. All of these can be given an interpretation based on known music theoretical principles:

1. consecutive unisons (or octaves), with the top voice (hence, both voices) moving down, implying parallel motion or voice crossing,
2. a diminished fifth followed by a perfect fifth, with any voice motions,
3. consecutive fifths, with the first fifth approached by a downwards movement in the upper voice, and with the voices both descending,
4. a major third followed by a minor seventh, with the top voice held. This implies a tritone melodic interval in the lower voice.

Regarding the third unword, it is known that Bach included parallel fifths (pattern {vint:P5} {vint:P5}) in certain contexts [9]. The reported unword is a specialization of this pattern to particular voice movements. Note that any generalization of the pattern (i.e. by dropping one or both of the voice movement features) will no longer be an unword.

3.2   Chord Sequences

The genre of uplifting trance [4] is used as a second case study for unword discovery. Trance chord sequences are tonal but permit some divergence from standard major/minor mode tonalities. They do not exist in isolation but must join together to form coherent structures, which imposes cyclic constraints between the last and the first chord of the loop.

A corpus of 100 uplifting trance anthem loops [15] is represented using two viewpoints: chord root movement (crm) and chord quality movement (major to major, major to minor, etc.) with the possible values {MM, mm, mM, Mm}. All loops are expanded once, so that the transition from the last to the first chord is observed and cannot be falsely reported as an unword.

Table 1 (bottom) shows a selection of highly significant unwords from the trance corpus. Most of these illustrate some modulation to different keys that is too rapid. For example, the second pattern moves from a triad (major or minor) to a major triad a fifth above, followed by another major triad, whereas a final minor triad would be more acceptable.

Table 1. Significant unwords in two corpora. Top: unwords in Bach chorale voice pairs. Bottom: unwords in trance anthem loop sequences. In the hypothetical trance instances, depending on context X refers to either any triad root, or either a major or minor triad.

pattern	λ	hypothetical instance
{vint:P1} {vint:P1,tvc:-}	77.9	
{vint:d5} {vint:P5}	53.9	
{vint:P5,tvc:-} {vint:P5,tvc:-}	45.1	
{vint:M3} {vint:m7,temp:bv-sw}	43.1	
{crm:m7} {cqm:mM}	29.5	CX B♭m XM
{crm:P5} {crm:M2,cqm:MM}	14.9	CX GM AM
{crm:M3} {cqm:MM}	14.3	CX EM XM
{cqm:Mm} {crm:P5} {cqm:Mm}	12.6	XM Cm GM Xm

4   Discussion and Conclusions

This paper presented new methods for unword representation (feature sets) and evaluation (using p-values). Unwords can be viewed as a specialization of *antipatterns*, patterns that occur less frequently than expected in a background corpus [3,6]. Here a statistical method for evaluating unwords was defined and applied to two music corpora as a proof of concept.

Unwords have several practical applications. Researchers have investigated the use of unwords for biological [2] and music [7] sequence comparison. The underlying idea is that each sequence determines a set of unwords, and two sequences are similar if there is intersection between their unword sets. Unwords can also be productively used for music generation [12]. Here one has a simple statistical model that somewhat under-fits the corpus, that is, generates with indistinguishable probabilities poor sequences in addition to stylistic ones. In this case one can filter any sequence which contains a significant unword.

The method developed in this paper can reveal prohibited structures, and it attempts to separate these from mere statistical absence in a corpus. To complement previous approaches which use unstructured sets of unwords, this paper showed that individual unwords can themselves be a productive endpoint of music corpus analysis.

Acknowledgments. Special thanks to Kerstin Neubarth for valuable comments on the manuscript.

References

1. CCARH: Digital encoding of 4-part chorales by J.S. Bach (2019). http://kern.humdrum.org/cgi-bin/browse?l=/185chorales. Accessed 15 Jan 2019
2. Chairungsee, S., Crochemore, M.: Using minimal absent words to build phylogeny. Theor. Comput. Sci. **450**, 109–116 (2012)
3. Conklin, D.: Antipattern discovery in folk tunes. J. New Music Res. **42**(2), 161–169 (2013)
4. Conklin, D.: Chord sequence generation with semiotic patterns. J. Math. Music **10**(2), 92–106 (2016)
5. Conklin, D., Bergeron, M.: Discovery of contrapuntal patterns. In: 11th International Society for Music Information Retrieval Conference, Utrecht, The Netherlands, pp. 201–206 (2010)
6. Conklin, D., Weisser, S.: Pattern and antipattern discovery in Ethiopian Bagana songs. In: Meredith, D. (ed.) Computational Music Analysis, pp. 425–443. Springer, Cham (2016). https://doi.org/10.1007/978-3-319-25931-4_16
7. Crawford, T., Badkobeh, G., Lewis, D.: Searching page-images of early music scanned with OMR: a scalable solution using minimal absent words. In: 19th International Society for Music Information Retrieval Conference, Paris, France, pp. 233–239 (2018)
8. Crochemore, M., Mignosi, F., Restivo, A.: Automata and forbidden words. Inf. Process. Lett. **67**(3), 111–117 (1998)
9. Fitsioris, G., Conklin, D.: Parallel successions of perfect fifths in the Bach chorales. In: 4th Conference on Interdisciplinary Musicology, Thessaloniki, Greece, pp. 1–10 (2008)
10. Hampikian, G., Andersen, T.: Absent sequences: nullomers and primes. In: Pacific Symposium on Biocomputing, Hawaii, USA, pp. 355–366 (2007)
11. Herold, J., Kurtz, S., Giegerich, R.: Efficient computation of absent words in genomic sequences. BMC Bioinform. **9**(1), 167 (2008)
12. Herremans, D., Weisser, S., Sörensen, K., Conklin, D.: Generating structured music for Bagana using quality metrics based on Markov models. Expert Syst. Appl. **42**, 7424–7435 (2015)
13. Pinho, A., Ferreira, P., Garcia, S., Rodrigues, J.: On finding minimal absent words. BMC Bioinform. **10**(1), 137 (2009)
14. Stefanowitsch, A.: Negative evidence and the raw frequency fallacy. Corpus Linguist. Linguist. Theory **2**(1), 61–77 (2006)
15. UTALC: Uplifting Trance Anthem Loop Corpus (2018). http://www.lacl.fr/~lbigo/utalc. Accessed 15 Jan 2019

Maths, Computation and Flamenco: Overview and Challenges

José-Miguel Díaz-Báñez[1]([⊠])(iD) and Nadine Kroher[2]

[1] Departamento de Matemática Aplicada II,
Universidad de Sevilla, Seville, Spain
dbanez@us.es
[2] MXX, London, UK
nadine@mxxmusic.com

Abstract. Flamenco is a rich performance-oriented art music genre from Southern Spain which attracts a growing community of aficionados around the globe. Due to its improvisational and expressive nature, its unique musical characteristics, and the fact that the genre is largely undocumented, flamenco poses a number of interesting mathematical and computational challenges. Most existing approaches in Musical Information Retrieval (MIR) were developed in the context of popular or classical music and do often not generalize well to non-Western music traditions, in particular when the underlying music theoretical assumptions do not hold for these genres. Over the recent decade, a number of computational problems related to the automatic analysis of flamenco music have been defined and several methods addressing a variety of musical aspects have been proposed. This paper provides an overview of the challenges which arise in the context of computational analysis of flamenco music and outlines an overview of existing approaches.

Keywords: Flamenco · Computational ethnomusicology · MIR

1 Introduction

The relatively young field of computational analysis of flamenco music has been explored in the scope of the COFLA research project [6] which aims at the development of genre-specific Music Information Retrieval (MIR) methods for flamenco music. Due to its improvisational and expressive nature, its unique musical characteristics, and the fact that the genre is largely undocumented, flamenco poses a number of interesting computational challenges. At the same time, its growing popularity, constant evolution and increasing presence in digital media calls for the development of computational tools to manage existing digital

This research has received funding from the Junta de Andalucía (project P12-TIC-1362), Spanish Ministry of Economy and Competitiveness (project MTM2016-76272-R AEI/FEDER, UE), and the European Union's Horizon 2020 research and innovation programme under the Marie Skłodowska-Curie grant agreement No. 734922.

M. Montiel et al. (Eds.): MCM 2019, LNAI 11502, pp. 344–351, 2019.
https://doi.org/10.1007/978-3-030-21392-3_29

content, allow a broad range of users access to the genre and to contribute to its preservation. In addition, flamenco poses no exception to the ongoing partnership between mathematics and music and the genre has recently been the focus of mathematical research. The development of MIR methods for flamenco, as well as music-theoretical concepts themselves, have given rise to new mathematical problems. A comprehensive elaboration on the synergies between mathematics and flamenco, can be found in [7] and a chapter in [23] provides a brief overview of flamenco music and its computational study in the context of mathematics. In each section of this paper, we introduce a set of research topics and the arising challenges, describe existing approaches and outlines open problems.

2   Prerequisites: Data Sets and Automatic Transcription

A fundamental necessity for computational studies is the creation of data corpora, in our case collections of music recordings, which are not only the basis for experimental evaluation, but are furthermore a valuable resource for data-driven exploratory studies. In the context of flamenco music, there are two well-established and available datasets. The $TONAS^1$ dataset contains 72 recordings of songs belonging to the *tonás* style family, together with their respective automatic and manual note-level transcriptions, and annotated style affinity. The *corpusCOFLA* [18], which has been developed specifically for computational studies, contains of over 1500 commercial flamenco recordings with manually curated meta-data and several manually annotated subsets. In addition to the audio recordings, the corpus contains editorial and manually curated meta-data, as well as several manually annotated subsets. In addition to audio collections, the knowledge base *FlaBase* [26], is a valuable resource for semantic data, including biographical and music-theoretical knowledge gathered from online resources.

The study of various aspects of flamenco singing requires the extraction of the singing voice melody from the audio signal. A comparison of several melody representations in the context of melody classification [17] has shown that note-level transcriptions have several advantages over other methods such as the fundamental frequency contour. Since manual note-level transcriptions are highly time consuming, their automatic extraction is an important research topic. A first approach towards computer-assisted transcription of a cappella flamenco recordings was proposed in [12] and later extended to recordings containing guitar accompaniment [13]. Recently, the *CANTE* algorithm, a novel method for the transcription of flamenco singing from monophonic and polyphonic recordings [22], has shown to yield an improvement compared to [12].

Open Problems: While automatic transcriptions have been successfully employed in a number of related MIR tasks, the problem can by no means be considered solved. Possible future directions of research include the crowd-sourced creation of a larger annotated dataset, which can then be exploited in the context of machine learning based approaches.

---

[1] https://www.upf.edu/web/mtg/tonas.

3   Melodic Analysis: Retrieval, Classification and Melodic Template Extraction

A frequently addressed aspect of flamenco music is the existence of melodic templates which set the basis for improvisational performances. In particular, a number of styles and sub-styles are characterized by a specific melodic movement which undergoes heavy ornamentation and variation during individual interpretations. It worth mentioning that this template remains implicit and does not exist in form of a musical score. From a computational perspective, we identify three challenges related to this music theoretical concept: Melody *classification*, *retrieval* and *template extraction*.

Melody classification aims at recognizing the template in a given performance which in turn allows to automatically identify the style or sub-style affinity. Based on the assumption, that performances with a common melodic template are similar to each other and dissimilar to performances based on other templates, the task has mainly been formulated as a *k-nearest-neighbour* classification task, where an unknown performance is labelled based on the labels of its most similar items in an annotated database. In this context, two components are crucial: the way the melody is represented and the employed distance metric. Early approaches have explored standard distance metrics between manually extracted global mid-level features extracted [24,25]. While these studies provided valuable insights into the criteria used by flamenco experts to distinguish styles, the need for manual annotations poses a major limitation. Studies targeting fully-automatic systems [10,11], explored *dynamic time warping* alignment between pitch sequences. Acknowledging the quadratic computational cost of this operation both studies investigated several contour simplification algorithms to reduce the sequence length. A systematic comparison of melody representations was conducted in [17], where the advantages of note-level transcriptions were demonstrated. The work furthermore explores unsupervised melody categorization and proposes a set of evaluation strategies, which provide deeper insight into system performance and scalability.

Melody retrieval refers to the task of automatically locating a given melodic sequence among a large number of candidates in a digital music collection. Such systems allow users to locate specific items based on their melodic content and furthermore provide the means to explore the evolution of melodic content from an ethno-musicological perspective. From a technical perspective, the retrieval problem focuses on the detection of sub-sections of melodies which are similar to a user query. To this end, [27] employed a modification of the *context-dependent dynamic time warping algorithm* on the fundamental frequency contour. Since the high amount of micro-tonal detail contained in this representation can distort similarity scores, [28] designed a gap-tolerant alignment method which operates on note-level transcriptions.

Melodic template extraction aims at approximating a the implicit underlying melodic template based on a set of interpretations of the same melody. In [3], the task is formulated as a geometric optimization problem where melodies are modelled as polygonal curves in the time-pitch space. The goal is to compute a new polygonal curve, representative of the template, which fits a fixed number p of similar items at each point in time. The particular challenge of this task is that the parameter p corresponds to an amount of melodies, but does not refer to a specific set of melodies. A second approach to the same computational task was proposed in [19] where a progressive multiple sequence alignment procedure is used to construct a graph model holding information on the frequency of notes and note transitions across performances. This model allows the extraction a melodic sequence which approximates the melodic template and allows the computation of a metric for melodic stability.

Open Problems: Given the limited amount of ground truth data, the creation of a large annotated audio collection is necessary step for the development of large, scalable melody analysis systems. This requires a significant amount of musicological effort, since a clear style taxonomy, in particular with respect to melodic templates, has so far not been established.

4 Detection of Phrase-Level Repetition

The structure of European folk music is heavily based on phrase-level repetition. The same observation can be made for certain flamenco styles, which are close to their folkloric origin. Consequently, detecting repeated sung phrases allows us to describe the structure of a performance and can furthermore aid related MIR tasks, such as query by humming and melody compression.

In the context of accompanied flamenco singing, a preliminary audio-based attempt to discover phrase-level repetition was proposed in [20]: Sung phrases are detected using a vocal detection algorithm. At a second stage, pair-wise alignment of chroma-based representations of the detected vocal segments is performed and groups of similar phrases were formed using a frame-centric clustering scheme. A more recent work [21], follows the following approach: Automatic transcriptions are segmented into phrases by exploiting certain musical properties typically encountered in folk songs. Then, all pair-wise melodic distances among the detected subsequences are computed, resulting in a distance matrix. Finally, a standard clustering algorithm receives the computed distance matrix and groups the phrases. As a result, each cluster corresponds to a prototypical melodic pattern and the members of the cluster to the occurrences of the pattern. This method yields convincing results and outperforms the approach in [20].

Open Problems: The musicological assumptions for the phrase segmentation algorithm of the current system do not generalize to all flamenco styles. In particular, many styles exhibit sung phrases which significantly vary in length. Consequently, a musicological study of phrase boundary characteristics in flamenco music and the development of a genre-tailored algorithm are logical directions for future work.

5   Rhythm and Its Mathematical Properties

Several attempts have been made to computationally model rhythm in flamenco music. In a first approach [8], a rhythmic pattern is represented as
binary sequences mapped to a circular lattice. Based on this representation,
mathematical measures can be used to characterize rhythmic similarity between
commonly occurring rhythmic patterns and to construct phylogenetic trees to
visualize their relationship [8,9], which in turn allow us to infer hypothetical
ancestral rhythms [4]. The latter study furthermore generalizes necessary conditions fulfilled by unknown nodes which are useful for computing the ancestral nodes. In [14], different rhythmic similarity measures are evaluated against
human judgements.

Mathematical models furthermore allow us to study rhythmic properties and
their ethno-musicological meaning. One such property, the rhythmic oddity [5],
describes patterns which do not have two beats that divide their span into two
intervals of equal duration which implies a notion of asymmetry. In circular
notation, this means that no two beats lie diametrically opposite each other on
the lattice circle. That is, no two vertices of the polygon are antipodal vertices.
The bulería pattern, which is referred to as an asymmetric rhythm in [2], as well
as an antipodal rhythm in [1], falls into this category.

Open Problems: While rhythm in flamenco has been analyzed with the used of
mathematical models, the automatic detection of beats, downbeats and rhythmic
patterns in flamenco recordings remains an open problem. In particular rhythmic
pattern detection could significantly improve automatic style detection, since
some styles are characterized by specific patterns.

6   Deep Learning Based Flamenco Analysis

In the context of audio and music processing, deep learning based methods
have shown to give promising results, and, in many cases, have been able to
outperform state-of-the-art methods. In recent years, several MIR tasks have
been approached from a deep learning perspective, including onset detection [29],
instrument classification [15] and music recommendation [30]. To the best of our
knowledge, the use of deep learning in the context of automatic content-based
description and discovery of flamenco music has been first addressed in [16],
where the focus is on a particular deep learning architecture, the Convolutional
Neural Networks (CNNs) and their application to two flamenco-related tasks,
singer identification in flamenco videos and *structural segmentation* of flamenco
music recordings.

The proposed image-based singer identification system relies of a number
of state-of-the-art image processing and computer vision technologies, which
are readily available in open source libraries. However, their application to the
task at hand goes beyond a trivial re-use of existing techniques, since problem-
specific adaptations were necessary and the integration of several processing

blocks required a certain level of domain-specific knowledge. The core of the framework is a pre-trained CNN which extracts an embedding with high discriminative power among faces from a given input image. This network was developed and trained for the particular purpose of being re-used in face recognition and authentication tasks, without the need to re-train on a problem-specific candidate set.

For the second task, a CNN-based system is proposed, which segments a flamenco recording into sections of consistent instrumentation. The method and has shown to outperform a baseline method which uses an ensemble of shallow classifiers. Moving towards the area of data mining, the segmentation backend was applied to the analysis of a large corpus of commercial flamenco recordings, exploring the resulting automatic annotations in a data-driven study. The goal is to enable musicological studies that would otherwise require time-consuming manual procedures, and verify, at a large scale, via computational means and a data-driven approach, existing musicological observations. This computational study, which revealed a number of trends and correlations, is the first of its kind in the context of flamenco music.

Open Problems: The work in [16] has demonstrated the potential of deep learning for the analysis of flamenco. Provided that sufficient amounts of annotated data exist, this methodology could be applied to other tasks in the context of flamenco, including beat tracking and automatic transcription.

7   Conclusions

We have outlined the ongoing research efforts towards the development genre-specific MIR methods for flamenco music. For each of the commonly addressed task, we have presented existing work and outlined current shortcomings, open problems and future extensions. Beyond the tasks described above, several domains of flamenco music have so far not been explored from an computational or mathematical viewpoint. Possible new lines of research could for example include the analysis of flamenco dance through computer vision or sensors. Furthermore, past approaches have mainly focused on the singing voice and less attention has been paid to the guitar accompaniment.

References

1. Aichholzer, O., Caraballo, L.E., Díaz-Báñez, J.M., Fabila-Monroy, R., Ochoa, C., Nigsch, P.: Characterization of extremal antipodal polygons. Graphs Comb. **31**(2), 321–333 (2015)
2. Barba, L., Caraballo, L.E., Díaz-Báñez, J.M., Fabila-Monroy, R., Pérez-Castillo, E.: Asymmetric polygons with maximum area. Eur. J. Oper. Res. **248**(3), 1123–1131 (2016)
3. Bereg, S., Díaz-Báñez, J.M., Kroher, N., Ventura, I.: Computing melodic templates in oral music traditions. Appl. Math. Comput. **44**(1), 219–229 (2019)

4. Caraballo, L.E., Díaz-Báñez, J.M., Pérez-Castillo, E.: Finding unknown nodes in phylogenetic graphs. In: Ortuño, F., Rojas, I. (eds.) IWBBIO 2015. LNCS, vol. 9043, pp. 403–414. Springer, Cham (2015). https://doi.org/10.1007/978-3-319-16483-0_40
5. Chemillier, M., Truchet, C.: Computation of words satisfying the rhythmic oddity property (after Simha Arom's works). Inf. Process. Lett. **86**(5), 255–261 (2003)
6. COFLA Homepage. http://www.cofla-project.com. Accessed 14 Mar 2019
7. Díaz-Báñez, J.M.: Mathematics and flamenco: an unexpected partnership. Math. Intell. **39**(3), 27–39 (2017)
8. Díaz-Báñez, M., Farigu, G., Gómez, F., Rappaport, D., Toussaint, G.T.: El compás flamenco: a phylogenetic analysis. In: Proceedings of BRIDGES: Mathematical Connections in Art, Music and Science, pp. 61–70. Southwestern College, Winfield(2004)
9. Díaz-Báñez, J.M., Farigu, G., Gómez, F., Rappaport, D., Toussaint, G.T.: Similaridad y evolución en la rtmica del flamenco: una incursión de la matemática computacional. La Gaceta de la Real Sociedad Matemática Española **82**, 489–509 (2005)
10. Díaz-Báñez, J.M., Kroher, N., Rizo, J.: Efficient algorithms for melodic similarity in flamenco singing. In: Proceedings of the 5th International Workshop on Folk Music Analysis (FMA), Paris, France (2015)
11. Díaz-Báñez, J.M., Rizo, J.C.: An efficient DTW-based approach for melodic similarity in flamenco singing. In: Traina, A.J.M., Traina, C., Cordeiro, R.L.F. (eds.) SISAP 2014. LNCS, vol. 8821, pp. 289–300. Springer, Cham (2014). https://doi.org/10.1007/978-3-319-11988-5_27
12. Gómez, E., Bonada, J.: Towards computer-assisted flamenco transcription: an experimental comparison of automatic transcription algorithms as applied to a cappella singing. Comput. Music J. **37**(2), 73–90 (2013)
13. Gómez, E., Bonada, J., Salamon, J.: Automatic transcription of flamenco singing from monophonic and polyphonic music recordings. In: Proceedings of the III Interdisciplinary Conference on Flamenco Research (INFLA) and II International Workshop of Folk Music Analysis (FMA), Seville, Spain (2012)
14. Guastavino, C., Gómez, F., Toussaint, G., Marandola, F., Gómez, E.: Measuring similarity between flamenco rhythmic patterns. J. New Music Res. **38**(2), 129–138 (2009)
15. Han, Y., Kim, J., Lee, K., Han, Y., Kim, J., Lee, K.: Deep convolutional neural networks for predominant instrument recognition in polyphonic music. IEEE/ACM Trans. Audio Speech Lang. Process. **25**(1), 208–221 (2017)
16. Kroher, N.: Flamenco music information retrieval. Ph.D. thesis, Universidad de Sevilla (2018)
17. Kroher, N., Díaz-Báñez, J.M.: Audio-based melody categorisation: exploring signal representations and evaluation strategies. Comput. Music J. **41**(4), 1–19 (2017)
18. Kroher, N., Díaz-Báñez, J.M., Mora, J., Gómez, E.: Corpus COFLA: a research corpus for the computational study of flamenco music. J. Comput. Cult. Herit. **9**(2), 10–21 (2016)
19. Kroher, N., Díaz-Báñez, J.M.: Modelling melodic variation and extracting melodic templates from flamenco singing performances. J. Math. Music (2019, to appear)
20. Kroher, N., Pikrakis, A., Moreno, J., Díaz-Báñez, J.M.: Discovery of repeated vocal patterns in polyphonic audio: a case study on flamenco music. In: Proceedings of 23rd European Signal Processing Conference (EUSIPCO), Nice, France, pp. 41–45. IEEE (2015)

21. Kroher, N., Pikrakis, A., Díaz-Báñez, J.M.: Discovery of repeated melodic phrases in folk singing recordings. IEEE Trans. Multimed. **20**(6), 1291–1304 (2018)
22. Kroher, N., Gómez, E.: Automatic transcription of flamenco singing from polyphonic music recordings. IEEE Trans. Audio Speech Lang. Process. **24**(5), 901–913 (2016)
23. Montiel, M., Peck, R.W.: Mathematical Music Theory: Algebraic, Geometric, Combinatorial, Topological and Applied Approaches to Understanding Musical Phenomena. World Scientific Publishing, London (2018)
24. Mora, J., Gómez, F., Gómez, E., Díaz-Báñez, J.M.: Melodic contour and mid-level global features applied to the analysis of flamenco cantes. J. New Music Res. **45**(2), 145–159 (2016)
25. Mora, J., Gómez, F., Gómez, E., Escobar, F.J., Díaz-Báñez, J.M.: Characterization and melodic similarity of a cappella flamenco cantes. In: Proceedings of the 11th Conference of the International Society for Music Information (ISMIR), Utrecht, Holland (2010)
26. Oramas, S., Gómez, F., Gómez, E., Mora, J.: FlaBase: towards the creation of a flamenco music knowledge base. In: Proceedings 16th International Society for Music Information Retrieval Conference (ISMIR), Málaga, Spain (2015)
27. Pikrakis, A., et al.: Tracking melodic patterns in flamenco singing by analyzing polyphonic recordings. In: Proceedings of the 13th Conference of the International Society for Music Information Retrieval, ISMIR, Porto, Portugal (2012)
28. Pikrakis, A., Kroher, N., Díaz-Báñez, J.M.: Detection of melodic patterns in automatic flamenco transcriptions. In: Proceedings of the 6th International Workshop on Folk Music Analysis (FMA), pp. 14–17 (2016)
29. Schluter, J., Bock, S.: Improved musical onset detection with convolutional neural networks. In: IEEE International Conference on Acoustics, Speech and Signal Processing ICASSP, Florence, Italy, pp. 6979–6983 (2014)
30. Van den Oord, A., Dieleman, S., Schrauwen, B.: Deep content-based music recommendation. In: Advances in Neural Information Processing Systems (NIPS), pp. 2643–2651 (2013)

Formalization of Voice-Leadings and the Nabla Algorithm

Isaac del Pozo[1]($\boxtimes$) and Francisco Gómez[2]($\boxtimes$) (iD)

[1] Getafe, Spain
isaacdelpozo92@gmail.com
[2] Universidad Politécnica de Madrid, Getafe, Spain
fmartin@etsisi.upm.es

Abstract. This work presents some concepts related to voice-leadings and proposes a formalization of them. The aim is to teach voice-leadings in a systematic way by using elements of mathematical music theory. Within this formalization, we defined the nabla distance of a chord progression. This distance is a measure of how close the voices are among them. One of its applications is to produce voice-leadings with nice properties, especially for jazz music. The nabla distance has been implemented in the form of an application, the ∇ application. This application computes the optimal voice-leading for a given chord progression.

Keywords: Voice-leadings · Chord progressions · Matrix algebra · Distance functions · Nabla distance · Optimal voice-leadings

1 Introduction

Voice-leading is the art and science of how to connect chords to one another. In the 20th century, Lewin [7] introduced Neo-Riemannian theory, which is based on the idea of connecting chords according to some definition of harmonic proximity [2]. This notion of harmonic proximity requires, in turn, a notion of a distance between chords. It is natural then to introduce at this point some mathematical formalism to address the question of how to measure the distance between two chords; see the work of Tymoczko [8–10], Hall and Tymocko [6], and Derfler [3], just to name but a few.

This work focuses on the pedagogical aspects of voice-leading in jazz music, a style where voice-leading is also an important feature. We would like to provide composers with a tool to understand and write voice-leadings by following criteria that are at the same time systematic and musically meaningful. On the mathematical side, we offer the musician a minimal but meaningful mathematical formalization of voice-leadings so that musical concepts are still recognizable in the formalization. The structure of this paper is as follows. We start by introducing some definitions, which will help build the formal framework

---

I. del Pozo—Independent researcher and musician.

© Springer Nature Switzerland AG 2019
M. Montiel et al. (Eds.): MCM 2019, LNAI 11502, pp. 352–358, 2019.
https://doi.org/10.1007/978-3-030-21392-3_30

(the musical universe). In Sect. 3, we study metric spaces in music and introduce the nabla distance, which is the distance to measure the size of a voice-leading. Section 4 contains the pedagogical applications of the nabla methodology.

2 The Musical Universe

We begin by defining the space of frequencies. In principle, it would be enough for our purposes to consider the set of audible frequencies, say, the interval $(20, 2 \cdot 10^4)$, when measured in Hz. However, for completeness we will consider the space of frequencies Φ as the real line (it is closed under product and sum of frequencies). Let x, y be two pitches described by their frequencies. We write $x \sim y$ if and only if $x = 2^k \cdot y$, for some integer k. Recall that two pitches are an octave apart when the quotient of the highest frequence to the lowest is 2. This relation identifies all the pitches that are apart any number of octaves as just one pitch.

From now on, we assume we are in the presence of the equal temperament. Given a fixed pitch class $[k]$, we define the circle of fifths $PC_k/\sim$ as the set $PC_k/\sim = \left\{ [k], \left[k \cdot 2^{\frac{7}{12}}\right], \left[k \cdot 2^{\frac{14}{12}}\right], \left[k \cdot 2^{\frac{21}{12}}\right], \ldots, \left[k \cdot 2^{\frac{77}{12}}\right] \right\}$. This definition is illustrated in Fig. 1. The pitch class of A was chosen as the base and then the circle of fifths is built up from it by multiplying the previous pitch by $2^{\frac{7}{12}}$, the distance of a fifth in terms of frequency.

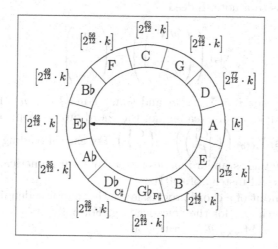

Fig. 1. The circle of fifths

A **chord** $X(q)$ is a subset of the pitch classes in $PC_k/\sim$. In Western tonal music, some chords are described by a **root** and a **quality**. A chord is an unordered collection of pitches. When we introduce the root and the quality, the pitches are then ordered. The root is the lowest pitch in the chord whereas the quality refers to labels given to chords. For example, a dominant seventh chord on C is the chord composed by C-E-G-B♭, in that order. The root of this chord is C and the quality dominant seventh. This label tells us that the first three notes form a major triad and that B must flat so that there is minor seventh between C and B. The quality of a chord is indicated by several symbols (m or lowercase for minor chords, + for augmented chords, etc.).

A **chord progression** is a sequence of chords. As such, chords in a progression are presented in a given order, which is the order they appear in time. A suitable way to deal with chord progressions is by considering the matrix of classes. If $P \in \mathcal{M}_{m \times n}(PC_k/\sim)$ is a chord progression of length n, then each chord is a vector of m notes and there are n chords in the progression. We can arrange the notes of the chord progression in a matrix as follows.

$$P = \begin{pmatrix} [\theta_{11}] & \cdots & [\theta_{1n}] \\ \vdots & \ddots & \vdots \\ [\theta_{m1}] & \cdots & [\theta_{mn}] \end{pmatrix}$$

To fix ideas, let consider the 2-note chord progression {E, C} to {F, E}, which from now on will be notated as {E, C}⟹{F, E}. Its matrix representation is $P = \begin{pmatrix} [E] & [F] \\ [C] & [E] \end{pmatrix}$.

Let Φ^+ be the set of positive frequencies. A **voicing** or a **voice-leading** of a chord is a mapping $V_{X(q)}$ from $\mathcal{M}_{m \times n}(PC_k/\sim)$ to $\mathcal{M}_{m \times 1}(\Phi^+)$. The mapping takes a given class to a note. Indeed,

$$V_{X(q)}\left(\begin{pmatrix} [\theta_{1j}] \\ \vdots \\ [\theta_{mj}] \end{pmatrix}\right) = \begin{pmatrix} \phi_{1j} \\ \vdots \\ \phi_{mj} \end{pmatrix}$$

where $\phi_{ij} \in [\theta_{ij}]$, for $i = 1, \ldots, m$ and some j in $\{1, \ldots, n\}$. Following with the previous example, a voice leading for the chord progression could be (among other possibilities) $V_{X(q)}\left(\begin{pmatrix} [C] \\ [E] \end{pmatrix}\right) = \begin{pmatrix} C4 \\ E4 \end{pmatrix}$. For ease of reading, we will notate the frequencies by their standard names instead of their numerical values. Therefore, we will write A4 instead of 440 Hz.

An **arrangement** of a chord progression is the mapping defining which notes of the chords are chosen for the voice-leading. Formally, it is a mapping $A_{C\sim}$: $\mathcal{M}_{m \times n}(PC_k/\sim) \to \mathcal{M}_{m \times n}(\Phi^+)$ written as

$$A_{C\sim}\left(\begin{pmatrix} [\theta_{11}] & \cdots & [\theta_{1n}] \\ \vdots & \ddots & \vdots \\ [\theta_{m1}] & \cdots & [\theta_{mn}] \end{pmatrix}\right) = \begin{pmatrix} \phi_{11} & \cdots & \phi_{1n} \\ \vdots & \ddots & \vdots \\ \phi_{m1} & \cdots & \phi_{mn} \end{pmatrix},$$

where $\phi_{ij} \in [\theta_{ij}]$, for $i = 1, \ldots, m$ and $j = 1, \ldots, n$. From now on, arrangements will be notated as $(\phi_1, \ldots, \phi_n) \longrightarrow (\phi'_1, \ldots, \phi'_n)$, that is, as bijections between sequences of notes; compare this notation to that of chord progressions above.

For the chord progression {E, C}$\Longrightarrow${D, G}, $A_{C\sim}$ could take on the form, among others, of $A_{C\sim}\left(\left(\begin{smallmatrix} [C] & [G] \\ [E] & [D] \end{smallmatrix}\right)\right) = \left(\begin{smallmatrix} C4 & G4 \\ E4 & D4 \end{smallmatrix}\right)$.

3 The Nabla Distance

It is possible to endow the musical space with a metric. The idea is to measure the distance between two notes and what follows is just a formalization of what our ears do in a natural way all the time; see [4] for more information on the cognitive aspects of music. We define a metric $\Delta : (\Phi^+)^2 \to \mathbb{R}$ as an integral.

$$\Delta(\alpha, \beta) = \left| \int_\alpha^\beta \frac{\Omega}{\phi} d\phi \right|,$$

where α and β are frequencies and Ω is a constant such that $\left| \int_1^2 \frac{\Omega}{\phi} d\phi \right| = 12$; see [1] for a relationship between this constant and the definition of cents. By working out the integral above, this distance can be expressed as $\Delta(\alpha, \beta) = \left| \Omega \ln\left(\frac{\alpha}{\beta}\right) \right|$. The value of the constant is $\Omega = 12 \cdot |\log_2(e)|$, which indicates that the octave is divided into 12 equal half-tones. This Δ function does hold the three properties of a metric, namely: positivity, $\Delta(\alpha, \beta) \geq 0$; symmetry, $\Delta(\alpha, \beta) = \Delta(\beta, \alpha)$; and the triangle inequality $\Delta(\alpha, \beta) \leq \Delta(\alpha, \gamma) + \Delta(\gamma, \beta)$.

The pair (Φ^+, Δ) is called the **musical metric space**. This metric can be extended to the spaces of pitch classes by just taking the minimum of the elements in each pitch class. For two classes $[\theta], [\tau]$ in $PC_k/\sim$, we have $\tilde{\Delta}([\theta], [\tau]) = \min\{\Delta(\alpha, \beta) \mid \alpha \in [\theta], \beta \in [\tau]\}$. See the work [5] of Forte for more information on distance functions. For example, $\Delta(C5, E4) = 8$ and $\Delta(C4, E5) = 16$, but $\tilde{\Delta}([C], [E]) = \min\{\Delta(\alpha, \beta) \mid \alpha \in [C], \beta \in [E]\} = 4$. Notice that the maximum value the distance $\tilde{\Delta}$ can take is 6.

Let $P \in \mathcal{M}_{m \times n}(PC_k/\sim)$ be a chord progression such that $P = ([p_{ij}])$, for $i = 1, \ldots, m$ and $j = 1, \ldots, n$. Consider σ, an element in the symmetric group $\mathcal{S}_m$ defined over the set of indices $\{1, 2, \ldots, m\}$. Then, we define $E(P)$, the **extension** of P, as those matrices $B = (b_{ij})$ in $\mathcal{M}_{m \times n}(PC_k/\sim)$ such the following two conditions hold: (1) For some values of j, $[p_{ij}] = [b_{ij}]$, for all $i = 1, \ldots, m$; (2) For the rest of values of j, $[p_{ij}] = [b_{\sigma_k(i)j}]$, for all $i = 1, \ldots, m$, where σ_k is a permutation in $\mathcal{S}_m$.

These conditions state that a column in B is either the same column in P or a permutation of some column of P. $E(P)$ is the set of such matrices. Consider again the matrix associated to the chord progression {E, C}$\Longrightarrow${F, A}. Then, the extension of P is

$$E(P) = \left\{ \begin{pmatrix} [C] & [A] \\ [E] & [F] \end{pmatrix}, \begin{pmatrix} [C] & [F] \\ [E] & [A] \end{pmatrix}, \begin{pmatrix} [E] & [A] \\ [C] & [F] \end{pmatrix}, \begin{pmatrix} [E] & [F] \\ [C] & [A] \end{pmatrix} \right\}$$

Next, we need to define the distance that a voice travels through a given chord progression. We will use the symbol $\tilde{\nabla}$ to define the **distance of a chord progression** P. Then, $\tilde{\nabla}(P)$ is defined as follows: $\tilde{\nabla}(P) = \sum_{i=1}^{m} \sum_{j=1}^{n-1} \tilde{\Delta}([\theta_{ij}], [\theta_{i(j+1)}])$. The value of $\tilde{\nabla}(P)$ is the sum of all the distances between consecutive notes of a voice over all voices in the chord progression.

The operator nabla can also be defined for the set $E(P)$ as follows: $\tilde{\nabla}(E(P)) = \left\{ \tilde{\nabla}(B) \mid B \in E(P) \right\}$. Notice that $\tilde{\nabla}(P)$ is a real value and $\tilde{\nabla}(E(P))$ a set of values. Let us compute $\tilde{\nabla}(P)$ for the chord progression $\{E, C\} \Longrightarrow \{F, A\}$. Indeed, $\tilde{\nabla}(P) = \sum_{i=1}^{m} \sum_{j=1}^{n-1} \tilde{\Delta}([\theta_{ij}], [\theta_{i(j+1)}]) = \tilde{\Delta}([E], [F]) + \tilde{\Delta}([C], [A]) = 1 + 3 = 4$ Actually, we don't need to consider all the matrices in $E(P)$ to compute $\tilde{\nabla}(E(P))$. It is enough to choose those where the first column is not rearranged. The nabla distances of the matrices in $E(P)$ are

$$\tilde{\nabla}\left(\left(\begin{bmatrix}[C] & [A]\\ [E] & [F]\end{bmatrix}\right)\right) = 1 + 3 = 4, \quad \tilde{\nabla} = \left(\left(\begin{bmatrix}[C] & [F]\\ [E] & [A]\end{bmatrix}\right)\right) = 5 + 5 = 10,$$

The nabla value of the extension of P is $\tilde{\nabla}(E(P)) = \left\{ \tilde{\nabla}(B) \mid B \in E(P) \right\} = \{4, 10\}$.

A **chord progression** is said to be **optimal** if $\tilde{\nabla}(P) = \min\left\{ \tilde{\nabla}(E(P)) \right\}$. In our example, the chord progression $\{E, C\} \Longrightarrow \{F, A\}$ was optimal as the nabla distance attained the minimum at that progression.

Analogously, the nabla distance can be defined for arrangements; it will be notated by ∇ (without tilde). If $A = (\phi_{ij}) \in \mathcal{M}_{m \times n}(\Phi^{+})$ is an arrangement, then the formal definition of ∇ is $\nabla(A) = \sum_{i=1}^{m} \sum_{j=1}^{n-1} \Delta(\phi_{ij}, \phi_{i(j+1)})$.

An **arrangement** A is said to be **optimal** if $\nabla(A) = \tilde{\nabla}(P_A)$, where P_A is the chord progression associated to A. Let us consider two arrangements associated to the chord progression $\{E, C\} \Longrightarrow \{F, E\}$, say, A_1:(E4, C4)$\longrightarrow$(F4, E4) and A_2:(E4, C4)$\longrightarrow$(F5, E5). Let us find which one is optimal by computing their nabla distances. We have $\nabla(A_1) = \Delta(E4, F4) + \Delta(C4, E4) = 1 + 4 = 5$ and $\nabla(A_2) = \Delta(E4, F5) + \Delta(C4, E5) = 13 + 16 = 29$. Therefore, the first arrangement is the optimal one.

Let us work out a larger example, with three voices and three chords in the progression. In the example below, we have removed the square brackets to simplify the notation as it is clear we are speaking of pitch classes. Since the extension of P is composed of all permutations of the columns of P, we can apply a sequence of permutations (the σ's below) to obtain a sequence of chord progressions reaching the minimum value.

$$P = \begin{pmatrix} A & D & G \\ F & B & E \\ D & G & C \end{pmatrix} \xrightarrow{\sigma_1 : D \leftrightarrow G} P_1 = \begin{pmatrix} A & G & G \\ F & B & E \\ D & D & C \end{pmatrix} \xrightarrow{\sigma_2 : G \leftrightarrow B} P_2 = \begin{pmatrix} A & B & G \\ F & G & E \\ D & D & C \end{pmatrix}$$

$$\tilde{\nabla}(P) = 31 \qquad\qquad \tilde{\nabla}(P_1) = 15 \qquad\qquad \tilde{\nabla}(P_2) = 13$$

$$P_2 = \begin{pmatrix} A & B & G \\ F & G & E \\ D & D & C \end{pmatrix} \xrightarrow{\sigma_3:G\leftrightarrow E} P_3 = \begin{pmatrix} A & B & E \\ F & G & G \\ D & D & C \end{pmatrix} \xrightarrow{\sigma_4:C\leftrightarrow E} P_4 = \begin{pmatrix} A & B & C \\ F & G & G \\ D & D & E \end{pmatrix}$$

$$\tilde{\nabla}(P_2) = 13 \qquad\qquad \tilde{\nabla}(P_3) = 11 \qquad\qquad\qquad \tilde{\nabla}(P_4) = 7$$

In this case, P_4 is the chord progression with minimum $\tilde{\nabla}$ distance.

Let us discuss now how to obtain the chord progression of minimum value. Assume we have a chord progression $P = ([\theta_{ij}])$, where $i = 1, \ldots, m$ and $j = 1, \ldots, n$. Each transition from a chord to the next can be thought of as a bijection between two sets of cardinal m. We know by elementary combinatorics that the total number of bijections is $(m!)^{n-1}$. If we assume that the number of voices is constant, then the size of $E(P)$ is exponential in n. However, constructing the whole set $E(P)$ is not practical. It is more interesting to design an algorithm to find the optimal chord progression through a set of operations performed on P. The example above could suggest that a possible algorithm would take the shortest distances between pitch classes and build the optimal sequence of chord progression (Fig. 2).

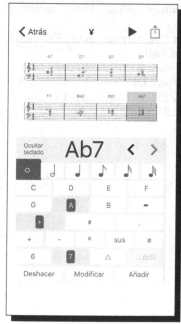

Fig. 2. The nabla application.

Alas, the previous statement is not true in general and the following little example disproves such a claim. Consider the chord progression $\{(C, E, B\} \Longrightarrow \{(B, F\sharp, A\}$. If we look for the shortest distances between the individual notes, we will obtain the bijection $C \leftrightarrow B, G \leftrightarrow F\sharp, E \leftrightarrow A$; the nabla distance of this bijection is 7. However, the bijection below gives a smaller nabla distance. which has $\tilde{\nabla}(P_1) = 1 + 5 + 1 = 7$ as its minimum value. Notice that the choice of $E \leftrightarrow A$ is forced by the choices of previous notes. However, the bijection $C \leftrightarrow B, E \leftrightarrow F\sharp, G \leftrightarrow A$ gives a smaller nabla distance: $\tilde{\nabla}(P_1) = 1 + 2 + 2 = 5$.

4   The Nabla Application

In this section we show how to use the idea of the nabla distance to teach voice-leadings in jazz music. Voice-leadings, contrary to what it might seem, are common in jazz music and part of a proper performance practice. In order to help the interested musician to understand and use the nabla approach to part-writing, we wrote an application, the ∇ app, which, from a sequence of chords input by the user, computes the optimal chord progression. The application is already available on Apple store and the interface is in Spanish, although it will be translated into English very soon. This application can be used to illustrate concepts of mathematical theory in the classroom. It may help the music student to familiarize themselves with mathematical formalization (all the concepts found in Sect. 2). Also, it allows the teacher to take a hands-on approach to part-writing in jazz or classical music.

References

1. Benson, D.: Music: A Mathematical Offering. Cambridge University Press, Cambridge (2006)
2. Cohn, R.: Audacious Euphony: Chromatic Harmony and the Triad's Second Nature. Oxford University Press, Oxford (2012)
3. Derfler, B.: Single-Voice Transformations: A Model for Parsimonious Voice Leading. Cambridge Scholars Publishing, Cambridge (2010)
4. Deutsch, D.: The Psychology of Music. Academic Press, Cambridge (1999)
5. Lewin, D.: The Structure of Atonal Music. Yale University Press, New Haven (1973)
6. Hall, R., Tymoczko, D.: Submajorization and the geometry of unordered collections. Am. Math. Monthly **119**(4), 263–283 (2012)
7. Lewin, D.: Generalized Musical Intervals and Transformations. Yale University Press, New Haven (1987)
8. Tymoczko, D.: A Geometry of Music: Harmony and Counterpoint in the Extended Common Practice. Oxford University Press, Oxford (2011)
9. Tymoczko, D.: The geometry of musical chords. Science **313**, 72–74 (2006)
10. Tymoczko, D.: Three conceptions of musical distance. In: Chew, E., Childs, A., Chuan, C.-H. (eds.) MCM 2009. CCIS, vol. 38, pp. 258–272. Springer, Heidelberg (2009). https://doi.org/10.1007/978-3-642-02394-1_24

Computational Music Therapy

Billie Sandak[1](✉), Avi Mazor[2], Amichay Asis[2], Avi Gilboa[2],
and David Harel[1]

[1] Department of Computer Science and Applied Mathematics,
The Weizmann Institute of Science, Rehovot, Israel
{billie.sandak,david.harel}@weizmann.ac.il
[2] Department of Music, Bar-Ilan University, Ramat Gan, Israel
avi.gilboa@biu.ac.il

Abstract. Free improvisation is a common technique in music therapy, used to express one's ideas or feelings in the non-verbal language of music. More broadly, music therapy is used to induce therapeutic and psychosocial effects; i.e., to help alleviate symptoms in serious and chronic diseases, and to empower the wellbeing and quality of life for healthy individuals and for patients. However, much research is required in order to learn how music therapy operates and to enhance its effectivity. Here we utilize our broad computational paradigm, which enables the rigorous and quantitative tracking, analyzing and documenting of the underlying dynamic expressive processes. We adapt the method, which we developed for the art and music modalities, to music therapy and apply it in a real-world experimentation. We study expressive emergent behaviors of clients directed by a therapist in a succession of sessions aimed at developing and increasing their expressivity through free improvisations. We describe our empirical insights, and discuss their implications in therapy and in scientific research arenas.

Keywords: Computational paradigm · Computer modeling · Music making · Arts therapies · Music therapy

1 Introduction

Music therapy is used in diverse populations and age groups to help alleviate symptoms and induce therapeutic and psychosocial effects in a wide variety of serious and chronic conditions, illnesses, mental disorders, disabilities, etc. [1–16]. For a patient or a healthy individual, the engagement with music also enhances one's well-being and quality of life, and is useful for research and practice in the social sciences, aimed at understanding and empowering individuals, groups and society [17–19]. Nevertheless, much research is required to reveal the underlying expressive behavioral mechanisms, by which music interventions work, and to enhance their effectivity [20–22].

The clinical setting, which consists of the musical work, the therapist and the patient, constitutes a rich dynamic environment of occurrences that is difficult to capture, driven by complex, simultaneous, and interwoven expressive behavioral processes, often considered intractable to human observers. Consequently, they are perceived and interpreted subjectively, and most often described verbally, thus

M. Montiel et al. (Eds.): MCM 2019, LNAI 11502, pp. 359–368, 2019.
https://doi.org/10.1007/978-3-030-21392-3_31

affecting the subsequent analyses and understanding. Our broad computational paradigm (CP), developed and utilized for the art and music modalities [23, 24], allows substantial barriers in the arts-based fields to be overcome, by enabling the rigorous and quantitative tracking, analyzing and documenting of the underlying dynamic processes, and allowing one to carry out exploratory, hypotheses-testing and – generating, and knowledge discovery investigations, which are empirically based. Our empirical infrastructure enables intra-/local-/micro- analysis, where the focus is on specific moments within the dynamics of an arts-based session, and inter-/global-/macro-analysis with reference to wider perspectives, across sessions, individuals and collectives; e.g., the discovery of demographic variation factors in artistic making [23, 24]. Past attempts to use computation to analyze music making were found to be limited ad-hoc implementations: recording of some particular parameters that were based on pre-determined hypotheses was carried out in [25], some featured tools were demonstrated on two single test cases [26], and in [27] extracted musical features of improvisations were used to predict the type of mental disorder of music therapy clients.

Musical improvisation is a common technique in music therapy used to express one's feelings or ideas in the non-verbal language of music. Directing patients or clients to improvise freely enables them to develop their creativity and expressivity, which is the basis of the study reported here. We adapt the CP and apply it to music therapy in a real-world experimentation aimed at improving one's expressiveness, yielding novel empirical insights to aid music therapists and researchers.

The CP captures emergent behaviors; i.e., arising properties and patterns of the behavioral processes, and it includes: *(1)* measuring and calculating exact time durations of occurrences within the music session; e.g., net idle time, in which the patient/client is not engaged in musical activity or pressing a key, total playing time and concurrent playing time, obtained from notes (keys) pressed in parallel; *(2)* tracking note use per time and per presses; e.g., net number of notes used, total number of notes pressed, their time durations and density, and their cluster formations, as well as note color preference (say, black and white keys on a piano keyboard); *(3)* capturing and analyzing preference profile of octave use and note intensity in the music making process; e.g., whether it is carried out in confined pitch (registers) and intensity levels (musical dynamics); *(4)* calculating transitions; e.g., crescendo, diminuendo, accelerando, ritardando and note color (for example, black to white, white to white, etc.); *(5)* profiling pitch classes; that is, the note use distribution collapsed onto an octave (C, C#, D,..., A#, B pitch); *(6)* pedal use; i.e., number of presses and time durations.

As described next, our setup involved human subjects participating in an experimental study that consisted of a series of sessions with a music therapist. We analyzed the dynamics of the emergent behaviors in their free improvisation playing, according to the parameters discussed above.

2 The Computational Paradigm and Its Use

The study reported upon in this paper is an application of our CP to understanding the effects of therapy in enhancing one's musical expression.

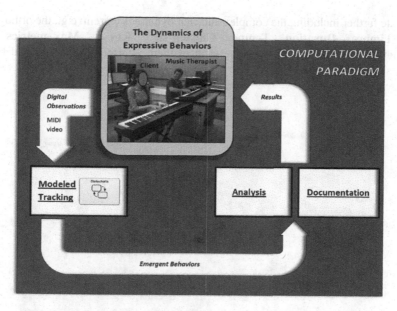

Fig. 1. The computational paradigm and its constituting components.

2.1   Music Room Modeling

Here we provide a brief description of the adaptation of the method for music therapy. We refer the reader to [23, 24] for a more detailed description of the methodology's architecture and modeling considerations for the various arts modalities. As seen in Fig. 1, digital observations of the system under study, i.e., musical work, are fed into the **Modeled Tracking** module, which captures the occurring events to yield emergent expressive behaviors. These are input to the **Analysis** and **Documentation** modules, the first of which outputs empirical insights into the field of study – music therapy, and the second transforms the behavioral dynamics to amenable descriptions therein. The **Modeled Tracking** module hosts the music room model, which is Statecharts-based [28]. Statecharts is a visual formalism [29], which enriches the basic state/event modeling approach with means for describing hierarchy (nested states) and multi-level transitions, as well as orthogonality (concurrent states), and more. We base our modeling on Statecharts, and use its underlying execution and analysis tools [30–32] to track and analyze the musical work system and the parameters therein. Three major entities comprise the music room: the musical work, the patient and the music therapist (see Fig. 2). The musical work (e.g., free improvisations), which is the center of attention here, is driven by events that transfer the system from state to state. For example, starting to play a musical note, and stopping it, pressing the piano pedal, entering an 'idle' state, etc. As such, and as seen in Fig. 2, the **Music_Work** subsystem state is decomposed into its exclusive substates, **Idle**, **Selecting**, and **Playing**, with the latter state further including the complex and rich dynamics therein; e.g., the orthogonal states **Timbre, Duration, Tempo, Cluster_size, Key_n, Max_metrics** and **Min_metrics** (see these in [24], where each of them is also further described by its substates).

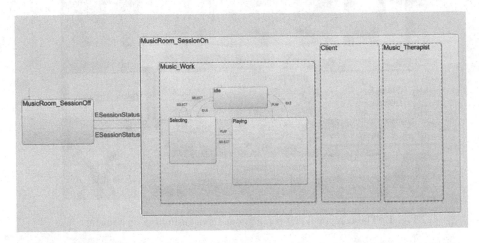

Fig. 2. Statecharts [28] modeling of the high-level state of the music room, with three concurrent/orthogonal states (dashed lines) specifying the entities therein: the **Music_work, Client** (patient) and **MusicTherapist**. The figure also shows the events that trigger the beginning of the therapy session and its termination, specified as mutually exclusive states, **MusicRoom_SessionOn** and **MusicRoom_SessionOff**, respectively (solid lines). Further details as to the nested states can be found in the text and in [23, 24].

2.2 Experimental Design

The study included a music therapist and four participants, or subjects, A, B, C, and D[1]. Each subject participated in six 50 min sessions, each of which began with a free improvisation and ended with one. That is, a total of 12 free improvisations for each subject. In between, the subjects were given exercises and tasks by the therapist, to execute either alone or accompanied by him. The participants were healthy/normal subjects, 22–35 years old, having had college-level musical education with several years of piano training (mostly during childhood) and modest experience in improvisations. The sessions were intended to develop the participants' expressive abilities.

The musical instrument used by the participants was a Casio MIDI piano keyboard controller (PX-160) and a pedal (sp-3). We employed the MIDI protocol [33, 34] for digital data collection. The improvisation data was recorded using Cubase9 [35] and was transformed by Max/MSP [36] to output script files. These were subsequently "read into" our Statecharts model and analyzed by the CP methodology.

---

[1] The research protocol was reviewed and approved by Bar-Ilan University's Ethics Committee. All participants signed a written informed consent.

For each of the subjects, the first and last improvisations (nos. 1 and 12) were extracted from the MIDI recordings, and were analyzed. The improvement of expressiveness should to be apparent in the sound (e.g., intensity, pedal use), physical (e.g., key color, octave range) and temporal (e.g., improvisation time) attributes of piano playing. Here we report on the results of Subject-B and then of Subject–A (additional results will be reported elsewhere).

3 Results

The results obtained from analyzing the first and last improvisations of Subject-B and Subject-A manifest enhanced musical expressiveness, whereas the empirical values of the musical parameters enable the rigorous comparison of the performances and the expressiveness change.

As seen in the top panel of Fig. 3A, the range of Subject-B's octave use grew, that is, the minimum octave used was no. 2 (marked by a green square) and the maximum octave value of 4 (in red) changed to the higher value of 5. The black square marks the most used octave in playing time, that is, from octave 4 to 3 in this case, whereas the exact distribution of the octave number use per the percentage of the playing time is depicted in the histogram appearing in the top left panel of Fig. 3B. The range of intensity values (dynamics) also grew. See the bottom panel in Fig. 3A, and the accompanying histogram showing the exact percentage of playing time for each intensity value (Fig. 3B top right panel). Interesting also to note is the increased use of the black keys (see Fig. 3C two bottom right panels for key color distribution of presses and their transitions, respectively). In addition, the pitch classes preference is shown in the bottom left panel of Fig. 3B; adding the notes E and F# to the repertoire of the last improvisation, "letting go" of the C note, and tending to more chromaticity overall. A meaningful change is also seen in the total time duration of the improvisation length, from 0.6 min of the first to more than four times in length, that is, to 2.7 min (Fig. 3C top left panel). In fact, all subjects increased the durations of their improvisations – feeling more comfortable in expressing themselves. Subject-B placed her foot statically on the pedal in the first improvisation (even before it started), whereas in the last one the pedal was freely used; 19 presses with 8.5 s average press throughout 91.6% of the improvisation time. Notable also is the concurrent playing time[2] (Fig. 3C top right panel), which grew from 214% to 264%, mostly owing to the larger cluster of keys pressed together (Fig. 3B bottom right panel) and almost 'doubling' the percentage of keys used doing so, from 29% to 50% (Fig. 3C top right 2nd panel). It is interesting to compare our detailed and precise approach with the therapist's written summary. The therapist described the first improvisation merely as "a short improvisation" and did not document the last one at all.

Subject-A's results are presented in Table 1. Notable is the use of the black keys in the last improvisation as compared to the first (almost all white), in terms of the

---

[2] Concurrent playing metric, quantifies the percentage of concurrent playing time per net improvisation playing time, yielded by keys pressed in parallel (e.g., three keys pressed throughout the session play time yield 300%).

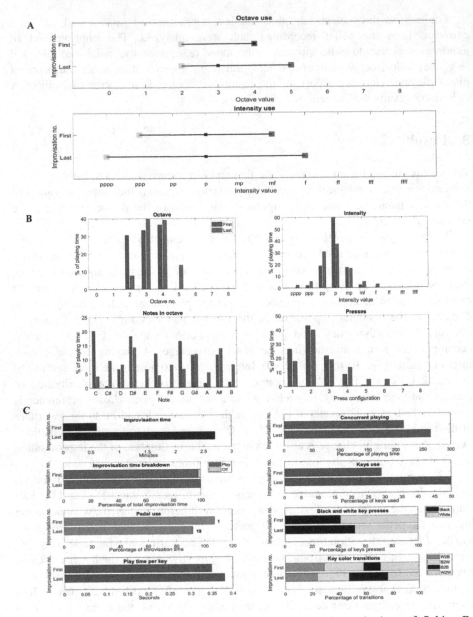

Fig. 3. Comparable empirical depiction of the first and last improvisations of Subject-B (extracted from the 1st and 6th sessions, respectively). Explanations are in the text. (Color figure online)

percentage of presses, the transitions (see '% black to black'), and the percentage of playing time distribution into pitch classes. This adds a more accurate aspect to the therapist's summary, including the use of the 'white' A note that was not captured by

Table 1. Parameter comparison of first and last improvisations of Subject-A.

Attribute	Parameter	First Impro	Last Impro
Time	% playing time	95.8%	76.2%
	% idle time	4.2%	23.8%
	% concurrent	237.1%	159.7%
	total (minutes)	1.5	3.6
Notes/ Keys	# of presses	425	905
	% used	51.3%	47.4%
	presses per key	10.9	25.1
	play per key (sec)	0.209	0.184
	% black presses	5.2%	97.9%
	% white presses	94.8%	2.1%
Intensity†	average	5	5
	lowest (minimum)	1	2
	highest (maximum)	9	9
	most used	5	4
Octave	average	4	4
	lowest (minimum)	1	0
	highest (maximum)	6	7
	most used	4	5
Cluster of notes	# of instances	814	1522
	max pressed*	6	4
	most pressed‡	2	1
	% most played§	36.5%	59.5%
Transitions	% diminuendo	49.9%	51.5%
	% crescendo	48.7%	45.3%
	% same intensity	1.4%	3.2%
	% accelerando	8.9%	2.3%
	% ritardando	91.1%	97.7%
	% white to black	5.2%	1.8%
	% black to white	5.2%	1.7%
	% black to black	0.0%	96.1%
	% white to white	89.6%	0.4%
Pitch Classes	% C	12.5%	0.0%
	% C#	0.7%	13.3%
	% D	16.8%	0.0%
	% D#	0.0%	35.2%
	% E	28.4%	0.0%
	% F	7.8%	0.0%
	% F#	0.0%	20.6%
	% G	5.4%	0.0%
	% G#	3.6%	15.7%
	% A	18.8%	1.5%
	% A#	0.0%	13.7%
	% B	6.1%	0.0%
Pedal	# of presses	23 (3.9sec)	47(4.6 sec)
	% of impro time	98.5%	97.4%

† 1-pppp ; 2-ppp ; 3-pp ; 4-p ; 5-mp ; 6-mf ; 7-f ; 8-ff ; 9-fff ; 10-ffff
* configuration of maximum number of keys pressed ;
‡ most pressed configuration ;
§ relative playing time of the most pressed configuration ;

the human observer, nor the durations of the improvisations and pedal use. The durations almost doubled from 1.5 min to 3.6 min, whereas pedal average duration grew from 3.9 s per press to 4.6 s.

We have found empirical evidence of change. For example: (i) enhanced octave use, which usually indicates that the patient has the ability to use more notes to express him/herself; (ii) enhanced range of intensity, which indicates the ability to express more varied emotional states; (iii) chromatic key transitions, which indicate more opportunities to express feelings and situations (at first, patients tend to "stick" to white keys or to black keys or to avoid chromaticity); (iv) frequent pedal use, which enables more shades of expression and thus indicates an improvement in expressive abilities; (v) enhanced concurrent notes use that requires playing with more than one finger at a time, which, again, enables broader expressive possibilities.

4 Discussion

Our CP tracks, analyses and documents the precise dynamics of emergent behaviors and change, and hence may: *(i)* complement the therapist's written subjective summary, adding empirical evidence and novel insights to missed and/or unreported occurrences; *(ii)* allow improvisation and session comparison, as well as retrieval, reproduction and sharing of information to be used in communication and understanding between specialists and communities of relevant fields; *(iii)* aid in the assessing and diagnosing of the patient/client and his or her progress, as well as the therapist's professional performance. Furthermore, the method facilitates comparison between clients, therapists, and collectives, differentiated by their performances and demographics [24], pathologies, etc.

Some of the future planned developments of the CP are: *(i)* to determine which of the parameters (as in Table 1) evaluate session progress and outcome; that is, to identify 'behavioral markers', such as those depicting change; *(ii)* to correlate the therapist's verbal description of the improvisation with the parameters/quantified occurrences obtained; e.g., "more freedom, more courageous, less fixation" could be correlated with octave and intensity range, and black and white key use; *(iii)* to track bodily and auditory dynamics narrating social interaction; e.g., facial expressions, body language, and therapist intervention (which can be done by modeling the patient and therapist entities; initial Statecharts-based models can be found in [23, 24]); *(iv)* to analyze the parameters for their musical syntax; e.g., harmony and structure (as here, we account for parameters that describe musical processes taking place in therapy amongst client populations for whom music-specific exposure in not common [37, 38]).

We believe that our approach has the potential of helping make significant progress in both scientific and clinical fields employing music, such as education, social work, psychology, healthcare and recreation.

References

1. Bruscia, K.E.: Defining Music Therapy, 3rd edn. Barcelona Publishers, Dallas (2014)
2. Bunt, L., Stige, B.: Music Therapy: An Art Beyond Words, 2nd edn. Routledge, London (2004)
3. Dileo, E.C.: Effects of music and music therapy on medical patients: a meta-analysis of the research and implications for the future. J. Soc. Integr. Oncol. 4, 67–70 (2006)
4. Burns, S., Harbuz, M., Hucklebridge, F., Bunt, A.A.: Pilot study into the therapeutic effects of music therapy at a cancer help center. Altern. Ther. Health Med. 7, 48–57 (2001)
5. Guzzetta, C.: Effects of relaxation and music therapy in a coronary care unit with presumptive acute myocardial infaction. Heart Lung. 18, 609–616 (1989)
6. Pacchetti, C., Mancini, F., Aglieri, R., Fundaro, C., Martignoni, E., Nappi, G.: Active music therapy in Parkinson's disease: an integrative method for motor and emotional rehabilitation. Psychosom. Med. 62, 386–393 (2009)
7. Hilliard, R.: The effects of music therapy on the quality and length of life of people diagnosed with terminal cancer. J. Music Ther. 40, 113–137 (2003)

8. Gold, C., Solli, H., Kruger, V., Lie, S.: Dose-response relationship in music therapy for people with serious mental disorders: systematic review and meta-analysis. Clin. Psychol. Rev. **29**, 193–207 (2009)
9. Hense, C., McFerran, K.S.: Promoting young people's musical identities to facilitate recovery from mental illness. J. Youth Stud. **20**, 997–1012 (2017)
10. Skeja, E.: The impact of cognitive intervention program and music therapy in learning disabilities. Proc. Soc. Behav. Sci. **159**, 605–609 (2014)
11. Chanda, M.L., Levitin, D.J.: The neurochemistry of music. Trends Cogn. Sci. **17**, 179–193 (2013)
12. Lindblad, F., Hogmark, Å., Theorell, T.: Music intervention for 5th and 6th graders—effects on development and cortisol secretion. Stress Health **23**, 9–14 (2007)
13. Smolen, D., Topp, R., Singer, L.: The effect of self-selected music during colonoscopy on anxiety, heart rate, and blood pressure. Appl. Nurs. Res. **15**, 126–136 (2002)
14. Kumar, A.M., Tims, F., Cruess, D.G., Mintzer, M.J., Ironson, G., Loewenstein, D., et al.: Music therapy increases serum melatonin levels in patients with Alzheimer's disease. Altern. Ther. Health Med. **5**, 49–57 (1999)
15. Zhao, K., Bai, Z.G., Bo, A., Chi, I.A.: Systematic review and meta-analysis of music therapy for the older adults with depression. Int. J. Geriatr. Psychiatry **31**(1), 188–1198 (2016)
16. Chang, Y., Chu, H., Yang, C., Tsai, J., Chung, M., Liao, Y., et al.: The efficacy of music therapy for people with dementia: a meta-analysis of randomised controlled trials. J. Clin. Nurs. **24**, 3425–3440 (2015)
17. Wang, C., Sun, Y., Zang, H.: Music therapy improves sleep quality in acute and chronic sleep disorders: a meta-analysis of 10 randomized studies. Int. J. Nurs. Stud. **51**, 51–62 (2014)
18. Ansdell, G., Stige, B.: Community music therapy. In: Edwards, J. (ed.) The Oxford Handbook of Music Therapy, pp. 595–621. Oxford University Press, NewYork (2016)
19. Tuastad, L., Stige, B.: The revenge of Me and THE BAND'its: a narrative inquiry of identity constructions in a rock band of ex-inmates. Nord. J. Music Ther. **24**, 252–275 (2015)
20. Wheeler, B.: Handbook of Music Therapy. Guilford Publications, NewYork (2015)
21. Greenberg, L.S.: The investigation of change: its measurement and explanation. In: Russell, R.L. (ed.) Reassessing Psychotherapy Research, pp. 114–143. The Guilford Press, New York (1994)
22. Juslin, P., Sloboda, J. (eds.): Handbook of Music and Emotion - Theory, Research, Applications. Oxford University Press, New York (2001)
23. Sandak, B., Huss, E., Sarid, O., Harel, D.: Computational paradigm to elucidate the effects of arts-based approaches and interventions: individual and collective emerging behaviors in artwork construction. PLoS One **10**(6), e0126467 (2015). https://doi.org/10.1371/journal.pone.0126467
24. Sandak, B., Cohen, S., Gilboa, A., Harel, D.: Computational elucidation of the effects induced by music making. PLoS One **14**(3), e0213247 (2019). https://doi.org/10.1371/journal.pone.0213247
25. Streeter, E., Davies, M.E.P., Reiss, J.D., Hunt, A., Caley, R., Roberts, C.: Computer aided music therapy evaluation: testing the music therapy logbook prototype 1 system. Arts Psychother. **39**, 1–10 (2012)
26. Erkkilä, J., Ala-Ruona, E., Lartillot, O.: Technology and clinical improvisation – from production and playback to analysis and interpretation. In: Music, Health, Technology and Design. Series from the Centre for Music and Health, vol. 8, pp. 209–225. NMH-publications, Oslo (2014)

27. Luck, G., Lartillot, O., Erkkilä, J., Toiviainen, P., Riikkilä, K.: Predicting music therapy clients type of mental disorder using computational feature extraction and statistical modelling techniques. In: Klouche, T., Nool, T. (eds.) MCM 2007. CCIS, vol. 37, pp. 156–167 (2007)
28. Harel, D.: Statecharts: a visual formalism for complex systems. Sci. Comput. Program. **8**, 231–274 (1987)
29. Harel, D.: On visual Formalisms. Commun. Assoc. Comput. Mach. **31**, 514–530 (1988)
30. Mathworks – Simulink - simulation and model-based design. http://www.mathworks.com/products/simulink. Accessed 1 Jan 2019
31. Mathworks - MATLAB - the language of technical computing. http://www.mathworks.com/products/matlab. Accessed 1 Jan 2019
32. Mathworks - Stateflow - model and simulate decision logic using state machine and flow charts. http://www.mathworks.com/products/stateflow. Accessed 1 Jan 2019
33. MIDI - Musical Instrument Digital Interface. http://www.midi.org/. Accessed 1 Jan 2019
34. MIDI Tutorial Part 2 - NOTE Messages. https://www.cs.cmu.edu/~music/cmsip/readings/MIDI%20tutorial%20for%20programmers.html. Accessed 1 Jan 2019
35. Cubase9 - digital audio workstations (DAW). https://www.steinberg.net/en/products/cubase/what_is_new_in_cubase_9.html#. Accessed 1 Jan 2019
36. Max/MSP – A visual programming language for audio and media. https://cycling74.com/products/max/#.WAhuCU27p9A. Accessed 1 Jan 2019
37. Gilboa, A., Bensimon, M.: Putting clinical process into image: a method for visual representation of music therapy sessions. Music Ther. Perspect. **9**, 32–42 (2007)
38. Letulė, N., Ala-Ruona, E., Erkkilä, J.: Professional freedom: a grounded theory on the use of music analysis in psychodynamic music therapy. Nord. J. Music Ther. **27**, 448–466 (2018). https://doi.org/10.1080/08098131.2018.1490920

Special Session on the Pedagogy of Mathematical Music Theory

Insiders' Choice: Studying Pitch Class Sets Through Their Discrete Fourier Transformations

Thomas Noll[✉]

Departament de Teoria, Composició i Direcció,
Escola Superior de Música de Catalunya, Barcelona, Spain
thomas.mamuth@gmail.com

Abstract. This contribution responds to a growing interest in the application of Discrete Fourier Transform (DFT) to the study of pitch class sets and pitch class profiles. Theoretical fundaments, references to previous work and explorations of various directions of study have been eloquently assembled by Emmanuel Amiot. Recent pioneering work in the application to music analysis and the reinterpretation of theoretical knowledge has been accomplished by Jason Yust. The intention of this paper is to show ways to make Yust's strategies and methods more easily accessible and reproducible for a broader readership, especially students. This includes the introduction of concepts as well as interactive experiments with the help of computation and visualization tools.

The theoretical starting point is the interpretation of pitch class sets in terms of their characteristic functions, i.e. as pitch class profiles with values 0 and 1. Apart from the magnitudes of the respective partials, the study of their phases is particularly illuminating. The paper shows how the contents of this approach can be made accessible in a four steps proceedure.

Keywords: Discrete Fourier analysis · Pitch class sets ·
Pitch class profiles · Two-phase-plots

1 The Diamond Jubilee: Lewin's Remarkable 1959 Article

The publication of Lewin's pioneering article [4] dates back precisely 60 years now. Although the condensed article presents an absolutely convincing application of Discrete Fourier Transform to a concrete music-theoretical problem it took the music-theoretical community nevertheless almost half a century in order to show an interest in this project. In fact, it was after Lewin's second go [5], that a small group of younger visionary theorists realized, that the special case of vanishing Fourier coefficients might just be the tip of an mathe-musical iceberg. Before immersing ourselves into the very basics, it is useful to recapitulate Lewin's original question.

© Springer Nature Switzerland AG 2019
M. Montiel et al. (Eds.): MCM 2019, LNAI 11502, pp. 371–378, 2019.
https://doi.org/10.1007/978-3-030-21392-3_32

If we have two chords (pitch class sets) X (of m tones) and Y (of n tones) we may form $m \times n$ tone pairs (x, y) with $x \in X$ and $y \in Y$. Each pair defines an interval $y - x \in \mathbb{Z}_{12}$. And the $m \times n$ interval-instances can be counted in terms of the interval function $IF(X, Y) : \mathbb{Z}_{12} \to \mathbb{N}$, where each index $IF(X, Y)(i) = \#\{(x, y) \in X \times Y \mid y - x = i\}$ is the multiplicity of i among the $m \times n$ interval-instances from X to Y. Figure 1 shows two such pairs, namely $X_1 = \{2, 5, 7, 11\}$ and $Y = \{0, 4, 7\}$ with the interval function $IF(X_1, Y) = [1, 1, 2, 0, 0, 3, 0, 1, 1, 1, 1, 1]$ and $X_2 = \{1, 5, 7, 11\}$ and $Y = \{0, 4, 7\}$ with the interval function $IF(X_2, Y) = [1, 1, 1, 1, 0, 2, 1, 1, 1, 1, 0, 2]$. It turns out that the chord $Y = \{0, 4, 7\}$ is uniquely determined by X_1 and $IF(X_1, Y)$, because there is no other chord $\tilde{Y}$, such that $IF(X_1, Y) = IF(X_1, \tilde{Y})$. This is different in the case of X_2 and $IF(X_2, Y)$, where there are seven other 3-chords, sharing the interval function from X_2 with Y: $IF((X_2, Y) = IF((X_2, \tilde{Y}_k)$ for $\tilde{Y}_1 = \{0, 1, 4\}, \tilde{Y}_2 = \{0, 1, 10\}, \tilde{Y}_3 = \{0, 7, 10\}, \tilde{Y}_4 = \{0, 4, 6\}, \tilde{Y}_5 = \{1, 6, 10\}, \tilde{Y}_6 = \{4, 6, 7\}$, and $\tilde{Y}_7 = \{6, 7, 10\}$.

Fig. 1. Left side: the chord $Y = \{0, 4, 7\}$ is uniquely determined by the chord $X_1 = \{2, 5, 7, 11\}$ and the interval function $IF(X_1, Y) = [1, 1, 2, 0, 0, 3, 0, 1, 1, 1, 1, 1]$. Right side: the chord $Y = \{0, 4, 7\}$ is *not* uniquely determined by the chord $X_2 = \{1, 5, 7, 11\}$ and the interval function $IF(X_2, Y) = [1, 1, 1, 1, 0, 2, 1, 1, 1, 1, 0, 2]$.

Lewin's elegant explanation for this different behavior takes advantage of the famous *convolution theorem* of Fourier theory (e.g. see [3] Theorem 1.10 on p.7). The discrete Fourier transform $\hat{f} : \mathbb{Z}_n \to \mathbb{C}$ of a complex-valued function $f : \mathbb{Z}_n \to \mathbb{C}$ is defined by virtue of $\hat{f}(k) = \sum_{j=0}^{n-1} f(j) exp(-2\pi i k j / n)$. The interval function $IF(X, Y)$ can be written as a convolution of the characteristic functions $\chi_X, \chi_Y : \mathbb{Z}_{12} \to \{0, 1\} \subset \mathbb{C}$, namely $IF(X, Y)(k) = \sum_{j=0}^{n_1} \chi_X(j) \cdot \chi_Y(k - j)$. The vanishing of one of the Fourier-coefficients $\widehat{IF(X, Y)}(k)$ of the interval function than implies the vanishing of the Fourier-Coefficient at that same index k of—at least—one of the two characteristic functions χ_X or χ_Y, and thereby provides freedom for the value of that coefficient for the other characteristic function. This is how the concrete ambiguities on the right side of Fig. 1 emerge, because $\widehat{\chi_{\{1,5,7,11\}}}(k) = 0$ for all odd indices k, while $\widehat{\chi_{\{0,4,7\}}}(k) \neq 0$, throughout.

Eventually Lewin's ideas initiate a gradual reclamation of the Fourier approach by music theorists. Several established music-theoretical concepts are being successively translated into the Fourier domain, and their interaction is being studied under new perspectives. This starts with the interpretation of the absolut values of the Fourier coefficients. A special case of the above discovery is the equation $IF(X, X)(k) = |\widehat{\chi_X}(k)|^2$ for $k \in \mathbb{Z}_{12}$, which Amiot ([3], p. 15) calls *Lewin's Lemma*. According to this formula two chords are Z-related (or belong to the same set class) if and only if the Fourier coefficients of their characteristic functions have the same magnitudes.

Avoiding the mathematical formalism Quinn [8] meets the challenge to interpret the vanishing of Fourier coefficients within a broader investigation of *chord quality* for a music-theoretical readership. The vanishing of a coefficient—a a *Fourier balance*—is often accompanied with high or maximal values of others. Amiot [1] undertakes systematic investigations into the link between the concept of *maximally even sets* of d tones and the maximality of the absolute value $|\widehat{\chi_X}(d)|$ among all d-chords X.

Recent exciting work is dedicated to the interpretation of the phases of Fourier coefficients. Traditional spaces of chords or tonal regions, such as Douthett and Steinbach's chicken wire torus or Weber's regional space maybe regained within tori of phases. This implies the possibility for robust analytical methods, because the Fourier coefficients of chords and scales of different cardinalities can be located in the same phase spaces and the interpretation of the notes of a score may freely switch between strict and fuzzy encodings through characteristic functions and pitch class profiles, respectively. These new developments are due to Amiot [2,3] and Yust [9–14]. Yust's analytical work entails new ideas about a generalized concept of tonality.

One may easily anticipate that this process will continue. Sooner rather than later it is desirable to let students of theory or composition participate in these new developments. So the question arises how one may suitably integrate carefully selected content into a theory class. The present paper offers a few proposals in this direction.

2   Step One: Partial Chords and Fourier-Prototypes

The present pedagogical approach complements that of the *Fourier Scratching*— an earlier attempt [6,7] to convey the nature of the Fourier transform through musical interaction in a predefined rhythmical playground. The Fourier Scratching deliberately covers the entire space of complex-valued functions $f : \mathbb{Z}_n \to \mathbb{C}$ for low dimensions n in a musically meaningful way, and the project intends to pique the players' curiosity for the complex numbers and the DFT. The Fourier Scratching addresses a general public and uses the musical rhythms as medium for the exploration of mathematical circumstances.

This is different here, where the main goal is to access the musical meaning of the Fourier coefficients of characteristic functions of pitch class sets. The applications mentioned in Sect. 1 use real-valued functions only, and therefore another approach lends itself for accessing the required knowledge, especially for the study of Yust's articles. Although the discrete Fourier Transform of functions $f : \mathbb{Z}_{12} \to \mathbb{C}$ is mathematically easier to handle than the case of continuous periodic functions $F : \mathbb{R}/\mathbb{Z} \to \mathbb{C}$, it appears that composition students usually bring a basic understanding of trigonometric functions and additive synthesis as a "dowry" from their knowledge in sound and signal processing, while they have seldom come across the complex exponential function.

It is therefore helpful to inspect continuous cosine functions over an octave periodic pitch domain $\mathbb{R}/12\mathbb{Z}$ and drag them along with their restrictions to $\mathbb{Z}/12\mathbb{Z}$. It is crucial though that the familiar association – say—of a periodic time-dependent movement of an air particle, a loudspeaker membrane, a Cello string etc. must be given up. It is only allowed to serve as a metaphor. There is no time parameter involved in this application.

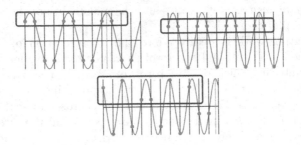

Fig. 2. The 3rd, 4th and 5th partial chords (with suitable phase shifts) corresponding to the periods $\frac{12}{3}, \frac{12}{4}$, and $\frac{12}{5}$, respectively. Their values are represented (1) as dots on the vertical lines of the $\mathbb{Z}_{12}$-grid and (2) as restrictions of (shifted) continuous cosine functions. The tones with positive values are framed. They form the associated prototypes: a hexatonic scale, an octatonic scale and Guido's hexachord respectively. The phases are chosen to orient these scales at the anchor tone $C = 0$.

The analogous transfer is indeed useful, as the *partial chords*—the DFT analogues to the partials of additive synthesis—are not musical chords in the usual sense. They can be visualized as discretized cosine functions and as such they have positive and negative values. It is important to bring the phase parameter into play and to understand that the range of the phase has to be adopted to the individual period of each partial chord, i.e. the period $\frac{12}{k}$ of the k-th partial. In visualizations the phase can be suitably shown in terms of a leftward shift of a cosine function. In Fig. 2 it is indicated through a vertical line; in Fig. 4 it is shown as a colored rectangle (in both cases measured from the right border of the graph in leftward direction). Figure 2 shows three partial chords, namely for $k = 3, 4$ and 5.

While the partial chords are still somewhat alien with respect to common musical intuition one obtains a link to prominent musical structures by inspecting the *Fourier prototypes*: the carrier sets of their positive values.

3   Step Two: Partial Decomposition

After having achieved some familiarity with the partial chords one may extend the analogous transfer to the inspection of additive synthesis. Here it is useful to have tools for interactive experiments.[1] Knowing the "right" parameters one

---

[1] The author developed little CDF-programs (Computable Document Format), which can be used with the free Wolfram CDF player.

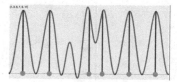

Fig. 3. Characteristic function $\chi_X = (0, 1, 0, 1, 0, 0, 1, 1, 0, 1, 0, 1)$ of the *Prometheus* chord $X = \{1, 3, 6, 7, 9, 11\}$. The (only auxiliary) continuous rendering arises from the superposition of the continuous partials.

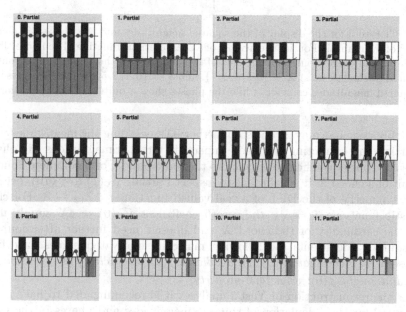

Fig. 4. Partial decomposition of the characteristic function of the *Prometheus* chord $X = \{1, 3, 6, 7, 9, 11\}$, see Fig. 3. The schematized keyboard layout within each partial-figure indicates the location of the 12 chromatic notes along the octave period. The gray/light rectangle on the right side below the keyboard indicates the size of the period, while the light part on the very right within it represents the phase shift.

may then re-synthesize the characteristic functions of given chords X in terms of superpositions of the appropriate 12 partial chords. Figure 4 shows the partials of the characteristic function $\chi_X = (0, 1, 0, 1, 0, 0, 1, 1, 0, 1, 0, 1)$ (see Fig. 3) of the *Prometheus* chord $X = \{1, 3, 6, 7, 9, 11\}$.

4 Step Three: Inspecting Fourier Coefficients

Careful exploration of the partial decompositions of various chords shows that the different partials typically have different impacts to the superposition. In Fig. 4 one can clearly observe a high impact of the sixths partial, whose prototype is the whole-tone scale.

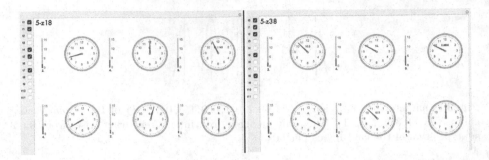

Fig. 5. CDF-tool for the display of the squared magnitudes and the phases (in a clock format) of the main six Fourier coefficients of a characteristic function. The figure allows the comparison of the Fourier coefficients of two chords with the same interval content (Z-related pitch class sets) $X = \{0, 1, 4, 5, 7\}$. and $Y = \{0, 1, 2, 5, 8\}$. One observes that the squared magnitudes coincide, while the phases show a quite different behavior.

At this stage one may go one step further: Disregarding the meanwhile familiar partials and extracting only their impacts in terms of magnitudes and phases brings the Fourier coefficients as such to the foreground. For a complete Fourier-portrait of a chord X it is sufficient to inspect Partials $\widehat{\chi_X}(1)$ to $\widehat{\chi_X}(6)$, because of the symmetry of the DFT of a real valued function $f : \mathbb{Z}_{12} \to \mathbb{R}$. For characteristic functions $f = \chi_X$ the zeroth coefficient $\widehat{\chi_X}(0) = \sharp X$ simply measures the cardinality of the chord X and doesn't need further attention. For the main six coefficients the following musically motivated names have been proposed: $\widehat{f}(1)$: *chromaticity*, $\widehat{f}(2)$: *dyadicity*, $\widehat{f}(3)$: *triadicity*, $\widehat{f}(4)$: *octatonicity*, $\widehat{f}(5)$: *diatonicity*, $\widehat{f}(6)$: *wholetone-property*.

For the reconstruction of Yust's analyses it is recommended to have a tool at disposal for the calculation of squared magnitudes and phases in the range between 0 and 12 (see Fig. 5).

5   Step Four: Analyzing Progressions in Two-Phase Plots

It is a common popular procedure in serval approaches to harmony to interpret chord progressions as trajectories in certain harmonic configuration spaces. Discrete Fourier analysis supports such an approach quite naturally. The consideration of two Fourier-phases at once takes place in a torus $\mathbb{R}/2\pi\mathbb{Z} \times \mathbb{R}/2\pi\mathbb{Z}$. Yust normalizes these spaces to a period of 12 in both dimensions.

The two sample analyses of chord progressions in Bach and Scriabin in Fig. 6 share an interesting characteristic: In both trajectories there is a more static and a more versatile coefficient. Interestingly, the Fourier coefficients change roles. Mobile octatonicity under static diatonicity is typical for traditional harmonic tonality (with seventh chords) and is exemplified by the progression in Bach. The Scriabin prelude exemplifies a form of mobile diatonicity under static octatonicity. It is an interesting proposal by Jason Yust to interpret a different activity allocation among the coefficients as a different type of tonality.

Fig. 6. The left figure shows a phase plot of the coefficients 4 (octatonicity) and 5 (diatonicity) of the trajectory formed by the first eight chords of the C-major prelude of the well-tempered piano (part I) by Johann Sebastian Bach (score above). The right figure shows a phase plot of the same coefficients for the first eight chords of Alexander Scriabin's prelude Op. 74 No. 2 (score below). In both windows the width and height of the rectangle around the location of chord no. 8 indicate the magnitudes of the 4th and the 5th Fourier-coefficients of this chord.

Acknowledgement. I thank my students of the course *Teoria musical dels segles XX i XXI* at ESMUC in Barcelona for their interest, commitment and feedback during the development of this material.

References

1. Amiot, E.: David Lewin and maximally even sets. J. Math. Music **1**(3), 157–172 (2007)
2. Amiot, E.: The Torii of phases. In: Yust, J., Wild, J., Burgoyne, J.A. (eds.) MCM 2013. LNCS (LNAI), vol. 7937, pp. 1–18. Springer, Heidelberg (2013). https://doi.org/10.1007/978-3-642-39357-0_1
3. Amiot, E.: Music Through Fourier Space: Discrete Fourier Transform in Music Theory. Springer, Cham (2016). https://doi.org/10.1007/978-3-319-45581-5
4. Lewin, D.: Intervallic relations between two collections of notes. J. Music Theory **3**(2), 298–301 (1959)
5. Lewin, D.: Special cases of the interval function between pitch-class sets X and Y. J. Music Theory **42**(2), 1–29 (2001)
6. Noll, T., Amiot, E., Andreatta, M.: Fourier oracles for computer-aided improvisation. In: 2006 Proceedings of the ICMC: Computer Music Conference. Tulane University, New Orleans (2006)
7. Noll, T., Carle, M.: Fourier scratching: SOUNDING CODE. In: SuperCollider Conference, Berlin (2010)
8. Quinn, I.: General equal-tempered harmony. Perspect. New Music **44**(2), 114–158, **45**(1), 4–63 (2006/2007)
9. Yust, J.: Schubert's harmonic language and fourier phase space. J. Music Theory **59**(1), 121–181 (2015)
10. Yust, J.: Distorted continuity: chromatic harmony, uniform sequences, and quantized voice leadings. Music Theory Spectr. **37**(1), 120–143 (2015)
11. Yust, J.: Applications of DFT to the theory of twentieth-century harmony. In: Collins, T., Meredith, D., Volk, A. (eds.) MCM 2015. LNCS (LNAI), vol. 9110, pp. 207–218. Springer, Cham (2015). https://doi.org/10.1007/978-3-319-20603-5_22
12. Yust, J.: Harmonic qualities in Debussy's 'Les sons et les parfums tournent dans l'air du soir'. J. Math. Music **11**(2–3), 155–173 (2017)
13. Yust, J.: Probing questions about keys: tonal distributions through the DFT. In: Agustín-Aquino, O.A., Lluis-Puebla, E., Montiel, M. (eds.) MCM 2017. LNCS (LNAI), vol. 10527, pp. 167–179. Springer, Cham (2017). https://doi.org/10.1007/978-3-319-71827-9_13
14. Yust, J.: Geometric generalizations of the Tonnetz and their relation to fourier phases spaces. In: Montiel, M., Peck, R. (eds.) Mathematical Music Theory: Algebraic, Geometric, Combinatorial, Topological and Applied Approaches to Understanding Musical Phenomena. World Scientific (2018)

Have Fun with Math and Music!

Maria Mannone$^{(\boxtimes)}$

University of Palermo, Palermo, Italy
mariacaterina.mannone@unipa.it, manno012@umn.edu

Abstract. If abstraction makes mathematics strong, it often makes it also hard to learn, if not discouraging. If math pedagogy suffers from the lack of engaging strategies, the pedagogy of mathematical music theory must deal with the additional difficulty of double fields and double vocabulary. However, games and interdisciplinary references in a STEAM framework can help the learner break down complex concepts into essential ideas, and gain interest and motivation to approach advanced topics. Here we present some general considerations, followed by two examples which may be applied in a high-school or early college level course. The first is a musical application of a Rubik's cube, the CubeHarmonic, to approach group theory and combinatorics jointly with musical chords; the second is an application of category theory to investigate simple musical variations together with transformations on a visual shape.

Keywords: Motivations · Groups · Categories

1 Introduction aka Motivations

"Mathematics is a monster!" exclaimed some students in a recent study [10,11] who had been asked to identify math with an animal, a wild thing, or a monster. Experiments showed that not only students were terrified by maths, but also some prospective teachers (of elementary school) were scared as well! Fear of math is an issue that may hinder learning and enjoyment of such a fruitful area of study. However, a new pedagogical approach highlighting the *aesthetic pleasure* we may get from the abstract sciences could help stu-

Fig. 1. A CubeHarmonic.

dents find the motivation to face difficulties that may arise during study. Also, specific activities and games can engage students and make the learning process more entertaining. This approach also applies to mathematical music theory. In this case, additional difficulties arise from the combination of two disciplines, each one with its own jargon, collection of practice, and thinking style. Using creative pedagogy [1], we can show students how they may receive inspiration from both maths in music making, and music in learning maths. In this paper,

---

M. Mannone is an alumna of the University of Minnesota, USA.

© Springer Nature Switzerland AG 2019
M. Montiel et al. (Eds.): MCM 2019, LNAI 11502, pp. 379–382, 2019.
https://doi.org/10.1007/978-3-030-21392-3_33

we present two ideas that can be proposed to students in their final year of high school, or first years of college. This paper is the short version of a book chapter [7].

2   Groups, Permutations, and the CubeHarmonic

Fig. 2. A pangolin.

Combinatorics and permutations have fascinated artists for centuries [13,17]. If topics such as permutations and group theory look 'abstract,' their embodiment in the form of a game may allow better understanding. This is the origin of the Rubik's cube, a toy as well as an object for mathematical study [2]. I thought of a musical application of the cube in 2013, and the *CubeHarmonic* has been currently developed as a working prototype [8,12]. The CubeHarmonic has notes on the face of each block—i.e., on each *facet*. Each face contains nine facets in the $3 \times 3 \times 3$ Rubik's cube. On each face there can be the notes of a chord, with some doublings, or the notes of a sequence of chords as in a cadence (Fig. 1 shows the original version with a 4-part harmony). By scrambling the cube, chords and chord sequences get mixed. The CubeHarmonic can remind us of a tonnetz [16]. On the unscrambled cube, Riemann's symmetries are locally verified—for example, we can consider two consecutive faces as a portion of the tonnetz, and the adjacent one as another portion of the tonnetz, cut and glued. Symmetries are also verified under rotations that go back to the initial configuration, called 'involutions.' With the Cube, combinatorics meets the tonnetz, two dense topics of interest for mathematical music theory. Music notation can be compared with the notation traditionally used to indicate moves on the cube. The original symmetries of the Rubik's group are broken if we assign a different note on each facet possessing the same color, making them distinguishable. We recover the symmetries if we play all the notes on a face at the same time, making the correspondence color = chord/cluster. Students can be asked to keep track of the rotations and of the musical combinations obtained, linking operations on the cube with musical transformations. Also, students can be asked to do the opposite, trying to perform a sequence of rotations and to hear the musical result of each.

3   Categories and the Pangolin

Another abstract topic is category theory [4,5], with its objects and arrows, and arrows between arrows, and nested structures. We can apply categories to make comparisons between musical sequences, visual shapes, and musical sequences and visual shapes[1] [6,9]. Here, we propose a categorical diagram based on the

---

[1] We should take care of some psychological studies on cross-modal correspondences [15] and Gestalt-derived theories [3], including the analysis of perceived correspondences between vertical motion and pitch variation [6,9,14].

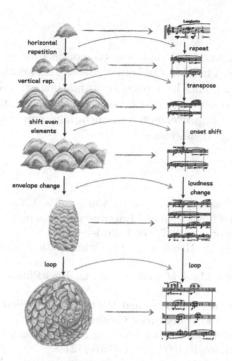

Fig. 3. Categorical scheme to study and sonify pangolin's armor. (Color figure online)

pangolin's armor. The pangolin (Fig. 2) is an endangered mammal; it defends itself from predators by closing in a ball (Fig. 3, bottom left), that, sadly, makes it easy prey for poachers. The (complex) image of the pangolin rolled in an armored ball may be produced from as a sequence of transformations starting with a single *armor scale*, that we can connect with a fragment of a *musical scale*. A category is constituted by objects and transformations between them, verifying associativity and identity. On the left of Fig. 3, we have a category[2] of visual shapes. On the right, we have a category of musical sequences. Horizontal arrows transform the armor's scales into musical sequences (straight arrows, red), and visual transformations into sound transformations (curved arrows, green). This is the action of a *functor*, that we can call a 'sonification functor.' If we have two different sonification strategies, we can define *natural transformations* between them. This scheme may be used as a pseudocode to compose, improvise, or program music. Students may enjoy developing algorithms to decompose complex structures into simpler objects, with transformations between them.

---

[2] A composition of scales still gives scales, as well as a composition of notes still gives notes, and the identity, when nothing changes.

4 Conclusion

In this paper, we proposed two simple ways to connect ideas, sounds, and images by using mathematics. The goal is to help students foster enthusiasm and engagement in learning maths, and, in particular, in mathematics as applied to music. Future developments of our work may investigate the reactions of students to this material, its continued improvement, and encourage new strategies for STEAM teaching. [Drawings by M. Mannone.]

References

1. Aleinikov, A.G.: Creative pedagogy. In: Carayannis, E.G. (ed.) Encyclopedia of Creativity Invention Innovation and Entrepreneurship, p. 327. Springer, New York (2013). https://doi.org/10.1007/978-1-4614-3858-8
2. Frey, A., Singmaster, D.: Handbook of the Cubik Math. Enslow Publishers, Hillside (1982)
3. Kubovy, M., Schutz, M.: Audio-visual objects. Rev. Philos. Psychol. 1(1), 41–61 (2010)
4. Lawvere, W., Schanuel, S.: Conceptual Mathematics: A First Introduction to Categories. Cambridge University Press, Cambridge (2011)
5. Mac Lane, S.: Categories for the Working Mathematician. Springer, New York (1978). https://doi.org/10.1007/978-1-4757-4721-8
6. Mannone, M.: Introduction to gestural similarity in music. An application of category theory to the orchestra. J. Math. Music 12(2), 63–87 (2018)
7. Mannone, M.: Can mathematical music theory be easily learnt and also be fun? In: Montiel, M., Gómez, F. (eds.) Theoretical and Practical Pedagogy of Mathematical Music Theory: Music for Mathematics and Mathematics for Musicians, From School to Postgraduate Levels, pp. 281–298. World Scientific, Singapore (2018)
8. Mannone, M., Kitamura, E., Huang, J., Sugawara, R., Kitamura, Y.: CubeHarmonic: a new interface from a magnetic 3D motion tracking system to music performance. In: Dahl, L., Bowman, D., Martin, T. (eds.) Proceedings of NIME Conference, Blacksburg, USA, pp. 350–351 (2018)
9. Mannone, M.: Networks of music and images. Gli Spazi della Musica 2(6), 38–52 (2017)
10. Markovits, Z.: Beliefs hold by pre-school prospective teachers toward mathematics and its teaching. Procedia - Soc. Behav. Sci. 11, 117–121 (2011)
11. Markovits, Z., Forgasz, H.: "Mathematics is like a lion": elementary students' beliefs about mathematics. Educ. Stud. Math. 96(1), 49–64 (2017)
12. Mazzola, G., Pang, Y., Mannone, M.: Cool Math for Hot Music. Springer, Heidelberg (2016). https://doi.org/10.1007/978-3-319-42937-3
13. Nolan, C.: On musical space and combinatorics: historical and conceptual perspectives in music theory. In: Sarhangi, R. (ed.) Bridges Proceedings, pp. 201–208 (2000)
14. Roffler, S., Butler, R.: Factors that influence the localization of sound in the vertical plane. J. Acoust. Soc. Am. 43, 1255–1259 (1968)
15. Spence, C.: Crossmodal correspondences: a tutorial review. Atten. Percept. Psychophys. 73, 971–995 (2011)
16. Tymoczko, D.: The generalized Tonnetz. J. Music Theory 1(56), 1–52 (2012)
17. Zweig, J.: Ars combinatoria. Art J. 3(56), 20–29 (2014)

Teaching Music with Mathematics: A Pilot Study

Andrew J. Milne[1]([⊠]) and Andrea M. Calilhanna[2]

[1] The MARCS Institute for Brain, Behaviour and Development,
Western Sydney University, Penrith, NSW 2751, Australia
a.milne@westernsydney.edu.au
[2] Sydney Conservatorium of Music, The University of Sydney,
Sydney, NSW, Australia
andrea.calilhanna@sydney.edu.au

Abstract. We detail a recently conducted teaching intervention involving the use of mathematics and associated software to teach rhythm and meter to Year 9 pupils. This intervention served as a feasibility and pilot study within a broader project related to the mutual teaching of mathematics and music. Causal conclusions cannot be made due to the lack of a control group, but questionnaires show that 81% of the pupils found interacting with software helped them to understand and visualize mathematical theories of rhythm and meter, and the same percentage think that mathematics and music are related. The two teachers who delivered the program enjoyed the experience and felt the software was beneficial.

Keywords: Music education · XronoBeat · STEAM education ·
Rhythm · Meter · Set theory · Maximal evenness · Modulo small ·
Cyclic graph

1 Introduction

In educational settings, there are widely reported correlations between mathematical and musical abilities [2,3,5,9,11,16,25] (including music theory [1,13–15,22]). These correlations remain after controlling for other factors such as general intelligence and academic aptitude [24]. Converging evidence suggests that both musical and mathematical skills are informed by core *geometric skills* for perceiving, recognising, and mentally manipulating spatial patterns [23].

The authors of this paper, in collaboration with Richard Cohn, Tara Hamilton, Courtney Hilton, and many others too numerous to mention, are conducting an ongoing applied research project called "Teaching Mathematics with Music and Music with Mathematics". We are developing a suite of educational materials including lesson plans and software designed to improve educational outcomes in both mathematics and music. To achieve this aim, we are (a) teaching mathematical and musical skills simultaneously; (b) using novel software applications that visualize musical structures with geometrical (typically, isomorphic) forms

© Springer Nature Switzerland AG 2019
M. Montiel et al. (Eds.): MCM 2019, LNAI 11502, pp. 383–389, 2019.
https://doi.org/10.1007/978-3-030-21392-3_34

that can be manipulated and sonified in musically appealing ways [17]; (c) using analogical comparisons between multimodal representations of the same underlying concept to help students draw out the commonalities of the musical and mathematical representations and generalize them [10,21].

This paper focuses on a recent pilot intervention at Sydney Grammar School that used music to teach mathematics – specifically rhythm and meter. It forms a counterpoint with two other recent pilot studies. One study was conducted at Andrea Calilhanna's private music tuition practice, and focused on the use of ski-hill graphs [6] and the associated SkiHill App [17] to teach and explain musical meter [4]. Qualitative results were detailed in [17] but, in summary, both students (aged 7 and 13) found the approach enhanced their understanding of meter as well as helping them to play previously challenging passages. The other intervention used musical rhythms to teach mathematics to Year 7 pupils in the second-lowest mathematics stream at Bankstown Girls High School (BGHS). This Western Sydney suburb has low socio-economic status (SES), and many of the pupils have English as a second language. For the three lessons, an adapted and simplified version of the music software application XronoMorph [18–20], called XronoBeat (developed by the first author, and pictured in [18]), was used to teach basic fraction skills – understanding what fractions are, and learning how to order them. The results were promising, with average test scores rising from 51% to 75% after just three lessons [12].

The study reported here provides a useful counterpoint to the BGHS study. Sydney Grammar is a private school for boys in central Sydney whose pupils are generally of high SES and, instead of teaching mathematics with music, we taught music with mathematics. In addition to XronoBeat, we used teaching materials specially developed by Richard Cohn, which were based on a rhythm-centred version of his "modulo small" teaching program [7,8].

2   Methods

The two classroom music teachers were provided with Cohn's lesson plans to teach to their Year 9 music students. There were a total of 28 boys, aged 14–15, who were all music pupils in the classes ordinarily taught by the two teachers. The lesson plans were designed for six 45-min lessons and comprised written descriptions of the lessons and explanatory diagrams and cyclic graphs. XronoBeat was installed on the computers in each classroom and there was one computer per child. This study was approved by the Human Research Ethics Committee of Western Sydney University. Below is a summary of the lessons:

Lesson 1 A 2-point cycle. A zero-based counting system for "beats". Basic set-theory relations: inclusion, rotation, and complementation. Basic musical terms: "time point" (="beat"), "pulse", "meter".

Lesson 2 A 3-point cycle. Application of basic terms learned last time. A 6-point cycle as a product of a 2-cycle and a 3-cycle. Exploration of hemiola and basic polymeter (3:2).

Lesson 3 Introduction to *maximally even* (ME) sets; how they apply to embeddings of the 2- and 3-cycle into the 6-cycle. The notation $ME(c, d)$. Explore $ME(8, d)$, that is, maximally even sets for an 8-point cycle but restricting to values of d that divide 8; that is, $ME(8, 2)$ and $ME(8, 4)$ (embedding of 2- and 4- point cycle within an 8-point cycle).

Lesson 4 The distinction between perfect and imperfect ME sets. Exploration of imperfect ME sets in an 8-point cycle: $ME(8, 3)$ and $ME(8, 5)$ – the Cuban *tresillo* and *cinquillo*. Rotation, inclusion, and complementation relations.

Lesson 5 The 12-point cycle. Perfect ME sets ($d = 2, 3, 4, 6$) and their interaction. A lesson on polyrhythms, building on Lesson 2. Imperfect ME sets in a 12-point cycle – $ME(12, 5)$ and $ME(12, 7)$. African bell patterns. Application of rotation, inclusion, and complementation relations, building on Lesson 4.

Lesson 6 Application of imperfect $ME(12, 5)$ and $ME(12, 7)$ in pitch: major and pentatonic scales. A 16-point cycle. The focus here is on imperfect ME sets, and their application to popular music. $ME(16, 5)$ yields the prime-generated double tresillo $(3, 3, 3, 3, 4)$; $ME(16, 7)$ yields the hyperdiatonic rhythm $(2, 2, 3, 2, 2, 2, 3)$; rock-n-roll examples of these.

3   Results

Students and teachers were assessed through questionnaires and observations made by both authors. This study was intended primarily to test the feasibility of the intervention and to obtain indications of possible effects bearing in mind that, due to the lack of a control group, causal claims cannot be asserted. The students were asked to write answers for seven post-test questions:

1. Which parts of the lessons did you enjoy the most or find the most interesting?
2. Which parts of the lessons did you enjoy the least or find the least interesting?
3. In what ways did you find the software help or hinder your learning of musical or mathematical concepts?
4. Which parts of the lessons or software did you not understand?
5. Did you learn anything that you had previously struggled to understand? If so, can you explain how?
6. Do you think mathematics and music are related subjects? Has your opinion changed since these lessons?
7. Do you have any suggestions for improving the lessons?

A statistical analysis of the questionnaires was undertaken by a research assistant not otherwise involved with the project. In summary, 73% of the pupils stated a general preference for computer interaction, and 69% expressed that the maths theory relevant to rhythms was the least interesting part of the lessons. However, 81% of the pupils stated that the interaction with the software helped with understanding and/or visualising the maths theory, and 23% of students understood complex rhythms more thoroughly as a result of the lessons. The majority of students (81%) thought mathematics and music were related subjects, with 42% of pupils expressing that they better understood the relation or saw a relation where they did not before as a result of the lessons. Although 38% of pupils did not express any difficulties with the lessons, 35% of pupils struggled with the theory, with 27% of pupils recommending more detailed explanations as a way of improving future lessons.

The teachers also filled in post-test questionnaires. Teacher A stated that the class were "at the strong end academically and musically" and taught the materials at length, extending some of the lessons to two lessons per written lesson. Teacher B expressed that it was challenging teaching new terminology to the students during the first lessons. However, both teachers expressed the efficacy of having XronoBeat in the classroom for students to interact with and to reinforce the concepts being taught. Teacher A explained that the students liked learning with XronoBeat because it was game-like. Teacher A noted how efficacious learning about mathematics and music could be in helping students with strong mathematical ability who were weak instrumental performers in that their new knowledge about mathematics and music would give those students a "leg up". Of particular interest to Teacher B was "applying the theory to existing musical examples, the mathematical aspects of the course and seeing the students brainstorm in a mathematical manner and explaining their ideas during discussions".

The teachers approached the pedagogy of rhythm and meter through applying visualizations and sonifications of the mathematical principles of basic set theory. In the classes, the students learned to identify rhythms and meter (sets and their relations) from experiencing polyrhythms and polymeter in Latin American, Afro-Caribbean, West African, Western art, and Western rock music. Both teachers drew cyclic graphs on the board, and cycles were also composed by the students using XronoBeat. The students of Teacher A used XronoBeat to produce rhythms in different tempos so as to observe, and comment on, the effect tempo can have on the perception of meter. Both teachers taught their students about different degrees of evenness (perfect evenness, maximal evenness, neither) in rhythms and the effect this has on the listening experience. For example, Teacher A's students reported that some rhythms, or sequences of rhythms, were "smooth" while others were "jarring" according to the amount of evenness and inclusion. Notably, neither teacher told the students how to hear the rhythms or meter; rather, the focus of lessons was on what the students heard and for them to bring to the class their observations of their own listening experiences. By mapping rhythms and meter to cyclic graphs to discuss inclusion, rotation and complementation, we observed students learned more deeply about why a piece of music has a certain "feel" or "groove".

Teacher A acknowledged that the students in their class knew "very little – both formally and informally – about Western popular musics," and added, "undoubtedly, this methodology provided a glimpse into that world and how it might be better comprehended academically." Both teachers saw the potential for XronoBeat to be included among the classroom music activities where theoretical materials were taught. Through applying visualizations and sonifications of mathematical music theory to their understanding of rhythm and meter, the students in both classes learned that, unlike traditional understandings, meter is not notation-based; rather, it is experienced and initially located in the mind of the listener. Students displayed impressive knowledge of the mathematics they had learned from prior classes in this pilot project and its relationship to their experience of music. Notably, students were focused, engaged, and eager when learning about mathematics of rhythm and meter through the application of set theory with visualizations and sonifications of cyclic graphs.

4 Conclusion

The results demonstrate that this type of music-teaching intervention, which integrates music software with mathematically based teaching materials, is feasible – the program ran successfully to completion over six weeks and both the pupils and teachers enjoyed the experience. It seems that the software helped the students to better understand mathematical concepts behind rhythm and meter, and they found it useful for providing immediate visualizations and sonifications of theoretical concepts as well as for exploring rhythms in a more creative way. One student noted "I legitimately learned so much just from trying out different combinations and ideas, 'what would happen if ...' and I think many other students would benefit from this powerful kind of learning". It is also interesting to note that such a high proportion of the students felt mathematics and music were related, with 42% of students suggesting that this intervention helped them to strengthen or to make new such connections. As with many novel interventions, there will always be practical difficulties related to integrating into standard curricula; however, given the desire in many education authorities for greater emphasis on inter-disciplinary activities and skills, we suggest that combining mathematics and music is a model that is both feasible and fruitful.

References

1. Bahna-James, T.: The relationship between mathematics and music: secondary school student perspectives. J. Negro Educ. **60**(3), 477–485 (1991)
2. Bahr, N., Christensen, C.A.: Inter-domain transfer between mathematical skill and musicianship. J. Struct. Learn. Intell. Syst. **14**, 187–197 (2000)
3. Brochard, R., Dufour, A., Després, O.: Effect of musical expertise on visuospatial abilities: evidence from reaction times and mental imagery. Brain Cogn. **54**, 103–109 (2004)
4. Calilhanna, A.: Teaching Musical Meter to School-Age Students Through The Ski-Hill Graph. Master's thesis, The University of Sydney. Chap. 4, pp. 92–179 (2018). http://hdl.handle.net/2123/19791
5. Cheek, J.M., Smith, L.R.: Music training and mathematics achievement. Adolescence **34**, 759–761 (1999)
6. Cohn, R.: Complex hemiolas, ski-hill graphs and metric spaces. Music Anal. **20**(3), 295–326 (2001)
7. Cohn, R.: Teaching atonal and beat-class theory, modulo small. MusMat: Braz. J. Music Math. **1**(1), 15–24 (2016)

8. Cohn, R.: Scaling up to atonality: the pedagogy of small cyclic universes. In: Montiel, M., Gómez, F. (eds.) Visualizing and Sonifying Mathematical Music Theory with Software Applications: Implications of Computer-based Models for Practice and Education, Chap. 6, pp. 127–149. World Scientific (2019)

9. Cox, H.A., Stephens, L.J.: The effect of music participation on mathematical achievement and overall academic achievement of high school students. Int. J. Math. Educ. Sci. Technol. **37**(7), 757–763 (2004)

10. Gentner, D., Loewenstein, J., Thompson, L.: Learning and transfer: a general role for analogical encoding. J. Educ. Psychol. **95**(2), 393–408 (2003)

11. Haimson, J., Swaina, D., Winner, E.: Do mathematicians have above average musical skill? Music Percept. **29**(2), 203–213 (2011)

12. Hamilton, T.J., et al.: Teaching mathematics with music: a pilot study. In: Proceedings of IEEE International Conference on Teaching, Assessment, and Learning for Engineering (TALE 2018). University of Wollongong, NSW, Australia (2018)

13. Harrison, C.S.: Relationships between grades in the components of freshman music theory and selected background variables. J. Res. Music Educ. **38**(3), 175–186 (1990)

14. Harrison, C.S.: Relationships between grades in music theory for nonmusic majors and selected background variables. J. Res. Music Educ. **44**(4), 341–352 (1996)

15. Harrison, C.: Predicting music theory grades: the relative efficiency of academic ability, music experience, and musical aptitude. J. Res. Music Educ. **38**(2), 124–137 (1990)

16. Helmrich, B.H.: Window of opportunity? Adolescence, music, and algebra. J. Adolesc. Res. **25**(4), 557–577 (2010)

17. Hilton, C., Calilhanna, A., Milne, A.J.: Visualizing and sonifying mathematical music theory with software applications: implications of computer-based models for practice and education. In: Montiel, M., Gómez, F. (eds.) Theoretical and Practical Pedagogy of Mathematical Music Theory: Music for Mathematics and Mathematics for Musicians, From School to Postgraduate Levels, Chap. 9, pp. 201–236. World Scientific (2019)

18. Milne, A.J.: XronoMorph: investigating paths through rhythmic space. In: Holland, S., Mudd, T., Wilkie-McKenna, K., McPherson, A., Wanderley, M.M. (eds.) New Directions in Music and Human-Computer Interaction. SSCC, pp. 95–113. Springer, Cham (2019). https://doi.org/10.1007/978-3-319-92069-6_6

19. Milne, A.J., Bulger, D., Herff, S.A.: Exploring the space of perfectly balanced rhythms and scales. J. Math. Music **11**(2–3), 101–133 (2017). https://doi.org/10.1080/17459737.2017.1395915

20. Milne, A.J., Herff, S.A., Bulger, D., Sethares, W.A., Dean, R.T.: XronoMorph: algorithmic generation of perfectly balanced and well-formed rhythms. In: Proceedings of the 2016 International Conference on New Interfaces for Musical Expression (NIME 2016), pp. 388–393. Griffith University, Brisbane, Australia (2016)

21. Richland, L.E., Zur, O., Holyoak, K.J.: Cognitive supports for analogies in the mathematics classroom. Science **316**, 1128–1129 (2007)

22. Rogers, N., Clendinning, J.P.: Music theory ability correlates with mathematical ability. In: Meeting of the Society for Music Perception and Cognition, Nashville, TN, US (2015)

23. Rogers, N., Clendinning, J.P., Ganley, S.H.C.: Specific mathematical and spatial abilities correlate with music theory abilities. In: Proceedings of the 14th International Conference on Music Perception and Cognition, pp. 537–543 (2016)

24. Rogers, N., Clendinning, J.P., Hart, S., Ganley, C.: Specific correlations between abilities in mathematics and music theory. In: Society for Music Theory: Fortieth Annual Meeting, Arlington, VA, US, November 2017
25. Schmithorst, V.J., Holland, S.K.: The effect of musical training on the neural correlates of math processing: a functional magnetic resonance imaging study in humans. Neurosci. Lett. **354**, 193–196 (2004)

Integrated Music and Math Projects in Secondary Education

Miguel R. Wilhelmi[1(✉)] and Mariana Montiel[2]

[1] Public University of Navarre, 31006 Pamplona-Irunea, Navarra, Spain
miguelr.wilhelmi@unavarra.es
[2] Georgia State University, 25 Park Place 1322, Atlanta, GA 30303, USA

Abstract. The introduction of projects involving music and mathematics in Secondary Education should allow the integration of these disciplines by non-specialists. In the present work we describe an experience carried out with future mathematics teachers with solid scientific-technical training, but little musical training. This pilot contributes with concrete orientations and results para the creation and development of STEAM activities, which can be found in [5].

Keywords: STEM · STEAM · Muthsics · Euclidean rhythms

1 STEM to STEAM

STEM is the acronym for Science, Technology, Engineering and Mathematics, used by authors worldwide in their research contributions for specialized journals (e.g., https://stemeducationjournal.springeropen.com/). Currently, there is a move towards including art to STEM disciplines (http://stemtosteam.org/), and for STEM projects to become STEAM projects.

"Muthsics" is the intentional combination of "mu-sic" and "(ma)th-s". Music and mathematics complement each other, as both disciplines contribute with their unique characteristics. Our postulate is that muthsics projects are a proper context for developing STEAM principles.

The problem lies in how to bring these creative experiences to schools and make them compatible with the established curriculum? How can we involve teachers without advanced studies in mathematics or in music, or those with monolithic training in one of the disciplines? Under what conditions is it possible to propose these projects in a controlled and evaluable manner for schools?

2 Experimentation

2.1 Mathematical and Musical Content

We will begin with a brief description of the mathematical content included and how the musical rhythms were employed to enhance the teaching of mathematics [1, 4]. The subjects included can be grouped into three general categories as follows:

(1) Euclid's Lemma and Euclid's algorithm, maximal evenness, and Euclidean rhythms.
(2) Clapping Music and cyclic permutations [3].
(3) Euclidean rhythms and mathematical calculations such as the greatest common divisor of two natural numbers. In terms of rhythm, it has been seen that the most common world rhythms are Euclidean rhythms [4].

In the mathematical context, there is growing interest for the incorporation of automatized procedures that mimic classical calculations ("maths by computer"). This perspective covers the learning stages at all levels, not only the university. According to the NCTM (http://www.nctm.org), technology determines, whether we like it or not, not only how to teach, but what to teach [2].

2.2   Context and Sample

Candidates for teaching at the middle and high School levels (12–20 years old) in Spain should pursue a Master's Degree in Teaching at the Secondary Level, which is a professional requisite. The applicants to the Master's program must have a Bachelor's Degree and the students who opt for the specialization in Mathematics come from different backgrounds. In Table 1, we show the student distribution by backgrounds and sex.

Table 1. Student distribution by backgrounds and sex.

School year	Total	W	M	Engin	Archi	Maths	Phys	Eco
1st	6	4	2	4	1	—	—	1
2nd	7	4	3	4	1	1	1	—

Key: W: Women; M: Men; Engin: Engineering; Archi: Architecture;
Maths: Mathematics; Phys: Physics; Eco: Economics

2.3   Instruments, Premises and Objectives

Before carrying out the activities the students answered a brief survey about their musical training. It can be said that the students had solid scientific-technical training, but little musical training; in this area, they were inexpert (*muthsics for clueless*). For this reason, we needed to teach musical terms (time span, pulses, notes, rests, rhythm, piece, etc.) before carrying out the actual activities relating music to mathematics.

The activities were distributed in two sessions of 1 h 45 min each, and alternated individual answers to proposed tasks with the collective discussion of their musical and mathematical content, as well as their relation to the school curriculum and the present tendencies concerning Secondary Education students and how they can acquire the knowledge and the skills mandated in the general program requirements. Due to space limitations, we will focus on activities 5 and 8 in session 1:

– S1.5 (5 min). The time period is divided in 12 pulses. It represents a rhythm as "even" as possible, with 4 notes (•) and 8 rests (—). The students produced rhythms of 12 pulses (4 notes and 8 rests). They were given a grid to facilitate an empirical search of flamenco rhythms (*fandango, soleá, etc.*) (Fig. 1).

– S1.8 (10 min). The time period is divided in 12 pulses. It represents a rhythm as "even" as possible, with 8 notes (•) and 4 rests (—) Once you have found a rhythm, try to show one that preserves regularity ("evenness"). The students, "on the march", were to apply the notion of "evenness". It was assumed that they would use musical or technical criteria, but that mathematical knowledge would not play a role in the activity, that is, they would not search for an algorithm based on the principles of maximal evenness and Euclid's algorithm.

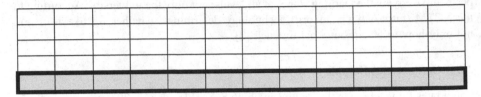

Fig. 1. Search for rhythms.

3   Results and Discussion

The proposed rhythms are formed by a longitudinal characteristic (the repetition of a pattern) or by symmetry with respect to the center (6 pulses "to the left" y 6 pulses "to the right"). In Table 2 all the proposed rhythms are shown.

Table 2. Rhythms proposed by the students, as "even as possible" (4 notes, •; 8 rest, —).

CUF	Rhythm	N°	G	Total
L	• — | • — | • — | • — — • | — • | — • | — •	5 1	C	6
CS	— • — — — • | • — — — • — • — — — • | — • — — — •	2 1	C&P	3
CS L	— — • • — | — — • • — • • — — — | • • — — —	1 1	C	2
SE	— — — • — — • • | • — — —	1	U	1
LRP	— • — • | — — • • | — • — • — — — • | — — • • | — — • •	1 1	Not	2

CUF: Characteristic used in forming. L: Longitudinal; CS: Central Symmetry; SE: Symmetry at the extremes; LRP: Longitudinal, with a maximum of repeated patterns
G: Grouping; C: Circular; P: Permutation; U: Unique; Not: Does not respond to the proposed rhythm

In situation 8, where they must represent an "even" rhythm with 8 notes (•) y 4 rests (—), the students contributed 28 timelines. Half of them (14 out of 28) are obtained by a repetition of the pattern that contains two notes and a rest (• • — /— • • /• — •) or combinations of these three patterns. This type of timeline is produced by 9 of the 14 students. On the other hand, 5 of 28 patterns are repetitions or combinations of the two patterns that contain four notes and two rests (• • • • — — /— — • • • •). The justification of the proposed "even" rhythms is not anecdotal. Several students make notes in the margins or the back of their notepaper that refer to the symmetry ("making groups, by symmetry, because they are in pairs") or groupings by divisibility.

Through the activity, the students come to realize that mathematics can model musical patterns and that this leads to different types of music (circular permutations) in a much more efficient manner than the trial and error method. Likewise, they see that "known" mathematical techniques (calculation of the GCD) in a specific context (arithmetic, by factorization) has not been easily extrapolated to an extra mathematical context. This supposes a very deep learning experience in terms of what "learning mathematics" and "using mathematics" means.

4 Conclusion

Muthsics is not a mere metaphor or play on words; it is a proposal for specific teaching and learning situations around mathematics and music that will allow students to learn new concepts in both areas by starting from their previous formal knowledge. The situations should allow the integration of the creative experience with the demands of the curriculum, even bettering the usual delivery of the disciplines. It is also essential that teachers without advanced training in mathematics or music, and whose focus is just one of the areas, are able to propose muthsics projects that can be controlled and evaluated.

Acknowledgement. This research work has been carried out within the framework of the project EDU2017-84979-R, of the Spanish State Program of R&D and Innovation Oriented to the Challenges of the Society.

References

1. Demaine, E., et al.: The distance geometry of music. Comput. Geom.: Theory Appl. **42**, 429–454 (2009)
2. NCTM: Executive Summary: Principles and Standards for School Mathematics. Autor, Reston (2017)
3. Reich, S.: Clapping Music for two performers (1972). http://earreader.nl/wp-content/uploads/2016/01/SteveReich-ClappingMusic.pdf. Accessed 01 Dec 2017
4. Toussaint, G.: The Geometry of Musical Rhythm. Chapman and Hall/CRC, London (2013)
5. Wilhelmi, M., Montiel, M.: Muthsics for clueless: an experiment with Euclidean rhythms. In: Montiel, M., Gómez, F. (eds.) Theoretical and Practical Pedagogy of Mathematical Music Theory: Music for Mathematics and Mathematics for Musicians, From School to Postgraduate Levels. World Scientific Publishing Co., Singapore (2018)

"Concerférences": of Music and Maths, for the Audience's Delight

Emmanuel Amiot[✉]

LAMPS, Université de Perpignan Via Domitia, Perpignan, France
`manu.amiot@free.fr`

Abstract. This paper describes a good way to put forward to a general public the relationship between maths and music: "concerférences", a French term coined to designate anything between a talk cum music and a concert cum fairly detailed scientific explanations. This format of exposition is quite versatile, and the content can be adapted to a wide range of publics. It has shown considerable pedagogical promise, some possible reasons are explored with examples taken from actual practice.

Keywords: Concerférences · Pedagogy · Math and Music

1 Introduction

There are several excellent reasons for the popularization of Math and Music. A pedagogical one is to show how many mysteries and complexities of music can be explained, modeled and re-created with appropriate mathematical concepts: though I, for one, believe than no computer program will ever emulate the genius of Mozart, I believe no less firmly that we can, and should, build the concepts and software for doing half as well, thus enhancing both understanding and creation of music. This involves a lot of mathematical work. Besides, as other speakers will show in this workshop, approaching mathematical concepts through musical questions is a wonderful pedagogical move, rejuvenating young students' interest in concepts that may seem stale and sterile in the classroom as well as exemplifying the interest **and fun** of a scientific approach. It is my firm belief as a maths teacher that some students whose *forte* is not conceptual intelligence will find interest in – nay, be thrilled by – mathematics, if their own type of intelligence is triggered.

The concept and practice of *"concerférences"* has been rapidly developing in recent years.[1] It originates perhaps on the one hand in those artists who break the traditional mutism on stage, and put in a few words of explanation alongside with their performance; and on the other hand in those among us who insist

---

[1] See references in [2], which covers the subject in greater depth and shows a variety of topics appropriate for a variety of audiences. The present talk focuses more on the general concept of concerference and its pedagogical interest.

© Springer Nature Switzerland AG 2019
M. Montiel et al. (Eds.): MCM 2019, LNAI 11502, pp. 394–398, 2019.
https://doi.org/10.1007/978-3-030-21392-3_36

on keeping some measure of artistic performance in their science, alleviating the sufferance of their knowledgeable but nonetheless perplexed audiences by musical interludes.

2   A Wide Choice of Topics

I will consider only two examples here: the arithmetic of notes with the circle $\mathbf{Z}_{12}$ and the *Tonnetz*.

2.1   Arithmetic of Notes: The Cyclic Ring $\mathbf{Z}_{12}$

Modular arithmetic is considered as an advanced topic and seldom taught, if ever, to young students. However, the cyclic model of pitch-classes (Kremer circles) is easy as Pi (or more precisely, as a clock). I have never had any difficulty in getting the point of equivalence modulo octave, I simply ask the audience to sing along some popular song ('Brother John' or 'Black Sheep'), showing by example how voices spontaneously settle an octave apart.[2]

Anticipating on the next section, it is of huge pedagogical interest to show in $\mathbf{Z}_{12}$ hitherto uninteresting features of $+$ and $\times$ (commutative, associative, opposite) taking on a new, unexpected splendor:

- The cyclic character of both operations is tickling: adding again and again the same number (class) eventually yielding the original starting point is surprising, so is the variable period of the phenomenon.
- The ring $\mathbf{Z}_n$ has new and exciting features, such as divisors of zero and numerous solutions to some equations (e.g. $1^2 = 5^2 = 7^2 = 11^2 \mod 12$). Compared to this new universe (which was actually there available all the time!), the old arithmetic of plain numbers looks so dull!
- As a conjunction of the two preceding points, the existence of non obvious generators (of the group) is intriguing, just as it is extremely meaningful (cycles of fifths, musical scales, etc.).

2.2   The Tonnetz

My favorite example in *concerférences* is without doubt the adventures of the *Tonnetz*.[3]

This makes a great story for any concerférencer, which spans almost three centuries.

---

[2] A Shepard-Risset never-ending scale, played while a Penrose stair (or Escher fountain) is shown, can help drive the idea home.

[3] Its topological structure is quite easy to grab when the audience follows a sequence of chords/notes going through one side and turning up on the opposite one, and there is a wealth of interesting videos using this model. A fantastic pedagogical tool is Louis Bigo's software HexaChord [3] which enables to follow chord progressions in real time.

Leonhard Euler invents the *Tonnetz* (and graph theory!) in 1739. The edges of the graph are the consonant pure intervals of fifth and thirds, the *dual* graph is made of the centers of the triangles, connected to their neighbors. These triangles are major or minor triads, and moving to a neighbor triads involves changing one note only, a 'parsimonious' operation with maximal simplicity. These three symmetries from one triangle to a neighbor[4] are the fundamental bricks of Otto v. Öttingen's and Bernhard Riemann's renewed theory of *Tonnetz* (1856). This grammar of transformations is taught nowadays as a powerful (and fashionable) tool for analysis of tonal music.

But much had been done with these symmetries even before they were even named. For instance, Beethoven wrote a suggestive sequence of triads in the third movement of his Ninth Symphony (1824). This was recognized as a cyclic sequence of parsimonious operations 172 years later by R. Cohn, who defined general P-cycles between pc-sets [5].

And Beethoven's cycle has one additional and remarkable quality: it passes through each of the 24 triads once and exactly once. Such a cycle in a graph, crossing each vertex exactly once, is a *Hamiltonian cycle*; the notion emerged around 1856 – simultaneously with the resurgence of the *Tonnetz*.

However, it took again a century and a half for researchers to come to grips with the obvious question: what are the other possible Hamiltonian cycles in the *Tonnetz* of triads? This requires some raw computer power, since finding Hamiltonian cycles is a NP-complete problem. This was tackled and solved in 2009, by Albini and Antonini [1] who found the 262 solutions. I was thrilled when I first encountered this result, which had just then become accessible with a personal computer (it takes about 2 h). The ultimate development of this exemplary sequence of mathemusical analysis was of course to use the new cycles for original compositions.[5] But the story moves on still, with an exploration of similar paths in a Tonnetz of seventh chords.[6]

3   Pedagogical Advantages

Clapping, singing, dancing,[7] counting: all of these musical operations are quite easy to execute with any audience. No need for professional orchestras, expensive

---

[4] P, L, and R respectively exchange C major triad with C minor, E minor and A minor.

[5] In *concerférences*, we sometimes use G. Albini's seminal variant https://youtu.be/rXR64vFcf-Q of Bach's first cello Suite, *Corale #4* which shows beautifully the parsimonious character of chord transitions. However, when I am privileged to share the stage with Gilles Baroin and Moreno Andreatta, the latter plays and sings live one of his own 'Hamiltonian songs' while the former projects his stunning graphics renderings in diverse geometrical models, for instance *Aprile* (https://www.youtube.com/watch?v=AB8By7ghTkU) on a moving poem by Gabriele d'Annunzio.

[6] See [4].

[7] https://www.youtube.com/watch?v=eUe1Ddkv2M4&t=1108s.

apparatus, etc. Also, it involves the participation of attendants, by far the best way to get them involved and understand what the *concerférencier* is talking about.

Unlike a classic maths course, a *concerférence* starts from everybody's personal experience. Since some of the mathematical notions are new material (graphs, modulo...), nobody begins in arrears. The freedom to choose material from outside scholarly curricula is invaluable (this would of course be true for other excursions, say in pictural arts or architecture, for instance).

The change of context not only induces a feeling of freedom, but enriches old (stale) notions which are given another look. For instance, the notion of parallel fifths may look strange on the pitch-class circle, but a movie with the *Pink Panther*'s theme stamps lastingly the notion of equivalence class [here the interval, appearing as a transpositional invariant]. It usually brings a rewarding light in the eyes of 14 years-old who have hitherto suffered on vectors and pairs of points and parallelograms.

I have mentioned modular arithmetic which provides a new light on old notions. It seems that such mind-openers reap clear benefits when the student returns to the curriculum, probably because the expanding of the field of knowledge stimulates interest and perhaps understanding.[8]

4 Adjusting to Different Audiences

Examples from pop music are mandatory for younger or more popular audiences. Fortunately they are as easily available (or even more) in illustrating nice math-emusical notions. For instance, journeying in the *Tonnetz* (or similar geometric musical spaces) illustrates well pop/rock/jazz music.[9]

It is a comfort and a pleasure to talk to peers (say doing a talk for a maths department), but in my experience greater rewards are reaped while talking to less expert audiences, which can be keen nonetheless. For instance, after I have explained the symmetries of the pentatonic scale, I love to show the most famous online picture of Jimmy Hendrix (while playing his best version of *Voodoo Child*, exemplifying how the best guitarists only use the 5 notes), and so far I have never been disappointed in that someone in the audience points out the symmetry bug in the picture... that shows Jimmy as right-handed! though of course the original is left-handed. I think that this collision of symmetries creates better and more enduring memory connections than many hours in the classroom.

In some cases a *concerférence* can be given at the invitation of some institution (high school, private association, university). There are then interesting possibilities of interaction, before or after the talk; there may be some follow-up of the *concerférence* in classes.[10]

---

[8] Recent experiments show particularly notable benefits for "lower performers" when subjected to artistic teachings [6].

[9] See examples with Paolo Conte or Frank Zappa at http://www.mathemusic4d.net/.

[10] For instance, if the concepts of musical inversions and retrogradations have been shown, students can be enticed to try them on their own musical compositions, for instance with synthesizers online like http://www.audiosauna.com/studio/.

5 Conclusion

Most publics are unfamiliar with 'the unreasonable efficiency of mathematics' and harbor a more romantic approach to the ineffability of music (which is a polite way of forbidding rational discourse on the topic). It is worthwhile to lower a bit Music from its pedestal while raising Mathematics in the opposite direction.[11]

More generally, *concerférences* have huge pedagogical interest, insofar as they establish unexpected connections—a romantic poet with modular algebra, Beethoven with graph theory, etc.—which strikes the public's attention, mobilizes their personal knowledge as something that can help them tread unfamiliar ground successfully, and creates/enhances synaptic connections, which is the acknowledged way for memorizing new notions.

When have you scheduled your next one?

References

1. Albini, G., Antonini, S.: Hamiltonian cycles in the topological dual of the tonnetz. In: Chew, E., Childs, A., Chuan, C.-H. (eds.) MCM 2009. CCIS, vol. 38, pp. 1–10. Springer, Heidelberg (2009). https://doi.org/10.1007/978-3-642-02394-1_1
2. Amiot, E.: "Concerférences", addressing different publics for mathemusical popularization. In: Montiel, M., Gómez, F. (eds.) Theoretical and Practical Pedagogy of Mathematical Music Theory, pp. 179–199. World Scientific Publishing (2019)
3. Bigo, L.: Hexachord, free software (Java). http://www.lacl.fr/~lbigo/hexachord
4. Cannas, S., Antonini, S., Pernazza, L.: On the group of transformations of classical types of seventh chords. In: Agustín-Aquino, O.A., Lluis-Puebla, E., Montiel, M. (eds.) MCM 2017. LNCS (LNAI), vol. 10527, pp. 13–25. Springer, Cham (2017). https://doi.org/10.1007/978-3-319-71827-9_2. https://www.researchgate.net/publication/317218582_On_the_group_of_transformations_of_classical_types_of_seventh_chords
5. Cohn, R.: Maximally smooth cycles, hexatonic systems, and the analysis of late-romantic triadic progressions. Music Anal. **15**(1), 9–40 (1996)
6. Klass, P.: Using Arts Education to Help Other Lessons Stick, NYT, 4th March 2019. https://www.nytimes.com/2019/03/04/well/family/using-arts-education-to-help-other-lessons-stick.html

---

[11] My usual answer to the teleological argument that Music, being the breath of Gods, is best left respectfully unstained by maths, is: "the better you know the person you love, the better you love him/her". The argument is usually well received.

Correction to: Mathematics and Computation in Music

Mariana Montiel, Francisco Gomez-Martin, and Octavio A. Agustín-Aquino

Correction to:
M. Montiel et al. (Eds.): *Mathematics and Computation in Music*, **LNAI 11502,**
https://doi.org/10.1007/978-3-030-21392-3

Maria Mannone was not given credit for the cover logo in the original version. This was corrected.

The original version of chapter 14, "Distant Neighbors and Interscalar Contiguities" was revised. This chapter was previously published non-open access. It was changed to open access retrospectively under a CC BY 4.0 license. The book has also been updated with the change.

The updated version of the book can be found at
https://doi.org/10.1007/978-3-030-21392-3_14
https://doi.org/10.1007/978-3-030-21392-3

M. Montiel et al. (Eds.): MCM 2019, LNAI 11502, p. C1, 2020.
https://doi.org/10.1007/978-3-030-21392-3_37

Author Index

Printed in the United States
By Bookmasters